REFERENCE

Short Stories for Students

National Advisory Board

Dale Allender: Teacher, West High School, Iowa City, Iowa.

Dana Gioia: Poet and critic. His books include *The Gods of Winter* and *Can Poetry Matter?* He currently resides in Santa Rosa, CA.

Carol Jago: Teacher, Santa Monica High School, Santa Monica, CA. Member of the California Reading and Literature Project at University of California, Los Angeles.

Bonnie J. Newcomer: English Teacher, Beloit Junior-Senior High School, Beloit, Kansas. Editor of KATE UpDate, for the Kansas Association of Teachers of English. Ph.D. candidate in information science, Emporia State University, Kansas.

Katherine Nyberg: English teacher. Director of the language arts program of Farmington Public Schools, Farmington, Michigan.

Nancy Rosenberger: Former English teacher and chair of English department at Conestoga High School, Berwyn, Pennsylvania.

Dorothea M. Susag: English teacher, Simms High School, Simms, Montana. Former president of the Montana Association of Teachers of English Language Arts. Member of the National Council of Teachers of English.

Short Stories for Students

Presenting Analysis, Context, and Criticism on Commonly Studied Short Stories

Volume 11

Jennifer Smith, Editor

GALE GROUP

Detroit
New York
San Francisco
London
Boston
Woodbridge, CT

Short Stories for Students

Staff

Editor: Jennifer Smith.

Contributing Editors: Anne Marie Hacht, Michael L. LaBlanc, Ira Mark Milne, Elizabeth Thomason.

Managing Editor: Dwayne D. Hayes.

Research: Victoria B. Cariappa, *Research Manager*. Cheryl Warnock, *Research Specialist*. Tamara Nott, Tracie A. Richardson, *Research Associates*. Nicodemus Ford, Sarah Genik, Timothy Lehnerer, Ron Morelli, *Research Assistants*.

Permissions: Maria Franklin, *Permissions Manager*. Jacqueline Jones, Julie Juengling, *Permissions Assistants*.

Manufacturing: Mary Beth Trimper, *Manager, Composition and Electronic Prepress*. Evi Seoud, *Assistant Manager, Composition Purchasing and Electronic Prepress*. Stacy Melson, *Buyer*.

Imaging and Multimedia Content Team: Barbara Yarrow, *Manager*. Randy Bassett, *Imaging Supervisor*. Robert Duncan, Dan Newell, *Imaging Specialists*. Pamela A. Reed, *Imaging Coordinator*. Leitha Etheridge-Sims, Mary Grimes, David G. Oblender, *Image Catalogers*. Robyn V. Young, *Project Manager*. Dean Dauphinais, *Senior Image Editor*. Kelly A. Quin, *Image Editor*.

Product Design Team: Kenn Zorn, *Product Design Manager*. Pamela A. E. Galbreath, *Senior Art Director*. Michael Logusz, *Graphic Artist*.

Copyright Notice

Since this page cannot legibly accommodate all copyright notices, the acknowledgments constitute an extension of the copyright notice.

While every effort has been made to secure permission to reprint material and to ensure the reliability of the information presented in this publication, Gale neither guarantees the accuracy of the data contained herein nor assumes any responsibility for errors, omissions, or discrepancies. Gale accepts no payment for listing; and inclusion in the publication of any organization, agency, institution, publication, service, or individual does not imply endorsement of the editors or publisher. Errors brought to the attention of the publisher and verified to the satisfaction of the publisher will be corrected in future editions.

This publication is a creative work fully protected by all applicable copyright laws, as well as by misappropriation, trade secret, unfair competition, and other applicable laws. The authors and editors of this work have added value to the underlying factual material herein through one or more of the following: unique and original selection, coordination, expression, arrangement, and classification of the information. All rights to this publication will be vigorously defended.

Copyright © 2001
Gale Group,
27500 Drake Road,
Farmington Hills, MI 48331–3535

All rights reserved including the right of reproduction in whole or in part in any form.

ISBN 0-7876-4263-0

ISSN 1092-7735

Printed in the United States of America.

10 9 8 7 6 5 4 3 2 1

Table of Contents

Guest Foreword
"Why Study Literature At All?"
Thomas E. Barden vii

Introduction ix

Literary Chronology xiii

Acknowledgments xv

Contributors xvii

And of Clay Are We Created
Isabel Allende 1

Battle Royal or The Invisible Man
Ralph Ellison 17

The Gilded Six-Bits
Zora Neale Hurston 39

A Good Scent from a Strange Mountain
Robert Olen Butler 60

The Grave
Katherine Anne Porter 78

Hands
Sherwood Anderson 94

Marriage á la Mode
Katherine Mansfield 115

Mrs. Plum
Es'kia (Ezekiel) Mphahlele . . . 130

Table of Contents

My Kinsman, Major Molineux
    Nathaniel Hawthorne 149

Roselily
    Alice Walker 169

Say Yes
    Tobias Wolff 188

The Sheriff's Children
    Charles Waddell Chesnutt 205

Silver Water
    Amy Bloom 228

The Snows of Kilimanjaro
    Ernest Hemingway 243

Storyteller
    Leslie Marmon Silko 256

Women in Their Beds
    Gina Berriault 284

Glossary of Literary Terms . . . 301
Cumulative Author/Title Index . 313
Nationality/Ethnicity Index . . 319
Subject/Theme Index 323

Why Study Literature At All?

Short Stories for Students is designed to provide readers with information and discussion about a wide range of important contemporary and historical works of short fiction, and it does that job very well. However, I want to use this guest foreword to address a question that it does *not* take up. It is a fundamental question that is often ignored in high school and college English classes as well as research texts, and one that causes frustration among students at all levels, namely—why study literature at all? Isn't it enough to read a story, enjoy it, and go about one's business? My answer (to be expected from a literary professional, I suppose) is no. It is not enough. It is a start; but it is not enough. Here's why.

First, literature is the only part of the educational curriculum that deals directly with the actual world of lived experience. The philosopher Edmund Husserl used the apt German term *die Lebenswelt*, "the living world," to denote this realm. All the other content areas of the modern American educational system avoid the subjective, present reality of everyday life. Science (both the natural and the social varieties) objectifies, the fine arts create and/or perform, history reconstructs. Only literary study persists in posing those questions we all asked before our schooling taught us to give up on them. Only literature gives credibility to personal perceptions, feelings, dreams, and the "stream of consciousness" that is our inner voice. Literature wonders about infinity, wonders why God permits evil, wonders what will happen to us after we die. Literature admits that we get our hearts broken, that people sometimes cheat and get away with it, that the world is a strange and probably incomprehensible place. Literature, in other words, takes on all the big and small issues of what it means to be human. So my first answer is that of the humanist—we should read literature and study it and take it seriously because it enriches us as human beings. We develop our moral imagination, our capacity to sympathize with other people, and our ability to understand our existence through the experience of fiction.

My second answer is more practical. By studying literature we can learn how to explore and analyze texts. Fiction may be about *die Lebenswelt*, but it is a construct of words put together in a certain order by an artist using the medium of language. By examining and studying those constructions, we can learn about language as a medium. We can become more sophisticated about word associations and connotations, about the manipulation of symbols, and about style and atmosphere. We can grasp how ambiguous language is and how important context and texture is to meaning. In our first encounter with a work of literature, of course, we are not supposed to catch all of these things. We are spellbound, just as the writer wanted us to be. It is as serious students of the writer's art that we begin to see how the tricks are done.

Seeing the tricks, which is another way of saying "developing analytical and close reading skills," is important above and beyond its intrinsic literary educational value. These skills transfer to other fields and enhance critical thinking of any kind. Understanding how language is used to construct texts is powerful knowledge. It makes engineers better problem solvers, lawyers better advocates and courtroom practitioners, politicians better rhetoricians, marketing and advertising agents better sellers, and citizens more aware consumers as well as better participants in democracy. This last point is especially important, because rhetorical skill works both ways—when we learn how language is manipulated in the making of texts the result is that we become less susceptible when language is used to manipulate us.

My third reason is related to the second. When we begin to see literature as created artifacts of language, we become more sensitive to good writing in general. We get a stronger sense of the importance of individual words, even the sounds of words and word combinations. We begin to understand Mark Twain's delicious proverb—"The difference between the right word and the almost right word is the difference between lightning and a lightning bug." Getting beyond the "enjoyment only" stage of literature gets us closer to becoming makers of word art ourselves. I am not saying that studying fiction will turn every student into a Faulkner or a Shakespeare. But it will make us more adaptable and effective writers, even if our art form ends up being the office memo or the corporate annual report.

Studying short stories, then, can help students become better readers, better writers, and even better human beings. But I want to close with a warning. If your study and exploration of the craft, history, context, symbolism, or anything else about a story starts to rob it of the magic you felt when you first read it, it is time to stop. Take a break, study another subject, shoot some hoops, or go for a run. Love of reading is too important to be ruined by school. The early twentieth century writer Willa Cather, in her novel *My Antonia*, has her narrator Jack Burden tell a story that he and Antonia heard from two old Russian immigrants when they were teenagers. These immigrants, Pavel and Peter, told about an incident from their youth back in Russia that the narrator could recall in vivid detail thirty years later. It was a harrowing story of a wedding party starting home in sleds and being chased by starving wolves. Hundreds of wolves attacked the group's sleds one by one as they sped across the snow trying to reach their village. In a horrible revelation, the old Russians revealed that the groom eventually threw his own bride to the wolves to save himself. There was even a hint that one of the old immigrants might have been the groom mentioned in the story. Cather has her narrator conclude with his feelings about the story. "We did not tell Pavel's secret to anyone, but guarded it jealously—as if the wolves of the Ukraine had gathered that night long ago, and the wedding party had been sacrificed, just to give us a painful and peculiar pleasure." That feeling, that painful and peculiar pleasure, is the most important thing about literature. Study and research should enhance that feeling and never be allowed to overwhelm it.

Thomas E. Barden
Professor of English and
Director of Graduate English Studies
The University of Toledo

Introduction

Purpose of the Book

The purpose of *Short Stories for Students* (*SSfS*) is to provide readers with a guide to understanding, enjoying, and studying short stories by giving them easy access to information about the work. Part of Gale's "For Students" Literature line, *SSfS* is specifically designed to meet the curricular needs of high school and undergraduate college students and their teachers, as well as the interests of general readers and researchers considering specific short fiction. While each volume contains entries on "classic" stories frequently studied in classrooms, there are also entries containing hard-to-find information on contemporary stories, including works by multicultural, international, and women writers.

The information covered in each entry includes an introduction to the story and the story's author; a plot summary, to help readers unravel and understand the events in the work; descriptions of important characters, including explanation of a given character's role in the narrative as well as discussion about that character's relationship to other characters in the story; analysis of important themes in the story; and an explanation of important literary techniques and movements as they are demonstrated in the work.

In addition to this material, which helps the readers analyze the story itself, students are also provided with important information on the literary and historical background informing each work. This includes a historical context essay, a box comparing the time or place the story was written to modern Western culture, a critical overview essay, and excerpts from critical essays on the story or author (if available). A unique feature of *SSfS* is a specially commissioned overview essay on each story, targeted toward the student reader.

To further aid the student in studying and enjoying each story, information on media adaptations is provided, as well as reading suggestions for works of fiction and nonfiction on similar themes and topics. Classroom aids include ideas for research papers and lists of critical sources that provide additional material on the work.

Selection Criteria

The titles for each volume of *SSfS* were selected by surveying numerous sources on teaching literature and analyzing course curricula for various school districts. Some of the sources surveyed include: literature anthologies, *Reading Lists for College-Bound Students: The Books Most Recommended by America's Top Colleges*; *Teaching the Short Story: A Guide to Using Stories from Around the World*, by the National Council of Teachers of English (NCTE); and "A Study of High School Literature Anthologies," conducted by Arthur Applebee at the Center for the Learning and Teaching of Literature and sponsored by the National Endowment for the Arts and the Office of Educational Research and Improvement.

Input was also solicited from our advisory board, as well as educators from various areas. From these discussions, it was determined that each volume should have a mix of "classic" stories (those works commonly taught in literature classes) and contemporary stories for which information is often hard to find. Because of the interest in expanding the canon of literature, an emphasis was also placed on including works by international, multicultural, and women authors. Our advisory board members—educational professionals—helped pare down the list for each volume. Works not selected for the present volume were noted as possibilities for future volumes. As always, the editor welcomes suggestions for titles to be included in future volumes.

How Each Entry Is Organized

Each entry, or chapter, in *SSfS* focuses on one story. Each entry heading lists the title of the story, the author's name, and the date of the story's publication. The following elements are contained in each entry:

- **Introduction:** a brief overview of the story which provides information about its first appearance, its literary standing, any controversies surrounding the work, and major conflicts or themes within the work.

- **Author Biography:** this section includes basic facts about the author's life, and focuses on events and times in the author's life that may have inspired the story in question.

- **Plot Summary:** a description of the events in the story.

- **Characters:** an alphabetical listing of the characters who appear in the story. Each character name is followed by a brief to an extensive description of the character's role in the story, as well as discussion of the character's actions, relationships, and possible motivation.

    Characters are listed alphabetically by last name. If a character is unnamed—for instance, the narrator in "The Eatonville Anthology"—the character is listed as "The Narrator" and alphabetized as "Narrator." If a character's first name is the only one given, the name will appear alphabetically by that name.

- **Themes:** a thorough overview of how the topics, themes, and issues are addressed within the story. Each theme discussed appears in a separate subhead, and is easily accessed through the boldface entries in the Subject/Theme Index.

- **Style:** this section addresses important style elements of the story, such as setting, point of view, and narration; important literary devices used, such as imagery, foreshadowing, symbolism; and, if applicable, genres to which the work might have belonged, such as Gothicism or Romanticism. Literary terms are explained within the entry, but can also be found in the Glossary.

- **Historical Context:** this section outlines the social, political, and cultural climate *in which the author lived and the work was created.* This section may include descriptions of related historical events, pertinent aspects of daily life in the culture, and the artistic and literary sensibilities of the time in which the work was written. If the story is historical in nature, information regarding the time in which the story is set is also included. Long sections are broken down with helpful subheads.

- **Critical Overview:** this section provides background on the critical reputation of the author and the story, including bannings or any other public controversies surrounding the work. For older works, this section may include a history of how the story was first received and how perceptions of it may have changed over the years; for more recent works, direct quotes from early reviews may also be included.

- **Criticism:** an essay commissioned by *SSfS* which specifically deals with the story and is written specifically for the student audience, as well as excerpts from previously published criticism on the work (if available).

- **Sources:** an alphabetical list of critical material quoted in the entry, with bibliographical information.

- **Further Reading:** an alphabetical list of other critical sources which may prove useful for the student. Includes full bibliographical information and a brief annotation.

In addition, each entry contains the following highlighted sections, set separate from the main text:

- **Media Adaptations:** where applicable, a list of film and television adaptations of the story, including source information. The list also includes stage adaptations, audio recordings, musical adaptations, etc.

- **Topics for Further Study:** a list of potential study questions or research topics dealing with the story. This section includes questions related to other disciplines the student may be studying, such as American history, world history, science, math, government, business, geography, economics, psychology, etc.

- **Compare and Contrast Box:** an "at-a-glance" comparison of the cultural and historical differences between the author's time and culture and late twentieth-century Western culture. This box includes pertinent parallels between the major scientific, political, and cultural movements of the time or place the story was written, the time or place the story was set (if a historical work), and modern Western culture. Works written after the mid-1970s may not have this box.

- **What Do I Read Next?:** a list of works that might complement the featured story or serve as a contrast to it. This includes works by the same author and others, works of fiction and nonfiction, and works from various genres, cultures, and eras.

Other Features

SSfS includes "Why Study Literature At All?," a guest foreword by Thomas E. Barden, Professor of English and Director of Graduate English Studies at the University of Toledo. This essay provides a number of very fundamental reasons for studying literature and, therefore, reasons why a book such as SSfS, designed to facilitate the study of literture, is useful.

A Cumulative Author/Title Index lists the authors and titles covered in each volume of the SSfS series.

A Cumulative Nationality/Ethnicity Index breaks down the authors and titles covered in each volume of the SSfS series by nationality and ethnicity.

A Subject/Theme Index, specific to each volume, provides easy reference for users who may be studying a particular subject or theme rather than a single work. Significant subjects from events to broad themes are included, and the entries pointing to the specific theme discussions in each entry are indicated in **boldface**.

Entries may include illustrations, including an author portrait, stills from film adaptations (if available), maps, and/or photos of key historical events.

Citing Short Stories for Students

When writing papers, students who quote directly from any volume of SSfS may use the following general forms to document their source. These examples are based on MLA style; teachers may request that students adhere to a different style, thus, the following examples may be adapted as needed.

When citing text from SSfS that is not attributed to a particular author (for example, the Themes, Style, Historical Context sections, etc.), the following format may be used:

> "The Celebrated Jumping Frog of Calavaras County." *Short Stories for Students.* Ed. Kathleen Wilson. Vol. 1. Detroit: Gale, 1997, pp. 19-20.

When quoting the specially commissioned essay from SSfS (usually the first essay under the Criticism subhead), the following format may be used:

> Korb, Rena. Essay on "Children of the Sea." *Short Stories for Students.* Ed. Kathleen Wilson. Vol. 1. Detroit: Gale, 1997, p. 42.

When quoting a journal essay that is reprinted in a volume of *Short Stories for Students,* the following form may be used:

> Schmidt, Paul. "The Deadpan on Simon Wheeler." *The Southwest Review* Vol. XLI, No. 3 (Summer, 1956), pp. 270-77; excerpted and reprinted in *Short Stories for Students,* Vol. 1, ed. Kathleen Wilson. (Detroit: Gale, 1997), pp. 29-31.

When quoting material from a book that is reprinted in a volume of SSfS, the following form may be used:

> Bell-Villada, Gene H. "The Master of Short Forms," in *Garcia Marquez: The Man and His Work* (University of North Carolina Press, 1990); excerpted and reprinted in *Short Stories for Students,* Vol. 1, ed. Kathleen Wilson. (Detroit: Gale, 1997), pp. 90-91.

We Welcome Your Suggestions

The editor of *Short Stories for Students* welcomes your comments and ideas. Readers who wish to suggest short stories to appear in future volumes, or who have other suggestions, are cordially invited to contact the editor. You may contact the editor via e-mail at ForStudentsEditors@galegroup.com. Or write to the editor at:

Editor, *Short Stories for Students*
Gale Group
27500 Drake Road
Farmington Hills, MI 48331-3535

Literary Chronology

1804: Nathaniel Hawthorne is born in Salem, Massachusetts.

1858: Charles Waddell Chesnutt is born in Cleveland, Ohio.

1864: Hawthorne dies on May 19.

1876: Sherwood Anderson is born in Camden, Ohio, on September 13.

1888: Katherine Mansfield is born Kathleen Mansfield Beauchamp in Wellington, New Zealand, October 14.

1890: Katherine Anne Porter is born on May 15 in Indian Creek, Texas.

1899: Ernest Hemingway is born July 21 in Oak Park, Illinois.

1903: Zora Neale Hurston is born January 7 in Eatonville, Florida.

1914: Ralph Ellison is born March 1 in Oklahoma City, Oklahoma.

1919: Es'kia Mphahlele is born on December 17 in Marabastad Township, Pretoria, South Africa.

1923: Mansfield dies January 9, at the age of thirty-four.

1926: Gina Berriault is born January 1 in Long Beach, California.

1932: Chesnutt dies November 15, in Cleveland, Ohio.

1936: Hurston wins a Guggenheim Fellowship, 1936 and 1938.

1941: Anderson dies on March 8.

1942: Isabel Allende is born August 2 in Lima, Peru.

1944: Alice Malsenior Walker is born on February 9 in Eatonton, Georgia.

1945: Robert Olen Butler is born January 20 in Granite City, Illinois.

1945: Tobias Wolff is born June 19 in Birmingham, Alabama.

1948: Leslie Marmon Silko is born March 5 in Albuquerque, New Mexico.

1953: Ellison wins the National Book Award.

1953: Hemingway wins the Pulitzer Prize for *The Old Man and The Sea*.

1953: Amy Bloom is born June 18 in New York City, New York.

1954: Hemingway wins the Nobel Prize for Literature.

1954: Hemingway receives an Award of Merit from the American Academy of Arts & Letters.

1960: Hurston dies January 28 in Fort Pierce, Florida.

1961: Hemingway commits suicide, July 2, Ketchum, Idaho.

1966: Porter wins the Pulitzer Prize.

1973: Walker wins the American Book Award for *The Color Purple*.

1977: Silko receives the Pushcart Prize for Poetry.

1980: Porter dies September 18 in Silver Spring, MD.

1983: Walker wins the Pulitzer Prize for *The Color Purple*, 1983.

1985: Wolff wins the PEN/Faulkner Award for Fiction.

1986: Porter wins the National Book Award.

1993: Butler is awarded the Pulitzer Prize.

1994: Ellison dies April 16 in New York City, New York.

1997: Berriault wins the Rea Award.

1997: Berriault wins the PEN/Faulkner award for *Women In Their Beds*.

1997: Berriault wins the National Book Critics Circle Award for *Women In Their Beds*.

1999: Berriault dies.

Acknowledgments

The editors wish to thank the copyright holders of the excerpted criticism included in this volume and the permissions managers of many book and magazine publishing companies for assisting us in securing reproduction rights. We are also grateful to the staffs of the Detroit Public Library, the Library of Congress, the University of Detroit Mercy Library, Wayne State University Purdy/Kresge Library Complex, and the University of Michigan Libraries for making their resources available to us. Following is a list of the copyright holders who have granted us permission to reproduce material in this volume of *Short Stories for Students (SSfS)*. Every effort has been made to trace copyright, but if omissions have been made, please let us know.

COPYRIGHTED MATERIALS IN *SSfS*, VOLUME 11, WERE REPRODUCED FROM THE FOLLOWING PERIODICALS:

American Indian Quarterly, v. 12, Winter, 1988. Copyright © 1988 by The University of Nebraska Press. Reproduced by permission.—*American Literature*, v. XLVII, January, 1977; v. LI, November, 1979. Duke University Press, 1977, 1979. Copyright © 1977 and 1979 by Duke University Press, Durham, NC. Both reproduced by permission.—*The CLA Journal*, v. 9, March, 1966; v. XXXV, March, 1992. Copyright © 1966 and 1992 by The College Language Association. Both reproduced by permission of The College Language Association.—*Freedomways*, v. 14, 1974. Freedomways Associates, Inc., 1974. Copyright © 1974 by Freedomways Associates, Inc. Reproduced by permission.—*Midcontinent American Studies Journal*, v. 3, Fall, 1962 for "The Ambiguity of Shrewdness in 'My Kinsman, Major Molineux'" by Bartlett C. Jones. Copyright © Mid-American Studies Association. Reproduced by permission of the publisher and the author.—*The Midwest Quarterly*, v. XI, Summer, 1970. Copyright © 1970 by *The Midwest Quarterly*, Pittsburgh State University. Reproduced by permission.—*The New England Quarterly*, v. 40, September, 1967 for "Allegory and 'My Kinsman, Major Molineux'" by John Russell. Copyright 1967 by *The New England Quarterly*. Reproduced by permission of the publisher and the author.—*Presence Africaine*, Fall, 1987. Reproduced by permission.—*The Women's Review of Books*, v. XIII, November, 1995, for "In the House of the Spirits," by Ruth Behar. Reproduced by the permission of the author.

COPYRIGHTED MATERIALS IN *SSfS*, VOLUME 11, WERE REPRODUCED FROM THE FOLLOWING BOOKS:

Barnett, Ursula A. From *DLB*. The Gale Group, 1993. Copyright © 1993 by The Gale Group.—Burbank, Rex. From *Sherwood Anderson*. The Gale Group, 1987. Copyright © 1987 by The Gale Group.—DeMouy, Jane Krause. From *Katherine Anne Porter's Women: The Eye of Her Fiction*. University of Texas Press, 1983. Copyright © 1983 by the University of Texas Press. Reproduced by permission.—Givner, Joan. From *DLB*. The Gale Group, 1991. Copyright © 1991 by The Gale Group.—Jaskoski, Helen. From *Leslie Marmon Silko: A Study of the Short Fiction*. Twayne Publishers, 1998. Copyright © 1998 by Twayne Publishers. The Gale Group.—Magalaner, Marvin. From *The Fiction of Katherine Mansfield*. Southern Illinois University Press, 1971. Copyright © 1971 by Southern Illinois University. Reproduced by permission.—Selke, Hartmut K. From *The Black American Short Story in the 20th Century: A Collection of Critical Essays*. B. R. Gruner Publishing Co., 1977. Reproduced by permission.

PHOTOGRAPHS AND ILLUSTRATIONS APPEARING IN SSfS, VOLUME 11, WERE RECEIVED FROM THE FOLLOWING SOURCES:

Allende, Isabel, photograph. AP/Wide World Photos. Reproduced by permission.—Anderson, Sherwood, photograph. The Granger Collection, Ltd. Reproduced by permission.—Berriault, Gina, May 17, 1997, photograph by Ken Cedeno. AP/Wide World Photos. Reproduced by permission.—Butler, Robert Olen, photograph by Jerry Bauer. Copyright © Jerry Bauer. Reproduced by permission.—Chesnutt, Charles Waddell, photograph. The Granger Collection, New York. Reproduced by permission.—Dix, Dorothea. Copyright © Bettmann/Corbis. Reproduced by permission.—DuBois, W. E. B., 1949 Paris Peace Conference, photograph. Bettmann. Reproduced by permission.—Elephants under Mt. Kilimanjaro, photograph by Wolfgang Kaehler. Copyright © Wolfgang Kaehler/Corbis. Reproduced by permission.—Ellison, Ralph, photograph. Archive Photos. Reproduced by permission.—Hemingway, Ernest, photograph. Corbis-Bettmann. Reproduced by permission.—Jackson, Jesse, Raleigh, NC, photograph. UPI/Corbis-Bettmann. Reproduced by permission.—Malan, Daniel F., 1948, photograph. Copyright © Bettmann/Corbis. Reproduced by permission.—Mansfield, Katherine, photograph. Corbis-Bettmann. Reproduced by permission.—Muslim with newspaper. Copyright © Bettmann/Corbis. Reproduced by permission.—Porter, Katherine Anne, photograph by Paul Porter. AP/Wide World Photos. Reproduced by permission.—Rescue workers, Columbia Floods, photograph by Oswaldo Paez. AP/Wide World Photos. Reproduced by permission.—Silko, Leslie Marmon, photograph by Nancy Crampton. Copyright © Nancy Crampton. Reproduced by permission.—Tarring and feathering. Copyright © Bettmann/Corbis. Reproduced by permission—View of crowded Fleet Street. Copyright © Bettmann/Corbis. Reproduced by permission.—Walker, Alice, 1989, photograph. AP/Wide World Photos. Reproduced by permission.—Wells, Ida, photograph. Copyright © Bettmann/Corbis. Reproduced by permission.—Wolff, Tobias, photograph. AP/Wide World Photos. Reproduced by permission.

Contributors

Greg Barnhisel: Barnhisel holds a Ph.D. in English and American literature and currently teaches writing at Southwestern University in Georgetown, Texas. Entry on *Snows of Kilimanjaro*. Original essay on *Snows of Kilimanjaro*.

Cynthia Bily: Bily teaches writing and literature at Adrian College in Adrian, Michigan, and writes for a variety of educational publishers. Entries on *And Of Clay We Are Created*, *Hands*, *Mrs. Plum*, *My Kinsman, Major Molineaux*, and *Roselily*. Original essays on *And Of Clay We Are Created*, *Battle Royal*, *Hands*, *Mrs. Plum*, *My Kinsman, Major Molineaux*, and *Roselily*.

Liz Brent: Brent has a Ph.D. in American Culture, specializing in film studies, from the University of Michigan. She is a freelance writer and teaches courses in the history of American cinema. Original essays on *And of Clay We Are Created*, *Battle Royal*, *Mrs. Plum*, *Roselily*, and *Say Yes*.

Jennifer Bussey: Bussey holds a master's degree in Interdisciplinary Studies and a bachelor's degree in English literature. She is an independent writer specializing in literature. Original essay on *Silver Water*.

Carol Dell'Amico: Dell'Amico teaches English at Rutgers, the State University of New Jersey, where she is currently working on a dissertation. Entry on *Storyteller*. Original essay on *Storyteller*.

Carole Hamilton: Hamilton is an English teacher at Cary Academy, an innovative private school in Cary, North Carolina. Original essay on *A Good Scent From a Strange Mountain*.

Sarah Madsen Hardy: Madsen Hardy has a doctorate in English literature and is a freelance writer and editor. Entries on *Gilded Six-Bits* and *Women in Their Beds*. Original essays on *Gilded Six-Bits* and *Women in Their Beds*.

Kendall Johnson: Johnson teaches American literature at the University of Pennsylvania where he recently received his Ph.D. Entry on *Battle Royal*. Original essay on *Battle Royal*.

Rena Korb: Korb has a master's degree in English literature and creative writing and has written for a wide variety of educational publishers. Entries on *A Good Scent From a Strange Mountain*, *Marriage á la Mode*, *Say Yes*, *Sheriff's Children*, and *Silver Water*. Original essays on *A Good Scent From A Strange Mountain*, *Marriage á la Mode*, *Mrs. Plum*, *Roselily*, *Say Yes*, *Sheriff's Children*, and *Silver Water*.

Jennifer Lynch: Lynch is a freelance writer living in northern New Mexico. Original essay on *Say Yes*.

Chris Semansky: Semansky publishes widely in the field of twentieth-century culture and literature. Original essays on *A Good Scent From a*

Strange Mountain, *Silver Water*, and *Women in Their Beds*.

Shaun Strohmer: Strohmer has a Ph.D. in English literature and has written widely on English, European, and American literature. Entry on *Grave*. Original essay on *Grave*.

And of Clay Are We Created

Isabel Allende

1989

Unlike many novelists, Isabel Allende did not train as a fiction writer by creating short stories before moving on to novels. Her first three works of fiction were novels, and she did not turn to the short story form until readers of *Eva Luna* asked to see the stories the title character refers to. ''And of Clay Are We Created'' was written specifically for the 1989 collection *The Stories of Eva Luna*.

The story is about a young girl who is trapped in a mudslide, and a reporter, Rolf Carlé, who is sent in his television helicopter to cover her rescue. Unable to maintain his reporter's objectivity, he joins in the unsuccessful rescue attempt, and then stays with the girl until she dies. As he talks with the girl over a period of days, Carlé remembers and begins to address his own youthful suffering, which he has repressed for many years. At a further remove, the girl and the reporter are being watched on television by the narrator, Carlé's lover, who experiences the pain of both.

Allende has often spoken about ''And of Clay Are We Created'' and its importance to her. The characters of the television reporter and his lover are both based on Allende's own experiences in journalism. In an interview with Marilyn Berlin Snell, she explains that the plot of the story is also based on fact: ''This story really occurred. In 1985, we saw her on every television screen in the world, the face of Omaira Sánchez, one of the thousands of victims of Colombia's Nevado Ruiz volcanic eruption. The

black eyes of that girl have haunted me. . . . She is telling me something. She is talking to me about patience, about endurance, about courage." Reviewers of *The Stories of Eva Luna* have praised Allende's ability to adapt historical events into fiction, as she does in "And of Clay Are We Created."

Author Biography

Although she has traveled around the world, and has lived in the United States for more than a decade, Isabel Allende considers Latin America her true home, and sets her fiction there. She was born on August 2, 1942, in Lima, Peru, where her Chilean father held a diplomatic post. After her parents divorced, Allende and her siblings went to live with her mother's parents in Santiago, Chile. She had no contact with her father for the rest of her life, but kept close ties to his family, including his cousin Salvador Allende, who became president of Chile in 1970.

As a child, Allende read eagerly and traveled widely. Her mother remarried, and the family lived in Bolivia, Europe, and the Middle East before returning to Chile when Allende was fifteen. Her life was rather ordinary for the next several years: she went to school, married, had two children, and worked as a journalist on television programs and documentaries, much like her character Eva Luna, the narrator of "And of Clay Are We Created." Years later she credited her journalism experience with helping develop her skills as a storyteller. In 1973, Salvador Allende was murdered and the military took control of Chile's government. For a time, Isabel Allende continued her journalism work and also worked secretly against the new government, but this became too dangerous and she moved to Caracas, Venezuela, in 1975.

Six years later, she received word from Chile that her grandfather was dying and sat down to write him a farewell letter. That letter eventually became her first novel, *La casa de los espíritus* (*The House of the Spirits*), 1982. The novel traces three generations in a Latin American family, focusing on the women, and draws heavily on Allende's own experiences. *The House of the Spirits*, like all of Allende's fiction, was written in Spanish and translated by others into English and other languages. It has sold over six million copies in Europe, Latin America, and the United States, and it has made Allende an international literary star.

Allende's second novel, a story of political killings in Chile, was *De amor y de sombra* (*Of Love and Shadows*), 1984. This was followed in 1987 by *Eva Luna*. Of all Allende's characters, Eva Luna is most like her: a feminist, a journalist, and a storyteller. In fact, the character Eva Luna often refers to stories that she never tells; it was readers' clamoring for those stories that led Allende to try her hand at short fiction and produce the volume *Cuentos de Eva Luna* (*The Stories of Eva Luna*), 1989, which includes "And of Clay Are We Created." She has repeatedly stated since then that she finds short stories much more difficult to write than novels, and her subsequent books have been in the full-length novel or memoir forms.

Plot Summary

The story opens abruptly, with a startling line: "They discovered the girl's head protruding from the mudpit, eyes wide open, calling soundlessly." As soon becomes clear, the girl is thirteen-year-old Azucena, one of thousands of villagers who lived on the slopes of a mountain in Latin America. A volcanic eruption has created enough heat to melt the ice on the mountain slopes, leading in turn to tremendous mudslides that have buried entire towns and killed more than twenty thousand people. The narrator, who is never named, watches pictures of the devastation on the television news, described by her lover, Rolf Carlé, the first television reporter on the scene.

Carlé and his assistant film the first attempts to rescue the girl, but when volunteers are unable to throw a rope to her, he wades up to his waist in the mud to tie the rope under her arms himself. He smiles a charming smile and assures her that she will soon be out. But when the volunteers begin to pull on the rope, Azucena screams in pain; the mud has created such a strong suction around her that she cannot be pulled free. She can feel some kind of debris holding her legs, and while others suggest that it must be the rubble from her crushed house, she insists that it is the bodies of her dead brothers and sisters.

The narrator has watched Carlé countless times as he has covered important stories, and she has always admired his ability to be strong and detached in the face of terrible events. This time, however, she can tell by watching his eyes and hearing his voice that his objectivity is slipping, and that he is responding emotionally to Azucena. The catch in his voice is one she has never heard before. Abandoning his task as a reporter, Carlé tries everything he can think of to get the girl free, but with no success. He manages to get a tire slipped under her shoulders so that she will not slip down any further in the mud. Finally he radios for a pump, with which he could drain the water around the girl, but none will be available until the next day. He stays beside the girl all night, giving her sips of coffee to warm her and telling her entertaining stories of his adventures to keep her calm.

Back in the city, the narrator keeps her watch, moving to the television station so that she can see Carlé's satellite transmissions unedited. She phones all of the important government and business people she can think of to try to locate a pump and makes appeals on radio and television, but to no avail. Watching the screen, she feels Carlé's pain and frustration, and weeps for the girl. She sees that Carlé has reached a kind of tiredness he has never reached before, and that he has "completely forgotten the camera."

Meanwhile, the story has been picked up by other news agencies, and a crowd of reporters and cameras has surrounded Azucena and Carlé, sending pictures of the girl to millions of people around the world. A doctor briefly examines the girl, and a priest blesses her, but no one in the crowd can do anything to help her. Although the area is littered with generators and lights and wires and other technical equipment for the television crews, no one can locate a pump.

As the second day closes, Azucena and Carlé are still together, talking quietly and praying. Carlé has run out of stories of his own, and turns first to the stories the narrator has told him, and then to Austrian folk songs he learned as a child. While he continues to talk to the girl, he remembers scenes from his youth that he has repressed for decades: burying bodies at a concentration camp, his father's abuse, his retarded sister's fear, his mother's humiliation. He does not share these memories with the girl, but turns them over in his mind and examines them as he has never done before. He realizes that like Azucena he is trapped, and that his brave adventures have been a way to escape his fear. His experience with the girl has exposed him to feelings he has pushed aside, and he is closer to her emotionally than he has ever been to anyone else.

On the morning of the third day, Azucena and Carlé are both cold, hungry, and exhausted. The

Isabel Allende

president of the Republic comes to be filmed with the girl. He praises the girl for being "an example to the nation" and promises to personally send a pump. But it is too late. As she watches on the screen, the narrator can tell the precise moment when the girl and the reporter give up hoping for a rescue, the moment that they accept the inevitability of death. For both, it is a moment of peace; they stop struggling. The narrator has managed to locate a pump and arranged a way to ship it, but on the third night the girl dies. Carlé takes the tire away from under her arms, and she slips down under the mud.

The last scene of the story occurs after Carlé has returned home. For some time he has not worked, but he has watched the film of himself and Azucena countless times, wondering what he might have done to help her. The narrator addresses him directly, assuring him that the wounds opened by his experience with the girl will heal in time.

Characters

Azucena

Azucena, whose name translated into English would be "Lily," is a girl who has been buried up to

Media Adaptations

- *The Stories of Eva Luna*, the collection from which "And of Clay Are We Created" is taken, was recorded in 1991 by Elizabeth Peña. The two-cassette set was produced by Dove Audio Books and is distributed by NewStar Media.

---

her neck in a mudslide. The rest of her village has been destroyed, and she says that the bodies of her dead brothers and sisters are holding her legs. As the story opens, the girl has just been found, and a rescue effort is underway. She has also been discovered by the national news media, and soon a crowd of television reporters comes to interview her on camera. While her story is broadcast around the world, she quietly talks with Rolf Carlé, the first reporter on the scene, about her life. Although she is thirteen years old, she has never traveled outside her small Latin American village, and she has never known love. She does not understand that she is being featured on international television, nor does she understand why the president of the Republic himself comes to call her "an example to the nation." After three days and nights trapped in the cold mud, she dies, and sinks away beneath the surface of the clay.

Rolf Carlé

Rolf Carlé is a middle-aged television reporter, the first reporter to reach Azucena's side. He has gone to her to cover the dramatic story of her rescue, but, for the first time in his career, he is unable to maintain his professional objectivity. He joins and then leads the attempts to rescue the girl; he stays beside her for three days and nights to keep her calm. As the reporter and the girl talk, Carlé begins to remember long-repressed memories: folk songs from his native Austria, his abusive father, and how he and his retarded sister lived their lives in fear. Just as he realizes that he is trapped in his pain just as Azucena is trapped in the mud, he also realizes that the girl will not be rescued. Before she dies, he tells her how important she has been to him. As the story ends he is grieving for Azucena and for his own wasted youth. But confronting the girl's death has shown him how to confront his pain and his healing has begun.

Female Narrator

The narrator (also known as Eva Luna) is Rolf Carlé's longtime lover, a woman who has many times said goodbye to him as he has gone off to cover important stories. Though she is never named in this story, readers of the entire collection from which the story is taken know that she is Eva Luna, a maker of television documentaries. As she watches Carlé on television, she can tell that the girl has touched him in a new way. She can read every emotion in his face and begins to feel what he feels. For three days she watches every bit of coverage she can, stopping only to make phone calls, trying to locate a pump to help with the rescue. She believes that she and Carlé can communicate through the screen. She knows when he begins to confront his past, and to tell the child things he has never told her or anyone else. She knows when he and the girl finally accept the reality of death. And, as she reveals in the last paragraph of the story, the only one addressed to Carlé, she knows that when he has recovered from the painful experience, he will be stronger than ever before.

Lily

See Azucena.

Eva Luna

See Female Narrator.

Themes

Memory and Reminiscence

For Rolf Carlé, the most important thing that happens during his days with Azucena is his confrontation with his long-buried memories. For years he has refused to think about the horrors of his own past: having to bury concentration camp prisoners, and living with an abusive father who sometimes locked young Rolf in a cabinet. Throughout his professional life as a journalist, he has taken extraordinary risks, choosing to cover wars and natural disasters and placing himself in danger. Talking with Azucena, he comes to realize that these risks have been attempts to build up his courage so that one day he might face his memories and his fears.

Topics for Further Study

- Find newspaper stories about the 1985 volcanic eruption of Colombia's Nevado Ruiz Mountain, the September 1999 earthquake in Taiwan, or another large-scale natural disaster. Look especially for stories about individual children trapped and rescued. Do you think the reporters writing these stories respect their subjects or exploit them? How emotionally involved do these reporters allow themselves to become?

- What can cause mudslides of the magnitude described in this story? Research the geography and the geology to find an explanation. What parts of the United States and Canada are subject to this danger?

- Most students know about the concentration camps run by the Germans during World War II, but fewer know much about Russian camps. Investigate these Russian camps. Who was held in them? What were conditions like? What happened to Russia during and after the war?

- Investigate the Roman Catholic Church and its teachings about humans being made from clay and returning to the clay after death—teachings that Azucena would have been exposed to. Find out about other cultures—there are many—that also have stories about the first human being created from clay.

The process of remembering is a painful one, bringing this brave, rugged man to tears. Azucena thinks he is crying because of her suffering, but he tells her, "I'm crying for myself. I hurt all over." The pain continues long after the girl's death. When Carlé returns home, he has no interest in working, or writing, or singing. He distances himself from everything he loves, including the narrator, and spends hours staring at the mountains and remembering. The narrator understands the process. She knows it will take time "for the old wounds to heal," but knows also that when the process is complete Carlé will return to her.

Individual versus Nature

The theme of people battling with nature runs through "And of Clay Are We Created." Time and again, humans set their smartest minds and their most advanced technologies against the indifferent forces of nature and each time humans are defeated. The story is set into motion by the tremendous eruption of the volcano. Using scientific instruments called seismographs, geologists have been able to predict that the mountain is about to erupt, but their technology can only take them so far. They cannot stop the eruption, they cannot say precisely when the eruption will occur, and they cannot convince the inhabitants of the mountain slope to believe their warnings. In spite of ever more sophisticated technology, the forces of nature are far more powerful than the forces of humans.

Allende makes the point clearer when Azucena is trapped. In spite of all the technology at their disposal, a large crowd of people cannot get one small girl free from the grasp of the mud. The news media can assemble an impressive collection of "spools of cable, tapes, film, videos, precision lenses, recorders, sound consoles, lights, reflecting screens, auxiliary motors, cartons of supplies, electricians, sound technicians, and cameramen," but they cannot deliver and operate one pump to get the girl out. The narrator phones every important person she can think of, and makes appeals on radio and television, but even her superior communications network produces no results. And while millions of people around the world are watching the girl's struggle on television, they are all helpless against nature.

Cycle of Life

From the beginning, Rolf Carlé is determined to rescue the girl, to "snatch her from death." But although she is trapped and can barely breathe, the girl does not struggle and does not seem desperate. She seems to know that she will die and to accept her fate. Some of her attitude may come from her Roman Catholic faith, which teaches that life and death are both gifts of God. Faith does not seem important to Carlé, who never mentions God or religion in his long talks with the girl, and he believes that he can defeat death.

Eventually, the adult man learns from and is consoled by the young girl. She teaches him to pray, and gradually he comes to accept her fate. When he leans over to kiss her goodbye, both are saved from despair, and they are figuratively "saved from the clay," or from the bounds of life and the earth. A few hours later, Azucena dies, and her body literally sinks back into the clay. Through the story, she has been in the clay, above it, and below it. The title's statement that "of clay are we created" holds out a promise that new life will be created from the same clay that took Azucena, and that the girl's slipping into the clay is part of the cycle of life.

Style

Point of View and Narration

Point of view is handled in an unusual way in "And of Clay Are We Created." The narrator tells most of the story in the first person, and yet most readers would say that she operates only on the edges of the action—she is an observer more than she is an actor. While it is common for a narrator to relate events she has witnessed, rather than participated in, it is unusual to have a narrator who reports what she has seen on television. On the one hand, the narrator shares with millions of others the experience of watching Azucena and Rolf Carlé on television; on the other hand, she has intimate knowledge of Carlé and access to unedited transmissions, and these set her apart from the other viewers. The television screen brings her closer to the reporter and the girl, and yet she is separated from them by hundreds of miles.

The final section of the story is told by the same narrator, but she speaks directly to Carlé, using the second person point of view. Again, the point of view is unusual. The narrator is telling Carlé things about himself that he surely already knows, recounting for him his recent actions and inactions, and there is no indication that he responds. Like the first-person point of view in the rest of the story, the point of view here creates an atmosphere that is at once intimate and distant. The narrator is physically close to Carlé now, but more distant emotionally than when she was watching him on television.

For Allende herself, point of view is one of the most important elements of "And of Clay We Are Created." In an interview with Farhat Iftekharuddin, she explains that when she first tried to write the story she told it from "an intellectual point of view" and focused on the girl Azucena. She eventually came to feel that this point of view was not presenting the proper story, and that her focus should be not on the girl but on Carlé. She wrote another draft of the story from the reporter's point of view, but found this unsatisfactory as well. Finally, she discovered that her focus should be on "the story of the woman who is watching through a screen the man who holds the girl," and she rewrote the story yet again, this time using the point of view of the unnamed female narrator.

Epilogue

An epilogue is a concluding section to a literary work, one that adds to the main composition and rounds it off. It would be possible to think of "And of Clay Are We Created" as complete as soon as Azucena sinks "slowly, a flower in the mud." If the story were concerned mainly with the girl or with the reporter, this would be a satisfying ending. But because Allende is concerned primarily with the development of the narrator throughout the story, she offers the final section, or epilogue, to bring the narrator back to center stage. The epilogue is set apart and dramatically different from the rest of the story: the time, the place, and even the point of view shift abruptly between the main story and the epilogue.

Dramatic Irony

As it is usually understood, dramatic irony is the contrast between what the characters in a story understand and the deeper understanding of the story's readers. Several instances of dramatic irony shape "And of Clay Are We Created." For example, it is ironic that a group of people who can assemble a tremendous collection of technical gear to show a trapped Azucena to the world cannot find a pump and get her out. With the exception of Rolf Carlé, the media people themselves do not see the irony; there is no hint that they find the situation remarkable or frustrating. The reader, guided by the narrator who repeatedly mentions the pump and describes the maze of cables and machines, sees the absurdity that the characters themselves do not see.

Another example of dramatic irony, which may or may not be seen by the narrator, is the fact that the narrator is closer emotionally to Carlé while she is watching him on television than she is when they are reunited. The effect of dramatic irony in this story is that the reader finds lessons in the story that the characters themselves do not see.

Historical Context

Latin America in the 1980s

Although the volcanic eruption on which "And of Clay Are We Created" is based occurred in Colombia in 1985, Allende does not specify the date and location in which the story is set. Like the rest of the collection *The Stories of Eva Luna*, the story is understood to take place somewhere in Latin America, sometime during the 1980s. The 1980s were a turbulent time for Latin America, the region encompassing approximately twenty nations in South America, Central America, Mexico, and the Caribbean where Romance languages are spoken.

Politically, Latin America was a region of great instability during this period. Many countries, including Argentina, Haiti, Panama, El Salvador, Grenada, and Guatemala, were under the control of repressive military dictators. In Colombia, armed guerillas challenged the government, which they accused of corruption, and were killed by the hundreds. Chile, Allende's native country, was ruled from 1973 until 1989 by General Augusto Pinochet, chief executive of the country and head of the armed forces. Pinochet held onto his power by torturing, killing, or banishing thousands of Chileans who opposed him. Books and magazines that were considered unfavorable to the government were banned or burned, and their authors were punished.

The effects of this political turmoil have been significant for writers and for Latin-American literature. Allende learned about the Colombian disaster the same way Eva Luna learned about Azucena—by watching the television news. Allende was living in California at the time, having been forced into exile shortly after Pinochet took control of the country by murdering Allende's uncle, Chilean President Salvador Allende. Her greatest novel, *The House of the Spirits*, is in part about the political situation in Chile, yet she wrote it while living in Venezuela. Similarly, other great Latin-American writers have produced important work while in exile. Nobel Prize-winning author Gabriel García Márquez wrote about Colombia while living in Mexico. Mario Vargas Llósa wrote about Peru from exile in Paris. Other writers have shared their fate, writing about homelands in struggle and homelands they could not return to.

The Boom and After

The period roughly covering the 1960s and the first part of the 1970s is often referred to as "The Boom" in Latin-American literature. Previously, Latin-American writing, particularly novels, resembled the European works on which they were patterned. During the Boom, writers including Carlos Fuentes, Gabriel García Márquez, Julio Cortazar, and Mario Vargas Llósa experimented with new dramatic forms specifically intended to reflect a Latin-American consciousness. García Márquez in particular became known for "magical realism," a combination of realism and fantasy through which fantastical events are narrated in calm, expressionless prose, as though the narrator had no idea that anything unexpected was occurring. Boom writers were overtly political, reflecting the shifting perceptions and instability of Latin American political and social life, and they were predominantly male.

Allende's early fiction is sometimes compared with the magical realism of García Márquez, but *The Stories of Eva Luna* reflects the writing of the post-Boom generation. The writers of this period include many women, and their writing is less political. The new works also tend to be less dense than works from the Boom, intentionally more accessible to the general reader rather than only the intellectual elite. They feature characters from a wide spectrum of social classes, and frequently focus on themes of love and relationships, and on issues facing women.

Critical Overview

Criticism about Allende's works has focused on the novels, especially on *The House of the Spirits*, her first novel, usually considered to be her best. Although most critics admired the magical realism and the passion of *The House of the Spirits* and found a new authentic voice in Allende's writing, some complained that the novel was an inferior imitation of the work of Gabriel García Márquez, the Colombian winner of the 1982 Nobel Prize for literature. The debate over García Márquez's influence and Allende's talent continued through the

Compare & Contrast

- **1985:** The eruption of the Nevado del Ruiz volcano in central Colombia kills more than 22,000 people and destroys more than 5,000 buildings. A large area is covered in mud and ash, making rescue of survivors nearly impossible.

    1990s: Colombia continues to be subject to volcanic eruptions and earthquakes, but none causes devastation equal to the Nevado del Ruiz eruption.

- **1980s:** There is a large gap between the poorest citizens of many Latin-American countries and the wealthiest citizens. Many of the wealthiest citizens are educated Europeans like Rolf Carlé, while the poorest tend to be of native or African descent.

    1990s: As in the United States, the gap between rich and poor continues to widen in Latin America. Colombia and other countries experience significant economic growth, but the pattern of income distribution means that poverty actually increases.

- **1980s:** The average per capita income in Colombia is nearly $1000, among the highest of the Latin-American countries.

    1990s: The average per capita income in Colombia is $1,650. The per capita income in the United States is over $22,000.

- **1980s:** In Colombia, over ninety percent of the citizens are Roman Catholic, a religion established there by European conquerors in the 1500s. Nearly ninety percent of Chileans are Roman Catholic. The numbers are similar for other Latin-American countries.

    1990s: Approximately ninety-five percent of Colombians are Roman Catholic, and ninety percent of all Latin Americans are Roman Catholic. Latin Americans who practice indigenous religions increasingly organize and work for official recognition.

- **1980s:** Many South American nations have autocratic governments led by military regimes and military dictators.

    1990s: The South American countries are led by democratically elected presidents. Chile's General Augusto Pinochet, forced out in 1989, is the last of the South American military dictators.

---

discussion of her next two novels, *Of Love and Shadows* and *Eva Luna*.

Another issue for critics has been Allende's feminism. She has been heralded for her strong feminine voice, but criticized for turning her male characters into stereotypes of traditional machismo and for creating women characters who desire dangerous or otherwise inappropriate men. The third major issue for Allende critics has been her status as a Latin-American writer, the label she prefers for herself. Although there is no formal criticism of "And of Clay Are We Created" other than mentions in reviews of *The Stories of Eva Luna*, these critical issues all surface repeatedly.

The foremost American critic of Allende's work is Patricia Hart, author of *Narrative Magic in the Fiction of Isabel Allende* (1989). In a review of the short stories, which she deems less successful than the novels, Hart finds three key elements: "lush, hyperbolic reality, a female sensibility and some none-too-subtle parodying of male stars of the Boom." Hart insists that Allende does not imitate Boom writers, but mocks them, turning their style to her own purposes. On the other hand, Suzanne Ruta's review reveals genuine irritation with Allende's echoes of the Boom, stating, "It's Allende's glib, sentimental treatment . . . and her cutesy allusions to other writers' inventions, that I dislike."

Critics have also divided over how well Allende handles the short story form. Louise Bernikow praises Allende's unique voice, drawing special attention to the stories' sense of place and visual imagery. In Bernikow's judgment, Allende "has only gotten better from one book to the next." Eleanor Bader finds the collection "touching, provocative, and entertaining," and the character of Carlé "memorable and captivating." Other reviewers were disappointed by *The Stories of Eva Luna*, feeling the short stories were too often melodramatic. Some observe that the short form did not give Allende room to create the rich characters and complex plots for which she had drawn praise. Dan Cryer describes the stories in the collection as "entertaining as long as you don't think much about them," and finds the plotting "energetic but given to soap opera."

Allende herself has admitted that she finds writing short stories much more difficult than writing novels, and less conducive to the "embroidery" she uses to steer and embellish her writing. Interviewed by Farhat Iftekharuddin she commented, "I would much rather write a thousand pages of a long novel than a short story. The shorter, the more difficult it is."

Although he judges the short stories as "some of [Allende's] finest work," Daniel Harris questions the author's political stance and her authenticity as a Latin-American writer. He describes her as "a gifted opportunist" who "shamelessly sentimentalizes the droll aborigines of primitive society," and "ransacks South America as if it were an insipid cache of folksiness." The risk in this stance, he explains, is that the horrors and atrocities described in the stories become mere clichés.

Although critics have not always been kind to Allende, the reading public has embraced her work enthusiastically. *The House of the Spirits*, originally written in Spanish as is all of Allende's work, has been translated into dozens of languages. It has sold over six million copies around the world, and been made into a film starring Meryl Streep and Jeremy Irons. Her subsequent books have also sold well, making her the most well-known and widely read female Latin-American writer in history.

Criticism

Cynthia Bily

Bily teaches writing and literature at Adrian College in Adrian, Michigan, and writes for a variety of educational publishers. In the following essay, she looks at the development of the narrator in "And of Clay Are We Created."

Isabel Allende's "And of Clay Are We Created" is the last story in her only collection of short stories, *The Stories of Eva Luna*. All of the twenty-three stories in the collection are narrated by Eva Luna, who was also the title character of Allende's third novel. Luna tells the stories while in bed with her lover, Rolf Carlé, drawing her inspiration from Scheherazade, who in the *Arabian Nights* saves her sister's life and her own by telling stories for a thousand and one nights. Readers who come to "And of Clay Are We Created" having already read *Eva Luna* and the rest of the short stories will understand all of this before they begin. They will be familiar with the characters Luna and Carlé and the relationship between them, and they will know the value Luna places on stories and storytelling.

For readers who encounter the story away from the context of the collection, however, the reading experience is a very different one. These readers do not know the name of the narrator, or that she is a writer of television dramas, or that she is a person to whom Carlé said, "You think in words; for you, language is an inexhaustible thread you weave as if life were created as you tell it." For these readers, it would be easy to ignore the narrator and to focus instead on the dramatic story of Azucena, the girl trapped in the mud, and the television reporter Rolf Carlé who tries to rescue her. The narrator's narration, certainly, focuses on Carlé and the changes he undergoes through his experience with the girl. Any mentions by the narrator of her own reactions and emotions are intended to help her audience understand her lover's ordeal.

Allende, however, has spoken frequently about her intentions for the story. For her, the story is about "the woman who is watching through a screen the man who holds the girl. This filter of the screen creates an artificial filter and terrible distance but also a terrible proximity because you see details that you would not see if you were actually there. And so, the story is about the change in the woman who watches the man holding the girl who is dying." If this is true (and we must give Allende credit for insight into her own work), what *is* the change in the narrator throughout "And of Clay Are We Created," as it can be observed by a reader of this story alone? If the story is meant to demonstrate what happens to a woman watching her lover from afar, what does it ultimately reveal?

What Do I Read Next?

- *The Stories of Eva Luna* (1991) is Allende's first collection of short fiction. Like Scheherazade, Eva Luna presents twenty-three interwoven stories to her lover Rolf Carlé, the male protagonist of "And of Clay Are We Created."

- *The House of the Spirits* (1985) is Allende's first novel. Three generations of a Latin-American family find strength through political and emotional struggle.

- *Leaf Storm and Other Stories* (1972) is by Gabriel García Márquez. In seven interwoven stories, wonderful and impossible things happen to the citizens of the Latin-American village of Macondo. García Márquez, a master of "magical realism," is the author with whom Allende is most frequently compared.

- *A Hammock Beneath the Mangoes: Stories from Latin America* (1992), edited by Thomas Colchie, is a collection of stories by twenty-six Latin-American authors, organized by country. Includes work by Allende, García Márquez, and Jorge Luis Borges, and also by newer and less well-known writers.

When Carlé leaves to cover the story, neither he nor the narrator understands what is to come. The narrator reports that she "had no presentiments." Carlé has often been the first on the scene, and has covered dramatic and dangerous stories before "with awesome tenacity." The narrator has watched him on television many times, and admired the way nothing seems to touch him or frighten him. She has learned over the years that his reporter's objectivity is really a protective mechanism that shields him from his own emotions. Knowing how unemotional he tries to hold himself, the narrator reacts strongly to the sound of his resolve slipping when he promises Azucena he will get her out: "I could hear his voice break, and I loved him more than ever."

Until Carlé's objectivity starts to give way, the narrator feels herself to be a part of the large audience watching him. Twice she refers to herself as part of the "we" who see Carlé and the girl on the screen. But after he begins to change his stance, her own changes as well. Now she moves from her home to the television studio, to be "near his world," and she refers to herself as his partner instead of as his audience. She has overheard his plea for a pump, and goes on radio and television "to see if there wasn't *someone* who could help us." Now the "us" she belongs to is Carlé and herself.

Ironically, the television screen both emphasizes the distance between the two and brings them closer together—at least, it brings the narrator close to Carlé, who is not thinking of her. It is a one-way closeness. Though the reporter surely knows that his lover will be watching on television for any sign he might send her, he has "completely forgotten the camera." Yet she feels the child's pain, and Carlé's frustration, and believes that she is "there with him." She tries the "frenzied and futile" gesture of sending him encouragement through mental telepathy. By the end of the first morning, she is reduced to tears and emotionally drained. On the second day the sensation is stronger: "I had the horrible sensation that Azucena and Rolf were by my side, separated from me by impenetrable glass." She can see them, but they cannot see her. She feels what they feel, but they are unaware of her.

On the morning of the third day, the narrator can see that "something fundamental" has changed in Carlé. "The girl has touched a part of him that he himself had no access to, a part he had never shared with me." The generous and loving part of the narrator is glad to see this change, but one wonders whether there is some jealousy when Carlé assures the girl that he loves her "more than all the women who had slept in his arms, more than he loved me, his life companion." There is more than compassion in the narrator's heart when she says that she "would have given anything to be trapped in that well in her place."

Although there is hardly enough evidence in this brief story to lead to an informed opinion about two human hearts, the relationship between the narrator and Rolf Carlé (she nearly always refers to him by his first and last name) seems unbalanced, as though the woman has no other purpose in her life other than to make things easier for the man—as though she is always watching him through a screen while he is unaware of her. When he is called away before dawn to cover the story of the mudslide, the narrator gets up to fix coffee while he packs, and they say goodbye as they always do. Once he is gone, she seems to be lost, a woman with nothing else to do even for one day: "I sat in the kitchen, sipping my coffee and planning the long hours without him, sure that he would be back the next day."

Of course, he is not back the next day, nor the day after that. The narrator, with no children to attend to, or friends to worry with, spends the time at the National Television studio because she cannot "bear the wait at home." She has "often spent entire nights" with her lover there, helping him with his work. At the end of the story, when Carlé has returned to her, she seems to have no responsibilities or desires other than to accompany him to the station to watch the videos again and again, and to stay beside him waiting as he sits "long hours before the window, staring at the mountains."

Carlé has passed through hell and back and is, the narrator believes, in the process of becoming more open and mature emotionally. The narrator sees this, telling him, "You are back with me, but you are not the same man." Are there ways in which the narrator is not the same woman as she was before? The changes are, at best, subtle, hard to see. Although clearly she has experienced a range of strong emotions throughout the ordeal, she does not seem to have taken much away from her experience of seeing her relationship reflected in the glass of the television screen. If Carlé has expanded his own vision of how he might live his life, the narrator seems to be satisfied with the status quo. Her wish in the final line is the rather bleak hope that "we shall again walk hand in hand, *as before*" (italics mine).

Critic Suzanne Ruta, commenting on the full collection of *The Stories of Eva Luna*, explains that through the telling of her stories to Carlé, Luna is "trying to help him break free of the cool, distant

> For her, the story is about 'the woman who is watching through a screen the man who holds the girl. This filter of the screen creates an artificial filter and terrible distance but also a terrible proximity because you see details that you would not see if you were actually there. And so, the story is about the change in the woman who watches the man holding the girl who is dying."

persona he's made for himself." The framework of "a troubled man and his helpful lover" gives structure to the collection, and leads naturally to "And of Clay Are We Created," in which "Scheherazade falls silent, acknowledging the limits of her power." For readers of this one story alone, there is no hint that the narrator's stories are intended to help Carlé, or that she feels herself to have a strength he does not have. Rather than presenting a woman who under extraordinary circumstances reaches the limits of her power, the story seems to present a woman with no power of her own.

Source: Cynthia Bily, in an essay for *Short Stories for Students*, Gale Group, 2001.

Liz Brent

Brent has a Ph.D. in American Culture, specializing in film studies, from the University of Michigan. She is a freelance writer and teaches courses in the history of American cinema. In the following essay, Brent discusses narration, point-of-view, and the theme of intimacy and distance, in Allende's story.

The short story "And of Clay Are We Created" by Isabel Allende is written from the perspective of a

Rescue workers remove victims of a Colombian mudslide. The plot of 'And of Clay Are We Created' revolves around the failed rescue of a young girl from the 1985 mudslide resulting from Colombia's Nevado Ruiz volcanic eruption.

woman whose "life companion," Rolf Carlé, a TV news journalist, has been sent on an assignment to a South American country to cover a catastrophic avalanche which has just taken place. The story is told from the *first-person point of view* of the narrator, as she learns only from television news coverage of Rolf Carlé's experiences at the site of the catastrophe. While there, he comes to the aid of a thirteen-year-old girl, Azucena, whose body is trapped up to her neck in mud. Rolf Carlé quickly drops his journalistic duties to attempt to rescue and to console the girl over a period of three days, until she dies, still trapped in the mud. In the process, the tragic situation of Azucena, and the compassion of the reporter who stays by her side, becomes an international media event. The narrator is thus able to learn of her lover's experience only through television broadcasts of the event. In the following essay, I discuss the relationship between the narrator and her far-away companion, Rolf Carlé, as experienced from her limited perspective on his life-changing experience, which occurs thousands of miles away from her.

"And of Clay Are We Created" is published in Allende's collection entitled *The Stories of Eva Luna*. Although it is a book of short stories, each one is based on the fictional character of Eva Luna, who appeared in Allende's novel *Eva Luna*. Thus, although the narrator of this short story is not named, the collection as a whole indicates that she is Eva Luna. A "Prologue" to the collection is written by the fictional character Rolf Carlé, Eva Luna's lover and "life companion." This "Prologue" is written from the *second-person point of view*, meaning that the narrator, Rolf Carlé, addresses his narrative to "you"—in this case, Eva Luna. Rolf Carlé describes a scene of passionate lovemaking between himself and Eva Luna. He represents the experience as one of intense emotional closeness that also allows for the experience of temporary emotional distance. He says that "We were too close to see one another, each absorbed in our urgent rite, enveloped in our shared warmth and scent." The idea that the lovers are "too close to see one another," implies that such intense intimacy involves a loss of perspective. He goes on to describe the experience of their lovemaking as one in which the lovers are so close that they experience solitude and distance from one another, which leads them back into a state of physical and emotional intimacy: "In the final instant we glimpsed absolute solitude, each lost in a blazing chasm, but soon we returned from the far side of that fire to find ourselves embraced amid a riot of pillows beneath white mosquito netting." This description portrays a relationship in which moments of emotional distance—"each lost in a blazing chasm"—are an integral element of the experience of emotional intimacy—"too close to see one another." He goes on to compare his experience of their relationship to that of a spectator looking at a photograph or painting of two lovers. He says that, "From an indefinite distance I am looking at the picture, which includes me." This continues the theme that their relationship is one characterized by both intimacy and distance, the distance reinforcing the experience of intimacy, and the intimacy allowing each the freedom to embark on their own solitary emotional "voyage." He continues that "I am spectator and protagonist"; As "protagonist" he experiences the painting, or the relationship, intimately, while as "spectator," he experiences the painting or relationship with a certain degree of distance. He goes on to describe the experience as one in which he simultaneously feels bonded with his lover, and alone, both close and distant: "I am there with you but also here, alone, in a different frame of consciousness."

The theme of a relationship built on the simultaneous experience of intimacy and distance, union and solitude, at the emotional, psychological, and physical level, as put forth in the "Prologue," sheds light on a parallel theme in the final short story of the collection, "And of Clay Are We Created." Throughout the story, the narrator, Eva Luna, bridges the temporary physical distance between herself and Rolf Carlé through drawing on the ongoing emotional and psychological bond between the two of them.

The narrator describes her experience of Rolf Carlé's preparations for leaving on the assignment in terms which indicate that the two routinely experience brief geographical separations throughout a relationship, which is otherwise characterized by togetherness. She explains that "When the station called before dawn, Rolf Carlé and I were together." Once he has prepared to leave, "we said goodbye, as we had so many times before." She is both used to these routine and brief separations, and used to his subsequent returns; after he leaves for the assignment, she "sat in the kitchen, sipping my coffee and planning the long hours without him, sure that he would be back the next day."

"Throughout the story, the narrator, Eva Luna, bridges the temporary physical distance between herself and Rolf Carle through drawing on the ongoing emotional and psychological bond between the two of them."

A *third-person*, objective, journalistic, sometimes scientific, point-of-view is utilized by the narrator in reporting the factual events surrounding the avalanche. This creates a feeling of great distance between the narrator and the faraway catastrophe, as if reading of it in the newspaper: "Geologists had set up their seismographs weeks before and knew that the mountain had awakened again. For some time they had predicted that the heat of the eruption could detach the eternal ice from the slopes of the volcano, but no one heeded their warnings. . . . The towns in the valley went about their daily life, deaf to the moaning of the earth, until that fateful Wednesday night in November when a prolonged roar announced the end of the world, and walls of snow broke loose, rolling in an avalanche of clay, stones, and water that descended on the villages and buried them beneath unfathomable meters of telluric vomit." She goes on to report that the assessment of the "magnitude of the cataclysm" included the calculation that "beneath the mud lay more than twenty thousand human beings and an indefinite number of animals," dead and decaying. Furthermore, "Forests and rivers had also been swept away, and there was nothing to be seen but an immense desert of mire."

Because all of the information the narrator receives about her lover's experience is gained through watching national television broadcasts of the disaster, she describes much of her experience of this reportage in the first person plural. Thus, although she is observing the experience of someone with whom she is personally intimate, she aligns her own perspective with that of the mass audience of TV news spectators, describing the experience as that of a collective "we." She explains that "We watched on our screens the footage captured by his assistant's camera, in which he was up to his knees in muck, a microphone in his hand, in the midst of a bedlam of lost children, wounded survivors, corpses, and devastation. The story came to us in his calm voice." However, even while watching him on TV, the narrator experiences the national broadcasts from the perspective of her intimate knowledge of Rolf Carlé: "He smiled at [the girl trapped in the mud] with that smile that crinkles his eyes and makes him look like a little boy." Even via poor television transmission, broadcast from thousands of miles away, the narrator notices intimate details of Rolf Carlé's emotional state, and experiences increased love and intimacy with him: "'Don't worry, we'll get you out of here,' Rolf promised. Despite the quality of the transmission, I could hear his voice break, and I loved him more than ever."

Eva Luna also describes Rolf Carlé's thoughts during his three days spent by the side of the little girl. The narrator could only have obtained this information from Rolf Carlé himself, having told her about his own experience of the event, once he had returned home: "Rolf Carlé, buoyed by a premature optimism, was convinced that everything would end well . . . Azucena would be transported by helicopter to a hospital where she would recover rapidly and where he could visit her and bring her gifts. He thought, She's already too old for dolls, and I don't know what would please her; maybe a dress. I don't know much about women, he concluded, amused, reflecting that although he had known many women in his lifetime, none had taught him these details."

Eva Luna experiences her relationship with Rolf Carlé as both geographically distant, and emotionally intimate. Her only contact with her lover is via the impersonal and public avenue of the television broadcast: "Many miles away, I watched Rolf Carlé and the girl on a television screen." However, even at this level of remove, she gets as close to him as possible by watching him on the TV screen from the station where he works: "I could not bear to wait at home, so I went to National Television, where I often spent entire nights with Rolf editing programs." This allows her to more intimately experience his feelings, although she has no direct contact with him: "There, I was near his world, and I could at least get a feeling of what he lived through during those three decisive days." Although her only contact with him is via the TV screen, she is able to bridge the geographical distance between them through their ongoing emotional intimacy with one another, and live through his experience at this emotional level: "The screen reduced the disaster to a single plane and accentuated the tremendous distance that separated me from Rolf Carlé; nonetheless, I was there with him. The child's every suffering hurt me as it did him; I felt his frustration, his impotence." She attempts to further bridge the distance between herself and her lover via some form of mental telepathy: "Faced with the impossibility of communicating with him, the fantastic idea came to me that if I tried, I could reach him by force of mind and in that way give him encouragement. I concentrated until I was dizzy—a frenzied and futile activity." She is able to maintain her emotional empathy for Rolf Carlé's experience, to the degree that she "would be overcome with compassion and burst out crying." Yet she cannot completely overcome the tremendous distance which remains between what Rolf Carlé is experiencing at the site of the disaster and what she experiences from watching it on TV thousands of miles away: "at other times, I was so drained I felt as if I were staring through a telescope at the light of a star dead for a million years." At this point, she experiences the distance at an exaggerated level: he seems to her to be not just on another continent, but on another star far out in the universe. This exaggeration causes her to feel removed from him by time, as well as by distance, looking at "the light of a star dead for a million years." These exaggerated feelings include the image of her lover, like the star, as long dead, and therefore much less accessible to her. Nonetheless, "even from that enormous distance," she can "sense" his private emotional state based on what she sees via national TV broadcast: "Rolf Carlé had a growth of beard, and dark circles beneath his eyes; he looked near exhaustion. Even from that enormous distance I could sense the quality of his weariness, so different from the fatigue of other adventures."

When equipment is brought in to produce "sharper pictures and clearer sound" on the television broadcasts, Eva Luna is brought into that much more intimate contact with her lover's experience: "the distance seemed suddenly compressed." Yet, while brought that much closer to the event via TV broadcast, she maintains the feeling of "impenetrable" separation from Rolf Carlé: "I had the horrible sensation that Azucena and Rolf were by my side, separated from me by impenetrable glass." With this increased quality in the broadcasting, she is at least able to experience more fully Rolf Carlé's actions throughout the incident: "I was able to follow events hour by hour; I knew everything my love did to wrest the girl from her prison and help her endure her suffering." Hearing only "fragments" of his conversation with the girl, Eva Luna knows him well enough to "guess the rest" of what he has said to her.

Try as he might, Rolf Carlé is unable to rescue the girl from the mud, and in the end can only console her. Eva Luna's emotional connection to him is so strong that, just based on what she sees him doing via TV broadcast, she intuits an almost magical knowledge of the consequences of this experience for Rolf Carlé's emotional life: "I, glued to the screen like a fortune-teller to her crystal ball, could tell that something fundamental had changed in him. I knew somehow that during the night his defenses had crumbled and he had given in to grief; finally he was vulnerable. The girl had touched a part of him that he himself had no access to, a part he had never shared with me. Rolf had wanted to console her, but it was Azucena who had given him consolation." From this great geographical distance, Eva Luna "recognized the precise moment at which Rolf gave up the fight and surrendered to the torture of watching the girl die." In spite of the distance, Eva Luna experiences herself as having bridged the gap between herself and her lover, feeling herself to be fully experiencing what he and the girl are experiencing together. She says "I was with them, three days and two nights, spying on them from the other side of life."

However, when Rolf Carlé returns home from this life-changing experience, the geographical distance between the two lovers is finally bridged, but an emotional distance has developed. Eva Luna, addressing Rolf Carlé directly through second-person narrative address, tells him, "You are back with me, but you are not the same man." The experience has caused him to emotionally withdraw from his lover, embarking on a "voyage" deep within himself. Eva Luna remains physically close to him, "beside you," waiting for his emotional "return" to their former intimacy, "walking hand in hand." In the final words of the story, she tells him, "Beside you, I wait for you to complete the voyage into yourself, for the old wounds to heal. I know that when you return from your nightmares, we shall again walk hand in hand, as before." As in the "Prologue," the second-person narrative address to "you" reaffirms the long-term intimacy between the two lovers, despite this temporary emotional distance.

"And of Clay Are We Created" is characterized by a shifting narrative point-of-view and address, which captures the experience of simultaneous intimacy and distance experienced throughout the relationship of the two lovers. The "Prologue" to the story collection describes a pair of lovers who are so physically and emotionally intimate that their lovemaking allows them the freedom to "glimpse absolute solitude, each lost in a blazing chasm," and yet "soon return to the far side of that fire," and find themselves in an intimate lovers' embrace. The use of second-person address in the prologue—Rolf Carlé addressing his lover directly as "you"—increases the feeling of intimacy between them, as if inviting the reader into the fold of their relationship. The narration of the story "And of Clay Are Created" describes the experience of emotional intimacy between the two lovers, despite great geographical distance and contact limited to that of a national television broadcast. The final paragraph describes the lover, returned home from this life-changing experience, to find himself emotionally distant from his "life companion," despite their physical proximity. The relationship, however, is one that thrives on such fluctuations between intimacy and distance, be it geographical or emotional, and always maintains the promise of renewed closeness, the assurance that, whatever the current distance between them, "we shall again walk hand in hand, as before."

Source: Liz Brent, in an essay for *Short Stories for Students*, Gale Group, 2001

Ruth Behar

In the following excerpt, Behar examines Allende's inspiration for writing "And of Clay Are We Created."

"And of Clay Are We Created" was inspired by the 1985 avalanche in Colombia that buried a village in mud. Among those trapped was Omaira Sánchez, a thirteen-year-old girl who became the focus of attention of news-hungry photographers, journalists and television cameras that fixed their curious and helpless eyes on the girl who kept her faith in life as she bravely met her death. In that horrid audience of onlookers, there was one man, a reporter, who made the decision to stop observing Omaira from the lens of his camera and lay down in the mud to offer her what comfort he could as her heart and lungs collapsed. Allende, who was obsessed by "the torment of that poor child buried alive," wrote her story from the perspective of a woman—and she was that woman—"who watches the televised struggle of the man holding the girl."

Allende assumed that once the story was published (in *The Stories of Eva Luna*), Omaira would disappear from her life. But Omaira she discovers, is

> a dogged angel who will not let me forget her. When Paula fell into a coma and became a prisoner in her bed, inert, dying slowly before the helpless gaze of all around her, I remembered the face of Omaira Sánchez. My daughter was trapped in her body, as the girl had been trapped in mud. Only then did I understand why I had thought about her all those years, and finally could decipher the message in those intense black eyes: patience, courage, resignation, dignity in the face of death.

She reaches a paradoxical conclusion: "If I write something, I fear it will happen, and if I love too much, I fear I will lose that person; nevertheless, I cannot stop writing or loving...."

Like the reporter who joins the girl in the mud, Allende, too, relinquishes the detached observer position. For her, this means exiling herself from the territory of fiction, which in the past has allowed her to invent the destinies of her characters and so removed reality to a safe and controllable distance.

Source: Ruth Behar, "In the House of the Spirits," in *The Women's Review of Books*, Vol. XIII, No. 2, November, 1995, p. 8.

Sources

Allende, Isabel, Prologue to *The Stories of Eva Luna*, translated by Margaret Sayers Peden, Bantam, 1991, p. 4.

Bader, Eleanor J., Review of *The Stories of Eva Luna*, in *Belles Lettres: A Review of Books by Women*, Vol. 6, No. 3, Spring, 1991, p. 60.

Bernikow, Louise, Review of *The Stories of Eva Luna*, in *Cosmopolitan*, Vol. 210, No. 1, January 1991, p. 22.

Cryer, Dan, "Unlucky in Love in Latin America," in *Newsday*, January 21, 1991, p. 46.

Gautier, Marie-Lise Gazarian, *Interviews with Latin American Writers*, Dalkey Archive Press, 1989, p. 8.

Harris, Daniel, Review of *The Stories of Eva Luna*, in *Boston Review*, Vol. 16, No. 2, April, 1991, pp. 28–29.

Hart, Patricia, "Boom Times–II," in *Nation*, Vol. 252, No. 9, March 11, 1991, p. 315.

Iftekharuddin, Farhat, "Writing to Exorcise the Demons" [Interview with Allende], in *Speaking of the Short Story*, edited by Farhat Iftekharuddin, Mary Rohrberger, and Maurice Lee, University Press of Mississippi, 1997, pp. 1–26; reprinted in *Conversations with Isabel Allende*, edited by John Rodden, University of Texas Press, 1999, pp. 353–54.

Ruta, Suzanne, "Lovers and Storytellers," in *Women's Review of Books*, Vol. 8, No. 9, June, 1991, p. 10.

Snell, Marilyn Berlin, "The Shaman and the Infidel" [Interview with Allende], *New Perspectives Quarterly*, Vol. 8, Winter, 1991, p. 57.

Further Reading

Allende, Isabel, "Writing As an Act of Hope," in *Paths of Resistance: The Art and Craft of the Political Novel*, edited by William Zinsser, Houghton Mifflin, 1989, pp. 39–63.
> Allende describes the violence, poverty, and beauty of Latin America, and explains that storytelling is the best medium for communicating its truths. "I write," she reveals, "so that people will love each other more."

de Carvalho, Susan, "*Escrituras y Escritoras*: The Artist-Protagonist of Isabel Allende," in *Discurso Literario*, Vol. 10, No. 1, 1992, pp. 59–67.
> An essay examining the character of Eva Luna, and how she uses storytelling as a means of self-examination. Although this essay refers to the novel *Eva Luna*, its insights may be profitably applied to the narrator of "And of Clay Are We Created."

Leonard, Kathy S., ed., *Index to Translated Short Fiction by Latin-American Women in English Language Anthologies*, Greenwood, 1997.
> An excellent guide through the dozens of anthologies that include, as the title indicates, English translations of short stories by Latin-American women. Useful for locating works by Allende, and also for finding available works by her peers.

Rodden, John, ed., *Conversations with Isabel Allende*, University of Texas Press, 1999.
> An extensive collection of interviews from various literary journals, originally published in English or translated from Spanish, German, and Dutch. The volume includes an index and annotated bibliography.

Rojas, Sonia Riquelme, and Edna Aguirre Rehbien, eds., *Critical Approaches to Isabel Allende's Novels*, Peter Lang, 1991.
> Although it deals only with Allende's first three novels, this collection reveals and explores the central critical issues in her fiction. The essays are in English and in untranslated Spanish. The Introduction, in English, is an excellent overview of the biographical and political sources of Allende's major themes.

Shaw, Donald Leslie, *The Post-Boom in Spanish American Fiction*, State University of New York Press, 1998.
> An analysis of Latin-American literature produced since the mid-1970s following the "Boom," a period that saw an explosion of internationally important works by Latin-American writers. Works written after the Boom tend to be more concerned with contemporary Latin-American society, especially with working-class and middle-class characters.

Battle Royal or The Invisible Man

Ralph Ellison
1947

"Battle Royal" is the name of the first chapter of Ralph Ellison's 1952 novel *Invisible Man*. This first chapter was originally published as a short story in the October 1947 issue of the English literary periodical *Horizon* and entitled "The Invisible Man." "Battle Royal" is the name adopted by subsequent anthologies to differentiate the story from the novel of the same name.

Ellison's novel won him fast and sustained acclaim as a major writer of the twentieth century. The story was well received upon publication and alerted many to Ellison's talent. "Battle Royal" presents a startling scene of violence, naiveté and economic power—a scene that implies the philosophical depth behind the institutions of racism and the pathos of asserting an identity in the shadow of historical tragedy.

Author Biography

With the publication of his novel *Invisible Man* in 1952, Ralph Ellison became a widely acclaimed author who is considered among the most important writers of the century. In addition to this novel, he published two collections of essays, *Shadow and Act* (1964) and *Going to the Territory* (1986) and throughout his life, he was a frequent contributor to literary and political journals including *New Masses*, *Nation*, and *American Review*. After his death,

Juneteenth, a novel he had been working on for many years but had not completed, was edited and published posthumously in 1998.

Ellison was born in Oklahoma City, Oklahoma, in 1914 and was named by his father after Ralph Waldo Emerson, the famous American transcendentalist writer of the nineteenth century. His father died when Ellison was four years old, and Ellison and his younger brother were raised by their mother who made sure her children had plenty to challenge them intellectually, socially, and culturally. Oklahoma was a source of inspiration to Ellison's later work. Growing up in the 1920s, he experienced the effects of racial prejudice, formulated in segregative practices of enduring Jim Crow laws. He also was drawn to the vibrant musical forms—jazz, gospel, classical, and folk—that pervaded the city.

In 1933, the nineteen-year-old Ellison left Oklahoma to attend Booker T. Washington's former college, Tuskegee Institute in Alabama, where he initially studied music. In 1936, before finishing his degree, Ellison moved to New York where he would eventually meet Langston Hughes, Alain Locke, and Richard Wright. Wright, in particular, played an important role in Ellison's early career. During the thirties, Ellison, like Hughes and Wright, was persuaded by the political and social critiques of the Communist Party. As Ellison's career continued, he disassociated himself from organized communism while continuing to critique economic exploitation and racism.

Before receiving a Federal Writers' Project grant in 1936 that allowed him to focus on his writing, Ellison performed many different kinds of jobs in New York: he worked as a freelance photographer, a receptionist, a stereo repairman, and a salesman. Ellison's first story was published in 1939, and many followed in the early 1940s. In 1942, he worked as managing editor of *Negro Quarterly*, and in 1944, he published two more stories, ''Flying Home'' and ''The Bingo Game.''

Ellison married Fanny McConnell in 1944 before serving in World War II as a cook in the merchant marines. When he returned to the States, he spent time on a farm in Vermont where he came up with the ideas that would become *Invisible Man*. In 1952, Ellison published *Invisible Man* and began to enjoy an enduring reputation as one of the century's most important writers. The novel was immediately characterized by many as a masterpiece, and reviews were positive even if critical of its political implications. In 1953, Ellison won the National Book Award, which would be followed by many other awards and honorary degrees throughout his life, including honorary doctorates from Harvard, Tuskegee, University of Michigan, and Brown University.

In 1967, a fire destroyed Ellison's summer home and much of his next major novel. He managed to rebuild the manuscript, which ran over a thousand pages. Ellison died in 1994 after battling cancer and was buried near his New York home in Washington Heights.

Plot Summary

The nameless, first-person narrator begins by suggesting that for the first twenty years of his life, he has looked to others to answer questions of self-definition. What he has discovered is that it is only he himself who can figure out who he is, but to do this, he must first ''discover that [he] is an invisible man!'' The story unfolds by narrating a scene in which those who are ''blind'' are not only the narrator, who literally wears a blindfold, but also those who abuse the narrator, sizing him up as mere stereotype, erasing his individuality and human dimension.

The narrator's question of self identity is not restricted to the mere twenty years of his own life but to the lives of his grandparents, who were born as slaves and freed eighty-five years before. This was a freedom that made them rhetorically part of a ''United'' States, but that in the social sphere kept African-Americans separate from whites like separate ''fingers on the hand.''

On his deathbed, the narrator's grandfather gives him odd and disturbing advice. The grandfather seemed to live a hardworking and conventional life, but his final words confirm his reputation as an ''odd man'' who might ''cause trouble.'' He tells the narrator that he has felt like a traitor and a spy his entire life and should have never given up his gun after Reconstruction (see historical notes, below). He advises the narrator to keep up a ''good fight'' by living with ''your head in the lion's mouth.'' The grandfather continues, ''I want you to overcome 'em with yeses, undermine 'em with grins, agree 'em to death and destruction, let 'em swoller you till they vomit or bust wide open.'' The grandfather's final fierce words are "Learn it to the younguns." This dying speech alarms the narrator's folks and haunts the narrator through the rest of the story, especially since the narrator feels so well liked and is even praised "by the most lily-white men of the town."

Although uneasy about the grandfather's final words, the narrator makes a very successful speech at his graduation in which he argues that humility is the secret to success. The speech is so well liked that he is invited to deliver it to "a gathering of the town's leading white citizens."

When the narrator arrives at the main ballroom of the hotel, he is told to participate with some of his schoolmates in a "battle royal." The fight is to take place in a large room with a portable boxing ring, around which chairs have been arranged for all the men with tuxedoes and cigars to sit as they watch. Riding with his schoolmates in the elevator to the room, the narrator feels superior to them, likening himself to a "potential Booker T. Washington" whose dignity might be tarnished through association with such rough characters.

Entering the room, the narrator is handed a pair of boxing gloves as he looks around. Through the haze of cigar smoke he sees all the prominent white men of the town—"bankers, lawyers, judges, doctors, fire chiefs, teachers, merchants"—getting drunk on whiskey. The narrator and his schoolmates are shuttled to the front of the ballroom and ringed by a crowd of menacing, curious and amused faces. At the front of the room, there is dead silence as the boys see "a magnificent blonde—stark naked" standing directly before them.

With the crowd of white men looking on, the narrator and his schoolmates do not know how to react. Some of the boys "lowered their heads, trembling," fearing the implied threat of being lynched if they demonstrate sexual interest in a white woman. The narrator feels forceful but contradictory feelings. A wave of "irrational guilt and fear" sweeps over him as his teeth chatter and his knees knock. He knows that it is dangerous to look at her, but cannot help but look. He wants to spit on her and touch her, "to love her and to murder her." The woman begins to dance provocatively and one of the narrator's schoolmates faints, another pleads to go home and yet another tries to hide his erection with his boxing gloves. The white men become a near-frenzied mob, chasing her and finally tossing her around as she tries to flee. Finally, some of the more sober men help her escape.

Ralph Waldo Ellison

Immediately after the woman flees, the ten young men are ordered to get into the ring to entertain their white audience by fighting each other, blindfolded. The narrator feels a "blind terror" in the darkness and hears shouts like "Let me at that big nigger!" from a voice that sounds like the school superintendent's. The fight is anarchic, cruel and bloody. At one point the narrator is able to begin peeking through his blindfold and is able to move carefully, avoiding blows and pitting one group of fighters against another.

Finally, the narrator is left alone in the ring with Tatlock, "biggest of the gang." All the other fighters planned to leave, setting the narrator up to get pummeled in the final showdown. The narrator attempts to strike a deal with Tatlock, proposing "Fake like I knocked you out, you can have the prize." Tatlock defiantly refuses, whispering back "I'll break your behind." The surprised narrator can only ask "For *them*?" Tatlock responds, "For *me*, sonofab—h!" Despite further attempts to buy Tatlock off, Tatlock batters the narrator, and the narrator worries about giving his speech. When the narrator hears the audience placing money on Tatlock, he is further confused about whether he should win the fight. Finally, the narrator is knocked out and pulled up into a chair after the count of ten.

After the fight, the "M.C." invites the boys to collect their money, which appears to be coins on a rug. The boys crouch over the rug, and, when told to start scrambling, they fight each other for the coins. As they do, electric shocks tear through their bodies. The narrator adapts to the shock by laughing, and he continues collecting as many greenbacks and coins as he can. Although the students try to avoid the rug, the drunk men push them on to the rug. One of the young men is lifted into the air and dropped, "wet back landing flush on the charged rug." After agonizing spasms, he manages to escape the rug and to burst out of the room. As the narrator works to avoid similar fate, he also tries surreptitiously to knock the chair of a drunk Mr. Colcord over, spilling him onto the rug. Mr. Colcord laughs and continues trying to push the narrator down. In the end, the coins turn out to be worthless slugs, brass tokens advertising an automobile.

After all of this, the narrator feels awful but is called in to make his speech. As the crowd's applause and laughter subsides, he determinedly begins, choking back blood and spit. His speech is about the importance of education. He recites a story about a ship that was lost at sea whose passengers suddenly sight a friendly vessel which tells the "unfortunate vessel" to "cast down your bucket where you are." Throughout the recitation, the crowd rudely makes fun of the narrator by interrupting him, asking him to repeat phrases. One of these phrases is "social responsibility" which he repeats a few times before accidentally yelling out "social equality" instead. After this slip, the narrator feels a rumble of displeasure and hears hostile remarks. Scared, he follows orders to repeat "social responsibility." A "small dry mustached man" asked if he was being "smart" and the narrator says "No, sir!" and explains that he made the mistake only because he was swallowing blood.

The narrator finishes to thunderous applause. He is presented with a prize by the Board of Education: a calfskin briefcase and a scholarship to a "state college for Negroes." The narrator is overjoyed as his eyes fill with tears. The next day his family and neighbors congratulate him. However, his grandfather haunts him, and the narrator has a disturbing dream that night. In the dream, the narrator goes to the circus with his grandfather who will not laugh at the clowns. The grandfather tells the narrator to open his briefcase and read the letter inside. The narrator tries but opens one envelope to find another inside, endlessly. The grandfather says "Them's years" and then he tells the narrator to open another envelope and to read it out loud. The narrator opens it and reads "To Whom It May Concern . . . Keep this Nigger-Boy Running."

Characters

Blonde Who Strips And Is Chased By The Audience

Before the ten classmates fight, they are forced to consider a "magnificent blonde—stark naked." The white men menacingly watch as the young men tremble with fear, knowing that in the time they live, a Black man who demonstrates sexual interest in a white woman risks being lynched. The narrator's description of the woman objectifies her into a "kewpie doll" as he tries to express his contradictory feelings of lust and fear. As the woman dances, the white male audience grows increasingly rowdy until they are literally passing her around over their heads. Finally, the woman escapes and the "battle royal" begins.

Classmates At The Smoker

When the narrator shows up at the hotel, expecting to give his speech, he is grouped with nine of his fellow classmates, all of whom are African American. The main event at the "Battle Royal" is the free-for-all fight between these ten young men who are blindfolded. Except for Tatlock, the story does not fill in individual characteristics for this group. In general, the narrator clearly looks down on them, feeling he is superior to what he perceives to be a rough bunch.

Mr. Colcord

An audience member with breath stinking of whiskey, Mr. Colcord tries to force the narrator on to the electrified rug. The narrator not only resists Colcord's efforts but responds by trying to topple Colcord onto the rug in ways that cannot appear obvious. In town, Colcord owns a chain of movie houses and "entertainment places."

M.C.

A nameless and faceless voice that directs the audience's attention from event to event and stirs up excitement. He is presumably white.

Narrator's Grandfather

A former slave who was freed about eighty-five years prior to when the story takes place. He and the narrator's grandmother lived a quiet, industrious life, "stay[ing] in their place and working hard." The grandfather was an "odd" man, however. On his deathbed, he tells the narrator some advice that haunts the narrator through the rest of story. In his last moments, the grandfather admits to feeling like a traitor and a spy, living in the "enemy's country." He wishes he had never given up his gun during the first days of Reconstruction. With his dying breath, he urges his grandson to "overcome 'em with yeses, undermine 'em with grins, agree 'em to death and destruction, let 'em swoller you till they vomit or bust wide open" and then "Learn it to the younguns." Later in the story, the narrator has a disturbing dream about attending the circus with his grandfather.

The School Superintendent

After the narrator's speech, the superintendent steps forward and congratulates the narrator saying, "some day he'll lead his people in the proper paths." In the name of the Board of Education, he presents the narrator with a prize consisting of a leather briefcase with a scholarship to the "state college for Negroes." Presumably, the superintendent has been watching the entire battle royal.

Small Dry Mustached Man

The "small dry mustached man" sits in the front row as the narrator delivers his speech. When the narrator accidentally says "social equality" instead of "social responsibility," the man interrupts and intimidates the narrator, asking the narrator to repeat what he has said. The man makes sure that the narrator insists it was an accidental slip of the tongue, and when the narrator acts subservient, the man seems satisfied.

Tatlock

The biggest and strongest of the narrator's classmates with whom he is forced to fight. By arrangement, the other fighters bow out of the ring, leaving the narrator in a final showdown with Tatlock. As the audience places bets on the winner, the narrator tries to make a deal with Tatlock. He proposes that Tatlock take a fall and in return the narrator will give Tatlock the winner's purse plus extra money. Tatlock, to the narrator's surprise, refuses with scorn. The narrator asks Tatlock whether he wants to pulverize him for the benefit of the white audience; Tatlock responds that he will beat the narrator up not for the audience but "For *me*, sonofab—h."

Topics for Further Study

- Do you trust the narrator's perspective? What are some different perspectives that might add to a fuller picture? How might the story be told through Tatlock's eyes? Through the eyes of the woman?

- In 1947, this story was first published as "The Invisible Man." Five years later, the novel was published under the title of *Invisible Man*. How does the absence of the article "The" change the title? How might one interpret the title and meaning of the book differently because of this change?

- The M.C. is a strange character. His voice steers the audience's and the reader's attention to particular scenes. Analyze the role the M.C. plays in the story. Why is there so little description of this character?

- There is a lot of laughing but it is difficult to discern what is funny. Why are so many of the men laughing? What kind of laughter is it and what does it mean?

- Why does the narrator give the speech at the end? Why doesn't he get angry and leave?

Themes

Racism

Through the grandfather's haunting words of advice, the story reaches to presumably the Emancipation Proclamation of 1863, issued in the midst of the Civil War. Eighty-five years later, in approximately 1949, the narrator must come to terms with his family's history. The story interweaves various levels of obvious and subtle racism in the projection of a nightmarish racial hatred. The offensive epithets speak for themselves. The economic structure of the spectacles implicitly criticize ways in which money and economic power sustain the expression of racial hatred. As the schoolmates fight each other for coins, trying not to get shocked, it seems that

Ellison is proposing a parody of what it is like to try to succeed in a segregated society. And, in this segregated world, economic success makes the African-American individual a target to both other African Americans and to whites who are threatened by such success.

More subtle commentary on racism emerges in questioning why the white men are so entranced by the spectacles of violence they stage. While everyone in the audience seems to enjoy commanding economic security, it might seem curious that they still are thrilled to see the narrator and his schoolmates demeaned and abused. What is the logic of the white men's fascination here?

Alienation and Loneliness of Growing into Adulthood

The narrator's experience at the smoker demonstrates that instead of feeling himself in mutual struggle with his schoolmates, he instead holds himself up as superior to them. Ellison also presents the narrator as naive, trusting in the institutions of education and in a conventional belief that one works hard to succeed in a land of democratic citizens, a color-blind meritocracy. The narrator's quest to be like Booker T. Washington reflects his ambition to be great and have people look up to him. In the midst of the battle royal, however, all the narrator can do is hope to salvage a piece of self respect. When the narrator is tearfully overwhelmed at the gift of the briefcase and scholarship, Ellison seems to mock his youthful optimism. The scholarship to the "Negro" college ironically confirms the narrator's sense of superiority to Tatlock and his other classmates. What the narrator grows to understand throughout the rest of the novel is that the scholarship was a reward for his subservience to the powerful white men at the smoker and to white people in general. The image of Booker T. Washington becomes an ironic symbol of greatness, reflecting the narrator's ability to garner self respect by pandering to the white community's sense of "responsibility" at the cost of friendship with other African Americans. Trapped in an illusionary feeling of achievement, the narrator's most intimate connection seems to be with his dead grandfather whose words haunt him.

The American Dream

The novel challenges some basic premises about how to succeed in the United States as an African-American man. The idea of the American Dream blends the notion of democracy and competitive business capitalism into a liberating optimism. Rhetorically, everybody has equal opportunity to advance in society by working hard, earning money and planning for the future. The Declaration of Independence asserts this optimism by declaring that "men are created equal" and have rights to "life, liberty and the pursuit of happiness."

Power of the Individual

Ralph Waldo Ellison was named after the transcendental philosopher Ralph Waldo Emerson. Emerson's essays, like "Nature" and "The American Scholar," invested the individual with a power to overcome and move beyond the past and to project a new, dynamic and liberating sense of the future. His essays looked to the natural world as an expression of the vibrant individual's power to realize his most optimistic and self-expressive visions of greatness. This vitality complemented a national desire in the United States to be exceptional by embracing principles of democratic brotherhood. The energy implied in Emerson's essays is powerful but hard to imagine in the real world. The narrator's sense of individual accomplishment highlights the potential shortsightedness of an Emersonian logic. In the South of the 1940s, it seems that the divisive effect of racial bigotry can only be "transcended" if one overlooks blatant expressions of hatred and systemic forces that concentrate economic power in the hands of dominant white society.

Style

Point of View and Narration

The narration is in first person, addressing the reader directly with a direct and honest tone implying a certain naiveté. The narrator is most capable of conveying his confusion. His sense of accomplishment is rendered pathetic by his constant inability to take offense at the inhumane treatment he endures at the hands of his "benefactors." By rendering scenes of physical and psychological violence to the reader in forceful detail and lyrical immediacy, one expects a statement of anger and resistance. Instead, the reader alone seems to understand the demeaning implication of the battle royal as the narrator progresses toward the ultimately triumphant scholarship award. The final mention of the narrator's dream suggests that this absence of indignation is indeed ironic, an irony that is wound more tightly in the novel as a whole.

Setting

The story takes place around eighty-five years after the Emancipation Proclamation of 1863, in approximately 1947. It is important that the narrator lives in the South, where slavery played a crucial role in sustaining the economic system of plantation farming until the Civil War. In the days after slavery's abolition, African Americans were prevented from becoming economically stable by the white community. The town of the story reflects a fundamental hierarchy in which white men are those with economic, political, judicial and educational authority. The hotel where the battle royal takes place represents the extent of this white power. It is significant that once inside the room where the events take place, one is either there as an audience member or an entertainer. The audience is composed only of white men being entertained by their perverse manipulation of the young African-American men and the "magnificent blonde" stripper.

Symbol and Images

The narrator's direct statement of the scene seems too simplistic given the frenzied events unfolding and the immediate impact of these events on the narrator himself. This incongruity invites the reader to see in these discrete images a broader significance, reaching to comment on the more general social dynamic that produces the story's violence.

The image of the circus occurs at the beginning and ending of the story. The grandfather urges the narrator to live his life with his head in the lion's mouth, and in the narrator's final dream he sits next to his grandfather at a circus. These images might symbolize the fundamental uncertainty of life. Whereas the conventional ideas of respectably working, earning and raising a family imply a clear logic, the circus is a spectacle that makes everything both funny and unpredictable. The circus is also a place of masquerade and of power reversals, where clowns enact skits that make those who are supposed to be in charge appear foolish. The circus is also a place that uses the illusion of danger—lions, canons, the tightrope—to dramatic effect. By equating life with a circus, the narrator's dreams seem to enforce the irony of his aspiration to be a respectable figure like Booker T. Washington.

The fight is a central symbol, representing the harsh reality of the marketplace for African Americans. The physical brutality reflects the reality of violence directed against Black men by white society in the North and the South. The scene of the schoolmates being confronted by the stripper represents the ways in which racism against African Americans was expressed sexually. The white, male audience's lurid interest in watching both the stripper and the young men's terrified reaction to her naked body are poignant and disturbing expressions of how deeply oppressive racism can be.

Structure

The story is presented as a retrospective, told from an unknown vantage point in the present, well after the narrated events have concluded. From this vantage point, the narrator remembers his life before he left for college in which two specific events occurred: the death of his grandfather and his participation in the battle royal. This reminiscence incorporates an historical depth by using the grandfather's life to reach back eighty-five years, thus connecting the narrated events to a national history of slavery's abolition and the eventual abandonment of Reconstruction. The reminiscence also suggests that the narrator may have grown into a more accurate understanding of these past events.

Historical Context

Slavery, Reconstruction and Plessy v. Ferguson *(1896)*

The Civil War was fought to keep the United States together as a single nation. While the *Declaration of Independence* asserted that it was "self-evident" that "all men were created equal," the subsequent formulation of the United States Constitution stipulated that slavery would remain legal. Because of the plantation system, the Southern states' economic livelihood depended on having a labor force which it could deny any legal, social or human rights. In the decades before the Civil War, the United States was held together through a series of compromises (*The Missouri Compromise (1820), The Fugitive Slave Act, Compromise of 1850, The Kansas-Nebraska Act (1854)*) that attempted to balance the political power of slave and free states. One of the most blatant statements of deprivation of Blacks' basic rights of citizenship and the attendant human rights was the Supreme Court's *Dred Scott* decision of 1857, which stated directly that no black person had rights any white man need respect. Under this ruling, no Black person was allowed claims to citizenship.

Compare & Contrast

- **1952:** Racial segregation is legal, upheld by the Supreme Court decision of 1896, *Plessy v. Ferguson*. Schools, housing and employment and businesses in the South maintain separate facilities for Black and white people.

   1954: The Supreme Court reverses the *Plessy v. Ferguson* decision with the decision, *Brown v. Board of Education, Topeka, Kansas*. Declaring that separate facilities are inherently unequal, the court ordered the desegregation of schools throughout the country.

   2000: Today, *de facto* segregation continues to frustrate the implementation of the court's 1954 decision.

- **1860:** About forty percent of African Americans living in the city of New York would have to move in order to achieve racial integration. In New Orleans, about thirty-six percent of African Americans would have to move. (Massey and Denton)

   1940: About eighty-seven percent of African Americans living in the city of New York would have to move in order to achieve racial integration. In New Orleans, about eighty-one percent of African Americans would have to move.

   1990: About eighty-two percent of African Americans living in the city of New York would have to move to achieve racial integration. In New Orleans, about sixty-nine percent of African Americans would have to move.

The Civil War began in 1861 as the North tried to keep the South in the national Union. Slavery was partially abolished by Lincoln's *Emancipation Proclamation* of 1863, which did not outlaw slavery in the border states between North and South in an attempt to keep those states aligned neutral in the war. After the Civil War, the Thirteenth Amendment (ratified 1865) outlawed slavery, the Fourteenth Amendment (ratified 1868) guaranteed the rights of citizenship to freed Blacks. The Fifteenth Amendment (ratified 1870) guaranteed the right to vote. While these were important steps, they did not prevent the further oppression of African Americans.

Reconstruction was a federal policy to engineer the inclusion of freed African Americans into the national—political, economic and social—framework. In the 1870s, the North had grown weary of the enterprise and more concerned with facilitating industrial and corporate development. Prejudice against African Americans in the North severely limited their employment opportunities while local laws and social practices in the former slave states intimidated African Americans, and effectively locked them from participation in the marketplace. Local laws like the Black Codes and Jim Crow as well as brutal Ku Klux Klan violence effectively prevented many African Americans from voting, working or living where they would have chosen.

The presidential election of 1876 marks the unofficial termination of federal attempts to reconstruct the South. The election motivated a political compromise that installed the Republican candidate, Rutherford B. Hayes, as president despite his failure to win a majority of electoral votes and his loss of the popular vote. The Democrats, who represented the interests of the former South, traded the presidency for assurances that under Hayes the last federal troops would be withdrawn from the South. Without the troops, the local governments in the South were able to follow with impunity programs of segregation and intimidation against African Americans. In 1896, the Supreme Court, in *Plessy v. Ferguson*, legally sanctioned separate Pullman cars for Blacks and whites, citing the segregation of public schools in Washington, D.C. as social precedent that demonstrated the social proclivity to segregate. The legal sanction of racial segregation structured the school system, employment opportunities and loan opportunities until *Brown v. Board of Education, Topeka, Kansas* (1954), which ruled that segregationist policies were inherently unequal. Ellison's novel is published just two years before the *Brown* decision.

African American Resistance and Leadership: Booker T. Washington and W. E. B. DuBois

In equating himself with his grandfather and with Booker T. Washington, the narrator recalls major figures who served to fight against the marginalization of African Americans, during and after the abolition of slavery. It is notable that the short story and the novel seem to use figures of men as leaders while women serve relatively minor roles. The narrator projects himself into a clearly empowered, masculine agency.

To understand the novel's irony regarding the narrator's reverence of Booker T. Washington, it is important to consider the context in which Washington became powerful. His autobiography, *Up From Slavery*, was published in 1901. It tells of his rise from his childhood status as a slave to being one of the most influential men of his time period. Following the legacy of Frederick Douglass, who in a previous generation had written of rising into social and political prominence after escaping slavery, Washington reached a wide audience with his message of African-American self-reliance and a seeming acceptance of the segregational boundaries in place throughout the United States. Washington founded the Tuskegee Institute, a school designed to educate African Americans in practical industries, vocations and trades. In speeches like the "Atlantic Compromise" that he delivered at the International Exposition in Georgia of 1895, he urged the uplift of African Americans while placating the white audience with a seeming endorsement of segregation. The narrator's speech echoes Washington's words to African Americans, urging them not to migrate to cities and seek integration but instead to "cast down your bucket down where you are."

W. E. B. DuBois was an African-American leader and critic of Booker T. Washington. In *The Souls of Black Folk*, DuBois urged African Americans to become central to the functioning of the United States through an education that stressed intellectual achievement. He proposed that a sole focus on vocational training perpetuated the disenfranchisement of the Black community and that if the "talented-tenth" of African Americans were allowed to exercise their mental capacities, it would self-evidently demonstrated that African Americans were crucial components of the national body. DuBois and Washington openly criticized each other's leadership.

DuBois' idea of "double-consciousness" is central to Ellison's novel. DuBois writes in the first chapter of *The Souls of Black Folk*: "It is a peculiar sensation, this double-consciousness, this sense of always looking at one's self through the eyes of others, of measuring one's soul by the tape of a world that looks on in amused contempt and pity. One ever feels his twoness—an American, a Negro; two souls, two thoughts, two unreconciled strivings; two warring ideals in one dark body, whose dogged strength alone keeps it from being torn asunder." DuBois' words seem particularly relevant to both the narrator and the grandfather's sense of divided identity.

The Philosophy of Ralph Waldo Emerson

Emerson was a famous American philosopher of the nineteenth century. His 1836 book *Nature* became a pillar of transcendental philosophy, a belief in the individual's fundamental agency in the world and potential to move beyond historical circumstance and local environment to fundamentally influence the world through the implementation of one's social vision. In according this power to the individual, Emerson borrows and reformulates within the democratic rhetoric of the United States the romantic energy espoused by the English romantic poets like Coleridge and Wordsworth as well as the dynamic idealism of Swedish philosopher Emanuel Swedenborg. Emerson's essay provides memorable quotations such as "Standing on bare ground—my head bathed by the blithe air and uplifted into infinite space—all mean egotism vanishes. I become a transparent eyeball; I am nothing; I see all; the currents of the Universal Being circulate through me; I am part or parcel of God." Ellison's blindfolded narrative "I" seems to comment ironically on Emerson's abstract and transcendent individual.

Naming Racial Categories

Invisible Man was published just before the Civil Rights movement of the 1950s began to gain momentum. In terminology used to name African Americans in the story, novel, reviews of the novel, and subsequent criticism, one can see the force of political and social conflict. When the novel was written, the popular press used the term Negro to name African Americans (see Irving Howe's review below). While intending a kind of respect, the term "Negro" is a clear enforcement of separate identity—a separation that included social, political and cultural implications but that was summed up in the simplistic description of one's skin color as black or "negro." The term "colored" also implied this difference. Although it was acceptable at the turn of the century (used to name the NAACP or National Association for the Advancement of Colored People), it developed a more pejorative sense in the 1950s, implying the segregationist practices of denying African Americans access to stores, lunch counters, and parks, as well as designating areas on buses or specific "colored" drinking fountains, separate from "white fountains," where African Americans were forced to drink. In contemporary conversation, the terms 'colored' and 'Negro' are both offensive, reflecting the deep prejudice of our nation's history.

The term "nigger" was deeply offensive, as the story demonstrates, touching a sense of white racial superiority and violence that stretched back to the practice of slavery. There is no indication that "nigger" has ever been a commonly acceptable term, free of its offensive implication of subordination and threat of violence. Even when used casually in fiction of the eighteenth and nineteenth centuries, it implies a deeply held belief in white racial superiority and disrespect of people it serves to name. The terms "black" and "Black" in the United States became acceptable ways of referring to African Americans as the political force of the civil rights movement took hold. The Black Arts Movement in the 1960s is one example of the way in which African Americans used the term Black to symbolize a cultural and communitarian solidarity and power. While its capitalized form is accepted today, the word "Black" can imply a clearer demarcation between people than exists culturally or biologically. While the forces of racism and prejudice have often enforced severe lines of demarcation in the social world, the reality of people's lives is often difficult to consider through the binary categories of "Black" and "white."

This essay uses African American to describe the narrator and his class mates. African American or African-American reflects the political tension of being a citizen of an American national culture that relied on slavery for two-hundred and fifty years and that extended slavery's effects through legally sanctioned social policies after the Civil War. The term emphasizes the cultural history of being Black and having ancestral connection to Africa and its many cultures.

The term "white" has been consistently acceptable, effectively naming a group of people with ostensibly various ethnic backgrounds. It is worth noting that no one's skin is literally white or Black, demonstrating that skin color is part of a system of representation, interpreted within social contexts. This strange consistency and effectiveness of the term "white" in the United States indicates perhaps that "whiteness" is not merely or mainly about one's literal skin tone, but about social (political, economic and cultural) power in the United States. The mere adjective "white" has seemed right for a long time, an often unnecessary descriptor of the "normal" American. This normalization of "whiteness" might provide an ironic index of the extent to which African Americans have been historically disenfranchised.

Civil Rights

This story was re-published as the first chapter of *Invisible Man* in 1952. Ellison's novel elucidated the social anguish of a society predicated on the social and legal principles of segregation in both the North and in the South. Two years after the novel was published, the Supreme Court issued *Brown v. Board of Education, Topeka, Kansas*, overturning *Plessy v.Ferguson* (1896), and declaring that the idea of "separate but equal" was inherently flawed. Segregation produced inequality of resources and opportunity. The Civil Rights movement in the South, led by religious leaders like Martin Luther King, Jr., would strengthen to a point that could no longer be ignored.

Critical Overview

Standing as the first chapter of Ellison's 1952 novel *Invisible Man*, "The Invisible Man" (a.k.a. "Battle Royal" or "Smoker") shares in critics' emphatic acclaim for the novel and the subsequent rise of the novel to fundamental literary importance. The story first appeared as "The Invisible Man" in the October, 1947 issue of the British literary periodical *The Horizon* (edited by Cyril Connolly). In adapting the story to the first chapter of the novel, Ellison made some minor alterations and added three final sentences to the story:

> It was a dream I was to remember and dream again for many years after. But at the time I had no insight into its meaning. First I had to attend college.

The critical review of the 1952 novel was immediately appreciative; Wright Morris reviewed the book in the *New York Times* on April 13, 1952, and wrote, "With this book the author maps a course from the underground world into the light. *Invisible Man* belongs on the shelf with classical efforts man has made to chart the river Lethe from its mouth to its source."

Irving Howe reviewed the novel for *The Nation*, giving it a generally favorable review while criticizing its facile appeal to an "unqualified assertion of individuality." Howe begins the review with a description of the opening chapter, "The beginning is nightmare. A Negro boy, timid and compliant, comes to a white smoker in a Southern town. Together with several other Negroes he is rushed to the front of the ballroom, where a sumptuous blonde tantalizes and frightens them by dancing in the nude. Blindfolded, the Negro boys stage a 'battle royal,' a free-for-all in which they pummel each other to the drunken shouts of the whites."

Saul Bellow, in his review of the novel in *Commentary*, mentions having read "The Battle Royal" scene in *Horizon* five years before. Bellow writes: "A few years ago, in an otherwise dreary and better forgotten number of *Horizon* devoted to a louse-up of a life in the United States, I read with great excitement an episode from *Invisible Man*. It described a free-for-all of blindfolded Negro boys at a stag party of the leading citizens of a small Southern town . . . This episode, I thought, might well be the high point of an excellent novel. It has turned out to be not the high point but rather one of the many peaks of a book of the very first order, a superb book."

Much criticism of the novel echoes Bellow's endorsement that Ellison shuns a "minority tone" in his writing. The last sentence of the novel's "Epilogue" draws attention to the universal reach of the narrator's voice: "Who knows but that, on lower frequencies, I speak for you." Saul Bellow's early review represents this approach in according Ellison a general, humanistic voice that speaks to more than just the experience of race. Bellow writes: ". . . keenly aware, as I read this book, of a very significant kind of independence in the writing. For there is a way for Negro novelists to go at their problems, just as there are Jewish or Italian ways. Mr. Ellison has not adopted a minority tone. If he had done so, he would have failed to establish a true middle-of-consciousness for everyone." While such a move toward humanistic value is possibly meant to be a compliment and to demonstrate the importance of the novel, there is an unsettling implication. To speak to a general audience, must one put aside the ideas of race? Is the "middle-of-consciousness" perspective a space that transcends racial conflict, racial identity and Bellow's idea of a "minority tone"? It might be more instructive to see how race is central to one's human experience.

Irving Howe noted this tendency in his consideration of the novel, writing, "Some reviewers, from the best of intentions, have assured their readers that this a good novel and not merely a good Negro novel." Howe continues by challenging this characterization and concludes his review, "But of course *Invisible Man* is a Negro novel—what white man could have written it? . . . To deny that this is a Negro novel is to deprive the Negroes of their one basic right: the right to cry out their difference." Surely the anguish of the first scene derives its power in presenting an African-American narrator who must face the smoker's vulgar racist structure as an object of manipulation; might it be that it is only through one's embrace of "minority tone" that a writer can touch common elements of a human experience?

There has been much critical work done on the novel as a whole in which the first chapter is closely considered. An early article in *Critique* by Jonathan Baumbach entitled "Nightmare of a Native Son: Ralph Ellison's *Invisible Man*" explores the way in which Ellison renders "profoundly all of us" through the "southern Negro" protagonist of the novel. The article continues by praising and interpreting the novel. An article called "Imagery in the 'Battle Royal' chapter of Ralph Ellison's *Invisible Man*" by Norman German in the *CLA Journal* explores the reach of animal imagery in the chapter. He observes that ". . . the animal imagery graphically highlights Ellison's theme that when one sex or race treats another as an object or animal, both become dehumanized or bestial."

There is much critical work considering Ellison's relationship to a literary and political heritage of American writing. Ellison's commentary on, reworking of, and critique of Emerson's transcendental individualism is explored in Kun Jong Lee's 1992 article in the *PMLA* entitled "Ellison's *Invisible Man*: Emersonianism Revisited." Lee argues that "Ellison's response to Emersonianism enacts a creative reading of the grandfather's advice: Ellison 'yesses' it to death (in an ironic version of the affirmative Emersonian position) until

Emersonianism chokes on him. In this way, like the narrator who reclaims his grandfather as his ancestor, Ellison brings Emerson into his own genealogy while subverting and expanding Emersonianism in the process." William Lyne, in the same issue of the *PMLA* as Lee, explores the valence of DuBois' trope "double-consciousness" in the article "The Signifying Modernist: Ralph Ellison and the Limits of the Double Consciousness."

The sexual politics of the novel are considered with insight by Daniel Kim in an article published in the Spring, 1997 issue of *Novel* entitled "Invisible Desires: Homoerotic Racism and its Homophobic Critique in Ralph Ellison's *Invisible Man*." Kim does a reading of the "Battle Royal" in pursuing his broader analysis of the novel. Kim argues that while Ellison offers a "far-ranging and subtle psychological account of white male racism," this account relies on the "presence of a disturbingly homophobic symbolism that undergirds it—for Ellison figures this homoerotically charged racial subordination, both directly and indirectly, as homosexuality." Kim's reading of the "battle royal" focuses on the way in which the "black male body" is both an object of the white men's physical violence and simultaneously an agent of violence, inflicting pain on other Black bodies. Kim draws attention to the way in which white men instrumentalize the "black male body" as a means of vicariously gratifying their own desires.

More general teaching guides and critical guides contribute greatly to an understanding of the history and literary aspects of the novel and the story. One helpful guide is a documentary companion entitled "Cultural Contexts for Ralph Ellison's *Invisible Man* (edited by Eric J. Sundquist) by Bedford Books of St. Martin's Press. Published in 1995, the collection reprints speeches, essays and Supreme Court opinions that greatly enhance an historical and thematic understanding of *"The Invisible Man."* These include Booker T. Washington's *Atlanta Exposition Address*, excerpts from DuBois' *The Soul of Black Folks*, and the Supreme Court brief ruling on *Brown v. Board of Education*.

Mark Busby's *Ralph Ellison* (Twayne Publishers, 1991) lends an overview on Ellison's life and literary achievement. In 1989, the Modern Language Association published Approaches to Teaching Ellison's *Invisible Man*. This collection of essays, edited by Susan Resneck Parr and Pancho Savery, includes discussion of the novel's first chapter. See especially "'Ball the Jack': Surreality, Sexuality, and the Role of Women in *Invisible Man*" by Mary Rohrberger and "Making *Invisible Man* Matter" by Walter Slatoff.

The Cambridge University Press' *New Essays on Invisible Man* assembles essays from Valerie Smith, John F. Callahan, Berndt Ostendorf, Thomas Schaub, and John S. Wright. Published in 1988, the essays address issues like Ellison's use of the mask trope, of jazz and notions of "primitive" and "cultured" artistic expression, and of the narrative structure of the novel.

Criticism

Kendall Johnson

Johnson teaches American literature at the University of Pennsylvania where he recently received his Ph.D. In the following essay, he discusses the parallels and differences between the Emersonian reflection of the ideal self and Ellison's "Battle Royal."

In 1846, Ralph Waldo Emerson's essay "Nature" elucidated the optimistic promise of American individualism. Emerson describes how the wilderness— "these plantations of God"—liberate the human spirit. He writes, "Standing on the bare ground— my head bathed by the blithe air and uplifted into infinite space; all mean egotism vanishes; I become a transparent eyeball; I am nothing; I see all; the currents of the Universal Being circulate through me; I am part or parcel of God." Emerson's reflection on the ideal self or "I" sets up contradictions that echo in Ralph Waldo Ellison's story "The Invisible Man." Throughout his ordeal, the narrator adopts an Emersonian optimism that enables him to keep looking ahead, thinking of himself as an ideal Booker T. Washington. The brutal scenes of violence test this optimism and suggest the limits that social forces, particularly racism, place on individuals. The following essay considers the narrator's detachment from his actual experience, arguing that this detachment reflects Ralph Waldo Ellison's qualification of an Emersonian optimism in light of the experiences of racial prejudice.

Emerson's metaphor of the "transparent eyeball" is complex. While it seems to imply a transcendent individual who is "part of parcel of God," it also implies a vanishing of individualism as "I become nothing." The metaphor of sight conveys this simultaneous inflation and erasure of the self.

Emerson's powerful notion of sight first reaches to the farthest horizon and then reduces the body to mere eyeball, finally dissolving the physicality of the "eyeball" in a liberating transparency. Emerson thus insists on a spiritual correspondence between the world and the individual and proposes a brilliant energy that wraps the individual and the seen world together in a formula for unity and cohesion.

Emerson's ideal "I" reacts to the decade of the 1830s when the United States was deeply divided over the practice of slavery and Westward expansion. While the transparency of Emerson's eyeball implies that it is a universal model, potentially representing all people, Ellison uses the term "invisibility" to counter this idealism. In the time Emerson wrote and published his essay, relatively few could hope to experience the liberating perspective it pronounced. Slavery implied a very different "plantation" than "Nature's wilderness"—a plantation fundamental to the economic stability of the South and the fabric of the nation as a whole. Ellison's narrator demonstrates that even if one believes himself capable of filling the world up with their vision, of dissolving "mean egotism" and becoming transparent, one is more likely limited by people's prejudices regarding race, gender, and social class. Ellison calls these limitations the effect of invisibility, suggesting that it is difficult to achieve the visionary capability of the "transparent eyeball" when one is being seen as a stereotype, rendered an object whose identity is reduced to the color of skin. When the narrator finally stands up to render his graduation speech at the hotel, Ellison ironically references "Nature's" metaphor of vision in describing the narrator: "There was still laughter as I faced them, my mouth dry, my eye throbbing."

In "The Invisible Man," the narrator looks around the room as if it were possible for him to expand into heroic self-fulfillment; however, the actual events brutally frustrate this elevation. But, even though the narrator never attains his heroic formula, he never concedes it to be impossible. This disjunction between the real events and the narrator's idealism is captured as the narrator reflects: I suspected that fighting a battle royal might detract from the dignity of my speech. In those pre-invisible days I visualized myself as a potential Booker T. Washington. But the other fellows didn't care too much for me either, and there were nine of them. I felt superior to them in my way, and I didn't like the manner in which we were all crowded together in

W. E. B. DuBois' idea of 'double-consciousness' and his emphasis on education for African Americans are both referenced in Ellison's 'Battle Royal.'

the servants' elevator." As the scared teenagers literally rise together to another floor, the narrator clings to Washington's image to elevate himself above the other African Americans. Instead of promoting a solidarity between the classmates who commonly endure the effects of white racism, the narrator sees Washington as a means of access into a higher class world that affords association with whites.

The real Booker T. Washington was born into slavery and eventually became the powerful president of Tuskegee Institute in Alabama. Under his leadership, Tuskegee became a powerful institution, training African Americans in vocational skills. Washington advocated a policy of economic self reliance for the African-American community, a policy that pleased powerful whites in the South whose social and economic power was maintained by the continuation of segregation. In his autobiography *Up From Slavery* (1901), Washington includes his address to the Atlanta Exposition of 1895 from which the narrator borrows key phrases in his speech. Speaking to a primarily white audience at

What Do I Read Next?

- *Autobiography of an Ex-Colored Man* (1912) by James Weldon Johnson. Unsigned on its publication in 1912, the novel was republished in 1927 with Johnson named as author. The story is a narrative about "passing," in which a young boy learns the rules of racially identifying and being identified as an African American at the turn of the nineteenth century. Raised by his African-American mother in the North and virtually abandoned (except for economic support) by his Southern, white father, the narrator ultimately decides to allow society to consider him white. The novel offers an ironic story of self-realization that both highlights and critiques the forces of racism.

- *The Big Sea* (1940) by Langston Hughes. The first volume of Langston Hughes' autobiographical novels, *The Big Sea* is a dynamic representation of learning what race means in New York, in Mexico, in the southern United States, and in Africa. The narrator uses humor, insight and a poetic sense of language to convey his experiences in learning to regard his racial identity and his cultural heritage as a source of strength from which he is able to understand himself as an individual in a complex world.

- *The Great Gatsby* (1925) by F. Scott Fitzgerald, is the story of Nick Carraway, a young man from Minnesota who moves to New York to become a stock broker. He tells of his friendship with Jay Gatsby, a man who has followed his first love for many years, trying to become rich enough to marry her.

- *Notes from the Underground* (1864) by Fyodor Dostoevsky. This book was a crucial influence on Ellison's full novel. Dostoevsky was a Russian novelist whose narrator in *Notes . . .* elucidates the feeling of anonymity, isolation and powerlessness that often characterized life in the increasingly industrialized cities of the nineteenth century.

- *The Souls of Black Folk* (1903) by W. E. B. DuBois. DuBois' essays present the enduring challenges facing African Americans in the South after the Civil War and at the turn of the century. He analyzes the political and historical implications of slavery and the courageous lives of those who had to fight for physical and intellectual survival.

- *The Street* (1946) by Ann Petry. The story of Lutie Johnson, a mother who struggles to raise her child in 1940s Harlem. The novel presents a variety of characters to depict the cruel effects of segregation and to analyze the relationship between race and socioeconomic opportunity.

---

the Exhibition, Washington said "In all things that are purely social we can be as separate as the fingers, yet one as the hand in all things essential to mutual progress." In promoting segregation, Washington mollified white fears of integration while emphasizing economic and social self-reliance of African Americans. Most pertinent to the narrator's speech is Washington's declaration that "The wisest among my race understand that the agitation of questions of social equality is the extremest folly."

It is important to consider that Booker T. Washington may have been manipulating his audience both in his autobiography and at the Atlanta Exposition. By knowing what the white power brokers wanted to hear, Washington could manipulate them with his words, performing an endorsement of segregation to gain economic and social power. As Houston A. Baker argues in *Modernism and the Harlem Renaissance*, Washington may be manipulating stereotypes to a purpose and "The Atlanta Exposition Address" chapter in *Up From Slavery* may be "a *how to* manual, setting forth strategies of address (ways of talking black and back) designed for Afro-American Empowerment." Despite this ironic dimension, the narrator of "The Invisible Man" seems to read and recite Washington's Exposition Address without any conscious irony. It is telling that even in the course of being physically beaten, the narrator still fixates on giving his speech. He remembers, "The harder we fought the more threatening the men became. And yet, I had begun to worry about my speech again. How would it go? Would they recognize my ability? What would they give me?" The final question here—"What would they give me"—indicates a potential agency in the narrator, but his concern about his audience recognizing his ability disturbs this pragmatism. As the narrator throws punches at Tatlock in "hopeless desperation," he "[wants] to deliver [his] speech more than anything else in the world" believing that "only these men could truly judge [his] ability."

When he finally renders for a second time the graduation speech, the narrator's one word slip from "responsibility" to "equality" precipitates a surprising effect. The boisterous, jeering laughter hangs "smoke-like in the sudden stillness" before "sounds of displeasure" fill the room. As the narrator has "hostile phrases" thrown at him, a "small, dry, mustached man in the front row blare[s] out, 'Say that slowly, son!'" When the narrator repeats "responsibility" instead of "equality," the mustached man asks, "You weren't being smart, were you, boy?"

The truly disturbing aspect of the narrator's "mistake" is not the mere statement of "social equality" but the idea that the narrator is being "smart"—making fun of the white audience. To be "smart" might imply that the entire speech is in fact a charade, covering over the narrator's actual belief in the necessity of social equality. It is important to realize that in extricating himself from that bind, the narrator is not expected to speak politically or philosophically to his understanding and endorsement of "social responsibility"; instead, he merely grovels, reinforcing the whites' comfortable belief—or illusion?—that he is a mere puppet that has simply uttered the wrong word.

Of course, the narrator's explanation of the mistake makes no logical sense. How would "swallowing blood" make him say one particular word instead of another? In fixating on the literal act of speaking and swallowing blood, the narrator distracts the audience from the deeper meanings of the word "equality." His "swallowing of blood" turns his "mistake" into a physical reflex and invokes the pathetic violence that the narrator had endured

> Emerson's metaphor of the 'transparent eyeball' is complex. While it seems to imply a transcendent individual who is 'part of parcel of God,' it also implies a vanishing of individualism as 'I become nothing."

before taking center stage to once again entertain his audience.

As the story ends, the narrator's safety depends on his ability to remain literal, speaking safely-scripted words that illustrate his lack of power. The small, mustached man concludes, "Well, you had better speak more slowly so we can understand. We mean to do right by you but you've got to know your place at all times. All right, now, go on with your speech." Here the hierarchy of power is clearly formulated. The pronouns "we" and "you" register a distinction that places the narrator in an inferior social category. By instructing the narrator to "know [his] place," the man emphasizes this inferiority; "do[ing] right by you" is another expression of white superiority, coded in a rhetoric of social responsibility. This differentiation and domination is reinforced, finally, by the demand on the narrator to "speak more slowly" and "go on with [his] speech." To conclude the speech, the narrator closes his ears and swallows blood.

In finishing his speech, the narrator reports that it "seemed a hundred times as long as before" and that he knows not to "leave out a single word." The speech is finally reduced to a mere string of stagnant words parroted to avoid impending violence. It sits in stark contrast to the expansive metaphors of Emerson's "Nature." When the narrator, with tears in his eyes, then accepts the leather briefcase and college scholarship, Ellison's story flattens Booker T. Washington into a one-dimensional image promoting capitulation to white authority. In these reductions—of the narrator to the excruciating recitation of the literal, and of Washington to a mere image of white acceptance—Ellison bridles Emerson's ebullient symbol of the "transparent eyeball." This graduate's eye literally throbs as he struggles to prove to his white audience that he is not "being smart."

Source: Kendall Johnson, in an essay for *Short Stories for Students*, Gale Group, 2001

Cynthia A. Bily

Bily teaches at Adrian College in Adrian, Michigan. In the following essay, Bily discusses Ralph Ellison's use of paradox to enhance an atmosphere of chaos in "Battle Royal."

Few rooms in literature are as vividly drawn as the fancy hotel ballroom in Ralph Ellison's "Battle Royal." Full of smoke, whiskey fumes, the red faces of howling drunken men watching a white woman dancing and a group of black boys fighting, the room calls to mind a chaotic vision of hell by Hieronymus Bosch. Ralph Ellison was fascinated by the chaos of the world, and saw confronting and depicting it as a writer's responsibility. In "That Same Pain, That Same Pleasure: An Interview," he explains, "I think that the mixture of the marvelous and the terrible is a basic condition of human life and that the persistence of human ideals represents the marvelous pulling itself up out of the chaos of the universe. In the fairy tale, beauty must be awakened by the beast, and the beastly man can only regain his humanity through love.... Here the terrible represents all that hinders, all that opposes human aspiration, and the marvelous represents the triumph of the human spirit over chaos."

The challenge in pulling oneself up is learning to make distinctions, to see individual details in a chaotic swirl of elements. Ellison's language consistently draws attention to the ballroom as a place where seeing is difficult, where vision is literally and figuratively clouded. The room is entered, like a carnival fun house, through a "big mirrored hall," and what is found inside is not to be trusted. The room is "foggy with cigar smoke" as the boys enter, and the white men are engrossed with something the narrator and his friends cannot see. Against the backdrop of the sensuous clarinet, the narrator repeats the idea that "the big shots were becoming increasingly excited over something we could not see." As the episode begins, the two groups are separated by what they can and cannot see.

The "big shots" eventually push the narrator forward, where the nude woman is dancing, "the smoke of a hundred cigars clinging to her like the thinnest of veils." Here the idea of seeing/not seeing becomes tangled on itself. The narrator wants to see her and yet not to see her: "I was strongly attracted and looked in spite of myself. Had the price of looking been blindness, I would have looked." The white men, having pushed the black teenagers forward, cannot decide how they should behave, and "some threatened us if we looked and others if we did not." What does it mean to look, and to see? What effect does looking have on the thing looked at? The dancer seems not to respond to the men's gaze, or to their drunken excitement, but retains "impersonal eyes" and a "detached look on her face."

After the dancer is carried from the room, the battle royal begins, and again the imagery of seeing/not seeing is insistent. As they are about to fight, the boys are literally "blindfolded with broad bands of white cloth," and the narrator feels a "sudden fit of blind terror." As the fight begins, the voices of the shouting men frighten the narrator, and he tries to move his blindfold aside because "I wanted to see, to see more desperately than ever before." But the blindfold is too tight, and the narrator comes to realize that a man who can't see is powerless. "Blindfolded, I could no longer control my motions. I had no dignity."

After a particularly hard blow to the face, the narrator discovers that his bandage has been knocked aside a bit and he has partial vision in one eye. Although the fighters are now out of control and hysterical, the narrator feels more in control, because "with my eye partly open now there was not so much terror." The rest of the boys are still "blind, groping crabs," but the narrator, with his limited vision, plays "one group against the other, slipping in and throwing a punch then stepping out of range." He believes now that his physical vision increases his control, but he soon finds that this is not the case. Although he is able to literally *see* what the other boys are doing around him, he does not *see* what they are planning as they exit the ring one by one and leave him to fight the "biggest of the gang."

The distinction between literal and figurative seeing is driven home (to the reader, if not to the narrator) when the boys are ordered to pick up their money where it is lying on the carpet. The narrator sees what the men want him to see: "I saw the rug scattered with coins of all dimensions, and a few crumpled bills. But what excited me, scattered here and there, were the gold pieces." Of course, the gold pieces are a trick, just as the electrified carpet is a trick.

Although the white men certainly bear a large portion of the blame for the boys' deception—they are, in fact, deliberately tricking the boys for their own amusement—Ellison makes it clear that the narrator's youth and inexperience, and his excitement at being asked to give his speech, also contribute to his situation. He is frequently distracted by the prospect of giving his speech. When the blindfolds are being put on the boys, the narrator does not at first realize what is happening to him, because "even then I had been going over my speech." He is thinking about his speech when the other boys start leaving the ring. When he is fighting Tatlock at the end of the battle royal, he thinks again of his speech, and he becomes "confused": "I wanted to give my speech more than anything else in the world"; "Should I try to win . . . ? Would not this go against my speech . . . ?" While his mind is thus occupied, Tatlock delivers the blow that knocks the narrator out.

Beyond the narrator's youthful eagerness, he is also subject to the same human weaknesses as his white tormenters. As he explained in a 1953 essay titled "Twentieth-Century Fiction and the Black Mask of Humanity," Ellison had found that American writers "seldom conceive Negro characters possessing the full, complex ambiguity of the human. Too often what is presented as the American Negro (a most complex example of Western man) emerges an oversimplified clown, a beast or an angel. Seldom is he drawn as that sensitively focused process of opposites, of good and evil, of instinct and intellect, of passion and spirituality, which great literary art has projected as the image of man." In creating the protagonist of "Battle Royal" and the novel *Invisible Man*, Ellison consciously tried to depict not an innocent victim or "angel," but a full, rich, complex human being, capable of making mistakes, and of learning and growing.

Ellison explained in *The Art of Fiction* that "the narrator's development is one through blackness to light; that is, from ignorance to enlightenment: invisibility to visibility." He was referring in this line to the whole novel, *Invisible Man*, of which "Battle Royal" was the first chapter. It should not surprise us, therefore, to find that this narrator is often blind, and in many ways ignorant. In many ways, his attitudes and behavior echo those of the white "big shots" in the ballroom.

> "The narrator is not at fault simply for participating willingly in his own humiliation. He also shares in the white men's feelings of superiority, and is himself capable of behaving as an oppressor. As he rides in the elevator toward the ballroom, he thinks about the boys with him, and thinks, 'I felt superior to them in my way, and I didn't like the manner in which we were all crowded together.'"

As brutal and humiliating as the battle royal itself seems to readers in the twenty-first century, Ellison does not entirely blame the white men for its existence. Most of the boys seem to take for granted that fighting this way is a good way to earn money, and the narrator has "some misgivings" only because he "didn't care too much for the other fellows who were to take part." Ellison wrote about the battle royal in *The Art of Fiction*, describing it as "a vital part of behavior pattern in the South, which both Negroes and whites thoughtlessly accept. It is a ritual in preservation of caste lines, a keeping of taboo to appease the gods and ward off bad luck. It is also the initiation ritual to which all greenhorns are subjected. This passage which states what Negroes will see I did not have to invent; the patterns were already there in society, so that all I had to do was present them in a broader context of meaning."

The narrator is not at fault simply for participating willingly in his own humiliation. He also shares in the white men's feelings of superiority, and is himself capable of behaving as an oppressor. As he rides in the elevator toward the ballroom, he thinks about the boys with him, and thinks, "I felt superior to them in my way, and I didn't like the manner in which we were all crowded together." As he fights Tatlock, he feels more on a par with the men than with the boy: "I felt that only these men could truly judge my ability, and now this stupid clown was ruining my chances."

The most disturbing example of the narrator's own capacity for cruelty and oppression comes when he watches the nude dancer. His description of the "magnificent blonde" strips her of all humanity, and reduces her to an object, a collection of body parts: "The hair was yellow like that of a circus kewpie doll, the face heavily powdered and rouged, as though to form an abstract mask, the eyes hollow and smeared a cool blue, the color of a baboon's butt." In watching her and dehumanizing her, the narrator is no different from the white men who are doing the same thing, and his response to her echoes the hatred the men feel for him: "I felt a desire to spit upon her as my eyes brushed slowly over her body." The atmosphere of chaos, of paradox, engulfs the narrator as he watches the dancer, and his feelings are contradictory and overwhelming: "I wanted at one and the same time to run from the room, to sink through the floor, or go to her and cover her from my eyes and the eyes of the others with my body; to feel the soft thighs, to caress her and destroy her, to love her and murder her."

When the dancer has been carried from the room, and the boys have toweled off and changed their clothes, the narrator does at last get to present his speech. As the men continue to drink and talk among themselves, the boy speaks eloquently about wisdom and patience and social responsibility. After all he has been through with these men, he is still taken in by their "thunderous applause." When they present him with a college scholarship, it makes up for everything: "I was overjoyed; I did not even mind when I discovered that the gold pieces I had scrambled for were brass pocket tokens."

Has the boy learned anything from his experience? There is no indication that he has. By presenting the ballroom as a chaotic world where nothing can be trusted, and by presenting the boy as fully human and flawed, Ellison makes a happy ending impossible. There is still too much for the boy to overcome, too much for him to learn. He does not yet know the difference between looking and seeing, and he does not understand that in a world of chaos, a piece of paper is no more to be trusted than a gold piece on a carpet. At the end of the story, though, there is some hope. The narrator is about to embark on a college education, and beyond that a life education. He has not yet pulled himself "up out of the chaos of the universe," but he is about to take the first step.

Source: Cynthia A. Bily, in an essay for *Short Stories for Students*, Gale Group, 2001.

Liz Brent

Brent has a Ph.D. in American Culture, specializing in film studies, from the University of Michigan. She is a freelance writer and teaches courses in the history of American cinema. In the following essay, Brent discusses figurative language in Ellison's story.

Ralph Ellison's short story, "Battle Royal," first published in 1947, describes an extremely disturbing event, organized by the local elite white men of a Southern town. This event involves the abuse and humiliation of several young black men for the purpose of entertaining a gathering of these prominent and outwardly respectable white men. The narrator of the story, a recent high school graduate, has been invited to repeat a much-celebrated speech he gave at his graduation, in which he emphasizes the importance of "humility" among African Americans. Instead, however, he is grouped with several of the toughest young black men from his high school, and forced to participate in a series of bizarre and grotesque activities as a form of entertainment for the white men. These young men are first forced into the frighteningly uncomfortable situation of being exposed to a beautiful, blonde white woman, who stands completely naked in the middle of the room, as the white men look on. This is an especially intimidating situation for these young African-American men, because they have been strictly taught by a racist Southern culture not to regard white women in a sexual way. The young men are then blindfolded and forced to fight one another in a bloody brawl. Finally, they are forced to scramble for loose change and dollar bills on a rug which has been charged with electricity, subjecting them to painful electric shocks at each point of contact. Only after being subjected to these cruel and horrible activities is the narrator allowed to give his speech. During the speech, however, he is made a laughingstock by the white men, after which he is presented with a leather briefcase containing a scholarship to the state Negro college. Throughout this narrative, Ellison makes use of figurative language to describe this disturbing experience. The following essay discusses the effectiveness of Ellison's use of figurative language in this story, focusing particularly on the recurring motifs of war, circus, and animal imagery.

The central figurative motif of Ellison's story is that of war. Racial relations between black and white in the United States are represented as a state of warfare. This war motif is most strongly asserted through the dying words of the narrator's grandfather, who tells his son that "after I'm gone I want you to keep up the good fight. I never told you, but our life is a war and I have been a traitor all my born days, a spy in the enemy's country ever since I give up my gun back in the Reconstruction." Racial relations in the United States, even after the end of the Civil War, and the era of Reconstruction, are described by the grandfather as an ongoing "war," and the struggle of African Americans to gain equality is referred to as "the good fight." The grandfather describes himself as a "traitor" to white people; he was "a spy in the enemy's country" in that he posed among white people ("the enemy's country") as the type of humble, subservient black man they wanted him to be, while secretly harboring rebellious ideas. The narrator admits that "I could never be quite sure of what he meant," but he nevertheless feels cursed by the statement. The narrator is particularly disturbed by his grandfather's description of himself as secretly a "traitor" to white people, although outwardly conforming to their wishes.

The story's title, "Battle Royal," suggests that the incidents described in the narrative are just one battle in this ongoing racial war. This battle, however, is not fought between black and white, but among the group of black "schoolmates." The narrator explains that "the battle royal was to be fought by some of my schoolmates as part of the entertainment." They are forced to blindly fight one another in a brutal fistfight, and then to fight one another again in the scramble for money on the electrified rug. This "battle royal" symbolizes the ways in which white society forces African Americans to fight amongst themselves, defeating one another, in a scramble for the limited resources provided them by white society. Instead of banding together to protest their racist treatment by the white men, the young black men find themselves turning against each other for the prize money, and then for the loose change on the rug.

> After describing the lives of African Americans as a 'war,' he goes on to assert his method of dealing with white society in terms which compare it to a lion tamer sticking his head into the mouth of a lion: 'Live with your head in the lion's mouth."

The figurative language of Ellison's story is further characterized by the recurring motif of comparing the experience to a circus. The circus imagery is significant to the story in several ways. A circus is a grandiose spectacle presented for the sole purpose of entertaining masses of people. A circus is also characterized by a variety of acts and events designed to arouse the awe and fascination of the crowds. The young African-American men in the story are forced to participate in a variety of events designed for the sole purpose of entertaining the crowd of white men who fill the hall.

In addition to circus imagery, Ellison's story includes the recurring motif of animal imagery. Sometimes the animal imagery is part of the circus imagery, a circus being characterized by various animal shows, such as lions, dogs, and seals. On one hand, the animal imagery implies that the treatment of African Americans by whites is animalistic and inhumane. On the other hand, the animal imagery in the story reinforces the message that the white men treat the African-American men as if they are no better than animals. Further, the circus animal imagery indicates that these young African-American men are being treated as *trained* animals—they are being taught by white society how to "perform," so to speak, for the entertainment and edification of white people. In the end of the story, the narrator realizes that, even his success as a high school student, and subsequent award of a scholarship to college, is simply further training for him to serve a role of subservience for the "entertainment" of white people.

The first mention of circus animal imagery in the story is uttered by the narrator's dying grandfather. After describing the lives of African Americans as a "war," he goes on to assert his method of dealing with white society in terms which compare it to a lion tamer sticking his head into the mouth of a lion: "Live with your head in the lion's mouth." The narrator's grandfather thus describes white society as a circus lion, a vicious beast in the presence of whom one is always in danger of being swallowed. Further, the grandfather's advice to "live with your head in the lion's mouth" implies that black people are at their best advantage symbolically "taming" the beast of white racist society by outwardly placating white people, while inwardly undermining their power. "I want you to overcome 'em with yeses, undermine 'em with grins, agree 'em to death and destruction, let 'em swoller you till they vomit or bust open." The grandfather's advice is to be so outwardly agreeable to white people, "let 'em swoller you," as to undermine white society from within by giving it what it thinks it wants, "till they vomit or bust open."

White society is described at several other points in the story, using figurative language which refers to animals. This imagery conveys the implication that the white men's treatment of the black men is animalistic and inhumane. As part of the circus motif, as mentioned above, white society is described as a circus lion. At the banquet hall, the white men, "all of the town's big shots," who attend the event, are described as voracious wolves, "who were there in their tuxedos, wolfing down the buffet foods, drinking beer and whisky and smoking black cigars." The image of white men as wolves indicates both their greed in exploiting black people and the vicious nature of their ardent racism. A wolf is a predator, and the racist white society preys upon the disempowered black community like a pack of wolves. The association of the white men with "howling" wolves is evoked later in the story, when the narrator is punched during a fistfight and, as he reels, sees the crowd of white men as, "howling red faces crouching tense beneath the cloud of blue-gray smoke." The white men in the crowd are later described as deadly snakes, animals almost always associated with evil, particularly by way of reference to the serpent in the Bible. After the narrator is blindfolded, and before he is forced to fight his fellow classmates, he explains that "I felt a sudden fit of blind terror. I was unused to darkness, it was as though I had suddenly found myself in a dark room filled with poisonous cottonmouths."

This reference to the "cottonmouth" snake is also appropriate because the mention of "cotton" recalls the use of black slaves in the South to pick cotton for white plantation owners. Although the story is written long after the abolition of slavery, the association suggests that even in the mid-twentieth century, white society's treatment of African Americans is little better than that of slave masters. Later in the story, when the young black men are forced to scramble for change on an electrified rug, one of the white men is heard to yell out, "like a bass-voiced parrot." Parrots are known for their ability to mindlessly mimic the words of human beings, without any comprehension of the meaning or significance of what they are saying. This image implies that the crowd of white men, shouting at the young black men, are no better than parrots, mindlessly repeating the racist words and deeds perpetuated by white society, without any thought or consideration.

The circus imagery continues with the description of the naked white woman in the middle of the room as having hair that is "yellow like that of a circus kewpie doll, the face powdered and rouged, as though to form an abstract mask." Here, the white woman is seen as occupying a similar social station to that of the young black men; like them, she is not treated as a human being, but as an inanimate object, a "doll," brought in as a toy or plaything, part of the circus-like entertainment for the enjoyment of the white men. Although the narrator ultimately seems to be sympathetic to the white woman, he also describes her in terms of animal imagery. He describes her eyes as "hollow and smeared a cool blue, the color of a baboon's butt." This is certainly an odd descriptive image. However, the association of the naked white women with "a baboon's butt" suggests both disgust and disdain. She is later described more sympathetically as a "bird girl," when the narrator states that, "She seemed like a fair bird-girl in veils calling to me from the angry surface of some gray and threatening sea." This image suggests that the narrator sees the woman as delicate, and vulnerable, indicating his feelings of sympathy for her, as she is also being humiliated and exploited by the roomful of white men, who appear intimidating as "some gray and threatening sea." One of the white men lasciviously ogling the naked white woman is described as an animal, "his posture clumsy like that of an intoxicated panda." This "creature" demonstrates the quality of the racist white men as no better than animals in their regard for, and treatment of, the white woman, as well as of the black men.

While the white men are described in terms of animals associated with viciousness, evil, and predatory behavior, the young black men are described as animals evoking very different associations. As they are forced to fistfight one another while blindfolded, the narrator describes the young African-American men as defenseless "crabs," doing their utmost to "protect" their vulnerable "midsections": "The boys groped about like blind, cautious crabs crouching to protect their midsections, their heads pulled in short against their shoulders, their arms stretched nervously before them." This description goes on to associate the young men with even more defenseless, "hypersensitive" creatures, "their fists testing the smoke-filled air like the knobbed feelers of hypersensitive snails." The narrator later associates himself with an animal, one that is delicate, vulnerable, and beautiful: a butterfly. As he lies knocked to the floor, he watches "a dark red spot of my own blood shaping itself into a butterfly, glistening and soaking into the soiled gray world of the canvas." Even in the moment of utter pain, humiliation, and defeat, the narrator maintains the sense of self-worth to envision himself as something beautiful. Further, butterflies are associated with change and rebirth, as the beautiful butterfly emerges from the plain cocoon. In some ways, this experience is a sort of "rebirth" for the narrator, as he gains a deeper, albeit more troubling, perspective on the nature of racism, and his own position in a white, racist society. When, in the next round of events, the young black men are forced to scramble for money on a rug charged with electricity, the narrator describes himself as a rat, when he describes the experience of being electrocuted on the rug: "A hot, violent force tore through my body, shaking me like a wet rat." Rats are generally considered among the lowest and most disdainfully regarded of creatures; the narrator here expresses the sentiment that white racist society looks down on African Americans as no better, and deserving no better treatment, than rats. Further, rats are scavengers, who survive by scrambling for whatever food they can find. Similarly, the young black men are made to scramble for the money on the rug, as if African Americans were given no dignified means of supporting themselves within the structure of white society.

Similarly to being treated like trained animals, the young black men are treated like "circus clowns," forced to makes fools of themselves for the entertainment of the white crowd. As the forced fistfight continues, the narrator finds himself one of two men left fighting. He attempts several times to work together with his fellow classmate in fooling the white men while avoiding actually hurting each other. But the other man is too caught up in the desire to win to appreciate this effort. The narrator then describes him as a "stupid clown" whom he felt was ruining his chances of making a positive impression on the white men. The young black men are further described as trained animals displayed for the purpose of entertaining the white crowd, as at a circus, when the narrator describes one of them "lifted into the air, glistening with sweat like a circus seal, and dropped, his wet back landing flush upon the charged rug." This description continues with further animal imagery, as the narrator describes seeing the young man, "literally dance upon his back, his elbows beating a frenzied tattoo upon the floor, his muscles twitching like the flesh of a horse stung by many flies." Here, the young black man is described as a horse, a beast of burden kept by humans to serve their own ends, just as black people have been used by white society as beasts of burden to perform grueling physical labor. The "many flies" which sting the horse describe the crowd of white men, the narrator implying that they are no better than flies, and perhaps dangerous only because they are "many" in number.

The circus imagery first evoked by the grandfather's advice comes full circle with the dream described by the narrator at the end of the story. The narrator describes a dream he had the night after being forced to participate in this series of events, and then being awarded a college scholarship. He dreams that he was at a circus with his grandfather, who "refused to laugh at the clowns no matter what they did." The clowns here represent African Americans, who are forced by white society to "perform" acts of self-humiliation for the entertainment and pleasure of white people. In the dream, the narrator's grandfather refuses to laugh at the clowns, because he knows that they are his own people, forced into such acts of submission. At the end of the dream, the grandfather has given the narrator a note that implies that white society will continue to make a clown of him, and that, by association, even the college scholarship is merely another gesture by white society meant to enforce the subservience and "humility" of black people.

Source: Liz Brent, in an essay for *Short Stories for Students*, Gale Group, 2001.

Sources

Baumbach, Jonathan, "Nightmare of a Native Son: Ralph Ellison's *Invisible Man*," in *Critique*, Vol. 6, No. 1, Spring, 1963, 48–65.

Bellow, Saul, "Man Underground: Review of Ralph Ellison's *Invisible Man*" in *Commentary*, June, 1952, pp. 608–610.

Busby, Marle, *Ralph Ellison*, Twayne, 1991.

Emerson, Ralph Waldo, "Nature," in *Selected Essays*, edited by Larzer Ziff, Penguin, 1985, pp. 35–82.

German, Norman, "Imagery in the "Battle Royal" Chapter of Ralph Ellison's *Invisible Man*," in *CLA Journal*, Vol. 21, No. 4, June, 1988, pp. 394–399.

Hoberek, Andrew, "Race Man, Organization Man, *Invisible Man*," in *Modern Language Quarterly*, Vol. 59, No. 1, March, 1998, pp. 99–119.

Holland, Laurence B., "Ellison in Black and White: Confession, Violence and Rhetoric in *Invisible Man*," in *Black Fiction: New Studies in the Afro-American Novel Since 1945*, edited by A. Robert Lee, Barnes and Noble Books, 1980, pp. 54–73.

Howe, Irving, "Review of Ralph Ellison's *Invisible Man*," in the *Nation*, May 10, 1952.

Kim, Daniel Y., "Invisible Desires: Homoerotic Racism and its Homophobic Critique in Ralph Ellison's *Invisible Man*," in *Novel*, Vol. 30, No. 3, Spring, 1997, pp. 309–328.

Lee, Kun Jong, "Ellison's *Invisible Man*: Emersonianism Revised," in *PMLA*, Vol. 107, No. 2, March, 1992, pp. 331–344.

Lyne, William, "The Signifying Modernist: Ralph Ellison and the Limits of the Double Consiousness," in *PMLA*, Vol. 107, No. 2, March, 1992, pp. 310–330.

Massey, Douglas S. and Nancy A. Denton, *American Apartheid: Segregation and the Making of the Underclass*, Harvard University Press, 1994.

Morris, Wright, *New York Times*, April 13, 1952.

Neal, Larry, *Visions of a Liberated Future: Black Arts Movement Writings*, edited by Michael Schwartz, Thunder's Mouth, 1989.

O'Meally, Robert, ed., *New Essays on "Invisible Man,"* Cambridge University Press, 1994.

Parr, Susan Resneck and Pancho Savery, eds., *Approaches to Teaching Ellison's "Invisible Man,"* The Modern Language Association, 1989.

Sundquist, Eric J., ed., *Cultural Contexts for Ralph Ellison's "Invisible Man": A Bedford Documentary Companion*, St. Martin's Press, 1995.

Further Reading

Branch, Taylor, *Parting the Waters: America in the King Years 1954–63*, Simon and Schuster, 1988.
> This Pulitzer Prize-winning history narrates the intensification of civil rights initiatives and the advent of a national movement that spanned across the North and South.

Ellison, Ralph, *Invisible Man*, Random House, 1952.
> The complete novel develops themes laid out in the short story. The plot follows the narrator to college and then to New York City where much of the novel takes place.

Kozol, Jonathan, *Savage Inequalities: Children in America's Schools*, HarperPerennial, 1991.
> This book offers accounts of the state of public education in the United States, demonstrating that racial segregation has endured since 1954, perpetuating inequalities in social and economic opportunity. The book blends insightful interviews of teachers and students with analysis of the current logic behind public policy.

Sundquist, Eric J., ed., *Cultural Contexts for Ralph Ellison's "Invisible Man": A Bedford Documentary Companion*, St. Martin's Press, 1995.
> This book offers fabulous excerpts from a wide range of documents, including Supreme Court decisions, literary essays, historical considerations and political essays. Serves to orient the novel in regard to the historical, political and social context in which it was written, published, and read.

The Gilded Six-Bits

Zora Neale Hurston

1933

Zora Neale Hurston's "The Gilded Six-Bits" was published in *Story* magazine in 1933, when Hurston was a relative newcomer on the literary scene. The well-known publisher Bertram Lippincott read the story and liked it so much that he wrote to Hurston and asked if she was working on a novel. She wasn't, but, eager for a book deal, she told him that she was, and, three months later, presented him with the manuscript of her first novel, *Jonah's Gourd Vine*.

Hurston, a noted talent and personality of the cultural movement known as the Harlem Renaissance, went on to greater success with the publication of her second novel, *Their Eyes Were Watching God*, in 1937, but later fell into obscurity and eventually died in poverty. Though it was pivotal to her career, "The Gilded Six-Bits" was not reprinted until renewed scholarly interest in Hurston led to the publication of a compilation of her short stories, entitled *Spunk*, in 1985. It is now considered one of Hurston's best stories.

"The Gilded Six-Bits" is a story of love, betrayal, and forgiveness. It playfully portrays the happy domestic life of two young newlyweds and shows the havoc that is wreaked when a slick and sophisticated outsider comes into their community and into their home. The story is typical of Hurston's fiction in that it offers a positive and affectionate vision of African-American life, that it is set in her native town of Eatonville, and that it reflects the rich oral traditions of that community. "The Gilded Six-

Bits," rich in metaphor and melodious dialect, is a meditation on the meaning of value and a celebration of emotional resilience and integrity.

Author Biography

Zora Neale Hurston was born January 7, 1903, in the all-black town of Eatonville, Florida. She was the daughter of John and Lucy Hurston. Her father worked as a preacher and a carpenter and also served as Eatonville's mayor. Her mother, a seamstress, was a powerful and positive influence in Hurston's life, encouraging her daughter to "jump at de sun." She died when Hurston was nine, her father quickly remarried, and Hurston was sent to boarding school. While still a child, Hurston worked at many odd jobs. A white employer eventually arranged for her to attend high school at Morgan Preparatory School in Baltimore, Maryland, where she graduated in 1918. Biographer Robert E. Hemenway writes that "the sources of the Hurston self-confidence were her home town, her family, and the self-sufficiency demanded of her after she left home for the world."

Hurston went on to Howard University, publishing her first stories while a student there. After receiving an Associate's degree, she struck out for Harlem, which had become a thriving center for black culture. The witty and outgoing Hurston took the town by storm, charming the black intelligentsia and white patrons of the blossoming artistic movement known as the Harlem Renaissance. She soon won a scholarship to attend the prestigious Barnard College, becoming its first black student. Here began her lifelong interest in anthropology. She received a B.A. from Barnard in 1928.

While studying, Hurston continued to publish short stories. In 1933, she published "The Gilded Six-Bits," and her first novel, *Jonah's Gourd Vine*, came out the following year. In 1935, she published *Mules and Men*, a collection of folklore gathered from her native Eatonville. Dividing her time between fiction and anthropology, Hurston began graduate studies in anthropology at Columbia University in 1935 and wrote what is widely considered her best novel, *Their Eyes Were Watching God*, (1937) while doing field work in the West Indies.

Ambitious and frank to a fault, Hurston made enemies as well as friends in Harlem. But, despite the fact that she had become a celebrated writer, she never lost her sense of humor or forgot her roots. The flamboyant and exuberant Hurston could talk to anyone, from rich benefactors to illiterate farmers. Her memories of the self-segregated Eatonville community stayed close to her heart, leading her to oppose school desegregation in the 1950s, against the rising tide of the Civil Rights Movement.

In her middle age, Hurston fell on hard times. She supported herself as a screenwriter and college drama instructor but was later reduced to working as a maid, a job she had never been good at in her youth. Hurston was married twice briefly and had no children. She suffered a stroke in 1959, and died in a public home the following year. She was buried in an unmarked grave at a segregated cemetery in Fort Pierce, Florida.

Plot Summary

The story opens with the description of a modest but cheerful house in an all-black community. Inside, Missie May, a young newlywed, rushes to bathe in anticipation of her husband Joe's return from work. She hears the sound of Joe throwing nine silver dollars in the door, signaling their playful weekly ritual. She pretends to be mad that he is throwing the money and chases him, then goes through his pockets to find little presents he has bought her.

As they eat dinner that night, Joe tells her that he is going to take her out to a new ice-cream parlor opened by a man from Chicago. They discuss this new man in town, whose name is Otis D. Slemmons. Slemmons appears to be rich and worldly. Joe admires his fine clothes, while Missie May comments on his big gut and suggests that he might be lying about his wealth and success. Joe cites a five-dollar gold piece that Slemmons wears as a stickpin and a ten-dollar piece he wears on his watch chain as evidence of his wealth. Joe has heard that women gave him all of his money, but Missie May continues to compliment her husband and deny Slemmons's attractiveness. Joe tells Missie May that he wants to show off his pretty wife to Slemmons.

When they return from the ice-cream parlor, they continue to talk of Slemmons and his gold. Joe tells his wife that he is happy without riches as long as he has her. A weekly trip to the ice-cream parlor becomes part of the happy couple's routine.

One night Joe is sent home from work early. As he walks home he fantasizes about having a son with Missie May. When he arrives home, he calls out to his wife to reassure her in case, hearing him, she fears an intruder. There is a loud noise in the bedroom. Joe imagines a robber or murderer is attacking Missie May. He enters the room and finds Slemmons in their bedroom half dressed. Slemmons pleads with Joe for his life, offering him money not to hurt him. Joe punches him and tells him to get out. As Slemmons flees, Joe hits him again and finds that his gold charm has broken off in his hand.

Joe's response is to laugh, while Missie May cries, telling Joe that she knows he doesn't love her anymore and explaining that Slemmons had offered her gold. Joe tells her he has gotten the gold piece for her. They spend the night awake in bed, not speaking. Missie May imagines that Joe will leave her, but Joe asks her to fix him breakfast, signifying some degree of normalcy between them. At breakfast she sees the gold piece that Joe has set down on the table. She cries, and he tells her not to think about the past.

Joe does not leave Missie May, but gone is the couple's loving playfulness. She often wonders where the gold coin is. One night Joe comes home from work complaining of a sore back. She rubs him—the first physical contact they have had since her betrayal. This leads to sex, which thrills Missie May until she finds the gold coin under Joe's pillow the next morning. She examines it and realizes that it is not a gold piece but a fifty-cent coin gilded with a thin layer of gold. She wonders if Joe thinks he has bought her. She puts the coin back in his pants pocket and leaves the house. But she soon runs into Joe's mother and resolves that no one should find out about the damage to her marriage.

One day Joe comes home from work and sees Missie May chopping wood. He tells her to stop, recognizing that she is pregnant. Missie May tells him that the baby will be a boy that looks just like him. Joe fingers something in his pocket—presumably the gold coin.

Six months later Missie May gives birth to a baby boy. Joe asks his mother, who has attended the birth, how his wife is, at first not asking about the child. His mother tells him that the baby looks just like him. For a week afterward, Joe goes to work and then comes home and stands at the foot of his wife's bed.

The next weekend Joe goes to the nearby city to do some shopping. He buys all of the regular staples, then asks how many molasses kisses he can

Zora Neale Hurston

get for fifty cents, throwing the gilded coin onto the counter. The clerk, who is a white man, asks him where he got it, and Joe tells him about a man who came through town pretending he was rich and trying to steal people's wives. The clerk asks if the man had tricked him, and Joe denies it. Joe asks for a full fifty cents worth of candy for his wife and new son. After he leaves the store, the clerk comments to the next customer that he wishes he could be like "these darkies," referring to Joe. The clerk says that they laugh all of the time and never worry about anything.

Joe goes back home and rolls fifteen silver dollars in the front door. Missie May, still recovering from childbirth, creeps to the door. She playfully tells Joe that when she gets her strength back, she'll get him back for doing such a thing.

Characters

Joe Banks

Joe Banks is Missie May's husband. Joe and Missie May are newlyweds who are demonstrably in love. Joe works the night shift at the local fertilizer plant, but he does not make very much

Media Adaptations

- "The Gilded Six-Bits," read by Renee Joshua-Porter, is included on an audiocassette entitled *Stories by Zora Neale Hurston*, recorded in 1996 by Audio Bookshelf.

---

money. When his week is over, he and Missie May enjoy a flirtatious game that begins with him rolling his pay in coins over their threshold. Their life is filled with "joyful mischief" and also genuine sweetness. "That was the best part of life—going home to Missie May." They represent domestic harmony, each happy in his or her role and routine, until the flashy stranger Slemmons enters their life. Joe is impressed with the man's apparent wealth and his stories of success with women. He wants to show off his wife to Slemmons. When Missie May betrays Joe by having an affair with Slemmons, Joe is shocked and uncommunicative. He leaves Slemmons's gilded trinket around the house as if to remind Missie May of her failing, but when she gives birth to a son who looks just like Joe, he is able to fully forgive her. He buys her molasses kisses with the gilded coin, which represents affection and sweetness winning out over blame.

Missie May Banks

Missie May Banks is Joe's newlywed wife. She is enraptured with her new role as his spouse and with their domestic routine. Missie May is content to take care of their modest house and looks forward each day to Joe's return. Part of the couple's rapport involves playful banter and "mock battles" that end with her searching his pockets for candy and trinkets. However, real conflict enters the relationship when Missie May agrees to have sexual relations with Slemmons, a pretentious outsider who promises her gold that she knows Joe admires but cannot earn. It is implied that Missie May wants the gold not for herself but for Joe. Missie May is bereaved when Joe discovers her with Slemmons, assuming he will never love her again. Joe tells Missie May not to dwell on the past, but he reminds her of her betrayal by leaving Slemmons's gilded trinket around the house. She resolves that she will stay in the marriage until Joe leaves her, which he does not do. Their domestic routine continues, but devoid of the joyful banter and affection in which they had both reveled. Joe finally forgives Missie May completely when she gives birth to a baby boy that looks just like him.

Clerk

A white clerk waits on Joe when he goes to Orlando to buy supplies after Missie May gives birth. He asks Joe about the gilded fifty-cent piece, and Joe tells him about Slemmons, not admitting that Slemmons tricked and cuckolded him. After Joe leaves, the clerk comments to the next customer, "Wisht I could be like those darkies." The clerk interprets Joe's story in terms of stereotypes about blacks being simple and happy.

Joe's Mother

Missie May runs into Joe's mother after she has left the house, having discovered the gilded gold piece under Joe's pillow. She knows that Joe's mother doesn't like her, and the encounter reminds her of her pride and makes her resolve to keep up the "outside show" of her marriage. Joe's mother also attends to Missie May when she is in labor. She had not approved of the marriage, but after Missie May gives birth to Joe's son, she tells her son that he made a good choice after all.

Otis D. Slemmons

Otis D. Slemmons is a sophisticated newcomer in the small, rural, all-black community of Eatonville. He has just opened an ice-cream parlor there. Joe meets him and is impressed with his tales of seducing women and making money, while Missie May tries to boost her husband's ego by pointing out Slemmons's big gut. However, Missie May is also impressed by his ostentatious gold jewelry, wishing that she could get some for her husband. Lured by promises of gold, she agrees to have a sexual relationship with Slemmons. Only after her husband discovers them together and takes Slemmons's watch chain does Missie May realize that Slemmons is a fake, and that the gold piece he wears is nothing but a gilded fifty-cent piece. Slemmons stands for the emptiness of material wealth and the inauthenticity of big-city sophistication.

Topics for Further Study

- What are Missie May's motivations for betraying Joe by sleeping with Otis Slemmons? Do you think Joe bears some of the responsibility for her mistake?

- "The Gilded Six-Bits" can be understood as an exploration of different ideas of value. What are some of the different kinds of value that an object or person can have other than monetary value? What, in Hurston's view, is most valuable?

- Hurston is famous for capturing the richness of African-American oral traditions in her writing. Hurston's characters speak in language that is full of metaphors. Identify as many metaphors as you can find in the quoted speech of the characters in "The Gilded Six-Bits." How do these metaphors relate to the story's larger themes?

- Do some research about all-black towns in the United States. Do you think that they are a good idea? How does Hurston's portrayal of one such community in "The Gilded Six-Bits" influence your opinion?

- The Harlem Renaissance writers who were Hurston's peers often represented Northern cities as places of freedom and the rural South as tied to the oppressive past of slavery. Find some other short stories written by blacks during the Harlem Renaissance and describe their representations of the customs and values of the city versus the country. How do they compare to Hurston's in "The Gilded Six-Bits"?

Themes

Appearances and Reality

Hurston introduces the theme of appearances and reality in the first lines of the story. On the surface of things, the couple's yard is nothing but a "Negro yard around a Negro house in a Negro settlement that looked to the payroll of the G and G Fertilizer works for its support." But Hurston goes on to welcome readers inside the couple's home, describing their playful battle and teasing affection. What appears on the outside to be modest and meager is, in fact, rich with love and joy in life.

Hurston makes the converse point through the character of Slemmons. He has seen the world and experienced life more broadly than Missie May and Joe have. He has the appearance of sophistication and riches, represented by the ostentatious gold pieces he wears as jewelry. Despite the fact that they enjoy the simplicity of their life together, Joe and Missie May are taken in by the image that Slemmons projects. The gold money he wears on his jewelry makes a particular impact on the young man and woman who have never seen luxury. It impresses them that he has enough extra money to wear some of it for show. They are naïve in believing that Slemmons is what he appears to be and that he has something that they might want. They eventually discover that the ten-dollar gold piece Slemmons wears on his watch chain is nothing but a fifty-cent piece covered with gold. While Slemmons is richer and more sophisticated than Joe and Missie May, his life lacks the authenticity of theirs. The fake gold piece represents the fake appearances Slemmons presents to the world. In reality, Slemmons has nothing that compares to the happiness that Joe and Missie May share.

Betrayal and Forgiveness

The plot of "The Gilded Six-Bits" pivots on Missie May's betrayal of her husband. The reason for her betrayal is complicated. She is deeply in love with Joe, but takes to heart his awe for Slemmons's apparent riches and his comment that "Ah know Ah can't hold no light to Otis D. Slemmons." When she suspects Slemmons of lying about his status, Joe holds up the gold stickpin and watch chain as evidence that he is as rich as he says he is. And when she says that the gold would look better on Joe, he replies that she's crazy and a poor man like him will never have gold money. Joe claims that he's satisfied with his life as long as he has her, but Missie May has picked up on his longing for Slemmons's wealth and social standing. She enters into a sexual relationship with Slemmons because he offers her gold—the very thing that Joe thinks he will never have. By trying to give Joe gold, she takes away something more precious—his trust in her.

When Joe discovers her with Slemmons, Missie May fears that his love for her died then and there. But Joe's response to her betrayal is ambivalent. He doesn't reject her, but he doesn't communicate with her about his feelings either. She takes some comfort in resuming their normal domestic routine, but is troubled by the absence of affection and openness between them. Joe tells Missie May not to dwell on the past, but he reminds her of her betrayal by leaving the gold trinket from Slemmons's watch chain out for her to see. This is the only way Joe communicates with her about her betrayal. When she gives birth to his son—one that clearly resembles him rather than Slemmons—Joe is finally able to put the past behind him. He trades the trinket for molasses kisses. The kisses are a symbol of forgiveness in that they represent the affection that has been lacking. Because they melt in the mouth, they also represent the dissolving away of Joe's grudge.

Love and Passion

"The Gilded Six-Bits" is, above all, a love story. Missie May and Joe's love may not seem dramatic from the outside, but they create drama by enacting mock battles that give them an excuse to tease and wrestle with each other. The opening scene, where Missie May receives Joe at the door, has strong erotic elements. The couple's sexuality is represented as positive, open, and playful. The character of Missie May is introduced sitting naked in the bath. When her husband arrives, she chases him, and they fall to the floor together, "a furious mass of male and female energy." Joe pretends to resist as she searches through his pockets for the little gifts she knows he has brought her, leading her to threaten to tear his clothes off. This healthy, joyful love is thwarted by the appearance of Slemmons who seduces Missie May by promising her the gold she covets out of love of Joe. Missie May's interaction with Slemmons appears to completely lack the eroticism of her relationship with her husband. She sees the affair as a transaction and, perhaps, a sacrifice. By the end of the story, the couple finds a way to heal through the domestic routine they both love, through the sexual passion that they can't repress ("youth triumphed and Missie exulted") and, most importantly, through the fruit of that passion, a baby boy.

Style

Setting

Hurston begins the story with description of its setting that uses the same adjective repetitively: "It was a *Negro* yard around a *Negro* house in a *Negro* settlement." Such deliberate emphasis underscores the 'blackness' of the community (which is later named as Eatonville, Hurston's real-life hometown), defining how it is seen from the outside. Once the story gets underway, the characters' race is not mentioned, though it remains implicitly significant. "The Gilded Six-Bits" takes place in a community that is all black, thus racial *difference* is not much of an issue—quite an exceptional situation in the United States, especially during the race-conscious 1930s when Hurston wrote. Instead, Hurston addresses the issue of race through celebrating the integrity and cultural richness of the all-black community. Because she often chose such happily segregated settings, Hurston's black literary peers sometimes criticized her for failing to address racism. The issue of the community's insularity is explored in "The Gilded Six-Bits" through the device of a disruptive worldly outsider, Slemmons, who is impressive to Missie May and Joe largely because he is from "spots and places—Memphis, Chicago, Jacksonville, Philadelphia and so on." Hurston also offers the nearby city of Orlando as a contrast to Eatonville. Joe goes there to shop and chats with a white clerk in a friendly way, only to be called a "darky" as soon as he leaves. Hurston portrays the small all-black town as a harmonious haven that shields its inhabitants from the deceptions and prejudices of the larger society.

Narration

"The Gilded Six-Bits" is narrated in the third-person, from the perspective of someone who is not a participant in the events. The narrator is omniscient, with access to some of Missie May and Joe's inner thoughts, though, for the most part, the story is narrated in a straightforward and objective way. Perhaps the most striking feature of the story's narration is Hurston's use of dialect in the quoted speech of her characters. This sets up a contrast between the standard English of the exposition and the imaginative, vivid language of the characters. While, in the history of American literature until that point, dialect had been used in a way that reduced its speakers to stereotypes of ignorance, Hurston gloried in the expressiveness of African-American oral traditions. As a folklorist, she appreciated her people's dialect as a unique and often beautiful aspect of their culture. Missie May's good clothes are ''Sunday-go-to-meetin' things'' and Slemmons is capable of lying because ''his mouf is cut cross-ways, ain't it?'' Hurston also shows African-American dialect as particularly rich with metaphorical expressions of love. ''God took a pattern after a pine tree and built you noble,'' says Missie May. ''Ah'd ruther all de other womens in de world to be dead than for you to have de toothache,'' Joe tells her. Dialect is central to the story's literary power.

Symbolism

The set of symbols Hurston employs in the story are connected through the concept of *value*. The story opens with Joe returning home with his weekly pay and a few small gifts for his wife. When he rolls the coins in the door, they stand not for Joe's economic earning power, but instead a playful and erotic ritual through which the couple celebrates the beginning of their free time together. The dollars Joe rolls in the door are a sign of the homecoming that he regards as the happiest aspect of his life and a symbol of how much he values Missie May. The candy kisses hidden in his pockets represent both affection and eroticism. In contrast, the coins that Slemmons wears as jewelry represent the display of wealth for wealth's sake. ''Whut make it so cool,'' Joe says, duly impressed with Slemmons's gold, ''he got money 'cumulated.'' But when Slemmons's coins enter the Banks's house (their surname itself being a pun on money), their happiness is disrupted. His coins, which he wields as a form of power, especially over women, end up being worthless. They do not win Missie May from Joe but remain as a sign of the mistake she made over what to value. When Joe trades Slemmons's gilded trinket for a huge quantity of candy kisses at the end of the story, this refers back to the celebratory opening scene and suggests that, with the baby, Joe's faith has been restored, and his joy has been redoubled. The candy kisses symbolize what is truly valuable to the happy couple.

Historical Context

Eatonville, Florida

''The Gilded Six-Bits'' is set in Eatonville, Florida, which was the first incorporated all-black town in the United States and also Hurston's real-life hometown. Such voluntarily segregated towns, growing out of a post-Civil War phenomenon known as ''race colonies,'' offered blacks the opportunity for political independence and some measure of freedom from the oppression of the wider racist culture. The area—now part of Orange County, Florida—was developed largely by white Northern veterans of the Civil War, with blacks coming there initially for work opportunities. A few progressive whites sold small parcels of land to African Americans with the purpose of allowing them to build their own, new community. Twenty-seven founders incorporated Eatonville as a town in 1887. It was designed with civic and community principles in mind, with a school and church at the town's symbolic center. Though racial segregation was the norm across the United States, Eatonville was exceptional because it was segregated by the choice of its own citizens, with the intention to empower them. In the words of Hurston biographer Robert Hemenway, Eatonville ''existed not as the 'black backside' of a white city, but as a self-governing, all-black town, proud and independent, living refutation of white claims that black inability for self-government necessitated the racist institutions of a Jim Crow South.''

Hurston lived in Eatonville only sporadically after age nine, but it remained central to her sense of self and to her vision as an artist. ''This community affirmed her right to exist, and loved her as an extension of itself,'' writes Alice Walker in her foreword to *Zora Neale Hurston: A Literary Biography*. Walker asks, ''For how many other black Americans is this true?'' Oral traditions thrived in Eatonville, where storytelling ''lying sessions'' on the porch of the general store were part of the texture of everyday life. Hurston made the oral culture of Eatonville the subject of her first anthropological study of folklore, *Mules and Men*. The tales, sensibilities, and language of Eatonville ''ly-

Compare & Contrast

- **1930s:** The U.S. economy suffers from a crippling economic depression. Older industries, such as the automotive, railroad, steel, textiles, and agriculture, are stagnant. New, service-based industries hold promise for economic development, but low wages and extremely high unemployment delay their growth. The national income is cut in half between the stock market crash (1929) and 1932.

    1990s: The country enjoys the longest period of economic growth in history. The Dow Jones Industrial Average breaks the ten-thousand mark for the first time. Unemployment is at a record low. A booming high-tech industry fuels the economy, leading to higher wages and more disposable income. This, in turn, supports a service-based consumer economy. Despite prosperity, consumer debt is at a record high. The average family spends more than it earns in a given year.

- **1930s:** The average family income in the United States is in the range of $500 to $1,500 per year. Most families have $20 to $25 per week to meet food, clothing, and housing expenses.

    1990s: At the end of the decade, the median family income is approximately $47,000 per year in the United States, leaving just under $4,000 per month for expenses.

- **1930s:** Men's roles are more disrupted by the Depression than women's, since men's status as breadwinners is undermined, while women's roles in maintaining the household remain largely intact. Relatively few women work outside of the home, even in working-class families. In the face of economic insecurity, most couples try to preserve traditional gender roles.

    1990s: A two-income family, with both husband and wife working, has become the norm in both middle-class and working-class families, for both social and economic reasons. The women's movement has led to greater opportunities for women in the workplace, and economic pressure makes two incomes necessary for most families.

- **1930s:** Discrimination against African Americans is generally accepted in the highly segregated mainstream American culture. Public spaces are segregated, many African Americans are deprived of the right to vote, and a dozen or more lynchings still occur each year. Politicians begin to identify the issue of civil rights as a national problem, but take little legislative action.

    1990s: In the aftermath of the Civil Rights Movement of the 1950s and 1960s, racism is much less overt in many sectors of American society. However, more subtle forms of racism still plague the nation. President Clinton names racism as a pressing national problem. Public spaces are integrated and the program of Affirmative Action has led to greater integration in the workplace as well, but blacks and whites often have separate cultural and social lives, and significant economic disparities still exist.

---

ing sessions" are also essential to her fiction. "Hurston came to know that her parents and their neighbors perpetuated a rich oral literature without self-consciousness," Hemenway writes, "a literature illustrating a creativity seldom recognized and almost universally misunderstood." Through both anthropology and fiction, Hurston preserved the unique oral creativity of the Eatonville community in print form and tried to make its value understandable to the wider world. "The Gilded Six-Bits" celebrates the integrity of the Eatonville community and the power of its indigenous form of expression.

The Harlem Renaissance

After college, Hurston headed for Harlem, a historically black neighborhood in New York City. She was part of a large demographic shift of African

Americans moving from the rural South to the urban North, and of a more specific cultural phenomenon that centered in Manhattan, known as the Harlem Renaissance. While "The Gilded Six-Bits" is set far from the sophisticated world of 1930s Harlem, the influences of the cultural movement afoot there contributed to the circumstances of its writing.

Harlem was referred to as "the Negro capital of America." Two-thirds of all black New Yorkers lived there, and it was a popular entertainment spot for blacks and whites alike. In the early stages of the Harlem Renaissance, starting about 1917, white artists and intellectuals began to collect, write about, and imitate African-American folk art forms. Later, in the 1920s, a small group of talented and well-educated blacks living in Harlem—often supported and promoted by white benefactors—became visible as they started to create art based on African-American folk culture for themselves.

Hurston was one such promising black talent when she came to New York in 1925. An extraordinary storyteller and wit, Hurston fit the image of the colorful and folksy Negro that had become so popular. She was embraced by members of the black and white intelligentsia alike as a representative of the 'New Negro.' But in the 1930s tensions between white patrons and black artists grew. Many black artists began to criticize the condescending and controlling attitudes of their white benefactors. Their writing became more overtly political, and they began to portray the psychological damage caused by racism in their works. Hurston was an exception to this trend, content to work the system for whatever benefits she could gain and continuing to write about the black experience in ways that, for the most part, did not focus on white stereotypes or oppression. Criticized by her peers during her lifetime, she was embraced by a later generation of black writers for representing a vision of African-American self-love and psychic health. A heartwarming story set in an all-black town where racism exists only at a distance, "The Gilded Six-Bits" is a clear example of these qualities.

Critical Overview

In 1933, when Hurston was a rising star of the Harlem Renaissance and an impoverished drama instructor at Bethune-Cookman College in Daytona, Florida, she showed her story, "The Gilded Six-Bits," to an English professor there. He liked it so much that he not only read it to his writing class, but took it upon himself to submit it to *Story*, a well-known literary magazine. Bertram Lippincott, a New York publisher wise to the black folk-art trend, then took it upon himself to write to Hurston, expressing interest in publishing any novel she might be working on. This led Hurston to begin and quickly finish her first novel, *Jonah's Gourd Vine*. Thus "The Gilded Six-Bits" was pivotal to her professional development as a fiction writer. (She was already on her way to establishing herself in the field of anthropology under the mentorship of notable anthropologist Franz Boas).

Hurston seemed to effortlessly charm and impress white mentors, and these mentors were some of the same people who wrote or influenced early reviews. Her reception in the mainstream American press was by and large very positive, while her black peers tended to be more critical. For example, a 1934 review of *Jonah's Gourd Vine* written by Martha Greuning for the mainstream *New Republic* cites Hurston's "zest and naturalness," calling her an "insider" who "shares with her hero the touch of 'pagan poesy' that made him thrill his hearers when he preached," and the *New York Times*'s Margaret Wallace calls the novel "the most vital and original novel about the American Negro that has yet to be written by a member of the Negro race." In contrast, Estelle Felton of the black periodical *Opportunity* says that "Hurston has not painted people but caricatures," and Andrew Burris of *The Crisis* deems the book a failure, claiming that "she has used her characters and the various situations created for them as mere pegs upon which to hang their dialect and their folkways." Black writers of an earlier generation found her fiction too crude and risque, while her peers wondered whether she capitulated too easily to white fantasies of happily humble black life. Throughout her career, fellow blacks accused Hurston of ignoring the realities of racism. Hurston disagreed, maintaining that a focus on how racism cripples American blacks was too limiting, and drawing on her idyllic all-black Eatonville as a model of a rich and un-degraded African-American culture.

From 1925 to 1945 Hurston was one of the most high-profile and acclaimed black writers in the country. In 1943 she appeared on the cover of the *Saturday Review of Literature* for being the first black author to win the Anisfield-Wolf Book Award. But she, like virtually all other black Harlem Renaissance writers, made very little money on her publications, and she had to work at a wide variety of jobs to support herself when white patronage dried up. By 1950 she was working as a maid, her books out of print. Ten years later she died in poverty and was buried in an unmarked grave.

In 1973 African-American novelist Alice Walker visited Eatonville and went on a pilgrimage to Hurston's grave. This period was the beginning of another 'renaissance' in African-American letters, this time centering on women writers. Walker wrote about the importance of Hurston's influence, one factor leading to a sudden rush of renewed interest in Hurston's writing. In his introduction to *Zora Neale Hurston: Critical Perspectives, Past and Present*, noted African-American scholar Henry Louis Gates, Jr., recollects first encountering Hurston's out-of-print work while teaching in 1976. ''An undergraduate student in a seminar at Yale demanded that I add her to our syllabus, and gave me her one dog-eared photocopy so that I could share it with our class.'' He goes on to say that in 1993, at the time of writing, ''at Yale alone, seventeen courses taught *Their Eyes Were Watching God!*'' Hurston fit onto American literature and women's studies syllabi self-conscious about the need to include more diverse authors, as well as in the courses of new African-American studies departments.

The publication of *Spunk*, in which ''The Gilded Six-Bits'' appears, can be attributed to the Hurston revival. This volume, collecting some of Hurston's best stories, was published in 1985. Brent Staples of the *New York Times* describes the book as ''splendid'' and ''energetic,'' as well as ''decidedly feminist.'' He credits ''The Gilded Six-Bits'' for ''hold[ing] up nicely after fifty-two years.''

Their Eyes Were Watching God remains Hurston's best-known work and is widely considered her strongest. Most of the considerable scholarly criticism of Hurston centers on this novel, though there is also notable academic interest in her anthropological writings. Many interpretations of Hurston's fiction combine attention to dialect with feminist concerns related to power and voice. Other recent critics refute Hurston's image as an artless folklorist, treating her work in terms of its historical context and political import. In ''Breaking Out of the Conventions of Dialect,'' Gayl Jones takes this approach in an analysis of ''The Gilded Six-Bits,'' defending Hurston against accusations of frivolity and discussing Hurston's dilemma—''How does one write of ordinary people without making the story seem trivial?''—in terms of her unconventional use of dialect.

In her lifetime, Hurston's reputation rose suddenly and dropped precipitously, only to rise to even greater heights after her death, thanks in large part to a new generation of black artists and writers who claimed her as a foremother. ''We are a people,'' writes Alive Walker in her foreword to *Zora Neale Hurston: A Literary Biography*. ''A people do not throw their geniuses away. If they do, it is our duty as witnesses for the future to collect them again for the sake of our children. If necessary, bone by bone.''

Criticism

Sarah Madsen Hardy

Madsen Hardy has a doctorate in English literature and is a freelance writer and editor. In the following essay, she discusses the significance of gender roles and economic power in ''The Gilded Six-Bits.''

Hurston begins her 1933 short story ''The Gilded Six-Bits'' with a scene celebrating the domestic bliss of a newlywed couple. She virtually leads readers by the hand up the path to the modest but cozy house, offering them an intimate glimpse into the couple's marital harmony. As the story opens, Missie May Banks, the young wife, readies the house and herself for her husband's return. Each Saturday the husband, Joe, announces his homecoming by rolling nine silver dollars across the just-scrubbed threshold. It is the end of his week at the fertilizer plant, and the nine dollars are presumably what is left of his paycheck after he has bought some basic supplies, as well as a few small treats for his wife. With the house in perfect order, Missie May relishes the teasing chase and flirtatious tussle she knows is to come, when she will tackle him and rifle through his pockets for the little gifts he has hidden.

The inclusion of this opening scene is crucial to the story, which goes on to show how the harmonious routine of the Banks household is disrupted by Otis Slemmons and the illusive temptation of his gold. First, the play fight offers a *contrast* with the real marital trouble to come. Second, it contains subtext about gender roles and economic power that *foreshadows* this same trouble. For, although Hurston portrays the homecoming ritual as a natural and exuberant expression of young love, it can be under-

What Do I Read Next?

- *Their Eyes Were Watching God* (1937), widely considered Hurston's finest work, is a novel concerning the life and loves of woman growing up in an all-black community. It offers an exuberant and affirmative picture of love and self-realization.

- *Mules and Men* (1935), is a collection of folktales that Hurston recorded from her native town of Eatonville, Florida. She shares them with an insider's appreciation of their social and philosophical messages and a storyteller's flare for language.

- *The Blacker the Berry* (1929), Wallace Thurman's Harlem Renaissance classic, tells the story of how intra-race color prejudice affects one family.

- *The Color Purple* (1983), by Alice Walker (an African-American novelist who contributed to Hurston's rediscovery and who was greatly influenced by her writing), portrays a woman overcoming oppression by men and discovering herself in the rural South.

- *Paradise* (1998), by Nobel Prize-winning author Toni Morrison, weaves a rich tapestry of history as she tells the story of an all-black town and the strange and powerful women who reside at a nearby nunnery.

- *Mama Day* (1989), a novel by Gloria Naylor, describes several generations of love, jealousy, and magic in a black community on a fictional island off of Georgia.

- *Sassafrass, Cypress, and Indigo* (1982), Ntozake Shange's novel about the experiences of three artistic African-American sisters, mixes traditional storytelling with innovation.

---

stood to be, like Slemmons's seduction scheme, the enactment of an economic exchange. In each exchange it is the man's role to provide money and the woman's role to compensate him for his offerings. The man's status derives from his earning power, while the woman's derives from her feminine charms. The first version of this exchange, taking place within the context of marriage, is depicted as balanced and healthy. The second, taking place outside of marriage, is depicted as exploitative and deceptive. However, close analysis of the opening scene suggests a correspondence between the two scenarios of exchange.

In the course of their affectionate banter that Saturday afternoon, Missie May and Joe have a dialogue about their roles as man and woman. Joe delivers the silver dollars to Missie May in a way she pretends to take offense to. "'Who dat chunkin' money in mah do'way?' she asks, spotting him hiding in the yard and then chasing him into the house. 'Nobody ain't gointer be chunkin money at me and Ah not do'em nothin,' she shouted in mock anger." While Joe is really handing over his hard-earned salary to his wife for the maintenance of their household, the assumption behind Missie May's mock anger may be the fact that to throw money at a woman is to call in question her sexual reputation, implying that she can be bought. This foreshadows her acceptance of Slemmons's offer of gold for sex. Later, after Joe catches them together, she must sincerely wonder if her husband thinks he can buy her like a prostitute when he leaves Slemmons's gold trinket under her pillow after they have sex. But, at the story's happy opening, such an unseemly implication is cause for jest between husband and wife, and also may add a kind of illicit excitement to their domestic routine.

After Missie May pretends to take offense at the coins, she goes on the offensive, rifling through Joe's pockets for gifts. She insists that he "gimme whateve' it is good you got in yo' pocket. Turn it go Joe, do Ah'll tear yo' clothes." Though Joe has hidden the presents to elicit just such a response, he pretends to resist, and telling her, "Move yo' hand.

> "Slemmons is disruptive to the Banks's marriage not so much because he represents a competitive love interest or a real sexual threat, but because he encourages Missie May to attempt to provide economically for Joe by 'earning' gold from him."

Woman ain't got no business in man's clothes nohow.'' Joe really wants her to search his pockets, not only so she will find the gifts he has bought for her, but also because it gives her an excuse to grope him and possibly tear his clothes. The scene combines a dynamic of economic exchange with a strongly sexual connotation. This is another instance of foreshadowing—Slemmons also lures her into having sexual contact with the promise of gifts. As the couple scuffles, Joe tells Missie May that, should she tear his clothes, ''you de one dat pushes de needles round heah,'' reminding her that it is her job as his wife to mend his clothes. In the context of marriage, sexual innuendo easily turns into teasing about household chores.

Thus, the mock battle and flirtatious banter of the opening scene not only provide evidence of Missie May and Joe's domestic happiness, they also subtly demonstrate the asymmetry of their economic power vis-á-vis their gender roles. In some sense, the gender roles in a traditional marriage of the 1930s—a marriage where the man has a job and the woman keeps house—echo the unseemly implications of throwing money at a woman. Marriage is a kind of exchange. A woman, with no economic power of her own, takes a man's money and gives him something in return—not only sex, as with prostitution, but also household labor, including childbearing and rearing. Sex and domestic work are what a man gets in exchange for passing his wages along to his wife. The couple's ritual plays on and revels in the rules of this arrangement.

From a contemporary perspective, Joe's commands to mend his clothes and cook for him may seem limiting or even demeaning, but Hurston portrays Missie May's self-respect as dependent on this very role. After the play fight, she has Joe's bath water ready, and when Joe tells her to have dinner on the table when he gets out of the tub, she reprimands him. ''Don't you mess wid mah business, man . . . Ah'm a real wife, not no dress and breath. Ah might not look lak one,'' she adds, referring perhaps to her part in their playful romp, ''but if you burn me, you won't git a thing but wife ashes.'' Though it comes in the form of waiting on her husband, Missie May asserts that the housework is her realm of control. Historians have noted that during the Depression, when the story takes place, most married couples tried to maintain their traditional gender roles, meaning that the husband worked and the wife kept house, even though men's status as family providers was threatened by the weak economy and high unemployment. Because work was scarce, women were less likely to work outside of the home. However, their role in maintaining the household became more important when money was scarce. The family budget depended on them to make up the difference for what their men might not be able to earn by cutting corners and making do, even though they had very little economic power of their own. This historical perspective may make it easier to understand why Missie May takes so much pride in her identity as a ''real wife,'' as defined through her mastery of housework.

Missie May doubtlessly loves Joe for his personal qualities, but, invested as the couple is in traditional gender roles, his value to her is tied to his earning power, as revealed by their playful ritual. Similarly, for Joe, part of Missie May's value to him can be attributed to her cooking and cleaning, and, as well, to her sexual attractiveness. He takes pleasure in showing her off to Slemmons, since in addition to flaunting his gold, Slemmons has cited his many women as evidence of his status. When Joe tells Missie May about having met Slemmons, he concludes that his wealth makes Slemmons attractive. He's got a ''mouth full of gold teethes'' and a fat belly that ''make 'm look lak a rich white man.'' Missie May retorts that he is ugly, ''got a puzzlegut on 'im and he so chuckle-headed, he got a pone behind his neck,'' going on to compliment Joe's physical appearance. But after she meets Slemmons herself, she begins to see things Joe's way, admitting, ''He'll do in case of a rush. But he sho' is got a heap uh gold on 'im . . . It lookted good on him sho' nuff.'' While women are attractive because of their physical beauty and caring attributes, men are attractive because of their economic power. Ironically, only when a man is already rich can he adorn himself with jewelry and accept gifts from the opposite sex without compromising his masculinity.

Missie May goes on to reassure Joe that the gold would "look a whole heap better on you," and begins to fantasize about somehow getting hold of such gold jewelry for him. Joe readily acknowledges that a "po man lak me" will never have access to such riches. This is because, lacking Slemmons's economic power and charisma, he will never convince rich white women to shower him with gifts, and because, rather than accumulating money, he gives it to his wife to run the household. Missie May doesn't admit to Joe that she wants to take matters into her own hands, speculating only that maybe someday they will find some gold along the road. In her wifely role, this is the only sufficiently passive way she can imagine to get hold of some gold with which to adorn her husband.

When Slemmons offers Missie May gold in exchange for sex, she steps outside of her cherished role as a "real wife," not only in that she is unfaithful to her husband but in that she attempts to take over Joe's own cherished role as the family breadwinner. Slemmons is disruptive to the Banks's marriage not so much because he represents a competitive love interest or a real sexual threat, but because he encourages Missie May to attempt to provide economically for Joe by "earning" gold from him. When this is revealed, Missie May and Joe's traditional gender roles are upset, and the domestic ritual with which they reinforced them can no longer be celebrated.

Though the story promotes openness and forgiveness, it envisions this only by means of a return to the asymmetrical economic arrangement that is arguably what led to the problem in the first place: that Missie May is economically powerless without a man. The morning after her betrayal, she is somewhat comforted when Joe asks her to make him breakfast and, later, when he succumbs to sleeping with her. But harmony is fully restored in the house only when she gives Joe a son—the ultimate symbol of her wifely value. At this point, Joe, once again secure in his status as husband, takes the trinket he wrested from Slemmons wrist and buys a little gift, offering it, with his wages, as a sign of his true love.

Source: Sarah Madsen Hardy, in an essay for *Short Stories for Students*, Gale Group, 2000.

Evora Evora Jones

In the following essay, Jones examines history as told through folk tales, in this case by opposing the simplicity of country life with the sophisticated and superficial life of the city.

The history of a people, recorded through folklore, reveals unique, significant, complex, and even virtuous behavior patterns of a culture. This kind of history is one of the contributions of Zora Neale Hurston, anthropologist and folklorist, and includes literature reflecting the pastoral and the picaresque. It also includes literature which maintains readability, relevance, and its rightful position among belles lettres. Characteristic of such history is Zora Neale Hurston's "The Gilded Six-Bits."

The term *pastoral* embodies many characteristics, the first of which is a "contrast between two worlds—one identified with rural peace and simplicity—the other with power and sophistication." This contrast pervades the story. While details of the story will be used later to indicate other pastoral qualities, an initial discussion of this characteristic is appropriate here for its overshadowing effect.

According to Robert E. Hemenway, "The Gilded Six-Bits" is an "ironic account of infidelity and its human effects." A young Southern, unsuspecting wife, anxious to earn a "gold coin," is seduced by an aggressive, pretentious, smooth-talking, city entrepreneur from Chicago who flaunts his superficial possessions and his dalliance with women. Missie May, the wife and central figure in the work, represents the simple and peaceful.

Hurston's three principal characters, Missie May, Otis D. Slemmons, and Joe, approach life variously. Joe, the husband of Missie May, represents the simple and the peaceful. Otis D. Slemmons, the city entrepreneur, symbolizes the powerful and sophisticated. While Joe is seemingly momentarily concerned with the interest that Missie May seems to have in Slemmons, and while Missie May is hopeful that she and Joe "will find" some gold, Missie May engages in an affair with Slemmons and is discovered by her husband in the process. The fleeting appeal of the city life is in contrast to the already pleasant security of rural life. Missie May hopefully tells Joe, "Us might find some gold long de road some time. Us could."

The simple life is exalted by Hurston when she gives significance not to the gilded coins but to the simple, natural entities of the earth. As Missie May

> "Hurston makes the rural South live through Missie May's enjoyment of it until new ideas and modes of behavior are introduced, altering the value system of the town and the people."

weeps in Joe's arms over her act of infidelity and her regrets about the act, Hurston writes:

> The sun, the hero of everyday, the impersonal old man that beams as brightly on death as on birth, came up every morning and raced across the blue dome and dipped into the sea of fire every evening. Water ran down the hills and birds nested. Nature's way of soothing the soul is symbolized and exalted in the sun. Nature tempers disappointments and pain.

The sophisticated city life is depicted with a kind of deceptiveness and shallowness in the conversation between Joe and the store clerk in the candy store in Orlando. When Joe throws the gilded half dollar on the counter, the clerk asks him where he got it, and Joe replies:

> Offen a stray nigger dat come through Eatonville. He had it on his watch chain for a charm—goin' round making out iss gold money. Ha ha! He had a quarter on his tie pin and it wuz all golded up too. Tryin' to fool people. Makin' out he so rich and everything. Ha! Ha! Trying to tole off folkses wives from home.

The gilded power and sophistication are elusive; the serenity and security of the simple life are desirable and attainable. The simple life is meaningful to the inhabitant, not to the observer, for as the clerk erroneously sums up Joe's life by saying that "[n]othin worries 'em," he fails to locate the true pulse of simplicity, serenity, and peace of mind inherent in the rural life of Joe and Missie May. The real pulse of simplicity is feeling—experience—sublimity.

A second characteristic of the pastoral is the presentation of situations of choice. From the time that Missie May meets the city businessman until she succumbs to his advances, she torments herself with thoughts of what life would be like with the glitter and prestige of owning gold coins. Because the reader is allowed to see immediately the temporary shallowness of the gold coins and the boastful talk, "the simple world is more intrinsically desirable." Missie May's need and desire to return to the simple life afforded by her husband, Joe, is found in the narrator's explanation of Missie May's behavior after her husband told her, "Missie May, you cry too much. Don't look back lak Lot's wife and turn to salt." The narrator continues, "Missie knew why she didn't leave Joe. She couldn't. She loved him too much, but she could not understand why Joe didn't leave her."

A third characteristic of the pastoral is the implication that the city (world) has "illusory, shallow rewards." Slemmons, symbolizing the city with its illusory rewards, is realistically depicted when the narrator describes the response of Missie May when she finds the piece of money under her pillow. The narrator explains:

> Alone to herself, she looked at the thing with loathing, but look she must: She took it into her hands with trembling and saw first thing that it was no gold piece. It was a gilded half dollar. Then she knew why Slemmons had forbidden anyone to touch his gold. He trusted village eyes at a distance not to recognize his stick-pin as a gilded quarter, and his watch charm as a four-bit piece.

Next, a manifestation of the pastoral in a literary work is in a peasant's need to be protected from corruption and temptation. Although Missie May is quickly aware of the likelihood of much exaggeration in the statements made by Slemmons, she is naïve and believing when alone with him. At one point, she tells Joe that "Dat stray nigger jes tell y'all anything and y'all b'lieve it;" yet, at another point, after she tells Joe, "Oh Joe, honey, he said he wuz gointer give me dat gold money and he jus' kept on after me." Missie May is aware, but she needs the protection of her husband.

The last pastoral quality in Hurston's short story is the revelation of "fundamental values." This story, while embodying many ideas, embodies best perhaps the idea that infidelity can be a cheap affair which tarnishes a marriage with the same deceptive shallowness found in the tarnish of Otis D. Slemmons's coin.

One of the pedagogical functions of folklore is to remind members of society of wise codes of conduct; Hurston's story serves this function. The deterioration of Missie May, caused primarily by worry and respect, evidences the need for society to adopt wise, accountable codes of behavior.

While extended definitions of the picaresque as a literary form abound, four characteristics of the picaresque lend themselves to Hurston's "The Gilded Six-Bits."

Initially, "picaresque," according to Robert Bone, "consists of a journey, which is not so much a spatial geographical excursion as a pilgrimage towards possibility, toward experience, toward spiritual freedom." Careful analysis of "The Gilded Six-Bits" reveals two of the characters, Missie May and Slemmons, on a "pilgrimage toward experience." For Missie May, the journey begins with the onset of supposing what life would be like for her and her husband if they owned the kind of "gold" that the city man flaunted; the journey ends with the realization that fleeting, gilded tokens are cheap, useless, and even damaging when one's life is traded for illusion. Darwin Turner surely had "The Gilded Six-Bits" in mind when he said that "most of Zora Neale Hurston's stories . . . seem to be quiet quests for self-realization." For Missie May learns to differentiate between the valued and the valueless. This, for Missie May, is a maturation process, a journey. For Slemmons, the journey begins with his stop in Eatonville, Florida, for the purpose of getting as much from the residents of this city as they will allow and by any means; the journey ends as "Slemmons was knocked a somersault into the kitchen and fled through the open door." This, for Slemmons, is a dying process, for the type of man symbolized by Slemmons is one who is ultimately defeated. The manipulative schemes, the flamboyant attire and accessories, bespeak an experience leading to defeat.

The second picaresque quality is the movement of the "picaresque hero from a static, hierarchical traditional society to a series of adventures on an open road." While Slemmons should not be labeled a hero, he can be seen as one who moves from traditional society to adventure. After all, when he settles in Eatonville, he is already being called "Mr. Otis D. Slemmons of spots and places—Memphis, Chicago, Jacksonville, Philadelphia and so on." The mobility of Slemmons indicates a series of adventures. Slemmons's haste in opening the ice cream parlor speaks of the ease with which he quickly settles in one place after the other. The adventuresome spirit is in direct contrast with Joe's life, since for Joe "[t]hat was the best part of life—going home to Missie May."

Another characteristic of the picaresque in literature is given by Robert Bone when he says:

This bastard is cut off from the past and from tradition; there is no ancestral fortune to sustain him; he is entirely on his own, and must survive as best he can.

Hurston brings Otis D. Slemmons into the story by showing him as a stranger to this quiet, rural town. The introduction of Slemmons is at once a contrast to the tone and quality of life into which Joe and Missie May have securely and so happily nestled.

Hurston does not give the readers any indication that this city-slicker is from the background of the Harlem Renaissance; she does, however, in her autobiography, *Dust Tracks on a Road*, say that people are products of their cultures. Since Eatonville, Florida, is clearly depicted as a specific cultural location by carefully recorded dialect, behavior, and descriptions, Otis D. Slemmons is cutoff from this tradition by the author's description of his previous residences and his behavior. Missie May even calls Slemmons "[d]at stray nigger" when she is warning Joe that this newcomer is bragging about many of his so-called dalliances with women and that this bragging may not contain all truth. The only words Hurston gives to Slemmons are those which are uttered through Joe as he tells what Slemmons asked and the pleas that Slemmons made for his life when he pleaded, "Please, suh, don't kill me. Sixty-two dollars at de sto'. Gold money." Joe says, "He asted me, 'Who is dat broad wid de forty shake?'"

Finally, the "picaresque journey is at the bottom a quest for experience." The experience is for all of Hurston's characters, but perhaps most meaningful for Missie May. The story is, at its core, one of a woman saved from destruction and tarnish with the birth of a son who looks like her husband, Joe, and by the forgiving heart of this husband.

"The Gilded Six-Bits" holds its rightful place among belle lettres in its realistic portrayal of life in the South. In his biography of Hurston, Hemenway says,

> Zora Hurston had known firsthand a culturally different esthetic tradition. While she and her classmates revered Beethoven, she also remembered the box playing of Eatonville's Bubber Mimms. She enjoyed Keats, but recognized the poetry in her father's sermons; she read Plato, but told stories of Joe Clark's wisdom. . . . Her racially different folk culture was tolerated . . . as a primitive mode of apprehending experience; yet she knew that . . . folk traditions enabled black people to survive with strength and dignity.

"Folklore," Hemenway adds, consists of unwritten traditions which cause people to perform in familiar ways," thereby creating reality.

Codes for conduct are evident in the consequences experienced by Missie May and Joe. Hurston's genius in presenting this is obvious. Her style unveils the short story within an even broader context than the literary qualities, pastoral and picaresque.

William Dean Howells praises the short story writer's use of "native sources" and "local color flavor of diction." On these two elements of the short story, he writes,

> I should, upon the whole, be disposed to rank American short stories only below those of such Russian writers as I have read, and I should praise rather than blame their free use of our different parlances, or "dialects," as people call them. I like this because I hope that our inherited English may be constantly freshened and revived from that native source which our literary decentralization will help to keep open, and I will own that as I turn over novels coming from Philadelphia, from New Mexico, from Boston, from Tennessee, from rural New England, from New York, every local color flavor or diction gives me courage and pleasure.

Hurston's mastery of the short story is evident. Her attention to the preservation of a culture is a universal technique which has been incorporated in numerous works.

Zora Neal Hurston's fiction provides a history of a people. It inculcates major elements in American fiction, and it does what one literary critic, William Dean Howells, suggests an American short story should do—revive a local dialect. Hurston's "The Gilded Six-Bits" is not only folklore; it is also great literature—the story of any people who would be momentarily disoriented by the glare and fleeting appeal of a false Utopia.

Zora Neale Hurston is unabashedly a writer of fine literature. A critical analysis of "The Gilded Six-Bits" affirms the genius of this writer in her skillful treatment of not only the pastoral and the picaresque but also fiction, narration, and folklore. Fiction is the shaping of a civilization through a certain construction of language. Hurston makes the rural South live through Missie May's enjoyment of it until new ideas and modes of behavior are introduced, altering the value system of the town and the people. The South represents that time and place in the lives of people, bound by cultural conditions. This time and this place are perfect complements for Joe and Missie May. People are their culture. A digression from the culture of a people is a digression from the reality of the people. Hurston's symbolic reference to illusion versus reality through the feigned significance of the gold coin is a direct reference to illusion versus reality in the altered behavior of people who have digressed from the moral tenor of their culture as a result of the temptations of the turpitude of other cultures.

The use of narration by Hurston is unsurpassed. Hurston's fiction is punctuated with philosophical truths throughout. Choices for analysis, treatment, and application are numerous. Through Missie May's character the need for attention to the spirit of the person and to the culture is evident. Through Joe's character the need for attention to the frailties of human nature, encouraged by strong forces of the modern world, is made clear. Through Otis's character the ever-present appeal of illusory qualities of a strange culture draws attention to the need to understand a given culture, not to embellish it. Through the use of her hometown, Eatonville, Florida, Hurston's narration projects unparalleled significance and strength, for she captures the nuances, scenery, language, tone, and a Southern code of behavior in what has been called her finest short story, "The Gilded Six-Bits."

Finally, Hurston's place in literature as a folklorist remains among the masters of creativity. Any variation on the theme of rural Southern life may be traced to Zora Neale Hurston's perception of it. Her story intensifies the history and the truth of Eatonville, Florida, a truth so complex that it could be of any time and any place. The author's mastery of myth, tale, and legend transcends Eatonville; it goes around the world without leaving the story's setting, for out of that setting is born an understanding of human nature and its culture.

Source: Evora Evora Jones, "The Pastoral and the Picaresque in Zora Neale Hurston's 'The Gilded Six-Bits'" in *The CLA Journal*, Vol. XXXV, No. 3, March, 1992, pp. 316–24.

Gayl Jones

In the following essay, Jones argues that through the use of dialect in the story the reader is brought inside the African-American community depicted in the story, which opens the possibility for a more complex examination of the characters.

Hurston's "The Gilded Six-Bits" (1933) takes us out of the conventional restrictions observed in Dunbar. This transformation is partly due to the shift in perspective: we are inside rather than outside the black community and there is not the same double-conscious concern with an exclusive white audience. Because there are not the same motives of the anti-lynching story or of the tradition of protest literature in general, Hurston can be concerned with the relationship between a man and woman in "a Negro settlement." She can expand the range beyond "humor and pathos" to a crisis-of-love story; there can be development and recognition, dilemma and resolution, delineated personality.

Critic George Kent has called this a "simple story." In an interview with Bell he says "that one [the story] suggests that really simple people could suddenly resolve all problems by suddenly forgiving each other very easily (...) I (...) recall that incident being very tediously resolved. I don't recall a really imposing short story by her (...)."

Though the story is about "simple people" whose relationship seems to be apparently simply resolved, in view of the problems manifest in Dunbar, it might be reviewed in a more complex light. Its shift in perspective (what Ellison would term "restoring of perspective"), its lack of preoccupation with audience, its sense that Southern rural black speech as dialect may contain any emotion in literature adds degrees of complexity not easily acknowledged or perceived in a cursory reading. Although there certainly is humor in places (as in all her work), it is the spontaneous good humor of fully realized characters in interaction and not that of dimensional minstrel humor. We laugh along *with* the characters in their happy moments; we go down into the depths with them during the "crisis of love"; we come out with them. We are brought beyond humor and pathos.

The focus is on relationships, interpersonal conflict and conflict of values. There are some elements of sophistication in the story (particularly in its many reversals) but the problem with Hurston (and this perhaps also accounts for Kent's reaction) is how does one write of ordinary people without making the story seem trivial, without making the writer's concerns seem likewise? The subject of Dunbar's story is perhaps a more "significant event" in socio-historical reality but, nevertheless, his Afro-American characters remain in the background in both their physical presence and psychological reality. On the other hand, Hurston's characters are pulled to the foreground in both these respects. Like most literary transitions, this does not appear to be of great note these days with contemporary Afro-American writers who automatically do the same, notwithstanding certain persistent (or recalcitrant) white critics who may still be asking the former whether they write about "black people or human beings?" and consider the Afro-American charac-

> "We laugh along *with* the characters in their happy moments; we go down into the depths with them during the 'crisis of love'; we come out with them. We are brought beyond humor and pathos."

ter's perspective "the broader perspective" and the significant one. However, it was an important transition and should be seen as an initial link between a literary technique (viewpoint) and its broader humanistic implications in the depiction of black humanity in literature.

We first meet Missie May and Joe in a ritual scene that occurs every Saturday morning when he throws nine silver dollars in the door "for her to pick up and pile beside her plate at dinner." He also brings her candy kisses. The beginning is full of happiness, "joyful mischief," "mock anger " and the "play fight."

Otis Slemmons, introduced shortly after this playful scene, becomes the center of a conflict of values and the latter, as the subject of much of Hurston's fiction, should be considered a worthy subject or what E. M. Forster would call a "noble" one. Nevertheless, Otis is from Chicago and "spots and places." In the initial dialogue between husband and wife we see the things that interest the couple about him: he has been places, he has gold teeth, he wears "up to date" clothes, his "puzzlegutted " build makes him "look like a rich white man," he has the attention of many women (including white ones up North) and he has gold pieces. These are the things that Joe notices and talks about. Initially, May's concerns seem not to be material but her love for Joe is uppermost; she loves him *as he is*. Joe, however, feels he "can't hold no light to Otis D. Slemmons" because he "ain't never been nowhere" and "ain't got nothing but you."

At first, May is not taken in by Otis or what he represents. Then there is a reversal. The next time we hear the couple talking together (after they have returned from seeing Otis at the local ice-cream parlor), Joe is expressing her earlier values and she is expressing his. We see then all the *things* she wants for him "because she loves him." Nevertheless, she wants them:

> Joe laughed and hugged her, 'Don't be so wishful 'bout me. Ah'm satified de way Ah is. So long Ah be yo' husband, Ah don't keer 'bout nothin' else'.

However, to get the gilded six-bits which the gold coins turn out to be, May betrays Joe with Otis. Joe comes home early from work and finds them together. There is a fine handling of emotional reactions here. He sees them and "open his mouth and laughs." Because this is not the expected response—the reaction and emotion seem contradictory—it deepens our sense of the emotion as "a howling wind [which] raced through his heart" and he "kept on feeling so much." He fights Slemmons, drives him away and the crisis of love begins. There is no more laughter or banter.

Kent calls the resolution easy. I think that it appears easy because Hurston handles all the emotional reversals and complications in narrative summary rather than in active dramatic scenes. One reads them quickly and so it seems that they are done quickly but these are real, subtle and difficult changes. Joe makes love to May then leaves a piece of Slemmons's "gold" with the bit of chain attached under her pillow. She then discovers that "it was a gilded half dollar." After the love making she thinks that "they were man and wife again. Then another thought came clawing at her. He had come home to buy from her as if she were any woman in the long house. Fifty cents for her love." She dresses and leaves the house, but she encounters her husband's mother and, so as not to "admit defeat to that woman," she returns home. Joe discovers she is pregnant, and when she has the child, he knows it is his (his mother even confirms that it looks like him so it must be his!) and they reconcile.

The story is perhaps resolved too simply at this point, the "baby chile" being a kind of *deus ex machina*. Nevertheless, Hurston's handling of their complications and reversals of emotion up to now has been superb and certainly adds more shadings of emotion than revealed in earlier dialect stories. Dialect itself is more complex and shows more literary sophistication. The links with the interior of the characters, the processes of emotional transformation, as well as the foreground presentation make it no "simple story" though it deals with "ordinary folks," yet it poses a challenge because it contains everything that was considered not the stuff of important fiction: it is regional, it focuses on the relationship between a black man and a black woman and it does not make interracial conflict its reason for being.

The problem of the "stuff of important fiction" of course transcends racial lines. A contemporary American white writer, Mary Gordon, has written an article entitled "The Parable of the Cave or In Praise of Water Colors" in which she speaks of Theodore Roethke saying that woman poets were "stamping a tiny foot against God" and that she has been told by male (but not female) critics that her work is "exquisite," "like a water color": "Water colors are cheap and plentiful; oils are costly; their base must be bought. And the idea is that oil paintings will endure."

Because Gordon's remarks are important in cross-sexual and cross-cultural criticism, I will quote her in full:

> There are people in the world who derive no small pleasure from the game of "major" and "minor." They think that no major work can be painted in water colors. They think, too, that Hemingway writing about boys in the woods is major; Mansfield writing about girls in the house is minor. Exquisite, they will hasten to insist, but minor. These people join up with other bad specters and I have to work to banish them. Let us pretend these specters are two men, two famous poets, saying, "your experience is an embarrassment; your experience is insignificant.
>
> I wanted to be a good girl, so I tried to find out whose experience was not embarrassing. The prototype for a writer who was not embarrassing was Henry James. "And you see," the two specters said, proffering hope, "he wrote about social relationships but his distance gave them grandeur.
>
> Distance, then, was what I was to strive for. Distance from the body, from the heart, but most of all, distance from the self as writer (. . .)
>
> If Henry James had the refined experience, Conrad had the significant one. The important moral issues were his: men pitted against nature in moments of extremity. There are no important women in Conrad's novels, except for *Victory*, which, the critics tell us, is a romance and an exception. Despite the example of Conrad, it was all right for the young men I knew, according to my specters, to write about the hymens they had broken, the diner waitresses they had seduced. Those experiences were significant. But we were not to write about our broken hearts, about the married men we loved disastrously, about our mothers or our children. Men could write about their fears of dying by exposure in the forest; we could not write about our fears of being suffocated in the kitchen. Our desire to write about these experiences only revealed our shallowness; it was suggested we would, in time,

get over it. And write about what? Perhaps we would stop writing.

"And so," the specters whispered to me, "if you want to write well, if you want us to take you seriously, you must be distant, you must be extreme.

I suppose the specters were not entirely wrong. Some of the literature that has been written since the inception of the women's movement is lacking in style and moral proportion. But so is the work of Mailer, Miller, Burroughs, Ginsberg. Their lack of style and proportion may be called offensive, but not embarrassing. They may be referred to as off the mark, but they will not be called trivial.

And above all I did not wish to be trivial; I did not wish to be embarrassing.

Most female writers (black and white) have experienced this from male critics. Black writers (male and female) have experienced it from (white) male critics and, ironically, given Gordon's remarks, from white female critics. The problem of writers dominated by literary standards of "significant events" (national, sexual, racial) is not only finding one's voice but of trusting it when one does find it; then finding the voice or voices that one most values and avoiding destruction of the creative spirit and discovering how one can most (as Kent would term it) "assert one's existence" and the existences of all the characters.

Kent himself feels that black women writers fail to explore real depth: "Often, the problem is that you don't get a deep enough definition of the things that the woman encounters which are her responses to power (...) I would say that black women writers that I've read don't seem to get much into subtle possibilities (...) I don't see much possibility and I'm not sure that there is always depth (...)." Yet, unlike most critics, he acknowledges that "it might be that male thing you were talking about."

This could be the "elliptical details" in the work for which a male critic would need more "analytical commentary."

But regardless of the "subtle possibilities" (of society, history, gender ?) that critics confuse with aesthetics, in the case of Hurston, dialect, as regional vernacular, can and does contain subject, experience, emotion and revelation. Two reasons for this new attitude and sense of possibility in character and dialect might be that she was born in the first incorporated all-black town of Eatonville, Florida, and that she was a folklorist possessing an exact as well as a creative ear. In her Foreword to *Their Eyes Were Watching God*, Williams speaks of her "command":

She had at her command a large store of stories, songs, incidents, idiomatic phrases, and metaphors; her ear for speech rhythms must have been remarkable. Most importantly, she had the literary intelligence and developed the literary skill to convey the power and beauty of this heard speech and lived experience on the printed page.

Hurston's evocations of the lifestyles of rural Blacks have not been equaled but to stress the ruralness of Hurston's settings or to characterize her diction solely in terms of exotic "dialect" spellings is to miss her deftness with language. In the speech of her characters, black voices—whether rural or urban, northern or southern—come alive. Her fidelity to diction, metaphor and syntax—whether in direct quotations or in paraphrases of characters' thoughts—rings, even across forty years, with an arching familiarity that is a testament to Hurston's skill and to the durability of black speech.

In "The Gilded Six-Bits" one sees the folklorist in the metaphors, images and descriptions in the dialogue: "He ain't puzzlegutted, honey"; "God took pattern after a pine tree and built you noble"; "You can make 'miration at it, but don't tetch it"; "Ah reckon dey done made him vast-rich." Certainly there is a difference between the metaphors used here and those in Melville's descriptive evaluation of Jube or Creelman's of Washington because we have individuality, range and elegance.

Oral tradition enters, complements and complicates character in the use "storytelling" or reported scenes to reinforce the dramatic ones. When May and Joe go to the ice-cream parlor and see Otis, they return and Joe retells the encounter:

On the way home that night Joe was exultant. "Didn't Ah say ole Otis was swell? Cain't he talk Chicago talk? Wuzn't dat funny whut he said when great big fat ole da Armstrong come in? He asted me, "Who is dat broad wid de forte shake?" Dat's a new word. Us always thought forty was a set of figgers but he showed us where it means a whole heap of things. Sometimes he don't say forty, he jes' say thirty-eight and two, and dat mean de same thing. Know whut be told me when Ah wuz payin' for our ice cream? He say, "Ah have to hand it to you, Joe. Dat wife, of yours is jes' thirty-eight and two. Yessuh, she's forty!" Ain't he killin'?

This description of the scene is important. Hurston does not take us to the ice-cream parlor directly and dramatically; she skips the scene and lets Joe's storytelling serve as a flashback and the story advances through the character's reactions to the moment. Therefore, the psychology of relationships is explored: there are complicating reversals and confusions of value, then the renewed and stronger affection.

Besides the use of storytelling dialogue, Hurston also moves "folk expressions" into the narrative while in most early fiction, and certainly the turn-of-the-century fiction of both Dunbar and Charles Waddell Chesnutt, it was confined to dialogue: "way after while," "make his market," "mess of honey flowers."

Here, the syntax, lexicon and expressive techniques of oral tradition break though to the narrative and alter it; this enlarges the scope of dialect to the modes of exposition. It is also possible for this extensible language to tell a story and Hurston offers a beginning here as well. Wideman speaks of this important "evolution":

> From the point of view of American literature then, the fact of black speech (and the oral roots of a distinct literary tradition—ultimately the tradition itself) existed only when it was properly "framed" within works which had status in the dominant literary system. For black speech, the frame was the means of entering the literate culture and the frame also defined the purposes or ends for which black speech could be employed. The frame confers reality on black speech; the literary frame was a mediator, a legitimizer. What was outside the frame—chaotic, marginal, not worthy of the reader's attention—becomes, once inside, conventionalized into respectability.
>
> The frame implies a linguistic hierarchy, the dominance of one language variety over all others. This linguistic subordination extends naturally to the dominance of one version of reality over others.

Hurston, in her use of dialect, was one of the first to initiate this breaking out of the frame—an important initiation for those writers committed to such linguistic explorations in fiction.

In "The Gilded Six-Bits," not only does the dialect have more functions but it is used in a story of greater complexity of character, greater thematic range and literary sophistication. Though the people themselves are "simple" in the sense of being "ordinary folks," their range is more than sentimental or comic emotion. Because the dialect here is given a fuller value and use, we move a step further toward a fuller exploration of black personalities in fiction but it will not be until *Their Eyes Were Watching God* that language, thought, experience, emotion and imagination will break through and add to the text like an apical bud, increasing the length of the stem or, to use Hurston's own image, "a peartree bud coming to flower." She fulfills the possibility of what dialect might do when moved beyond the literary conventions and allowed more of the magic and flexibility of authentic folk creation.

Source: Gayl Jones, "Breaking Out of the Conventions of Dialect: Dunbar and Hurston" in *Presence Africaine*, No. 144, Fall, 1987, pp. 39–46.

Sources

Burris, Andrew, Review, reprinted in *Zora Neale Hurston: Critical Perspectives, Past and Present*, edited by Henry Louis Gates, Jr. and K. A. Appiah, Amistad, 1993, pp. 6–8.

Felton, Estelle, Review, reprinted in *Zora Neale Hurston: Critical Perspectives, Past and Present*, edited by Henry Louis Gates, Jr. and K. A. Appiah, Amistad, 1993, pp. 4–5.

Gates, Henry Louis, Jr., Introduction to *Zora Neale Hurston: Critical Perspectives, Past and Present*, edited by Henry Louis Gates, Jr. and K. A. Appiah, Amistad, 1993.

Greuning, Martha, Review, reprinted in *Zora Neale Hurston: Critical Perspectives, Past and Present*, edited by Henry Louis Gates, Jr. and K. A. Appiah, Amistad, 1993, pp. 3–4.

Hemenway, Robert E., *Zora Neale Hurston: A Literary Biography*, University of Illinois Press, 1977.

Staples, Brent, "In Short," in *New York Times Book Review*, August 11, 1985.

Walker, Alice, Foreword to *Zora Neale Hurston: A Literary Biography*, Robert Hemenway, University of Illinois Press, 1977.

Wallace, Margaret, Review, reprinted in *Zora Neale Hurston: Critical Perspectives, Past and Present*, edited by Henry Louis Gates, Jr. and K. A. Appiah, Amistad, 1993, pp. 3–4.

Further Reading

Gates, Jr., Henry Louis, and K. A. Appiah, eds., *Zora Neale Hurston: Critical Perspectives, Past and Present*, Amistad, 1993.
   This volume collects reviews and criticism on Hurston's work from 1934 to 1992, offering a useful historical perspective on Hurston's literary reputation. Some of the more recent scholarly essays may be too specialized for the general reader.

Hemenway, Robert E., *Zora Neale Hurston: A Literary Biography*, University of Illinois Press, 1977.
   Hemenway offers an authoritative account of Hurston's life based on sensitive insights on her various writings. This scholarly book is long and detailed, but accessible to the general reader.

Hurston, Zora Neale, *Dust Tracks on a Road*, with an introduction by Maya Angelou, HarperCollins, 1992.

Hurston's breezy and possibly inaccurate memoir, originally published in 1942, describes the author's rise from poverty and her experiences as a darling of the Harlem Renaissance.

Lewis, David Levering, *When Harlem was in Vogue*, Oxford University Press, 1981.

This thorough and readable analysis of the cultural phenomenon that was the Harlem Renaissance offers a useful context for Hurston's work.

Nathiri, N. Y., ed., *Zora! A Woman and Her Community*, Sentinel Books, 1991.

Editor Nathiri, a fellow native of Eatonville, takes a personal approach to Hurston's life and work, creating an adoring "family album" for her. Includes biographical information, interviews with her relatives, and background on Eatonville.

A Good Scent from a Strange Mountain

Robert Olen Butler

1992

Robert Olen Butler had already published five novels—most of them concerning Vietnam during the war era—when he brought out his collection *A Good Scent from a Strange Mountain* in 1992. This volume of short stories—all of which featured unique narrators but were set in Louisiana among Vietnamese immigrants—drew immediate critical applause and won the Pulitzer Prize in 1993.

Reviewers praised many of the fifteen stories, but one, the title story, was also selected for inclusion in *The Best American Short Stories* of 1992. This story, which is told by a man close to a century old, obliquely discusses several of the different types of people affected by the troubles in Vietnam. There are the narrator's son-in-law and grandson, who get involved in the murder of a fellow immigrant who speaks out in favor of cooperating with the present government in Vietnam. There is his daughter, who represents holding on to the traditions that have long been part of the Vietnamese family. There is Ho Chi Minh, the nationalist who led his country to independence and communism. And there is the narrator himself, Dao, who chose the difficult route of remaining uninvolved and peaceful through the long years that Vietnam struggled and fought. Dao's reminiscences and attempts to bring harmony to his own life at the moment he approaches his death lend a definitive closing note to this volume, which one reviewer said "offers tales of heroism not in corporeal battle but in the spiritual struggle for faith and hope in the face of betrayal and impossibility.''

Author Biography

Robert Olen Butler was born January 20, 1945, in Granite City, Illinois, and spent the majority of his childhood in a small steel mill town in that state. His father, a retired actor, helped inspire his interest in books, movies, and theater, and his mother's stories about Granite City during the Depression inspired the content for his fifth novel, *Wabash*.

Butler excelled in high school, serving as president of the student body and graduating as co-valedictorian. He enrolled at Northwestern University, where he planned to major in theater. In his sophomore year, however, he transferred to oral interpretation, which is an approach to literature through performance. This focus drew Butler increasingly to writing. After graduating *summa cum laude* in 1967, he attended graduate school at the University of Iowa, where he earned an M.F.A. in playwriting.

Believing he would be drafted for the Vietnam War, Butler signed up for a three-year enlistment in return for a guaranteed position in counterintelligence. He spent a year learning Vietnamese from a native speaker, and was then assigned to serve in Vietnam as an administrative assistant and interpreter. His time in Vietnam had a profound effect on Butler, and he would return to this past many times in his writings.

After returning to the United States in the early 1970s, Butler worked alternately as a reporter, a high school teacher, and a freelance writer in Granite City, Illinois; Chicago; and New York City. During the 1970s, Butler continued to pursue his dream to be a writer and worked on his first novel. In 1979, he began to take creative writing courses again.

His first novel, *Alleys of Eden*, was published in 1981 and is one of three novels that make up a loose Vietnam trilogy. Since the early 1980s, Butler has regularly published. His first five books, though widely praised, did not register outstanding sales.

In the 1980s, Butler took a job teaching fiction writing at McNeese State University in Lake Charles, Louisiana. There he became acquainted with Vietnamese immigration to the area, and he began to write stories about the displaced people. The collection *A Good Scent from a Strange Mountain* had its inspiration in National Public Radio's request for Butler's contribution to a series on writing. Butler looked at the more than thirty short stories he had previously written and rediscovered an interest in Vietnamese folkways.

With the success of *A Good Scent from a Strange Mountain*, Butler became far more well-known. The book won the Pulitzer Prize in 1993 as well as numerous other national awards. Based on the book's strength, Butler also was awarded a Guggenheim Fellowship. Butler continues to work as a writer and a teacher.

Plot Summary

The story takes the form of an old man's memories and final attempts to deal with the past as he nears his own death. Dao, almost 100 years old, is a Vietnamese man living in New Orleans, Louisiana. Believing that his death approaches, Dao summons the important people from past, including the ghost of his old friend Ho Chi Minh, the communist nationalist instrumental in winning Vietnam's independence from France.

In 1917, Dao and Ho Chi Minh, then going by his given name of Nguyen Ai Quoc, were both young men living in London and Paris. In London, Ho worked as a pastry cook, and Dao worked as a dishwasher. Now, when Ho appears before Dao, his hands are covered with sugar because he is trying to make a special glaze. However, he is having trouble remembering how to make it properly.

Dao has reached the point in his life where, as is Vietnamese custom when a person is very old, he takes a "formal leave-taking" of his family and friends, who all come to visit him. It is also Vietnamese tradition to have a close family, but, sitting in his chair in the living room, Dao can see that some of his family have become too Americanized.

He overhears a conversation between his son-in-law Thang and his grandson Loi. Both served in the South Vietnamese army in the war. They think he is asleep while they discuss the murder of a fellow immigrant. The man owned a newspaper and wrote an article expressing that it was time to accept the communist government in Vietnam and to work with its leaders. He was murdered for voicing these

Robert Olen Butler

opinions, assassinated as he sat in his Chevrolet pickup truck, which Dao sees as a symbol of his Americanization. Thang and Loi seem to be speaking in code as they mention that no murder weapon has been found. Lam, Dao's daughter, who is married to Thang, also seems to be communicating in code as she speaks of how terrible the man's death is. Dao deliberately pretends to be sleeping. He does not want to say anything about what he has heard, for he is a Buddhist and he believes in the value of familial harmony.

During his first visit, Ho asked Dao if he was still a Hoa Hao Buddhist. Dao became a Buddhist when the two men were in Paris in 1918. Dao believes that in Paris he embraced the past—the Buddhism of his ancestors—while Ho embraced his future. He recalls how Ho rented a dark suit and a bowler hat to wear as he paced the halls of Versailles, hoping to speak with Woodrow Wilson. He wanted to speak to the U.S. president, who was in the midst of the peace accords that officially ended World War I, about helping Vietnam get representation in the French Parliament—at the time, Vietnam was a French colony. In returning to the topic of Dao's Buddhism, Ho notices the Chinese characters on Dao's prayer table. They mean ''A good scent from a strange mountain.'' This is the saying of the Hoa Hao Buddhists. The Hoa Haos believe in simplicity, as expressed by this saying.

After Ho leaves that evening, Dao calls his oldest daughter to see if the doorknob that Ho touched is sticky. It is. After his daughter says good night, Dao recalls all the people who were important to him but who are now dead, including his wife and his firstborn son. In this village square, where the dead congregate, Dao smells a wonderful sweet smell from a strange mountain. Dao tries to explain to his daughter that the doorknob is sticky from Ho's hand, but he is too sleepy.

The next night, Ho returns. The men talk of Ho's attempts to make the pastry glaze, and then Dao asks if he has seen his wife, but Ho has not. Dao asks if Ho is disappointed that Dao did not become involved in Ho's struggle, but Ho absolves Dao of any guilt he might feel. Dao knows that Ho is not at peace, and Ho explains that it is not over his inability to make the glaze. Dao tells him he should be at peace, after all, he won their country back from the French, but Ho replies that there are no countries in the afterlife.

The next day, Thang and Loi continue to talk about the murdered newsman. This makes Dao recall Ho's talk the night before, of how the Vietnamese were fools to trust the Americans, who also fought against the Japanese in World War II. Dao speaks of the need for harmony, and he is reminded of the conversation he overhears between Thang and Loi. They also talk bitterly of foolishly trusting the Americans. It is clear from what they say that they were involved in, if not present at, the murder of the newsman. Listening to their talk, Dao suddenly wishes for death, believing that he has lived too long.

When Ho comes to visit for the third time that night, Dao suggests the two men pace, as they did in Paris, and talk about Marx and the Buddha. The two men walk, and Dao tells Ho of his suspicion that Thang and Loi are involved in the political killing. As he waits for Ho to speak, Dao recalls holding Loi as a baby and being repulsed by the sour smell of milk on his breath. He remembers Thang across the room, wanting Lam to take Loi away from him. Ho reminds Dao that he has never done anything political. Dao asks if there are politics in the afterlife. Ho does not answer. Instead, the sweet smell of the sugar on his hands grows stronger and stronger as Dao feels Ho close to him. He does not see Ho, but he feels as if Ho was passing through his body. Then he hears the door open and close softly. Dao is about to return to bed. He knows that Ho is right: he will never speak to his grandson about what he knows. He also remembers the recipe for the glaze that Ho has been so unsuccessful in making.

Characters

Dao

Dao is the narrator of the story. Nearly 100 years old, he has lived in many places outside his native Vietnam: London, Paris, and now New Orleans. Dao was in Vietnam during the war, and though it is not explicitly stated, must have fled the country after the fall of South Vietnam to the communists. He is living his final years with his family.

While in Paris many decades ago, Dao became a Hoa Hao Buddhist, and thus he values "harmony among all living things, especially the members of a Vietnamese family." Dao comes to understand that his son-in-law and grandson are involved with the assassination of a fellow immigrant who supported acceptance of the idea of communist rule in Vietnam. Through his discussions with Ho, Dao, who "has never done a political thing," decides to overlook this knowledge to preserve his family. However, the conversations with Ho also serve as a subtext, for Dao is looking for absolution for the fact that he did nothing to help his country win freedom from France. With Ho's help, he finds peace within himself and takes his final steps toward death.

Lam

Lam is Dao's daughter and Thang's wife. She appears to have knowledge of the involvement of her husband and her son in the assassination of Le. In conversation, she subtly reminds them not to allude to the incident in front of her father.

Nguyen Bich Le

Dead before the story opens, Le was a Vietnamese immigrant in New Orleans who published a Vietnamese newspaper. Le embraced his new culture, and he enraged people like Loi and Thang with his paper. Although he maintained he was still a patriot of South Vietnam, he wrote an article in which he stated his belief that it was time to accept the reality of the communist government in Vietnam and to work with them. He was murdered for publicly expressing these beliefs.

Loi

Loi is Thang's son and very like his father. He served in South Vietnam's army as a lieutenant. He is involved with the assassination of a fellow immigrant who supported acceptance of the idea of communist rule in Vietnam. Like his father, he knows where the murder weapon is, and there is the implication that he was present at the murder as well. Loi is bitter about the exile of his people as well as about the role the Americans took in the Vietnam War, and he and his father discuss these topics often.

Ho Chi Minh

The character of Ho (also known as Nguyen Ai Quoc) is based on a real person: Ho Chi Minh, who led the fight for Vietnam's freedom from France in the 1940s and 1950s, and who became the leader of independent North Vietnam. Ho was a learned man, speaking both French and English as well as his native Vietnamese. In the earlier part of the 1900s, he traveled throughout Europe, where he became a nationalist and a Marxist. Ho returned to Vietnam in 1940 to lead the fight against the Japanese invaders.

In the story, Ho appears to Dao as he was at the time of his death, even though Dao did not know him then. The two friends spent time together in Paris and London. When Ho visits Dao, despite his manner of dress, he talks about less-worldly issues that would have concerned him when the two were friends, such as making a pastry glaze. The conversation between the two men reveals deeper meanings, however. Ho's appearance to Dao is a manifestation of Dao's own subconscious, which is looking to find peace with the actions that form his life.

Oldest Daughter

Dao favorably compares his oldest daughter to Lam. He considers her a "good girl," one who understands the importance of harmony within the Vietnamese family. She obeys and helps her father without question.

Nguyen Ai Quoc

See Ho Chi Minh

Thang

Dao's son-in-law is a former colonel in South Vietnam's army. Thang has some involvement with the assassination of a fellow immigrant who supported acceptance of the idea of communist rule in Vietnam; he knows the murderers and may have even been part of the killing. Thang is bitter about the exile of his people. He believes that the South Vietnamese should never have trusted the Americans and should have handled the problems with their government leaders on their own. Dao believes that Thang is "insincere."

Themes

War

The problems of the Indochina War and the Vietnam War are themes in the story, though Dao does not refer to them directly. Dao brings up the Indochina War—the war between the Vietnamese nationalists and the French, which took place from 1946 to 1954—when he asks Ho whether he is disappointed that Dao did not join him in this struggle. Ho further expands upon this topic when he talks of the mutuality of the Vietnamese and the Americans, both of whom wanted to stop the spread of the Japanese empire. Ho's feelings connect him and the people who joined in this first struggle with the Vietnamese who fought in the Vietnam War and their struggle, both in the war and with the division of their country afterward. Ironically, Ho's comments link him directly to Thang and Loi, who fought on the opposing side in the Vietnam War.

Dao, who appears not to have been directly involved in that war, still evokes it in several different ways. Thang and Loi both served in South Vietnam's army as a colonel and a lieutenant, respectively. They remain bitter about their exile from their country after the fall of South Vietnam, and in part, blame the Americans. Dao also recalls how he and his wife lived through the Tet Offensive in 1968 and listened to the bombs falling outside. Such evocations underscore the struggle the Vietnamese have undergone in the latter half of the twentieth century.

Memory and the Past

As he approaches death (though he is not sick, he is almost 100 years old), Dao focuses increasingly on his memories of the past and how they reflect upon his perception of the present. The story begins with the visitation of Ho, whom Dao has not seen for decades. It soon becomes clear that there are many reasons that Dao sees Ho now. Foremost, Dao is experiencing the inner struggle of how to handle the problems within his family. He knows that Thang and Loi are involved in a political murder, yet his religious beliefs and his culture demand that he try and maintain familial harmony. Furthermore, Dao has never, as Ho puts it, "done the political thing." Dao's focus on the past is also manifested in his vision of the village square, populated by those people who have died before him. In this afterlife, Dao hopes to find the people who have meant so much to him: his wife, his firstborn son who died as a baby, the first person to call Ho "monsieur" ("mister"), and the Dakar natives sent to their deaths in shark-infested waters by the French colonial officials. Dao projects his feelings about his upcoming death onto Ho. Dao questions Ho about whom he has met in the afterlife, and Ho evokes the images of those whom Dao does not even think of, such as the young Vietnamese men who wanted their country's respect from the European powers.

Family

The bonds of family play an important part in the Vietnamese culture and in the story. Dao follows Vietnamese tradition, and, as he is now very old, he gathers his family around him to bid them a final farewell. This custom is followed to allow the older person time to tell the "people of your life . . . your feelings, or try at last to understand one another, or simply say goodbye." The members of Dao's family come to pay their final calls over a series of days. His "insincere" son-in-law, Thang, and his grandson Loi, however, mar what should be a time of peaceful leave-taking. He discovers that his family is governed by a web of lies and deceit with the understanding that the two younger men took part, on some level, in the murder of a Vietnamese newsman who spoke of accepting the unified country. Dao's daughter Lam also keeps this secret—she reminds them not to speak in front of her father—signifying her comprehension and perhaps even her acquiescence. Only Dao's oldest daughter, whose name is not revealed, plays out a satisfactory role. She is kind, caring, and dutiful. Despite the inadequacies of some of his family members, Dao still holds onto his belief in the family's importance. His decision at the end to not reveal anything of what he knows about the news-

Topics for Further Study

- Read *The Deuce*, Butler's novel about a half-Asian, half-American boy living in the United States. How does Thanh-Tony's experiences compare with Dao's? How are their perceptions of Vietnam and America alike and different?

- Dao's son-in-law and grandson hold very different points of view than Dao, both toward their native land and toward Americanization. Imagine that you are telling the story of the newsman's murder from the point of view of either of these other characters. What would you include in the story? What would this character feel about his actions?

- Conduct research to find out more about the Vietnamese immigrant experience in the United States. Investigate how they came here, where they live, what types of communities they form, and how they have adjusted to life here.

- Find out more about Ho Chi Minh. What role did he play in his country's history? How do you think the fate of Vietnam would have been different if Ho had not done what he did?

- Do you think it is fair of Dao to have refused to take part in the political troubles that embroiled his country for decades? Why or why not? What kinds of difficulties would fighting have presented for a man like Dao? What kinds of problems would he face for remaining uninvolved?

- What do you learn about Vietnamese culture and tradition from the story? What would you like to know more about, and why?

- Read another story from *A Good Scent from a Strange Mountain*, and compare its narrator to Dao.

- Find out about the ways that ordinary Vietnamese were affected by the Vietnam War. Choose one segment of society to focus on. Summarize your findings.

---

man's murder is done in part to maintain harmony in the family.

Style

Point of View

The story is told from the first-person point of view. Dao tells the story so the reader is privy to only his thoughts, feelings, and observations. Because of this point of view, a limited and obscured view of the tumultuous events that have taken place in Vietnam over the past decades is presented—as aptly reflects Dao's limited involvement. A Hoa Hao Buddhist, Dao values harmony, which he seeks to impose on his surroundings. Since returning to the religion of his forefathers as a young man in Paris, Dao has upheld these values, thus, unlike Ho, Thang, and Loi, he has remained uninvolved in Vietnam's political strife. Living through these times, however, Dao has a sharp awareness of the difficulties that beset his country and continue to beset his countrymen, even though they are "in exile," and his musings make constant references to the problems faced. Because of this limited point of view, an understanding of the history of Vietnam in the twentieth century is essential to fully appreciate the story.

Setting

The story takes place in New Orleans, Louisiana. Many South Vietnamese refugees settled in the area after they fled their homeland. As Butler told Sybil Sternberg in an interview with *Publishers Weekly*, as he flew to the area for the first time, he saw below him from the plane window a landscape that looked like the Mekong Delta: "There was the same calligraphy of waterways, the rice paddies, the subtropical climate, the French influence." The many Vietnamese immigrants formed a tight-knit Vietnamese community. In the story, memories and reminders of home surround Dao and the other immigrants. For instance, they read a local Vietnamese-language newspaper, which features items of concern to many, such as the events that have taken place in Vietnam since its reunification in the 1970s. The story also shows the efforts of the older immigrants, such as Dao, to hold fast to their traditions and culture.

Structure

The story shifts between Dao's evenings talking with Ho and his days listening to the conversation of Thang and Loi. The nighttime events and the daytime events reflect upon each other; what happens in the night reminds him of what happens in the day and vice versa. This structure emphasizes the relentless interaction of the past, present, and future. What happened in the past in Vietnam has a very real effect on what is happening right now in Louisiana. For instance, the newsman is murdered because he expresses ideas about how to deal with present-day Vietnam that offend some of the exiles.

Dao, though uninvolved in this event, focuses on it as symbolic of Vietnam's past and his limited role in the struggles. Indeed, at this stage in his life, Dao cannot truly separate the past and the present. The fluidity of Dao's thoughts, as he moves back and forth between nights with Ho and days with his family, makes it difficult to separate the two periods, which is the point of this style and structure. Dao's fluidity also allows him to slip into the future—the afterlife—showing his movement toward death.

Imagery and Symbolism

Butler makes use of a number of images and symbols in the story. Dao readily explains some of them. The murdered newsman had become Americanized. This is clear to Dao because the man had chosen to purchase a Chevrolet pickup truck; a Chevrolet "is a strongly American thing," and the pickup truck made him "also a man of Louisiana, where there are many pickup trucks." The newsman chose not to "purchase a gun rack for the back window, another sign of this place," which ironically might have saved him by blocking the assassin's bullet. Dao's musings on this topic show the gun's power as both a peacekeeping object and an object of extreme violence, reflecting on its role in the wars of Vietnam.

Clothing also symbolizes different things. When Ho comes to Dao at night, he is dressed in "the dark clothes of a peasant and the rubber sandals, just like in the news pictures." But when Ho tried to get a meeting with the European and American leaders at Versailles, he took on their appearance, renting a dark suit and a bowler. Ho further evokes the image of young Vietnamese nationalists taking on the costume of the Western world in their effort to gain the West's respect and support. In Ho's afterlife are "a million souls . . . the young men of our country, and they are all dressed in black suits and bowler hats."

Historical Context

A Brief History of Twentieth-Century Vietnam

In 1859, France began to make inroads in Southeast Asia, and by the end of the century was the dominant power in the region, which became known as French Indochina—present-day Vietnam, Cambodia, and Laos. Despite the efforts of Vietnamese nationalist groups, the French maintained control of the region until around the outbreak of World War I.

Ho Chi Minh had become the most important nationalist in Vietnam. In 1930 and 1931, he helped organize strikes, demonstrations, and peasant uprisings against the colonists. The French exiled him to the Soviet Union and China, but after the Japanese invasion in 1940, he returned home to organize a communist resistance movement to fight both the Japanese and the French colonial government. After the defeated Japanese withdrew in 1945, Ho proclaimed independence for Vietnam, but no major government recognized this declaration. France tried to reclaim Indochina the following year and soon had regained much of the land. When France agreed only to make Vietnam a free state within the French empire, fighting broke out between France and Ho's Viet Minh. The Indochina War lasted from 1946 until the Viet Minh's victory in 1954.

The ensuing peace treaty, the Geneva Accord, called for the withdrawal of all French troops and also temporarily divided Vietnam into two zones at the seventeenth parallel. Ho Chi Minh controlled the northern section (which he did until his death in 1969), but an election was set for 1956 that would choose one government for the entire country. While the north embarked on a program of industrialization, problems arose in the south, where political chaos, a poor economy, and refugees hampered the new government of Ngo Dinh Diem. Diem managed to return order to South Vietnam only through dictatorial rule. When it came time for the proposed elections, Diem refused to hold them. His government became increasingly repressive, and opposition grew.

In North Vietnam, the Viet Minh formed the communist National Liberation Front (NLF) with the goal of overthrowing Diem and reuniting Vietnam. The NLF supported guerilla activity in the south. As the situation worsened, Diem was assassinated by army officers, who then took over the government in 1963.

The two sides began to engage in war, and by the mid-1960s, the U.S. military had become involved. The Vietnam War was a long and deadly conflict. When it finally ended in 1975, with North Vietnam's victory, it claimed as many as two million Vietnamese casualties and also significantly affected neighboring countries Laos and Cambodia. The country was officially reunited in 1976 under a communist government. More than one million South Vietnamese fled the country, some because they feared punishment by the North Vietnamese, others because of food shortages, but most because they did not want to live under a communist government. Around 725,000 of these immigrants settled in the United States.

America in the 1990s

In the 1990s, the United States strove to develop and maintain better relationships with countries around the world. The United States also worked to promote world peace, often through the United Nations. By 1992, thousands of United Nations forces were working on peacekeeping missions throughout the world.

At home, the United States saw a new wave of immigration. The Immigration Act of 1990 increased the number of immigrants allowed in the United States and doubled the number of skilled workers. In the first part of that decade, more new immigrants came to the United States than in any other decade since 1910. The majority of these immigrants—more than eighty percent—came from Asian, Latin American, and Caribbean countries. Some native-born Americans were alarmed by this increase, but supporters of immigration believed that such movement revitalized urban areas and strengthened the economy.

The World in the 1990s

Overall, the 1990s saw a dramatic rise in democracy throughout the world, as well as the development of increasingly global economies. Many countries—including most in Eastern Europe—overthrew their communist governments. Some governments, however, continued to rule in an authoritarian manner, most notably those of China, Cuba, North Korea, and Vietnam. In these countries, the communist government remained firmly entrenched.

The Vietnam War had taken its toll on the country, and Vietnam struggled economically for years after the war ended. In 1993, Vietnam was ranked among the world's poorest countries. Then the government of Vietnam, like many other communist governments, began to restructure the country's economy, adding some elements of free trade. Under this program, the country experienced an economic revival. Foreign trade expanded, as did foreign investment in Vietnam. Diplomatic relations between Vietnam and democratic countries, such as the United States, also were restored. Vietnam's government loosened certain restrictions, and more visitors were allowed to enter the country, including former Vietnamese residents and American Vietnam veterans.

Critical Overview

Even before publication of *A Good Scent from a Strange Mountain*, Butler had already established his reputation as a writer of Vietnam fiction. Such categorization displeased the author, who stated, ''Artists get at deeper truths.'' Some of Butler's earlier works had also drawn criticism because he told the stories from a point of view that was not his own—that is, he took on the role of a Vietnamese person. Several short stories were even rejected by magazines on these grounds.

With the publication of *A Good Scent from a Strange Mountain* in 1992, which went on to win the Pulitzer Prize the following year, Butler silenced his critics. In this collection of fourteen short stories and a novella, critics and readers all agree on the power of Butler's prose and his haunting evocation of the Vietnamese voice. Most critics favorably commented on Butler's skillful and caring manipulation of the language. Richard Eder, in his review for the *Los Angeles Times Book Review*, notes that ''Butler writes essentially, and in a bewitching translation of voice and sympathy, what it means to lose a country, to remember it, and to have the memory begin to grow old. He writes as if it were his loss too.'' According to Cynthia McCown in *America*, it is Butler's ''familiarity with the Vietnamese language [that] gives this work its narrative conviction as Butler takes on the personas of expatriate Vietnamese from an aging bargirl to an Amerasian teen to a 100-year-old man who dreams of his friend Ho Chi Minh.'' Jon Anderson, writing in the *Chicago Tribune*, notes further praise for Butler's work: ''the stories in his new book . . . are so delicately phrased that they sound as if they had been written in Vietnamese and translated.''

The stories take place in Louisiana, where a large immigrant population settled in the post-Vietnam War years. They all feature a Vietnamese exile as the narrator. Butler brings to life North Vietnamese and South Vietnamese, Buddhists and Catholics, men and women, those who succeed in America and those who suffer. His stories span the gamut of topics, drawing on his narrators' experiences in Vietnam and during the war, as well as exploring their current lifestyle in Louisiana and their perception of America. The narrators offer a variety of perspectives on the Vietnamese experience. Some stories take place in Vietnam, while others take place in the United States. The stories demonstrate the difficulties that the immigrants have in the new country and explore reasons for these difficulties, such as the language barrier, which can lead to misinterpretations. Although the stories all stand alone, they also draw power from their collection. As Madison Smartt Bell says in the *Chicago Tribune*, the collection has ''a sort of novelistic unity, enhanced by his [Butler's] sharp insight into their [the Vietnamese] ways, their beliefs and their reaction to life among strangers in a strange land.''

At the time of the book's publication McCown did voice one concern: ''*A Good Scent from a Strange Mountain* is calculated to be positive, even uplifting. It is a Vietnam story unlike any that has been popularized by the dark perception of our own collective American loss. As such, it may reflect too much of the romantic for some tastes. This work celebrates courage and dignity, but not in the face of ultimate defeat. Rather it expresses the essence of old Dao's main religious tenet: 'The maintenance of our spirits is simple, and the mystery of joy is simple.'''

Readers and critics quickly were drawn to the title story of the collection. ''In a collection so delicate and so strong,'' declares Eder, ''the title story stands out as close to magical.'' The story has been noted for strong images and its unity of recollection. Says McCown, ''Ho's sugar-scented hands open the casement of memory for Dao: the Carlton Hotel in London, 1917, Ho as a retoucher of photographs in Paris, and as a political leader, still 'painting the blush into the faces of Westerners.'''

Since publication of this collection, Butler has written several more novels, yet *A Good Scent from a Strange Mountain* still stands out as one of his most remarkable works. It is already being studied in college and adult-education classes, and its stories appear in numerous anthologies.

Criticism

Rena Korb

Korb has a master's degree in English literature and creative writing and has written for a wide variety of educational publishers. In the following essay, she explains how Ho Chi Minh's nighttime visits are Dao's attempt to bring harmony to his family before he dies.

''A Good Scent from a Strange Mountain'' is the title story from Robert Olen Butler's 1992 collection, which includes fourteen stories and one novella, all told from the points of view of Vietnamese immigrants living in Louisiana. The different narrators created by Butler are also similar in that they are undergoing the process of reconciling their past lives with their present lives. As such, the influence of the tumultuous events that have shook Vietnam in the past several decades make its importance on the Vietnamese psyche clear.

The narrator of the story, Dao, is almost 100 years old, and he feels that he is approaching the end of his life. As is Vietnamese tradition, he calls his family and close friends around him for a ''formal leave-taking.'' At this point, Dao also takes stock of what he has and hasn't done in his life, especially as contemporary circumstances force him to evaluate the choices he has made. Dao's old friend Nguyen Ai Quoc, better known to the world as Ho Chi Minh, comes to visit and say goodbye. Their conversations reflect upon Dao's past, present, and future and help him make the resolutions he needs to move on to the next step in his life: death.

What Do I Read Next?

- Tim O'Brien is another writer of Butler's generation who served in Vietnam. He has also written a collection of interconnected stories, *The Things They Carried*. These stories focus on a platoon of foot soldiers, recounting their experiences in Vietnam and afterwards.

- The author of the screenplays for *Apocalypse Now* and *Platoon*, Michael Herr covered the Vietnam War for *Esquire* magazine. Many people consider his book *Dispatches* (1991) to be the best account of the Vietnam War.

- Henry Roth's 1934 novel *Call It Sleep* tells of the experience of a young Jewish immigrant living in a ghetto in New York. After years of going unnoticed, critics and scholars rediscovered the book in the 1950s, and today it is viewed as a modern classic.

- Le Ly Hayslip's *When Heaven and Earth Changed Places* (1993) details her experiences during the Vietnam War, describes her journey to the United States, and chronicles her return to her homeland in 1986 to search for her family. Hayslip recounts the terrible ordeal that she underwent during this period and also demonstrates the strength that got her through it.

- *Sorrow of War* (1996) by Bao Ninh is the first novel to tell about the war from a North Vietnamese perspective. This quasi-autobiographical story tells about a North Vietnamese infantryman who is trying to purge his horrible memories through the act of writing.

- Le Minh Khue's short stories are collected in *The Stars, the Earth, the River* (1997). These are fourteen stories that center on the Vietnam War. It is the first volume in the *Voices from Vietnam* series.

- *The Other Side of Heaven: Post-War Fiction by Vietnamese and American Writers* (1995), edited by Wayne Karlin et al., gives alternate views of the war and its effect on the Vietnamese and the American societies, residents, and cultures.

Because so much of the story rests upon events that shook Vietnam in the twentieth century, a basic understanding is necessary to truly appreciate the narrative's power. Ho Chi Minh is Vietnam's most famous nationalist, and his actions were pivotal in winning the country's freedom from France, who had colonized Vietnam since the end of the 1800s. Ho made his first attempts toward obtaining some measure of independence as early as the 1910s, when he was in Paris. Back in Vietnam in the early 1930s, Ho incited demonstrations, protests, and peasant uprisings, and the colonial government banished him from the country. In the upheaval of World War II, however, when Japan invaded French Indochina—present-day Vietnam, Laos, and Cambodia—Ho returned to his homeland, organized the Viet Minh, and led the successful fight against the French colonizers. After this victory, Ho took charge of the government of North Vietnam, a position that he held until his death in 1969. The Indochina War left Vietnam divided into north and south sectors. The government in the south resisted efforts to reunite the country, and the Viet Minh began a campaign of guerrilla warfare to achieve this goal. By the mid-1960s, the country was officially at war. After South Vietnam fell to the communist north, many South Vietnamese fled the country. Dao and his family were among the emigrants.

Since the time they spent together in London and Paris, the lives of Dao and Ho have widely diverged. While Ho became a revolutionary leader who condoned acts of violence, Dao became a Buddhist who prized harmony and peace above all else. Ho now inhabits the world of the afterlife. Ho's presence is forewarned by "a sweet smell about him, very strong in the dark," for Ho has been trying to remember how to make the pastry glaze he

> "Suddenly, Ho moves toward Dao and seems to pass through him. 'He was very close and the smell was strong and sweet and it was filling my lungs as if from the inside.' This shows Dao at the essence of his harmony; he has actually become that treasured 'good smell from a strange mountain.'"

learned as a pastry chef under the great Escoffier while Dao and Ho were in London. This smell emerges as a key focus throughout the story. Long ago, in Paris, Ho embraced a sect of Buddhism known as Hoa Hao. Their mantra is "A good scent from a strange mountain"; the basis of their religion is that life should be harmonious and "the maintenance of our spirits is very simple, and the mystery of joy is simple, too."

Dao's family in Louisiana does not follow these same precepts he holds dear. The main thrust of the present-day drama centers on Dao's realization that his son-in-law, Thang, and his grandson, Loi—both of whom served in the army of South Vietnam—are involved in the murder of a fellow Vietnamese immigrant, a newsman. Nguyen Bich Le had recently printed an article in his local Vietnamese newspaper in which he wrote that "it was time to accept the reality of the communist government in Vietnam and begin to talk with them." He believed that they "had to work now with those who controlled our country." Despite these strong words, Mr. Le still considered himself a patriot. "I believed him," thinks Dao. "If anyone had asked an old man's opinion on this whole matter, I would not have been afraid to say the Mr. Le was right." Not everyone in the community agreed, however, and Mr. Le was assassinated.

As Dao comes to realize the role his son-in-law and grandson have played, he wonders if he should let his knowledge affect his desire to achieve harmony within himself, and within his family, before he dies. Further complicating the issue is his understanding that his daughter, Lam, who is Thang's wife, is also cognizant of the same actions. Whenever the two men discuss the affair in Dao's presence (he feigns sleep), it is Lam who reminds them to be careful of what they say. Once she "said in a very loud voice, with her eyes on me, 'That was a terrible thing, the death of Mr. Le,'" to which her husband and son responded in the affirmative. Dao struggles with whether he should reveal his knowledge.

This dilemma seems to be a crucial impetus for Ho's visit, for Ho took the political path and Dao took the peaceful path, paralleling Dao's role in relationship to Thang and Loi's. Dao's conversation with Ho eventually convinces him to let matters be. Ho does not fault him for not doing the "political thing," an absolution that relieves Dao's self-imposed guilt. Dao's consciousness also affirms the importance of things outside of the political. The primary way he resolves this issue is through Ho's inability to remember how to make the pastry glaze. In the afterlife, this problem is what concerns Ho, not the problems of a nation. Dao thinks that Ho wants to accomplish this task for Escoffier, but he is incorrect, which is revealed when Dao asks if Ho is at peace in the afterlife. Dao thinks that Ho's inability to make the glaze—thus Escoffier's displeasure—leads to Ho's disturbed state of mind, but Ho tells Dao, "I have not seen him. This has nothing to do with him, directly." Even Ho doesn't understand what causes him to lack peace. Dao tells him, "You won the country. You know that, don't you?" This response shows that Ho should be satisfied with his life, for he has accomplished something great. Ho, however, is not convinced. "There are no countries here," he says, implying that the act of freeing a country is not all that matters in the grand scheme of things. Perhaps, he seems to say, living in harmony with one's memories—as Dao is attempting to do—counts for even more.

Richard Eder writes in the *Los Angeles Times Book Review* that Dao "has lived spiritually apart from his country," which causes him confusion. Ho, on the other hand, never learned to make the pastry glaze; doubtless, political concerns and worries took up his mind. Dao, however, did listen to Escoffier's instructions, and he knows why Ho cannot make the glaze correctly. Eder writes, "Butler holds the two failures in equilibrium. To neglect a revolution and to neglect a glaze are two aspects of human limits."

What Dao deems important, in contrast to what Ho finds important, shows the basic tenets of his beliefs. As he concludes the story, "I was only a washer of dishes but I did listen carefully when Monsieur Escoffier spoke. I wanted to understand everything. His kitchen was full of such smells that you knew you had to understand everything or you would be incomplete forever." This hearkens back to Dao's Buddhism. Dao cherishes what is simple and brings harmony—a prayer table, a caring daughter, a pastry glaze. When Dao thinks of the afterlife that he is quickly approaching, he thinks of a village square in Vietnam and a room he shared with his wife in Saigon. "[T]he room was full of a wonderful *scent* [emphasis mine], a sweet smell," which makes him think that "a *mountain* [emphasis mine] of emerald had found its own scent." Dao makes the connection even clearer: "I crossed the room to my wife and we were already old, we had already buried children and grandchildren that we prayed waited for us in that village square at the foot of the *strange mountain* [emphasis mine]." This passage illustrates Dao's intrinsic trust in what is important in life: the ties of family. As he says, "a Vietnamese family is extended as far as the bloodline strings us together, like so many paper lanterns around a village square. And we give off light together. That's the way it has always been in our culture." Many of the immigrants, however, have let the old Vietnamese ways slip, for they "have been in America for a long time." Of the people who surround him, only his oldest daughter, who is a "smart girl," has this understanding "about Vietnamese families."

When Dao confirms his suspicions that Thang and Loi are involved in the murder of the newsman, he does not know how to react. In the past, whenever the two men spoke bitterly of the war and of the foolish trust the South Vietnamese put in the Americans—"We should have taken matters forward . . . and done what needed to be done," they remonstrate—they quickly apologized to Dao. "We're sorry, Grandfather," they would say. "Old times often bring old anger. We are happy our family is living a new life." Dao had always accepted this lie, "glad to have the peace of the family restored." This time, however, Dao cannot deny their true feelings. Loi says to his father, "I would be a coward not to know," most probably referring to knowing the location of the murder weapon, which has been a central topic of their conversation. "Thang laughed and said, 'You have proved yourself no coward.'" This is the point at which Dao embraces the idea of his death. "I wished to fall asleep," he says, "and let go of life somewhere in my dreams and seek my village square."

The night after this event, Ho comes to visit Dao for the third time. Dao gets out of bed to pace with Ho and talk of important ideas and issues, as they did as young men in Paris. Dao confesses his suspicions to Ho. Ho's response to Dao's dilemma about Thang and Loi helps Dao clarify the importance of his obligation to establish harmony in his family, but there is a price Dao must pay for this enforced peace, for he cannot readily live with his knowledge. Suddenly, Ho moves toward Dao and seems to pass through him. "He was very close and the smell was strong and sweet and it was filling my lungs as if from the inside." This shows Dao at the essence of his harmony; he has actually become that treasured "good smell from a strange mountain." He lies down to sleep, prepared for his journey to death. That Dao will die that night is indicated by his pulling down the window shade, one of the story's final actions. This contrasts with one of the story's first actions: "My oldest daughter leaves my shades open, I think so that I will not forget that the sun has risen again in the morning. I am a very old man. She seems to expect that one morning I will simply forget to keep living." Dao states that he "could never die from forgetting." Indeed, Dao's final moments in the story indicate that he can live with his memories of how he has chosen to live his life, but that he cannot live with the knowledge of how his family has chosen to live theirs.

Source: Rena Korb, in an essay for *Short Stories for Students*, Gale Group, 2001.

Chris Semansky

Semansky publishes widely in the field of twentieth-century culture and literature. In the following essay, he discusses the different kinds of knowing represented in "A Good Scent from a Strange Mountain."

Robert Olen Butler's story, "A Good Scent from a Strange Mountain," focuses intently on the last phase of an old man's life. In it, we see a character, Dao, tempted away from the Buddhist beliefs that have determined his actions since he was a young man. Butler takes a piece of history—Ho Chi Minh's time working in a hotel in London—and uses it as a conceit in the story, making Dao the friend who went to Europe with him. The story unfolds as a long intermittent dream, with episodes of illusion followed by reciprocal episodes of reality. All the episodes are given equal weight so that, with Dao, the reader must search for as much meaning in the hallucinations as in the waking actions. The story encourages readers to examine the idea that important questions can be approached only through the intellect and its interaction with the tangible world. Through the character of Dao, we see the possibility that deeper meaning resides as much in the symbolic world of dreams as it does in the waking world of concrete things. Most significantly, Dao's sense of smell is used to indicate the presence of truth and beauty, or its absence, as he seeks to understand the final fragments of life left to him.

Dao, who has lived "almost a century," is engaging in the last custom that Vietnamese culture demands of him. It is the custom of taking a week or two to see family and old friends who are still alive so that a formal, final leave-taking can be accomplished before one's death. This ritual presupposes relatively ideal relationships: "A Vietnamese family is extended as far as the bloodline strings us together, like so many paper lanterns around a village square. And we all give off light together." But Dao's real relationships with his daughters, son-in-law, and grandson are problematic. Towards his oldest daughter, with whom he lives in New Orleans, he feels frustration but also gratitude—it is significant that she is the only family member who smells pleasantly of "lavender and fresh bedclothes." Throughout the story, they struggle over the window shades that she insists on keeping open so that the light will be a reminder to him "to keep living." But he bristles at such reminders and retaliates by suggesting she worry more about herself. His younger daughter is more distant, serving primarily to bring her husband and son into Dao's orbit—an orbit that they dramatically threaten by their violent political acts. Specifically, their politics are represented by the Vietnamese Party for the Annihilation of Communism, and Dao becomes convinced that his son-in-law and grandson may be responsible for the murder of a newspaperman whose accepting views of the communist government in Vietnam enraged them. The realization that they might be involved troubles the Buddhist Dao greatly, and he is not happy to have stayed out of the main fray of political conflict for his entire life only to be tempted, at the very end, by an issue of justice that reaches out for him to address.

The anticommunist politics of Dao's immediate family function as counterpoint to the political figure who dominates Dao's hallucinatory nights: Ho Chi Minh. Dao was, or claims to have been, a friend of Ho Chi Minh's in his youth. They went to Europe together and worked in a London kitchen, Dao as a dishwasher and Ho Chi Minh as an apprentice pastry cook under the great Escoffier. It was there, Dao tells us, that the two of them paced the floors of their rooms together, spoke of Marx and Buddha in equal measure, and saw snow fall for the first time. Ho Chi Minh serves as a foil to Dao in the story; the political against the spiritual, a life of action and intervention against a life of acceptance and peace. Now, as Dao dies in New Orleans, Ho Chi Minh, long dead himself, begins to appear nightly, his hands covered with sugar, his mind distressed over the minutiae of forgotten recipes he once knew perfectly in the days when he worked in Escoffier's kitchen.

His presence can be read as a reference intended to raise the specter of ideological division that comes between Dao and his other male family members. Ho Chi Minh's communist regime marked the return of Vietnamese rule in Vietnam after French colonialism. His rise, and the resulting upheaval, represent the world of human action which Dao's life has eschewed. The life of his senses has always been of primary importance to him, and his son-in-law and grandson, caught up in—and spiritually impaired by—their passionate political beliefs, represent a world that he will not miss. When Dao reminds Ho Chi Minh that he did in fact win the country over, his friend merely shrugs, "There are no countries here," he says, indicating that in death there are no antithetic forces. Nevertheless, the politics of Dao's family and formerly of Ho Chi Minh create a context in which Dao's struggle resounds. Is he right not to become involved? In point of fact, his grandson always smelled wrong to him: "I could smell his mother's milk, sour on his breath . . . the boy sighed on my shoulder and I turned my face away from the smell of him." In this way we see evidence of Dao's repressed political self: he rejects the grandchild who will eventually and vehemently reject the communist political agenda Dao himself witnessed Ho Chi Minh solidifying.

Although Dao hesitates to become involved in the world as a political person, in his final days he is forced to see how political ideology has stripped some of his family members of their humanity. He comes up against the limitations of his spiritual beliefs and engages in elliptical conversations with the ghostly Ho Chi Minh in an attempt to find out if in fact he himself has chosen the wrong path. Ho Chi Minh mirrors his own dismay: Ho is unable to remember the things he once knew effortlessly, caught mid-process with sugar-coated hands and unable to do the next step in the recipe. The Ho Chi Minh that appears to Dao seems to have no understanding of why the political world once intrigued him so utterly. The man who once had "eight simple requests for the Western world concerning Indochina" is helplessly covered in a simple syrup glaze and beseeches Dao to tell him whatever he can remember of the fondant recipe. During these scenes, a powerfully sweet smell never leaves Dao's nostrils; a smell the reader might eventually ascribe to friendship or even love between the two men.

Even before Dao begins to suspect his son-in-law and grandson of murder, Dao's idea of harmonious family life had been ruptured, in particular by the losses of his wife and a beloved infant son. A village square referred to early in the story as a prayed-for meeting place after death, where families' lights might burn together, is evoked after Ho Chi Minh's first visit to Dao. "I crossed the room to my wife and we were already old, we had already buried children and grandchildren that we prayed waited for us in that village square at the foot of that strange mountain . . . I want to be with her in that square and with the rest of those we'd buried, the tiny limbs and the sullen eyes and the gray faces of the puzzled children and surprised adults and weary old people who have gone before us, who know the secrets now." The sweet smell that is present to Dao whenever Ho Chi Minh appears, attributable to the sugary glaze on his hands, floods Dao as he remembers a night with his wife. It was a night when they were still in Vietnam, and bombs were falling and the air should have smelled of tar and motorcycle exhaust and cordite, but instead smelled, impossibly, of "a wonderful scent, a sweet smell that made her sit up, for she sensed it too." In this lyrical passage we see Dao's love for his now-dead wife, and their love for their lives, made all the more intense by the threat of bombs falling near them. The presence of death ratchets up the intensity of what they are experiencing, and Dao's wife becomes for him a piece of that fleeting energy as he clings to her. He remembers that the smell "had nothing to do with flowers, but instead reminded us that flowers were always ready to fall into dust."

As a Hoa Hao Buddhist, Dao believes that the mystery of joy is very simple, and can be expressed by four Chinese characters that mean "a good scent from a strange mountain." In some sense, the story is an explanation of these words. Dao's most meaningful, most joyful moments were those he shared simply with the wife he loved, and those he spent in

> "The presence of death ratchets up the intensity of what they are experiencing, and Dao's wife becomes for him a piece of that fleeting energy as he clings to her. He remembers that the smell had nothing to do with flowers, but instead reminded us that flowers were always ready to fall into dust."

friendship with Ho Chi Minh. His wish now is to be with them, and with others whose actions in his life moved him. In his mind's eye, he gathers them all together in the village square:

> [T]he Vietnamese boy from a village near my own who died of a fever in the Indian ocean and the natives in Dakar who were forced by colonial officials to swim out to our ship in shark-infested waters to the moorings and two were killed before our eyes without a French regret. Ho was very moved by this and I want those men in our square and I want the Frenchman too, who called Ho "monsieur" for the first time. In these images we see the four Chinese characters put in terms of relationships. Out of strangeness, out of love for the other, comes beauty. It is not the mountain one knows but the mountain one is not familiar with that strikes at the heart.

In the final scene in the story Ho Chi Minh visits Dao for the last time and Dao reveals his anxiety about the "political killing" he believes his son-in-law and grandson are involved in. Ho reminds Dao that he has never "done the political thing" when choosing to act. A sudden, strong scent of sweetness fills the air, and Ho disappears for the last time. Dao purposefully closes the shade that his daughter has left up and "slipped into bed, quite gracefully, I felt, I was quite wonderfully graceful, and I lie here now waiting for sleep." The permeating sweet scent and the sense of grace tell us that Dao has found that his path is the right one—he will never say a word to anyone about his suspicions about his son-in-law and grandson, and he has, until the end, managed to gracefully elide being involved

"For me, Vietnam is simply a metaphor in which I'm able to explore the human condition. Whatever Americans' attitudes are about Vietnam, historically or politically, are of no consequence to me or my writing." Certainly, the title story of his collection *A Good Scent from a Strange Mountain* seems to contain none of the didactic ghastliness that Americans have come to associate with literature about the Vietnam War. The story alters reality, portraying one of the key players of the Vietnam War, Ho Chi Minh, in a most puzzling and provocative way, as one who returns from the dead to take his old friend Dao to the afterworld. Ho is like Charon of Greek mythology, who ferries the dead across the river Styx—the river of hate—to the afterworld, except Ho has an odd preoccupation with trying to remember a recipe. His obsession begins and ends the story, yet has only a tenuous connection to Dao and his real-life concerns. Nevertheless, as Dao gets into bed and contemplates his passage to the afterlife, he thinks about the recipe:

> He and I will be together again and perhaps we can help each other. I know now what it is that he has forgotten. He has used confectioners' sugar for his glaze fondant and he should be using granulated sugar. I was only a washer of dishes but I did listen carefully when Monsieur Escoffier spoke. I wanted to understand everything. His kitchen was full of such smells that you knew you had to understand everything or you would be incomplete forever.

Dao's peaceful Buddhist mind has recalled the details that his violent former friend has forgotten, and both of them have succeeded in putting the Vietnam War behind them. "A Good Scent from a Strange Mountain" is not about the war itself, but about its aftermath, the diaspora of Vietnamese families and their struggle to recover tranquility and harmony, to cross, in effect, the river Styx, and to move beyond hate. The story's art consists in showing that it is possible to bury the horrors of war beneath a patina of lyrical beauty.

Butler's portrayal of Ho Chi Minh stands in stark contrast to the Ho Chi Minh of historical memory. Ho Chi Minh was a ruthless and fearsome leader who sacrificed millions of Vietnamese lives for the sake of a free and unified Vietnam. He began with a war of attrition against France in the 1950s, boasting, "You can kill ten of my men for every one I kill of yours, yet even at those odds, you will lose and I will win." In 1954, he won a decisive battle at Dien Bien Phu, having sustained more than twice as many losses as France suffered. Then, when political measures failed to reunite Vietnam under communism, Ho conducted another war of attrition in

Ho Chi Minh (pictured here) appears in ghostly form to an aging Vietnamese man who is the protagonist of "A Good Scent from a Strange Mountain."

in things he believes can end only in despair. He recalls Ho's lost fondant recipe in its particulars, and knows that when he joins his friend he will have something for him. As if "a mountain of emerald had found its own scent," Dao is filled with certainty and joy—that very soon he will know whether his lost son, waiting in the village square for him, will come on tottering infant's legs, or as a man, eager to greet him.

Source: Chris Semansky, in an essay for *Short Stories for Students*, Gale Group, 2001.

Carole Hamilton

Hamilton is an English teacher at Cary Academy, an innovative private school in Cary, North Carolina. In this essay she examines how violence and death are subsumed under lyrical beauty in Robert Olen Butler's "A Good Scent from a Strange Mountain."

Robert Olen Butler has asked not to be categorized as a "Vietnam writer." "I'm a Vietnam novelist in the way Monet is a lily-pad painter," he insists.

which approximately three million North and South Vietnamese soldiers lost their lives. Butler's Ho Chi Minh, however, is a changed man. Having lost his political fervor, he now recognizes the futility of human strife.

Dao's imminent death lies at the heart of the story. It is a story told with beauty and grace, through the vehicle of Dao's undeclared battle with his daughter Lam over the window shade. His daughter wants it open all night, so that he "will not forget that the sun has risen again in the morning." Lam thinks that he may "simply forget to keep living," so she opens the shade to bring light and life to her aging father. Never in the story does Lam display outright fear or grief about her father's death, though her love and sympathy are obvious when she wordlessly strokes his head as he cries about old memories. They have a traditional Vietnamese family relationship, full of dignity and respect, where every gesture matters and is enacted with grace and care. Because of this attention to gesture, Dao understands the symbolic significance of his daughter's determination to open the shade.

Looking at the shade triggers Dao's memory, taking him back to a time he had held his infant grandson Loi. He remembers having turned his head away from the baby's sour breath, a gesture of rejection. His son-in-law Thang had noticed his averted face and wanted his wife to take their son away from Dao. Now guilt and a rekindling of his Buddhist desire for family harmony cause Dao to realize that he "will never say a word" about his son-in-law and grandson's involvement in Mr. Le's murder, thus resolving a conflict that would have marred Dao's peaceful exit from life as well as perpetuated the disruption in the Vietnamese community.

At the end of the story, Dao closes the shade before slipping into bed, feeling "quite wonderfully graceful" and implicitly ready for death. In shutting out the world, Dao enters the tranquil state of mind necessary to leave his life. Mr. Le's fate slips from his mind as murder and hate take a back seat to repose. Dao's death promises good things—release from sadness, revival of his lost friendship with Ho Chi Minh, and the chance to see his wife and other lost loved ones in "that village square at the foot of the strange mountain." His relatives will accept the passing of a man nearing one hundred years old. When the symbolic shade is drawn indicating Dao's readiness for death, the reader senses relief and acceptance through the medium of Butler's serene language and images that lend beauty and transcendence to death.

> "The symbol of the sugar-coated hands and lost recipe allude to the craft of art, a craft that demands understanding 'everything' so that the artist can take ingredients from reality--lily pads or the Vietnam War--and transform them into something sensuously beautiful."

The shade may also carry symbolic meaning in the realm of writing and art, since it acts as a medium that filters what is seen. All art is a distortion of reality, projected through the artist's lens. Some critics have disparaged Butler's literary lens as having too soft a focus, ignoring art's role to promote social change. Reviewer Boyd Tonkin writing for *New Statesman & Society* notes that in Butler's collection "a whiff of sentiment drifts like incense through the book," but "precious little bluntness," implying by this that Butler's delicate stories lack the expected intensity, as though the stories miss their point. However, Robert Olen Butler's writings do not espouse a political or social agenda. He comments in an online chat that "The 'point' an artist makes is to articulate a vision of the world not through ideas but through the reshaping of moment-to-moment sensual experience into an organically whole and resonating object that is a novel or story." Although he chooses the tormenting reality of the Vietnamese Diaspora as his subject, he transforms it into moments of sensual beauty, not a manifesto. The shade that filters vision symbolizes what he has to do to accomplish this.

The conflict over Dao's awareness that his son-in-law and grandson participated in the murder of Mr. Le involves another kind of "covering" that filters vision: the eyelid. In this case, Dao somewhat deceitfully pretends to sleep, his eyes half closed, while actually listening to and observing his family discuss the details of the murder. Dao narrates, "I had stopped listening to the small talk of these people and I had let my eyes half close, though I could still see them clearly and I was very alert." Under the guise of sleeping, Dao hears the minutest inflections of voice and perceives through half-closed eyelids the subtle facial gestures his family uses to invite each other to "listen beneath" the words for coded messages.

The family would not want him to hear their talk, because they know his sympathies lie with the dead man, who had "recently made the fatal error . . . of writing that it was time to accept the reality of the communist government and begin to talk with them." Dao agrees with this spokesman of the politically divided North and South Vietnamese communities in his Louisiana town. He says, "I would not have been afraid to say that Mr. Le was right." Dao's daughter Lam clearly knows of her father's sympathies, for she tries to cover up her husband and son's discussion of the murder weapon by saying loudly, "that was a terrible thing, the death of Mr. Le." Dao's support of Mr. Le is a huge concession for a Hoa Hao Buddhist, who were militant supporters of a democratic Vietnam. Factions of Hoa Hao Buddhists had participated in guerrilla resistance to France during its long period of colonization in Indochina; and when the communists entered South Vietnam, Hoa Hao Buddhists resisted them as well. This sect of Buddhism espoused patriotic loyalty, and although they tended to concentrate among the agricultural part of the populace and to advocate a socialistic agenda for the poor, Hoa Hao Buddhists opposed communist rule in South Vietnam because of China's dominance in communist Asia. Dao holds fast to his Hoa Hao political leanings, but he also recognizes, with Mr. Le, that to regain a unified Vietnam, it will be necessary to end the hatred against communists and seek harmony through cooperation.

The image of Dao eavesdropping with half-closed eyes recalls the meditating Buddha, the epitome of tranquility. This image combined with Dao's impassive narration transform the telling of a potentially volatile situation into a graceful scene. Dao exercises a great deal of Buddhist self-control to keep from responding angrily to his own family involvement in killing a man he liked and whose political realism he approved. But Dao narrates the tale in lyrical simplicity, like a fairy tale, adding poignant details about the way the newspaperman had embraced American culture by buying a Chevrolet pickup truck. He defuses the anger of the story and makes his family's culpability the key issue. His decision to remain quiet about it gets portrayed as a triumph of Buddhist harmony. It is as though he can repair his family by overlooking this crime, just as Mr. Le had suggested that the rift in larger Vietnamese family can only be repaired by overlooking the war crimes of Vietnam's recent past. Dao's view through half-closed eyes blocks out the brutality of the murder, drawing the reader's attention instead to the slow dance of family gestures and the importance of maintaining family harmony.

Another time that Dao chose harmony over action occurred when he followed the Buddhist path while Ho followed the path of politics. Now, eighty years later, Ho forgives Dao for parting with him, saying softly, "You felt that you'd taken action. I am no longer in a position to question another soul's choice." When Dao informs Ho (who had died before South Vietnam fell to his forces) that his communist program had "won the country," Ho merely shrugs in response, "There are no countries here." Ho's statement reads like a passive polemic against war, and it affirms Dao's chosen path. The symbol of half-closed eyes that filters out bad things represents a path toward tranquility, just as the closed shade represents a way to transcend worldly cares completely, through death.

Cynthia McCown, reviewing the collected stories of *A Good Scent from a Strange Mountain* for *America* in 1993 observes that the stories are "calculated to be positive, even uplifting," and she warns readers that "it may reflect too much of the romantic for some tastes." McCown's tactful criticism suggests that Butler's stories romanticize ugly truth into undue beauty. The hauntingly evocative, almost blithe title story portrays a touching friendship, far removed by the Vietnam War, yet deeply affected by it. The narrator voices its central philosophy when he says, "The Hoa Hao believes that the maintenance of our spirits is very simple, and the mystery of joy is simple, too." Ho Chi Minh seeks to recover joy through remembering the glaze recipe, in an effort to recapture his lost past and the simple joy of making pastry glaze. Dao, with his Buddhist approach to life, eventually remembers details that Ho has forgotten because Dao was alive to the joy even then. Although he was only "a washer of dishes," he listened carefully and now he seems to "understand everything." He follows the dictate of Hoa Hao Buddhists to live the simple life, smelling the "good scent from a strange mountain."

The scent of sugar on Ho symbolically represents the joy of simple pleasures, including the pleasure of creating. Dao's philosophy, to live simply but observe carefully, echoes in the advice Robert Olen Butler recently offered to young writers, "You need to ravenously store up sense impressions and then call them up in a trancelike state of creation, working from the dream space and not the analytical mind." Like Dao, Butler too chose the path of trying to take everything in, to listen, to observe, and to understand.

Robert Olen Butler's story puts esthetic concerns for harmony and grace in direct competition with political loyalty and action, and esthetics wins. Politics, war, anger, death, and murder are subsumed under art, coated in sugar, in effect, like Uncle Ho's hands. Through the images of the shade and half-closed eyes, Butler suggests that art must filter life and obscure or transform what is not harmonious. The symbol of the sugar-coated hands and lost recipe allude to the craft of art, a craft that demands understanding "everything" so that the artist can take ingredients from reality—lily pads or the Vietnam War—and transform them into something sensuously beautiful. Butler's story, "A Good Scent from a Strange Mountain" gently reminds the reader that living with and creating harmony are more necessary than fueling old angers.

Source: Carole Hamilton, in an essay for *Short Stories for Students*, Gale Group, 2001.

Sources

Anderson, Jon, "Inside Stories," in the *Chicago Tribune*, March 22, 1992, p. 3.

Barnes & Noble, eds., *Barnes & Noble.com Chat Transcripts* [chat with Robert Olen Butler], http://www.barnesandnoble.com/community/archive/transcript.asp?userid=1P0WU126YR&eventId=1202 (June 28, 2000).

Bell, Madison Smartt, Review of *A Good Scent from a Strange Mountain*, in the *Chicago Tribune*, February 23, 1992, Books section, p. 3.

Busbee, James, "The Devils of *The Deep Green Sea*" [book review], in *Weekly Wire*, http://weeklywire.com/ww/03-02-98/memphis_book.html (June 28, 2000).

Eder, Richard, Review of *A Good Scent from a Strange Mountain*, in the *Los Angeles Times Book Review*, March 29, 1992, p. 3.

Karnow, Stanley, "Ho Chi Minh," *Time 100: Leaders & Revolutionaries*, http://www.time.com (accessed June 30, 2000).

McCown, Cynthia, Review of *A Good Scent from a Strange Mountain*, in *America*, December 11, 1993, p. 18.

Sternberg, Sybil S., PW Interviews: Robert Olen Butler, in *Publishers Weekly*, January 3, 1994, pp. 60–61.

Further Reading

Haines, David W., ed., *Refugees as Immigrants: Cambodians, Laotians, and Vietnamese in America*, Rowman & Littlefield, 1989.
    A collection of pieces on the Indo-Chinese experience in the United States.

Karnow, Stanley, *Vietnam: A History*, 2d ed., Penguin, 1997.
    A definitive history of the Vietnam War including personal tales, and political and military events.

Nordgren, Joe, "Robert Olen Butler," in *Dictionary of Literary Biography*, Vol. 173, Gale, 1996.
    An essay on Butler's writings.

Thomas, C. David, ed., *As Seen By Both Sides: American and Vietnamese Artists Look at the War*, University of Massachusetts Press, 1991.
    This unique book looks at the Vietnam War through artistic renderings.

The Grave

Katherine Anne Porter

1935

"The Grave" was first published in 1935 in the *Virginia Quarterly Review*, although it would receive more attention as part of a collection of stories published in 1944, *The Leaning Tower and Other Stories*. That collection was generally well received by critics, who admired Porter's elegant, understated style, although her light touch won praise for subtlety even as it was criticized for lacking warmth and vitality. "The Grave" appears as part of a group of stories within *The Leaning Tower* called "The Old Order." Taken as a whole, the stories present the family history of a young girl named Miranda: each very short tale depicts a scene from their past in a nostalgic, poetic tone that is nonetheless tinged with a vague sense of darkness. The last story of the group, "The Grave" begins with Miranda, nine years old, playing with her brother Paul in the empty graves that formerly contained many of the relatives from the earlier stories.

The earlier stories are not necessary to understanding "The Grave," however. In fact, although it is last in "The Old Order," it was the first "Miranda story" to be published. Even without the added context of the family's aristocratic, slave-owning Southern past, the story touches lightly on issues of race, gender, and class. In its portrayal of Miranda and Paul's discovery of unborn baby rabbits within the womb of a rabbit they shoot while hunting, "The Grave" also offers a feminine coming-of-age story. Through the eyes of Miranda, the story not only conveys a sense of the changing

social standards for women in the first part of the twentieth century, but also transcends its historical setting with its nuanced understanding of the wonder and the worry inherent in learning about the reproductive powers of one's own body.

Author Biography

Katherine Anne Porter was born Callie Russell Porter in Indian Creek, Texas, on May 15, 1890. As with her pen name, Porter frequently embellished, exaggerated, or entirely fabricated biographical facts, so the precise truth of her life story remains uncertain. She took her name from her paternal grandmother, Catherine Anne Porter; Porter's grandmother cared for her son Harry's family at her Texas home following the death of Porter's mother. Some critics have observed similarities between Porter's life and the life of Miranda, the principal character in "The Grave." Thomas F. Walsh suggests that the story is influenced by how "Porter's own father had created in her the desperate need to cling to the innocence he ironically had denied her by plunging her into early guilt over her mother's death."

Porter's writing career began in journalism, and she worked in Denver, New York, and Mexico—the latter often providing a setting for her short stories. Her time as a journalist undoubtedly contributed to her realistic style and her use of "truth-telling" as a literary technique. Porter's first collection of short stories, *Flowering Judas and Other Stories*, was published in 1930.

From 1933 to 1936, Porter lived abroad on a Guggenheim fellowship; her time in Berlin provided the foundation for her short story "The Leaning Tower," which was published along with "The Grave" in a 1944 collection of stories. In 1945, Porter began work on her only novel, *Ship of Fools*, which won her both popular and critical acclaim when it was published in 1962.

Not until 1965, however, did Porter receive serious recognition for her achievements in the genre for which she is now famous. That year, *The Collected Stories of Katherine Anne Porter* was published, and subsequently received the Gold Medal for Fiction awarded by the National Institute of Arts and Letters, the Pulitzer Prize, and the National Book Award. In 1966, Porter was appointed to the American Academy of Arts and Letters.

In her later years, Porter's political interests became a more important focus of her writing. In 1977, three years before her death, she published *The Never-Ending Wrong*—a kind of personal memoir about the Sacco-Vanzetti trial and execution. The work received mixed reviews, but even her harshest critics acknowledged the importance of her earlier work. Porter died September 18, 1980, in Silver Spring, MD, of cancer.

Plot Summary

The story begins in the family cemetery of the heroine, Miranda. Then nine years old, she and her twelve-year-old brother, Paul, pass through the cemetery on their way to go hunting; they set down their rifles and climb the fence to explore the now-empty graves. The bodies had been removed to the public cemetery so the small plot of land, a portion of Miranda's grandmother's farm, could be sold to provide money for other relatives. Miranda and Paul play among the graves with little thought of the coffins and dead bodies they once held. Digging in the grave of her grandfather, Miranda discovers a small silver dove—she announces proudly to Paul that he must guess what she has found. Paul, too, has found something, and they play at guessing what the other has unearthed. Unable to guess, each reveals their treasure: Paul displays an engraved gold ring, Miranda shows him the dove, and they trade. Paul is especially pleased; his silver dove is the screw head for a coffin.

Miranda is satisfied with the ring, and they decide to leave, continuing the hunt for rabbits, birds, and other small prey. Miranda has never been particularly interested in hunting—a trait that her brother finds exasperating—and she is not attentive today either. Her brother tells her that the first dove or rabbit should be his to shoot, and she asks without concern whether she can have the first snake. Her mind is on the ring, which contrasts sharply with her overalls, straw hat, and sandals. Despite criticism from neighbors for wearing boys clothes, Miranda had never been bothered by it, and had always accepted her father's explanation: the overalls were perfectly suited to playing on the farm, and wearing them would save her dresses for school. The ring seems to change Miranda's mind: she begins to think about turning back, going home for a bath, and dressing up in her finest dress. She nearly turns back without telling Paul, she has fallen so far behind him

Katherine Anne Porter

in their walk, but decides to catch up with him and inform him that she is going home.

As she catches up to Paul, they spot a rabbit, and he shoots, killing it with one shot. Paul begins skinning the rabbit; Miranda's Uncle Jimbilly could turn the skin into a fur coat for one of her dolls. Miranda admires her brother's skill in skinning the animal. Then Paul lifts the rabbit's belly—it was pregnant. He cuts the tiny rabbits from the mother's womb, and Miranda is rapt with wonder and excitement. Touching one of the unborn bunnies, Miranda feels vague stirrings about her own body's reproductive abilities. She feels as though she has discovered something that she had, in another way, always known. The more she thinks about it, the more troubled she becomes. She tells Paul she doesn't want the fur, so he puts the little rabbits back inside their mother's body, then wraps the fur around them and hides them in the bushes. At some length, Paul commands Miranda never to tell anyone about what they have seen. Miranda, unnerved by the incident, never tells a soul.

Miranda eventually forgets the rabbits entirely, and does not remember them for nearly twenty years. Then, while in a foreign marketplace, a vendor presents her with a tray of sugared candies shaped like little animals, including lambs, birds, and rabbits. She is startled by the sudden remembrance of the dead rabbits and is briefly frightened by her recollection. That memory fades, and instead she pictures her brother, standing in the sun and admiring the silver dove she had found.

Characters

Miranda

Miranda is the main character in the story; through most of it, she is nine years old, but the story concludes with the adult Miranda, perhaps nearing thirty, reflecting on her memories. She lives on the farm of her grandmother, now dead, with her father, Harry, her brother, Paul, and her older sister, Maria. Although her family once had money and social status, her grandmother had slighted her father Harry in her will, leaving them "in straits about money." Miranda thus has an awareness of both her family's grand past and their current difficulties; she has a "powerful social sense, which was like a fine set of antennae radiating from every pore of her skin." Lacking the guidance of a woman—either her mother or grandmother—Miranda's father dresses her in boys clothes: "dark blue overalls, a light blue shirt, a hired-man's straw hat, and thick brown sandals." To neighbors, Miranda's odd dress reflected both their family's fall from grace and the disorder of a motherless household, and Miranda senses their scorn. At the beginning of the story, Miranda seems innocent, "scratching around aimlessly and pleasurably as any young animal." When she sees the bodies of unborn rabbits, pulled from the womb of the mother rabbit her brother had shot, she feels she has received forbidden knowledge—a feeling that haunts her even twenty years later, when she suddenly recalls the incident.

Paul

Paul is Miranda's twelve-year-old brother. He takes Miranda hunting with him reluctantly and instructs her on how to handle her gun, although she listens poorly and displays little interest. By contrast, Paul is almost too involved with the sport: "She had seen him smash his hat and yell with fury when he had missed his aim." When Paul discovers the unborn rabbits in the body of a rabbit he kills, he seems surprised, although Miranda suggests that he is not as innocent as she was: "Her brother had spoken as if he had known about everything all along. He may have seen all this before." Nonetheless, Paul seems concerned about exposing Miranda to this new knowledge of the birth process. Usually impatient and condescending toward Miranda, he approaches her "with an eager friendliness, a confidential tone quite unusual in him," instructing her never to tell what they've seen. When Miranda remembers the image of the rabbits as an adult, immediately it is replaced by a vision of Paul, "whose childhood face she had forgotten, standing again in the blazing sunshine, again twelve years old, a pleased sober smile in his eyes, turning the silver dove over and over in his hands."

Media Adaptations

- "The Grave" was recorded as an audiocassette by Audio Partners in 1989, along with three other stories from *The Collected Stories of Katherine Anne Porter*. The stories are read by Porter's lifelong friend actress Siobahn McKenna.

Themes

In "The Grave," Porter's use of symbolism allows a very short story to express a variety of themes. The ring and dove found by Miranda and Paul in the family cemetery, the rabbits, Miranda's clothing—all of these elements contain many shades of meaning.

Coming of age

Only nine years old during the main part of the narrative, Miranda is not yet interested in the stuff of womanhood, like her older sister Maria's violet talcum powder or wearing pretty dresses. When she puts on the ring her brother Paul finds among the empty graves in their family's cemetery, however, she begins to feel differently. Before, she had been content to play in overalls and a hired-man's hat, "scratching around aimlessly and pleasurably as any young animal"; now, wearing the ring, she suddenly feels an urge to "put on the thinnest, most becoming dress she owned, with a big sash, and sit in a wicker chair under the trees." It is as if she starts the transformation from child to woman.

That transformation is pushed further along when Miranda sees the pregnant belly of the rabbit her brother shoots. Paul takes the unborn baby rabbits from their mother's womb, and Miranda is filled with curiosity and excitement. Looking at the babies, she learns more about what it means to be female: "She understood a little of the secret, formless intuitions in her own mind and body, which had been clearing up, taking form, so gradually and so steadily she had not realized that she was learning what she had to know." Although Miranda won't be a woman for several years, she is already changed by the incident. Before, she might have wanted the skin of the rabbits for her dolls' fur coats, but not anymore. Without fully knowing why or what has happened, Miranda puts a part of her childhood innocence away forever.

Redemption

Although the story begins in a grave and ends with the death of a pregnant rabbit, it also celebrates a triumph over the grave, especially through the use of Christian symbolism. It begins with empty graves, no longer the resting place of dead bodies, but a playground for young children—new life in the face of death. In the grave of her grandfather, Miranda finds a silver dove—the screw-head for a coffin. Even in the context of the story, the dove acts as a Christian symbol of rebirth, for that is why it is used to decorate the coffins of the dead.

Playing among the graves, Miranda and Paul seem to be in a kind of Eden; they are in a "garden of tangled rose bushes and ragged cedar trees and cypress." We can guess that there will be a fall, however, when Miranda asks if she can "have the first snake" in their hunt, suggesting the snake that led Eve to eat from the tree of knowledge. Shortly thereafter, Miranda has her first taste of forbidden knowledge, as well. Upon seeing the bodies of the unborn baby rabbits, Miranda's innocence transforms instantly into an irreversible awareness of both birth and death: "Having seen, she felt as if she had known all along. The very memory of her former ignorance faded, she had always just known this."

If the story of the rabbits suggests a kind of fall for Miranda, the end of the story holds out the possibility of redemption. When, twenty years later, she remembers the event, it happens like a resurrection: "the episode of that far-off day leaped from its

Topics for Further Study

- Although it was initially published on its own, "The Grave" was later published as the last in a group of stories called "The Old Order," all of which describe the life of Miranda's family. Porter gives fuller descriptions of Miranda's grandmother, her father Harry, and her Uncle Jimbilly, who are mentioned only briefly in "The Grave," and of the family's slave-owning past. Read the stories that precede "The Grave" and see how your interpretation of the story changes. Does knowing the full family history add to your understanding of Miranda's "vague stirrings" for the past? What kind of family memories and secrets were buried in the grandmother's cemetery?

- Critics frequently suggest that the character of Miranda, who appears in several of Porter's short stories, is closely related to Porter herself. Read parts of one of Porter's biographies with Miranda in mind. How does Porter compare to the ideal of Southern womanhood Miranda dreams about? Can you make a connection between her interest in creating an illustrious Porter family tree and Miranda's memories of her family's grand past?

- Porter's work is often considered as part of a body of literature by Southern women writers, including Eudora Welty and, later, Flannery O'Connor. Read some of their works, comparing and contrasting them to Porter's. How do they depict Southern women? How do they depict the South itself? Are there certain elements of their work that characterizes Southern women's writing?

- The Reconstruction period was a particularly dark one for the South. Plantations and families that had relied on free slave labor were often lost, unable to run their farms or their households. Find an account of a family or families that struggled with this transition. What hardships did they face? What hardships did their freed slaves face? How did the fall of the plantation system change Southern society?

- Miranda seems shocked but intrigued by the womb of the mother rabbit and her unborn babies. She knows a little bit about reproduction, but Porter suggests that this is forbidden knowledge. What was education for women like in 1903? How do you think Miranda would be likely to learn about sex and reproduction? How has education for women and sex education changed in the last century?

- Porter makes much of Miranda's clothing in "The Grave"—both the overalls and sandals she is wearing and the fancy dress she'd like to wear. The old neighbors suggest that Miranda's clothing was inappropriate. What would a young Southern girl be likely to wear in 1903? How would it vary depending on her social status?

- Critics often discuss the symbolism of various objects in "The Grave," including the ring. Adrienne Rich's poem "Aunt Jennifer's Tigers" also describes a ring that seems to be very symbolic. After reading Rich's poem, can you see any similarities in how Rich and Porter use the ring as a symbol? In what ways does Porter's use of symbolism seem, as critics have suggested, especially "poetic"?

---

burial place." Then, the vision of dead rabbits fades into a memory of Paul, "standing again in the blazing sunshine—the silver dove over and over in his hands." The image of Paul in the bright light suggests a revelation—perhaps even the epiphany of the apostle Paul on the road to Damascus. The focus of that revelation is the dove, another symbol of rebirth; resurrected from her memory, Miranda's fall from innocence and her vision of death are redeemed by the possibility of salvation.

Social order

Without a mother to guide them, Miranda's family adopts practices that contradict prevailing social standards. Miranda's boyish dress—"dark blue overalls, a light blue shirt, a hired-man's straw hat, and thick brown sandals"—raises eyebrows among the neighbors. "Ain't you ashamed of yoself, Missy?" they ask her. "It's aginst the Scriptures to dress like that." Her older sister Maria "rode at a dead run with only a rope knotted around her horse's nose." As the story explains, such unfeminine behavior is a serious affront: "it was making a scandal in the countryside, for the year was 1903, and in the back country the law of female decorum had teeth in it."

Behavioral standards determined by gender are closely tied up with other kinds of social order in "The Grave." Although the neighbors ask Miranda about her clothes, they are at least as concerned with her father's slipping social status, the result of being snubbed in Miranda's grandmother's will: "Some of his old neighbors reflected with vicious satisfaction that now he would probably not be so stiff-necked, nor have any more high-stepping horses either."

Thus when Miranda puts on the old ring, she feels a desire not only for feminine trappings, but also for a return to her family's grand past: "she had vague stirrings of desire for luxury and a grand way of living which could not take precise form in her imagination but were founded on family legend of past wealth and leisure." At once, the ring seems to symbolize a standard of femininity and an aristocratic social status, suggesting that perhaps the two ideals are closely related.

Style

Symbolism

"The Grave" is rich with symbolism that can be interpreted in many different ways; such symbols can be called "multivalent." For example, the ring Paul finds in the empty graves and gives to Miranda seems to symbolize for her both an ideal of femininity and the now-lost wealth of her family. The rabbit Paul shoots was pregnant; her dead body thus reflects both death and life, and for Miranda, it marks both a fall from innocence and an initiation into womanhood. Finally, Miranda's visit to the foreign marketplace twenty years later suggests the power of symbolism. Seeing a tray of sugar sweets shaped like baby birds and rabbits—animals she and Paul hunted that day—the full force of that incident immediately returns, making her temporarily immobile. The symbolic power of those little candies brings the entire incident to life for her again.

Modernism

Porter's writing style in "The Grave" shares some characteristics with modernism, a literary movement that occurred after World War I. While not as radically experimental as the works that frequently are associated with modernism—James Joyce's *Ulysses* or T. S. Eliot's *The Waste Land*, for example—"The Grave" exhibits modernist tendencies in its spare but poetic style, its avoidance of a strictly linear plot, and its emphasis on fluid boundaries. Modernism was not only a literary but also a cultural movement, which stood in opposition to older Victorian social standards and practices, particularly its rigid hierarchies of class, race, and gender. Modernism was particularly important in the American South, which was also engaged in a conflict between its plantation past and a newly developing, less stratified social order. In this sense, too, Porter's writing shares modernist concerns: in her depiction of Miranda's transgression of feminine standards, in allusions to her family's fall from a grand past, and in the graphic and ambiguously positive representation of feminine reproductive power.

Epilogue

The final scene in "The Grave," in which an older Miranda suddenly recalls the image of the dead rabbits, functions as a kind of epilogue to the story. Normally, we might expect the epilogue to assist the reader in interpreting the events of the story better, particularly since we first understand them through the eyes of Miranda as a nine-year-old child. This epilogue is remarkable in that it seems to make the meaning of the story less clear, or more ambiguous; Porter's conclusion emphasizes Miranda's contradictory feelings—"like the mingled sweetness and corruption she had smelled that other day"—rather than providing a kind of closure. Similarly, the epilogue contrasts two very different images from Miranda's memory of the day: "the bloody heap" of the rabbits and "her brother—again in the blazing sunshine—turning the silver dove over and over in his hands." The epilogue thus compels the reader to consider the relationship between these two images, and to wonder what that day really meant to Miranda.

Setting

The Southern setting of "The Grave" provides the reader with a great deal of background information not explicitly stated in the story. Porter announces that the year is 1903, so the story happens in Texas not long after the Civil War and Reconstruction had devastated the South. Thus the "family legend of past wealth and leisure" evokes images of plantations and a Southern aristocracy destroyed by both the war and the economic decline it caused. Miranda's "powerful social sense" and concern with seeming "ill-bred" reflect not merely an individual personality trait, but a Southern sense of humiliation and disgrace. The Southern setting also colors Porter's depiction of feminine stereotypes. When she describes Miranda's desire to "put on the thinnest, most becoming dress she owned, with a big sash, and sit in a wicker chair under the trees," the story evokes not just any ideal of womanhood, but a Southern belle. As a result, Miranda's desire to return to the house suggests a nostalgia for the South's pre-War greatness, although the ambiguity of the story does not allow that nostalgia to remain.

Historical Context

Reconstruction Era in the South

The period following the Civil War in the South was a tumultuous one. Although Abraham Lincoln had favored a more forgiving approach to reuniting the states, following his assassination more radical Republicans took over, eventually managing Southern state governments by military rule. Already defeated in the Civil War, the South was further humiliated by the continued forcible domination of the North. By 1890, just a decade before the setting of "The Grave," the South was ranked last in every category when compared to other regions: lowest in per capita income, lowest in public health, lowest in education. For Southerners who could remember the glory of the South before the Civil War, this was a great blow to their pride.

Women's Movement

In the early twentieth century, the women's movement picked up steam with the push to give women the vote. The suffrage movement had been growing since the mid-1800s, beginning with the 1848 Seneca Falls Convention on women's rights headed by Lucretia Mott and Elizabeth Cady Stanton. That movement was closely related to the abolitionist movement—women who supported civil rights for African Americans also began to demand civil rights for themselves. Not until 1914, however, did the voting rights amendment have any realistic chance of succeeding, and from then until its eventual ratification in 1920 the question of women's rights was one of the most hotly debated topics in public discourse. Having gained the right to vote, women were still considered second-class citizens in both domestic and professional life, although some outspoken women—who were often vehemently chastised—continued to work for increased freedom for women. For example, Eleanor Roosevelt, during her twelve years as First Lady (1933–1945), insisted that only female reporters cover her, to extend opportunities for female journalists.

Socialism

In the 1920s and 30s, as Porter began her fiction-writing career, artists and intellectuals in the United States increasingly moved to the left politically, allying themselves with socialism, communism, and sometimes the Communist Party, and with the growing labor movement of the early twentieth century. Communism was also a force in the political upheavals of Mexico, which Porter documented as a journalist, marked by a concern for the Indian laboring classes. Socialist rhetoric of the area was characterized by class antagonism and frustration with the power of an entrenched establishment—an old order—versus laborers and small-scale farmers, such as Porter's father. Flirtation with radical politics was quite common among the cultural elite of the period, but by the end of the 1930s it was waning significantly; the surge of patriotic sentiment occasioned by World War II then struck a decisive blow. For Porter personally, the corruption of the new government established in Mexico, which she felt had betrayed the lower classes of Indian Mexicans, contributed to her disillusionment.

Literary Trends

Although specific dates are difficult to determine, the artistic movement referred to as modernism began in earnest after the First World War and "ended," or was supplanted by, postmodernism after the Second World War. Major works in the modernist canon were published in 1922, including James Joyce's *Ulysses*, T. S. Eliot's *The Waste Land*, and Virginia Woolf's *Jacob's Room*. Other artists associated with modernism include authors Gertrude Stein and Ezra Pound, painter Pablo Picasso, and composers Igor Stravinsky and Arnold

Compare & Contrast

- **1900s:** Natural childbirth—without the use of drugs, anesthesia, or other devices—is the norm for most women. Home birth is common, particularly in rural areas.

    1930s: Grantly Dick-Read publishes *Natural Childbirth*, proposing childbirth techniques that would later be adapted by natural childbirth advocates such as Ferdinand Lamaze. Nonetheless, the trend toward increasing medical intervention continues as labor and delivery is treated like an operation.

    Turn of the Millennium: The rate of Caesarian—or surgical—birth is at an all-time high of 25 to 30 percent in some hospitals, particularly those serving well-insured white women. At the same time, the increasing popularity of birthing centers and nurse-midwives offers women the opportunity to deliver naturally, with medical assistance standing by in case of emergency.

- **1900s:** In 1902, Elizabeth Cady Stanton dies, never having achieved her lifelong goal of winning the right to vote. In her final years with the National American Women's Suffrage Association, Stanton is censured by the increasingly conservative organization for her radical feminist views.

    1930s: First Lady Eleanor Roosevelt takes an active, often unpopular role in advancing the status of women. In 1933, she holds the first-ever press conference called by a First Lady, inviting only female journalists. In 1934, she assists her female friend Caroline O'Day in her successful campaign for Congress. Eleanor Roosevelt frequently arranges meetings for civil rights and women's rights leaders to gain access to FDR.

    Turn of the Millennium: Although the Equal Rights Amendment was declared dead in 1982, women still make small gains in public life. Elizabeth Dole, wife of former Senate majority leader and Republican presidential candidate Bob Dole, becomes one of the serious major-party candidates for president. She drops out of the race frustrated by the pressure to fundraise.

- **1900s:** The South is just coming out of a violent and difficult period of Reconstruction. Meanwhile, the United States as a whole is just coming out of a depression. Redistribution of land ownership and labor shortages following the abolition of slavery keep the South lagging behind the economic recovery of the North, which was fueled by the Industrial Revolution.

    1930s: Following the stock market crash of 1929, the whole country plunges into the Great Depression, which peaks in 1933. The labor movement of the industrialized North was echoed in the organizing of poor whites and blacks of the largely rural South, who were hit especially hard.

    Turn of the Millennium: Although the South has regained political power, rural areas of the region remain some of the poorest in the country.

- **1900s:** The period from 1865 to 1900 can be termed the Realistic Period in American Literature, marked by novels from such authors as Mark Twain and Henry James. The first decade of the century marks a turn toward what is often called the Naturalistic Period, characterized by such authors as Jack London and Theodore Dreiser. Twain's humor aside, these authors often took a dark view of the natural and cultural challenges confronted by American men.

    1930s: Post-war disillusionment contributes the rise of modernism. American modernists of the 1930s often reflected the tumultuous, class-conscious politics of the era, especially William Faulkner, Thomas Wolfe, and John Steinbeck.

    Turn of the Millennium: Postmodern writing of the late twentieth century is characterized by more extreme manifestations of the counterculture tendencies of modernism. The postmodern movement reflects attempts to supplant so-called high culture with mass media: television, popular music, movies. Postmodern literature demonstrates a resistance to the notion of genre and an interest in popular culture.

Schoenberg. Because the features of modernism vary with the artists, a cohesive definition is impossible to create, but it can be characterized by the attempt to break from traditions of the past, especially those of social structures and conventional morality. Formally, modernist art of all genres tended to violate norms of realistic representation, coherence, straightforward structure, and proper syntax.

Critical Overview

"The Grave" was first published in the *Virginia Quarterly Review* in 1935, but it did not receive much critical attention until it was published again in 1944 as part of a collection of stories, *The Leaning Tower and Other Stories*. In this collection, "The Grave" was grouped with a smaller collection of short stories focusing on the character of Miranda, called "The Old Order."

Early reviews of *The Leaning Tower and Other Stories* were mainly positive, hailing Porter as a careful stylist and an important contributor to the genre of the American short story. In *The Saturday Review*, Howard Mumford Jones admired the stories' "smooth literary texture" and the "exquisite rightness" of her style. However, he also criticizes her for an "approach [that] sometimes reminds one of a cat stalking its prey with unnecessary caution," suggesting that her roundabout storytelling methods decrease the stories' dramatic power. Similarly, Joseph Warren Beach, while admiring Porter as a "truth-teller" who was "refreshingly free from self-consciousness," cautioned that the "deceptive quietness in her tone . . . may lead us to do less than justice to her writing." Writing for the *Kenyon Review*, Marguerite Young claimed that "Miss Porter's great service to the short story has been . . . that in her hands it acquires a new stature and significance."

Later critics would most frequently discuss symbolism in her work, finding "The Grave" in particular a story amenable to a formalist approach—a critical approach that emphasizes studying the story as a discrete whole, apart from considerations of the author's biography or her other works. Such critics therefore considered "The Grave" without considering the context of "The Old Order" or any of the other stories in which Miranda was a central character. The ring and the dove found in the graves, the rabbits, and the grave itself have each been explained by a variety of different interpretations. William Prater interprets Miranda's exchange of the dove for the ring as "symbolizing her unconscious willingness to trade her childhood innocence for the knowledge that the gold wedding ring represents," adding that the grave represents "the 'burial place' of her mind in which she represses an unpleasant but meaningful experience." In response to scholars' attempts to fix meanings for the various symbols in the story, Dale Kramer suggests that the symbolism of "The Grave" works on both intellectual and subliminal levels. His reading of the story thus emphasizes the unconscious, and he argues, like others, that the form and symbolism of the story indicate Miranda's psychological repression of "the fuller implications of sexual knowledge" contained in the vision of the unborn rabbits.

Some critics suggested that despite Porter's alleged atheism (alleged because some say Porter was Catholic), the symbolism of "The Grave" was predominantly Christian, and subsequently offered Christian interpretations of the story. In a defense of his formalist methodology, George Cheatham dismisses the importance of Porter's own beliefs to argue that the story should stand on its own. In that context, Cheatham proposes that the dove "unquestionably symbolizes the resurrection of man's immortal soul through the power of the Holy Spirit." In a later essay, Cheatham adds to this reading of the symbolism of the grave, arguing that "Miranda rejects all inherited structures of meaning—the past, the mythic, and the sacred (all suggested by the silver dove)—for the freedom of existence unmediated by structure—for the present, the personal, and the profane (all suggested by the rabbit)." Constance Rooke and Bruce Wallis also interpret "The Grave" in terms of Christian symbolism, claiming that "criticism [of the story] has continued to neglect the story's paradigm of our most primal racial myth, that of the fall of man, which is itself the pattern of a primal experience in the life of each individual." They see Miranda's grandmother's garden as the fallen Garden of Eden, a reading they buttress with Miranda's mention of the snake, Miranda's and Paul's names, the neglect of the trees and rose bushes, and more. Thus they do not read Miranda's later vision of the rabbits, quickly replaced by a vision of Paul, as a symptom of repressing sexual knowledge, but rather as a sign of her knowledge of the possibility of redemption and resurrection. "With its end in the 'blazing sunshine' of such new knowledge, this is decidedly not the story of a willful self-blinding, but rather of an epiphany of the first water."

More recent essays have taken a turn away from the formalist practice of basing an interpretation only on the story itself, and have looked at "The Grave" in terms of the other "Miranda" stories, emphasizing the theme of truth. At the same time, recent criticism has also focused on gender issues. Janis P. Stout looks at the Miranda stories together, finding Miranda, like Porter, to be a "truth-teller in a world of false speakers." Kaye Gibbons looks at how Miranda's sense of truth develops throughout the stories, seeing "The Grave" as a kind of conclusion. In it, she argues, Miranda learns to stop digging beneath the surface for the truth and allow it to come to her instead. Judith Kegan Gardiner asks how Porter's writing in "The Grave" might reflect a "female esthetic," arguing that the story illustrates "wider possibilities for the female artist than initially seem to be available to the [story's] hero."

Criticism

Shaun Strohmer

Strohmer has a Ph.D. in English literature and has written widely on English, European, and American literature. In the following essay, she discusses Porter's use of the grotesque in "The Grave."

Many of Katherine Anne Porter's Miranda stories present grotesque images, especially grotesque interpretations of female bodies. In those misshapen and sometimes tortured bodies, we can see the results of restrictive and sometimes fatal cultural codes for Southern women. However, these stories also depict grotesque images of women that suggest the possibility of escaping these roles by re-creating the grotesque, not as deformed or unspeakable, but as beautiful and worth celebrating. In these stories, Porter inverts grotesque images of women that have suppressed them and reinvents those images to give women power.

"The Grave" provides a clear example of how Porter adapts the grotesque to her own unique purposes. In this final story from "The Old Order," Miranda and her brother Paul are hunting rabbits when Paul discovers that he has killed a pregnant mother rabbit:

> Brother lifted the oddly bloated belly. "Look," he said, in a low amazed voice. "It was going to have young ones." Very carefully he slit the thin flesh from the center ribs to the flanks, and a scarlet bag appeared. He slit again and pulled the bag open, and there lay a bundle of tiny rabbits, each wrapped in a thin scarlet veil. The brother pulled these off and there they were, dark gray, their sleek wet down lying in minute even ripples, like a baby's head just washed, their unbelievably small delicate ears folded close, their little blind faces almost featureless.

The body of the pregnant rabbit conforms closely to the interpretation of grotesque bodies outlined by Russian literary theorist Mikhail Bakhtin, in his important and widely read *Rabelais and His World*. For Bakhtin, the grotesque body is a body in the process of rebirth and renewal, a body that contains multiple bodies—just like the body of the pregnant rabbit. Yet for Bakhtin, the pregnant body is a degraded body. In the passage above, however, Porter's description of the pregnant body of the rabbit re-creates it as an elevated body. The children treat the body with reverence, kneeling before it in near-religious awe. Miranda seems even to receive an almost divine revelation from her vision of the mother rabbit: "She understood a little of the secret, formless intuitions in her own mind and body, which had been clearing up, taking form, so gradually and steadily she had not realized that she was learning what she needed to know." The image of the grotesque female body attracts Miranda. She wants to see, she wants to know; she is filled with "shocked delight" when confronted with the power of her own body. She embraces the ambiguous, multifarious nature of the rabbit body for herself.

Yet the framing of her revelation suggests what she leaves behind in order to claim that grotesque—really, her own feminine power. Just before she sees the rabbit, Miranda decides she wants to return to her family's legendary aristocratic past. She has been wearing masculine clothing—overalls and a hired man's hat—but looking at the ring she found earlier makes her want to take them off. For Miranda, the ring symbolizes the mythic Southern past, in particular mythologized Southern womanhood, as the ring shines "with the serene purity of fine gold." The qualities of serenity and especially purity represent the essence of what it was to be an ideal Southern woman. The gold evokes a memory of a golden age from Miranda's family's past, an age from which the South has fallen, and its incon-

What Do I Read Next?

- *A Curtain of Green and Other Stories*, (1941) by Eudora Welty. Porter wrote the foreword to this classic collection of short stories by another major Southern woman writer. Like Porter's work, Welty's stories often deal with women and families, and are Southern in setting and style. One of the most famous stories in the collection, "Why I live at the P.O.," resembles Porter's style in its light touch and its undercurrent of darkness that is never fully explained.

- *Pale Horse, Pale Rider*, (1939) by Katherine Anne Porter. This collection of three "short novels," as Porter calls them, offers more insight into the character of Miranda in "Old Mortality" and "Pale Horse, Pale Rider." In the contrasting characters of Aunt Amy and Cousin Eva from "Old Mortality," Porter offers a striking critique of the ideal of Southern womanhood. "Pale Horse, Pale Rider" presents Miranda as an adult; the story is much different in tone from the nostalgic stories of Miranda's childhood.

- *Katherine Anne Porter: A Life*, by Joan Givner. Porter hand-picked Givner to write her biography. Although Givner's is the "official" version, she makes a clear effort to distinguish fact from fiction, despite Porter's admitted penchant for exaggeration, half-truths, and poetic license. The book details Porter's extensive travels, her writing career, her teaching, and her criticism, using extensive quotations from interviews with Porter, her family, and her literary contemporaries.

- *Recollections of a Southern Daughter: A Memoir by Cornelia Jones Pond*, (edited 1999). This memoir recounts the social adjustments that came about as a result of the Civil War and Reconstruction in the South, tracing the subject's plantation childhood through to "starting over" in post-war society. As an account of an actual Southern woman, the memoir offers the opportunity for comparison and contrast with Porter's depiction of a fallen South.

- *The Unvanquished*, (1938), by William Faulkner. Set in Mississippi, this fictional story of the Sartoris family follows them through the Civil War, defeat, and Reconstruction. Like Porter, Faulkner was a Southern modernist; his vision of the South after the war provides a kind of masculine counterpart to Porter.

- *In the Land of Dreamy Dreams*, (1989) by Ellen Gilchrist. A contemporary Southern woman writer, Gilchrist demonstrates how the short story and regional fiction have developed since Porter's time.

---

gruity with Miranda's "grubby" appearance suggests the impossibility of truly returning to that age. The image of the ring itself—a closed, encircling band—also suggests the confinement inherent in the gender roles of the old order.

Nevertheless, Miranda begins to long for a lost Southern past upon looking at the ring, almost instinctively:

> She wanted to go back to the farmhouse, take a good cold bath, dust herself with plenty of Maria's violet talcum powder... put on the thinnest, most becoming dress she owned, with a big sash, and sit in a wicker chair under the trees.... These things were not all she wanted, of course; she had vague stirrings of desire for luxury and a grand way of living which could not take precise form in her imagination but were founded on family legend of past wealth and leisure.

Miranda wants to feminize herself, but in this passage, she must achieve that feminization by being clean, white, bounded, and unmoving. She wants to become feminine by becoming the statue-like ideal of Southern mythology. In the context of Bakhtin's theories of the body, she envisions herself as a classical, closed body. Covered in talcum powder, Miranda cannot even sweat. She is bound by a sash, a symbol of femininity much like the ring that precipitated this feminine fantasy. But the origin of the ring—the grave—implies again the impossibility of achieving this ideal. The ring comes not only from the past, but a past that is dead and buried. It is a part of the old order.

Although Miranda thinks of "turning back," to both a mythic past and home, she stops and realizes that she must continue moving forward for now, if only to catch up with her brother, Paul. At the moment Miranda decides to keep going, she comes upon the rabbits, and is confronted with a very different image of what it is to be female. In this interpretation of femininity, the color of female is not ghostly white but bloody scarlet: the rabbits' flesh is scarlet, the womb is scarlet, the rabbit fetuses are each wrapped in a "scarlet veil." The female body is not bounded, but open. Where the living female of the old order seems nearly dead in her statuesque classicality, the dead female here contains the process of life. By employing grotesque imagery that depicts the mother rabbit as more natural than the Southern feminine ideal, Porter inverts the hierarchy of classical and grotesque bodies to establish the grotesque female body as an ideal in itself.

Miranda does not celebrate her revelation, however; her delight in recognizing the rabbit's feminine power is cut with a fear of having transgressed the boundaries of acceptable knowledge. She begins to tremble without knowing why, and she realizes she now knows something that Paul had known all along. Miranda has taken possession of a knowledge that had traditionally been held by men. Porter's description of Paul's response to the scene confirms his control of this knowledge: he speaks in a low voice, "as if he were talking about something forbidden." He tells her, "They were just about to be born," dropping his voice on the last word. By Paul's placing a kind of reverse emphasis on the word "born" through the low, passive voice, Porter suggests that the female body made grotesque by childbirth is considered by male authority to be unspeakable and an inappropriate sight for a woman. Finally, when they are leaving the woods, Paul confronts Miranda about her transgression of this gendered boundary of knowledge: "Don't you ever tell a living soul you saw this. Don't tell a soul. Don't tell Dad because I'll get into trouble. He'll say I'm leading you into things you ought not to do. He's always saying that." Paul's admonitions also reveal the masculine possession of sexual knowledge, for their father controls it. Yet Paul also implies that his own knowledge is acceptable, as long as he does not share it with Miranda. Consequently, Miranda does not tell anyone, fearing punishment for her transgressive knowledge.

> Very carefully he slit the thin flesh from the center ribs to the flanks, and a scarlet bag appeared. He slit again and pulled the bag open, and there lay a bundle of tiny rabbits, each wrapped in a thin scarlet veil."

Thus Miranda finds the female grotesque body both terrifying and appealing. She can hardly bring herself to voice her understanding of it in human terms. When Paul explains to her what she has seen, she asserts that she knows, but she hesitates to relate her knowledge to her own body: "'I know,' said Miranda, 'like kittens. I know, like babies.'" Both Miranda's phrasing, first making the analogy with kittens before extending it to her own species, and Porter's writing, inserting a dialogue marker ("said Miranda") in her assertion, slow Miranda's process of accepting what she knows. When she finally does accept it, she becomes "quietly and terrible agitated." Notably, the once delicately beautiful, feminized rabbit is transformed into a "bloody heap." Having seen the positive but transgressive potential for a female grotesque, having internalized and acknowledged it, she allows Paul to bury the evidence—of her potential and of her knowledge. She seems to reject that view of feminine power. Yet she also refuses the rabbit's skin, which she would normally give to Uncle Jimbilly to make fur coats for her dolls. In that, she seems to reject traditional forms of feminine adornment—forms she might associate with the old order.

Thus through Miranda, Porter reclaims the grotesque as a sign of feminine creative power, but she does so ambivalently. Through that ambivalence, Porter can both embrace and deny the freeing yet frightening changes in gender roles that accompany the downfall of the old order.

Source: Shaun Strohmer, in an essay for *Short Stories for Students*, Gale Group, 2001.

Joan Givner

The following excerpt describes the relationship between Porter and the character of Miranda in "The Grave."

In "The Grave," through her fictional representative Miranda, Porter describes an incident which had happened about the time her grandmother died in 1901. Porter was accompanying her brother on a rabbit-shooting expedition when he shot and eviscerated a female rabbit carrying young. In the story Miranda is just experiencing the first stirrings of her female destiny. She is growing tired of being a tomboy and yearns for the trappings of femininity: pretty clothes, jewelry, and perfumes. The knowledge thrust upon her so crudely and abruptly when her brother lays open the womb of the dead rabbit is a shock. Yet this knowledge of the other, more dangerous, side of female destiny seems something she has really known all along (Miranda's mother, like Porter's own, had died as a result of childbearing).

The rabbit incident is powerful enough to stand alone as a complete story, but Porter adds another dimension by placing it in the context of Miranda's whole life, showing that the effects of this small event are neither trivial nor transient and that the past is not easily sloughed off. She tells of Miranda years later walking through the marketplace of a strange city in a strange country; a Mexican-Indian vendor shows her a tray of dyed sugar sweets. Suddenly the sights and sounds converge to bring back to her mind, from where it has long lain buried, the memory of her brother and the rabbit. The memory horrifies her, reinforcing the frightening nature of the incident and showing the capacity of past experiences to lie dormant and make an unexpected ambush.

Source: Joan Givner, "Katherine Anne Porter," in *DLB*, Gale, Vol. 102, 1991, pp. 223–47.

Jane Krause DeMouy

In the following essay, DeMouy examines Miranda's inner conflict in "The Grave."

In "The Grave," all the ghosts of the Old Order are gathered up and Miranda begins to understand what ancestry will require of her. In a paradigm of the separation from the bosom of her family that she will eventually achieve, this story focuses on the removal of several caskets from the family graveyard, which are then laid to rest "for eternity" in a public cemetery. After the coffins have been disinterred from the farm's graveyard, Miranda and her brother Paul play in the empty trenches and find treasure in the pungent soil, a legacy from their dead ancestors. Later, Paul shoots a rabbit, and together they discover tiny fetuses in the dead rabbit's womb.

Once again the mysteries of birth and death revolve around the matrix of sex; the conjunction of these creates an epiphany so fearsome to nine-year-old Miranda that she will repress it for many years. Once again a story is a window on a psychological trauma, although most readings emphasize the initiation itself and ignore the fact that the adult Miranda remembers the experience only with horror and dread. "The Grave" focuses on Miranda's stifled fears about her womanhood, raising a simple story about sexual knowledge to the social and philosophical level, as Cleanth Brooks has pointed out. On the social level, we can observe again a fragile, traditional femininity approved by Miranda's society warring with the sturdy individualism in Miranda's psyche. Sex complicates this struggle. Miranda's dim awareness of sexuality and fertility among the farm animals expands to include an understanding of the reproduction of human life. For both her and Paul, birth is a forbidden knowledge. After carelessly intruding on this mystery they both feel guilt and shame. But Miranda is not traumatized until her quick mind sees the link between her femaleness and the precarious, bloody ritual of birth. Giving life means risking death. This is her true legacy from her grandmother and her society.

The personal story related here achieves philosophical significance because it parallels Adam and Eve's archetypal fall from innocence in the Garden of Eden. Miranda's first sexual knowledge is not only forbidden and shocking, but carries with it guilt and the danger of expulsion as well as the sure knowledge of her own mortality. Remembering that some ethnic versions of Genesis make the sin of Adam and Eve a sexual one, we can better appreciate how the primal images here create the story of one young girl's repulsion at sexual knowledge or ultimately the story of male/female disaffection.

The use of symbols which invoke simultaneously—and often ironically—all three levels of meaning is, as always, deft. The central symbol of the grave is a good example. It is, of course, a burial place and most often associated with death. However, placed in context with the death of the pregnant rabbit, the grave is also a womb, suggesting a beginning rather than an end. It connotes not only burying, but the possibility of unburying, of resurrecting. This becomes particularly significant in its third meaning, for the grave also suggests the subconscious, where Miranda constantly buries and unburies her secrets and fears.

Aside from the overriding significance of the grave as symbol, Porter uses the Eden archetype to underscore the primal importance of the children's experience in the graveyard. First of all, the story begins with one of the narrator's infrequent references to her grandfather, whose bones her grandmother has unearthed three times to ensure that they will be buried together. It is the only time we are reminded that Miranda is descended from a male as well as a female ancestor. This pairing reminds us therefore that "male and female He created them," as does the pairing of Miranda and her brother Paul as they play in the open graves. In every other mention of Miranda's siblings, her older sister Maria is also included. Maria's absence from the graveyard reinforces the pairing essential to the continuation of life.

In addition, the cemetery is secluded, a small plot "in a corner" of their grandmother's first farm. It is a pleasant if neglected "garden of tangled rose bushes and ragged cedar trees and cypress, [and] uncropped sweet-smelling wild grass," Edenic in an unpretentious way. The earth smells "sweet" and "corrupt," suggesting not barrenness and death, but fruitfulness and continued life, which the children also represent, as the second generation to issue from the dead whose graves they play in. The children are themselves ignorant of the potency of the earth and find the graves rather commonplace: "when the coffin was gone a grave was just a hole in the ground."

Nevertheless, Miranda and Paul find silver and gold in these graves, in the form of a dove-shaped coffin screw head and a gold wedding band, "carved with intricate flowers and leaves," redolent of the peace and natural beauty which is the real value of the garden graveyard. Miranda and Paul echo the first man and woman, too, in that they owned the garden formerly, but no longer do. Thus, when they pocket their talismans, Miranda suggests they ought to leave before somebody sees them and tells; feeling like trespassers where they were once at home, they quit the place to hunt.

The act of hunting joins the Edenic images in the first part of the story and the sexual symbolism that occurs throughout. The earth, of course, is nurturing and feminine, and the open graves in the fecund soil suggest the womb, as we have noted.

"But Miranda is not traumatized until her quick mind sees the link between her femaleness and the precarious, bloody ritual of birth. Giving life means risking death. This is her true legacy from her grandmother and her society."

When Miranda and Paul leap in and out of the holes, they unwittingly mimic the birth they have received from the ancestors whose bones have rested in the graves.

They are equally unaware of the role identity they exhibit in claiming the treasure they have found in the graves. Paul is "more impressed" with the silver dove Miranda has unearthed, while she is "smitten" by the thin gold ring he has found. His choice of the dove "with spread wings" associates him with the free flight of the bird and the hunt, since doves are one of the prey the children seek. Ambiguity of image is again utilized here since it is live birds that ordinarily entice Paul, but the silver dove he claims is not only without life itself, it is a death emblem, a screw head for a coffin. Significantly, it is as lifeless as the doves Paul will shoot if he can find them.

The Winchester rifles the children carry are phallic, and the use of them an indicator of masculine potency. Paul has had more experience with the rifle, and Miranda defers to him. He wants a shot at the first dove or rabbit they see; and evoking simultaneously the primacy of Eden and the phallus, Miranda responds, "What about snakes? ... Can I have the first snake?"

Miranda's inadequacy with the rifle ensures that she is no threat to Paul's masculinity; it demonstrates as well that her tomboyishness is not a pervasive masculinity. On the contrary, her desire for the gold ring and the fact that it fits her thumb perfectly suggest just the opposite. Miranda is a female through and through, although her appearance—in a period and culture which set store by appearance—might suggest otherwise. The overalls, shirt, and sandals she wears for play are identical to her brother's. She and her sister are accustomed to riding bareback astride their horses. All this seems agreeable and comfortable to Miranda since her father approves.

But her "powerful social sense, which was like a fine set of antennae radiating from every pore of her skin" makes her feel ashamed when she recognizes that her tomboy clothing shocks the old women who respected her grandmother—even if the clothes are practical and comfortable, and the old women themselves backbiting hypocrites. This is perhaps the clearest statement in Porter's fiction of the paradoxical emotions behind Miranda's warring impulses: Grandmother and her social standards can inflict shame even in the face of a rational understanding that a new standard makes more sense.

Now with the gold ring on her dirty thumb, she is linked to everything it symbolizes: the unbroken circle suggests the preciousness of her virginity as well as the security, love, and honor she will derive from a respectable marriage. She wishes to put aside her overalls in favor of a totally impractical—but ideal—femininity: "She wanted to go back to the farmhouse, take a good cold bath, dust herself with plenty of Maria's violet talcum powder . . . put on the thinnest, most becoming dress she owned, with a big sash, and sit in a wicker chair under the trees. . . ." It is perhaps because her reverie is interrupted at precisely this point that the climactic moment has such an impact for her. In the next instant, Paul kills a rabbit precipitously and with one shot. Miranda's romantic image is supplanted by the realistic one of Paul with a phallic knife, expertly skinning the rabbit's bloated, pregnant body. Miranda is too naïve to consciously register that a male has killed this special rabbit, but the point is not lost on her unconscious mind. Even if rabbits were not fertility symbols, the image of the tiny fetuses, "dark gray, their sleek wet down lying in minute even ripples, like a baby's head just washed, their unbelievably small delicate ears folded close, their little blind faces almost featureless," would be sufficient to suggest burgeoning life aborted.

Accustomed to seeing dead animals, Miranda reacts as she does to Great-Aunt Eliza's telescope: "She looked and looked . . . filled with pity and astonishment and a kind of shocked delight in the wonderful little creatures for their own sakes, they were so pretty." However, her reaction shifts abruptly and without explanation when she sees that "there's blood running over them." In that moment of pity and fear, she sees the tragic implications of birth. She begins to tremble with a new insight, understanding at once "a little of the secret, formless intuitions in her own mind and body," understanding distantly that the female prize she has wished to be could not remain dressed in organdy and seated in a wicker chair; she would be claimed in marriage to bear bloody babies who are sometimes aborted and who sometimes bring death to their mother, even as they seize life for themselves.

The story does not state that Miranda remembers the death of her own mother in childbirth, but certainly she recognizes for the first time the blood rites of womanhood, even though she does not recognize words like menstruation, intercourse, and parturition. She feels "terribly agitated" and, significantly, has taken the masculine rifle again under her arm. Whereas the fetuses were before "wonderful little creatures," they are now a "bloody heap." Miranda wants nothing to do with the rabbit skin, a prize she usually claims. Paul, whose guilt already shows in his voice, makes a grave of the mother's body for the young and furtively hides them all away. At last he makes a secret of what they have seen, adding to Miranda's agitation the sense that they have trespassed.

She worries, is confused and unhappy, and then finally represses the experience until, twenty years later, she is halted in a foreign marketplace by a vendor carrying a tray of sugar sweets shaped like baby rabbits. It triggers the image of that earlier sight and, we are told, she is "reasonlessly horrified" by the "dreadful vision," lest we doubt the psychological shock of the original experience. In repressing her earlier memory, Miranda has refused to relinquish her ghost; and, failing that, she has not been able to exorcise it.

Her reasonless horror is finally dissolved by the thought that she and Paul had, that day, "found treasure in the opened graves." But it is not the gold ring which hangs in her mind's eye nearly twenty years later. It is the image of Paul, his face lit by the sun, full of potency and possibility, handling the silver dove which was hers first, before she ignorantly traded it away.

This time she trades her ignorance, reclaiming the dove in its positive image: the spirit's ability to fly free. With that knowledge, Miranda expects to resurrect her own freedom, but even more complex epiphanies await her.

Source: Jane Krause DeMouy, *Katherine Anne Porter's Women: The Eye of Her Fiction*, University of Texas Press, 1983, pp. 139–44.

Sources

Bakhtin, Mikhail, *Rabelais and His World*, translated by Helene Iswolsky, Indiana University Press, 1984.

Beach, Joseph Warren, "Self-Consciousness and its Antidote," Review in *The Virginia Quarterly Review*, 21, 1945, pp. 292–93.

Cheatham, George, "Death and Repetition in Porter's Miranda Stories," in *American Literature*, 61, 1989, pp. 610–624.

———, "Literary Criticism, Katherine Anne Porter's Consciousness, and the Silver Dove," in *Studies in Short Fiction*, 25, 1988, pp. 109–115.

Gardiner, Judith Kegan, "'The Grave,' 'On not Shooting Sitting Birds,' and the Female Esthetic," in *Studies in Short Fiction*, 20, 1983, pp. 265–270.

Gibbons, Kaye, "Planes of Language and Time: The Surfaces of the Miranda Stories," in *The Kenyon Review*, 10, 1988, pp. 74–79.

Jones, Howard Mumford, "A Smooth Literary Texture," Review in *The Saturday Review*, 30, September, 1944, p. 15.

Kramer, Dale, "Notes on Lyricism and Symbols in 'The Grave,'" in *Studies in Short Fiction*, 2, 1965, pp. 331–336.

Prater, William, "'The Grave': Form and Symbol," in *Studies in Short Fiction*, 6, 1969, pp. 336–338.

Rooke, Constance, and Bruce Wallis, "Myth and Epiphany in Porter's 'The Grave,'" in *Studies in Short Fiction*, 15, 1978, pp. 269–75.

Stout, Janis P., "Miranda's Guarded Speech: Porter and the Problem of Truth-Telling," in *Philological Quarterly*, 1987, pp. 259–78.

Walsh, Thomas, "From Texas to Mexico to Texas," in *Katherine Anne Porter and Texas: An Uneasy Relationship*, Texas A & M University Press, 1990.

Young, Marguerite, "Fictions Mystical and Epical" (review), *Kenyon Review*, 1945, pp. 149–54.

Further Reading

Clark, William and Clinton MacHann, eds., *Katherine Anne Porter and Texas: An Uneasy Relationship*, Texas A & M University Press, 1990.

This collection of essays presents diverse views on Porter's status as a Southern writer. Several essays examine links between Porter's stories and events from her life.

Jones, Anne, *Tomorrow is Another Day: The Woman Writer in the South, 1859–1936*, Louisiana State University Press, 1981.

Jones discusses how the ideal of Southern womanhood was an obstacle to women with literary aspirations. Jones's suggestion that the ideal Southern woman was like a work of art—fragile, lovely, and inanimate—resonates both with Porter's description of Miranda in "The Grave" and with descriptions of Porter by her contemporaries and admirers.

Hilt, Katherine, ed., *Katherine Anne Porter: An Annotated Bibliography*, Garland Publishing, 1990.

This book-length bibliography is current to 1990, and collects interviews, book reviews, and criticism on Porter's works. The first section also offers an extensive list of first and subsequent publications of Porter's fiction, journalism, letters, poems, and more, including foreign language publications.

Singal, Joseph, *The War Within: From Victorian to Modernist Thought in the South, 1919–1945*, University of North Carolina Press, 1982.

Singal's book suggests that by the time Porter was writing, "Modernism had been firmly installed as the predominant style of literary and intellectual life" in the South. The study looks at modernism as a cultural rather than a merely artistic movement, making connections between literary style and the historical transformations of the period.

Yeager, Patricia, "The Poetics of Birth," in *Discourses of Sexuality: From Aristotle to AIDS*, University of Michigan Press, 1992, pp. 262–96.

Yeager discusses birth imagery and the politics of reproduction in "The Grave" and Eudora Welty's short story "The Wide Net."

Hands

Sherwood Anderson

1916

First published in the March 1916 issue of *Masses*, a Chicago literary magazine featuring avant-garde writing, Sherwood Anderson's "Hands" became the first story in his first and most important collection *Winesburg, Ohio*. Although he had published two novels already, Anderson had difficulty finding a publisher for his collection. The editor who had published his novels thought the stories were too dark to attract readers. In fact, *Winesburg, Ohio* sold well and was widely reviewed. Most critics admired the book for its insight and honesty, but others labeled it crude and disgusting.

The stories all featured "grotesques," or psychologically isolated people who live in the small post-Civil War town of Winesburg. The central character of "Hands" is Wing Biddlebaum, a man who was a schoolteacher in another town until his attentions to his students were misunderstood as being erotic. Now he lives alone in Winesburg, afraid to get close to people for fear his hands will betray him again. The suggestion of sexuality, and particularly of homosexuality, was unusual in 1919, and readers and critics reacted strongly. Nearly all contemporary reviewers compared the book to *The Spoon River Anthology*, Edgar Lee Masters' 1915 collection of poems about different figures in a small town. Some said that the two authors depicted similar characters and debated over whose approach to the characters was gloomier.

Anderson often said that he created "Hands" in one sitting in 1915 and never changed a single word. Now that scholars have access to Anderson's handwritten manuscripts, it is clear that this legend is untrue, that the story reached its final form through a combination of inspiration and careful revision.

Author Biography

Considered one of the most important literary voices to come out of the American Midwest, Sherwood Anderson was born in Camden, Ohio, on September 13, 1876. For the next several years the family moved from one small Ohio town to another, finally settling in Clyde in 1884. At the time, small-town America was still recovering from the Civil War, and had not yet been changed forever by industrialization. Clyde, the town Anderson used as a model for his fictional town of Winesburg, Ohio, was a small town set in the middle of farming country and had little to offer a young man who did not wish to be a farmer or a merchant.

Anderson's family was poor. His father was a harness maker, when he worked at all, and the demand for his skill lessened as industrialization grew and harnesses could be made quickly and inexpensively by machine. Anderson helped the family by taking any job that came along, from running errands to running numbers. He went to school irregularly, but like many young people who later become writers, he read everything he could. In 1896, when he was twenty, Anderson went to Chicago and found a job in a warehouse. By 1900, he was working as a writer of sorts, writing and selling advertisements in Chicago. He returned to Ohio in 1906, married, and started a paint business. Quietly, he also wrote novels but did not publish them. In 1912, he was found wandering the streets of Elyria, Ohio, in a daze. He never went back to his business, and he left his wife and children and returned to Chicago, determined this time to be a writer.

Anderson made the acquaintance of other writers in Chicago and became a part of the "Chicago Renaissance." His first novel, *Windy McPherson's Son* (1916), finally found a publisher after two years of rejections, and at the age of forty he was at work on an interwoven collection of short stories. They were published in Chicago literary magazines and eventually gathered together as a book, *Winesburg,* *Ohio*, in 1919. The first story in the collection, "Hands," is about a lonely and misunderstood man in a small Midwestern town. Both books were well received, as were two others Anderson produced in subsequent years. His stories of isolated and damaged people, whom he called "grotesques," touched a nerve with readers, and he became financially secure and a critical success.

Anderson remained a popular writer and lecturer for the rest of his life, although most critics believe that the quality of his work declined during the 1920s and 1930s. As he became more successful and more sophisticated, he could no longer write as movingly about his one true subject: the hearts and minds of simple people in small-town America. Anderson died on March 8, 1941, on his way to South America to meet and write about the common people there.

Plot Summary

The story opens with a sentence that establishes the setting and the main character: "Upon the half decayed veranda of a small frame house that stood near the edge of a ravine near the town of Winesburg, Ohio, a fat little old man walked nervously up and down." As he stands alone and looks out over the fields, he sees a wagon full of young people returning home from berry picking. They are laughing and enjoying each other's company, and one of them yells across to the man, mocking him for his baldness.

The man is Wing Biddlebaum, a loner who is "forever frightened" and who has almost no connection with the people of Winesburg, although he has lived near the town for twenty years. To the townspeople, he is a mystery, someone to ignore or to mock. But Wing has befriended George Willard, the local newspaper reporter, who walks out to Wing's house occasionally to visit. George is about twenty years old, and Wing, although he looks sixty-five, is about forty. As Wing paces on his porch, he looks down the road, hoping that George will come to talk. When he is not with George, he is alone and afraid. With George, he is confident and talkative, and he is able to express the ideas that he has developed over the lonely years.

Wing's most striking physical characteristic— the one that gave him his nickname—is his hands. They are in constant motion, gesturing while he talks, waving about. When Wing first came to

Sherwood Anderson

Winesburg, he worked as a field hand, and with his quick, sure hands he once picked a legendary hundred and forty quarts of strawberries in a single day. George has noticed that frequently Wing seems to become suddenly aware of his hands and snatches them behind his back or shoves them into his pockets. He has wanted to ask about it, but as he comes to know Wing better and to respect him more, he finds he cannot invade his privacy by asking.

George remembers one day when he nearly asked. The two men were walking in the fields and Wing had talked "as one inspired." Wing was adamant that George should make something of his life, and not get tied down like the people of Winesburg. "You are destroying yourself," he cries to George. "You have the inclination to be alone and to dream and you are afraid of dreams." As he talks, he lays his hands on George's shoulder, urging him again to move beyond the ordinary, and dream. Suddenly, he looks horrified and snatches his hands away. With tears in his eyes, he abruptly leaves for home, leaving George standing in the field alone and confused. George resolves not to ask about Wing's hands, which obviously contain some painful secret.

The secret has to do with Wing's former life, when he was about George's age. He was a schoolteacher in rural Pennsylvania, and his name was Adolph Myers. He was a truly gifted teacher, dedicated to education and to the boys in his charge. He was "meant by nature to be a teacher of youth." With his students, Myers sat in the evenings and talked as he does now with George, and as he talked he rubbed the boys' shoulders or rumpled their hair.

Under the influence of Myers's gentle voice and gentle hands, the boys began to dream. One boy, however, "imagined unspeakable things" about himself and Myers, and told his parents that Myers had sexually abused him. Swiftly, the parents took action. One man came to the school and beat Myers, and the teacher was driven from town. Passing through Ohio, Myers saw the name "Biddlebaum" on a packing crate, and when he arrived in Winesburg, he took the new name.

No one in Winesburg knows what happened. Wing himself does not know what went wrong in Pennsylvania, only that somehow his hands were the cause of the trouble. Now he lives alone, has no friends, and tries to keep his hands to himself. As he paces on the porch of his house, he hopes that George Willard will come and relieve his loneliness. But George does not come this night, and Wing passes another evening alone.

Characters

Wing Biddlebaum

Wing Biddlebaum (also known as Adolph Myers) is a bald, fat recluse who lives in a small house outside the town of Winesburg, Ohio. He is bent, and looks like an old man, but he is only forty years old. His most distinguishing feature is his hands. They are active, expressive hands that move about in rapid gestures while he talks. Their movement has earned him the nickname "Wing." When Wing was a young man, still using his birth name Adolph Myers, he was a schoolteacher in rural Pennsylvania. He was a gifted teacher who inspired his students to learn, and who showed affection for them freely, rubbing their shoulders and ruffling their hair. When a "half-witted boy" took Myers's touches for sexual advances, Myers was run out of town. Now he lives alone in Winesburg, using a false name and avoiding people. Only with his friend George Willard is he able to talk and relax a bit, and to try to use his gift for inspiring young men. He urges George to follow his own inclination to dream. But when he forgets himself and lays his hands on George's shoulders, Wing panics and runs away.

Henry Bradford

Henry Bradford is a saloon-keeper in Pennsylvania, whose son is a student of Adolph Myers'. Suspecting that Myers has made improper sexual advances to his son, Bradford comes to school one day and, finding him in the school yard, beats and kicks Myers.

Half-witted Boy

One of Adolph Myers's students is a "half-witted boy" who develops a crush on his teacher. The boy fantasizes about sexual contact with his teacher and reports his fantasies as fact. The boy's stories confirm the "hidden, shadowy doubts" that the men in town had already held about the gentle Adolph Myers.

Adolph Myers

See Wing Biddlebaum

George Willard

Wing Biddlebaum's only friend in the town he has lived in for twenty years is George Willard, the reporter for the *Winesburg Eagle*. George occasionally visits Wing in the evening, and as the story opens, Wing is pacing on his porch hoping George will appear. In the past, the two have taken walks together, in town or out in the country, and Wing has tried to encourage George to follow his dreams. George has been curious about Wing's hands, noticing that he alternately waves them about and hides them away, but out of respect for his friend he holds his questions back.

Themes

The Grotesque

"Hands" is the first of twenty-three stories in *Winesburg, Ohio*, and they are all preceded by an introduction of sorts titled "The Book of the Grotesque." In this section, an old man dreams of a series of men and women passing by, a "procession of grotesques." He gets out of bed and writes down their stories. The narrator of "Hands" and the other

Media Adaptations

- Two unabridged audio versions of the complete *Winesburg, Ohio* have been released recently. In 1995, Audio Bookshelf issued a version read by Terry Bregy. The set includes four cassettes running a total of six-and-one-half hours, including an introduction to Anderson and his work. Recorded Books issued another version in 1997, read by George Guidall. Its five cassettes run seven-and-one-half hours.

stories has never seen the old man's writing, but it has inspired him to tell his own stories of grotesques.

The word "grotesque" has been used in art and literature to describe fantastical distortions of human and animal forms. Typically, something that is called "grotesque" is abnormal, ugly, strange. But Anderson is using the term in a special way, and the old man of *"The Book of the Grotesque"* sees that his grotesques are "not all horrible. Some were amusing, some almost beautiful."

Wing Biddlebaum is a grotesque, a man damaged and distorted by his treatment in Pennsylvania, but the term should not be understood as an indication that he is evil. His hands, which have caused him so much trouble, have made "more grotesque an already grotesque and elusive individuality," but the fault lies in the world around Wing, not in what is inside him.

Alienation and Loneliness

The central theme of the story is Wing Biddlebaum's loneliness. The first image of the story is of him pacing alone on his porch, hoping his only friend will come to call. From his porch, he can see a group of people laughing and playing, but his only contact with them is when they make fun of him. The last image of the story is of Wing, on his knees picking up bread crumbs, still alone. Between these two images are memories and scenes of loneliness and isolation. Wing has lived alone, outside of town, for twenty years, and almost no one in town

Topics for Further Study

- Using the Oxford English Dictionary and a dictionary of literary terms, investigate meanings of the word "grotesque," especially as it is used as a noun. Learn how the meanings have changed over time. In what ways is Wing Biddlebaum a grotesque?

- Look at a few paragraphs from short stories by Nathaniel Hawthorne, Herman Melville, Edgar Allan Poe, Mark Twain, or other nineteenth-century American writers. Compare individual sentences in these writers' works with sentences in "Hands." How do the styles compare? What new things was Anderson attempting to do with his prose?

- Some early reviewers of Anderson's short stories wrote that the author was cold and distant and created characters even he did not care about. Based on "Hands," do you think this assessment is accurate?

- Look closely at the passages in "Hands" where Adolph Myers' relationship with his students is described. Do you think his physical contact with the students is appropriate? How would such contact be viewed in your community?

- The half-witted boy's accusations confirm "hidden, shadowy doubts" in the minds of the men in town. What might have contributed to these doubts?

- Readers and critics have disagreed over the years about whether or not Wing Biddlebaum was sexually attracted to his young students. Does it make a difference to how you read the story? Discuss the ways in which the meaning of the story—and of Wing's friendship with George Willard—is affected by Wing's sexual orientation.

---

knows anything about him except that he is a quick berry picker.

With George Willard, Wing is a little less alone, although even with him he cannot truly be himself. He is always holding something back, afraid. He desperately wants to see George on the evening of the story's opening, but he can do no more than hope for a visit. He is incapable of calling on George himself and must wait for his friend to take the initiative. Once he crosses a field and looks down the road, but even this frightens him, and he retreats to his porch. A man who is so afraid will not be able to climb out of his loneliness.

Yet Wing's alienation has not made him bitter toward humanity. He does not enjoy his isolation, and dreams of sitting under a tree in a garden and having young men gather around to talk to him. He needs George because he needs and still desires human connection. George is "the medium through which he express[es] his love of man."

Appearances and Reality

Because Wing Biddlebaum has so little contact with the people of Winesburg, they know him only by his external appearances. In fact, he is not what he appears to be. His name is not really Wing Biddlebaum, but Adolph Myers. He looks sixty-five, but he is only forty years old. He is known in town as a skilled field laborer, but he is also educated and intelligent enough to have been a schoolteacher. By pointing out the differences between appearance and reality in Wing's character, Anderson raises the question about whether the appearance of impropriety in Wing's behavior toward his students was based in fact. The parents reject Myers because of the appearance of homosexuality, but as the story shows, appearance and reality can be quite different.

Sex

The cause of Wing's trouble is sex, or the idea of sex. Specifically, the parents of his students come to believe that Wing is a pederast, and that his touching of the boys' shoulders and hair had an inappropriate element of sexuality. Anderson is intentionally indirect in his depiction of Wing's sexuality. At times, the narrator seems to be hinting that Wing is homosexual, as when he states that "in their feeling for the boys under their charge such men are not unlike the finer sort of women in their love of men." Other times the narrator attributes the parents' suspicions to a "rare, little-understood" power that gifted teachers have.

Whether or not he is actually homosexual, Wing himself does not understand what he has done wrong. He feels no guilt or shame in his relationship with the boys, yet he learns that others find something shameful in his hands. The narrator endorses Wing, saying that he was "meant by nature to be a teacher of youth." Whether or not Wing is gay is not the issue that the story addresses. Instead, the story demonstrates what happens when people come to believe a man is homosexual, when they respond in anger and fear.

Style

Point of View and Narration

"Hands" is told in the third person, by an unseen narrator who does not participate in the story and who has only a limited ability to see into the characters' thoughts and feelings. For example, the narrator observes closely as Wing Biddlebaum paces up and down on his veranda and knows that Wing is hoping for a visit from George Willard. But when the young woman on the wagon mocks Wing's baldness, the narrator does not report any emotional reaction from Wing. Does the remark hurt his feelings? Does he share in the joke? The narrator reports only the physical manifestation of Wing's response, saying that Wing's "nervous little hands fiddled about the bare white forehead as though arranging a mass of tangled locks." Similarly, when Henry Bradford beats Myers, there is no description of Myers's pain or shock. The narrator describes only what can be seen: "the frightened face of the schoolmaster."

For most of the story, the narrator focuses on Wing as though from above, but for the scene in which George almost asks about Wing's hands, the narrative stance shifts slightly. The focus is still on Wing, but now the narrator reports what George saw and heard in the fields that day. There is no indication of George's responses through most of the scene. Presumably, he is listening with rapt attention as Wing launches into a "long, rambling talk." There is no hint that he finds anything objectionable in Wing's advice to him, or in Wing's hands on his shoulders. Wing's reactions are again depicted through what can be seen: his "look of horror," his "convulsive movement," and the tears in his eyes. When Wing is gone, however, the narrator directly quotes George's internal monologue, and states that George is "touched by the memory of the terror he had seen in the man's eyes." It is the only time in the story that thoughts are reported so precisely.

After this scene, the narrator moves back to the further distance for the rest of the story. Wing's thoughts and feelings are given only in the vaguest phrases. As he moves through his lonely evening, he seems to be an automaton, going through the motions of eating and cleaning and undressing while feeling nothing.

Symbol

When one image is repeated throughout a story and comes to represent an abstract idea, that image may be called a symbol. In his discussion of "Hands" in *Sherwood Anderson: A Study of the Short Fiction*, Robert Allen Papinchak examines the imagery of hands in the story. Of course, the title indicates the importance of the image, and Papinchak reports that the words "hand" and "hands" occur thirty times in the brief story. The hands stand for everything that is unusual about Wing Biddlebaum; they are his "distinguishing feature" and the things that make him grotesque.

They are the source of his fame when he uses them to pick strawberries, and the cause of his downfall when he uses them to caress his students. Most of all, they are the symbol of what Wing does not understand about himself and about the world. His hands seem to operate under a power of their own, alarming him, and he looks "with amazement at the quiet inexpressive hands of other men." Of course the hands of other men have not always been inexpressive: one man's hands became fists to beat Wing with, and another came at Wing with "a rope in his hands."

Images of hands being used against Wing, and Wing's determination not to use his own hands to touch his friend, highlight Wing's isolation and loneliness. As the narrator explains, "The story of Wing Biddlebaum is a story of hands." The use of a repeated image to make it take on a symbolic meaning has become a common element of short fiction, but according to Papinchak, Anderson was one of the first American writers to experiment with it.

Episodic Plot

Beyond the issues of sex and obscenity, the feature of the stories in *Winesburg, Ohio* that gave critics the most difficulty was the plot structure. Generally, the plot of a story is thought of as the pattern into which characters and their actions are arranged. A story that is plot-driven is a story in which what *happens* is the most important element, and inner or psychological development of the characters is less important. Individual scenes or episodes occur in a particular order to provide or withhold information about events. A mystery story, for example, might please its readers by providing an exciting story line, though its characters may be only standard, "cardboard" figures.

Many readers of "Hands" have come to the conclusion that there is no plot at all, that nothing really happens during the story. At the beginning and at the end, Wing is alone at home, wishing George would come. In between, the narrator reflects on the friendship between Wing and George, recounts from George's point of view a walk the two took together, and tells the story of Adolph Myers in Pennsylvania. Myers never learns how George felt about their walk, and George never learns Wing's history. In terms of action and consequence, the episodes are not related. The sections fit together in creating a dominant impression, a psychological whole, but not a plot in the usual sense of the word. This type of structure is called an episodic plot, or an episodic structure. Anderson believed that this kind of structure, in which the connections between events is not always apparent, best echoed the structure of human life.

Historical Context

The Chicago Renaissance

For much of the twentieth century, New York City has been the literary center of the United States, but around the time of the First World War that distinction was held by Chicago. Sherwood Anderson was part of a group of writers and editors, called the Chicago Renaissance or Chicago Group, who flourished from about 1910 to about 1925.

Other writers in the group included the poets Carl Sandburg and Edgar Lee Masters, and the novelist Theodore Dreiser. At first, these writers focused on Midwestern themes and reached mainly a Midwest audience, but their influence quickly spread.

Chicago was the home of *Poetry: A Magazine of Verse*, edited by Harriet Monroe. Founded in 1912, it was one of the first so-called little magazines, or noncommercial literary magazines dedicated to innovative writing. It was in the pages of *Poetry* that Pulitzer Prize-winning poet Carl Sandburg had his first publication, and the magazine also published early work of Ezra Pound, Marianne Moore, and T. S. Eliot. Down the street from Monroe's office were the offices of Margaret Anderson (who was not related to Sherwood Anderson), editor of *The Little Review*. In its fifteen-year run, it became one of the most important of the little magazines and after a few years was published out of New York and then Paris. In 1918 the *Little Review* began the first American publication of James Joyce's *Ulysses*, which was so controversial that issues of the magazine were seized and burned by the United States Post Office. Sherwood Anderson had contributed to the first two issues of the *Little Review* in 1914. The short story "Paper Pills," which follows "Hands" in *Winesburg, Ohio*, was first published in the *Little Review* in 1915.

Anderson was living and writing in the midst of this exciting time in Chicago. He and the other Chicago Group writers and editors knew each other socially, worked together, read aloud to each other, contributed to each other's projects, and discussed theories of politics and art. They rejected what they saw as the stuffy forms that writing had taken in the nineteenth century and worked on poetry in free verse and fiction that was not constricted by the formal demands of plot. They disagreed with "genteel" nineteenth-century writers who said that optimistic themes and healthy characters should take center stage, and instead they experimented with unhappy and damaged characters engaged in impolite behaviors.

Among the fiction writers of the Chicago Group, Anderson took the greatest risks with subject matter and with form, according to Welford Dunaway Taylor's *Sherwood Anderson*. Not only did he write about sex with a frankness that shocked his contemporaries, but he insisted on episodic structures for his fiction. Taylor writes that even the editor of *Masses*, the progressive magazine in which *"Hands"* first appeared, "is said to have felt that some of the

Compare & Contrast

- **1890s:** The "public highway" running between town and the berry fields of Winesburg, Ohio, is a dirt road. Field workers travel by wagon, and goods are shipped by train.

  1990s: Although there are still unpaved highways and freight trains in the rural parts of the Midwest, they have mostly been replaced by paved roads on which trucks pass.

- **1890s:** Strawberries are grown throughout the country and picked by hand by day laborers who are mostly local. The fictional Wing Biddlebaum picks one hundred and forty quarts in a day.

  1990s: Most large-scale strawberry farms are in California. The berries are still picked by hand, because they bruise easily, but the picking is done by migrant workers, many of them from Mexico.

- **1890s:** Most schools, like Adolph Myers' school in the story, have only one teacher for all the grades, and the teachers have little direct supervision.

  1990s: Except in the most remote areas, American schools are larger, with more teachers in each building and with large bureaucracies to hire, supervise and, if appropriate, to discipline teachers.

- **1890s:** The fictional *Winesburg Eagle*, like many small-town papers, is put out by two men: an owner/editor and a reporter.

  1990s: Even most small-town papers have larger staffs, and most small papers have been put out of business or been purchased by large multimedia corporations. The Internet, however, allows small groups of people to produce online periodicals, and to achieve much wider circulations than the small, print newspapers of a century before.

Winesburg stories were formless. After publishing two, the magazine stopped accepting them."

Arriving in Chicago at the right time, Anderson was able to find a supportive and talented group of friends to help him shape his own art and career. Along with his colleagues, he was able to straddle two worlds, writing about issues and ideas with big-city sophistication, but planting his work firmly in the small-town Midwest.

Psychology

Just before Anderson and his companions were attempting to revolutionize literature during the early part of the twentieth century, Sigmund Freud was revolutionizing the understanding of human psychology. His many books, including *The Interpretation of Dreams* (1900) and *Three Contributions to the Theory of Sex* (1910), were widely read and discussed in Europe by both professionals and general readers, and by 1914 or so Freud's ideas had even reached the Midwest. Anderson and the others in the Chicago Renaissance discussed the latest psychological theories, just as they discussed socialism and literary criticism.

The combination of the arrival of a new set of controversial theories and the publication of a collection of unconventional short stories was beyond the power of critics to resist. Critics who could see no other explanation for his interest in mentally unstable characters quickly labeled Anderson a "Freudian." For his own part, Anderson insisted all his life that he had never actually read Freud. Rex Burbank concludes in his book *Sherwood Anderson* that "Anderson repeatedly rejected Freudian formulas, for he resisted what he regarded as the oversimplification of the human mind and heart." Nevertheless, because Freud and Anderson both wrote about neurotic people, readers of Anderson's works have often associated him with Freudianism.

Critical Overview

Though it has been widely anthologized since its publication, there is little substantive criticism of "Hands" as a separate work. The story first appeared in a small Chicago literary magazine called the *Masses*, where it attracted some attention from the literary elite in that city, but the magazine did not enjoy a large body of readers. Typically, the story is studied as one integral part of the whole book that is *Winesburg, Ohio*. Perhaps because "Hands" is essentially the first story of the larger work, it is frequently discussed as it introduces themes, techniques, and characters found throughout the larger work.

Anderson often complained toward the end of his life that the early reviews of *Winesburg, Ohio* were too harsh, but in fact they were largely favorable. The book's success brought "Hands" to readers all across the country, and reviews were published in New York, San Francisco, and every important newspaper and magazine in between. One of Anderson's goals was to create a new form for the short story, to free it from the confines of being as plot-driven as most nineteenth-century short stories had been. One critic who appreciated the new form was the influential editor and critic H. L. Mencken. In a 1919 review, he describes the stories in *Winesburg, Ohio* as "half tale and half psychological anatomizing, and vastly better than all the kinds that have gone before." Other critics agreed that Anderson had attempted something new and worthy in the book, and that his new emphasis on honestly revealing the psychology of characters instead of on tracing their actions called for new forms.

Some critics felt that Anderson was perhaps too honest in the book, revealing things that were better left hidden. Rather than seeing in Anderson any tenderness and compassion for his characters, these critics saw the author as cold and unfeeling. Many thought that there was too much emphasis on sex. Though it may be difficult for readers at the turn of the twenty-first century to understand, Anderson's stories were considered quite daring, even obscene, when they were published in the first part of the twentieth century. The anonymous reviewer for the *New York Sun* was not alone in feeling disgusted by the perverted characters in *Winesburg, Ohio* and their "nauseous acts." In fact, the hints at sex and sexuality in the book are never more direct than those in "Hands."

For decades, critics hinted at but did not frankly discuss a central question raised by the story: Is Wing Biddlebaum homosexual, or just misunderstood? Since the 1960s, critics have weighed in on this issue, but have not reached a consensus. Some critics argue, as Rex Burbank does in his *Sherwood Anderson* volume for Twayne, that Biddlebaum was not homosexual, and that "his caresses were interpreted as homosexuality by stupid, insensitive townspeople." Welford Taylor, in another book titled *Sherwood Anderson*, concludes that the townspeople "have made an innocent man an unfortunate victim."

As the general public has become more comfortable with the idea of homosexuality, and as more has been learned about Anderson's own curiosity about homosexuality, critics have become more willing to consider that Biddlebaum is gay. According to these readings, Biddlebaum's contacts with his students might have had a taint of inappropriate sexuality, and his fear of touching George Willard is a fear of his sexual urges. Judy Jo Small's *Reader's Guide to the Short Stories of Sherwood Anderson* summarizes this line of reasoning, but adds the caveat that even eighty years after Anderson wrote, "sexuality in general and sexual orientation in particular is still far from being well understood."

The collection as a whole is frequently read as a *Bildungsroman*—a German literary form that focuses on a character during his developmental years. In their view, the stories in *Winesburg, Ohio* trace the development of the repeated character George Willard. Therefore much criticism of "Hands" gives more emphasis to George's development than would be given him if the story were studied alone. Small, for example, identifies George as "the central figure of the book," though it is a stretch to see him as the central figure of "Hands." Walter Rideout analyzes *Winesburg, Ohio* in an essay in *Shenandoah*. He finds that "Hands" provides a statement of the central theme of the book: the conflict between "the world of practical affairs" and "the world of dreams." Through the rest of the stories George explores the two choices, and finally resolves the conflict for himself. In this analysis, and others like it, "Hands" functions more as a chapter in a novel than as a story.

After the reviews that appeared shortly after the book's publication, criticism of *Winesburg, Ohio* appeared infrequently for about thirty years, although the book never went out of print. The 1960s and 1970s were a time of renewed interest in Anderson, and especially in *Winesburg, Ohio*, and many books and articles about Anderson were published before interest began to fade again. His reputation has waxed and waned, but for fifty years he has been generally considered the author of several bad books and one great one.

Criticism

Cynthia Bily

Bily teaches writing and literature at Adrian College in Adrian, Michigan, and writes for various educational publishers. In the following essay, she examines Sherwood Anderson's use of repeated imagery in "Hands."

When Sherwood Anderson wrote fiction in the early 1900s, he was consciously experimenting with new short-story forms and with a new kind of written language to fit the new forms. In *Sherwood Anderson: A Study of the Short Fiction*, Robert Allen Papinchak describes Anderson's style as "less cluttered with lengthy sentences and multisyllabic words than that of Irving, Hawthorne, Poe, and other American writers to that time. Instead, Anderson used short, direct sentences, frequent modifications of nouns, series of prepositional phrases, and the repetition of phrases and ideas, which often depend on a structural circularity." Papinchak asserts that in "Hands," all of Anderson's stylistic qualities may be observed. In this essay I examine one of these qualities—the use of repeated phrases and ideas.

Walter B. Rideout, in an article in *Shenandoah*, traces several elements that run through the entire *Winesburg, Ohio*. These repetitions contribute to a sense that "the seemingly artless, even careless, digressions are rarely artless, careless, or digressive.... If this is simplicity, it is simplicity—paradox or not—of a complicated kind."

The most obvious example is the word "hand," which by Papinchak's count occurs in the singular or the plural thirty times in the story, which runs just over 2,350 words. The image of Wing Biddlebaum's fluttering, fiddling, nervous hands is repeated so many times that it becomes a symbol of his alienation and loneliness, as thoroughly documented by Papinchak and others. More interesting is the repetition of the idea of *beating* hands—not yet another look at the movement of nervous hands, "like unto the beating of the wings of an imprisoned bird," but the picture of Wing as he "closed his fists and beat them upon a table or on the walls of his house."

This beating, which seems so out of character for a man "forever frightened and beset by a ghostly band of doubts," actually makes Wing feel more comfortable. He seems unable to talk without something to beat on. If he and George Willard are out walking, and he feels the urge to speak, he finds "a stump or the top board of a fence and with his hands pounding" he talks easily. The images of the hands like a bird and the beating hands come together the day Wing and George are in the field: "By a fence he had stopped and beating like a giant woodpecker upon the top board [he] had shouted at George."

It must be difficult for the first-time reader to imagine where this beating comes from. The narrator repeatedly points out that Wing's hands are expressive, that he talks with his hands. He looks "with amazement at the quiet inexpressive hands of the other men," but he cannot control his own. This begs the question, What are the hands expressing? What can Wing be saying to George when he beats the walls or pounds a stump? We know part of the answer. He is urging George to dream.

But why should this advice require such strong gesturing? The ideas of dreams and dreaming form another cluster of repeated phrases in the story. After his outburst to George, Wing settles down and for a short time he is able to talk softly, forgetting his hands, "speaking as one lost in a dream." "You must try to forget all you have learned," he tells George. "You must begin to dream." As the reader soon learns (but George does not), Wing has spoken of dreams before. When he was Adolph Myers, a schoolteacher in Pennsylvania, he went for walks with his students and talked while he was "lost in a kind of dream." In those days, his voice was always soft, and his hands did not beat the fence tops but only gently touched the boys' shoulders or hair. The gentle voice and the gentle touch were "part of the schoolmaster's effort to carry a dream into the young minds." Under his touch, the boys lost their "doubt and disbelief" and "they began also to dream."

Ironically, it is a dream that is Wing's undoing. One of his students imagines "unspeakable things and in the morning [goes] forth to tell his dreams as facts." And once the image of the dream is corrupted, the image of the beating hands snaps into focus. When Henry Bradford comes to the school yard, the imagery of the beating is insistent: "he began to beat him with his fists"; "his hard knuck-

What Do I Read Next?

- *Winesburg, Ohio* (1919), by Sherwood Anderson, is the highly acclaimed collection that includes "Hands." In each of the twenty-three stories, young George Willard establishes a connection with one of the lonely, isolated people in his small town.

- *The Spoon River Anthology* (1915), by Edgar Lee Masters, is a collection of verses in which the men and women of Spoon River tell their stories from the grave.

- *The Women of Brewster Place* (1980), by Gloria Naylor, is a collection of stories that won the American Book Award. It gives voice to seven African-American women in seven interconnected short stories.

- *Ethan Frome* (1911), by Edith Wharton, depicts a farmer with a poetic soul who struggles with poverty, loneliness, and a bad-tempered wife in rural New England.

- *Everything that Rises Must Converge* (1965), by Flannery O'Connor, is a collection of stories of grotesque characters confronting religious questions in the backwoods of Georgia.

- The *Collected Poems* (1950) of Carl Sandburg, a friend of Anderson's and another voice of the Chicago Renaissance, celebrates American agriculture and industry and the American people.

---

les beat down into the frightened face''; ''tired of beating the master, [he] had begun to kick him.''

The beating gestures are tied up in Wing's mind with the dreams and the horrible mistake and the father's wrath. When he calls up one, he calls up them all. Because he never understood at the time what all the fuss was about, he does not know how to separate them twenty years later. The imagery of beating hands links Wing Biddlebaum and Henry Bradford together.

Another set of repeated phrases reinforces this connection. Wing is ''beset by a ghostly band of doubts.'' When he is not with George, he has a ''shadowy personality, submerged in a sea of doubts.'' Before the tragedy, it was Wing who cast ''doubt and disbelief'' from the minds of his students, but now he himself is filled with doubts. What does he doubt? Again, the imagery links him to the students' fathers. When the half-witted boy tells his story, ''Hidden, shadowy doubts that had been in men's minds concerning Adolph Myers were galvanized into beliefs.'' The men have doubted Myers's sexual orientation. Does Wing share the same doubts about himself? Again, Anderson does not answer, but the imagery clearly links Wing with the other men.

A third set of repeated phrases arises out of the few paragraphs describing the accusation against Myers. The community's reaction to the boy's accusation is immediate: ''Through the Pennsylvania town went a shiver.'' It is the shiver of fear that the men experience upon identifying a homosexual man in their midst. Just five paragraphs earlier, Wing has run away from George after touching his shoulder. George gets up and goes home ''with a shiver of dread.'' Does George also have doubts about Wing's sexual orientation? '''There is something wrong,''' he says, '''but I don't want to know what it is.'''

One effect of the repeated images and phrases is to add a subtle bit of shading to what is generally considered to be a major theme of *Winesburg, Ohio*, alienation and loneliness. There is no doubt that Wing Biddlebaum is lonely, friendless, isolated. But his feelings and emotions are essentially human. In his gestures, in his doubts, and in his love of the boys who are sons and students, he is very like the fathers, the very men who might seem to be as unlike him as is possible. The Wing Biddlebaums of the world might not be so isolated if we were all more attuned to the things we share as humans.

Early readers of "Hands" struggled with the structure and organization. There seemed to be no reason for the order of the different scenes, and no sense that one scene was the cause of the next. A clue to Anderson's method of organization might be found in another series of repeated phrases. The narrator, in the manner of an epic poet, twice calls upon a poetic muse to help him tell the story. "The story of Wing Biddlebaum's hands is worth a book in itself," says the narrator, but "It is a job for a poet." The narrator cannot adequately explain Myers's power over his students, because "it needs the poet there."

If the story of "Hands" is read as a poem instead of as a conventional, plot-driven short story, the organization makes more sense. In this way of reading, the impressions created by the imagery are more important than the sequence of action. The images appear and reappear and all come together in one climactic scene. They create echoes between characters and between situations, and they provide structure for the story. David D. Anderson, analyzing *Winesburg, Ohio* in an article in *Critical Studies in American Literature*, describes Anderson's "intuitive approach" to his characters' deepest secrets. Anderson's "intuitive perception," he writes, is "accomplished not through analysis but through empathy, and his purpose is not to diagnose and to cure but simply to understand and to love."

Source: Cynthia Bily, in an essay for *Short Stories for Students*, Gale Group, 2001.

David Stouck

In the following excerpt, Stouck discusses Anderson's continued pattern of "loneliness and frustration" in "Hands."

In *Winesburg, Ohio* the idea of death does not signify only the grave, but more tragically it denotes the loneliness and frustration of the unlived life. As in *Poor White* we are aware in *Winesburg, Ohio* of movement as characteristic of American life, but here it is the restlessness of the individual who grows increasingly oppressed by his loneliness and his inability to express himself to others. In each story when the character reaches an ultimate point of insupportable frustration or recognizes that he can never escape his isolation, he reacts by waving his hands and arms about, talking excitedly, and

> These repetitions contribute to a sense that 'the seemingly artless, even careless, digressions are rarely artless, careless, or digressive.... If this is simplicity, it is simplicity--paradox or not--of a complicated kind."

finally running away. In a very stylized pattern almost every story brings its character to such a moment of frenzy where he breaks into something like a dance.

The introductory sketch, "The Book of the Grotesque," is either ignored by critics or dismissed as a murky and confusing allegory. That Anderson intended it to carry significant weight in relation to the rest of the book is clear when we remember that "The Book of the Grotesque" was the publication title Anderson first gave to the whole collection of stories. In its oblique and terse fashion the sketch defines the relationship of the artist to his characters. The subject is an old man who is writing a book about all the people he has known. The first thing we notice is that the writer is preoccupied with fantasies about his failing health. When he goes to bed each night he thinks about his possible death, yet paradoxically that makes him feel more alive than at other times; thoughts of death heighten his awareness to things. In this state the old writer has a waking dream in which all the people he has known are being driven in a long procession before his eyes. They appear to the writer as "grotesques," for each of these characters has lived according to a personal truth which has cut him off from the others. These are the characters of Anderson's book. The procession they form is like a dance of the dead, for as mentioned above most of these people from Anderson's childhood are now dead. The youth in the coat of mail leading the people is the writer's imagination and also his death consciousness—his memory of the past and his awareness that loneliness and death are the essential

> "In each story when the character reaches an ultimate point of insupportable frustration or recognizes that he can never escape his isolation, he reacts by waving his hands and arms about, talking excitedly, and finally running away."

"truths" of the human condition. We are told in this sketch that the old carpenter, who comes to adjust the height of the writer's bed and who instead weeps over a brother who dies of starvation in the Civil War, is one of the most lovable of all the grotesques in the writer's book. Just such a character apparently befriended Anderson's lonely mother in Clyde, Ohio; this detail indicates both the personal and the elegiac nature of the book.

The first story, "Hands," tells about Wing Biddlebaum whose unfulfilled life typifies the other life stories recounted in the book. From his little house on the edge of town Wing can watch life pass by: "... he could see the public highway along which went a wagon filled with berry pickers returning from the fields. The berry pickers, youths and maidens, laughed and shouted boisterously. A boy clad in a blue shirt leaped from the wagon and attempted to drag after him one of the maidens, who screamed and protested shrilly. The feet of the boy in the road kicked up a cloud of dust that floated across the face of the departing sun." With its archetypal images of the public highway, youths and maidens, the berry harvest, and the cosmic image of the sun, the scene Anderson has created is a tableau depicting the dance of life. By contrast Wing Biddlebaum ventures only as far as the edge of the road, then hurries back again to his little house. He lives in the shadows of the town. Yet, like the berry pickers, his figure is always in motion, walking nervously up and down his half decayed verandah. His hands especially are always moving and are compared to the beating wings of an imprisoned bird.

Source: David Stouck, "'Winesburg, Ohio' As a Dance of Death," in *American Literature*, Vol. XLVIII, No. 4, January, 1977, pp. 532–33.

Barry D. Bort

In the following essay, Bort examines "Hands," the first story in Winesburg, Ohio, *by tracing the recurrent theme of loneliness and desperation born of the failure to communicate.*

A recurrent theme of the literature of recent times has been the difficulty and even impossibility of communication . . .

Sherwood Anderson's *Winesburg, Ohio* is vitally concerned with the difficulty of understanding. The characters in that work are all desperately trying, in a strange variety of ways, to make meaningful contact with someone or something outside themselves. The opening chapter, "The Book of the Grotesque," explains how each tried to live by one or perhaps several truths and closed his eyes to the immense world of reality beyond the margins of that province.

These distortions of reality labelled truths immure each character within the isolation of his selfhood but they do not preclude an attempt to escape from this inner loneliness. Any passion, any ideal, however genuine or commendable, is liable to the distortion that can destroy its living malleability. Even the man who understands this may fall victim to the rigidity of his conception.

Winesburg, Ohio opens with "Hands," the story of ultimate frustration. Wing Biddlebaum sees himself reaching out to others, his marvelous hands complementing the truth of his words. As a school teacher he had "walked in the evening or had sat talking until dusk upon the schoolhouse steps lost in a kind of dream. Here and there went his hands, caressing the shoulders of the boys, playing about the tousled heads." . . . But a half-witted boy imagines "unspeakable things" and Biddlebaum narrowly escapes lynching by fleeing to his aunt's farm near Winesburg. George Willard, the town reporter and the unifying figure in most of the sketches, watches his hands perform the lovely ritual of their movement.

"A few stray white bread crumbs lay on the cleanly washed floor by the table; putting the lamp on a low stool he began to pick up the crumbs, carrying them to his mouth one by one with unbelievable rapidity. In the dense blotch of light beneath the table, the kneeling figure looked like a priest engaged in some service of his church.''... The ritual has but one celebrant and the church no communicants.

Source: Barry D. Bort, "'Winesburg, Ohio': The Escape from Isolation," in *The Midwest Quarterly*, Vol. XI, No. 4, Summer, 1970, pp. 443–56.

Carol J. Maresca

In the following essay, Maresca shows how different symbols in the story "Hands" are used to portray or reveal hidden meanings.

Dialogue, a common vehicle for characterization and theme in fiction, is conspicuously limited in Sherwood Anderson's *Winesburg, Ohio*. The characters rarely indulge in conversation with one another and rarely debate a problem within themselves. Thus, the novel, which attempts to study the isolation of mankind, achieves a success of the highest order by isolating the reader from the characters at least on the verbal level. Anderson's message, however, is *not* that man can never learn to know his fellow man, but rather that conversation is, at best, an elementary and often a false indication of a man's personality. Kate Swift, the school teacher in *Winesburg*, tells reporter George Willard that he must learn "to know what people are thinking about, not what they say." To learn what a man is "thinking about," then, the more perceptive person will study a man's exterior being, his actions and his appearance.

Anderson uses both eyes and hands to reveal meaning in *Winesburg*, but in particular he makes the reader aware of the hands of his characters. Where "they fought" would convey meaning adequately, he deliberately writes they "fought *with their fists* on Main Street...." (underscoring added).

The first function of the hand images appears to be a substitution for lengthy character description. "Hands," the first story in the collection, explicitly reveals Anderson's conscious intention: "Wing Biddlebaum talked much with his hands. The slender expressive fingers, forever active, forever striving to conceal themselves in his pockets or behind his back, came forth and became the piston rods of his machinery of expression."

In and of themselves, the hands of Anderson's characters may indicate the character's state in life. The knuckles of Doctor Reefy's hand remind the storyteller not only of the twisted, yet delicious apples in the Winesburg orchard, but also of the doctor's own life, his courtship, and his short mar-

> "Tom Foster's industrious and aged grandmother has hands which are 'all twisted out of shape' and Elizabeth Willard's white hands, 'dropping over the ends of the arms of the chair,' betray the secret of her unsuccessful life."

riage. Tom Foster's industrious and aged grandmother has hands which are "all twisted out of shape" and Elizabeth Willard's white hands, "dropping over the ends of the arms of the chair," betray the secret of her unsuccessful life.

Hands assume wider significance as symbols, however, when they are used to express a character's emotions or passions. When a character in *Winesburg* expresses anger, he does so with his hands and, in particular, with his fists. George Willard's mother, for example, "clenched her fists" when she thought of her own failure in life and vowed to return from death, if necessary, to keep defeat from her son, though God might "beat her with his fists." When Belle Carpenter, a young milliner in Winesburg, felt anger and frustration, she wished she could "fight someone with her fists" and Ray Pearson longed to "shout or scream or hit his wife with his fists" when he realized that he was caught in life's web of responsibility. The large fists of Belle Carpenter's boy friend, Ed Handby, were the bartender's most characteristic feature (his surname enforces this association) and once "with his fist he broke a large mirror in the wash room of a hotel." And when the Reverend Curtis Hartman succeeded in overcoming his temptation to sin, he joyfully shouted to George Willard, "The strength of God was in me and I broke the window with my fist."

Flying arms indicate high excitement in Anderson's characters. The town baker, chasing a meddlesome grey cat, "swore and waved his arms about." Similarly, Elmer Cowley, who thought himself "queer," was eager to explain himself to a farm hand, whom he greeted by "making motions with his long arms," and to George Willard. As Elmer talked, "his arms began to pump up and down" and later started to "flay the air."

Experiencing the sense of confusion which occurs before maturity, three young boys in *Winesburg* thrust their hands into their pockets. With this gesture, which is more subtle than clenched fists or flying arms, Elmer Cowley walks away from town feeling friendless, Seth Richmond releases Helen White's hand and, to indicate his maturity, declares he is going to leave home to find work, George Willard helplessly listens to Elmer's problems, and in "An Awakening" he, too, uses the gesture while asserting his maturity.

But it is at the point where the characters express love that gestures, in addition to revealing character, begin to illuminate the theme of the novel. In the expression of this theme, two impulses stimulating the gesture of touch are important: the offering of love, by which a character reaches out to comfort another, and the need for love, by which a character reaches out to grasp.

Jesse Bentley needed love and, being a religious person, he sought this love from God. He prayed for a sign from God and felt that God "might at any moment reach out his hand, touch him on the shoulder, and appoint for him some heroic task to be done." Jesse's daughter, Louise, was lonely but not religious, and she turned to man to satisfy her cry for love. "Sometimes it seemed to her that to be held tightly and kissed was the whole secret of life." When John Hardy did not hold her, Louise put her head on the shoulder of her father's farm hand and hoped that he would caress her.

Alice Hindman was extremely sensitive to the sense of touch and refused to have anyone move the furniture in her room. After Ned Currie deserted her she sometimes dated the drug clerk and occasionally "she put her hand out and touched softly the folds of his coat." In her darkest moment of isolation she wanted "to find some other lonely human and embrace him."

The sense of touch, of course, often involves sexual love in the novel. Yet we are less aware of the love gesture as an expression of desire than as an expression of the lover's own isolation. George Willard "wanted to touch Louise Trunnion with his hand.... Just to touch the folds of the soiled gingham dress would, he decided, be an exquisite pleasure." Seth Richmond imagined his arm around Helen White, Ed Handby pressed Belle Carpenter to him tightly, Kate Swift held George Willard by the shoulders, and Enoch Robinson married because, in his loneliness, he wanted "to touch actual flesh and bone people with his hands."

The most meaningful gesture in *Winesburg*, however, is stimulated by the attempt to comfort and to offer love, and seems to originate in a Christian concept of love. Only after the Reverend Curtis Hartman chipped the bell tower window, which pictured the figure of Christ laying his hand on the head of a child, did he begin his life of sin. He later told his congregation, "I have been tempted.... It is only the hand of God, placed beneath my head, that has raised me up." Clearly, the communication of love gives man the strength and courage he needs in life.

Many examples of love gestures between characters in the novel involve a parent-child relationship, recalling and perhaps receiving inspiration from the Christ-child image. David Hardy thought his mother must be a new person when, relieved to find the boy she believed was lost, she "clutched him eagerly in her arms. Having experienced love, David was able to impart it and at his grandfather's farm he "wanted to embrace everyone in the house" and made his great-aunt "ecstatically happy" by caressing her face. In a later incident David's terror left him only when his grandfather held his head "tenderly against his shoulder." Tom Hard tried to comfort his crying daughter by "taking her into his arms" and Ray Pearson, having thought of his children and having "in fancy felt their hands clutching at him," could not advise Hal Winters to escape marriage.

When the love gesture is used outside the family circle, as in the stories of Elizabeth and George Willard, it includes all of mankind and illuminates Anderson's central theme which is too often misinterpreted as one of isolation. Isolation is present and is part of the human condition, but man can release himself from that isolation by reaching out his sympathies, his understanding, his very selfness, until he forgets self and becomes one with the person he is reaching toward. In this way, gestures not only convey meaning but also cause meaning, for they take man out of himself and into the heart of another.

As a young woman, Elizabeth Willard had wanted to escape her isolation. She often dated the men who stayed in her father's hotel and when "they took hold of her hand, she thought that something unexpressed in herself came forth and became a part of an unexpressed something in them." Had the traveling men experienced a reciprocal release of love, Elizabeth would have known happiness. Years later, shortly before her death, Elizabeth remembered these men and how she was "forever putting out her hand into the darkness and trying to get hold of some other hand." Her description of human isolation is pathetically accurate.

Elizabeth's son, George, achieved the happiness which his mother was denied. Like his mother, George wished to express his love through touch, but he also wished to be touched. Man must give and accept love, he must join in a mutual exchange of understanding and affection. George was fortunate in loving Helen White for she, too, comprehended the nature of love. Significantly, "Sophistication," the last story in *Winesburg* (for "Departure" is a statement of conclusion), relates that Helen ran from home to find George at the same moment that George was walking to the White home, causing them to meet each other halfway. Together they walked to the fair grounds. They "held each other tightly and waited. In the mind of each was the same thought. 'I have come to this lonely place and here is this other.'...."

Embrace has been responded to by embrace, understanding by understanding. Man has escaped, at least for a short time, the isolation of his own being.

Source: Carol J. Maresca, "Gestures as Meaning in Sherwood Anderson's 'Winesburg, Ohio,'" in *CLA Journal*, Vol. 9, No. 3, March, 1966, pp. 279-83.

Rex Burbank

An American critic and scholar, Burbank has written studies of Thornton Wilder, Jane Austen, and early American literature. In the following excerpt from his Sherwood Anderson, *Burbank discusses the significance of the unconventional narrative sequence used in* Winesburg, Ohio.

In 1914, the famous exhibition of post-Impressionist paintings was held in the Chicago Armory, where Anderson went ... on afternoons to see the works of Cezanne, Van Gogh, Gauguin, and others among the "French moderns." Like such "Impressionists" as Monet, Renoir, and Degas before them, these painters portrayed the impressions of experience upon the consciousness of the artist, or of an observer with whom the artist identified himself, rather than the external appearances of events and objects. But they went even beyond the Impressionists in attempting to convey not only the subjective experience of the artist or observer but the abstract structure beneath natural forms....

Van Gogh deliberately distorted his figures, used violent splashes of color, and swirled his brush across his canvasses to signify his own tumultuous feelings. Gauguin, the one-time stockbroker who, like Anderson abandoned business for art, drew his Tahitian natives with bold colors restrained by simple but clear lines, thereby synthesizing complex and powerful inner feelings with external forms.

Anderson's interest in painting at this time was more than casual: he himself painted.... [The] techniques of composition in Impressionist and post-Impressionist art ... offered possibilities in form and texture for fiction that were agreeable to his own views of life and art. More specifically, the new art suggested the shaping of a narrative sequence in accordance with the flow of feelings and thoughts, or impressions, of the narrator rather than according to time: according to psychological instead of chronological time. This meant that form would develop in two ways: first, from within the narrative (as Van Gogh saw nature's form as essentially an inner thing), which required that the traditional "plot" sequence of action (Anderson particularly despised the highly plotted stories of O. Henry) would be abandoned for a form that moves with the mind and feelings; and, second, because both mind and feelings operate in a continuum of time, following moods, attitudes, or ideas rather than a chronological order, form would grow by means of a series of disconnected images which are thematically and symbolically related and coalescent like the paintings of the French impressionists....

Though he deeply admired Dreiser (who himself had broken away from the neatly plotted story) for the uncompromising honesty with which he drew his characters, Anderson moved away from Dreiser's graceless journalistic style and from his brand of stark Naturalism and surface realism in favor of techniques that permitted him to penetrate the external forces of Naturalistic fiction, to bypass the ponderous collection of external social facts, and to get to the feelings and the irrational impulses of his characters, their innermost struggles.

The style and structural techniques of Impressionism and Symbolism lent themselves admirably to these aims, and so did the stylistic practices of Gertrude Stein, whose *Tender Buttons* and *Three Lives* Anderson read ... in 1914.... In his *Memoirs* he declared that, through Stein, he adopted the

"Van Gogh deliberately distorted his figures, used violent splashes of color, and swirled his brush across his canvasses to signify his own tumultuous feelings. Gauguin, the one-time stockbroker who, like Anderson abandoned business for art, drew his Tahitian natives with bold colors restrained by simple but clear lines, thereby synthesizing complex and powerful inner feelings with external forms."

conscious stylistic intention of capturing the color and cadence of his own Midwestern speech, to lay word against word "in just a certain way" in order to convey the feelings (as distinguished from the facts) of life by means of "a kind of word color, a march of simple words, simple sentence structure."

The influence of the post-Impressionists and of Gertrude Stein may best be demonstrated by perusal of "Hands," one of the best tales in *Winesburg*, in which Anderson's technique of constructing the tales around epiphanies can be seen in the portrayal of Wing Biddlebaum, whose deeply creative nature has been thwarted and perverted, through a central image of hands whose restless, bird-like activities expend themselves in random and trivial actions. The incidents of the story are clustered about this image, intensifying it and in turn being unified by it. As the incidents charge the image with meaning, the narrative proceeds to a climactic epiphany which reveals Biddlebaum's defeat to be that of the innermost self.

The narrative opens with an objective, scenically rendered paragraph showing Biddlebaum's alienation from the town and suggesting a relationship between his alienation and his "nervous little hands." It then moves in succeeding paragraphs to a generalized exposition of his more intimate acquaintance with George Willard and Willard's curiosity about the hands. Another short-view scene follows, revealing the connection between Biddlebaum's thwarted, imaginative nature and his fear of his hands. Establishment of Biddlebaum's fear shifts the narrative to a review of the events that caused him to flee from Pennsylvania to become a recluse in Winesburg. In that review we see that his hands were his means of expressing love and that the nature of this love was creative, for it found its outlet in communicating to schoolboys, through his gentle caresses, his own tendency to dream. But his caresses were interpreted as homosexuality by stupid, insensitive townspeople, and he was driven from the town. In Winesburg, he has withdrawn from the lives of others; and, unable to find creative outlet for his imaginative life, he has become a human fragment, a grotesque. The hands change from image to symbol as the narrative progresses and the themes of alienation, fear, love, and shame become in turn associated with them; and as the symbol gathers its meanings the narrative builds toward the final symbolic act, the epiphany. The epiphany occurs after Willard leaves, and the full ironic meaning of Biddlebaum's life is felt in the discrepancy between his religious posture, as he kneels, and the meaningless drumming of his fingers as they pluck bread crumbs from the floor: Biddlebaum is a kind of defeated, strangely perverted priest of love.

The narrative structure thus follows the course of the omniscient author's mind as he explores various times in the past, probes into his characters' minds, relates bits of descriptive detail, and cites scraps of dialogue—all of which add up to the final symbolic scene in which Biddlebaum's defeat is seen in the fullness of its nature. As in the best stories of Chekhov and of Crane—Anderson's Impressionistic forebear—the final scene of "Hands" is anticlimactic, for nothing happens to Biddlebaum." If the story has a "climax," it comes at the point—about half way through—in which Biddlebaum urges Willard to leave Winesburg. By deliberately violating a straight time sequence, Anderson avoids the traditional, and often artificial, plot of clear-cut cause and effect actions culminating in a decisive action, and at the same time he gains an almost tragic irony. Nothing in Biddlebaum's life can be climactic any more. His life is characterized by disillusionment, futility, and defeat; and both the anticlimactic structure and the muted tone of reminiscence support the vision of an inner life quietly but desperately submerged, and of a static, imprisoned external life. The stasis of his life, the impasse between social repression and need for expression, can be seen in the following paragraph, in which the feeling of Biddlebaum's seething but frustrated passions is rendered by what Gertrude Stein approvingly termed "clear and passionate" sentences: sentences with simple diction and structure whose passion is conveyed by the contradictory effects of emotional balance and antithesis. We should notice how the terms *beat, action, desire, sought,* and *pounding* are subdued and counterpointed by *comfortable* and *ease*: "When he talked to George Willard, Wing Biddlebaum closed his fists and beat with them upon a table or on the walls of his house. The action made him more comfortable. If the desire to talk came to him when the two were walking in the fields, he sought out a stump or the top board of a fence and with his hands pounding busily talked with renewed ease."

Not all the tales in *Winesburg* are so felicitously constructed and executed as "Hands," but the best of them, like the book as a whole, convey the feeling of isolation, loneliness, and defeat through grotesque characters. Though the tales are self-contained and complete in themselves and may be read individually with enjoyment, they gain an added and very important dimension when read consecutively as episodes in a single narrative; for *Winesburg* as a whole presents a unified portrayal of the growth to maturity and consciousness of young George Willard, who develops as the symbol of the "whole" man against whom the grotesques stand as fragments.

Like Dickens' *David Copperfield*, Meredith's *The Egoist*, and Joyce's *Portrait of the Artist as a Young Man*, *Winesburg* is—in addition to being a collection of tales—a *bildungsroman*, a story of a boy growing to manhood and becoming involved in the perplexing world of adults. Though he does not appear in all the tales, Willard shares importance in the narrative with the grotesques, to whom he is the symbolic counterpoint....

In George Willard, Anderson presents the *making* of an artist of life. Willard wants to become a writer, but before he can do so he must serve his apprenticeship to life itself. In his development we see Anderson's implied belief that the solution to the "terrifying disorder" of life, the alternative to grotesqueness, is the kind of absorption of other lives that is seen in George and in the old man in the prologue. While the artist is the archetype of the psychologically and socially liberated person, liberation is not confined to the artist; for Willard achieves freedom before he becomes a writer, and the old writer never writes his book about the grotesques.

By contrast, the grotesques are so because for one reason or another they have (willfully or because of circumstances they cannot control) become isolated from others and thus closed off from the full range of human experience. Where the old writer has accepted isolation and opened his mind and imagination to the truth of all human experience, they have attempted to embrace a single truth to live by (often, because their alternatives are limited, they have *had* to), thereby closing off other possibilities of experience and compounding their loneliness and becoming enslaved by it. The writer himself is saved by the "young thing" inside him; his imaginative receptiveness to all human feelings....

The structural form of the narrative from prologue to epilogue is psychological and episodic rather than linear; the tales are built about these moments of consciousness or revelation instead of following a simple sequence of time or causality. For Willard, those moments follow a pattern of progression toward increasing consciousness as he absorbs the experiences of the grotesques. On the other hand, these symbolic moments reveal the psychic limitations, confinement, or defeat of the grotesques whose lives are in a state of arrest. The narrator emphasizes in "The Book of the Grotesque" that the grotesques are not all horrible. Joe Welling in "A Man of Ideas," is comical; Dr. Reefy, in "Paper Pills" and in "Death," is a man of insight and understanding; Louise Trunnion, in "Nobody Knows," is simply pathetic.

All, however, are characterized by various types of psychic unfulfillment or limitation owing in part to the failure of their environment to provide them with opportunities for a rich variety of experience and in part to their own inability or reluctance to accept or understand the facts of isolation and loneliness. The nature of their psychic unfulfillment is revealed in the tales by epiphanies. Their development may roughly be compared to the action of a fountain which, fixed at its base and therefore moving toward nothing, suddenly overflows—as the pressure within builds up—and shows what has remained hidden from view. Just as a fountain retains the contents that have overflowed and returns them to their source, so the briefly revealed inner lives of the grotesques return unchanged to their imprisonment or defeat.

Like Joyce's Stephen Daedelus, Willard is the nascent artist serving his apprenticeship to life; but the important fact about him is that, while he is subject to the same environmental restrictions as the grotesques, he grows toward maturity and ultimately frees himself from Winesburg, while the grotesques do not. Like McPherson and McGregor of *Windy* and of *Marching Men*. Willard is a prototype of the man who is liberated from the confinement of a narrow and oppressive environment. But he differs from those earlier heroes in that he leaves at a point in his life when he has gained an intense love for the people of the town of his birth and youth, and his departure is prompted not by rejection of the town and hope for success but by a determination to broaden the range of his imaginative experience. . . .

Willard grows from passive observer of life to active participant, from aimlessly curious boy to intensely conscious adult. . . .

At the death of Elizabeth Willard in "Death," his adolescent resentment at the inconvenience caused by his mother's death in keeping him from seeing Helen White gives way to realization of the finality of death and to consciousness of the tragic beauty his mother represented. His full awareness of life's paradoxes comes in "Sophistication," when he becomes conscious of the "limitations of life" and of "his own insignificance in the scheme of existence" while at the same time he "loves life so intensely that tears come into his eyes."

With this ephiphany, which is also the climax of the book, Willard "crosses the line into manhood" as "voices outside of himself whisper a message concerning the limitations of life," and as consciousness of the condition of man's isolation and loneliness is followed by his beginning "to think of the people in the town where he had always lived with something (illegible line-note in report) and confused, overlapping feelings; to distinguish passion from compassion, for instance. . . .

George Willard achieves maturity when he realizes and accepts loneliness as the essential human condition and understands the value of all human suffering. Understanding comes, paradoxically, only when he has emancipated himself from this Winesburg influence. . . . [He] can understand that all men are alone with their feelings and that only through sympathy and compassion toward others do those feelings have any meaning or, to put it another way, those feelings are the only really meaningful things in life. The grotesques are people whose instinctive desires, aspirations, and deepest emotions have no meaning because they have no "other" who will impose a meaning upon them; thus they are drawn to the receptive aspiring writer Willard, who accepts and will ultimately give meaningful expression to their feelings, or in the case of Dr. Reefy and George's mother, to each other.

Those grotesques who are the most sensitive and articulate find their desires and aspirations thwarted by a repressive conventionalism that offers little opportunity for fruitful human relationships. . . .

In the portrayal of all these defeated people a vision of American small-town life emerges in which we see a society that has no cultural framework from which to draw common experiences; no code of manners by which to initiate, guide, and sustain meaningful relationships among individuals; no art to provide a communion of shared feeling and thought; and no established traditions by which to direct and balance their lives. They live in the midst of cultural failure.

The theme of cultural failure rises by suggestion from background images of decay and decomposition. The town is a wasteland ruled by dull, conventional people. Its religion has deteriorated into an empty moralism; its people have lost their contact with the soil. While Anderson uses his images sparingly, interweaving them subtly with narrative and dialogue, they evoke an atmosphere of desolation which impinges with crushing effect upon the lives of the grotesques; and, as the images recur, they become symbolic of a culture which, as Waldo Frank has said, has reached the final stages of deterioration. Rubbish and broken glass clutter the alleys and streets and of the village. . . . Dr. Reefy's office is located off a "dark hallway filled with rubbish"; Belle Carpenter lives in a "gloomy old house" in which the "rusty tin eaves-trough had slipped from its fastenings . . . and when the wind blew it beat against the roof of a small shed, making a dismal drumming noise that sometimes persisted all through the night"; and Wing Biddlebaum's small frame house offers a view of a "half decayed veranda." . . .

[Though] the characters who embody convention are shadowy or fragmentary, their power over the lives of the grotesques is felt as an intangible but decisive, sinister influence. They present a background of moral decay, calculation and artifice, of a rampant egoistic individualism. George Willard's father (''Mother'') and John Hardy (''Surrender'') embrace the religion of success; Wash Williams' mother-in-law and Helen White's mother (''Sophistication'') exploit sex with varying degrees of crudity and subtlety to draw men to their daughters. Collectively, the citizens of Winesburg torture Wing Biddlebaum with shouts of deprecation. The Hardy sisters crush the sensitive Louise Bentley with hypocritical and degrading conventional courtship rites characterized by crafty use of sex.

In such an atmosphere the grotesques typically isolate themselves in rooms as barren of joy as the town itself, emerging—often at night—to walk alone or with George Willard, in whom they confide. In the darkness or within their rooms, their secret inner lives ''show forth'' in an epiphany, an outburst of emotion, or in a casual, unguarded remark and reveal the full extent of their psychic defeat....

The point of view of the omniscient author—of the mature George Willard, recalling tenderly but with detachment of time and place his small-town youth—softens the tone; it permits the town and the grotesques to emerge as objects of compassion rather than of attack, as they are in Masters' *Spoon River* and in Lewis' *Main Street*. Tone and point of view thus effectively and almost imperceptibly become thematic in themselves—in the manner of lyric poetry.

While Anderson later wrote individual tales that are superior to the stories in *Winesburg*, he never again wrote a long work that combines with such felicity the penetrating insights into the impoverished inner lives of broken, sensitive people; the sustained, pervasive mood of social degeneration; and the quiet, unforced portrayal of a hero liberating himself from the confines of his limited environment as *Winesburg* does. It is his most complete and authentic plea for freedom of expression of the inner life and for sympathetic receptivity to the needs of the human heart. Written at the dawn of an era of revolt against American provincialism and against the romanticized stories of idyllic and virtuous village life, it has outlasted both the nostalgic, sentimental romances and most of the iconoclastic satires about village life written before and since, precisely because it goes well beyond both of those oversimplified extremes to acknowledge both the worth and the tragic limitations of life in the small Midwestern towns and—by easy geographical extension—of all human life....

Source: Rex Burbank, *Sherwood Anderson*, Twayne Publishers, Inc., 1964, pp. 61–77.

Sources

Anderson, David D., *Critical Studies in American Literature*, The University of Karachi, 1964, pp. 108–131; reprinted in *Critical Essays on Sherwood Anderson*, edited by David D. Anderson, G. K. Hall, 1981, p. 167.

Burbank, Rex, *Sherwood Anderson*, Twayne, 1964, pp. 65, 117.

Frank, Waldo, ''Winesburg, Ohio, After Twenty Years,'' in *Story*, Vol. 19, No. 91, September–October, 1941, pp. 29–33.

''A Gutter Would Be Spoon River,'' *New York Sun*, June 1, 1919, p. 3.

Mencken, H. L., ''Novels, Chiefly Bad,'' in *Smart Set*, Vol. 59, August, 1919, p. 142.

Papinchak, Robert Allen, *Sherwood Anderson: A Study of the Short Fiction*, Twayne, 1992, pp. 8–9.

Rideout, Walter B., ''The Simplicity of *Winesburg, Ohio*,'' in *Shenandoah*, Vol. 13, Spring, 1962, pp. 20–31; reprinted in *Critical Essays on Sherwood Anderson*, edited by David D. Anderson, G. K. Hall, 1981, pp. 146, 150–151.

Small, Judy Jo, *A Reader's Guide to the Short Stories of Sherwood Anderson*, G. K. Hall, 1994, p. 37.

Taylor, Welford Dunaway, *Sherwood Anderson*, Frederick Ungar, 1977, pp. 29, 37.

Further Reading

Howe, Irving, *Sherwood Anderson*, William Sloan Associates, 1951.
   A highly readable critical biography by a man who admired Anderson's early works, and who was strongly disappointed by the later ones. Howe does not address ''Hands'' separately, but devotes a chapter to the influences and themes of *Winesburg, Ohio*. Still the most important book-length Anderson study.

Papinchak, Robert Allen, *Sherwood Anderson: A Study of the Short Fiction*, Twayne, 1992.
   A thorough analysis of all of Anderson's short fiction. Papinchak uses ''Hands'' as an example to illustrate Anderson's ''representative stylistic technique,'' citing the use of hands as a repeated symbol, and the author's clean and direct sentence style.

Small, Judy Jo, *A Reader's Guide to the Short Stories of Sherwood Anderson*, G. K. Hall, 1994.
   In a useful chapter on ''Hands,'' Small outlines circumstances of composition of the story, Ander-

son's sources and influences, the publication history, some connections between the story and other Anderson works, and a review of important criticism.

White, Ray Lewis, ed., *The Merrill Studies in "Winesburg, Ohio,"* Charles E. Merrill, 1971.
A small but important compilation of background information and critical pieces, including an analysis of Anderson's writing process by William L. Phillips; several contemporary book reviews; and brief and accessible critical articles on themes, imagery and symbolism.

———, *Sherwood Anderson: A Reference Guide*, G. K. Hall, 1977.
An annotated list of more than 2,500 pieces of criticism published between 1916 and 1975, including criticism written in non-English languages. Includes citations with brief summaries of twenty-three reviews of *Winesburg, Ohio* from 1919.

Marriage á la Mode

Katherine Mansfield

1920

"Marriage á la Mode," published in 1921 as part of the collection *The Garden Party, and Other Stories*, was the last of Katherine Mansfield's stories dealing with the shallow London bohemian art world, a world which Mansfield knew all too well. The story has often been compared to the better-known "Bliss," published the previous year. Like its predecessor, "Marriage á la Mode" satirizes the shallow denizens of the art circles, while presenting an unfolding (apparently irretrievable) domestic drama.

In "Marriage á la Mode," Mansfield creates a world ruled by parasitic, immature, and unfulfilled adults. Both the characters themselves and Mansfield's choice of imagery convey the essential hollowness of these people's lives. Every detail in the story adds to this impression, from a strawberry bonnet to conversational quirks. Again, Mansfield demonstrates her talent for keen characterization and subtle observation.

Mansfield also delves into the psychology of her main protagonists—the husband and wife—by giving voice to each character. While these characters, both the victim and the victimizer, may hardly be likable people, their evocation at Mansfield's skillful hand leads to a clear picture of them, the world they inhabit, and the way they want to live. The brief story could be called a "slice of life," yet Mansfield, as she does in so many of her works, chooses a significant period, one that will inevitably lead to profound change.

Mansfield's contemporary readers remarked on the clarity of vision in *The Garden Party*. Though in many stories, the incidents were slight, perhaps even commonplace, this in no way detracts from their power; indeed, Mansfield's genius derives from her unsentimental way of drawing attention to the day-to-day events which add up to the sum of a life.

Author Biography

Katherine Mansfield was born Kathleen Mansfield Beauchamp in Wellington, New Zealand, October 14, 1888. She began writing at a young age, and her stories appeared in school publications when she was only nine years old. From a prosperous family, Mansfield was sent to school in England while still a teenager. She published stories in the *Queen's College Magazine*. After the completion of her education, she returned to New Zealand, but Mansfield found life in her native country unexciting and provincial. She longed to return to England, and she eventually persuaded her parents to allow her to go back as well as provide her a small allowance. Thus, at nineteen she made her home in England. After a hasty and short-lived marriage, Mansfield went to a German health spa, where she got the ideas for many of the stories that comprised her first collection, *In a German Pension* (1911). These stories focused on themes of sexual relationships, female subjugation, and childbearing, and critics have found in them some of her most effective portrayals of the female psychology. *In a German Pension* also established her reputation as an important new writer.

Mansfield had returned to London to write *In a German Pension*, and she continued to work on her short stories over the ensuing years. Between 1911 and 1915, she published short stories and book reviews in numerous magazines. She also met the editor and critic John Middleton Murry. He helped get her stories published in a magazine he edited. Further, Mansfield and Murry worked together editing the *Blue Review* and *Rhythm*. The couple married in 1918. The two were a part of London's literary scene, and Mansfield counted among her friends such important writers as Virginia Woolf.

While many of Mansfield's stories reflect the contemporary London world, the death of Mansfield's brother in 1915 reinforced her resolve to incorporate childhood memories and experiences in her fiction. Her next two collections, *Bliss, and Other Stories* (1920) and *The Garden Party, and Other Stories* (1922), contain many of her most well-known New Zealand stories, such as "Prelude" and "At the Bay." The success of these volume established Mansfield as a major talent.

By 1918, Mansfield had been diagnosed as having tuberculosis. After suffering a bout of the disease in the early 1920s, she was forced to leave England and her husband and friends for warmer climates. Mansfield disliked this enforced isolation. Despite her illness, Mansfield wrote almost continuously. She died January 9, 1923, at the age of thirty-four. After her death, Murry edited her private papers and published additional short stories, contributing to the enhancement of Mansfield's literary reputation. Over the decades, Mansfield's stories (including some she did not want published and some unfinished stories), letters, and journals have been published, and she continues to be a widely read author.

Plot Summary

The story opens with William on his way to the train station in London. He is on his way to see his wife and children, who live outside the city. William remembers that he has not brought a gift for his children, and this realization causes him to reflect on the changes that his life has undergone recently as his wife Isabel has come to embrace more modern attitudes and friends. William purchases a melon and a pineapple for his sons and boards the train. Though he tries to concentrate on papers he brought from the office, William cannot stop his thoughts from drifting to Isabel and the way things used to be between them. While William thought they were happy in their small city house, Isabel was in reality lonely and pining for new company and contemporary friends. After she made friends with Moira Morrison, Isabel began her self-transformation, which included the acquisition of the house in the suburbs.

When William arrives at the station, he is pleased to find Isabel waiting for him alone, but as they exit, he sees her menagerie of friends: Bill, Dennis, and Moira. The three adults, including Isabel, have a distinctly childish air, crying out loudly and usurping the fruit William has brought for the children. The adults pile into the taxi. Then another of Isabel's friends, Bobby, comes out of a store with his arms full of packages. Immediately thereafter, the shop owner also emerges; Bobby neglected to pay for his purchases, but Isabel does so.

That afternoon, Isabel and her friends go for a swim, but William stays behind to spend time with the children. Unfortunately, they are asleep, and William spends the time alone. From the garden, William hears the conversation of Isabel and her friends as they come up the road: they are talking about who will look after William.

That evening, the adults dine together but then afterwards everyone is so tired that they all go to bed. It is not until the next afternoon, as he is waiting for his taxi to take him to the train station, that William finds himself alone with his wife. She notes that she has not seen much of him, nor have the children (they had a previous engagement). Then the taxi arrives, and William leaves his home.

The next day finds Isabel and her friends lounging outside. The postman brings a fat letter for Isabel, from William. She opens it, surprised to find pages and pages of correspondence. Isabel reads the first line—"*My darling, precious Isabel*"—and feels suffused with emotion: confusion, excitement, fright. She decides that the letter is ridiculous. Her laughter attracts the attention of her friends, who want to know what is so funny. She tells them she has received a love letter from William and then proceeds to read it aloud. After she has finished, Bobby wants to reread it. Isabel, however, surprises them by withdrawing into the house with the letter in hand.

Alone in her bedroom, Isabel recognizes how vile her own behavior was. She pictures herself and her friends ridiculing William, and she wonders why and how she could have read his letter aloud. She realizes that she has become a shallow, vain person. From outside the voices of her friends call her to go swimming. Isabel knows she must make a decision, either go with them or stay alone and write William back. Although she knows she should stay, she decides to go with her friends and vows to write William later.

Characters

Dennis Green

Dennis is the least distinguished of Isabel's friends. He seems quieter than the rest, and he is apparently a writer.

Katherine Mansfield

Bill Hunt

Bill Hunt, another of Isabel's friends, is apparently a painter, although he refuses to paint the friends around the dinner table because the "light's wrong."

Isabel

Isabel is one of the main characters in "Marriage á la Mode." She is the object of her husband William's desire, as well as the cause of his frustration. At the time the story begins, Isabel has already firmly ensconced herself in a shallow lifestyle. She has chosen to trade in their former, quaint way of life for one in which she surrounds herself with thoroughly modern friends and attitudes. Her fixation on contemporary values presents itself through her parenting ideas—she gets rid of the children's old toys because they were "so 'dreadfully sentimental'"—as well as her exchange of her old-fashioned husband for her modern friends.

Isabel has already made this change by the time the story opens; William refers to her as the "new Isabel." Through the course of the story, however, Isabel undergoes an even more significant transformation. When she receives William's letter, she feels a wave of mixed emotions; she is confused, frightened, but "more and more excited." Unable to process her own reaction, she instead turns William's declarations of love into an object of ridicule to be shared with her friends. Though Isabel experiences a pang of regret, recognizing her own "vile, odious, abominable, vulgar" behavior, she still chooses to go swimming with her friends instead of responding to William's heart-wrenching letter. By the end of the story, Isabel has firmly committed herself to this form of life, one in which genuine affection and emotion are jettisoned in favor of the facile; her transformation is clearly indicated by the story's final sentence: "And, laughing in the new way, she ran down the stairs."

Bobby Kane

Isabel's friend Bobby's most obvious characteristic is his lack of money, which could be construed as his leeching off Isabel and thus William. He comes out of the shop with his arms full of packages, but "'They're none of them paid for.'" Isabel quickly pays the shopman, and Bobby's frightened face is transformed into one of radiance. He also fulfills the role of the effeminate man, one that Mansfield frequently has in her stories; he is flamboyant and active, both in his physical actions and his verbal expressions.

Moira Morrison

Moira is Isabel's friend, the one who, in her words to William, would "rescue your wife, selfish man." Through Moira, apparently, Isabel was introduced to her new set of friends. Moira seems shallow and foolish, both in her appearance (she is dressed in a hat that looks like a huge strawberry), in her conversational topics, and her tastes.

William

The majority of the story is presented through William's eyes. William is a self-proclaimed sentimentalist. Ill at ease among Isabel's new friends, William longs to return to the past, when he and Isabel were happy (or so he believed) in their simpler life. By the time the story opens, William exists in a state of extreme isolation. This is indicated in many aspects of the story: he spends only one day out of the week with his family and the rest of his time is spent working and living in London; he hardly sees his two young children as they are either asleep or whisked off to a previously planned activity; he is deserted by Isabel and her friends the afternoon he arrives; he spends no time alone with his wife until he is about to leave them at the end of the weekend. Such isolation distinctly contrasts to his perception of the life he and his family used to lead; he recreates a scene from the past with his children and Isabel that indicates his delight in being part of a close-knit family. Yet, evidently, his delight was not shared by his wife.

William's motivation for writing to his wife is unclear. While Isabel characterizes it as a "love letter," the only line quoted from it—"God forbid, my darling, that I should be a drag on your happiness"—shows that William recognizes his lack of importance in Isabel's current life, and would seem to indicate a willingness to withdraw from her life if that is truly what she wants. However, this topic is little explored. More definite is Isabel's lack of response to William's letter, and that William will get very little satisfaction in that regard.

Themes

Marriage and Family

The theme of marriage is perhaps the most important in "Marriage á la Mode," for the story raises the question of what a marriage should be and also points out that, unfortunately, two people may have different needs and expectations of the marriage. By the 1920s, when the story was written, women had begun to demand more equality and take a more dynamic role in their relationships. Thus, in one sense, Mansfield describes a truly modern marriage as Isabel gets what she wants from the relationship: the house by the shore, the unconventional friends, the lack of commitment to her family. Yet, the marriage described in "Marriage á la Mode" hardly constitutes any relationship, let alone a relationship supposed to embody one of the closest bonds that two people can form.

William and Isabel have little affinity for each other, let alone time to spend with each other. It is hard to imagine them as happy as William believed they once were, and the question arises of how William managed to be deluded for so long. Did he trick himself into believing they were happy, or did Isabel pretend to be happy? Or perhaps was Isabel happy then, and only later did she long for a more modern lifestyle and friends? Mansfield never answers these questions, but the story also makes clear that the reasons behind the present state of the relationship between William and Isabel do not matter—only the present has relevance. Also, while

Topics for Further Study

- Read one of Virginia Woolf's short stories, such as ''The New Dress,'' and compare her style and the feelings she evokes to Mansfield's work.

- Choose one of the artistic movements of early twentieth-century England, such as cubism or dadaism, to investigate. Then imagine you are a journalist, and write an article about this movement.

- Read one of Katherine Mansfield's ''New Zealand'' stories, such as ''A Doll's House,'' ''Prelude,'' ''At the Bay,'' or ''The Garden Party.'' How do the characters, situations, and settings in these stories compare to those in ''Marriage á la Mode''? Which type of story do you prefer, and why?

- Moira Morrison is involved in the contemporary London art scene. Conduct research to find out more about that period in London art. What kind of art do you think Moira is most interested in? Why?

- Critics have disagreed about William's character. Some find him effeminate, some find him dull, while others merely find him unbelievable. Analyze William's character in terms of his love for Isabel, his alienation from the group, and the believability of his actions.

- Critics such as Marvin Magalaner have commented in detail about Mansfield's use of food imagery in ''Marriage á la Mode.'' Conduct research to find out the psychological implications inherent in these images and in the group's voracious appetites. Then decide if you think Mansfield uses these images to full effect.

- Mansfield biographer Jeffrey Moore categorized the satire in ''Marriage á la Mode'' as ''facile.'' Do you agree or disagree? Why or why not? How do you think Mansfield could have better satirized Isabel and her friends? Rewrite one of the group scenes, using satire.

William seems to truly love his wife, it is difficult to know whether he loves the real Isabel—who is the ''new'' Isabel—or whether he loves his idealized vision of her.

Isabel's relationships with her immature friends in a real sense are in direct opposition to the supposed relationship between a husband and wife; her bonds to the friends are based on shallowness, superficiality, parasitism, and triviality, while the bonds between a husband and wife should be based on true feelings of affection, mutual respect, and the willingness to give to the other. In one sense, however, Isabel's relationships with her friends does mockingly resemble the marriage relationship in their collective ostracism of William.

While Isabel is comfortable in an environment in which true love, passion, and friendship do not exist, William cannot fit it. This is partially because he has no ability for the facile, as do Isabel and her friends, but partially because he loves his wife and wishes to fulfill their earlier dreams of marriage—a marriage in which husband and wife maintain closeness and create a family. William holds onto more traditional ideas of marriage and family, yet that Isabel and the children have moved outside of London—which means he only sees them over the brief weekend—demonstrates his willingness that Isabel should be happy, even at his own expense.

Change and Transformation

Although by the time the story opens up, Isabel has already changed into this new ''shallow, tinkling, vain'' creature, the theme of change and transformation is still important to ''Marriage á la Mode.'' Isabel's transformation is what has brought the current state of misery to William's life. Instead of surrounding herself with family, Isabel chooses to immerse herself in a host of friends as shallow as herself. Further, Isabel's change reflects the drive towards the modern and away from anything that speaks of the traditional or old-fashioned. As such, the children are deprived of their old toys because Isabel finds them "dreadfully sentimental." Isabel believes that the boys' exposure to anything old fashioned—from toys to the Royal Academy—will give the boys poor taste, which they will only have to unlearn later.

The "new" Isabel (as Mansfield repeatedly refers to her) appears to have undergone an even more permanent change in regard to her relationship with William. She reads his love letter aloud to her friends, but immediately thereafter recognizes how "vile, odious, abominable, vulgar" were her actions. Instead of turning this low point into a positive—and writing to William and reestablishing a connection with him—Isabel chooses to further affiliate herself with her friends and go swimming. More than anything else, this choice seems to affirm Isabel's embrace of her new lifestyle, for she actively allies herself with the people she had just harshly judged, who ridicule her husband—thus she becomes one of them herself.

Friendship

Although Isabel's newly acquired friends are shallow and superficial, they are important to understanding the story because of the power they hold over Isabel. For the friendship of the likes of Moira, Bobby, Bill, and Dennis, Isabel is willing to make her husband miserable and virtually ignore her children. More importantly, Isabel is willing to turn herself into a person she herself does not even like. When she shares in their coarse laughter at William's letter, Isabel clearly demonstrates that she has joined their ranks.

Many readers may find Isabel's liking for these friends inexplicable, for they show few admirable traits except perhaps for their ability to put up with each other. The story also subtly points out that the bonds of these friendships seem to rest as much on monetary attraction as on mutual liking. For instance, Bobby Kane relies on Isabel to pay the candy store clerk, instead of purchasing his own treats. Isabel even alludes to their leeching off her household when she "couldn't help wondering what had happened to the salmon they had for supper last night. She had meant to have fish mayonnaise for lunch and now . . ." Clearly, part of Isabel recognizes that her friends are taking a good deal from her. Unfortunately, she is not willing to recognize just how much she is giving them.

Style

Point of View and Narration

"Marriage á la Mode" is told primarily from William's point of view, but the story does shift to Isabel's point of view to make its final statement. The story opens with William's thoughts as he boards the train in London. He is concerned with buying a gift for his children and wonders about his upcoming meeting with Isabel. Such an opening clearly demonstrates that family is most important to William. This long scene can be compared to his meeting with Isabel, whose conversation revolves more around her friends. In a sense, Isabel even negates the children by refusing to give them the fruit William purchased for them, instead keeping it to share with her friends. The brief weekend continues to be funneled through William's point of view, which is effective because it allows Mansfield to depict William as he truly is amongst Isabel's circle: alone and on the outside.

The end of the story, however, switches to Isabel's point of view. There is no artistic way to avoid this shift, for in order to effect the proper ending, readers need to see Isabel's (and her friends') reaction to William's letter and her subsequent actions. Isabel's alliance with her friends against William marks the story's culmination. Stylistically, however, Isabel's and William's points of view reflect Mansfield's writing style and are fairly indistinguishable. Both sections, as well, never delve too deeply into the thoughts of the characters. Instead, Mansfield's narration presents William's and Isabel's major concerns and reactions to situations and then depicts both of them embarking on a set course of action.

Satire

"Marriage á la Mode" satirizes—or uses humor, wit, or ridicule to criticize—the pretentious, phony bohemian art society in which Isabel has chosen to involve herself. While Mansfield's story makes no grand pronouncements on this shallow segment of society, her disdain for Isabel and her immature friends is clear. The group speaks in childish exclamations and conducts pointless conversations; once the verb "childishly" is used to describe Bobby's words. They indulge in no meaningful activities—it is alluded that Bill is a painter, but he refuses to paint the friends at the dinner table. They are self-obsessed and full of self-importance. Ironically, they are determined to keep William out of their inner circle, a circle of which he has no interest in being a part.

Physically and emotionally, Mansfield makes them appear foolish and ridiculous. Moira is first introduced wearing "a bonnet like a huge strawberry" and jumping up and down, giving a reader the image of a giant, jumping strawberry, not a woman at all. As a group, the friends reject traditional adult behavior. None of them apparently have anything better to do on a Monday than laze around Isabel's house. All of them appear content to sponge off of Isabel (and thus William). Bobby is presented as the most childlike of them all with even his very moods dependent on others. When the candy shopman comes after him as Bobby neglected to pay for his purchases, Bobby looks "frightened," but a moment later, after Isabel has taken care of the bill, he "was radiant again."

Symbolism and Imagery

Mansfield's primary symbols and images used in "Marriage á la Mode" revolve around food. William brings home a melon and a pineapple for the children; Moira's hat looks like a strawberry; the day's purchases include fish and candy; the friends are depicted around the dinner table, eating voraciously. Overall, these images, such as Bill "stuffing his mouth with bread," imply both the selfishness of Isabel and her friends—for instance, dining on fruit at the expense of the children—as well as their spiritual emptiness. As Isabel says, "We're all starving. William's starving, too." Indeed, they are all hungry for something that cannot be fixed by eating a large meal. Although they do not know it, Isabel and her friends lack a purpose or greater meaning in their lives. William, on the other hand, is hungry for the simple life he and Isabel once shared.

Historical Context

Postwar Art

After the devastation of World War I, in which millions of people died, artists expressed their disillusionment with society. Art that emerged in the postwar period showed a marked departure from past forms. Artists rejected traditional ways of expressing their ideas, and dramatists, novelists, and poets all took bold new steps. In the plays of Bertolt Brecht, characters would often step out of their roles and directly address the audience. In painting and sculpture, artists turned to expressionism—using shapes, line, and color to communicate complex emotions to the audience. Spanish painter Pablo Picasso, who worked in Paris, helped create a style of art called cubism, which used shapes to show the abstract structures of the objects they painted instead of accurately depicting their physical appearances.

The Bloomsbury Group

The Bloomsbury group was one of London's foremost intellectual and artistic circles. Members of this group—who included writer Virginia Woolf, painter Vanessa Bell, novelist and essayist E. M. Forster, art critic Roger Fry, and economist John Maynard Keynes—rejected Victorian ideas on religious, artistic, social, and sexual matters. Such literary luminaries as George Bernard Shaw and William Yeats also could be found in attendance at the Bloomsbury group's regular Thursday night meetings. In 1917, Leonard Woolf, Virginia Woolf's husband, set up the Hogarth Press. It published Sigmund Freud's works in English, T. S. Eliot's poetry, and Mansfield's short stories, among other pieces.

The British Economy

In late 1920, Britain headed into a cycle of economic depressions, which only ended during World War II. Unemployment quickly reached 1.5 million, where it remained for most of the decade. The upper classes, which predominated in finance, demanded the restoration of a free market, cuts in spending, and balanced budgets. With such restraints, the government was able to afford little relief to the unemployed. Working-class people, in particular, who were more subject to the ups and downs of the trade cycle, were adversely affected.

The Modern British Woman

During World War I, many women had joined the ranks of male workers. They were needed in the factories, as men went to war. Millions of British women entered government departments, factories, and private offices. They worked in capacities ranging from doing clerical jobs to producing munitions. Such increases in economic opportunity for women presented an important opportunity for women's emancipation, as well. By 1918, the Franchise Act gave all women over the age of twenty-eight the right to vote (all men over the age of twenty-one were given this right by the same law). Soon the first British female sat in the House of Commons. Women, however, did not have equal voting rights as men

Compare & Contrast

- **1920s:** London's population is around 7.4 million.

    1990s: London's population is around 7.0 million.

- **1920s:** Cubism, dadaism, and surrealism are all new artistic movements that develop among European painters, and these movements influence other artistic fields. Cubism relies on geometric forms, shapes, and designs; dadaism denounces conventional artistic standards; and surrealism draws from the unconscious and the world of dreams.

    1990s: The field of visual arts offers many formats and incorporates multiple media, such as words and television images. Some artists implement modern technologies and create interactive pieces.

- **1920s:** British women over the age of twenty-eight have the right to vote (since 1918). Not until 1928 will women be made equal to men in terms of voting.

    1980s and 1990s: Women hold important political positions in Great Britain. Margaret Thatcher served as the country's prime minister from 1979 to 1990.

- **1910s and 1920s:** The average British household has three children.

    1990s: The average British household has less than two children.

- **1910s:** During World War I, only about a third of the native Germans who have made their homes in Britain remain in the country.

    1990s: Immigrants from Australia, New Zealand, Canada, and South Africa—some 253,000 people—come to reside in Britain.

---

until 1928, when the Representation of the People Act, known as the "flapper act," was passed.

As in the United States, young British women made stylistic changes that reflected their freedoms, such as wearing shorter skirts and bobbing their hair. Despite these advances, most married women remained dependent on their husbands. Working women were paid less than men for equal labor and did not have equal opportunity for employment. For instance, women were not to be found as the heads of large companies, as judges, or as university professors.

The Modern World

The decade of 1910 was a period of great technological change. Before World War I, telephones were the convenience of the upper classes. In 1918, wall telephones were considered the height of modernity. By the early 1920s, wireless sets (radios) were being installed throughout England. Radio broadcasting in England began in 1922 and became a popular form of entertainment, as did attending talking movies. Also, automobiles, which prior 1914 were only enjoyed by the wealthy, became much more common.

Critical Overview

"Marriage á la Mode" is often compared by critics to another of Mansfield's stories, the more well-known "Bliss." In both works, Mansfield sets a domestic drama against the satirical background of the pretentious English bohemian art crowd. While both stories were characterized in 1949 by John Middleton Murry, Mansfield's husband, as "semi-sophisticated" failures concerning "quite simple women who have taken up with the stupider *intelligensia*," the majority of critics see neither story as a failure. "Marriage á la Mode" is only one of Mansfield's stories set against the London art crowd of which Mansfield was a rather reluctant participant.

"Marriage á la Mode" was first published in December 1922 and was included in Mansfield's collection, *The Garden Party, and Other Stories*. Early critics generally enjoyed the volume, seeing it as a solid addition to Mansfield's body of literary work. D. K. Laub, writing for the *Detroit News*, calls her a "genius" and comments on her "refreshing originality—both in point of view and literary style . . . it is superb." The reviewer for *The Nation and the Athenaeum* particularly applauds her way of recreating the ordinary world. "In none of her stories are we left with the feeling that the subject has been picked up, examined, and set down completely known. . . . We have the impression rather of being for a few moments privileged spectators of lives that were going on before we observed them, and that will continue when our attention has been drawn elsewhere." The reviewer for the *Spectator* actually preferred this collection to the previously published *Bliss, and Other Stories*. "Nothing happens in any of the stories [in *The Garden Party*]. . . . This shows a more surer self-knowledge than the author displayed in "Bliss," where events were often allowed to intrude."

Malcolm Cowley, who reviewed *The Garden Party* for *Dial*, readily asserted that Mansfield's stories had "literary qualities" and "was almost as good as 'Bliss,'" but pointed out some limitations, namely Mansfield's reliance on certain stock characters or situations. "There is a woman: neurotic, arty, hateful, and a good, stupid man whom she constantly torments," writes Cowley, "He suffers and she laughs, and he loves her still." One notable exception to the general praise earned by the book was Conrad Aiken's *Freeman* review: "The delight that many of these stories afford on the first reading is intense; it wanes a little on the second, and we notice the cleverness—fatal sign! And on the third reading—but is there a third. One can not dine on the iridescent?"

Contemporary critics rarely see "Marriage á la Mode" as one of Mansfield's most significant stories, yet it still holds importance in the body of her work. As Saralyn R. Daly points out in *Katherine Mansfield*, with this story Mansfield "moved to the condemnation of groups," or, as described by Marvin Magalaner in *The Fiction of Katherine Mansfield*, "the flamboyant, articulate, utterly silly pseudo-bohemian set is the target of Mansfield's scorn." Mansfield knew of the world she wrote about. The poet Elizabeth Bowen writes in her introduction to the 1956 edition of Mansfield's *Stories* that these very types that she ridiculed in "Marriage á la Mode" were those who preyed upon Mansfield and her husband. Jeffrey Meyers, in *Katherine Mansfield, A Biography*, also finds the story to be important for what it demonstrates about her relationship with Murry and about her ideas on marriage in general. While Meyers discounts the satire as "far too facile," he finds that the story highlights Mansfield's attitude toward the sanctity of marriage. As Mansfield once wrote, "To know *one other* seems to me a far greater adventure than to be on kissing acquaintance with dear knows how many."

Criticism

Rena Korb

Korb has a master's degree in English literature and creative writing and has written for a wide variety of educational publishers. In the following essay, she discusses the characters' attributes in "Marriage á la Mode."

Despite her early death at age thirty-four, Katherine Mansfield produced a prodigious body of work, one which continues to bring her acclaim to the present day. She first came to the public eye with her "New Zealand" stories—stories that drew on her childhood. The American writer Willa Cather wrote in her discussion of contemporary writers, "To my thinking, she never measured herself up so fully as in the two remarkable stories about an English family in New Zealand, "Prelude" and "At the Bay." But Mansfield lived out her adult life in Europe—in England and on the Continent—and her connections there brought her into close contact with the blooming literary and artistic world populated by such illustrious artists as Virginia Woolf and D. H. Lawrence. It is not surprising, then, that in several of her stories Mansfield focused her energies and talent on examining this world filled, in addition to artists of true talent, with those who only held artistic pretensions. Such stories, like "Marriage á la Mode" and "Bliss" have been grouped together by critics for their similar satirical condemnation of the artistic sub-world of the London intelligentsia and for their portrayal of the problems of married life. Indeed, Cather's assessment of Mansfield—"It was usually [her] way to approach the major forces of life through comparatively triv-

What Do I Read Next?

- "Bliss" by Katherine Mansfield, published a year earlier than "Marriage á la Mode," is one of the author's most well-known and anthologized stories. Like "Marriage á la Mode," it concerns a domestic drama played at against a background of ridiculous, artsy Londoners. Critics often compare these two stories.

- The French writer Colette's 1910 novel *The Vagabond* depicts a modern woman trying to achieve social and artistic independence.

- Virginia Woolf's *Mrs. Dalloway* (1925) examines one day in the life of Clarissa Dalloway, an upper-class Londoner.

- Keri Hulme, a contemporary New Zealand writer, explores the dynamics of a cobbled-together family in her novel *The Bone People* (1983). The winner of England's Booker Prize in 1985, it was praised for its evocation of the Maori people—the original inhabitants of New Zealand.

- Evelyn Waugh's 1945 satirical novel *Brideshead Revisited* follows the family and friends of a wealthy English family.

- F. Scott Fitzgerald's *The Great Gatsby* (1925) explores the jazz era generation that emerged in the United States during the 1920s. This novel reveals the new morals and cynical attitude of younger Americans.

- Anton Chekhov's short story "Misery" was considered by Mansfield to be a masterpiece, and she used a similar approach in her own story "The Lady's Maid."

---

ial incidents. She chose a small reflector to throw a luminous streak out into the shadowy realm of personal relationships"—applies equally to "Marriage á la Mode." Taking place over a period of little more than one day, this story displays the grim shell of a marriage—what remains after the wife has chosen to ignore her husband and children in favor of her superficial and trivial friends.

Sylvia Berkman writes in her study of the writer's work that "Mansfield had no affection for the modern metropolitan young woman. Almost without exception the young women she presents are callous, temperamental, selfish, and unreasonable." Berkman's description aptly fits Isabel, the young wife in "Marriage á la Mode." As the story opens, Isabel's husband, William, already knows where her loyalties lie, yet he continues to cling to the hope that the "new Isabel" will give way to the old Isabel, the woman with whom he had previously shared a life. That Isabel had seemed content to take holidays on a farm and romp with their small children. William "hadn't the remotest notion in those days that Isabel wasn't as happy as he." Now William has been demoted from playing any part in Isabel's happiness; instead he has been relegated to the solitary role of provider, enabling Isabel to have a house by the sea, which seems to primarily serve as a lazy setting for her to entertain her equally lazy friends.

Mansfield succinctly sets the stage for the domestic drama about to unfold. As the story opens, William's thoughts focus on his wife and children. He wonders if Isabel will meet him at the station, but what he wants most is to see his wife alone. He imagines her "at the station, standing just a little apart from everybody else" or "sitting in the open taxi outside." His wish seems to come true when he first arrives, but subsequent events immediately make clear that William will not get what he wants from Isabel; though she is standing "apart from the others, and ... she was alone," the taxi waiting outside is surrounded by her friends. This scene sets the tone for the rest of the weekend, which is a continual perversion of William's true desires.

Isabel and her friends have little use for William. This sad truth is first demonstrated by their conversation in the taxi, which revolves around their co-opting of the pineapple and melon William has brought as gifts for the children. Later that day, they ridicule him behind his back. When Moira declares they ought to have a gramophone that plays "The Maid of the Mountains"—an extremely popular musical production of the time—Isabel attempts to defend him, but as are all her efforts, they are superficial. "That's not fair to William," she cries. "Be nice to him, my children! He's only staying until tomorrow evening." Instead of defending her husband, she is merely defending his presence to her friends. Her choice of words—the reminder that they must suffer his company for a scant time—also subtly indicates how small a role he plays in their lives.

Various scholarly criticism of William hardly defends the man either; Berkman contends that "his unhappy soliloquies . . . are scarcely masculine," Saralyn R. Daly asserts in *Katherine Mansfield*. She also writes that he is a "neutral figure who wins sympathy only because the group which causes his misery is cruel and tasteless." Mansfield biographer Jeffrey Meyers characterizes him as "plodding." An exploration of William's plight and his reactions to it, however, lead to a more thorough understanding of the symbols and message of the story as a whole.

Marvin Magalaner in *The Fiction of Katherine Mansfield* points out that "William is particularly drawn to the world of childhood in his revulsion from the perverse adult world of his wife's pals." While going to the train station and on the train, William thinks of his own small sons and the gifts that he will bring them. He acknowledges the differences between the way he would raise them and the new way Isabel wants to raise them. While she feels it is necessary for them to have "Russian toys, French toys, Serbian toys" instead of the "old donkey and engines," William admits that when he was a child he "used to go to bed hugging an old towel with a knot in it." Looking out the train window, William sees the landscape with fields and animals, but what most captures his attention is a river "with naked children splashing in the shallows." Even his descriptions of Isabel bring him back to the state of childhood innocence and naiveté. He pictures Isabel as the rosebush of his childhood garden, and "he was still that little boy" who delighted in shaking the rain-soaked petals upon himself. He now rejects images of the adult Isabel, instead preferring to remember her when

> "William 'hadn't the remotest notion in those days that Isabel wasn't as happy as he.' Now William has been demoted from playing any part in Isabel's happiness; instead he has been relegated to the solitary role of provider, enabling Isabel to have a house by the sea, which seems to primarily serve as a lazy setting for her to entertain her equally lazy friends."

they were on vacation, when "Isabel wore a jersey and her hair in a plait; she looked about fourteen."

William's retreat into childhood—though in one sense, pitiable—makes sense as a counterbalance to the distorted world in which Isabel now lives, in which the adults take on the roles of greedy, mean children; they are horrifying in their refusal to grow up. Mansfield constantly characterizes Isabel's friends as childlike—Moira jumps around in a hat that looks like a "huge strawberry," and at one point Bobby Kane even speaks "childishly." The group of friends deny all adult conventions—none of them seem to work nor set out to accomplish anything meaningful with their lives.

The only actual children present, William and Isabel's sons, serve as a counterpoint to William's wish for the past with Isabel—which he in turn views through the fantasy lens of a child—and the group's childish behavior. But the children are never seen. They are asleep when William arrives on Saturday, and the next day their governess whisks them away on a previously arranged activity. Thus, they only exist in William's recollection of them playing in their former London home. Then they acted like real children, "having rides on the leopard skin thrown over the sofa back, or . . . playing shops with Isabel's desk for counter." The minimal

A scene of London circa 1920, which provides the setting for Mansfield's "Marriage á la Mode."

role played by the real children highlights their usurpation in Isabel's world by her childlike friends. Instead of mothering her children, Isabel nurtures her adult friends.

Mansfield also makes use of imagery and symbolism to define the group. For instance, Moira calls Isabel "Titania," who is the queen of the fairies of Shakespeare's *A Midsummer Night's Dream*. In Shakespeare's play, Titania is bewitched by a half-man, half-animal creature, just as Isabel is bewitched by her grotesque companions. Isabel's companions also sponge off the fruits of William's labor. This is aptly illustrated when Bobby Kane leaves Isabel to pay the shopkeeper for the candies he has chosen. The metaphor of the group's voracious and parasitic nature is also carried to the physical level, as Mansfield describes the scene at the dining table, where they all eat "enormously" of the food made available through William's work. In contrast, William only feels a "dull, persistent gnawing." Magalaner points out that this "seems clearly to be a pang of psychological hunger. His marital situation allows for no nourishment either for the children or for himself."

Isabel's lack of empathy—indeed, her lack of interest—for William's feelings is made abundantly clear by the last scene of the story. While the story had previously been told from William's point of view, Mansfield shifts to Isabel's point of view. This is the only time readers get any sense of what Isabel really thinks, but it only serves to emphasize her attraction to her friends, her forsaking of her family, and the group mentality that dominates her life. Much of the scene's dialogue is not even attributed to any specific character, which gives the message that all the characters are alike and thus interchangeable. While Mansfield has given different characters specific characteristics, for instance, Bill is a painter and Dennis is a writer (though no evidence of their artistry is evident), they all react in the exact same manner, sharing along with Isabel in the mockery of William.

In the final scene, the adults are again portrayed as a group of children in their aimless questions and in Moira's recent discovery of the blissfulness of sleep. More importantly, the group responds to an adult situation with the cruelty of children. Isabel receives a letter from William. Although the contents of the letter are not revealed, with the exception of one telling sentence, "God forbid, my darling, that I should be a drag on your happiness," clearly William has sent to his wife what he perceives to be an accurate picture of their marriage, its problems, and perhaps ways to fix it. Instead of recognizing the seriousness of the situation, Isabel's friends, and Isabel herself, only ridicule William. "It's the most marvelous find," says one, and Isabel invites them to "Gather round," for a reading of it.

The group responds abysmally to the letter, reveling in its expression of feeling and mocking William's lover-like declarations. Isabel surprises herself by withdrawing from her friends. At this point, she recognizes how "vile, odious, abominable, vulgar" was their behavior. J. F. Kobler in *Katherine Mansfield, A Study of the Short Fiction* asserts that Isabel "honestly struggles with the question [of whether to write William or rejoin her friends to go swimming]," however, Isabel's "struggle" seems almost too short-lived to so deem it. Despite her knowledge that she should stay in and respond to William, she chooses to join her friends, telling herself that "I shall *certainly* write." Unconsciously, Isabel is firmly allying herself with her friends, and defending her actions. In so doing, writes Kobler, "Isabel demonstrates that her real nature—her inborn qualities—may be at work." While Isabel, indeed, may have better qualities than she demonstrates in the story, by its end, she has firmly allied herself against her husband and even more ominously, demonstrates her ability to defend her indefensible actions. With such a devastating ending, Mansfield hardly portends a happy outcome for William and Isabel.

Source: Rena Korb, in an essay for *Short Stories for Students*, Gale Group, 2001.

Marvin Magalaner

In the following essay, Magalaner contrasts Mansfield's use of "domestic tragedy" with "broad social satire" in "Marriage á la Mode."

"Marriage à la Mode" is in the tradition of "Bliss," both stories in which a domestic tragedy is played out against a background of broad social satire. In both instances, the flamboyant, articulate, utterly silly pseudo-bohemian set is the target of Mansfield's scorn though in the former story they play a greater role in the personal catastrophe than in the latter. Both Bertha Young and her husband, though they enjoy the company of people like Eddie Warren and the Norman Knights, maintain a distance from the circle—observers rather than participants. And the character who brings down their flimsy marital structure, Pearl Fulton, is instantly recognizable as another outsider. In "Marriage," it is precisely that the husband cannot be seduced into the bohemian circle while his wife Isabel is charmed away from reality by its members which produces the rupture. Though Isabel has a momentary epiphany of a sort before the charm takes hold again, it is the husband's turn, in this story, to recognize the impossibility of life with his wife so long as she is unable to free herself from its pernicious influence.

The author makes clear that, to William at least, life before the advent of the bohemians had been idyllic. Even in urban London, he had been able to grow petunias and to revel in the innocent joy of his young love for Isabel—for him similar in retrospect to the sublime experience of the boy in "Something Childish But Very Natural." William is particularly drawn to the world of childhood in his revulsion from the perverse adult world of his wife's pals. As he looks out of the train window, what attracts him is "a wide river, with naked children splashing in the shallows." His thoughts on the train are of his own children and the gifts he would bring to them. Though it is painful to think of his grown-up Isabel, he can remember with pleasure his wife on vacation in the old days, wearing "a jersey and her hair in a plait; she looked about fourteen." Even he himself, in reverie, is "still that little boy" who used to shake the rain-soaked rosebush over himself.

This freshness and natural beauty of childhood acts as a sustaining force in William's life when he is unable to bear the present state of his marital affairs. He will not bring anything mechanical or sophisticated to his children; rather he chooses a pineapple and a melon, the delights of nature, to please them. His worry is that even this simple gift may be diverted to the bohemians who surround his wife. "Isabel's friends could hardly go sneaking up to the nursery at the children's mealtimes. All the same, as he bought the melon William had a horrible vision of one of Isabel's young poets lapping up a slice . . . behind the nursery door."

By nightmare juxtapositions of this kind, Mansfield balances the fresh beauty of childhood and nature with another view of childhood, ugly and grotesquely perverse. "Be nice to him, my children," says Isabel *not* to Paddy and Johnny but to her bohemian circle. And the group is, without doubt, painted as a pack of horrible children whose freshness is utterly missing and whose relationship to nature is hardly pastoral. William has good reason to worry that the fruit intended for his little ones will be diverted by the clownish, insatiable adults. Moira

> "Though it is painful to think of his grown-up Isabel, he can remember with pleasure his wife on vacation in the old days, wearing 'a jersey and her hair in a plait; she looked about fourteen.' Even he himself, in reverie, is 'still that little boy' who used to shake the rain-soaked rosebush over himself."

Morrison's bonnet is "like a huge strawberry," a perversion of nature, and she "jumped up and down" like a youngster. The effeminate Bobby Kane buys children's candy from a shop and, childlike, forgets to pay for it. Bill Hunt, like a perverse, overly imaginative child, imagines that the packages containing the fruits really conceal "de-cap-itated heads!" These are people playing at being children and failing to carry off the pretense. Their encounter with nature at the water (so different from the view of the naked children bathing that William sees from the train window) is capped by their visit to a pub for "sloe gin."

As she does in "Bliss," Mansfield makes full use of the imagery, and perhaps the symbolism, of food. Usurpers not only of William's hearth and his wife, the bohemian crew figuratively eats William out of house and home. Even the title of the story hints at the motif of eating. The displacement of one set of children by the other is dramatized by the fate of the love offering William brings to his family—the pineapple and melon rejected for his own offspring by Isabel and turned over by her to the outsiders.

Imagery of food abounds, from the sweets of Bobby Kane to the fish which the group must accept if it wishes to have ice. They speak of anointing themselves with butter. They dine on sardines and whiskey. And even when the talk turns to the color of one's legs under water, Moira describes hers as of "the palest, palest mushroom colour." All eat "enormously" except, apparently, William, the "stranger" to the group and, now, to his own wife. Within him, instead, there is a "dull, persistent gnawing," now grown "familiar," which abates only when William is able to get his mind off his marriage. This gnawing sensation, though not attributed to a specific bodily source in the story, seems clearly to be a pang of psychological hunger. His marital situation allows for no nourishment either for the children or for himself. Isabel has turned her attention elsewhere. His choice of the fruits as gifts had been his way, unconsciously, of offering at least to the deprived children (and he is, as has been noted, one of them) the nourishment of love, but even these had gone to fatten the usurpers of his contentment.

Freudian implications aside, Mansfield's concentration on the imagery of food and eating represents an appropriate rendering of the "vile, odious, abominable, vulgar" presence of grossness in the band of usurpers: a grossness now beginning to rub off on Isabel. As in "Bliss," all the pseudo-sophisticated small talk of the ballet, of aesthetic considerations, and the like cannot hide the elemental coarseness of the bohemians. Their role as destructive parasites is thoroughly established. As a consequence, they are stamped with the parasite's symbolic mark and made voracious eaters of the substance of another creature. Indeed, the reference to the "mushroom" quality of Moira's legs under water is less obscure when one realizes that the mushroom is a parasitic fungus. No less interesting in this regard is Bobby Kane's last name, reminiscent of another Cain who lived at the expense of his brother.

A Midsummer Night's Dream is invoked too in the story through Moira's habit of calling Isabel "Titania." That Isabel should be queen of the fairies is doubly meaningful in "Marriage à la Mode." That she should be estranged from her husband also fits the pattern. Most significant is the bewitching of Titania in Shakespeare's play so that the exquisite queen finds Bottom a handsome and desirable companion. She cannot see the ass's head as gross and grotesque nor does she recognize how far she has fallen from her usual high standards. Bewitched, Titania offers the absurd Bottom "what thou desirest to eat," and Bottom, half man, half animal (like bohemians) chooses to "munch your good dry oats." Ironically for the modern couple, William is no Oberon nor is the idea of bewitching Isabel his. It is left for the less noble and exalted William to deplore the charm that has been placed upon Isabel but to be unable except for a brief moment to break the spell. The modern Titania never entirely wakes from the dream and her husband, therefore, must seek to escape the nightmare through renunciation and flight.

Meaningfully, in the picture of midsummer that Mansfield offers, both protagonists live in dream: William seeking relief in the fantasy of his childhood past and his married life before the descent of the bohemians; Isabel in the nightmare spell itself cast by her companions. There is evidence, however, that the wife has invited her bewitched state— that she had never been truly content with the idyll of normal marriage and motherhood. Perhaps the reader is to see the bohemian clan as merely the expression of Isabel's inner state, dramatized for fictional presentation. As Bertha Young in "Bliss" finds in Pearl Fulton both a nemesis and a secret sharer, so in this story Moira Morrison may function both as enchantress and as the expression of Isabel's deepest nature, evoking in the wife what Isabel most wishes to have evoked. Perhaps the presence of both elements in Isabel explains the painting that William sees in the sitting room:

> On the wall opposite William some one had painted a young man, over lifesize, with very wobbly legs, offering a wide-eyed daisy to a young woman who had one very short arm and one very long, thin one. . . .

William's simple, natural offer of love is made to a woman whose aspect is distorted and grotesque—a combination of two persons of varying appearance. The auguries for a successful marriage are not auspicious.

Source: Marvin Magalaner *The Fiction of Katherine Mansfield*, Southern Illinois University Press, 1971, pp. 86–91.

Sources

Aiken, Conrad, Review of *The Garden Party, and Other Stories*, in *Freeman*, June 21, 1922, p. 357.

Berkman, Sylvia, *Katherine Mansfield, A Critical Study*, Yale University Press, 1951.

Bowen, Elizabeth, Introduction to *Stories*, by Katherine Mansfield, Vintage Books, 1956, pp. v–xxiv.

Cather, Willa, *Not Under Forty*, Alfred A. Knopf, 1936.

Cowley, Malcolm, Review of *The Garden Party, and Other Stories*, in *Dial*, August 22, 1922, p. 230.

Daly, Saralyn R., *Katherine Mansfield*, Rev. Ed., Twayne Publishers, 1994.

Kobler, J. F., *Katherine Mansfield, A Study of the Short Fiction*, G. K. Hall, 1990.

Laub, D. K., Review of *The Garden Party, and Other Stories*, in the *Detroit News*, July 16, 1922, p. 7.

Magalaner, Marvin, *The Fiction of Katherine Mansfield*, Southern Illinois University Press, 1971.

Meyers, Jeffrey, *Katherine Mansfield, A Biography*, New Directions Press, 1978.

Murry, John Middleton, *Katherine Mansfield and other Literary Portraits*, Peter Nevill Ltd., 1949.

Review of *The Garden Party, and Other Stories*, in *The Nation and the Athenaeum*, March 25, 1922, pp. 949–950.

Review of *The Garden Party, and Other Stories*, in *The Spectator*, March 18, 1922, p. 342.

Further Reading

Bell, Quentin, *Bloomsbury Recalled*, Columbia University Press, 1995.
   This memoir written by the son of Vanessa and Clive Bell, members of the Bloomsbury group, recalls the notable people involved in that dynamic scene.

Boddy, Gillian, *Katherine Mansfield, The Woman and the Writer*, Penguin Books, 1988.
   This overview of Mansfield's life includes numerous photographs and discussions of the major short stories.

Mansfield, Katherine, *The Journal of Katherine Mansfield*, edited by John Middleton Murry, Ecco Press, 1983.
   These selections from Mansfield's journals are edited by her husband.

———, *Selected Letters of Katherine Mansfield*, edited by Vincent O'Sullivan, Clarendon Press, 1989.
   These are selected letters written by Mansfield.

———, *Selections, Critical Writings of Katherine Mansfield*, edited by Clare Hanson, St. Martin's Press, 1987.
   Mansfield's non-fiction writing includes essays and book reviews.

Tomalin, Claire, *Katherine Mansfield, A Secret Life*, Alfred A. Knopf, 1988.
   This is a biography of Mansfield.

Mrs. Plum

Es'kia (Ezekiel) Mphahlele

1967

First published in Mphahlele's 1967 short story collection *In Corner B*, "Mrs. Plum" was written during the early 1960s while the author was living in Paris. The collection, which includes stories about life in Nigeria and South Africa, was published by the East African Publishing House in Nairobi, Kenya, though the author had taken a teaching position in Denver, Colorado, by that time. Such was the life of this homeless writer. Mphahlele's work had been banned in his own country of South Africa, and *In Corner B* was not available there until the banning order was lifted in 1979.

"Mrs. Plum," makes up four chapters, by far the longest story in the collection, and is sometimes considered a novella rather than a short story. It depicts the changing relationship between Karabo, a black South African cook from the village of Phokeng, and her employer Mrs. Plum, a white liberal living in the suburbs of Johannesburg during the years of apartheid. As Karabo observes Mrs. Plum's conduct over three years, she comes to realize that Mrs. Plum's attitude toward blacks is hypocritical, and that her belief in the equality of blacks and whites is shallow.

"Mrs. Plum" was heralded upon publication as an indictment of white liberal South Africans who claimed that they could bring about political change in the country by working within the system. This is a theme that the author had explored in other stories, including "The Living and the Dead" (1958) and

"We'll Have Dinner at Eight" (1961). It is still considered one of Mphahlele's best and most important stories and has been included in several widely distributed anthologies of African and world fiction. Mphahlele himself included it in a later short story collection, *Renewal Time*, (1981) and called it "the best thing I ever pulled off."

Author Biography

Es'kia Mphahlele was born on December 17, 1919, in Marabastad Township, Pretoria, in the strictly segregated country of South Africa. His father was a messenger, and his mother a housemaid, like the character Karabo in "Mrs. Plum." His childhood was not a happy one, and Mphahlele learned to admire strong, resourceful women who survived in spite of domestic violence, poverty, and an oppressive government. His mother, for example, kept her children fed and clothed, and even sent them to good schools, by working as a domestic.

In 1945, Mphahlele began working as a high school teacher and married Rebecca Mochadibane, who became the mother of his five children and his supporter over more than fifty years. An avid reader, he had begun writing short stories and published his first collection, *Man Must Live*, in 1946. Mphahlele was a devoted teacher, but in the early 1950s the government made new laws requiring blacks and whites to attend separate and unequal schools. When Mphahlele protested this change, he was fired. In 1957 he was given permission to leave South Africa to teach and write in Nigeria, only on the condition that he never return.

Mphahlele's early years are described in the first volume of his autobiography, *Down Second Avenue*, a sometimes angry account of life in the black townships. The story of racial segregation in South Africa was a revelation to readers around the world. The book became an international success, and it led to Mphahlele being one of several writers officially banned in South Africa in 1961. This meant that it was illegal to sell—or even to quote—his work.

Mphahlele taught at different African universities, then moved to Paris to work with the Congress for Cultural Freedom. While in Paris, he published a collection of essays, *The African Image* (1962), and wrote several short stories set in Africa, including "Mrs. Plum," which was published in the collection *In Corner B* (1967). By then, Mphahlele was teaching and writing in Denver, Colorado, widely recognized as a major fiction writer and social critic.

After twenty years of exile, Mphahlele returned to South Africa in 1977 with the permission of the government. Two years later, the ban on his writing was lifted, and Mphahlele's next several books, including the novel *Chirundu* (1979) and the second volume of his autobiography, *Afrika My Music* (1984), were published in South Africa.

Mphahlele was given the name Ezekiel at birth, but changed his name to Es'kia when he returned from exile. Both names appear on his writings. In all, Mphahlele has written or edited more than twenty books of fiction and essays. As a chronicler of injustice, he helped bring about change, and he was witness to the end of apartheid and the creation of democracy in South Africa in the 1990s.

Plot Summary

The story opens with Karabo, a young woman from the black South African township of Phokeng, describing her white "madam," Mrs. Plum. In the suburbs of Johannesburg where Karabo works for Mrs. Plum, all of the homeowners are wealthy and white, and all of the servants are black and poor. This is South Africa under apartheid, the system of laws that kept whites, blacks, Indians, and mixed-race people or "coloreds" in separate places ("apart") to protect the power of the white minority.

Mrs. Plum is not like any employer Karabo has ever heard of. She uses Karabo's African name, instead of giving her a "white" name like Jane. She encourages Karabo to improve herself by giving her books and newspapers to read, teaching her to follow recipes, and paying for dance lessons. She praises Karabo when she does well. She even makes Karabo join her for meals at the table, which makes Karabo uncomfortable. No other whites invite blacks to sit at their table, and the food Mrs. Plum eats is not what Karabo is used to.

Mrs. Plum has a daughter, Kate, just Karabo's age. Kate confides in Karabo about her mother, her love life, her dreams, telling Karabo "many things a white woman does not tell a black servant." Karabo gets used to hearing Kate's confidences, but never shares her own. Although Mrs. Plum and Kate ignore Karabo's place in the social order, Karabo never forgets. Mrs. Plum is an author, who writes books and articles calling for the end of apartheid, and who participates in public demonstrations at government buildings. Karabo, who knows nothing of national politics, does not understand what Mrs. Plum is trying to accomplish, or why Mrs. Plum thinks she can speak for black people. But as she reads the newspapers, Karabo learns more about the position of blacks in South Africa and comes to see that beatings, arrests, and other mistreatment are part of a national pattern.

Karabo is also learning at the Black Crow Club. There, she chats with other servants, joining in making fun of their employers' strange ways. From these conversations, it is clear that whites and blacks live in completely separate worlds, although they inhabit the same space. Karabo and her friends do not understand the actions of the whites, especially the way they devote so much attention and money to their pets, and the servants are angry about the disrespect they are shown by their employers. Mrs. Plum is delighted that Karabo goes to the Black Crow Club to learn sewing and knitting and has no idea that Karabo is also listening to lectures by an anti-apartheid activist who urges the women to keep a wall of mistrust between themselves and their employers.

Mrs. Plum has two dogs, who sleep in beds with pink linens in her bedroom. They are looked after by Dick, the gardener and housekeeper, who feeds, brushes, and perfumes the dogs daily. Mrs. Plum is fond of the dogs to the point of foolishness, and she does not trust Dick to look after them properly. Actually, Dick is so afraid of white people that he would never dare do less than his duty. He knows that if he displeases his employer, she can dismiss him and mark his pass, the document that all black South Africans were required to carry at all times under apartheid, and he will be sent home.

During Karabo's third year with Mrs. Plum, the mild unease in the house becomes great tension, and Karabo becomes more confused about her employer. Mrs. Plum is accustomed to having dinner parties and inviting liberal whites and educated blacks together. Both Karabo and Kate fall in love with the same guest, a black doctor. Kate and the doctor make plans to leave the country and marry, because a marriage between people of different races is illegal in South Africa. Karabo never mentions her feelings to Kate or to the man, but pulls away from Kate in anger and hurt. Mrs. Plum, who has always spoken of equal opportunity for whites and blacks, is appalled that her daughter would consider marrying a black man. After a great deal of shouting, the marriage is called off. Soon after, the police begin house-to-house searches, looking for servants without the proper passes allowing them to be in the district. When the police come to search Karabo's and Dick's rooms, Mrs. Plum turns the hose on the police and makes them leave. The next day, she is arrested. Refusing to pay the small fine, she goes to jail for two weeks, hoping to call attention to the unfairness of the pass laws.

A few weeks later, Karabo's best friend Chimane discovers she is pregnant and has an abortion because her family cannot afford for her to be unemployed while she tends a baby. Dick reveals that he works to support a younger sister, who could not attend school if he lost his job. Karabo considers in a new way how hard the lives of blacks are because of apartheid, and she finds herself disliking everything about Mrs. Plum. One morning, when she goes to wake Mrs. Plum, she hears strange noises. Looking through the keyhole into the bedroom, she finds Mrs. Plum holding one of the dogs close to her while she masturbates. Karabo says nothing, but adds the disturbing scene to her collection of impressions.

When a rumor spreads that servants are planning to poison the white people's dogs, Mrs. Plum fires Dick. Soon after, Karabo's uncle dies, and Mrs. Plum refuses permission for her to travel to Phokeng to mourn him. Karabo has had enough. She quits her job and goes home. A week later, Mrs. Plum arrives in Phokeng and asks Karabo to return. She is just as uncomfortable in Karabo's home as Karabo has been in Johannesburg, a fact that interests Karabo. Karabo agrees to come back, but not before she negotiates a raise and more vacation time. She understands Mrs. Plum entirely now, and cannot be surprised or hurt by her again.

Characters

Chimane

Chimane is Karabo's closest friend. She is from Karabo's hometown, and works for the white family next door to Mrs. Plum. When their duties permit, Karabo and Chimane meet in the backyard to share the latest gossip and remark on the strange behavior of their employers. On their Thursday afternoons off, they dress up and go to town together to shop and to see their friends at the Black Crow Club. When Chimane becomes pregnant, she worries that her family will suffer if she quits work to tend a baby, and she gets an abortion.

Dick

Dick works for Mrs. Plum, tending the garden, cleaning the house, and caring for the dogs. He uses his earnings to send his sister to school. He is a good worker and too afraid of whites to break any rules. Although he is the first to know Mrs. Plum's secret, he does not reveal it to anyone. Still, when a rumor is spread that the blacks are going to poison the white people's dogs, Mrs. Plum sends Dick away.

Karabo

The female narrator of the story, Karabo is from the black township of Phokeng, near Rustenburg. Like many black South Africans, she has come from her town to work as a domestic for white families in the Johannesburg suburbs, and she sends money back to her family every month. Karabo ages from nineteen to twenty-two years old during the course of the story and learns a great deal about herself and the world during those three years. When she begins working for Mrs. Plum, she knows her "place" as a servant in a white suburb, and she knows that all of the employers are white and the employees black. But she does not have a sense of the political and social standing of blacks and whites throughout the nation, and she has no idea that there are people working for systemwide change. As she becomes more sophisticated politically, and more sure of herself, she comes to resent Mrs. Plum's condescending attitude and eventually stands up for herself and demands higher wages. She is still Mrs. Plum's employee at the end of the story, but her approach to her job and to her relationship with Mrs. Plum is clear-eyed and confident.

Lilian Ngoyi

Lilian Ngoyi was an actual person. She was a member of the African National Congress, a political party campaigning against the unfair treatment of black South Africans. In the story, she lectures the women at the Black Crow Club about the relationships between blacks and whites and urges them to preserve their dignity as much as possible while they are employed by whites. From her, Karabo learns to place her own individual situation in a larger political context.

Kate Plum

Mrs. Plum's daughter, Kate, is the same age as Karabo, and tries to be her friend. At the beginning of the story, she is off at boarding school during the week and comes home on the weekends. After she graduates, she becomes "wilder," playing loud music, staying out late at night, and falling in love with a black doctor. She tries to explain her mother to Karabo but becomes impatient when Karabo does not understand.

Mrs. Plum

The title character of the story is a widow living in the Johannesburg suburb of Greenside. She is a complex and, for Karabo, a confusing character. She is a member of South Africa's privileged white minority but also an author and activist campaigning for better treatment for the black majority. Mrs. Plum entertains whites and blacks in her home and goes to jail rather than have her black servants searched under the conditions of the pass laws but is adamantly opposed to her daughter marrying a black doctor whom Mrs. Plum invited to several dinner parties. She forces Karabo to eat at the table with her but does not try to learn about the food Karabo likes. She tries to help Karabo improve herself by offering her reading material and paying for dancing lessons, but she can be petty as an employer and refuses Karabo a few days off to mourn her uncle's death. Mrs. Plum is typical of the white liberal in South Africa under apartheid: she likes the Africans as a people but does not try to know them as individuals.

Themes

Civil Rights

Although they are the vast majority of the population of South Africa, the black Africans in the story do not share the personal rights that members of the white minority enjoy. The blacks are required to carry an identification document called a "pass" at all times, and they can work and travel only in the areas specified on the pass. Dick does his best to please his employers, because he knows that they could sign his pass at any time and force him to leave the district. When the police come to search for black servants who do not have the proper passes, they do not need a warrant or any reasonable cause to search Dick's and Karabo's

Topics for Further Study

- Read a few overviews of apartheid in South Africa and of Jim Crow laws in the United States. In what ways were they similar? How did they differ?

- Find a description of the British educational system. Karabo states that she has completed Standard Six. How much education is that?

- Investigate the role that the United States played in urging South Africa to end apartheid. How did the United States explain its role? Which other countries took similar positions? Which countries disagreed with the U.S. position?

- The United States has sometimes established or supported economic sanctions against a nation that has not guaranteed the civil rights of its own people. Most recently, the United States has supported economic sanctions against South Africa and Iraq. What is the philosophy behind such a tactic? How effective has it been?

- Read some recent accounts of life in South Africa. How have conditions changed for workers like Karabo since apartheid was dismantled?

---

rooms, and the servants have no right to refuse the search.

When Karabo is at the Black Crow Club, she listens to lectures by Lilian Ngoyi, who points out the injustices of South African minority rule. Ngoyi urges her followers to work toward a day when the government represents all the races and classes of South Africa, and when all South Africans are citizens with equal rights. Karabo finds Ngoyi's dreams of a united and equal South Africa intriguing. But because blacks do not even have the right to vote during the time of the story, the idea of them sharing political power seems impossible.

Public versus Private Life

The more Karabo learns about Mrs. Plum, the more Mrs. Plum seems "like a dark forest which one fears to enter, and which one will never know." Mrs. Plum is enigmatic because her public and private lives are so different. Publicly, she is an activist for equal treatment for blacks, writing books and articles and letters to the editor, and wearing a black armband as she demonstrates outside government buildings. She openly invites whites and blacks to the same gatherings at her house. She even goes to jail rather than submit to an unjust law. Mrs. Plum seems—and believes herself to be—a just and fair person who believes in equality.

But in her heart, and in her home, Mrs. Plum is not as free from the taint of her privileged upbringing as she seems to be. Though she makes a point of calling Karabo by her true name, she persists in referring to Dick and other adult male servants as "boy." She welcomes black men into her home, but refuses to allow her daughter to marry one. She encourages Karabo to expand and learn but will not tolerate Karabo challenging her authority. She seems to love Africans as a group, but not as individual people.

Most damning of all is Mrs. Plum's secret perversion involving the dogs. Mphahlele intends her secret to be alarming and frightening. A woman like that cannot be trusted and cannot be good.

Growth and Development

As she ages from nineteen to twenty-two, Karabo is continually learning and growing. Mrs. Plum sponsors some of her education. She learns to cook according to recipes and to look after guests. She improves her skills at reading, writing, and speaking English. Mrs. Plum even pays for Karabo to take dancing lessons at the Black Crow Club.

Karabo also learns things Mrs. Plum does not know about and would not approve of. At the Black Crow Club, she learns to look at her own situation in a wider, more political context. Listening to Mrs. Plum and Kate talk about politics, she learns that white people do not know everything about important matters. Karabo's refrain throughout the story is "I was learning. I was growing up." Finally she gains enough confidence to make demands of Mrs. Plum, and when her demands are not met, she stands up for herself and leaves Mrs. Plum's employ. When Mrs. Plum comes after her and asks her to return, Karabo negotiates a new contract. As the two drive back toward Mrs. Plum's home, Karabo reports that "I felt sure of myself, more than I had ever done."

Style

Setting

The setting of "Mrs. Plum" is important not only for the location in which the story takes place, but for the time period as well. The story takes place in the white suburb of Greenside, outside Johannesburg, South Africa's largest and most populous city. Johannesburg was, in the 1960s as it is now, a modern city with skyscrapers and industry in the center, pockets of poverty to the south and west, and wealthy suburbs to the north. During the time of the story, South Africa was strictly segregated, and only white people with large homes and black servants to take care of them inhabited the suburb of Greenside. The servants lived in simple quarters on their employers' property. Most of them, like Karabo and Chimane, left their families behind in small farms or towns far away, and sent money back whenever they could. Normally, they would visit their families back home only once a year.

Mphahlele assumes his readers will know something of apartheid and includes references to laws, locations, and people without explanation. For him, Mrs. Plum and Karabo represent typical people in South Africa during the 1960s. However, his focusing on Karabo's character means that readers who are not familiar with South African history will nevertheless be able to understand her growth and development even if the setting is unfamiliar to them.

Point of View

The story is told in the first person by Karabo, speaking to an unseen reader or listener. Everything that happens, therefore, is filtered through Karabo's consciousness. She reports what she sees and hears, and describes her own reactions to events in the story. But Karabo is not an introspective person, and her reactions tend to be impressions or actions rather than long passages of rational analysis. For example, she reports that when her former employer's cousin touched her inappropriately, she "asked the madam that very day to give me my money and let me go." She does not reflect on her compromised dignity or her position but lets her actions speak for themselves. Other characters, including Mrs. Plum and Kate, are presented only through their speech and action; the reader is not privy to their thoughts.

Telling the story from Karabo's point of view makes her the most well-rounded character in the story and helps the reader establish a sympathetic connection with her immediately. Mphahlele's work was banned in his own country, and books are expensive throughout Africa. The first readers of "Mrs. Plum" would have been educated and relatively wealthy Africans and Europeans. Because they would not have shared Mphahlele's experiences living in segregated poverty, his manipulation of point of view was important for building a relationship between his readers and his character and for helping them see the world through her eyes.

Bildungsroman

A *bildungsroman* is a story about a young person growing up, becoming an adult. The term comes from German and may be translated as "education novel." A number of critics have described "Mrs. Plum" as a *bildungsroman* because it is the story of Karabo's development of a "total awareness of self" by the end of the story. Her repetition of the statements "I learned. I grew up" and Lilian Ngoyi's and Mrs. Plum's encouragement of Karabo's education point to the importance of Karabo's growth and development. Not only does Karabo see more and more of the peculiar white society in which she lives temporarily, but her understanding of what she sees deepens, as well. Mrs. Plum is not a better person at the end of the story, but Karabo is a wiser one. She returns to Mrs. Plum's home, but this time it is with her eyes wide open.

Historical Context

South Africa and Apartheid

Mphahlele wrote "Mrs. Plum" while he was living in Paris, in exile from South Africa. He had left his country because he could no longer live and work under the restrictions of the system of laws called apartheid.

Records show that various dark-skinned peoples have inhabited the land that is now South Africa since the eleventh century. The first Europeans arrived in 1488, and by the middle of the seventeenth century, Dutch settlers called Boers had begun farming and establishing towns. By 1779, there were fifteen thousand whites living in South Africa and millions of blacks of different ethnic groups. The blacks had complicated systems of kingship and lived mostly by herding and farming. Their lack of sophisticated technology, especially modern weapons, meant that they could not

Compare & Contrast

- **1948:** South African Prime Minister D. F. Malan introduces apartheid, a system of laws that restrict the rights of blacks to preserve the power of the white minority.

  1961: As South Africa declares independence from Great Britain and Malan is replaced by Hendrik Verwoerd, apartheid becomes even more restrictive. Blacks are forbidden to live in the white cities and towns but may travel to the cities to provide cheap labor for whites. They do not have the right to vote.

  1990: South African President F. W. de Klerk announces that apartheid will be dismantled, and calls for a new bill of rights and a new system of government under which every adult will vote. Four years later, South Africa elects its first democratically chosen president, the black activist Nelson Mandela.

- **1949:** The passage of the Prohibition of Mixed Marriages Act makes marriage between whites and other racial groups illegal.

  1990: Along with most other restrictions under apartheid, the Prohibition of Mixed Marriages Act is repealed.

- **1950s:** When the South African government makes mixed race people or "coloureds" ineligible to vote, a group of white women called the Women's Defense of the Constitution League protests. The group, also called the Black Sash, stages silent protests over racial injustice, and offers assistance to victims of oppression for the next forty years.

  1990s: Women continue to work for equality in South Africa. Approximately one-third of the members of the post-apartheid parliament are women.

- **1960s:** Abortion is illegal in South Africa. A woman in Chimane's position who feels she must obtain one must undergo a dangerous "back alley" procedure, usually performed in unhygienic conditions by a woman with no formal medical training.

  1990s: Abortions are legal in South Africa (since 1977), though it is discouraged. Abortions may now be administered under safe conditions by doctors and midwives.

---

retain their lands and their power against the white settlers. British settlers arrived in 1820, and at the turn of the century a war between the British and the Boers ended with South Africa becoming a self-governing colony of Great Britain. The new colony was established in 1910 for the good of the British, and the black residents were seen mostly as an inconvenience.

At first, blacks could serve in the parliament of the new colony if they were nominated by whites, but racial segregation was strongly encouraged. In 1948, a Dutch Reformed Church minister named D. F. Malan became prime minister, and segregation, called apartheid, became law. Malan hoped that the blacks who had moved to the cities would move back to their homelands and stay there, leaving the cities for the whites, who now made up approximately twelve percent of the population. Blacks, Asians, and mixed-race people called "coloureds" were restricted to separate entrances at public buildings, including post offices and train stations. Separate restaurants and movie theaters were established for the different groups. Marriage between whites and nonwhites became illegal.

Between 1950 and 1957, the year Mphahlele left South Africa, the restrictions became tighter. All citizens were forced to carry identity documents called "passes," on which their race was marked. Blacks were not allowed to live in white areas and could work in only the areas specified on their passes. If a black worker in a white area lost her job, she had only six days to find new work or she would have to leave the district. Under the Bantu Education Act, separate schools for the separate races were created, but all students were required to learn English and to study English history and literature instead of their own traditional cultures. In some areas, blacks had their farmland taken away, and they were forced to live in townships with no means of support other than sending family members to the cities to work for whites.

Within South Africa, the responses to this oppression varied. Some blacks formed political parties and tried to overthrow the system of apartheid. Opposition leaders were jailed, and writers who opposed government policies found their work banned. As blacks became poorer and weaker, many whites enjoyed becoming richer and more powerful. But many whites opposed apartheid, including liberals like Mrs. Plum who believed that the system could be changed by working within the law. Other whites, who worked outside the law and committed acts of civil disobedience, found themselves jailed or banned.

African Humanism

Because Africa has for so long been under the influence of European colonizers, generations of Africans grew up learning only about European culture in school, and African art, forms of government, and social structures became more and more Europeanized. As African nations gained independence in the 1960s, African intellectuals tried to identify what was essentially African underneath the layers of Western thought and culture. Through *The African Image* (1962) and other critical writings, Mphahlele emerged as one of the most important scholars articulating a definition of what came to be called "African humanism."

In an interview with Richard Samin, Mphahlele outlined the common values that inform African humanism as he defines it: a belief in ancestral spirits and the importance of elders, a strong sense of community that informs human relationships, a strong connection between human nature and nature outside human control, and a continuity between living and nonliving things. These beliefs stand Africans outside Western consumer culture, but consumer culture can encroach upon and weaken African humanism.

Critic Ruth Obee finds all of Mphahlele's fiction to be informed by this system of belief, as she discusses in her 1999 book, *Es'kia Mphahlele: Themes of Alienation and African Humanism*. According to Obee, Karabo's strong desire to go home to mourn her uncle and pay respects to her aunt is an example of Karabo's own African humanism, which "stands in dramatic contrast to Mrs. Plum's materialism."

Critical Overview

Mphahlele was living in Paris in the mid-1960s when he sent his manuscript of *In Corner B*, the collection in which "Mrs. Plum" first appeared, to the East African Publishing House in Kenya, East Africa. He wanted to support an African publisher rather than a European one—a decision he came to regret for purely practical reasons. Kenya was a new nation, having achieved independence only in 1963, and did not have efficient systems in place for producing books or other goods. The manuscript languished for three years before being published, and when the book was issued, there were no high-profile media outlets for promotion. The audience for the book built gradually, mostly by word-of-mouth, and although the book is now recognized as important and of high quality, contemporary reviews were few. In South Africa, Mphahlele's work was banned, and the book was not available there until 1979.

Those who were able to read *In Corner B* upon publication praised it for presenting a more confident voice than the author's earlier work. Lewis Nkosi, for example, notes that "Mphahlele's writing has become tighter, more solid and assured as he acquires a more properly synthesized vocabulary to deal with the stresses of South African life." Several contemporary critics singled out the narrative voice in "Mrs. Plum" for special notice.

The story has met with almost universal approval. In a letter quoted by Ursula Barnett, Mphahlele himself called the story "the best thing I ever pulled off." Gerald Moore, in *Twelve African Writers* (1980), does not choose "Mrs. Plum" as one of the strongest stories in *In Corner B*, but describes it as the author's "most ambitious story to date." Norman Hodge, in a 1981 article in *English in Africa*, called it "the summit of the author's achievements in shorter fiction to date."

Mphahlele has frequently articulated his definition of African humanism, and his treatment of that humanism has drawn the attention of critics. In a 1980 article for *Journal of Commonwealth Literature*, Samuel Omo Asein examines the author's humanism. Asein describes ''Mrs. Plum'' as a conflict between Karabo's humanism and Mrs. Plum's liberalism. Ruth Obee also calls Karabo a humanist. Obee writes that, in her attempts to help Chimane through her pregnancy and abortion, ''Karabo exemplifies the compassion of the practicing African humanist.'' She concludes, '''Mrs. Plum' stands as one of Mphahlele's most definitive statements on African humanism, as both a philosophy and as a way of life.''

Several critics have focused on Karabo's development as the most important thread in the story. Norman Hodge wrote about the story in an article published in the South African journal *English in Africa* in 1981, two years after the ban on Mphahlele's work was lifted. He called the story a ''bildungsroman,'' or a story of education and maturation, and traced Karabo's growth through her experiences with the white and black worlds. By the end, he writes that Karabo has moved ''from a basic ignorance of white urban realities to a relatively complete and comprehensive understanding of both the social situation and her position in this society.'' Her pattern of development is a common and universal one. Other writers have agreed with Hodge's assessment but explored the unique details of a bildungsroman in the particular political setting of South Africa under apartheid.

Most critics have seen Mrs. Plum as hypocritical, and the story as a condemnation of her as the worst sort of white liberal. Ursula Barnett, in *Ezekiel Mphahlele* (1976), was more sympathetic. She acknowledged Mrs. Plum's willingness to go to jail for her beliefs and saw some kindness in her treatment of Karabo. She wrote of Karabo and Mrs. Plum, ''Here are two people, each representing her race in some of its better qualities, who genuinely try to understand each other, and fail miserably.''

More than thirty years after the publication of *In Corner B*, Mphahlele is considered one of the most important of the African writers, and his work is studied in high schools and colleges and universities in the United States, in Europe, and throughout Africa. As the end of apartheid brings a new era in scholarly study of African writers in South Africa, and as an improved economy makes books available to a larger South African readership, Mphahlele will finally be studied by South Africans and in the context of a large body of freely available South African writing.

Criticism

Cynthia Bily

Bily teaches writing and literature at Adrian College in Adrian, Michigan, and writes for various educational publishers. In the following essay, she examines the concept of family in Mphahlele's story.

While it is certainly a story of politics, and a story of growing up, Es'kia Mphahlele's ''Mrs. Plum'' is also a story of family. Mphahlele's own family has always had a strong influence on him, and he has drawn throughout his life on the strength of women. Raised by his grandmother and then by his single mother, Mphahlele has been married to his wife Rebecca for over fifty years. By all accounts, his relationships with his children are based on love and respect. The author's mentions of humble family matters in his two volumes of autobiography demonstrate the importance he places on the family bond. In ''Mrs. Plum,'' the author uses the states of his characters' families to suggest their moral worth.

Like many of the servants she knows, Karabo has come to Johannesburg from her rural hometown to work for white people. She sends part of her earnings home to her family in Phokeng, and sets some more aside for supplies to take with her when she visits. She is allowed only one trip home each year, at Easter, when all the servants go ''for a long weekend to see our people and to eat chicken and sour milk and *morogo*—wild spinach. We also [take] home sugar and condensed milk and tea and coffee and sweets and custard powder and tinned foods.'' During their time apart, Karabo and her family exchange frequent letters. When the servants get together on their Thursday afternoons off, they ''talk and talk and talk: about our people at home and their letters; about their illnesses; about bad crops; about a sister who wanted a school uniform and books and school fees.''

Dick, who does the housecleaning and watches over Mrs. Plum's dogs, has a situation much like Karabo's. His family is in Orlando Township, and he sends his salary back to them so that his younger sister can stay in school. She wishes to become a nurse and midwife, which will require years of schooling, but Dick has been unable to hold any job very long. Still he will not abandon her. He borrows

What Do I Read Next?

- *In Corner B* (1967), by Ezekiel Mphahlele, is a collection of twelve short stories that draw on the author's experiences in Nigeria and South Africa. It includes ''Mrs. Plum.''

- *Afrika, My Music: An Autobiography 1957–1983* (1984), by Es'kia Mphahlele, is the second volume of Mphahlele's autobiography. It covers the two decades of his exile in Africa, Europe and the United States, and his return to South Africa in 1977.

- *The Penguin Book of Southern African Stories* (1985), edited by Stephen Gray, is a well-received anthology of thirty-nine short stories from South Africa, Botswana, Lesotho, Malawi, Namibia, Swaziland, and Zimbabwe.

- *When Rain Clouds Gather* (1967), by Bessie Head, is an ultimately optimistic novel about racial and gender oppression in Africa. Head was classified as mixed race when born in South Africa, and like Mphahlele she found her true voice as a writer only after leaving South Africa.

- *My Traitor's Heart* (1990), by Rian Malan, is a horrifying account of apartheid by a white reporter who left South Africa because of the atrocities he had seen, and who returned to confront and try to understand his native land. The author has been widely praised for his honesty and courage in writing this book.

- *The Land and People of South Africa* (1990), by Jonathan Paton, is an illustrated overview of the country. Although it was written before the end of apartheid, it provides a thorough examination of the period during which ''Mrs. Plum'' takes place.

---

money from other servants ''to pay his sister's school fees, to buy her clothes and books.'' But since he is gone to the city to earn money, the sister has had to assume extra responsibilities at home: ''she looked after his old people, although she was only thirteen years of age.'' For Karabo and Dick, supporting their families is a duty and a source of pride.

By contrast, Mrs. Plum's family has fallen apart. Her husband killed himself before Karabo joined the household. Her daughter Kate is wild, undisciplined. Kate listens to music too loudly and stays out too late at night, and falls in love with people Mrs. Plum feels are wrong for her. Karabo reports that after a particularly nasty disagreement, ''they were now openly screaming at each other. They began in the sitting room and went upstairs together, speaking fast hot biting words.'' Perhaps to compensate for the loving family she does not have, Mrs. Plum lavishes her affection on her dogs, who live in more comfort than many servants do. They are washed and brushed, they sleep on pink linen, they wear doggie sweaters. As Karabo eventually learns, Mrs. Plum's affection for her dogs extends to the point of perversion. Mrs. Plum is depicted as a shocking and dramatic example of the warped values of South African whites.

Chimane's white employers are not a happy family, either. The husband's mother comes to visit, and the wife treats her with disdain. While Chimane cooks for the rest of the family, the mother-in-law is not invited to share their food. She cooks for herself when the family meal is over. If the family cat is sitting on the only available chair, the mother-in-law is not allowed to move it and sit down herself. Chimane and Karabo do not know what to make of this kind of treatment of a family member. They can only conclude that ''white people have no heart no sense.''

Because whites have so little regard for their own families, it is not surprising that they do not respect the families and the family values of their servants. For Karabo, Chimane, and Dick, trying to sustain a family from such a great distance is

> "Because whites have so little regard for their own families, it is not surprising that they do not respect the families and the family values of their servants. For Karabo, Chimane, and Dick, trying to sustain a family from such a great distance is difficult and worrisome. But under the laws of apartheid, there is little they can do."

difficult and worrisome. But under the laws of apartheid, there is little they can do. Their families are prohibited by law from moving to Greenside, Mrs. Plum's suburb; it is an area for whites only, and for their servants. Black families must live where they are told to live, but their wage-earning children must live where there are jobs.

The system is particularly hard on Chimane. When she learns she is pregnant, her immediate reaction is despair. Although she would love to be a mother and the wife of the baby's father, she feels trapped. If she takes time off work to have the baby and care for it, her family will have no income. She moans, "What shall we be eating all the time I am at home? It is not like the days gone past when we had land and our mother could go to the fields until the child was ready to arrive."

Chimane decides to have an abortion, a risky and painful process. It is painful, both physically and emotionally, but she feels she has no choice. Her aunt comes to help her recover and to mourn the lost child. She complains, "If she had let the child be born I should have looked after it or my sister would have been so happy to hold a grandchild on her lap." Then Timi, the father of the unborn child, rejects her because of the abortion. Apartheid forced Chimane to choose between feeding her family and saving her baby. In choosing the abortion, she wounded her aunt and lost her lover. But in choosing the baby, she would have taken food out of her parents' mouths. Chimane's employers, the beneficiaries of apartheid, never even know about Chimane's struggle.

For Karabo, the time for making a choice comes when her uncle dies. For months, she has been receiving letters from home, telling of various deaths from a mysterious illness. Africans feel a kinship with large extended families, and Karabo's mother keeps her informed about her father, her sisters, the mother-in-law of her sisters' teacher, and even "a woman she does not think I remember because I last saw her when I was a young girl[—] she passed away in Zeerust[—]she was my mother's greatest friend when they were girls." Now it is her uncle, her mother's brother, who has died. Karabo asks Mrs. Plum for a few days off to take "tears and words of grief to his grave."

For Mphahlele, Karabo's wish to go home is not extraordinary, although he knows that Mrs. Plum does not understand the request. Ursula Barnett explains in *Ezekiel Mphahlele* that a mother's brother is "a relationship considered closer by Africans than that of any other uncle." Before writing this story, Mphahlele described a typical situation in *The African Image*: "A man asks his employer for leave to go home in some reserve two hundred miles or so away, because his aunt's cousin's husband (spoken of as a direct uncle) is dead. The employer often doesn't understand why a man should travel two hundred miles to see a corpse. He doesn't know what it means to his 'boy' in terms of human relations and communal living." Mrs. Plum does not understand and denies the request.

Karabo decides that she must go anyway, and that she cannot continue in Mrs. Plum's employ. She quits her job and takes the bus home. At last the reader gets to meet Karabo's family, to determine whether they are worth all the worry. They are. When Karabo tells her father she has no job, he replies, "So long as you are in good health, my child, it is good." The talk between Karabo and her parents is respectful, and she defers to them when Mrs. Plum asks her to return: "You must ask my father first." When the parents are consulted, the father replies lovingly, "It goes by what you feel my child." There is no evidence that Mrs. Plum notices the remarkable contrast between this civil and kind conversation and her own screaming arguments with Kate, but the reader cannot help but see.

As demonstrated by the families described in "Mrs. Plum," the social structure imposed by apartheid is detrimental to black families, yet these black families stay strong. Ironically, the white families, who seem to have every advantage, are full of conflict.

Source: Cynthia Bily, in an essay for *Short Stories for Students*, Gale Group, 2001.

Liz Brent

Brent has a Ph.D. in American Culture, specializing in film studies, from the University of Michigan. She is a freelance writer and teaches courses in the history of American cinema. In the following essay, Brent discusses the significance of the dogs in Mphahlele's story.

In the 1972 short story "Mrs. Plum," Ezekiel (or Es'kia) Mphahlele addresses issues of black-white relations during the era of apartheid in South Africa through the narrator's focus on the white peoples' treatment of their pet dogs. Karabo, the narrator, is a young black South African woman working as a maid in the home of Mrs. Plum, a white woman active in organizing for the rights of blacks. Although Mrs. Plum is a liberal and makes many gestures toward treating Karabo fairly, she nevertheless harbors many racist attitudes toward blacks and continues to treat her black employees in a demeaning and unfair manner. Karabo's narrative focuses on Mrs. Plum's two pet dogs, Monty and Malan, in describing the racial relations between herself and her employer.

Mrs. Plum's treatment of her dogs is an insult to her black African employees because she to some extent equates her pets with her servants. As the story opens, Karabo makes the statement that Mrs. Plum "loved dogs and Africans," which were two of the "three big things in Madam's life." The irony here is that, while Mrs. Plum sees herself as someone who "loves" Africans, this "love" is an insult to her servants because she sees it as on a par with her "love" for dogs. The implication is that, to her mind, black Africans are no better than animals—even if they are beloved pets. This equation of the status of black servants with that of animals is further indicated by the fact that the black servants are even fed the same meat as the dogs. The expression "dog-meat boys" is used to describe the boyfriends of the domestic maids, because, as Karabo explains, "A boy who had a girlfriend in the kitchens, as we say, always told his friends that he was coming for dog's meat when he meant he was visiting his girl. This was because we gave our boyfriends part of the meat the white people bought

> After hearing a white man call his dog 'Rusty,' Karabo thinks, 'Dogs with names, men without.'

for the dogs and us." At other points in the story, as well, the oppressed status of black Africans in South Africa is equated to that of animals. Karabo is told by Lilian Ngoyi, her teacher, "Remember your poor people at home and the way in which the whites are moving them from place to place like sheep and cattle." Karabo later thinks of herself as a herd of defenseless "sheep" in comparison to a white person who is a predatory "fox that falls upon a flock of sheep at night."

Karabo and her friends are also disdainful of the white peoples' habit of talking to their dogs as if they were human beings. Again, this is an insult to the black Africans because the dogs are given equal, or higher, status than black Africans, although they are in fact human beings, while the dogs are not. Dick, who works as Mrs. Plum's gardener, is particularly disdainful of this habit; he exclaims to Karabo, "These things called white people! ... Talking to dogs!" Karabo comments that, "Monty and Milan became real dogs again," only when Mrs. Plum went out of town on vacation; in other words, with the white owner away, the black servants have the luxury of treating the dogs like animals, rather than like spoiled humans.

The black African servants resent their employers' treatment of their pet dogs. The underlying reason for this resentment is due to the fact that these animals are treated far better and provided with far more creature comforts, than the impoverished servants working to support their families. After hearing a white man call his dog "Rusty," Karabo thinks, "Dogs with names, men without." She is referring to the fact that white people often call black African men "boy," or "Jim," and are not interested in the real African names of their servants, but simply call them any convenient name. The black Africans are also disdainful of the various ways in which the whites treat their pet dogs like "gentlemen," fed "tea and biscuits" like honored guests, while they themselves are treated worse than animals. Karabo describes Mrs. Plum's royal treatment of her dogs with great disdain: "They are to be washed often and brushed and sprayed and they sleep on pink linen. Monty has a pink ribbon, which stays on his neck most of the time. They both carry a cover on their backs. They make me feel fed up when I see them in their baskets, looking fat, and as if they knew all that was going on everywhere." The pink sheets and pink ribbon indicate the frivolous nature of the extent to which the white people pamper their pets; the color pink is associated with a certain degree of prissiness and frivolity. The linen sheets and clothes provided for the dogs are a particular insult to Karabo, because she and her friends have very limited resources to buy dresses and stockings for themselves, while the dogs are privileged to luxurious outfits. The dogs are "fat," of course, from being well fed, while the servants are given little more than scraps to eat, and must send most of their earnings home to support their families who are living at a subsistence level.

Dick, who takes care of Mrs. Plum's dogs, is equally disdainful of the frivolous outfitting of the dogs, in part because of the added work it represents. He jokes with Karabo that "One day those white people will put earrings and toe rings and bangles on their dogs. That would be the day he would leave Mrs. Plum. For, he said, he was sure that she would want him to polish the rings and bangles with Brasso." This overdressing of the dogs, while the black servants have little resources for clothing, is particularly insulting to Karabo when Mrs. Plum's dogs ruin her stockings, and Mrs. Plum ultimately blames her rather than the dogs. Karabo explains that, "Once one of the dogs . . . tore my stocking—brand-new, you hear—and tore it with its teeth and paws. Then I told Madam about it, my anger as high as my throat, she gave me money to buy another pair. It happened again. This time she said she was not going to give me money because I must also keep my stockings where the two gentlemen would not reach them." The pet dogs of white people are even given the status of "masters and madams," when their owners are on vacation, and the black servants must wait hand and foot on the dogs. Karabo explains that, "In winter so many families went away that the dogs remained masters and madams. You could see them walk like white people in the streets. Silent but with plenty of power. And when you saw them you knew that they were full of more nonsense and fancies in the house."

The living conditions of dogs in African communities, compared to those of white communities, represent the contrast between the lives of African people and white people. Chimane tells Karabo a funny story about a dog belonging to an African man in which the dog jumps out of its master's arms to get at a pot of meat cooking in a market. This anecdote, which contrasts the behavior of an "African dog" with a dog owned by white people, symbolizes the difference between the living conditions of black Africans and the "spoiled" lives of white people. Chimane concludes the story by stating, "That is a good African dog. A dog must look for its own food when it is not time for meals. Not these stupid spoiled angels the whites keep giving tea and biscuits." Karabo goes to see her friend Chimane in an impoverished black area, which she describes as "that terrible township where night and day are full of knives and bicycle chains and guns and the barking of hungry dogs and of people in trouble." Whereas the dogs in the white neighborhoods are "fat," the dogs in the black neighborhoods are "hungry."

Dick, the gardener for Mrs. Plum, also points out the differences between the black Africans' relationship to their animals and that of the whites. For the Africans, in their rural homelands, animals are not spoiled pets, but are used as tools for subsistence living gained through hard work. He points out to Karabo the difference between the ways in which Africans talk to their oxen and the way in which white people talk to their dogs: "at home do you not know that a man speaks to an ox because he wants to make it pull the plow or the wagon or to stop or to stand still for a person to inspan it. No one simply goes to an ox looking at him with eyes far apart and speaks to it." The pampered treatment of pet dogs by white people is later contrasted with the use of animals by traditional black African society for ritual sacrifice. At a party thrown by a black African while his employers are away, one of Karabo's friends announces that he and a friend have won a lot of money from betting on a horse. He comments that "At home I should slaughter a goat for us to feast and thank our ancestors."

Having to care for these overprivileged animals is often highly unpleasant for the servants of the white people. One of Karabo's friends describes the big pet rat of a child of her previous employers, which made her housework particularly distasteful: "He puts it on his bed when he goes to school. And let the blankets just begin to smell of urine and all the nonsense and they tell me to wash them. Hei, people . . . !" Karabo and other black servants occasionally assert themselves against either the pets, or their employers' expectations of them in caring for these pets. These moments of resistance represent a form of rebellion in that, at least in some small way, they are able to assert their own right to be treated like human beings, rather than being treated worse than animals. Sometimes these moments of rebellion are enacted against the pets when the white people are not around to find out. Even a small kick to one of the dogs by a black servant demonstrates a form of resistance to white oppression. One of Karabo's friends tells her that "Me, I take a master's bitch by the leg, me, and throw it away so that it keeps howling. . . . I don't play about with them, me." Other times, the black servants refuse to carry out certain tasks in caring for their employers' pets, another way of asserting their rights against white authority; another of Karabo's friends explains that "They wanted me to take their dog out for a walk every afternoon and I told them I said, It is not my work, in other houses the garden man does it. I just said to myself I said, They can go to the chickens. Let them bite their elbows before I take out a dog, I am not so mad yet." Dick even goes so far as to allow Mrs. Plum's dogs to run out into the street, nearly getting hit by a car, when she is not around. Through his carelessness, perhaps deliberate, Dick expresses a certain level of resentment against Mrs. Plum's treatment of the dogs compared to him.

Karabo and her friends are particularly insulted by the white peoples' plan to build a cemetery for their dogs. The dog cemetery represents a variety of ways in which the white people are far more concerned with their dogs than with the difficult lives of their underpaid black servants. The immoral nature of this discrepancy is expressed by Karabo's friend Chimane, who says that, "These white people can do things that make the gods angry. More godless people I have not seen." The idea of the dog cemetery further reinforces their resentment of dogs being treated like humans while they themselves are treated worse than animals. Karabo tells Chimane, "By my mother one day these dogs will sit at table and use knife and fork. These things are to be treated like people now, like children who are never going to grow up." Chimane adds that the white people prefer to spend their resources on their dead pets than on the basic needs of their black servants; she comments, "why do they not give me some of that money they will spend on the ground and on gravestones to buy stockings! I have nothing to put on, by my mother." Mrs. Plum's concern "that Monty and Milan could be sure of a nice burial" is particularly insulting to Karabo after she receives notice of her uncle's death and Mrs. Plum argues that there is no need for her to go home, since the funeral has already occurred. Thus, while she is greatly concerned with the burial of her dogs, Mrs. Plum is completely unsympathetic to Karabo and her family in mourning the death of a close relative. Mrs. Plum denies Karabo the right to take a day off in order to "take my tears and words of grief to his grave and to my old aunt." Karabo's decision to quit working for Mrs. Plum in order to go home is an assertion of her right to the human compassion Mrs. Plum reserves only for her dogs.

After her dogs have been stolen, and probably killed, Mrs. Plum appears at Karabo's home asking her to return to her employ. Karabo is for the first time able to assert herself in demanding from Mrs. Plum an increase in wages and more paid time off. Karabo has the realization that, for Mrs. Plum, she herself is just a substitute for the companionship of the dogs; she asks herself, "did this woman come to ask me to return because she had lost two animals she loved?" As the story closes, Karabo sees clearly that Mrs. Plum's "love" for Africans, which she equates with her love for dogs, is false, to the extent that she does not see the African people she knows and who work for her, such as Karabo and Dick, as individuals with the rights of human beings.

Source: Liz Brent, in an essay for *Short Stories for Students*, Gale Group, 2001.

Rena Korb

Korb has a master's degree in English literature and creative writing and has written for a wide variety of educational publishers. In the following essay, she discusses Karabo's growing realization of the hypocrisy of Mrs. Plum's liberalism and her corresponding growth of her own independence.

With publication of such influential works as the autobiography *Down Second Avenue* and the novel *The Wanderers*, Ezekiel Mphahlele came to be widely viewed as one of Africa's most important twentieth-century writers. He has lived in his native South Africa, and after his exile in the 1950s, he lived in other African countries as well as in the United States. His most important works, however, have centered on the plight of Africans in racist South Africa, many during the years of apartheid. Like his longer works and his essays, his short stories also reflect these important issues. Published between 1946 and 1967—several in *Drum* magazine, which was the launching point for many noted South African writers—these stories introduce the themes that governed black African life: life in the townships, the politics of protest, and black urban existence.

Reviewers praised his second collection of stories, *In Corner B*, and, along with the author, saw in it significant development. Ursula Barnett writes in the *Dictionary of Literary Biography* that in these stories "Mphahlele's creative skills have matured" from his earlier collection. Along with the title story, Barnett singled out "Mrs. Plum": "There is an economy of words and a conciseness of imagery lacking before. They [the stories] mark the height of his creation of short fiction." Considered one of his most successful stories, both for its tacit exposure of the hypocrisy of white South African liberals and its realistically stultifying backdrop of typical black life in the white suburbs, "Mrs. Plum" is noteworthy for other reasons as well. Mphahlele, notes Finuala Dowling in her discussion of his short stories in *Reference Guide to Short Fiction*, believed the story to be "the best thing" he "ever pulled off." Additionally, its length—almost that of a novella—inspired Mphahlele to undertake new projects. As he told Cosmo Pieterse in 1968:

> [W]hen I wrote "Mrs Plum" this was a kind of finger exercise to see what I could make of the long story or the novella, and once having done that I felt more confident; so I got into the novel and I have now finished a novel which is in the hands of the publishers [The Wanderers], . . . I'm not going to go back to the short story I think. I want to, I simply want to go on with the novel.

"Mrs. Plum" takes the forms of a young black servant's recollections of her mistress. Karabo comes to work for Mrs. Plum in her suburban Johannesburg home. At first, Karabo is surprised at her treatment in her new place of employ; Mrs. Plum insists on treating her with a real measure of equality. Over time, however, as Karabo learns her own self-worth, she comes to understand the shallowness of Mrs. Plum's liberalism. Her assertion of independence at the end of the story is both an indictment of Mrs. Plum and a strong statement of her value as an individual.

The story opens with a simple characterization of Mrs. Plum. According to Karabo, "She loved dogs and Africans and said that everyone must follow the law even if it hurt." These were the three main principles of Mrs. Plum's life: she loves her dogs because she is a lonely woman and they give her affection; she loves Africans because her championing their cause allows her to maintain a view of herself as a good person; and she believes in the law because she does not delve deeply into any of the issues that she claims plague her. Mrs. Plum only cares for these things for what they can give her, not for any of their own innate characteristics.

At first, however, Karabo only notes how different Mrs. Plum is from previous employers. Mrs. Plum insists on calling her by her African name, in striking contrast to Karabo's former families, where she was called either "Jane" or "You Black Girl." When Karabo first meets Mrs. Plum, she is impressed because she "spoke as if she knew a name is a big thing. I knew so many whites who did not care what they called black people as long as it was all right for their tongue. . . . [T]he only time I heard the name [Karabo] was when I was at home or when my friends spoke to me." Mrs. Plum also teaches Karabo how to cook and how to treat guests; helps her learn to speak and write better English; and wants Karabo to eat at the table with her and her daughter Kate. She also pays the fee for Karabo's Thursday afternoon Black Crow Club, where she will learn such skills as sewing, knitting, and dancing.

In so doing, however, Mrs. Plum unwittingly fosters the development of Karabo's self-will; for at the club, Karabo is exposed to the ideas of Lilian Ngoyi, who is a teacher there. Ngoyi was an important member of the African National Congress, which led the decades-long struggle against apartheid. Ngoyi, and her quest for true understanding and equality, becomes a counterpoint to Mrs. Plum, whose reform measures would only assuage the economic inequities of South Africa and not better the actual status of black Africans.

In her books, newspaper articles, and editorials, Mrs. Plum does call for changes in South African governmental policy toward blacks. She asks the government "to be kind to" Africans. They "should be treated well, be paid more money." Thus Africans who have attended school—meaning they have been taught to read and write—should be able to participate in the government by choosing "those who [they] want to speak for them." The reality of Mrs. Plum's plan is that only "a few of your people" would "one day be among those who rule." Ngoyi, by contrast, not only calls for a South Africa in which blacks are part of the government, but believes that "[T]he power should be given to the Africans." Blacks "shall be more than they" in this new government "as we are more in the country." The difference between the two women is also pointed out in Ngoyi's assertion that "A master and a servant can never be friends." As she notes, "You are not even sure if the ones you say are good are not like that because they cannot breathe or live without the work of your hands."

Before attending Ngoyi's classes, Karabo had demonstrated her comprehension of the inherent wrongness of Mrs. Plum's setting herself up as spokesperson for the black people. When Kate first tells Karabo that Mrs. Plum goes to meetings "[F]or your people," Karabo wonders why. Her own people "have mouths" too.

> Why does she want to say something for them? Does she know what my mother and what my father want to say? They can speak when they want to.... [Kate says] I don't say your people—your family only. I mean all the black people in this country. I say Oh! What do the black people want to say?

Through her classes with Ngoyi, however, Karabo comes to understand her own source of discomfort with the role that Mrs. Plum takes for herself—she comes to understand the hypocrisy of women in Mrs. Plum's position. As Karabo confesses,

> I always thought of Madam when Lilian Ngoyi spoke.... Now Lilian Ngoyi asked she said, How many white people can be born in a white hospital, grow up in white streets, be clothed in lovely cotton, lie on white cushions; how many whites can live all their lives in a fenced place away from people of other colours and then, as men and women learn quickly the correct ways of thinking, learn quickly to ask questions in their minds, big questions that will throw over all the nice things of a white man's life? How many? Very very few.

Karabo's understanding that Mrs. Plum does not have, as Ngoyi puts it, "both feet in our house" grows over time. Mrs. Plum notices that Karabo is changing, which does not please her. "What else are they teaching you at the Black Crow, Karabo?" she asks, showing her suspicion that Karabo's education is surpassing her intended boundaries. Karabo no longer wants to read Mrs. Plum's white newspapers because they contained "pictures of white people most of the time." Karabo reports that "they talked mostly about white people and their gardens, dogs, weddings and parties. I asked her if she could buy me a Sunday paper that spoke about my people. Madam bought it for me. I did not think she would do it." Karabo's surprise indicates her growing comprehension that Mrs. Plum pays only lip service to the needs and rights of blacks.

Barnett points out that "Mphahlele dislikes this type of liberalism intensely because it lacks the one characteristic that is his own ruling passion—a

> " I asked her if she could buy me a Sunday paper that spoke about my people. Madam bought it for me. I did not think she would do it.' Karabo's surprise indicates her growing comprehension that Mrs. Plum pays only lip service to the needs and rights of blacks."

feeling of compassion for one's fellow human beings." That Mrs. Plum is such a person is seen in many different ways, for instance, her discomfort with Karabo's changes, her distrust of the garden man Dick, and her adherence to the law. Mrs. Plum gets arrested for obstructing police business when two officers come to the house to make sure that the pass laws, which determine which blacks may leave the townships and visit the cities, are being followed. Mrs. Plum bypasses paying a five-pound fine, which she can easily afford, and elects to go to jail for two weeks as her punishment. Instead of appreciating Mrs. Plum's gesture, Karabo again compares her to Ngoyi: "I thought of what Lilian Ngoyi often said to us: You must be ready to go to jail for the things you believe are true and for which you are taken by the police. What did Mrs. Plum really believe about me, Chimane, Dick and all the other black people, I asked myself? I did not know." Mrs. Plum had chosen jail over the fine "to show that she felt she was not in the wrong," words that significantly reveal that Mrs. Plum's protests stem from her own set of beliefs and not from any definitive knowledge or understanding of the African people. She never sees the black Africans who surround her as individuals, only as representatives of South Africa's unfair system. So even though Mrs. Plum does make efforts to help Karabo, it is not because of *who* Karabo is but because of *what* she represents: the repressed black South African underclass.

Over time, Karabo comes to possess a more thorough understanding of the inequities that South

Daniel F. Malan, the former South-African prime minister under whom apartheid became law.

African policy visits upon black Africans. Her friend Chimane must decide what to do about an unplanned pregnancy. Chimane doesn't feel that she can take time off from working to get married and have the baby because she will be unable to feed her family during this period. Karabo realizes that in a system that takes all rights from people, "Luck and the mercy of the gods" is all that saves her. Karabo comes to feel disgust for the trappings of Mrs. Plum that she has taken upon herself. Sitting on her bed she "smelled Madam" and quickly realized that it came from her own perfume. "I used the same cosmetics as Mrs. Plum's. . . . why have I been using the same cosmetics as Madam. . . . And then I took all the things and threw them into the dustbin. I was going to buy other kinds on Thursday; finished!" Even after this purging ritual, Karabo is still unsettled.

> I could not sit down. I went out and into the white people's house. I walked through and the smell of the house made me sick and seemed to fill up my throat. I went to the bathroom without knowing why. It was full of the smell of Madam. Dick was cleaning the bath. I stood at the door at looked at him cleaning the dirt from Madam's body. . . . To myself I said, Why cannot people wash the dirt of their own bodies out of the bath? . . . *Ag*, I said again to myself, why should I think about it now when I have been doing their washing for so long and cleaned the bath many times when Dick was ill. I had held worse things from her body many times without number.

Karabo's shift in regard for Mrs. Plum culminates in the scene in which, peeping through a keyhole, she sees her employer sexually gratifying herself with one of her much loved and pampered dogs. Karabo and other black servants had already showed disdain for the white people's dogs. At the Black Crow Club, the women display their suppressed rage at their treatment by whites through discussion of their dogs. One dog is "Big in a foolish way." Another maid takes "a master's bitch by the leg, . . . and throws it away so it keeps howling." Chimane and Karabo draw comparisons between white dogs and African dogs. "A [African] dog must look for its own food when it is not time for meals. Not these stupid spoiled angels the whites keep giving tea and biscuits."

That the white people's dogs are a focus of black anger is apparent—the dogs invariably are better treated than the servants. When a story begins to spread through Johannesburg that the servants were going to poison the dogs, Mrs. Plum shows typical South African white bias in her assumption that Dick—who believes that it was wrong to hold animals accountable for the sins of their masters—poses a danger to her dogs. She asks Karabo for her opinion on Dick's trustworthiness, and Karabo sees a face on Mrs. Plum she has never seen before: "The eyes, the nostrils, the lips, the teeth seemed to be full of hate, tired, fixed on doing something bad; and yet there was something on that face that told me she wanted me on her side." Instead of contributing to Mrs. Plum's bigotry, after Mrs. Plum fires Dick, Karabo quits Mrs. Plum's employ. A week later, Mrs. Plum comes to Karabo's township to ask her to return. Karabo's assents after negotiating shrewdly. In the car on the way back to Mrs. Plum's house, Mrs. Plum tells Karabo that she no longer has the dogs, for they were stolen the day after Karabo left. Karabo asks herself, "did this woman come to ask me to return because she had lost two animals she loved?" Before she can explore this question in her mind, Mrs. Plum says, "You know, I like your people, Karabo, the Africans." Karabo wonders, "And Dick and me?" The story closes on this scene, succinctly demonstrating Mrs. Plum's bitter dismissal of the individuality of Africans and Karabo's understanding of this truth.

Source: Rena Korb, in an essay for *Short Stories for Students*, Gale Group, 2001.

Ursula A. Barnett

The following excerpt provides an overview of Mphahlele's "Mrs. Plum" and discusses the main character's liberal views.

[Mphahlele's] best-known story, of almost novella length, is "Mrs. Plum." It concerns a liberal, white widow who lives in a suburb with her daughter, her servants, and her dogs. Karabo, the female domestic worker who narrates the story, finds Mrs. Plum's liberalism puzzling but accepts it at first as one of the eccentricities of the white race: "my madam . . . loved dogs and Africans and said that everyone must follow the law even if it hurt. These were three big things in Madam's life." That is how the story opens. Relations between them deteriorate when there is trouble in the neighborhood. At first Mrs. Plum supports her servants against the police to the extent that she goes to jail. Karabo is impressed, but among her friends and at her home in Phokeng there is only poverty and tragedy; suddenly she is sickened by the smell of the cosmetics she secretly shares with Mrs. Plum, by the dogs, and by Dick, the other servant, who cleans out the dirt of Madam's body from the bathtub. Dick is suspected of poisoning dogs in the neighborhood, and Mrs. Plum dismisses him. In protest Karabo leaves her employ. The story ends when Mrs. Plum visits Karabo in her home village and asks her to return. She tells Karabo that two pet dogs have died. Did this woman, Karabo wonders, come to ask her to return because she had lost two animals she loved? "You know, I like your people, Karabo, the African," Mrs. Plum says. Karabo wonders if Mrs. Plum likes her as an individual.

In the course of the story readers gradually realize that while Mrs. Plum's liberalism is quite genuine, unlike that of Miss Pringle in "We'll Have Dinner at Eight," it is completely impersonal. Mphahlele dislikes this type of liberalism intensely because it lacks the one characteristic that is his own ruling passion—a feeling of compassion for one's fellow human beings. By bringing into the story a historical character, the black leader Lillian Ngoyi, as a teacher in a women's club Karabo attends, Mphahlele shows the white liberal as irrelevant to the education and maturity of a young black girl. Only by sharing a common cause with other women in her position can Karabo become conscious of her worth as a black woman.

Source: Ursula A. Barnett, "Es'kia Mphahlele," in *DLB*, Gale, Vol. 125, 1993, pp. 89–108.

Sources

Asein, Samuel Omo, "The Humanism of Ezekiel Mphahlele," in *Journal of Commonwealth Literature*, Vol. 15, No. 1, 1980, p. 45.

Barnett, Ursula B., *Ezekial Mphahlele*, Twayne, 1976, p. 106, 110.

Hodge, Norman, "Dogs, Africans and Liberals: The World of Mphahlele's 'Mrs. Plum,'" in *English in Africa*, Vol. 8, No. 1, 1981, p. 33, 36.

Moore, Gerald, *Twelve African Writers*, Indiana University Press, 1980, p. 58.

Mphahlele, Ezekiel, *The African Image*, Faber & Faber, 1962, p. 212.

Nkosi, Lewis, *Home and Exile*, Longman, 1965, p. 131.

Obee, Ruth, *Es'kia Mphahlele: Themes of Alienation and African Humanism*, Ohio University Press, 1999, p. 130, 143, 148.

Samin, Richard, Interview in *Research in African Literatures*, Vol. 28, Winter, 1997, pp. 182–200.

Further Reading

Akosu, Tyohdzuah, *The Writing of Ezekiel [Es'kia] Mphahlele, South African Writer: Literature, Culture and Politics*, Mellen University Press, 1995.
  This book is an important overview of the critical reception of Mphahlele's work and an assessment of his literary achievements. Akosu claims that aesthetic questions about African writing are inappropriate, and that Mphahlele's work should be analyzed from a functionalist stance—that is, how it works as literature.

Barnett, Ursula A., *Ezekiel Mphahlele*, Twayne, 1976.
  Although published before Mphahlele's return to South Africa from exile in 1977, this volume is still the best introduction to Mphahlele's early and middle life and work. It includes a chronology, biography, and close reading of his major writings, including "Mrs. Plum."

Egejuru, Phanuel Akubueze, *Towards African Literary Independence: A Dialogue with Contemporary African Writers*, Greenwood Press, 1980.
  These pieces are interwoven interviews with several important writers, including Mphahlele, on the importance of African literature for Africans and for Westerners. Mphahlele discusses the challenges of being both an African and an exile, and of writing for an African audience but being published and read by Westerners.

Hodge, Norman, "Dogs, Africans and Liberals: The World of Mphahlele's 'Mrs Plum,'" in *English in Africa*, Vol. 8, No. 1, March 1981, pp. 33–43.

Hodge's text is a close reading of ''Mrs. Plum,'' emphasizing the indictment the story makes of white liberals in South Africa under apartheid.

Manganyi, N. Chabani, *Exiles and Homecomings: A Biography of Es'kia Mphahlele*, Ravan Press, 1983.

This insightful biography was written by a clinical psychologist with full cooperation from Mphahlele and his family. This biography is unusual in using a first-person narrative voice.

Obee, Ruth, '''Mrs Plum': The Authoritarian Personality and Black Consciousness,'' in *Es'kia Mphahlele: Themes of Alienation and African Humanism*, Ohio University Press, 1999.

Obee studies the psychological context for Mrs. Plum's embracing of morally bankrupt laws and Karabo's African humanism.

Ruth, Damian, ''Through the Keyhole: Masters and Servants in the Work of Es'kia Mphahlele,'' in *English in Africa*, Vol. 13, No. 2, October 1986, pp. 65–88.

This essay is an examination of the theme of the white employer and black employee in South Africa under apartheid, as it plays out in three of Mphahlele's short stories. In each case, the white employer is blind to the humanity of the employee, while the employee is able to see and to grow.

Woeber, Catherine, and John Read, *Es'kia Mphahlele: A Bibliography*, National English Literary Museum (Grahamstown, South Africa), 1989.

This text is a thorough but unannotated compilation of Mphahlele's publications in journals and books, and of critical articles and reviews of his work.

My Kinsman, Major Molineux

Nathaniel Hawthorne

1832

"My Kinsman, Major Molineux" was first published in the 1832 issue of *The Token*, an annual collection of fiction, poetry, and essays generally bought as a Christmas present. It was one of four stories by Nathaniel Hawthorne in the issue, but like all of the pieces in the magazine, it did not carry the author's name. The story was not a favorite of the author's, and it drew no special attention from readers. It was not included in either of Hawthorne's first two collections of short stories, *Twice-Told Tales* (1842) and *Mosses from an Old Manse* (1846). Finally in 1851 it was published in the collection *The Snow-Image and Other Twice-Told Tales*. The story was not especially popular during Hawthorne's lifetime, being greatly overshadowed by the novels that the writer produced in the 1850s.

In the second half of the twentieth century, however, the story took on a new life. Appreciated for its gentle irony and its glimpse at life in colonial New England, "My Kinsman, Major Molineux" has been widely anthologized, and has become a staple of literature courses at the high school and college levels. The story of a young man from the country who goes to the city to find his relative is typical in many ways of early nineteenth century American literature. "My Kinsman, Major Molineux" is held as an example of the themes, styles, and techniques of the period, and as a sample of the talents of one of America's most important writers.

Author Biography

When Nathaniel Hawthorne was born in Salem, Massachusetts, in 1804, the United States was new and unformed. In New England, where his family lived, the somber influence of the Puritan settlers was still strong, and Hawthorne's life and fiction were always marked by undertones of a brooding pessimism. His father was a sea captain who died in Dutch Guiana when his son was four years old. Nathaniel was raised by his eccentric mother in the homes of various relatives, and he spent most of his time alone.

After graduating from Bowdoin College in 1825, Nathaniel was determined to make his way as a writer. For ten years he lived with his family and devoted himself to reading, and to writing allegorical and historical tales of life in colonial New England. During this time, he changed the spelling of his family name from "Hathorne" to "Hawthorne" in an attempt to distance himself from an ancestor deeply involved in the prosecution of the Salem witch trials of the 1690s. His first publication was a novel, *Fanshawe* (1828), published anonymously at his own expense. It tells the story of a college student who falls in love, gives the young woman up to another man, and dies. As most first novels are, the work was semi-autobiographical and immature. When Hawthorne recognized the failings of his first novel, he bought up all the unsold copies and burned them.

He next turned his energies to short stories, exploring the nature of moral decay. Several were purchased, for a few dollars each, by S. G. Goodrich, the editor of an annual miscellany, *The Token*. The 1832 edition of *The Token* included four Hawthorne stories, including "My Kinsman, Major Molineux," although the author's name did not appear. Goodrich preferred to leave the stories unsigned so his readers would not know how much of his material had come from one writer. Several of the *Token* stories were later gathered into Hawthorne's collection *Twice-Told Tales* (1837), which proudly bore the author's name, but "My Kinsman, Major Molineux" was not published again until 1851, in a collection titled *The Snow Image*.

Hawthorne tried for twelve years to earn a living as a writer before he was forced to find other employment. He married in 1842, at the age of thirty-eight, worked as a surveyor at the Custom House in Salem, and continued to publish short stories. When he lost his job in 1849, he settled down to write what became his greatest work, *The Scarlet Letter* (1850). This well-received novel was soon followed by *The House of the Seven Gables* (1851), *The Snow Image*, and *The Blithedale Romance* (1852). For the rest of his life, Hawthorne was free from worries about money, and he was able to concentrate on writing, traveling, family life, and his friendships with other writers of the day, including Herman Melville and Henry Wadsworth Longfellow. He died in his sleep on May 19, 1864.

Plot Summary

The story opens with the narrator addressing the reader directly, setting the scene. The story takes place in New England "not far from a hundred years ago," that is, approximately 1730. The colonies had not yet become independent of Great Britain, and passions were running high. At nine o'clock on a moonlit evening, a young man of eighteen lands by ferry at an unnamed city. His name is Robin, and, by the look of his clothes and manner, the ferryman can tell he has never been to the city before. Robin carries a "wallet," which is a small knapsack, and a cudgel, or a short club. Paying the ferryman with almost all of his money, he sets off eagerly toward town.

As he walks through the outskirts of the city, it occurs to Robin that he does not know where he is going. Apparently, he is seeking the home of a relative, but none of the houses he passes seems grand enough to be his kinsman's home. He continues walking, and gradually the houses become more elegant. Seeing a well-dressed man on the street, Robin grabs his coat and asks whether the man knows where "my kinsman, Major Molineux" makes his home. As soon as Robin asks this question, the barbers in a nearby shop stop their work, and the other man's expression turns angry. Robin does not notice these reactions, and when the man refuses to help him, Robin attributes the refusal to the man's country manners. Clearly this man is not well-bred enough to deal civilly with a stranger.

As Robin walks on, the smell of tar is in the air. He finds an inn full of people, and asks the crowd whether anyone can direct him to Major Molineux. When they also turn silent and angry, he attributes their reaction to the fact that he has no money. Returning to the streets, he finds them full of gaily dressed people, and looks at every face to see whether he can recognize his relative. A woman in a scarlet petticoat tries to lure Robin into her house, assuring him that she is the Major's housekeeper, but when a watchman passes by she runs into her house and shuts the door. As he wanders, Robin shows himself to be completely unprepared for the city and the city people, although he remains unaware of his naivety.

As he walks the streets with no plan, hoping to somehow stumble upon the Major's house, he grows hungry and desperate. He sees a large hurrying man covered with a cloak, and demands to be told where his kinsman is. This stranger stops, and tells Robin, "Watch here an hour, and Major Molineux will pass by." Taking off his cloak, he reveals his face, which is painted red on one side and black on the other. Robin is astonished, but asks no questions. Instead, he sits on the steps of a church, determined to wait for the Major.

As he waits, Robin is vaguely aware of a murmuring sound coming from far away. No more people pass by, and he grows melancholy thinking of his family back home. Finally another man passes by, and when Robin asks him for information he responds with genuine kindness and concern. He encourages Robin to tell him why he is looking for Major Molineux, a person this man knows something about. Robin explains that he is the second-oldest son in the family. His older brother is following their father in running the farm, and Robin is expected to make his own way in the world. Some time before, Major Molineux visited the farm and showed an interest in the boys, promising to help them one day. Robin has come to the city to begin a career, hoping for the assistance of his wealthy relative.

The kind stranger is intrigued by the story, and sits down with Robin to wait. He agrees that Major Molineux will soon be passing by, and he is eager to see the reunion. The two chat for a short time, and then the murmuring turns into shouting. A crowd of people comes pouring down the street, some playing musical instruments, some carrying torches. A horseman leads them, waving a sword, with his face painted half red and half black. At the end of the procession is a cart bearing Major Molineux. He has been tarred and feathered, probably because he is a Major in the British military in a town that is moving toward independence.

Robin and his kinsman make eye contact, but do not speak. As the Major passes by, Robin seems

Nathaniel Hawthorne

to see every stranger he has encountered this night, and every one is laughing. The laughter is contagious, and Robin finds himself laughing more loudly than any of the others. When the procession has disappeared out of sight, Robin asks the kind stranger to show him back to the ferry. He has decided not to stay in the city after all. The stranger refuses, encouraging him to stay a few days. He believes that Robin will be able to make his own way in the city, even without the help of his kinsman.

Characters

Gentleman

The last person Robin meets during his night of encounters and misdirections is a gentleman of "open, cheerful, and altogether prepossessing" looks, who speaks the only kind words Robin hears in the city. Curious to see how Robin will react to seeing his relative in disgrace, he joins the young man on the church steps, and chats with him while they wait.

Major Molineux

Little is known about Major Molineux, the kinsman whom Robin is seeking. He never speaks a

Media Adaptations

- "My Kinsman, Major Molineux" was recorded on an audiocassette by Jimcin Records in 1983. The story is also included on Volume 7 of Jimcin's audio anthology *Great American Short Stories: A Collection* (1984).

word in the story, and Robin's questions about him are met with stony silence. First cousin to Robin's father, and a man with wealth and no children, he has expressed a desire to help Robin establish himself in a career. Molineux is a major in the British military, serving in what is still a British colony. Although he is tarred and feathered at the end of the story, there is no hint of what he may have done wrong. Even in his disgrace, the narrator describes Molineux as "an elderly man, of large and majestic person, and strong, square features, betokening a steady soul."

Robin Molineux

Robin is the story's protagonist, a young man of nearly eighteen who has come from the country to find his relative, Major Molineux. Robin is the son of a country minister who maintains a small farm. Because the older brother will inherit the farm, Robin hopes Major Molineux can help him find another occupation. This is Robin's first trip to the city, and everything about him—his clothes, his way of speaking, and the club he carries—identifies him as a country boy out of his element. At home, Robin is considered a "shrewd youth," but in the city he misinterprets everything he sees. Time after time he asks people to help him find his relative, and they turn away or mutter angrily. Each time he attributes their unwillingness to help to their own ignorance, rudeness, or low status. Robin never understands, until he sees his relative in tar and feathers, that the people bear a grudge against Molineux. Realizing the depth of his ignorance, Robin decides that his best course of action might be to return home.

Themes

Coming of Age

Many critics have seen "My Kinsman, Major Molineux" as the story of Robin's passage from child to adult. Robin's journey follows the conventional pattern: he travels from his home to a distant land, where he meets strange people and has exciting adventures. Each encounter leaves him a little wiser than he was before. By the end of the story he has learned enough to survive on his own, or, in the words of the kind gentleman, to "rise in the world without the help of [his] kinsman, Major Molineux." Robin himself is not aware of his growth and development, but the gentleman is sure of it. The story, then, opens with the ferryman's view of Robin, as a rough and unready youth, and ends with the gentleman's view of Robin as a "shrewd youth."

Order and Disorder

The biggest problem facing Robin is that he cannot make sense of anything that is happening around him. He cannot find his way around the crooked and meandering streets; the architecture of the houses is "irregular"; the people behave strangely, dress alarmingly and say incomprehensible things; and the quality that he hoped would open doors for him—his relationship with Molineux—has the opposite effect. Where he expected to find order, a pattern for his life, he finds only disorder, chaos.

But it is not just from his point of view that the world is in disorder. The narrator, too, describes a world gone mad, a mob carrying on "in senseless uproar, in frenzied merriment." The chaos is a "contagion" spreading through the crowd, and it reaches even Robin, who can know nothing of the politics that led the mob to their actions. Robin's experiences in the city are contrasted with his memories of home, and of an ordered life centered on "his father's custom" of daily worship. His challenge will be that of all young people who start out on a new life: to find a way to make sense of what is new and strange.

Politics

In the long paragraph that opens the story, Hawthorne's narrator introduces the historical setting: the story takes place in New England in or near the 1730s. Although the Revolutionary War is still some four decades in the future, the people of the Massachusetts Bay Colony have already begun to rebel against British rule. They have driven away or imprisoned four of the previous six appointed governors, and lower-ranking members of the "court party," or those loyal to the King, have also been tormented. Robin's kinsman, Major Molineux, is a part of the British forces maintaining rule in the colony, and it is in this role that he is tarred, feathered, and paraded through the town.

Writing in the early 1830s, Hawthorne was grateful for the results of the Revolution, but as John P. McWilliams, Jr., has explained in an article for *Studies in Romanticism*, he was not sympathetic to the kind of mob mentality that could inflict cruelty on individual loyalists. There is no mention in the story of any particular wrongs committed by Molineux. His only crime seems to be that of fulfilling his duty at a time of "temporary inflammation of the popular mind."

City versus Country

One of the most frequently seen themes in literature, particularly in the literature of the United States during the eighteenth and nineteenth centuries, is the conflict between the city and the country. Stories of young men from the city venturing out into the country and being confounded by the wilderness are as common as stories presenting the situation found in "My Kinsman, Major Molineux," a young man from the country being overwhelmed by his first trip to the big city. Everything that happens to Robin happens because he is in a new place, because he does not know how to read the signs.

Robin is so "evidently country-bred," the ferryman can tell it just by looking at him, and can tell that Robin has never been to town before. For one thing, Robin carries a club, which might be useful for confronting animals in the wilderness but is hardly the appropriate tool to have at hand in the city. Though he thinks of himself as "shrewd," Robin in fact does not understand anything he sees or hears, and just as a person from the city might become lost and confused on a winding path through the woods, Robin becomes "entangled in a succession of crooked and narrow streets." Looking into the church, in many ways the center of the town, he feels "a sensation of loneliness stronger than he had ever felt in the remotest depths of his native woods." His instinct is to go back home, feeling "weary of a town life."

Topics for Further Study

- Investigate the political climate in the American colonies during the first half of the eighteenth century. When did the colonists start to talk and write publicly about seeking independence? How common were minor acts of rebellion like that committed against Major Molineux?

- Find one or two descriptions of medieval religious pageants. How is the procession in the story like these pageants? What is the significance of the similarity?

- Research the methods and materials used in tarring and feathering. Is the punishment physically harmful, or primarily humiliating? Where and when has it been used?

- Make a list of stories in which a young man from the country comes to the city on a quest. How is this story like and unlike the others? In how many of the stories does the young man find what he has come for?

Style

Irony

The term "irony" refers to a difference between appearance and reality, or between what someone says is true and what is actually true. The narrator in this story is being ironic when he continually refers to Robin as a "shrewd youth." Robin certainly believes himself to be shrewd, and tells the kind gentleman that he has a reputation at home for shrewdness, but the fact remains that Robin is remarkably *not* perceptive or intuitive. For example, when Robin meets his first town-dweller and asks about his kinsman, the man answers him rudely, and even threatens him. Robin ponders this response for a moment, and then, "being a shrewd youth," he guesses wrongly that the man must be a newcomer who is unacquainted with Molineux. As Robin passes through town he misinterprets everything he sees and hears, and the narrator greets every misinterpretation with an ironic comment about Robin's shrewdness.

The effect created by this irony is to add light humor. The narrator and the reader know more than Robin does, and poke fun at him for his inability to see what is before him. But the mocking is gentle. Robin is not stupid, or someone to despise because of his own inflated sense of self. Instead, the quiet irony demonstrates that Robin is a young man who might rightfully have expected to do well in the city, but who finds himself in over his head.

Setting

A story's setting is the background against which the action occurs, and is usually thought of as the time and place. In "My Kinsman, Major Molineux," the narrator outlines the setting in the opening chapter. The story takes place "not far from a hundred years ago," or around the late 1720s or early 1730s, in the Massachusetts Bay Colony, which encompassed most of what is today Massachusetts and New Hampshire. During that time, rural families like Robin's were relatively unaffected by politics, but colonists in the cities were beginning to rebel against British control. It would be four decades before the American Revolutionary War would begin, but minor acts of rebellion and civil disobedience, such as the tarring and feathering of Major Molineux, had begun to break out.

Romanticism

Hawthorne is generally considered one of the first and greatest writers of the romantic period in American literature, and "My Kinsman, Major Molineux" exhibits some of the characteristics of romanticism that Hawthorne would develop further in his novels. Romanticism was a movement in the eighteenth and nineteenth centuries away from neoclassicism, the strictly formal kinds of literature and art that attempted to echo classical Greek and Roman cultures. In American fiction, romantic writing reflected the bursting confidence and mystery surrounding the growth of a new nation.

"My Kinsman, Major Molineux" demonstrates several elements of romanticism. European romantic writers often set their stories in medieval Europe, peopled with knights and kings, but Hawthorne and others found the same inspiration in the historical period before American Independence. The dreamlike atmosphere of the story, the somber tone, and the fact that the events occur in dim light are also romantic elements. Finally, the focus on Robin and his psychological state, rather than on action and physical conflict, was a new development of the romantic period.

Allegory

An allegory is a story in which the characters and actions can be thought of as standing for larger issues and ideas. Certain characters in an allegory might stand for abstract qualities, as in the story of the Grasshopper and the Ant in which one character stands for laziness and the other for hard work. In an article in *Sewanee Review*, Q. D. Leavis suggests that "My Kinsman, Major Molineux" should be read as an allegory, and that a proper subtitle for the story would be "America Comes of Age." According to her reading, Robin personifies "the young America," brought to the point of deciding how to set a course for the future. When Robin joins in the laughter at his uncle's expense, he represents America realizing that it must cast off British influence and strike out on its own.

Historical Context

The Romance and the Tale

Writing "My Kinsman, Major Molineux" in the late 1820s or early 1830s, Hawthorne looked primarily to European writers for his models. For readers and writers of the nineteenth century, the forms of writing called "the novel" and "the romance" were distinct in style and in theme. Hawthorne found that most readers and critics favored the novel, but that the romance suited his own artistic temperament better.

Romance did not have the meaning it came to have in the late twentieth century: a story mainly concerned with romantic love between a beautiful heroine and a dashing, heroic man. Instead, the word originally applied to the languages derived from Latin (the Romance languages), including Spanish, French, and Italian. The term was later applied to stories written in French, and later still to a specific type of French story dealing with knights and castles and adventures. Romances were popular in Europe through the nineteenth century, and often used medieval settings, royalty, and chivalry, and fantastic spirits and dragons.

For Hawthorne and others, the term *Romance* was used to distinguish more imaginative literature from the novel, which was considered more realistic. Hawthorne frequently wrote about these terms,

Compare & Contrast

- **1828:** Andrew Jackson is elected president. His emphasis on the rights and responsibilities of the common man in governing a democratic nation help create an era of enthusiastic patriotism.

   1990s: After decades of well-publicized scandals involving top government officials, public interest in national affairs is weak.

- **1830s and 1840s:** Handsomely printed and bound annual collections of essays, short stories, and poems are popular Christmas gifts in England and the United States. They provide a strong market for short fiction. Although most pieces are published anonymously, the annuals enable several important writers, including Hawthorne, to establish a reputation with publishers.

   1990s: Short fiction is published in popular and literary magazines, but does not sell as well in book form as the novel. Fiction writers frequently gain practice by writing short fiction, but build an audience through the publication of novels.

- **1700s:** With no motorized vehicles and no paved roads, travel from country to town is slow. It has taken Robin five days to come from one part of the Massachusetts Bay Colony to another, a distance of no more than one hundred ninety miles.

   1990s: A car can cross Massachusetts in about three hours, traveling at normal highway speeds. The Concorde airliner travels faster than the speed of sound.

- **1700s:** Boston is the largest settlement in New England, and is probably the town where Molineux lives. In 1790, the earliest year for which records are available, the population is 18,320.

   1830: Boston is the largest city in New England. Its population is 61,392.

   1990: Boston is still the largest city in New England. Its population is 574,283.

---

especially in the prefaces to his longer works. In the preface to *The House of the Seven Gables*, he explained the difference as he saw it: "When a writer calls his work a Romance, it need hardly be observed that he wishes to claim a certain latitude, both as to its fashion and material, which he would not have felt himself entitled to assume, had he professed to be writing a Novel." The writer of romance, if he wished, might "manage his atmospherical medium as to bring out or mellow the lights and deepen and enrich the shadows of the pictures." It is in this spirit that Hawthorne set many of his tales, including "My Kinsman, Major Molineux," in darkness, twilight, and shadow.

Two difficulties presented themselves to the American writer of romance in the early part of the nineteenth century: there was little demand for this kind of imaginative literature, and America had no medieval past and no royalty to establish the proper atmosphere. This lack of demand caused reviewer Benjamin in 1836 to predict that if Hawthorne could collect his magazine stories into a book he could have a success "certainly in England, perhaps in this country." Hawthorne commented throughout his life that he felt burdened by the difficulty of creating romantic fiction in a country that had not yet developed a taste for it.

He dealt with the problem of having no medieval past by substituting the best American equivalent: the period from the original Puritan settlement to the time just before the Revolutionary War. Here he found heroes and enemies, grand issues and ideas. In the period just after Andrew Jackson was elected president of the United States, the country was energetically patriotic and celebratory. The decades before the Revolution, the historical setting of "My Kinsman, Major Molineux," were far enough in the past to have acquired the patina of legend and mystery. The story's narrator establishes the setting in the first paragraph, and then begins the second with a line straight out of a medieval tale: "It was near nine o'clock of a moonlight evening, when a boat crossed the ferry with a single passenger." Moonlight, Hawthorne writes in the "Custom House" section of *The Scarlet Letter*, "is a medium most suitable for a romance-writer to get acquainted with his illusive guests."

Roughly equivalent to the terms *romance* and *novel* as used to distinguish two types of long fiction are the terms *tale* and *short story*, used to distinguish two ways of thinking about short fiction. Tales are less bound by constraints of realism than are short stories. Hawthorne thought of his book-length works, including *The Scarlet Letter* and *The Blithedale Romance* as romances. His shorter works were gathered into collections with titles including *Twice-Told Tales* and *Snow-Image, and Other Twice-Told Tales*. For Hawthorne, the terms were used carefully, to mark out what he describes in *The Scarlet Letter* as a "neutral territory, somewhere between the real world and fairy land, where the Actual and the Imaginary may meet, and each imbue itself with the nature of the other."

Critical Overview

"My Kinsman, Major Molineux" was first published in the 1832 edition of *The Token*, an annual book of essays, poetry, and short fiction to which Hawthorne contributed several pieces over the years. The story was published anonymously, and it was not until 1836, when journalist Park Benjamin wrote a review of that year's *Token*, that the reading public came to know Hawthorne's name. Having read "a sufficient number of his pieces to make the reputation of a dozen of our Yankee scribblers," he praises Hawthorne's style, and his modesty in remaining anonymous. "If Mr. Hawthorne would but collect his various tales and essays into one volume," Benjamin notes, "we can assure him that their success would be brilliant—certainly in England, perhaps in this country." Hawthorne did issue a collection the next year, and it did sell well, but it did not include "My Kinsman, Major Molineux." The story did not appear again until 1851, in the collection *Snow-Image*.

When *Snow-Image* appeared in 1851, it was quickly overshadowed by Hawthorne's great novel, *The Scarlet Letter*, published in the same year. By this time, Hawthorne was widely recognized as an important writer, both in the United States and in England, as Benjamin had predicted. Edgar Allan Poe and Herman Melville had reviewed his stories with approval. In what may be the first published overview of Hawthorne's work, Henry T. Tuckerman describes the stories in terms that seem especially appropriate for "My Kinsman, Major Molineux": "He always takes us below the surface and beyond the material; his most inartificial stories are eminently suggestive; he makes us breathe the air of contemplation, and turns our eyes inward. It is as if we went forth, in a dream." Tuckerman did not mention "My Kinsman, Major Molineux" specifically in his article, nor did Henry James in his 1879 book-length study of Hawthorne.

In an article published in 1957 in *Nineteenth-Century Fiction*, Seymour Gross observes, "It is one of the peculiarities of the study of American literature that, despite the abundance of critical effort expended on Hawthorne's fiction, what is perhaps his most powerful story, "My Kinsman, Major Molineux," has been until only recently all but completely ignored." At the time, Gross was unable to identify a single anthology of American literature or of short stories that included "My Kinsman." But the 1950s saw the publication of several critical articles on the story, and although the number of publications has tapered off in the intervening decades, the story continues to be popular.

Most twentieth-century critics have read the story as a psychological examination of Robin, with the historical setting as mere background. Several have used Freudian psychology to examine Robin's search for a father figure, or for independence. In a 1959 article in *Criticism* tellingly titled "Robin Molineux on the Analyst's Couch," Roy Harvey Pearce explains that Robin gains freedom only by participating in the guilty act of mocking his father figure. Roy R. Male, in *Hawthorne's Tragic Vision* (1957), demonstrates that each man Robin meets in town is a distorted father-figure. He draws on "the Freudian theory of dream interpretation, which asserts that visions of the father figure may commonly be split into two or more images."

Other critics have read the story as primarily concerning history. For some, it is a historical allegory. Q. D. Leavis, in a 1951 article for *Sewanee Review*, proposes "America Comes of Age" as a suitable subtitle for the story, and suggests that the story is easiest to understand as a "poetic parable in dramatic form." In her reading, Robin represents young America, coming to adulthood by casting off dependence on the authority figure Molineux/England. John P. McWilliams, Jr., agrees that history is at the center of the story, but disagrees with Leavis about the theme. He argues in a 1976 article in *Studies in Romanticism* that Robin does not in fact "come of age," nor show any signs of learning. McWilliams suggests that Hawthorne appreciated Independence but did not fully approve of all the means used to achieve it. Robin might stand for "those readers who, even when confronted with the violence and demagoguery of the Revolution, prove unwilling or unable to recognize them."

Criticism

Cynthia Bily

Bily has a master's degree in English literature and has written for a variety of educational publishers. In the following essay, she discusses Hawthorne's use of imagery of light and darkness.

Nathaniel Hawthorne's short story "My Kinsman, Major Molineux" was one of his earliest publications, appearing anonymously in the 1832 edition of *The Token*. It waited more than one hundred years to gain its current position as one of the author's most widely anthologized and studied short stories, although it is built on many of the same themes and techniques as Hawthorne's better-known stories and novels. Images of light and darkness, for example, are used in this story to illuminate (pun intended) the theme, just as these images provide insight to "Young Goodman Brown," "The Birthmark," and other stories.

A central question for readers of "My Kinsman, Major Molineux" has been whether or not Robin, the "shrewd youth," actually learns anything from his experiences in town and, if so, what might that new knowledge be. Seymour Gross is among those who see the story as one of growth and maturity. In an article for *Nineteenth-Century Fiction*, he points out Hawthorne's "masterly manipulation of lights and darks" in this story and in others. He finds that "the light-dark device is more significant in this story because, where in the other stories it is used as a kind of thematic signpost, here the motif is the theme itself: the journey from dark innocence to painfully illuminated knowledge." But John P. McWilliams, Jr., is one of several critics who claim that "Hawthorne never confirms that Robin has changed or learned anything.... The ending of the tale, evidence of Robin's maturing to so many critics, can more plausibly be regarded as evidence of his persistent naiveté."

Has Robin learned and grown during his ordeal? Has he, as Gross claims, moved from darkness to light? Or has he remained in darkness, as McWilliams believes? I believe the truth is closer to McWilliams' reading than to Gross'. Robin has learned something, but he has learned to accept a falsehood. Educated under an artificial light, he has accepted an artificial truth.

When Robin Molineux steps off the ferry at the end of a five-day journey from his country home to the city, it is "near nine o'clock of a moonlight evening." The moon is bright enough to get around by, apparently, since Robin carries no light source with him and intends to find his way through town. The ferryman carries "a lantern, by the aid of which, and the newly risen moon, he took a very accurate survey" of Robin. Leaving the landing and approaching the town, Robin examines the first buildings he sees and he, too, makes an accurate survey by moonlight: "yonder old house, where the moonlight enters at the broken casement" cannot be his relative's house, for Molineux is a man of means and position. To this point, Robin's judgment is sound, with the notable exception that he did not think to ask the ferryman for directions. He has not made any missteps yet.

But something peculiar happens the first time Robin approaches a man to ask for help. As Gross points out, Robin sees the man of two successive hems from a small distance, and reaches him "just when the light from the open door and windows of a barber's shop fell upon both their figures." Now Robin makes his first mistake—not in asking about the Major, which is a reasonable thing for him to do, but in misinterpreting the man's refusal to help him as a sign of the man's backwardness. In the moonlight, Robin makes reasonable guesses, but in his first encounter under city lights he does not. Will the pattern hold?

Wandering further, Robin becomes "entangled in a succession of crooked and narrow streets." Above the rooftops "the masts of vessels pierced the moonlight" and Robin is able to read street signs and learn that he is near the business district. There is no reason to think that his efforts at reading street signs are misplaced. But soon he enters the brightly lit tavern, and again he misjudges. The tavern owner greets him courteously, with a low bow, and Robin concludes, "The man sees a family likeness!" When Robin mentions the Major's name,

What Do I Read Next?

- "Young Goodman Brown" (1835) is another Hawthorne short story of a young man on a journey. Brown leaves his wife and sets out through the forest, where he stumbles upon a witches' coven and finds his wife among them. He returns to Salem a gloomy man who has lost his faith in the goodness of humans.

- Hawthorne's "The Birthmark" (1843) is an allegorical tale in which a scientist marries a woman who is perfectly beautiful except for a tiny birthmark on her cheek. Determined to remove the mark, the scientist tries several methods, finally finding a potion that erases the birthmark and kills his wife.

- *The Scarlet Letter* (1850) is Hawthorne's great novel about the suffocating influence of Puritanism. Hester Prynne is made to wear a scarlet letter "A" on her breast as punishment for adultery, while her lover keeps his sin a secret and suffers the torment of guilt.

- "Bartleby, the Scrivener" (1853) is Herman Melville's tale of a Wall Street attorney who cannot establish a connection with his new scribe. The young employee answers every request with "I should prefer not to."

- *Great Expectations* (1860–61) is Charles Dickens' novel of the village boy Pip who goes to the city with the expectation of finding wealth and love.

- Henry David Thoreau's "Civil Disobedience" (1849) is an essay that asserts "that government is best which governs least." It is an individual's responsibility, Thoreau explains, to refuse to obey unjust laws.

- Mason Weems's *History of the Life, Death, Virtues and Exploits of George Washington* (1800) is a fictionalized history of the Revolutionary period, popular in the nineteenth century and read by Hawthorne. The 1806 edition contains the first account of Washington and the cherry tree.

- *Nathaniel Hawthorne: A Critical Biography* (1949), by Mark Van Doren, is a biography that frankly reveals the affection the author feels for Hawthorne, yet still presents an even-handed criticism of Hawthorne's work.

"there was a sudden and general movement in the room, which Robin interpreted as expressing the eagerness of each individual to become his guide." But things are not what they seem to be.

As Robin moves through town, he encounters more people in lighted places. By "the light of the moon, and the lamps from the numerous shop-windows" he sees well-dressed figures promenading on the streets. Turning down a side street, he comes to a row of houses, and "the moonlight fell upon no passenger along the whole extent," but he sees a woman's garment within a lighted entryway. When she steps "forth into the moonlight" Robin is able to see her for who she is. She would like to draw him into her lighted house, but Robin knows to avoid that temptation. Interestingly, Robin encounters a man with a painted face as he is passing through the shade of the church steeple. Neither in the light of the tavern nor in the shade of the steeple does Robin learn anything from this man, but when he steps "back into the moonlight" Robin learns that his relative will pass by in an hour.

Robin passes the next hour alone. First he examines the street, "and the moon, creating, like the imaginative power, a beautiful strangeness in familiar objects, gave something of romance to a scene that might not have possessed it in the light of day." After a while, Robin climbs to a window frame and looks into the church, where "the moonbeams came trembling in, and fell down upon the deserted pews, and extended along the quiet aisles. A fainter yet more awful radiance was hovering around the pulpit, and one solitary ray had dared to rest upon the open page of the great Bible." Hawthorne writes elsewhere of the imaginative powers of moonlight, as in the "Custom House" section of *The Scarlet Letter*. For Hawthorne, imagination is not the same thing as untruth. Instead, it can be the key to a greater truth. In Robin's case, it takes him home.

Under the influence of the unadulterated moonlight, Robin dreams of his family back in the country. He imagines the great tree where his father conducts worship services "at the going down of the summer sun . . . holding the Scriptures in the golden light that fell from the western clouds." Back home, God was worshiped in the open air, in natural light, but Robin can't go home again.

Now he meets the last stranger, the one who will treat him kindly. Significantly, he first becomes aware of this man by "the sound of footsteps along the opposite pavement." He cries out to the man, and the man responds "in a tone of real kindness." The light is dim, the shadows are oblique, and Robin must trust his ears instead of his eyes. By doing so, he wins the only friend he will find this night.

Now the procession begins, and it brings its own light. "A redder light disturbed the moonbeams" as torches pass by, "concealing, by their glare, whatever object they illuminated." As the painted man passes Robin and releases him from his gaze, there are more torches "close at hand; but the unsteady brightness of the latter formed a veil which he could not penetrate." Soon, "traces of a human form appeared at intervals, and then melted into the vivid light." Finally comes the sight Robin was meant to see: "There the torches blazed the brightest, there the moon shone out like day, and there, in tar-and-feathery dignity, sat his kinsman, Major Molineux!"

Robin is at a crossroads. What will he see? The torches compete with the moonlight as both shine on Molineux; there is a wrong way and a right way to look at him. Under the influence of the torches and the torchbearers, Robin could join in the "bewildering excitement" and contribute his "shout of laughter" to the "senseless uproar." Or he could see what the narrator sees, unaffected by the crowd: "an elderly man, of large and majestic person," with "a head grown gray in honor." He could see that he is part of a "frenzied merriment, trampling all on an old man's heart." We do not know what the kind gentleman sees, nor whether he joins in the laughter. But we know that Robin falls to the "contagion" of merriment.

> "Hawthorne was attracted to the idea that things seen by artificial light (and by twilight, another repeated theme of Hawthorne's) are not to be trusted."

What has Robin learned? If he has learned that his relative deserves pain and humiliation, he has learned a cruel untruth. Molineux has been nothing but kind to Robin, a relative whom he barely knows. Robin knows nothing of the political situation that brought Molineux to such a bad end. "I have at last met my kinsman," Robin says, but in fact he knows nothing about the man. The vision of the prisoner on the cart amid the "unsteady brightness" of the torches is not a vision to be trusted.

Hawthorne was attracted to the idea that things seen by artificial light (and by twilight, another repeated theme of Hawthorne's) are not to be trusted. In "The Birthmark," Aylmer's gaze is drawn to Georgiana's birthmark under these conditions. "With the morning twilight Aylmer opened his eyes upon his wife's face and recognized the symbol of imperfection; and when they sat together at the evening hearth his eyes wandered stealthily to her cheek, and beheld, flickering with the blaze of the wood fire, the spectral hand that wrote mortality where he would fain have worshipped." Not until the end of the story, when he has administered the potion that will soon kill her, does Aylmer look at his wife in full light: "He drew aside the window curtain and suffered the light of natural day to fall into the room and rest upon her cheek." Under artificial light the birthmark appears large and important; under natural light, Aylmer sees how foolish he has been, and what damage he has caused.

In "Young Goodman Brown," the title character also sees strange things that trouble him. As he passes through the woods trying to escape the devil, he looks up to pray. Suddenly the available natural light is blotted out: "a cloud, though no wind was stirring, hurried across the zenith and the brightening stars." Soon the only light is that cast by "four blazing pines, their tops aflame, their stems untouched, like candles at an evening meeting." Goodman Brown is not sure he should trust his own eyes as he gazes around at the people before him: "Either the sudden gleams of light flashing over the obscure field bedazzled Goodman Brown, or he recognized a score of the church members."

Robin, like young Goodman Brown, has been "bedazzled" by what the firelight has shown him; like Brown, he makes the mistake of trusting what he has seen. When the procession has passed by, Robin is ready to return home. He knows, or thinks he does, what his uncle really is, and he is "weary of a town life." The gentleman, however, knows that reality is more complicated than Robin thinks. He refuses to escort Robin back to the ferry, "not tonight at least," and encourages him to stay a few more days, to see what he can learn in the light.

A research study conducted in 1999 seemed to demonstrate that schoolchildren score higher on standardized tests when they are sitting in natural rather than artificial light. While Hawthorne cannot have anticipated electricity and fluorescent lighting, he did have a sense that to learn the truth about something, people need to examine it in the light of day.

Source: Cynthia Bily, in an essay for *Short Stories for Students*, Gale Group, 2001.

John Russell

In the following essay, Russell looks at Hawthorne's use of allegory within "My Kinsman, Major Molineux."

At five-year intervals, beginning in 1954, Professor Roy Harvey Pearce has encouraged Hawthorne critics to descend with the writer into history rather than pull away and judge his tales in psychological contexts where history is not given first importance. He has brought "My Kinsman, Major Molineux" forward as his chief example because of a recent, almost exclusive concentration on Robin, his dream-experience, and the initiation rites the boy apparently goes through. One of the contributors to that criticism, Seymour Gross, later summed it up rather interestingly by referring to an *American Imago* article written by a psychiatrist. This specialist felt that Robin at the end of the story was about to regress—to return to his woods—and as Gross remarks, "The psychiatrist stands alone; in the dozen or so other interpretations of the story . . . all agree that some *rite de passage* has been effected." This is a temperate way of disagreeing, and ought to be, for readers will remember that Hawthorne left the outcome debatable. Robin did express a wish to go home, but Hawthorne let the last words lie with the old gentleman who seemed to be acting as the boy's mentor. "Some few days hence, if you wish it," the man had said, "I will speed you on your journey. Or, if you prefer to remain with us, perhaps . . . you may rise in the world without the help of your kinsman, Major Molineux." The "if's" and "or's" show that neither regression nor psychological growth can be proved.

Proof is not necessary to criticism, and it is certainly true that the figure of young Robin is tremendously arresting. But the unresolved ending and other features of the story make me feel that its elemental quality owes much more to Hawthorne's art than to Robin's depth, and that Pearce's corrective is valid: the story ought to be looked at more intently as the illumination of an historical phenomenon.

Everyone agrees that the narrative, set firmly in pre-revolutionary days, has political relevance—that the rebellion which ousts Major Molineux is a "type" of the American Revolution—but vagueness over the allegory after that has actually preempted much psychological criticism of the tale. Gross felt, for instance, that "If the sole explanation for the action is made in terms of the historical incident . . . then the great bulk of the tale, Robin's quest, remains sheer Gothic mystification." Not, however, if the first paragraph is kept carefully in mind; and memorable as the opening is, it requires partial quotation because of some details in the middle:

> After the kings of Great Britain had assumed the right of appointing the colonial governors, the measures of the latter seldom met with the ready and general approbation which had been paid to those of their predecessors, under the original charters. . . . The annals of Massachusetts Bay will inform us, that of six governors in the space of about forty years from the surrender of the old charter, under James II, two were imprisoned by a popular insurrection; a third, as Hutchinson inclines to believe, was driven from the province by the whizzing of a musket-ball; a fourth, in the opinion of the same historian, was hastened to his grave by continual bickerings with the House of Representatives; and the remaining two, as well as their successors, till the Revolution, were favored with few and brief intervals of peaceful sway. The inferior members of the court party, in times of high political excitement, led scarcely a more desirable

life. These remarks may serve as a preface to the following adventures, which chanced upon a summer night, not far from a hundred years ago.

Why we should tend to "go vague," after a start as precise as this, happens I think because we are Americans and, identifying ourselves with Robin as we do, and with our own national origins, we tend to start off by assuming that Robin represents young America. More than one critic has done this, and I would hazard a guess that tens or hundreds of students have done it when asked in classrooms what Robin represents. If the answer that comes, "Young America," is not qualified, the fatal step will have been taken, and readers will have forced themselves into a psychological or mythic rather than historical interpretation of the allegory.

The easiest way to see why Robin cannot represent young America in general is to observe that all his *antagonists* perform this representation. Singly or in groups as they appear—and Hawthorne provides a great variety—they are a rough-and-ready lot, reeking of self-sufficiency and, though menial or of otherwise questionable breeding, obviously are not to be trifled with where their independence is concerned. The early description of the occupants of the tavern is one of the best places to catch overtones of the recent and muscular self-sufficiency of the colonies:

> ... the larger part ... appeared to be mariners. ... Three or four little groups were draining as many bowls of punch, which the West India trade had long since made a familiar drink in the colony. Others ... had the appearance of men who lived by regular and laborious handicraft. ... [Some] had gotten themselves into the darkest corner of the room, and heedless of the Nicotian atmosphere, were supping on the bread of their own ovens, and the bacon cured in their own chimney smoke.

The emphases here, on staples conspicuously "their own," and on the rum and tobacco, seem unmistakably to point out a raw but capable America. And it is *against* these types that Robin brushes. He is clearly not of them and must signify something else—why this has not been emphasized seems to involve an elementary problem in reading allegory. For it is invariably concluded that because Robin is young, Hawthorne must be writing about youth in some definite respect. Yet it would take a rather infertile allegorist to devise a tale in which a young man represents youth. Almost in deference to Hawthorne, a reader ought not to stumble in haste and make a misidentification: I think it is made in fact because of the rush to bypass the historical *nature* of the story.

> "Major Molineux himself remains the symbol of British rule, of the efficacy of the crown. Thinking of Robin as the composite Old Whig-Tory, we can think of Molineux's name as the prerogative that ought to carry sway, from the newcomer's point of view."

The question hanging now is, of course: What *does* Robin represent? The answer will be abrupt when it comes, yet there may be a way of gliding into it. This would involve deciding how readers actually feel toward the character Robin. Arresting as he is, I think readers are not essentially feeling *with* Robin and groping along as bewildered as he; rather, I feel they are like spectators at tragedy whose urgent question is not "What is going on here?" but rather, "Why don't you *see*?" This I feel to be true even after the central transition, when, it will be remembered, Robin has asked for his kinsman Major Molineux and been rebuffed by a watchman and an elderly citizen, tricked by a courtesan, and turned out of doors by an innkeeper. "He now roamed desperately, and at random, through the town, almost ready to believe that a spell was on him. ..." Even here, where commentators come down hard for a terrifying "dark night of the soul," I believe the reader is not so much caught up in this and is still saying, "Why don't you see that when you mention the Major's name they are turning on you?"

If this premise about the reader's attitude is valid—if one tends to feel like a spectator wishing a fatal obtuseness would be dispelled for the poor benighted "shrewd youth"—it becomes easier to say that in this allegory, specifically, Robin represents the six governors of Massachusetts Bay Colony between the years 1686 and 1729.

Perhaps, since the statement may seem startling or even high-handed in its limitation, I ought to say what indication in the text at least caused the first step to be taken toward this interpretation. It was the watchman saying to Robin, "'Home, or we'll set you in the stocks by peep of day!'" Earlier, the old citizen who made such a to-do about his "authority" had also threatened Robin with the stocks, and now Hawthorne underscored the point: "'This is the second hint of the kind,' thought Robin. 'I wish they would end my difficulties, by setting me there to-night.'" Out of the opening paragraph about the governors came the echo—"two were imprisoned"—and a connection seemed intended.

Now it is interesting that this country youth, "one of whose names was Robin," has six encounters during this telescoped evening, and asks of six people the haunting question as to the whereabouts of "my kinsman, Major Molineux." And it does turn out that the six encounters correspond to the fates of those royal appointees, the governors Hawthorne read about in Thomas Hutchinson's history. (Though none of them had a Robin to his name, Hutchinson does employ the phrase "round robin.") For instance, one, according to that author, "was driven from the province by the whizzing of a musket-ball." Military violence lowers here—or the next thing to it. And so, when Robin accosts the muffled-up man with the red and black face, demanding to hear of his kinsman, the man comes back with, "Let me pass, I say, or I'll strike you to the earth!" And then he reveals his features, which Hawthorne explains at the climax: "his fierce and variegated countenance, appeared like war personified; the red of one cheek was an emblem of fire and sword; the blackness of the other betokened the mourning that attends them."

The most insidious of Robin's encounters are the two that correspond with the "brief intervals of peaceful sway" accorded two of the six governors. For the poignant problem of the loyalists as a whole—which, I suppose, may be what the story is finally describing—was that none could profit by the experience of others before them. Consistently we run across, in Thomas Hutchinson, the description of the reception given by the Massachusetts Bay colonists to each new governor after these colonists had hounded out the preceding one. The descriptions are all the same. The story's widest application seems at last the sad one, showing that human beings, especially when persuaded they are in legitimate circumstances, cannot read the handwriting on the wall no matter how imposing and fresh it may be. "Mr. Dudley was received with ceremony and marks of respect...." "Mr. Burnet was received with unusual pomp." Twenty pages on: "The governor's friends observed the effect the controversy [with the House of Representatives] had upon his spirits. In a few days, he fell sick of a fever and died at Boston...." "The beginning of an administration in the colonies is generally calm and without ruffle."

Now consider Robin's reception at the inn, and notice Hawthorne's care with language in the allegory:

... he was accosted by the innkeeper, a little man in a stained apron, who had come to pay his professional welcome to the stranger....

"From the country, I presume, sir?" said he, with a profound bow. "Beg leave to congratulate you on your arrival, and trust you intend a long stay with us. Fine town here, sir, beautiful buildings, and much that may interest a stranger. May I hope for the honor of your commands in respect to supper?"

Small wonder that Robin's response is, "The man sees a family likeness! the rogue has guessed that I am related to the major!"—shortly after which he is just about hurled out on his ear.

Of the other brief interval of peaceful sway, that with the prostitute, we may perhaps say that she also had profit in mind and let it go at that, for Hawthorne seems to have outdistanced his mentor Hutchinson here. That is, the historian gives only a few hints that the aristocratic governors or other members of the king's party lived more loosely than the new world Puritanical stock. But a touch of culpability is brought in by Hawthorne in this way. One may ponder also the phenomenon that mistresses and courtesans so often prove comforting to leaders whose empires are tottering—from Mark Antony to Mussolini.

By this time other counters in the allegory may have already seemed to fall in place. Major Molineux himself remains the symbol of British rule, of the efficacy of the crown. Thinking of Robin as the composite Old Whig-Tory, we can think of Molineux's name as the prerogative that ought to carry sway, from the newcomer's point of view. (Hutchinson speaks frequently of "prerogative men" in the various governors' entourages at Massachusetts Bay, and Robin has this sort of confidence in his uncle's name.) It also should be seen that the "country" Robin is from—significantly separated by water from the New England town—is England, and that Robin is not symbolic of a Yankee bumpkin. The excellence of Hawthorne's choice here is that the supposedly shrewd English gentry are found naïve in this crucial political respect. And so an assertive, sturdy, but finally dim *juvenile* is chosen to represent royalists; rather than youthfulness itself, it is the special youthful qualities—overconfidence, obstinacy, obtuseness—that go into the making of Robin. Think of the faith he has in his cudgel. Hutchinson describes the second governor, Sir William Phips, in a Robin-like action in this regard. Phips got cantankerous when a certain Captain Short seemed insubordinate: "and meeting Captain Short in the street, warm words passed, and at length the governor made use of his cane and broke Short's head."

That the cudgel was "formed of an oak sapling" from his native woods shows why Robin has faith in it. Woods represent England in the allegory. They come into play several times, the most interesting being in connection with the last of Robin's six encounters, at which point Hawthorne delivers his stroke of genius.

The allegory has not been diagrammatic; the fates of the governors have not been paraded in order. It does happen, though, that the last governor, Burnet the bishop's son, was the one "hastened to his grave by continual bickerings with the House of Representatives." Hawthorne allegorizes this controversy in a novel way by using in Robin's last encounter a house instead of a man. The episode occurs during the nightmare sequence when Robin pauses by a church across the street from a great house with balcony and imposing pillars. "Perhaps this is the very house I have been seeking," he thinks. He falls into a reverie now, in which the peaceful religious ways of his home are contrasted with the austere, grave-ringed New England church. "Am I here, or there?" he cries, coming out of the reverie and trying to fix his eyes on the house across the way:

> But still his mind kept vibrating between fancy and reality; by turns, the pillars of the balcony lengthened into the tall, bare stems of pines, dwindled down to human figures, settled again into their true shape and size, and then commenced a new succession of changes. . . . A deeper sleep wrestled with and nearly overcame him, but fled at the sound of footsteps along the opposite pavement.

These are the footsteps of the kindly man who gives Robin a civil answer to his sixth and last enquiry about Major Molineux, and who then volunteers to wait with him for the Major's expected "arrival." He is the voice of reason and moderation, as opposed to that wild ringleader with the red and black face; he is also the one who reminds Robin, "You must not expect all the stillness of your native woods here in our streets," and then asks him, "May not a man have several voices, Robin, as well as two complexions?"

This ameliorating figure seems placed here to soften the jars, not only of insurrection madness, but even of the bickering of hot legislators—who make the house rock before Robin's eyes between loyalty ("the tall, bare stems of pines" indicate this) and the rights of man (the columns dwindle to human figures). As for the equation between the pines and loyalty, the native-forest symbolism would be enough to warrant it. It is worth adding, though—perhaps we have an insight here to Hawthorne's working methods—that Hutchinson actually reported one governor's fight with the house over the cutting of pine trees in Maine, the governor maintaining these were "his majesty's" trees, "reserved by the royal charter . . . for the royal navy."

Robin's mentor thus could foreshadow genuinely reasonable debate and the call for redress of grievances. Though Hawthorne's sympathies in the story are for the sadly unrooted Tory mind, he is of course partial to the final revolution and evolution of America. As Daniel Hoffman maintains, writing of this late-found friend of Robin, "The implication is that the forces of Order and Stability do in the end prove stronger than those of Destruction and Misrule which dethrone them."

We are, however, left in this tale with the terrible impression of the foaming Major Molineux, tarred and feathered. Hawthorne's famous ambiguity is much in evidence at the end. Even this, to my mind, becomes more richly appropriate when we look at the allegory of Robin as reflecting the predicament of the "composite" Tory. The young kinsman's laugh, for example, coming when he is surrounded by the jeering acquaintances of the earlier evening, as all watch Molineux pass—is it a curing, sanative laugh or an hysterical, traumatic laugh capping full despair? Both, I would answer: for different people in the predicament, the climax might have cured and might have killed. Robin is a composite person. Hence in the logic of the allegory we are not permitted to know whether Robin will stay in the town he says he is weary of, or whether he will make his way back across the water. Both alternatives were taken by those involved who were loyalists during and after the upheavals of our revolutionary times.

The magnificent thing is that Hawthorne could have fleshed out what might have been purely diagrammatic, could have felt so strongly as to have kept his attention (and consequently ours) drilled to

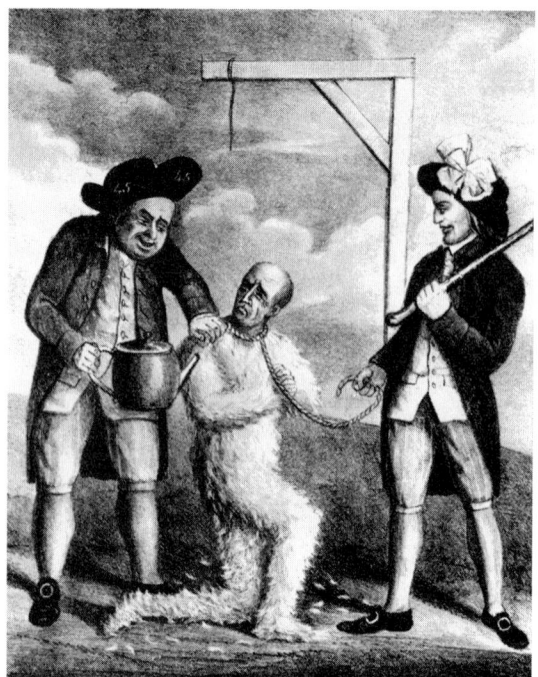

An illustration of American Revolutionists tarring and feathering a British loyalist in eighteenth-century Boston. The title character of 'My Kinsman, Major Molineux' suffers this same fate.

one character put through a composite ordeal before our eyes. His art and sympathy and his *clarity*, more than any irresolute or Kafkaish ambiguity on his part, earn him plaudits in this early story. What terrible shortsightedness on the part of those eminent men and their retainers, succeeding one another because the colonists would not abide them—and still, each of them so confident on arrival of being able to administer affairs for his "loyal" fellowmen. But after all, each would have seen the equivalent of what Robin saw—for example, "the broad countenance of a British hero swinging before the door of an inn." Why shouldn't they expect coöperation? All this evokes more legitimate pathos, perhaps, than the pathos which I for one have a time responding to: that of some everyman cutting away from one or more father figures, undergoing assault from the "powers of darkness," emerging self-created, and all the rest.

In the *Centenary Essays* published in 1964 to commemorate Hawthorne's death, Lionel Trilling's essay, "Our Hawthorne," spoke of the admiration writers like Henry James had for Hawthorne's "surface aesthetic." Trilling grew nostalgic over the fact that this kind of interest has lapsed. "Of this surface aesthetic," he said, "the modern critics . . . say little. Their concern is with an aesthetic of depth. . . ." But honoring the surface of an allegory may be doing as much justice to Hawthorne's work as pouring deep into its sub-basements all that we have come to suppose goes into our own predicament (breaking from adolescence, for instance)—ours, and by extension, everyman's. Trilling's nostalgia seems an appropriate way for one to remember the artist Hawthorne, rather than displacing him with oneself, just as Hawthorne would remember people of the past rather than displacing them with himself.

Source: John Russell, "Allegory and 'My Kinsman, Major Molineux,'" in *The New England Quarterly*, Vol. 40, No. 3, September, 1967, pp. 432–40.

Bartlett C. Jones

In the following essay, Jones explores Hawthorne's vagueness surrounding his meaning of "shrewdness" in "My Kinsman, Major Molineux."

Nathaniel Hawthorne's tale of mid-eighteenth century Massachusetts, "My Kinsman, Major Molineux," is woven around an ambiguous use of the term "shrewd." Five sets of oppositions, or tensions, are established in the opening pages, developed throughout the narrative and contrasted in a climactic scene. Robin's shrewdness, if proven beyond reasonable doubt, resolves these tensions in his shout of laughter and brings the story to a successful conclusion. Recent criticism has stressed sub-conscious factors when explaining Robin's laugh. My analysis indicates that his motivation is primarily conscious, that his decision represents a complex historical development. As such the story assumes a new dimension, a biting commentary on a human nature too prone to choose the expedient.

The Colonial reaction against Royal officials and the court party in Massachusetts prior to the American Revolution is the tale's first opposition. A boy like Robin Molineux, coming into so charged a political atmosphere, must ultimately choose between the rival factions. Contrasting the country and the town, a second tension, is politically significant. The story is laid in Boston, cradle of Massachusetts insurgency. Historically, leaders like Sam Adams had to overcome the loyalist sentiment of the back country before plunging the Bay State into a fight for independence. A third opposition, rough clothing compared with fashionable attire, follows from Robin's country origin. His coarse coat, leather breeches, home knit stockings, cudgel and the wallet he carries on his back set him off from the townsmen. The "courteous" innkeeper sees that he is from the uncommitted back country before any words pass between them.

The theme of youth struggling against the world is quite evident in Robin's situation. His parchment three-penny is not enough to buy a meal at the inn. Robin's elder brother is to receive the family farm. The youth is seeking his affluent kinsman, Major Molineux, who has offered to aid one of his impoverished cousin's two sons. Finally, illegal personal force is pitted against socio-legal repression. When Robin grabs the skirt of the old man's coat, he is threatened with imprisonment in the stocks. The innkeeper sardonically reads descriptions of runaway bond servants and the reward for their recapture, before saying, "Better trudge, boy; better trudge." The night watchman frightens Robin's temptress, "the lady of the scarlet petticoat," back into her quarters and commands him to go home or face the stocks. Robin's cudgel becomes the recurring symbol for illegal, personal violence, just as the stocks represent social coercion Robin wants to smash the old man's nose and break the innkeeper's head. He longs to wreak vengeance on the men who laugh at him. Robin considers forcing someone to direct him to the Major by brandishing his cudgel and, later, he tries to intimidate a pedestrian in that fashion. He feels "an instinctive antipathy towards the guardian of midnight order." Growing desperate from fatigue and hunger, Robin thinks of personal retribution when faced with social repression. He is more analytic when confronted with illegal, personal force—perhaps because he embodies it and familiarity has brought a measure of understanding.

The temptress nearly succeeds in luring Robin into her rooms before the appearance of the night watchman. Despite this narrow escape, Robin distrusts her at once. He doubts whether "that sweet voice spoke Gospel truth," and ultimately reads "in her eyes what he did not hear in her words." There is no question that the temptress represents an illegal force after her flight from the watchman. (Later, when law and order breakdown completely, she ventures into the street with impunity.) Before this encounter, Robin invariably draws the wrong conclusions each time he tries to interpret his experiences. Previous references to his shrewdness, when he mistakes the old man for a country representative

> "Robin is called 'shrewd' when he flees from the temptress, after the watchman disappears. And this action *is* shrewd, since the 'good youth' has already learned that he cannot resist the scarlet woman's gentle persuasion."

and when he infers that his light purse outweighs the name of Major Molineux, seem clearly ironic. Hawthorne tells us that Robin replied "cunningly" to the temptress after she said that the Major was inside her house. Robin says, "But I prithee trouble him to step to the door; I will deliver him a message . . . and then go back to my lodgings at the inn." This reply *is* cunning. It contains a lie, for Robin has no lodgings; but it gives him a pretext for remaining outside and provides for the contingency that the Major is within. Robin is called "shrewd" when he flees from the temptress, after the watchman disappears. And this action *is* shrewd, since the "good youth" has already learned that he cannot resist the scarlet woman's gentle persuasion. Robin's conduct at this point is important; it foreshadows his climactic act.

In the middle of the story, between Robin's flight from the temptress and the appearance of the lynching mob, certain tensions are reinforced while others become blurred. Robin's loneliness and isolation from the rest of the world grow more intense before the appearance of the kindly gentleman, an urbane, detached observer who is never directly involved in the story. The contrast between town and rural life is heightened by the comparison of the town church with a country religious observance, as Robin remembers it. The gentleman, however, speaks to Robin "in a tone of real kindness," a conspicuous departure from the townsmen's previous practice. He also holds the skirt of Robin's coat, an act which seemed boorish when Robin detained the old man in that way. Still, the tension between the town and the country remains. When an uproar is heard in the distance, the gentleman says "You must not expect all the stillness of your native woods here in our streets." Robin predicts that the disturbers of the peace will be set in the stocks, thereby mentioning a symbol twice invoked against him. He seems, however grudgingly, to accept social repression as a necessity. The discrepancy between Robin's clothing and the townsmen's grows weak, partly because the gentleman's clothes are not described. The youth also meets individuals "in outlandish attire" and the man with the twofold complexion "muffled in a cloak." Just before the mob arrives, "Half-dressed men hurried towards the unknown commotion." An examination of the climactic scene and the denouement explains why Hawthorne made several oppositions less rigid.

The mob sweeps by and the cart carrying the Major, "in tar-and-feathery dignity," stops directly in front of Robin. "The double-faced fellow" and the Major, presumably a Royal official, have both stared at him. (These stares are significant because Robin had been able to read the truth in the eyes of his temptress and correct "what he did not hear in her words.") Gripped by a feeling which Hawthorne describes as a "mixture of pity and terror," Robin is compelled to make a crucial decision. He still represents the country vs. the town; youth vs. the world; and, at least symbolically, loyalty to England vs. rebellion. As foreshadowed in the middle of the tale, however, Robin's position is now inverted with respect to the other oppositions. He now represents socio-legal repression opposing the personal violence of the townsmen. He could be a witness at their trial, for example. Also, his clothing is now relatively fashionable compared with that of certain townsmen. Some of the mob are described as "wild figures in the Indian dress, and many fantastic shapes without a model." The innkeeper has an apron over his head, while the old man whose fashionable appearance was contrasted with Robin's crudeness at the beginning of the story, has become a caricature. The old man is:

> ... wrapped in a wide gown, his gray periwig exchanged for a nightcap, which was thrust back from his forehead, and his silk stockings hanging about his legs. He supported himself on his polished cane in a fit of convulsive merriment, which manifested itself on his solemn old features like a funny inscription on a tombstone.

It is indisputable that Robin's immediate problems are allayed by his laugh, although his motivation is not simple. Previous scholarship has attributed his shout of laughter, "the loudest there," to many factors. Robin has been under a strain and needs an emotional outlet. As he says in the middle of the story, "I have laughed very little since I left home, sir, and should be sorry to lose an opportunity." He laughs because the crowd's laughter is contagious and because the scarlet woman's touch provokes, we may guess, tingling sensations of a pleasant yet unfamiliar nature. But his laugh is also prompted by shrewdness, expediency, the desire for self-preservation. Robin has seen many of the lynch mob at close range and is related to its victim. He must side with the mob or, at least, seem to applaud its work. Otherwise he might well be thrown into the cart and, perhaps, put to death. (Death is a reality to Robin, as revealed in his thoughts inspired by the graves around the town church.) If the element of conscious shrewdness partially explains Robin's laugh, the tensions are all resolved. Robin accepts the town, the ways of the world, and the spirit of colonial rebellion—with its illegal, personal force and the rough, outlandish clothing of its adherents. He has matured, or retrogressed—depending on the viewpoint—enormously. The critic must reject Mark Van Doren's conception that Robin, at the end of the story, is "much as he had been, except that he knows he has no prospects."

Two important clues suggest that expediency is one stimulus to Robin's climactic laugh. If Robin acts shrewdly when contending with the illegal force of the temptress, it is logical, in terms of his character development, that he will meet the overwhelming physical strength of the mob in the same way. Hawthorne refers back to the temptress when he plants the second clue. When Robin comments on the distant shouting, the gentleman says, "May not a man have several voices, Robin, as well as two complexions?" Then: "'Perhaps a man may; but Heaven forbid that a woman should!' responded the shrewd youth, thinking of the seductive tones of the Major's housekeeper." This exchange is apparently linked to Robin's climactic laugh through similarity of language and metaphor. (One indication is that the gentleman's question and Robin's answer are provoked by shouts, and Hawthorne twice calls Robin's laugh a shout. Another indication concerns the attitude of "Heaven" toward deception through the voice. Immediately after Robin's laugh, Hawthorne depicts the indifference of the "cloud spirits" and the "Man in the Moon." This animism reflects ironically upon an activity divorced from Christian ethics. The Heaven, which is called upon to prohibit two-voiced women, is ambivalent.) In any case, Robin's admission that a man may have two voices is pertinent when discussing the reasons for his laugh. Like the mob's shout, a laugh may be deceptive. Full recognition that the voice may deceive, plus a strong motive for siding with the mob, suggests that Robin laughed, in part, to save himself. The other emotional factors contributed to his successful shout, "the loudest there."

Oversubtle interpretation is an obvious danger here. The youth's request to be shown the way back to the country implies that his future course is not fixed; but it should be noted that he does not protest when the gentleman orders him to remain in town for a few days. Robin goes so far as to call the mob and the onlookers "my other friends." Shrewdness does not connote clairvoyance, sophistication, worldly wisdom, will power or higher spiritual values; it is a quality men share with lower animal forms. Robin's bewilderment, false inferences, gaucheries and irresolution do not prevent him from acting shrewdly when the situation demands it. Hawthorne apparently provides sufficient clues to clarify the ambiguity surrounding the term. Formulating a final sentence which illuminates the meaning of an entire work is a recognized literary device. The last sentence of the story, in which the gentleman addresses Robin, reads:

> Or, if you prefer to remain with us, perhaps, as you are a shrewd youth, you may rise in the world without the help of your kinsman, Major Molineux.

Earlier, when Robin said that he had a reputation for shrewdness, the kindly gentleman replied, "I doubt not that you deserve it." In context, the gentleman is taking a wait and see position. Now, he has observed Robin in the great crisis of his life. The most satisfactory dramatic reading of the last sentence demands heavy emphasis on the "are." This motivational pattern may be extended legitimately to rural Massachusetts, which finally chose a comparable solution to a dilemma like Robin's. Through him we see the back country join the drive for independence.

Source: Bartlett C. Jones, "The Ambiguity of Shrewdness in 'My Kinsman, Major Molineux,'" in *Midcontinent American Studies Journal*, Vol. 3, No. 2, Fall, 1962, pp. 42–46.

Sources

Benjamin, Park, Review of *The Token* and *Atlantic Souvenir*, in *American Monthly Magazine*, Vol. 2, October, 1836, pp. 405–07; reprinted in *The Recognition of Nathaniel Hawthorne*, edited by B. Bernard Cohen, University of Michigan Press, 1969, p. 5.

Gross, Seymour, "Hawthorne's 'My Kinsman, Major Molineux': History as Moral Adventure," in *Nineteenth-Century Fiction*, Vol. 12, September 1957, pp. 97–109; reprinted in *Casebook on the Hawthorne Question*, edited by Agnes Donohue, Thomas Y. Crowell, 1963, pp. 51–52, 59.

Hawthorne, Nathaniel, Preface to *The House of the Seven Gables*, 1851; reprinted, Norton, 1967, p. 1.

———, *The Scarlet Letter*, 1850; Bantam, 1965, pp. 34, 35.

Leavis, Q. D., "Hawthorne as Poet," part 1, in *Sewanee Review*, Vol. 59, Spring, 1951, pp. 179–205; reprinted in *Nathaniel Hawthorne's Tales: A Norton Critical Edition*, edited by James McIntosh, Norton, 1987, p. 367.

Male, Roy R., *Hawthorne's Tragic Vision*, Norton, 1957, p. 49.

McWilliams, John P., Jr., "'Thorough-Going Democrat' and 'Modern Tory': Hawthorne and the Puritan Revolution of 1776," in *Studies in Romanticism*, Vol. 15, Fall, 1976, pp. 549–71; reprinted in *Nathaniel Hawthorne's Tales: A Norton Critical Edition*, edited by James McIntosh, Norton, 1987, pp. 377–78, 379.

Pearce, Roy Harvey, "Robin Molineux on the Analyst's Couch," in *Criticism*, Vol. 1, 1959, p. 87.

Tuckerman, Henry T., "Nathaniel Hawthorne," in *Southern Literary Messenger*, Vol. 17, June, 1851, 344–49; reprinted in *The Recognition of Nathaniel Hawthorne*, edited by B. Bernard Cohen, University of Michigan Press, 1969, pp. 56–57.

Further Reading

Cohen, B. Bernard, ed., *The Recognition of Nathaniel Hawthorne: Selected Criticism since 1828*, University of Michigan Press, 1969.
  Starting with an overview of trends in Hawthorne, this collection of forty-three reviews and critical articles includes reviews by Henry Wadsworth Longfellow, Herman Melville, Edgar Allan Poe, William Dean Howells, and T. S. Eliot. "My Kinsman, Major Molineux" is not specifically mentioned.

James, Henry, *Hawthorne*, 1879; reprinted, edited by Dan McCall, Cornell University Press, 1998.
  This first book-length critical study of Hawthorne is still in print in several editions, and still highly regarded. James appreciates Hawthorne's genius, but he has been accused of overemphasizing the "provincial" qualities of American life and of Hawthorne's own life and outlook.

Male, Roy R., *Hawthorne's Tragic Vision*, Norton, 1957.
  Male traces moral growth as the primary concern of all of Hawthorne's important works. "My Kinsman, Major Molineux," he finds, is the story of Robin's quest for a father. Only when he breaks free of his dependence on the illusory authority figure is Robin ready to be a man.

Martin, Terence, *Nathaniel Hawthorne*, Twayne, 1965.
  This is an introduction to the life and work of Hawthorne for the general reader. Martin examines Haw-

thorne in the context of an early nineteenth-century culture that did not look favorably on imagination and had no great body of imaginative literature. He includes a chronology and annotated bibliography.

Mellow, James R., *Nathaniel Hawthorne in His Times*, Johns Hopkins University Press, 1998.

Winner of the 1983 National Book Award, this is the standard biography of Hawthorne. At nearly seven hundred pages it is comprehensive but thoroughly readable by a general audience.

Pennell, Melissa McFarland, ed., *Student Companion to Nathaniel Hawthorne*, Greenwood Press, 1999.

This examination of Hawthorne is intended for students at the high school and college levels. The chapter on "My Kinsman, Major Molineux" includes material on the setting, plot, themes, and historical context.

Roselily

Alice Walker
1973

"Roselily" was first published as the opening story in Alice Walker's first collection of short stories, *In Love and Trouble: Stories of Black Women* (1973). The collection won the Rosenthal Award of the National Institute of Arts and Letters, and was widely and favorably reviewed. "Roselily" has been included in several important literary anthologies, including *Calling the Wind: Twentieth-Century African-American Short Stories* (1993).

The story of a rural African-American woman from Mississippi who is about to escape poverty and disgrace by marrying a man she barely knows, a Muslim from the North, it received praise from critics for giving a voice to a segment of the population that has seldom been represented in fiction. The central character is an unmarried woman with three children, aged three, four, and five, and Walker depicts her with respect and compassion.

The prospects for Roselily finding happiness in her loveless marriage seem dim; she is one of the many female characters in *In Love and Trouble* who suffer not only from financial hardship but also from the imbalance of power between men and women. In part because of her own disillusionment with the inequalities that she faced when the Civil Rights Movement did not lead to a significant increase in equality for African-American women, Walker's work is frequently concerned with women's struggles and misguided loyalties. In an interview published in the prose collection *In Search of Our*

Mothers' Gardens, Walker described the central characters in *In Love and Trouble*: "thirteen women—mad, raging, loving, resentful, hateful, strong, ugly, weak, pitiful, and magnificent—try to live with the loyalty to black men that characterizes all of their lives. For me, black women are the most fascinating creations in the world."

Author Biography

Born and raised in a poor community in the rural South, Alice Malsenior Walker may have seemed an unlikely candidate to become such a significant writer in the twentieth century. Yet it was her experiences among poor black folk, her ear for their language, and her respect for their dignity, that gave her the material and the reason for her writing. She was born on February 9, 1944, in Eatonton, Georgia, the eighth child in a family of sharecroppers. When she was eight, one of her brothers accidentally shot her in the eye with a BB gun. The resulting scar left her shaken and shy, and she began to spend more time alone, reading.

Walker graduated at the top of her high school class, earning a scholarship to Spelman College, a college in Atlanta for African-American women. After two and a half years there, she transferred to Sarah Lawrence College in New York, where she was one of only six black students. When she returned from a summer trip to Kenya in 1964 and discovered she was pregnant, she fell into a depression that nearly drove her to suicide. Her father had said that his daughters would be turned from the family if they had children out of wedlock. Instead of killing herself, she procured an illegal abortion, and turned to writing poetry to relieve the pressure of her anxieties. These poems became her well-received first collection, *Once: Poems* (1968).

Between the writing and the publication of *Once*, Walker graduated from college and began to work with the Civil Rights Movement, helping African Americans register to vote in Georgia and Mississippi. It was then that she met a white lawyer from New York, Mel Leventhal, whom she later married. She was pregnant with her husband's child when she attended the funeral of Martin Luther King, Jr. One week later, she suffered a miscarriage. The next year, 1969, saw the birth of her only child, a daughter Rebecca.

Walker's first novel, *The Third Life of Grange Copeland*, was published in 1970, followed three years later by *In Love and Trouble* (1973), the collection that includes "Roselily." Both books drew on her own background as a black woman struggling with poverty, sexism, and racism—a theme that would turn up again in *The Color Purple* (1982). For that novel, Walker won the National Book Award, and became the first black woman to win the Pulitzer Prize for fiction. She has continued to write and publish fiction, poetry, and essays, and is one of the most popular and critically acclaimed writers of her generation.

Plot Summary

The story begins with the opening words of the traditional wedding ceremony, "Dearly Beloved." The two words, italicized, hang above a paragraph of prose, with no explanation. Following the paragraph are a few more words from the ceremony, "we are gathered here." The brief story is arranged this way throughout. A paragraph or two of prose is followed by a bit of the minister's words, until two sentences from the wedding are complete: "Dearly Beloved, / we are gathered here / in the sight of God / to join this man and this woman / in holy matrimony" and "If there's anybody here that knows a reason why / these two should not be joined / together, / let him speak / or forever hold / his peace."

The eleven prose sections are spoken in the third person by a narrator who can see into the mind of Roselily, the central character. Each section reports what Roselily thinks and observes as she is being married. There is no dialogue and no real action, but simply the meandering thoughts of the central character. The story opens with Roselily daydreaming through her own wedding, seeing herself in her mother's wedding gown. It is obvious immediately that this is not the story of a joyous wedding day. The wedding party stands on the porch of Roselily's house, and the man she is marrying (he is never named) does not approve of the location.

Throughout the ceremony, cars can be heard passing by on the highway. White people drive the cars, and the men in the crowd keep looking at the passing cars in a "respectful way." For the groom, Roselily can tell, the distraction caused by the white people, and the fact that these country people in

Panther Burn, Mississippi, follow the "wrong God," ruins the wedding. Roselily, who has three children, wonders what it would be like to not have them, and instantly her guilt is mixed in her mind with the guilt of not quite believing in the Christian God, and not believing in the minister's authority.

The groom, who lives in Chicago, is a Muslim, a member of the Nation of Islam. Roselily does not know much about his religion, except that she will have to cover her head and sit in a separate section for women at his place of worship. When she thinks of his religion, she imagines "ropes, chains, handcuffs." But to give her children a chance at respectability, she is willing to change her life. She had earlier pinned her hopes on the father of her fourth child, a married Harvard graduate from New England who had come to Mississippi to work in the Civil Rights Movement. He had been unable to adapt to life without Bach and chess, and had returned to New England with his son, telling his wife that he had found the child. Roselily wonders how her son will fare in the North.

She feels distant from her future husband. His religion and his manner seem to carry "stiff severity," and she wonders whether she will be a new person when she is made to wear a veil. If she becomes a new person, what will become of her memories? Remembering her dead mother, the hard life of her "gray old" father who stands before her, and her grandparents in the cemetery, she feels them all pulling her back. She feels too old for big changes. When she reaches Chicago she will have an entirely new life. She will not have to work in a factory any more, but will be expected to stay at home and raise more children. She wonders whether that kind of life will be full enough.

Now she wishes she had asked more questions before agreeing to marry this man. Perhaps she was too impatient for a new life in a new place. She was eager to be "Respectable, reclaimed, renewed. Free!" Yet she worries now about the kind of freedom she will find "in robe and veil." Her future husband loves her, or he loves what he will turn her into, but she does not know whether she loves him. Is she moving toward freedom, or toward a new kind of entrapment? She does not know what she feels.

When the wedding is over there is a kiss, and the sound of firecrackers and car horns. As the witnesses cheer and give their congratulations, the groom turns his attention inward, away from the crowd and away from his wife. She imagines how it will be later, when they are driving through the

Alice Walker

night to Chicago. She feels ignorant, inadequate, but he offers no reassurance: "He is standing in front of her. In the crush of well-wishing people, he does not look back."

Characters

Husband

The man to whom Roselily is being married is never named. He is a Black Muslim from Chicago, who will take Roselily and her children back with him after the wedding and remake them. He has agreed to a country wedding on Roselily's front porch, but he looks down on the people of Panther Burn because of their simple ways and their subservience to whites. Roselily wonders whether he also looks down on her.

Roselily

Roselily is the protagonist of the story, and everything in the story is seen through her eyes. She has lived all her life in Panther Burn, Mississippi, the daughter of poor but hard-working parents. Roselily herself knows what it is to work hard: she is unmarried and raising three children alone on what she earns picking cotton and sewing in a factory.

Marrying and moving to Chicago is her best chance to attain respectability at last, and she is willing to take that chance for the sake of her children, even though it means marrying a man she does not love. As she half-listens to her wedding ceremony, she reflects on how she has arrived at this state, and wonders how she will take to the strict confines of life as the wife in a Black Muslim home.

Themes

Alienation and Loneliness

An unwed mother in a small town, Roselily lives a lonely life. As she stands beside her future husband filled with doubt, there is no one in the crowd who senses what she is feeling. She feels no connection to the people she is leaving or to the man she is leaving with. She has no friends, although she has known the same women since they were girls together; as a single woman she has been a threat, especially when the other women's husbands made passes at her. She has a demanding job at a sewing plant, and is raising three children alone, so she has little time for anything else. The only person she feels "joined" to is her mother, who is dead. She does not think she loves her husband, and the fact that he loves her "makes her completely conscious of how unloved she was before."

Change and Transformation

Roselily is a woman who is seeking to change, to be transformed. In her current life, she is unwed, the mother of four children by at least three fathers. She works long hours in a sewing factory, and still lives in the same small town where her family has lived for generations. Although she had a lover from New England and is marrying a man from Chicago, she knows nothing about life beyond her small community. Her children will grow up "underneath the detrimental wheel," with the same limitations, unless she can make a change.

Although she has serious misgivings about her marriage, it does offer her the chance for a new life. His life as a Black Muslim has already worked a transformation in her husband. The old women at the wedding can sense that he was once one of them, but in some way that they cannot name, he is "still a son, not a son. Changed." Roselily knows that she will change, too. She will move to Chicago and live in a larger house on the South Side. She and her husband and children will "live and build and be respectable and respected and free." This chance to have her husband "redo her into what he truly wants" is both exciting and terrifying. When she has been transformed, will she have lost herself? For the sake of her children, she is willing to take the risk.

God and Religion

One of the central conflicts of the story is between Roselily's wavering belief in Christianity and her husband's devout faith as a Black Muslim. Roselily has been raised a Christian, and she is the bride in a Christian wedding, but she does not really believe in God. To her, the minister is more intimidating than any image of God she has ever held. Although nominally a Christian, she also has learned some of her family's folk beliefs, of which she is both "ashamed and frightened." Her husband's religion also seems more intimidating than comforting. She will be made to wear a robe and veil, to stay home and raise more children, to sit apart in worship services. Although she knows more about his faith than the wedding guests, who "cannot understand that he is not a Christian," she has only small images and pieces of information.

Walker has expressed her own doubts about the ability of Christianity and Islam to serve African-American women. In other stories, she has examined Christianity as an imperialist weapon used against Africans. "Roselily," as she explains in *In Search of Our Mothers' Gardens*, reflects the fact that she is "intrigued by the religion of the Black Muslims, by what conversion means to black women, specifically, and what the religion itself means in terms of the black American past: our history, our 'race memories,' our absorption of Christianity, our *changing* of Christianity to fit our needs. What will the new rituals mean?" Roselily, on the day of her wedding, is about to learn the answer.

Style

Point of View

"Roselily" is told in the present tense by a limited third-person narrator. The narrator is not Roselily, but reports only what she thinks and sees. Everything is seen through her eyes, and interpreted through the filters of her own experiences. Because Roselily is not paying close attention to her own wedding but daydreaming, the images and thoughts presented by the narrator are meandering, some-

Topics for Further Study

- "Roselily" was removed from a statewide reading test in California because many people believed the story to be antireligious. What message, if any, do you think the story presents about religion? Write a letter to a newspaper editor or school administrator explaining why you think "Roselily" should or should not be taught in your local high school.

- Investigate the beliefs of the Nation of Islam, especially those regarding the proper roles for men and women. Does Roselily seem to have an accurate idea of what her new life will be like?

- Women in Arabic Islam countries often wear a veil, or *purdah*. Learn what you can about this custom, and find some accounts by women who wear the veil. Why do many Muslim women see the *purdah* as freeing, rather than confining?

- Roselily supports herself and three children on her wages as a sewing machine operator in a factory. Find out how much she might earn at this job, and calculate her expenses for food, shelter, and daycare. Do the math. How much of a factor in her decision to marry is her economic situation?

- Look at some accounts of the Civil Rights Movement of the 1950s and 1960s. How many educated white men and women from the North came, like Roselily's married lover, to help with the movement? What kinds of work did they do?

---

times sharply in focus and at other times only vague impressions. It is possible that the husband truly loves Roselily and feels tenderness for her and her children. Perhaps he is nervous about the marriage himself. But there is no attempt to reveal his thoughts, except as Roselily tries to read them through his clothing and his manner. Telling the story from this point of view puts the focus squarely on Roselily and on her feelings during the few minutes of the ceremony. Walker is not interested in giving the plot details of a wedding and what happens after it, but in giving a voice to one woman at one moment in her life.

Setting

The setting of a story includes the time and place in which it occurs, and also the spiritual and even economic background of the characters. "Roselily" takes place in the rural town of Panther Burn, Mississippi. The time is probably during the 1960s, since the child that Roselily gave to his civil-rights-worker father is no older than two. The residents of Panther Burn are poor and black. Roselily's father has earned a meager living trapping animals and selling their skins to Sears, and Roselily herself has worked picking cotton, and now supports three children by operating a sewing machine in a clothing factory. All of the cars driving by on the highway have white drivers.

People who are born in this small town tend to stay, there being no reason and no opportunity to get out. Roselily has lived there all her life, along with all the girls she knew in school. Her mother and grandparents are buried there. They are all Christian, but retain some echoes of traditional beliefs in ghosts and curses as well. Roselily is clearly intelligent, but she is not well educated. Her language and that of her people is not "good enough" for her Harvard lover, and her tastes do not run to Bach and chess. More significantly, she knows nothing about the world of the North. She supposes that New England is far different from Mississippi, but does not really know. All she knows for sure about Illinois is that Abraham Lincoln lived there. The idea that she will be going to a completely new setting is what thrills and frightens her.

Narrative

The term *narrative* is generally taken to mean a telling of an event or a series of events. These events might be actions, or conversation, or other elements of plot that are related to each other by a web of cause and effect. Often, the details are arranged in chronological order, but the order may be varied for particular effects. "Roselily" is not a narrative in the conventional sense. There is no direct action and no talk, except for the ritual speech of the minister. The time passed during the "present" of the story may be as little as five minutes, or perhaps as many as fifteen. Presumably, the wedding party and guests are speaking and moving about, but the only actions that pass before the reader's mind are those that Roselily remembers from the distant past or imagines about her future. In this non-narrative construction, "Roselily" is more like a poem than like a conventional short story.

Stream of Consciousness

The term for the non-narrative structure of the story is *stream of consciousness*. The term applies to writing that seeks to capture the way the human mind really works: not logically and sequentially, in full sentences and developed paragraphs, but in a rush of interwoven thoughts, impressions, and memories. By reading the entire story, one can piece together a sequential narrative of Roselily's life, but the details are not presented chronologically. Roselily's movements from idea to idea are triggered by the minister's words, by outside noises, by physical sensations, and by memories connecting to other memories.

Historical Context

African-American Women Writers

Walker has often commented that when she was studying English in college in the early 1960s, nearly all of the writing discussed in her classes was written by white men. Later, when classes in black literature were formed, nearly all of the writers studied were black men. No works by African-American women were being taught, and few were even in print. As a reader and a writer, Walker hungered for models that would be more appropriate to her own life. In an essay titled "Saving the Life That Is Your Own: The Importance of Models in the Artist's Life," she recounts a story about another African-American writer: "It has often been said that someone asked Toni Morrison why she writes the kind of books she writes, and that she replied: Because they are the kind of books I want to read." Taking Morrison's comment one step further, Walker explains, "I write all the things *I should have been able to read*."

Readers since the late 1960s and early 1970s, when Walker was writing the stories in *In Love and Trouble*, have not had such difficulty finding a variety of models. The period saw a tremendous flowering of writing by African-American women that was recognized for its literary quality and that sold well. In addition to Walker's early volumes of poetry and fiction, there appeared Nikki Giovanni's poetry collection, *Black Feeling, Black Talk* (1968); Maya Angelou's first volume of autobiography, *I Know Why the Caged Bird Sings* (1970); Audre Lorde's black feminist lesbian poetry collection, *The First Cities* (1970); Toni Morrison's novels, *The Bluest Eye* (1970) and *Sula* (1973); and Gayl Jones's novel, *Corregidora* (1975). These women wrote about women's experiences from a woman's point of view. Although they found some resistance to their writing, especially from African-American male critics, they also found a large and eager audience.

Black Muslims

Roselily's husband is a Black Muslim, an adherent to the religion called the Nation of Islam. The religion was founded in the 1930s in Detroit, Michigan, by Wallace D. Fard, who proclaimed himself "the Supreme Ruler of the Universe." At first, one of the goals of the religion was to work toward a separate African-American nation, which would come to fruition after the white race and Christianity were destroyed. Later, emphasis shifted to working toward social justice in a multicultural world. Black Muslims took their teachings both from the Islamic Holy Book, the Qur'an, and from the Christian Bible, to create a religion that only loosely resembled either mainstream religious tradition. Religious practice is founded on obedience and discipline. Black Muslims follow strict dietary rules based on Islamic belief, and maintain clearly defined and separate roles for men and women.

In 1934, Fard was replaced by Elijah Muhammad, who was proclaimed a "Prophet." Muhammad led the Black Muslims until 1975, gradually building the movement into a large and well-organized body of black separatists, clustered mainly in large Northern cities like New York, Detroit, and Chicago. During the Civil Rights Movement of the 1960s, the Nation of Islam was generally opposed to the nonviolent strategies of Dr. Martin Luther King, Jr., believing that a more aggressive and confrontational approach would be more successful in gaining equal rights for African Americans. But the Nation of Islam was not merely angry and

Compare & Contrast

- **1970:** Alice Walker first hears of the writer Zora Neale Hurston, a long-forgotten African-American writer of the Harlem Renaissance. She comes to admire Hurston's gift for giving voice to poor black women, and determines to read all her work.

  Today: Because of Walker's efforts, Hurston biographer Robert Hemenway, and others, all of Hurston's work is in print, and widely anthologized and taught.

- **1973:** The United States Supreme Court declares that forbidding abortion during the first trimester of pregnancy is unconstitutional. Prior to this, abortions are illegal and often unsafe "back-alley" operations. Walker herself has undergone such an operation, but for most women the procedure is unavailable.

  Today: Abortions are safe and widely available for American women who wish or need to limit the size of their families. Contraception is also inexpensive and easy to obtain.

- **1967:** Walker's husband, the attorney Melvyn Leventhal, is one of many educated whites from the North who have come to Mississippi to work in the Civil Rights Movement. Walker publishes an essay entitled "The Civil Rights Movement: What Good Was It?"

  Today: Laws protecting the power of wealthy whites have been erased, but institutional racism is still widespread. While many individual African Americans have made economic strides, there are still large pockets of poverty in black inner cities. No movement on the scale of the Civil Rights Movement has arisen to confront remaining issues of race and class.

- **1967:** When Walker and her white husband move to Jackson, Mississippi, it is illegal for an interracial couple to share a home, even if they are married.

  Today: The population of Mississippi is approximately two-thirds white and one-third black. Segregation laws do not exist, and the races have closer, yet still uneasy, relationships.

---

aggressive. When the boxer Muhammad Ali, a Black Muslim, was drafted in 1967 to fight in Vietnam, he refused to go because of his religious beliefs and was forced to give up his title as World Heavyweight Champion.

Critical Overview

Having already made a name for herself with her first book of poems, *Once: Poems* (1968), and her first novel, *The Third Life of Grange Copeland* (1970), Walker found herself the center of a great deal of critical attention when *In Love and Trouble* came out in 1973. Louis Pratt and Darnell Pratt list twenty-nine reviews in their annotated bibliography, *Alice Malsenior Walker*, far more than usual for a first volume of short stories. The reviews were almost unanimously favorable, although a few reviewers found the stories uneven in quality.

One issue for writers of fiction at the end of the twentieth century is whether fiction that does not revolve around white men can be considered "universal." Often, books about white men are thought of as representing the "human condition," while books about women are thought to represent women, and books about black women are thought to represent black women. Some early reviewers praised Walker for drawing on her own experiences in the rural South to portray the particular situations of black women. Barbara Smith, in a review for *Ms.*, admires Walker's skill at exploring "with honesty the texture and terrors of Black women's lives." In a review for *The Crisis*, the magazine of the NAACP, Mercedes Wright argues that Walker's characters face their particular conflicts because they live in a racist and sexist society.

Other earlier reviews acknowledged that Walker's characters are, as the title states, black women, but felt that their stories were more widely applicable. Writing for *Bestsellers*, Oscar Bouise reports that Walker had enabled him to appreciate the experiences of these women, and praises her as a "master of style." V. S. Nyabongo praises Walker in *Books Abroad* for presenting a collection of stories which, through women's stories, reflect on themes that are significant for all people.

"Roselily" remained a much-admired but seldom-discussed story after the first rush of reviews, receiving renewed notice after Walker's winning of the 1983 Pulitzer Prize and American Book Award for *The Color Purple* gave rise to a reevaluation of her earlier work. In her groundbreaking essay "Walker: The Achievement of the Short Fiction," Alice Hall Petry demonstrates that the situations that keep Walker's women "in love and trouble" are not of their own making. "Certainly marriage offers these women nothing, and neither does religion, be it Christianity, the Black Muslim faith, or voodoo." Mary Helen Washington agrees, in "An Essay on Alice Walker," that Roselily is "trapped and cut down by archaic conventions, by superstition, by traditions that in every way cut women off from the right to life."

After the publication of *The Color Purple*, it became something of a cliche to charge that the male characters in Walker's fiction are portrayed in too negative a light, and her women, while downtrodden, are invariably resilient. Two critics have noted, however, that Roselily displays no special pluck in her current situation. In an essay titled "Zora Neale Hurston and Alice Walker: A Spiritual Kinship," Alma Freeman compares Roselily with Janie Crawford, the protagonist in Hurston's *Their Eyes Were Watching God*, and finds that, unlike Janie, Roselily accepts her entrapment. Donna Haisty Winchell agrees that Roselily is an example of the women in *In Love and Trouble* who are not seen "fighting back successfully against preconceived, stultifying, and restrictive notions of women's roles."

Critics have also discussed the experimental qualities of the story. Hall finds the irony of alternating Roselily's thoughts with the words of the wedding ceremony "heavy-handed," but concludes "the device does work in this story." Barbara Christian, in "The Contrary Women of Alice Walker," notes the narrator's use of the third person pronoun *she* to represent Roselily's own thoughts, and suggests, "even in Roselily's mind, the being who wonders about, questions this day of triumph, is both herself, and yet not herself."

In 1994, "Roselily" suddenly attracted national attention again, when the California Department of Education ordered the story removed from a statewide reading test. The call for removal came from a group called the Traditional Values Coalition, which labeled the story antireligious. They worried that Roselily's admission that she does not believe in God, the fact of her husband's belief in Islam, and the implied questioning of marriage itself would raise improper questions for the tenth graders taking the test. Supporters of the story's inclusion spoke of the need for state tests and curricula to include challenging, thought-provoking material that deals with real-world issues. Ironically, during the same year as the "Roselily" controversy, Walker was honored by California's governor as a "state treasure" for her contributions to literature.

Walker has collected the text of "Roselily" and two other censored pieces of her own writing, letters to the editor in support of and opposed to "Roselily," and transcripts of the State Board of Education hearings on the matter into a book called *Banned*. As is the case with most cases of book removal, the removal of the story from the California test served to create renewed interest in the story, and to bring it to the attention of a new generation of readers.

Criticism

Cynthia Bily

Bily has a master's degree in English literature and has written for a variety of educational publishers. In the following essay, she discusses the poetic qualities of Walker's story.

Over three decades of continuous productivity and acclaim, Alice Walker has earned a place as one of the most important American writers of the twentieth century. She has published six novels, two collections of short stories, two collections of essays, five volumes of poetry, and several books for children. Ten million copies of her books have been sold around the world. She was the first African-American woman to win the Pulitzer Prize for fiction, for her novel *The Color Purple*, and several

What Do I Read Next?

- Walker's first short-story collection, *In Love and Trouble: Stories of Black Women* (1973), includes ''Roselily'' and other stories of vulnerable women looking for dignity and love.

- *The Color Purple* (1982) is Walker's novel about Celie, a woman who finds inner strength after a life of abuse and abandonment. It won both the Pulitzer Prize and the American Book Award.

- *In Search of Our Mothers' Gardens* (1983) is Walker's collection of ''womanist prose,'' or essays, about women and art.

- Zora Neale Hurston's *Their Eyes Were Watching God* (1937) was one of the first novels to use the voice of a poor Southern African-American woman. It is the story of Janie Crawford, who refuses to be limited by bitterness and pain.

- *Cane* (1923) is by Jean Toomer, a major writer of the Harlem Renaissance. The first section of the book contains several stories of Southern black women in prose and verse.

- *The Black Muslims* (1996) is an objective history of the black nationalist organization to which Roselily's husband belongs.

---

of her other books have been as well-regarded by critics and scholars as by the buying and reading public.

Walker has come so far from the young writer struggling to find her voice, it is easy to forget that she was a poet before she was a fiction writer, and that she inverted the normal order of things by publishing a novel, *The Third Life of Grange Copeland*, before issuing her first collection of short stories, *In Love and Trouble: Stories of Black Women*. Early in her career, Walker turned to poetry at her lowest moments. The poems in her first collection, *Once: Poems*, for example, were written in one desperate week just after an abortion. In an interview with John O'Brien, collected in *In Search of Our Mothers' Gardens*, she explains, ''all of my poems ... are written when I have successfully pulled myself out of a completely numbing despair, and stand again in sunlight. Writing poems is my way of celebrating with the world that I have not committed suicide the evening before.'' But the lines between genres have always been a bit blurred for her. Essays are likely to contain bits of verse, some of the poems read like prose, and some stories, like ''Roselily,'' read like poems. It could be believed that ''Roselily'' *is*, in fact, a poem, or can profitably be read as one.

Walker herself has hinted at the appropriateness of this type of reading. In the John O'Brien interview she discusses her attempts to ''try to figure out what I am doing in my writing, where it is headed, and so on,'' and concludes, ''I almost never can come up with anything.'' But if she cannot articulate a plan for work in progress, she knows which finished pieces please her: ''I like those of my short stories that show the plastic, shaping, almost painting quality of words. In 'Roselily' and 'The Child Who Favors Daughter' the prose is poetry, or prose and poetry run together to add a new dimension to the language.'' It is exactly the ways that ''prose and poetry run together'' in the story that will be considered.

Of course, anything can be read as a poem, and a writer can call a collection of words anything she wishes. The idea behind the exercise of looking for ''found poems'' is that a poem is a poem if the reader thinks it is, even if someone else thinks it's a phone book. Walker has planted small poetic treasures through ''Roselily,'' to reward those who wish to find a poem in it. In doing so, she has created a piece of writing that resembles the swirl of impressions and sensations of Roselily's mind.

The structure of the story is nonlinear, a collection of short paragraphs or stanzas that float as

> "Of course, anything can be read as a poem, and a writer can call a collection of words anything she wishes. The idea behind the exercise of looking for 'found poems' is that a poem is a poem if the reader thinks it is, even if someone else thinks it's a phone book."

freely as Roselily's consciousness. They are not chronological, nor are they arranged in a sequence shaped by cause and effect. Some of the passages respond directly to the bits of wedding ceremony that come before them, but many do not. The paragraphs accumulate in the reader's mind like pieces of a collage or a stained-glass window. The whole is greater than the sum of its parts, but the parts themselves could be gently shifted, rearranged.

Of all of Walker's writings, "Roselily" most resembles, in the way it is put together, a poem called "Mornings / Of An Impossible Love," from *Once: Poems*. "Mornings" is composed of five brief passages written in paragraph form. It presents five musings by a woman whose lover is getting ready to leave her. Like "Roselily," it gains its poetic power by accumulation, by layering, by repetition. It does not attempt to tell a story so much as to put on the page the thoughts and impressions in a woman's mind.

To direct readers to focus on sensation or atmosphere rather than on plot or action, poetry exploits sound. Poetry, more than prose, is concerned with "what it is like" rather than "what happened next," and readers must be made to slow down, to linger over lines and experiences. In Roselily's short, stanza-like passages of thought, Walker uses some of the sound tools of the poet, including alliteration, repetition, and rhythm, to heighten the emphasis on particular lines and phrases. Most of this heightening is subconscious, but readers, especially experienced readers, pick up clues from the sounds of words in addition to their meanings.

Alliteration is the repetition of initial consonant sounds in words that come right after each other or closely together. For example, the first line of the story after "Dearly Beloved" begins: "She dreams; dragging herself." The repetition of *dr* is hard to pronounce, making something of a tongue twister. The small difficulty in pronouncing "dreams; dragging" makes the reader slow down, linger over the words, and this gives them added emphasis. In this briefly extended moment, the reader is forced to confront what is surely a surprise at the beginning of the story: After a lovely flower name, and the beginning of a wedding ceremony, and the sweet thought "she dreams," there is the word *dragging*. The reader thus learns right away that this story will have surprises, and that one must pay attention to the individual words. Right away, the reader is encouraged to make a small shift and begins to read the story like a poem.

Other lines elevate their emotional content by the inclusion of alliteration. Thinking of the respectability she will soon have, Roselily imagines her new position: "What a vision, a view, from up so high." Here the *v* sound echoes, but it does not slow the line down. The repetition of synonyms emphasizes the soaring feeling, as all the consonants fit smoothly together into one long line.

Near the end of the ceremony, Roselily reflects, in short, choppy lines, on what is ahead for her. "Proposal. Promises. A new life! Respectable, reclaimed, renewed. Free!" Here again, the consonant combinations are hard to pronounce smoothly, and the punctuation between words slows down the reading even further. "Proposal. Promises." Roselily is holding on to these words, remembering why she is about to make this big change. The marriage was not her idea; she is beyond thinking her way out of her situation. But her husband has suggested this marriage, and now it is happening. Like a chant, she repeats and remembers. "Proposal. Promises." And what will she gain? She will become "respectable, reclaimed, renewed." This, too, sounds like words she has repeated to herself many times, shaping them through trial and error to an alliterative and rhythmic chant. She is not thinking in full sentences or big ideas any more, but forcing herself to focus on the essential: "Respectable, reclaimed, renewed."

In addition to using repetition of consonant sounds for emphasis, Walker also repeats whole words and phrases, creating a rhythm that is more poetry than prose. This happens most often in the second half of the story, after the minister asks whether anyone "knows a reason why." For example, the words "wonders" and "thinks" are repeated far more frequently than would be necessary for exposition. At one point, "She wonders how to make new roots. It is beyond her. She wonders what one does with memories." A bit later, "She thinks of her mother, who is dead. Dead, but still her mother." And a bit later, "She wonders what it will be like. Not to have to go to a job. Not to work in a sewing plant. Not to worry about learning to sew straight seams." The rhythmic qualities of the repeated lines keep repetitions like this from sounding silly or dull. Interestingly, the frequency of this kind of repetition increases as the story goes along, as though Roselily's thinking becomes less rational and more impressionistic as she gets closer to being a wife.

There are lines in the story that read like puzzles, or like tangled balls of line that must be untangled to be examined. Like the alliterative lines, these lines force the reader to stop and linger, to sort out the meaning. The first "stanza" includes such a line: "The man who stands beside her is against this standing on the front porch of her house." At the halfway point, when the minister begins his second sentence, there is this: "*If there's anybody here that knows a reason why* / But of course they know no reason why beyond what they daily have come to know." Teachers of expository writing and even fiction writing encourage their students to avoid lines like this, under the assumption that readers of prose do not expect to be challenged at the sentence level. Ideas may be complex, but sentences should be clear. Poetry revels in such word games, in demonstrating on the page the non-linear qualities of thought and emotion.

Others have discussed the story's use of repeated images. As Donna Haisty Winchell demonstrates in *Alice Walker*, Roselily's "mother's white robe and veil" is transformed into the robe and veil that protect and segregate Muslim women. Roselily never explicitly makes the connection, but the repetition of the image and the language (the image of the robe and veil occurs four times in this very brief story) connect and confuse the two meanings in the reader's mind. In "An Essay on Alice Walker," Mary Helen Washington identifies several "fleeting images" of entrapment that "inadvertently break through" Roselily's mind: "quicksand, flowers choked to death, cotton being weighed, ropes, chains, handcuffs, cemeteries, a cornered rat." To use imagery so insistently in such a small space seems again to be more poetry than prose.

This is not to say that qualities such as sound, rhythm, word play, and repeated imagery are not to be found in prose. Nothing is gained by debating whether "Roselily" and "Mornings" are short stories or poems. Literature is more than message; it is also the medium, the way a message is conveyed. Is "Roselily" a short story or a poem, perhaps the type of lyric poem called a dramatic monologue? It is both, and draws power from each tradition. But if a reader is willing to bring to this story some of the serious playfulness that poetry draws out, she will be twice blessed.

Source: Cynthia Bily, in an essay for *Short Stories for Students*, Gale Group, 2001.

Liz Brent

Brent has a Ph.D. in American Culture, specializing in film studies, from the University of Michigan. She is a freelance writer and teaches courses in the history of American cinema. In the following essay, Brent discusses the theme of "personal spirits" in Walker's story.

The short story "Roselily," by Alice Walker, is written as the internal monologue of a woman, Roselily, while she stands at the altar taking her wedding vows. Through this internal monologue, Roselily expresses a strong current of ambivalence about the marriage that is taking place. Furthermore, as she hears each phrase of the wedding vows, spoken by the preacher, Roselily interprets it in her own way, as an expression of her true feelings about the impending marriage.

A closer look at one of the opening epigraphs to *Women in Love and Trouble*, the short story collection in which "Roselily" appears, helps to illuminate the nature of Roselily's ambivalence. This passage, from *The Concubine*, by Elechi Amadi, describes a young girl whose parents engaged her to marry when she was only eight days old. It is explained that the girl's irrational behavior and frequent crying is attributable to her *agwu* her "personal spirit": "Of course the influence of *agwu* could not be nullified overnight. In fact it would never be completely eliminated. Everyone was mildly influenced now and then by his personal spirit." Thus, the girl's "personal spirit," which "could never be completely eliminated" represents the assertion of her own individual will against the restrictions placed on her by her role in society.

> With each phrase of the sermon, Roselily's internal monologue twists the words into an expression of her own 'personal spirit'—a spirit at odds with the traditionally intended meaning of the wedding vows."

Having been promised by her parents to marry without her choice or consent, the girl's internal impulse toward rebellion can only be expressed through her "personal spirit." The implication is that, even under the most oppressive conditions, the individual will, or "personal spirit" of any person will find a way to assert itself.

The second epigraph to this story collection complements the first. An excerpt from *Letters to a Young Poet*, by the poet Rainer Maria Rilke, this passage asserts that it is human nature to "be oneself," no matter what difficulties one encounters to do so, "at all costs," and "against all opposition": "everything in Nature grows and defends itself in its own way and is characteristically and spontaneously itself, seeks at all costs to be so and against all opposition."

Together, these two passages illuminate the meaning of Roselily's inner monologue during her wedding ceremony. As the snippets of the traditional Christian wedding sermon intrude upon her thoughts, Roselily's inner monologue represents the assertion of her "personal spirit," despite the restrictions placed upon her by her impending marriage. Although, unlike the girl in the first epigraph, Roselily has freely chosen this marriage, her position as a poor, Southern, black woman, a single mother of four children (one of them living with his father), has severely limited the options from which she has had to choose. And, although she outwardly conforms to the expectations of her community and her husband-to-be, Roselily's internal monologue expresses the impulse to be herself, if only in her mind, even "against all odds." With each phrase of the sermon, Roselily's internal monologue twists the words into an expression of her own "personal spirit"—a spirit at odds with the traditionally intended meaning of the wedding vows.

Even as the wedding ceremony begins, "Dearly Beloved," Roselily's private thoughts break free from the restrictions being imposed upon her by this marriage: "She dreams. . . ." Her thoughts struggle to take her far away from where she stands at the altar, "dragging herself across the world." Although she is about to marry a man whom she will be expected to obey, her thoughts take her to a place where she specifically does something he disapproves of: "The man who stands beside her is against this standing on the front porch of her house. . . ."

As the sermon continues, Roselily's inner monologue continues to express the assertion of her "personal spirit" against the restrictions of her subordinate position in society, as represented by her impending marriage. As the preacher says, "We are gathered here . . ." Roselily mentally finishes his sentence, "like cotton to be weighed." Roselily sees her own role in the wedding as that of an item in a monetary exchange; she feels like a bale of cotton, being weighed and evaluated for the purposes of someone else's profit. This thought expresses Roselily's sense of her role in the wedding and marriage as little more than a material possession of the man she is marrying in an exchange that will ultimately benefit only him.

Roselily's rebellious thoughts during the wedding ceremony go so far as to enter the realms of murder and blasphemy. She expresses a wish that she could be free of her three children: "She dreams she does not already have three children." But her inner desire for freedom from her societal role in the family goes even farther, to the extent that she envisions killing her children. The flowers in her hand symbolize her children, who are presumably three, four, and five years of age, as she thinks "a squeeze around the flowers in her hands chokes off three and four and five years of breath." But Roselily is aware of herself outwardly conforming to societal expectations while inwardly rebelling against them. After imagining killing her own children, Roselily makes an outward gesture of faith to the preacher, as she "forces humility into her eyes, as if she believes he is, in fact, a man of God." Yet, while conforming to the preacher's expectations through this outward gesture, Roselily's true beliefs run counter to those represented by the preacher and traditional religion.

Roselily imagines her own version of God, different from that of the preacher: "She can imagine God, a small black boy, timidly pulling the preacher's coattail."

Roselily envisions her marriage to this man as a form of bondage, or slavery. She associates the phrase "to join this man and woman," as indicating that she will be tied, chained, or handcuffed to him as if against her will: "she thinks of ropes, chains, handcuffs. . . ." Yet, she has chosen the marriage because she imagines it will be a ticket to freedom from economic oppression for herself and her children: "Respect, a chance to build. Her children at last from underneath the detrimental wheel. A chance to be on top. What a relief, she thinks. What a vision, a view, from up so high." Roselily is thus of two minds about the marriage. But her reasons for going into it are born of economic hardship and limited options for herself and her children. Her "personal spirit," however, continues to rebel against the marriage.

Despite Roselily's positive expectations regarding her new life with her new husband in the northern city of Chicago, she also associates the city with the oppression of her "personal spirit." In imagining the city, "she thinks of the air, the smoke, the cinders. Imagines cinders big as hailstones; heavy, weighing on the people. Wonders how this pressure finds its way into the veins, roping the springs of laughter." Roselily thus associates the city with oppressiveness, as expressed through the image of the cinders, "weighing on the people." She imagines the effect of city life almost as that of a disease, which "finds its way into the veins," again associating it with images of bondage that will effectively crush her spirit, "roping the springs of laughter."

Upon hearing the preacher's words, "If there's anybody here that knows a reason why," Roselily feels that she herself doesn't know the "reason why" she has chosen to marry this man. The only reason she can think of is that he represents a life different from, hopefully better than, the impoverished life she and her children have known up to this point: "But of course there is no reason why beyond what they daily have come to know." The impending marriage, which is meant to unite a man and woman into a family, feels for Roselily like the beginning of a separation from her man and her children. Already she "feels shut away from him because of the stiff severity of his plain black suit."

And, imagining their new life, "it is as if her children are already gone from her." Roselily imagines that her new life with this man will not make room for her own "personal spirit," restricting even her right to her own memories, for "she wonders what one does with memories in a brand-new life. This had seemed easy, until she thought of it." The "brand-new life" represents for Roselily a sacrifice of her past, her "memories," and thus of some part of who she is.

The traditional wedding statement, "If anyone here knows a reason why these two should not be joined together, let him speak or forever hold his peace," becomes fragmented in Roselily's mind, taking on very different, if not contrary, meanings to its original intent. The phrase, "these two should not be joined," taken out of the context of the complete sentence, expresses Roselily's inner feeling that she and this man should *not* be joined. Roselily feels that her marriage to this man is "absurd," meaningless, and imagines that her sisters, too, can see this: "They giggle, she feels, at the absurdity of the wedding." Although Roselily has chosen to marry this man for the sake of starting a "new life," she now begins to doubt her desire for "something new." She thinks that it is her sisters who are "ready for something new," and that it would be more appropriate for one of them to marry him. Again, Roselily associates the word "joined" with bondage and slavery; she feels "yoked." While this marriage represents a "new" life, Roselily begins to feel the urge to be "joined" to her past: "An arm seems to reach out from behind her and snatch her backward." Roselily associates the word "joined," not with her new husband, but with her dead relatives. She feels "joined" to her mother, although she is dead. She also associates the word "joined" with her ancestors, her grandparents, the "ghosts" of the past, rather than the newness of her future: "She thinks of cemeteries and the long sleep of grandparents mingling in the dirt. She believes that she believes in ghosts." Roselily feels rooted, or "joined," through her ancestors, her family, and her personal past, to the "soil" upon which she has always lived. The "soil" represents her rural Southern roots, as opposed to the "cinders" of the northern city to which she is moving. Roselily thinks of this "soil" as having something to offer her, for she believes "in the soil giving back what it takes." All of these thoughts confirm Roselily's feeling that she and this man "should not be joined."

As the preacher says, "together," Roselily's internal monologue finishes the sentence, "together

... in the city." Yet Roselily's strong connection to the past, to her "memories" conflict with the promise of a "new" life and "new" self associated with the city. Roselily's husband-to-be "sees her in a new way," but she is not sure she is capable of shedding her connection to the past to become "new enough." While the wedding represents the "new," Roselily maintains a stronger emotional tie to the past, to "memories." She even associates her wedding dress with a restriction on her personal freedom, as "even now her body itches to be free of satin and voile, organdy and lily of the valley." And, while the "new" represents loss of freedom, the past represents freedom from such restrictions: "Memories crash against her. Memories of being bare to the sun." Roselily's memories of freedom are clearly in violent conflict with the new restricted life represented by the wedding dress. The memories "crash against her," with the force of violent impact.

As Roselily hears the preacher's words, "let him speak," she thinks that maybe she should have let her husband-to-be "speak" to her more about what their life together would be like: "She wishes she had asked him to explain more of what he meant." Yet, Roselily had been eager to marry him because he represented a new life and promise of "freedom." She was "impatient to see the South Side, where they would live and build and be respectable and respected and free. Her husband would free her.... A new life! Respectable, reclaimed, renewed. Free!" However, as she stands at the altar, Rosemary's current thoughts about the marriage undercut her original dreams of freedom.

As the wedding draws to a close, Roselily's "personal spirit" begins to assert itself all the more ardently against the marriage and the restrictions it represents. She imagines herself, her "personal spirit," in the marriage as a rat trapped in a cage: "Something strains upward behind her eyes. She thinks of the something as a rat trapped, cornered, scurrying to and fro in her head, peering through the windows of her eyes." At this point, Roselily's "personal spirit" rebels against the marriage through her desire "to live for once." Because he has sanctified the marriage, Roselily begins to see the preacher himself as a force standing in the way of her "freedom," her need to assert her "personal spirit": "The preacher is odious to her. She wants to strike him out of the way, out of her light, with the back of her hand. It seems to her he has always been standing in front of her, barring her way."

With the closing words, "his peace," the wedding ceremony is completed. In Roselily's mind, the marriage will not represent *her* peace, but only "his" peace—that of her husband. She thinks of being "joined" to this man as being imprisoned, feeling that "her husband's hand is like the clasp of an iron gate." And, while she is imprisoned by the marriage, her husband remains "free" within the marriage, as he holds out a "free hand" to the people crowding around him after the ceremony. And, while she before saw the preacher as the one "standing in front of her, barring her way," it is now her husband who "is standing in front of her."

Source: Liz Brent, in an essay for *Short Stories for Students*, Gale Group, 2001.

Rena Korb

Korb has a master's degree in English literature and creative writing and has written for a wide variety of educational publishers. In the following essay, she discusses Roselily's impending entrapment through marriage, and its relationship to the epigraphs that open the collection.

Two epigraphs drawing from vastly different cultures and time periods introduce Alice Walker's 1967 collection of short stories, *In Love and Trouble*. These epigraphs provide a subtle commentary on the stories to come, particularly "Roselily," the story that opens the volume, which traces the dreamlike state of a poor southern African-American woman on the verge of making her marriage vows to a Black Muslim who will take her and her children to a new life in Chicago.

The first epigraph is excerpted from *The Concubine*, a novel published in 1966 by noted Nigerian author Elechi Amadi. Amadi writes of the young Ahurole, who has over the past year or so erupted into "unprovoked sobbing" from time to time.

> But though intelligent, Ahurole could sometimes take alarmingly irrational lines of argument.... From all this her parents easily guessed that she was being unduly influenced by *agwu*, her personal spirit.... [T]he influence of the agwu could not be nullified overnight. In fact it would never be completely eliminated. Everyone was mildly influenced now and then by his personal spirit. A few like Ahurole were particularly unlucky in having very troublesome spirits.

Then, at the end of the selection, Amadi reveals the reason for the child's anxiety: "Ahurole was engaged to Ekwueme when she was eight years old."

The second selection comes from an early twentieth-century collection of the German poet Ranier Maria Rilke.

> People have (with the help of conventions) oriented all their solutions toward the easy and toward the easiest side of the easy; but it is clear that we must hold to what is difficult; everything in Nature grows and defends itself in its own way and is characteristically and spontaneously itself, seeks at all costs to be so and against all opposition.

In an article published in *The Black Scholar*, Barbara Christian refers directly to both of these epigraphs. She raises the crucial question the story poses in her introduction to "Roselily."

> The form of her [Roselily's] story, itself a marriage ceremony, is a replica of the convention, the easy solution to which she has been oriented. As a poor black woman with four illegitimate children, she is, it seems, beyond redemption. Thus, her wedding day, attended as it is by satin voile, and lily of the valley, is from any number of viewpoints a day of triumph. But *she*, how does she see it?

Throughout the ceremony, Roselily's subconscious mind constantly questions her "triumph." As Christian points out, Walker uses only the pronoun "she" throughout the ceremony, never "I"; it is "as if Roselily is being seen from an external point of view. . . . It is as if even in Roselily's mind, the being who wonders about, questions this day of triumph, is both herself, and yet not herself." Though Roselily successfully distances herself from her own realization of the truth, the story clearly shows her double awareness that she has made the easy choice and that she is troubled by it.

Marriage will offer for Roselily a life of relative ease, for her children greater opportunities, and for the family, respectability for the first time. Up until this moment, Roselily's life has consisted of "doing everything for three children, alone" (the fourth she gave to his father in the North because he "had some money"). She supported them through her work in a sewing factory, where she constantly worried about "learning to sew straight seams in workingmen's overalls, jeans, and dress pants." She has "prayed for" a chance to rest, but her thoughts as the preacher utters the words "*to join this man and this woman*" show that much of her inclination to marry comes because of desire to better her children's lives. She sees the marriage as a union between her and her children and the man. In Chicago, the children will have "a chance to build . . . at last [be out] from underneath the detrimental wheel. A chance to be on top." At the end of the ceremony, the children look at their stern stepfather with distaste and awe, because he is different from everyone they have known, but also with hope for the future they know he can bring them to.

> When the preacher utters the words 'to join this man and this woman' Roselily's mind immediately jumps to 'ropes, chains, handcuffs."

The marriage also offers Roselily respectability for the first time in her life. The girls she has grown up with are married to men who are "hanging around her, already old, seedy." In Panther Burn the fathers of her children drive by, "waving, not waving" as the mood hits them. They are only "reminders of times she would just as soon forget." She has the self-awareness that she "does not even know if she loves" her new husband, but she is certain that she "loves his sobriety. . . . She loves his pride. She loves his understanding of her *condition*."

Though Roselily tries to convince herself that she is pleased at "finally being married, like other girls," her *agwu* will not be so accepting. Like Ahurole, who is unwittingly and unhappily engaged, Roselily's impending fate causes her deepseated anxiety. As Christian notes, Roselily's *agwu*, which is "troubled by change," expresses its feeling "only in her dreaming." Still this spirit makes itself known—both to the reader, and more importantly, to Roselily, who already understands that her marriage will not provide freedom but entrapment. As the story opens and the preacher welcomes the guests to the ceremony, Roselily dreams she is a child standing with "knee raised waist high through a bowl of quicksand soup." This is only the first of many images of entrapment presented in the story. Roselily's *agwu* continues to bring her impending fate to her through images of physical restraints. She thinks of her father's occupation, a trapper who sold the skins of wild animals to Sears. When the preacher utters the words "*to join this man and this woman*" Roselily's mind immediately jumps to "ropes, chains, handcuffs." Her very clothes represent her bondage, and "her body itches to be free of satin and voile, organdy and lily of the valley." She knows she is "[y]oked" to a future that does not appeal to her. She will be forever held in "her husband's hand [which] is like the clasp of an iron gate."

Her husband's religious beliefs provide the main basis for her entrapment. As Christian explains the precepts of the Black Muslims, "to the man she is marrying, God is Allah, the devil is the white man, and work is building a black nation." He looks down on Roselily, her family, and her community members for following the "teachings from the wrong God"—the white man's Christian God. Instead, Roselily will be forced to embrace Islam, a religion that traditionally segregates women. During worship, women are "required to sit apart with covered head." The *purdah*, which religious law requires all Islamic women to wear in public, becomes symbolically the marriage veil that she now wears. In her book-length study *Alice Walker* Donna Haisty Winchell explains, "The marriage veil has been transformed into the purdah, the outward sign that in her womanhood she is inferior and that marriage is a binding, not a freeing." Roselily also recognizes that she is submitting her children to her husband's ideology. She thinks of her new "lifetime of black and white. Of veils. Covered head. It is as if her children are already gone from her." Her husband will place them "exalted on a pedestal" as new members of the black nation. This stalk, she thinks, "has no roots," because her children will lose all contact with their background and where and who they come from.

To her husband, this is preferred. He looks down upon Roselily's people for their rural southern background. "She knows he blames Mississippi for the respectful way the men turn their heads up in the yard, the women standing waiting and knowledgeable." He does not understand the "country black folks." Instead, he will take her to Chicago, which becomes, for Roselily, yet another symbol of entrapment. In Chicago, she will see for the first time a cinder, "which they never had in Panther Bluff." She sees her neighbors as "clean," but Chicago as filled with "black specks falling, clinging, from the sky," which itself will oppress her. "She thinks of the air, the smoke, the cinders. Imagines cinders big as hailstones; heavy, weighing on the people." These ashes—symbols of the spent city—become ropes that will choke off "the springs of laughter."

Instead of looking ahead to the future, throughout the entire ceremony, Roselily's *agwu* draws her to her past. "She thinks of her mother, who is dead.... She thinks of cemeteries and the long sleep of grandparents mingling in the dirt. She believes that she believes in ghosts." The dead relatives become a part of her *agwu* as well. They provide the "arm [that] seems to reach out from behind her and snatch her backward." She cannot think of her and her husband's life "*together*" but rather of her own memories, which "crash against her." She has "[m]emories of being bare to the sun" because she knows that soon she will spend her life covered in the robes and veils of religion. She will be forced to hide her body and its sexuality, except for in its procreative function. For she knows "[t]hey will make babies.... They will be inevitable.... Babies. She is not comforted."

Where, she wonders, does a person put her memories in a "brand-new life"? She particularly recalls the father of her fourth child who was "a good man but weak." Its placement in the story—coming as the preacher speaks the words "*in holy matrimony*"—implies that he was the man Roselily wanted to marry and a contrast to the man she is now marrying. For the northerner, classical music and chess are more important than the basic, primal draw of religion. He came to Mississippi during Freedom Summer of 1964 "to try to right the country's wrongs" by registering rural African-American voters, while Roselily's husband seemed to come to the South—a region for which he has no fondness—simply to find who he could "redo ... into what he truly wants." The husband will attempt to build a separate African-American society, while the northerner tried to integrate Roselily and her people into white society.

By the end of the story, before the final moment when she must speak those irrevocable words that accept the marriage, Roselily has become the rat that is "trapped, cornered, scurrying to and fro in her head, peering through the windows of her eyes." Significantly, she attempts to distance herself from this image: she only feels *something* behind her eyes—she does not see herself as the rat. She has the realization that she "wants to live for once. But doesn't quite know what that means." She wonders if she has ever really loved, "[i]f she ever will." The immediate rage she then feels toward the preacher, wanting to "strike him out of the way," feeling that he has always been "barring her way," shows her subconscious knowledge that she never will. It also shows her impotent urge to strike against her fate.

Though Roselily only acknowledges this truth through a dreamlike state, she clearly understands, as Winchell says, "the price she is about to pay for financial security and a future for her children." Winchell, however believes that the "search for psychological wholeness is at the heart of 'Roselily'." Realistically, the title character has little ability to achieve this. Triply disenfranchised—being poor, African-American, and female—life presents Roselily with few appealing options. Thus "Roselily" demonstrates the themes raised by Walker's choice of epigraphs. Instead of holding on to what is difficult, Roselily makes the convenient choice in her marriage, but is vastly disturbed by her actions. After she is irrevocably bound to her husband through marriage, the "worried" Roselily "feels ignorant, *wrong*, backward."

As Christian points out, however, Roselily's "dreaming is as separate from her external behavior as this Mississippi country church is from her future home.... But at least she can, in her imagination, know her confinement to be troublesome and recognize in a part of herself that this change is not the attainment of *her* fulfillment." As such, "Roselily" is an apt story to open this collection, significantly subtitled, "Stories of Black Women," for it raises issues that haunt the remaining stories—and the lives of African-American women.

Source: Rena Korb, in an essay for *Short Stories for Students*, Gale Group, 2001.

Carolyn Fowler

In the following review, Fowler presents an overview of the story "Roselily."

Alice Walker is an exceptionally good writer. More than that, she has the artist's insight into the quiet dramas enacted in the inner lives of those who are anonymous and ineffable: most of us. All of which adds up to a young writer of great promise and great potential.

The promise—and the potential—are manifest in Ms. Walker's first volume of short stories, *In Love and Trouble: Stories of Black Women*. The stories take in a wide spectrum of the black woman's experience in America. We are afforded glimpses of the young rural Southern woman without a husband ("Roselily,", "Strong Horse Tea"), the bored, upper class educated housewife who wanders into a love affair with a stranger ("Really, Doesn't Crime

A member of the Black Muslims sells papers featuring leader Elijah Muhammad in 1960s Chicago. The Islamic religion figures prominently in 'Roselily,' as the title character marries a Black Muslim, moves north, and contemplates how conversion to Islam will change her life.

Pay?"), the deeply religious old woman who "stood with eyes uplifted in her Sunday-go-to-meeting clothes" ("The Welcome Table"), the black campus co-ed strangely relating to the strange white professor of French ("We Drink the Wine in France"), the conjuring tradition ("The Revenge of Hannah Kemhuff").

I have the impression that the author has first-hand knowledge of many of the different life-styles she portrays in these stories. But love is not at issue in all of them. Rather, the authentic Heart of a Woman at the core of most of them shines through to pierce the surface of our caring. Yet, it is always the poignant, sad and unfulfilled heart, and primarily as it manifests itself in the rural South, which is revealed to us. The one story not set in blackamerica ("The Diary of an African Nun") does show the same lonely biding visible in most of the other women portrayed, but would probably have been better situated in a subsequent volume. And Ms.

Walker's talent for affecting our sensitivities is often badly served by the tinge of cynicism she projects into many of her dénouements. All of which goes to say that *In Love and Trouble* is a book of great sensitivity, but a sensitivity not yet completely, fully realized.

Yet, these stories do succeed for the most part in creating a mood on which the reader is transposed to a state of being which, for want of more precise labels, we may call the esthetic experience. Thus, they hover in the vague no-man's-land where poetry pervades the atmosphere and obliges the world of reason to yield before the spiritual realities of the soul's yearning after more than it has. So it is that almost all of these stories focus on the most intimate reaches of the inner lives of the characters. But the purity of the esthetic experience is often marred by obvious contrivances, as in the story which opens the collection ("Roselily" —an unfortunate choice for first place, perhaps). Roselily stands beside the vaguely outlined figure of the man who will take her from her rural southern past and roots into the big city with her illegitimate children, and snatches of her conflicting thought alternate with the minister's recitation of the marriage ceremony. The device soon becomes tedious, and the experiencer of the story (the reader) soon becomes in spite of himself the critical observer of the writer's craft.

Source: Carolyn Fowler, "Solid at the Core," in *Freedomways*, Vol. 14, No. 1, 1974, pp. 59–60.

Sources

Bouise, Oscar A., Review of *In Love and Trouble*, in *Bestsellers*, Vol. 33, No. 14, October 15, 1973, p. 335.

Christian, Barbara, "The Contrary Women of Alice Walker," in *The Black Scholar*, Vol. 12, No. 2, March–April 1981, p. 23.

Freeman, Alma S., "Zora Neale Hurston and Alice Walker: A Spiritual Kinship," in *Sage*, Vol. 2, No. 1, Spring, 1985, pp. 37–40.

Hall, Mary Washington, "An Essay on Alice Walker," in *Alice Walker: Critical Perspectives Past and Present*, edited by Henry Louis Gates, Jr. and K. A. Appiah, Amistad, 1993, p. 42.

Nyabongo, V. S., Review of *In Love and Trouble*, in *Books Abroad*, Vol. 48, No. 4, Autumn, 1974, p. 787.

Petry, Alice Hall, "Walker: The Achievement of the Short Fiction," in *Alice Walker: Critical Perspectives Past and Present*, edited by Henry Louis Gates, Jr. and K. A. Appiah, Amistad, 1993, pp. 194, 205.

Pratt, Louis H. and Darnell D. Pratt, *Alice Malsenior Walker: An Annotated Bibliography: 1968–1986*, Meckler, 1988, pp. 51–58.

Smith, Barbara, "The Souls of Black Women," in *Ms.*, Vol. 2, February, 1974, pp. 42–43.

Walker, Alice, "From an Interview" [with John O'Brien], *In Search of Our Mothers' Gardens*, Harvest/Harcourt Brace Jovanovich, 1983, pp. 249, 251, 263–64, 265.

———, "Saving the Life That Is Your Own: The Importance of Models in the Artist's Life," in *In Search of Our Mothers' Gardens*, Harvest/Harcourt Brace Jovanovich, 1983, pp. 7, 13.

Winchell, Donna Haisty, *Alice Walker*, Twayne, 1992, p. 31.

Wright, Mercedes A., "Black Woman's Lament," in *The Crisis*, Vol. 81, No. 1, January, 1974, p. 31.

Further Reading

Petry, Alice Hall, "Walker: The Achievement of the Short Fiction," in *Alice Walker: Critical Perspectives Past and Present*, edited by Henry Louis Gates, Jr. and K. A. Appiah, Amistad, 1993, pp. 193–210.
  This is the first serious critical appraisal of Walker's short stories. Petry is harshly critical of *You Can't Keep a Good Woman Down*, because it does not live up to the power and insight of *In Love and Trouble*.

Pratt, Louis H. and Darnell D. Pratt, *Alice Malsenior Walker: An Annotated Bibliography: 1968–1986*, Meckler, 1988.
  For the years mentioned in the title, this is a thorough annotated bibliography of works by Walker, and of critical articles, biographical articles, reviews and essays about Walker and her work. As the authors explain, the helpful annotations are descriptive, rather than evaluative.

Walker, Alice, *Banned*, Aunt Lute Books, 1996.
  This is an analysis of some of the controversies surrounding Walker's fiction. The book also reprints the short stories "Roselily" and "Am I Blue?" and the first chapter of *The Color Purple*, all of which have been criticized or restricted.

Washington, Mary Helen, "An Essay on Alice Walker," in *Alice Walker: Critical Perspectives Past and Present*, edited by Henry Louis Gates, Jr., and K. A. Appiah, Amistad, 1993, pp. 37–49.
  This essay examines Walker's "preoccupation" with writing about black women. After a brief history of the situations of black women in the United States since the eighteenth century, Washington demonstrates how Walker's fiction and poetry trace a history of psychological development from slavery to enlightenment.

Winchell, Donna Haisty, *Alice Walker*, Twayne, 1992.

This overview examines Walker's life, and analyzes all of her published work through *The Temple of My Familiar*. Winchell examines survival and the search for wholeness as Walker's central theme, and demonstrates the theme's handling in ''Roselily.''

Say Yes

Tobias Wolff

1985

Tobias Wolff is perhaps best known by the American reading public for his memoir *This Boy's Life*, which was later made into an acclaimed movie, but his literary reputation was first established on the merit of his short stories. He is still primarily known for these short stories, in which he depicts many characters' voices and a wide range of emotions. Since the early 1980s, Wolff has produced several collections of short stories. These fictions focus on the important relationships and the moral choices in everyday people's lives: men and women, husbands and wives, parents and children. As scholar Marilyn C. Wesley writes in the *Dictionary of Literary Biography*, Wolff writes ''about the basic needs of Everyman, written with a respect that Everyman deserves.''

Wolff has often been likened to other writers of his generation such as Raymond Carver and Richard Ford. In his short stories, Wolff practices a direct, even nondramatic, style of writing. This is certainly the case in his story ''Say Yes,'' which takes as its backdrop an average evening in the life of a married couple. When the conversation delves into an issue on which the couple do not agree, the relationship experiences a newfound rockiness. The husband's reaction to this argument demonstrates the secret undercurrents that run through relationships.

Author Biography

Tobias Wolff was born in 1945 in Alabama. His parents divorced when he was a boy. Wolff's mother retained custody of him, while his brother Geoffrey—who also became a writer—lived with their father. As a child, Wolff traveled with his mother, Rosemary, to the Pacific Northwest, where she remarried. This period of Wolff's life is recounted in *This Boy's Life: A Memoir*, which was later made into a film.

Wolff briefly attended preparatory school on the East Coast, but he was expelled. From 1964 through 1968, Wolff served as a lieutenant with the U.S. Army Special Forces (Green Berets) in Vietnam. He later recounted his wartime experiences in the memoir *In the Pharaoh's Army: Memoirs of the Lost War*.

Wolff earned his B.A. in 1972 and then his M.A. from Oxford University three years later. That year, his first book, *Ugly Rumours*, was published in London. Also that year, he won a prestigious Stegner Fellowship from Stanford University. From 1975 through 1978, he worked as a Stegner lecturer at Stanford, and in 1978, he received a second M.A.

Wolff began publishing regularly with the 1981 appearance of the short story collection *In the Garden of the North American Martyrs*. Over the next four years, Wolff published two more short story collections. His stories also appeared in numerous magazines, and several have been selected for inclusion in the O. Henry Prize Stories series. Wolff has also been awarded numerous grants, such as those from the National Endowment for the Arts, and has won national prizes.

In 1980, Wolff and his family moved to New York State, where he became a writer in residence for Syracuse University. Wolff remained there for seventeen years, until he was offered a position at Stanford University as the head of the graduate writing program. Wolff has lived in northern California since then, where he continues to work primarily on short stories.

Tobias Wolff

Plot Summary

The unnamed husband and his wife, Ann, are washing and drying the dishes when they begin to discuss interracial marriages. The husband says that he thinks it is a bad idea for African Americans and whites to marry. His wife wants to know why he thinks so, and the narrator immediately believes that she is implying he is a racist. She responds that she doesn't think he is racist, but she just doesn't see what is wrong with interracial marriage. The husband says that whites and African Americans come from different cultural backgrounds, so they can never really know and understand each other. He also believes that foreigners should not marry Americans, because they come from a completely different background.

Ann, clearly upset by the conversation, cuts her hand when she plunges it back in the water to continue washing dishes. The husband runs to the bathroom to get first-aid equipment. He cleans out the cut, which turns out to be shallow and fairly superficial. He feels he has done something good by reacting to the accident so quickly, and he hopes that she will return the favor by not picking up the conversation again. Ann, however, states that he wouldn't have married her if she were African American. The husband avoids answering by telling her that if she were, in fact, African American, the two probably wouldn't have even met because they would have traveled in different social circles. Ann persists in her line of hypothetical reasoning, imagining that she were African American, and they did meet, and they did fall in love. The husband responds with what he considers to be reason: that if Ann were African American, she wouldn't be her. Ann acknowledges this to be true but continues with her questioning, wanting to know if he would still marry her if she were African American. The husband says he is thinking about it, but Ann says that she knows he won't marry her. When pressed, he admits that he wouldn't marry her. Ann thanks him for answering and then goes to the living room and reads a magazine.

The husband knows that his wife is angry, and her feigned indifference to him hurts him. He decides he must show his own indifference to her, so he cleans up the kitchen and takes out the garbage. Outside, looking at the lights of the town, he feels ashamed that he let his wife get him into a fight. He thinks about how close they are and how well they know each other. He even does not bother to throw rocks, as he usually does, at the dogs that had knocked over the garbage can.

When he goes back inside, the house is dark, and Ann is in the bathroom. He stands outside of the door and apologizes, promising he will make it up to her. She asks how he will do that. Not expecting this question, he whispers that he will marry her, knowing he had to come up with the right answer. She says, "We'll see," and tells him to go on to bed. He gets into their bed, and then hears her say from the hallway to turn off the light. He does so, and the room goes dark. He hears Ann move across the room, but he can see nothing. The room is silent, as he listens for another sound—the sound of a stranger.

Characters

Ann
See Wife

Husband
The husband in the story is generally an unsympathetic character. He appears to have racist feelings and seems to be dishonest with himself. He claims to appreciate the stability his life with Ann provides him, but he still makes efforts to undermine it. He refuses to take responsibility for his actions. Throughout the evening, he is seen to be less than a genuine person; he does things for effect rather than out of a genuine, sincere desire. Within the confines of the story, his most significant trait is his rejection of his wife, which she takes quite seriously, much to his surprise. By the end of the story, the husband demonstrates yet another shift in mood: excitement as he realizes that, in certain ways, his wife is unknowable to him. The final scene has him awaiting his wife in their darkened bedroom, imagining that she is a stranger—a fact that he seems to embrace, as demonstrated by the excited pounding of his heart.

Wife
The wife in the story, Ann, gets angry at her husband when he says he would not marry her if she were an African American. Ann demonstrates what she feels and thinks through her actions. When she is angry at what she perceives to be her husband's racism, her discomfort shows as she thoughtlessly plunges her hands into the dishwater and cuts her thumb. After she retires to the living room, after her husband says he wouldn't marry her, she makes her feelings clear by deliberately scrutinizing the pages of her magazine. When she goes to bed, she makes clear the deep wound her husband has inflicted upon her by refusing to answer his knock on the bathroom door and not responding to his subsequent apology. By the end of the story, though he has said he would marry her, she does not commit to forgiving him. She even indicates that she might not accept "his offer" of marriage. She does venture into their bedroom, where her husband is already in bed, but only on the condition that her husband turn off the light. This request seems to indicate her alienation from him: she may not want him to see her, since he can't *truly* see her; or she may not want to see the man she married.

Themes

Racism
The idea of racism is a theme in the story, for the implication of the husband's racism is what causes the couple to quarrel. The wife dislikes her husband's beliefs that African Americans are different from whites. He maintains that it is not that he is prejudiced against African Americans, but that they come from a different culture than white people— "they even have their own language." His protestation that "I *like* hearing them talk"—because it makes him feel happy—reveals much about his personality: his belief that African Americans are inherently foreign to whites, his condescending attitude, and his sense of otherness from himself—

he needs something completely unlike himself to bring him pleasure.

The husband's negative response to Ann's question of whether he would marry her were she African American indicates the pervasive and destructive nature of his racism. Though the story provides no other context against which to view his relations with people who are not white, his instance of refusing to marry his wife shows that he thinks that African Americans are not like he and his wife, but perhaps more importantly, that for him, love does not go deeper than skin color—deeper than the superficial. Though he claims that he can only love her if she is white because otherwise "you wouldn't be you," the implication is that he wouldn't love a black Ann. The husband's actions successfully negate his pretensions to their close relationship. They also show that the narrowness of looking at people through eyes that only register exteriors, such as skin color, can cut people off from others.

Love and Marriage

The husband in the story believes that he and his wife enjoy a close relationship, one based on years of being together. As the story opens, they appear to be working compatibly in the kitchen, she washing the dishes and he drying; they seem to be partners. The husband's self-congratulations about helping his wife, however, indicate that he is not truly comfortable in this role. The husband also is culpable of getting them involved in the discussion that leads to the argument, for he sees that she is getting upset, yet he keeps pushing the issue. Indeed, the conversation about African Americans and interrelationships calls into question the crux of their marriage. The husband's refusal to marry his wife if she were African American shows how little true affection is involved in this relationship. That the reader does not see the couple make up further affirms the relative isolation that people can live in even within a supposedly secure marriage.

The fact that the husband, in all of his ruminations on the fight, never mentions his love for his wife is significant. Instead, he thinks about "how close they were" and "how well they knew each other." When he apologizes to his wife, and tells her he would marry her, even then he does not speak of love. Only Ann mentions the word *love* during the conversation. When Ann says, "'Let's say I am black and unattached and we meet and fall in love,'" the husband does not even respond to the idea of the emotion; instead, he repeats, "'If you were black you wouldn't be you.'" His response

Topics for Further Study

- How do you think the husband and wife will resolve their situation? Do you think they will resolve it? Write a scene that takes place the following day.

- Analyze the husband in terms of whether or not he is a racist character.

- Unlike many stories, "Say Yes" lacks any significant interior drama. What do you think the characters are thinking while their argument is taking place and afterwards? Write a paragraph on this topic.

- Write a counterargument to the husband's statement that African Americans "don't come from the same culture" as whites.

- The husband says to his wife in defense of his position on interracial marriages, "'Don't take my word for it. Look at the statistics. Most of those marriages break up.'" Conduct research to find out statistics of how many interracial marriages versus same-race marriages break up. Can you come up with a hypothesis for your findings?

shows that he is more attached to the *idea* of Ann—what Ann represents for him—than to being in love with Ann.

Alienation

Although he does not recognize it, the husband depicted in "Say Yes" is alienated both from his wife and from himself. He perceives that they have a close relationship, yet he cannot even imagine marrying his wife if she were African American because then she would not be the same woman he first met. That he sees his feelings for his wife as intrinsically linked to skin color demonstrates that he does not appreciate her as a complete, whole being—rather, he cares for those aspects of her that he believes he can understand. Under such circumstances, it is not possible for the husband to have a full and truly loving relationship with his wife.

A suggestion is made at the end of the story as to from where this inability to embrace his "complete" wife stems: his own desire for that which is strange and unknown. Lying in bed, in the darkness, he hears his wife move through the room. He reacts to these auditory cues in the same way he would react if he heard a noise echoing in the house—the noise of an intruder. The excitement he feels at hearing his "unknown" wife shows his alienation from himself, for he has not even readily acknowledged his own desire for something or someone different; it takes a bad argument to point out this facet of himself.

Style

Narration and Construction

The story is told chronologically, and the story takes place over a brief period of time: the space of one evening. The narration is relatively straightforward; the narrative voice does not delve into the thought processes of the characters. Readers never even learn the name of the husband, and only learn the wife's name after she has cut her hand, almost halfway through the story.

The story's construction is relatively simple: A husband and wife engage in an argument about a specific topic. The problem of the story, in part, however, derives from the fact that what they are arguing about is an important issue: Do you love someone for what they are or who they are? While the husband would argue that he does both, that his wife would not be who she is without being what she is, the ending shows that even his perception of his relationship with his wife is not as simple as he pretends. As the husband is excited to welcome the "stranger"—his wife—to his bed his reactions bring a new complexity to their relationship and to the story itself.

Point of View

The point of view of "Say Yes" is the third-person, limited point of view. Jonathan Penner writes in the *Washington Post* that such a "narrative mode permits an exterior view of even the central figure, which seems to be why Wolff employs it. He's disinclined to tell stories from the inside out, to present a world through the thoughts and feelings of a viewpoint character. Instead, Wolff tries to create windows on the soul through speech and action."

The husband's point of view is made clear by what he says: that he believes that people of different races are different from himself, a white man. This revelation, around which the story centers, indicates a great deal about the character of the husband, as does the ways he expresses these ideas. His wife's reactions to his declaration that he would not marry her were she African American are also clear, although even less about her is revealed than about the husband. Her anger is apparent through her measured turning of the magazine pages, and her feeling of disconnection from her husband is made clear when she wants him to turn the light off before she enters their bedroom.

Imagery

The story is quite short and straightforward, yet it still contains a few important images. When the husband squeezes Ann's injured thumb, "a single drop of blood welled up, trembling and bright, and fell to the floor''; this drop of blood stands for the tears that Ann does not shed. When the husband goes outside, he sees two "mutts" who live down the street knocking over his garbage can. The dogs, who are not fighting, still are portrayed with an edge of violence: "One of them was rolling around on his back, and the other had caught something in her mouth. Growling, she topped it into the air, leaped up and caught it, growled again and whipped her head from side to side.'' The controlled intensity of the scene mimics the one that has just taken place between the husband and the wife. The husband seems to recognize this truth, for instead of heaving rocks at them, like he usually does, he lets them go away unharmed.

Historical Context

The Republican Years

The 1980s was a decade led by Republican thinking and policy. Ronald Reagan took office as president of the United States in 1980, and he served two terms, after which his vice president, George Bush, was elected to the nation's top office. Reagan held conservative political beliefs, both on the domestic front and when it came to foreign policy. Although his economic programs brought the national inflation rate down, they also seemed to favor the wealthy. During the Reagan era, many middle-

Compare & Contrast

- **1980s:** At the beginning of the 1980s, nine percent of all United States households are made up solely of a married couple. There are over forty-eight million married couples in the United States.

  1990s: At the end of the 1990s, only three percent of all United States households are made up solely of a married couple. There are close to fifty-five million married couples in the United States.

- **1980s:** In 1980, 67.2 percent of the white American population is married, and 51.4 percent of the African-American population is married.

  1990s: While more than half of the American population continues to marry, the percentages for both whites and African Americans has decreased in the past ten years. In 1997, 62.1 percent of the white American population is married, and 42.4 percent of the African-American population is married.

- **1980s:** In 1980, there are 651,0000 interracial couples in the United States. Of these couples, 167,000 are made up of a white and a black American.

  1990s: The number of interracial couples has risen a great deal in the past ten years. In 1990, there are 1,264,000 interracial couples in the United States. Of these couples, 311,000 are made up of a white and a black American.

- **1980s:** In 1980, of a total of just over forty-nine million married U.S. couples, almost half do not have children under the age of eighteen.

  1990s: In 1997, of a total of almost fifty-four million married U.S. couples, close to twenty-nine million do not have children under the age of eighteen.

- **1980s:** In 1980, the marriage rate in the United States is 10.6 per 1,000 people, and the divorce rate is 5.2 per 1,000.

  1990s: In the mid-1990s, both the marriage and divorce rates have fallen over the past ten years. In 1995, the marriage rate in the United States is 9.7 per 1,000 people, and the divorce rate is 4.4 per 1,000.

---

class Americans saw their personal income shrinking, while the richest of Americans increased their wealth.

By the 1980s, the cold war, led by superpowers the United States and the Soviet Union, had been ongoing for almost forty years. Reagan, an ardent opponent of communism, encouraged his administration to greatly increase military spending. As the United States and the Soviet Union built up a stockpile of nuclear weapons capable of destroying the earth several times over, many Americans came to fear the possibility of a nuclear war. By the end of the 1980s, however, U.S.-Soviet relations had thawed dramatically, primarily as the Soviet government began to initiate greater political and economic freedoms. As countries throughout Eastern Europe also renounced or rebelled against their communist governments, cold war tensions dissipated.

A Changing America

During the 1980s, Americans were increasingly spending more money on leisure and entertainment activities, such as sporting events, movies, and health clubs. However, although many sociologists had proclaimed their belief that people would have more leisure time, this did not come to fruition; instead, most people worked more hours but had less money to show for it.

In the 1980s, more blue collar workers were slipping through to the lowest layers of the middle or even to the lower class. Unemployment reached as high as twenty percent among factory workers. African Americans and Hispanics had a harder time getting and keeping jobs than did white Americans; they were often the last hired and the first fired. More than thirty percent of African Americans—or nine million people—were classified as poor.

In contrast, the 1980s saw the rise of the Yuppie—young, urban professionals. Yuppies were usually white men and women between college age and forty. They often worked in middle management, banking, the law, or the high-tech fields. They had extraneous income to spend on household extravagances. Books such as Tom Wolfe's *Bonfire of the Vanities* satirize and depict these Yuppies, portraying them as leading spiritually empty lives.

The 1980s was also when the fatal disease AIDS first came to public awareness. It had surfaced in Central Africa in the mid-1970s, but was not discovered in the United States until early the next decade. The number of reported AIDS cases rose dramatically throughout the 1980s, reaching over 50,000 by mid-decade.

Race Relations

During the 1980s, civil rights policies and legislation from previous years were attacked and sometimes reversed. Many African Americans became discouraged, and a *Newsweek* poll conducted in 1988 showed that seventy-one percent of the African Americans surveyed believed that the federal government was doing "too little" to help African Americans.

The 1980s were riddled with racial incidents. The decade opened with riots in Miami, following the acquittal of four white police officers in the beating death of an African-American man and ended in 1989 with the fatal shooting of a sixteen-year-old African-American boy by young white men. In between these incidents came attacks by Neo-Nazis and members of the Ku Klux Klan. In the 1980s, David Duke, a former grand wizard of the Klan, also won a seat in the Louisiana legislature, elected by a virtually all-white suburb of New Orleans. This victory was a disgrace to the Republican Party, as Duke ran on that ticket. The decade also saw a rise in racially motivated incidents on college campuses.

The 1988 Presidential Elections

African-American leader Jesse Jackson ran for president in 1984 and again in 1988. He sought to unite a "Rainbow Coalition"—a diverse group of voters representing all races, classes, and creeds. His candidacy drew many African-American voters to the polls. Although Jackson won more votes in the 1988 Democratic primary than any other candidate, Massachusetts' governor Michael Dukakis won more delegates, and he ran for president against George Bush. Race issues played into the campaign, as Bush's campaign focused on an African-American convicted murderer who had attacked a couple while out of jail on a weekend pass under a Massachusetts prison program; some critics charged that the ads were racist, that they played on white America's fear of black criminals.

Critical Overview

Wolff's first short story collection, *In the Garden of the North American Martyrs*, was published in 1981. When *Back in the World*, which collected "Say Yes," was published four years later, many reviewers commented on how it differed from its predecessor. Mona Simpson writes in the *New Republic* that she finds the second batch of stories to be "in a more somber mode." They "feel omniscient," she says, "universal, with biblical resonance." She continues, "In these new stories, Wolff works with the same thematic concerns, the same passion for moral questions, but his fictional canvas is sparer and simpler.... He has chosen more dramatic, emblematic characters." These characteristics, according to Simpson, add a new power to Wolff's work. She sums up *Back in the World* as a collection of "stripped-down moral fables."

Geoff Dyer, writing for the *New Statesman*, finds this collection far superior to the first, calling the stories "better and more expansive than those in Wolff's impressive but uneven first collection." Dyer proclaims that this collection lifted Wolff to the top ranks of American writers; "With this new volume," Dyer writes, "he rivals Raymond Carver as the finest male short story writer now working in America."

Many critics focused on Wolff's eye for detail, or in the words of *New York Times* critic Michiko Kakutani, "his gift for meticulous observation." In a review for the *Los Angeles Times*, Richard Eder praises Wolff's "lavish display of skill." Matthew Gilbert, writing for *Boston Review* notes the depth to which Wolff pays attention to the details of his stories; "Wolff also invests the settings of these

In the 1980s, the time during which 'Say Yes' was published, African-American leader Jesse Jackson ran twice for president and founded his 'Rainbow Coalition' organization.

stories with a life of their own. They embrace the main action and subtly become essential to the story. In 'Say Yes,' the kitchen utensils seem to participate in the argument between husband and wife.''

David Montrose of the *Times Literary Supplement* generally liked the collection, finding that Wolff "excels at creating people and moods," which he does "by showing, accreting detail, rather than telling." At times, however, some critics felt that this technique stifled Wolff's voice. Writes Jonathan Penner for the *Washington Post*, "Not even a writer as good as Wolff can eschew *he thought* and *he felt* forever," and concludes that "only a partial humanity percolates through action and speech."

Not all reviewers, however, lauded the collection. Russell Banks, in his review for the *New York Times Book Review*, states that the collection was "a considerable falling off for Mr. Wolff," and that it did not "measure up" to his previous published works. "Whereas the earlier stories used digression to build a dialectic, to make something *happen*, these seem to meander into narrative cul-de-sacs." The criticism of Thomas DePietro, of the *Hudson Review*, was similar to Banks's; DePietro finds fault with the "minimalist" mode in which Wolff works, noting particularly a "conspicuous absence of subject matter" in the stories. DePietro finds the shorter stories to end in a "pseudo-epiphany" and the longer stories to end "washed out and proud of it." Banks, however, demonstrates a keen awareness of Wolff's writing talent, noting the "brilliant moments" scattered in the stories, which made him "await Mr. Wolff's next book with all the more eagerness." Kakutani, who admits that there "is not a lot of hope" for Wolff's characters, nevertheless finds in their presentation "the promise of some kind of redemption in their fumbling efforts to connect with one another."

Since its publication, "Say Yes" has appeared in several anthologies. In many ways, it is highly representative of Wolff's short fiction, which tends to center on the human relationships and their inherent instability. As Marilyn C. Wesley states in her article on Wolff for the *Dictionary of Literary Biography*, Wolff's "is a genuinely humanistic fiction—both human and humane." Over the years, Wolff's reviewers have generally perceived this leaning. Relatively little explicit criticism about the story exists, however, one of its few specific references was negative: Montrose writing in the *Times Literary Supplement* believes that "Say Yes" was among the "least noteworthy" among Wolff's "generally admirable" collection of stories. Dyer, writing in the *New Statesmen*, states that "Wolff's characters never feel quite sure what's happening to them," a statement that seems to apply to "Say Yes," in which the husband reacts with bewilderment about the argument he finds himself in with his wife: "His stories are about people who don't know how they're going to end." Indeed, the closing lines of *"Say Yes"* demonstrate that uncertainty, as the husband listens for the sounds of his wife moving through their dark bedroom the same way he would listen to a stranger moving through their house.

Criticism

Rena Korb

Korb has a master's degree in English literature and creative writing and has written for a wide variety of educational publishers. In the following essay, she discusses how well the husband and wife truly know each other.

In writing an introduction to the short story collection *Matters of Life and Death*, Tobias Wolff, in his role as the editor, attempted to explain why he chose the stories for inclusion: "They [these writers] speak to us without flippancy, about things that matter. They write about what happens between men and women, parents and children. They write about fear of death, fear of life, the feelings that bring people together and force them apart, the costs of intimacy. They remind us that our house is built on sand. They are, every one of them, interested in what it means to be human." As Marilyn C. Wesley points out in her article on Wolff in the *Dictionary of Literary Biography*, with these words, Wolff "provided a definition of the guiding principles behind his own stories." She continues, "What his reviewers have consistently understood, and what Wolff himself implies, is that his is a genuinely humanistic fiction—both human and humane."

Wolff's short story "Say Yes" is very brief—only a few pages long—yet it takes place at a key moment in the relationship between a couple. They are given the opportunity to face each other and their truest feelings. After a chance conversation, one that comes about when they "somehow got on the subject of whether white people should marry black people," the couple get into an argument that will have repercussive effects in the important issues it raises between them: how much do they really know about each other, and more importantly, how much do they want to know?

While these questions cannot be fully answered based on such a brief text, the night in question does illustrate the deliberate "lies" under which a marriage can function. The husband has an image of himself that can best be defined as that of the "good" husband—one who helps out his wife, wants to understand her, and tries to make her happy. This image, however, does not hold up against the evidence of the husband's actions and motivations. For instance, the story opens with the husband and wife doing the dinner dishes but the husband immediately undercuts their partnership when he admits that for him "Helping out with the dishes was a way of showing how considerate he was" rather than an action undertaken sincerely. Similarly, the husband's later act of scouring the kitchen derives from his desire "to demonstrate his indifference" to his wife—in response to her indifference to him. The husband takes what should be acts of genuine kindness and turns them into statements about the marital relationship.

In addition to this duplicitous behavior, the husband, with deliberation and cognizance, provokes his wife into the argument. During the conversation, he notices his wife's reaction to his statement that white people and black people should not intermarry: "Sometimes his wife got this look where she pinched her brows together and bit her lower lip and stared down at something. When he saw her like this he knew he should keep his mouth shut, but he never did. Actually it made him talk more. She had that look now." These words show that the husband has a history, a pattern even, of bringing up and pursuing topics that his wife finds distasteful—most likely distasteful in their reflection upon her husband. After the fight, he denies any personal responsibility as he muses that he "felt ashamed that he had let his wife get him into a fight." Although in this instance he demonstrates remorse, he also erroneously blames his wife for initiating the quarrel. While these thoughts strengthen his claims of knowing his wife so well, they also reinforce that such awareness of another person can have a negative outcome: clearly, the husband understands that the expression he sees on her face

What Do I Read Next?

- Wolff's *This Boy's Life: A Memoir* is a riveting, autobiographical account of the author's teen years. Brought to the Pacific Northwest by his divorced mother, young Toby soon is forced to endure life under his strict and cruel stepfather. Toby's efforts to get away from his stepfather lead to his self-transformation.

- Wolff's second memoir, *In the Pharaoh's Army*, and his novella, *The Barracks Thief*, both evoke his experiences in the Vietnam War.

- Wolff's brother, the novelist Geoffrey Wolff, wrote a memoir of his childhood with the boys' father, *The Duke of Deception* (1979).

- Ann Beattie's short story ''Weekend'' (1978) explores the relationship between a husband and wife after the husband's repeated affairs.

- Short story writer Andre Dubus's ''The Fat Girl'' tells about the important relationships in a woman's life: to the food she eats and the people she loves. In the story, Louise, the fat girl, fights against her weight but also comes to accept that most people will judge her for how she looks on the outside, not for who she is on the inside.

- Richard Ford's collection of three novellas, *Women and Men*, depict turning points in the relationships of their central characters and explore universal truths and questions about how men and women—and people in general—get along.

- Raymond Carver is credited as a major force in the revitalization of the short story in the late twentieth century. His 1976 collection *Will You Please Be Quiet, Please?* established his reputation. In the title story of his 1988 collection *Where I'm Calling From*, Carver tells the story of a man searching for a meaningful connection.

- Annie Dillard, an American writer best known for her reflective essays, has written her autobiographical narrative, *An American Childhood* (1987).

---

derives from her dislike at his words and beliefs. Despite this comprehension, he continues to pursue the conversation.

Why he does so is unexplained by the text, but what is significant about the ensuing argument is the complete fallacy upon which he builds his side of it. According to the husband, marriage should be a union between people who think alike and can thus know each other well, and his argument against interracial marriage rests on the assumption that people of different races are quite dissimilar and thus do not belong together. '''How can you understand someone,''' queries the husband, '''who comes from a completely different background?''' This question takes on an ironic quality, though he doesn't understand it as such, for he and his wife evidence quite dissimilar opinions on the subject of interracial marriage. The husband's logic, then, would imply that he and his wife don't really belong together. As he tells his wife of African Americans and whites, '''A person from their culture and a person from our culture could never really *know* each other,''' but their disagreement aptly demonstrates that although people can come from a similar cultural background, they still might not be able to understand each others' viewpoints or belief systems.

The husband's insistence on sticking with his side despite the clear lack of logic suggests that, if, as he claims, he is not a racist, there is something else at stake in this argument. The most obvious suggestion is that the husband is deliberately, although perhaps subconsciously, trying to subvert the companionship that he claims he and his wife have built. As already mentioned, he is at fault for prolonging the argument, and once involved in it, he seems to make no effort to get himself and his wife to gracefully acquit themselves. The wife eventually forces her husband to answer this question:

> "After a chance conversation, one that comes about when they 'somehow got on the subject of whether white people should marry black people,' the couple get into an argument that will have repercussive effects in the important issues it raises between them: how much do they really know about each other, and more importantly, how much do they want to know?"

"'[Say] that I'm black, but still me, and we fall in love. Will you marry me?'" Here Ann, the wife, gives her husband the perfect opportunity to opt out of the argument; she is laying down the conditions that although she is black she is the same Ann he now knows. Under such circumstances, her husband has no reason not to marry her, but he still "thought about it" before turning her down. The husband refuses to use Ann's choice of words to allow him to salvage the evening and satisfactorily close the argument. This action strikes an incongruous note for a character who congratulates himself on acting out the role of the model husband.

The husband comes to regret this decision, recognizing that "[I]n another thirty years or so they would be both be dead. What would all that stuff matter then?" This moment of reflection leads him to apologize to his wife. But she doesn't react as he expected. Instead of forgiving him, she wants to know how he will make his rejection up to her. He realizes "from a sound in her voice, a level and definite note that was strange to him . . . that he had to come up with the right answer," so he says that he will marry her, which may or may not be a truthful answer. The tone of her voice is apparently the husband's first inclination that he cannot accurately read or predict his wife.

This distancing on the part of his wife has another effect, however, whether desired or not: she has become an unknown quantity. As the husband waits in their bed for his wife to come, he hears her moving across the room and suddenly his "heart pounded the way it had on their first night together." This sexual memory is then surrounded with fear and alarm and even a threat to personal safety as the husband further extends the metaphor, comparing the beating of his heart to the way it pounded "when he woke at a noise in the darkness and waited to hear it again—the sound of someone moving through the house, a stranger." The husband's likening of his wife to an intruder indicates how unexpected and potentially damaging is her behavior to him. He finally understands that he does not understand her as well as he has always believed he does. He also feels excitement, wanting to hear the noise again because it reminds him of his wife's otherness.

The husband's behavior at this moment adds support to the idea that he may have attempted to create a rift between them, or at least welcomed it. In part because of the brevity of the story, a reader cannot hope to fully understand the husband's reactions to the argument or his complicated feelings after it. However, the text indicates that the couple does not truly know each other as well as the husband would claim—despite "the years they had spent together, and how close they were." Further and perhaps more importantly, the story shows that sometimes it is best to not know another person fully. The conversation of the evening, for Ann, has the effect of making her feel estranged from and rejected by her husband. In contrast, her husband is excited by the realization that his wife still is capable of surprising him. Ironically, if he knew her as well as he claimed, he would not feel this good anxiety that he does at the end of the story. The ending lines of the story indeed affirm the positive aspects of what Marilyn C. Wesley has called a "healthy defamiliarization," a "bit of unknowability in even the most intimate relationships."

Source: Rena Korb, in an essay for *Short Stories for Students*, Gale Group, 2001.

Jennifer Lynch

Lynch is a freelance writer living in northern New Mexico. In the following essay, she discusses the disparity between ideas of normalcy and actual events.

Characteristic of the work of Tobias Wolff, "Say Yes" displays an everyday event and turns it inside out, illustrating the machinations of normalcy. In the course of an argument between a married couple, he makes explicit the disparity between the individual's idea of what is happening and actual events. Rather than dissect the human self-concept, Wolff displays the gap between self-image and behavior. He achieves the effects of both intimacy and simple directness through his use of lean, simple subject-verb sentence construction (in which the verb follows the subject) and few adjectives, adverbs, and descriptions. The simplicity of the sentences precludes explicating causal relationships; these are left to the reader to deduce, demanding active participation on the part of the reader. Surface normalcy is viewed through the lens of a third-person narrator who has limited access to the protagonist's thoughts, feelings, and sensations. The narrative takes place from a middle distance, which takes into account a limited amount of reaction and motivation on the part of characters, but provides enough distance from them so that the reader recognizes the absurdity inherent in the seemingly normal. Through such narrative, Wolff explodes preexisting ideas of normalcy and reveals the craziness in everyday life.

"Say Yes" opens with a conversation between a man and his wife while they wash and dry dishes, told with an eye to the man's point of view. Although at one point the man, effectively the protagonist, calls his wife Ann, they are essentially he and she, and in their anonymity they are any married couple, in their familiarity every married couple. Washing and drying the dishes and a series of other domestic evening tasks map the course of the evening, and reveal both the man's self-concept and the relationship between the couple. In the first sentence, the man is drying dishes while his wife washes. In the following sentence, it is reported that the husband washed dishes the previous evening. No causal relationship is made explicit between the two sentences through use of a word such as "because," but it is implied that the man is drying this evening because he washed the night before. From these first two sentences in the story, it is clear that the narrator has an emotional investment in being fair and doing what he thinks right. He refers to a time when his wife's friend congratulates her on having such a considerate husband, and his response is "*I try.*" In his own estimation he is "considerate," and his goal in helping out with housework is to show it. From this first paragraph, it is evident that the

> "When he encounters two neighborhood dogs in the trash, he chooses not to throw rocks at them the way he normally would, but lets them go, returned to his self-concept as a nice, considerate guy, but alerting the reader to the disparity between his real and imagined selves."

narrator is invested in being a nice guy; he seeks approval as much out of self-image as good intentions. Thus, his character is open to scrutiny from the beginning of the story.

Because of the narrator's self-proclaimed consideration, it comes as somewhat of a surprise when the narrative moves from his account of their conversation to the actual dialogue. Put on the defensive when his wife questions why he thinks black people and white people shouldn't marry, he tells her not to infer he is racist. Because he responds this way rather than answering her question, he comes across as defensive and hotheaded, in contrast to his self-image introduced a half page earlier. As the dialogue continues, he does answer her, reasoning that people from different cultures can never really know each other. His argument relies upon his conviction that he and his wife, apparently both white and from the same culture, know and understand each other in a deep way. His wife repeats his assertion to call it into question, suggesting that she does not share his conviction that he knows her so well. As the argument escalates, her husband notices that she washes the dishes carelessly, leaving many of them dirty. His attention to the domestic task at hand illustrates his displaced focus; he wants to be the good husband, do all the right things, but his attention is on the dishes when they are having a discussion that is clearly important to his wife. In her distraction and haste the wife cuts her thumb on a knife, interrupting the task which ties the argument together.

When the narrator's wife cuts herself, her husband rushes to her aid, running upstairs for alcohol and a Band-Aid. He asserts to himself that "He'd acted out of concern for her, with no thought of getting anything in return, but now the thought occurred to him that it would be a nice gesture on her part not to start up that conversation again, as he was tired of it.'' Clearly, he is attached to the idea of coming to his wife's rescue, and despite his disclaimer, wants to be rewarded for his behavior, again seeking approval. Rather than acquiesce, however, his wife chooses to dry dishes, throwing off the pattern of fairness established at the opening of the story, and increasing the tension. Ann poses the central question of the story, wondering whether her husband would have married her if she had been black. As he sidesteps the question, he washes the silverware with nearly antiseptic care, his urgent cleaning a counterpoint to the metaphoric mess created by this argument with his wife. As she presses him, Ann's eyes get bright, then brighter, as if with excitement, and although "He had won the argument . . . he still felt cornered." A shift takes place in the dialogue as the tension between the two builds; although the conversation is theoretical, their speech shifts to make it immediate. She asks, "Will you marry me?" and he responds, "Let's not move too fast on this. . . . We don't want to do something we would regret for the rest of our lives." The immediacy of the language lends urgency to the conversation, and an importance greater than a theoretical discussion, as if their marriage is truly at stake in this moment. Ann's stimulation, as indicated by her brightening eyes, and the mention of winning, lend themselves to the sense that this is a game, with high stakes. When her husband finally answers "No," his answer is as much about their mutual antagonizing as the question.

Once she receives this answer, Ann withdraws to the living room, and her husband feels punished by what he sees as her deliberate show of indifference. He feels he has "no choice but to demonstrate his own indifference to her" by continuing to clean the kitchen. The obligatory nature of the couple's behavior supports the image of a game with a prescribed set of rules. "Quietly, thoroughly," the husband finishes the dishes, wipes the counters, cleans up the blood from Ann's cut, and mops the entire floor. His cleaning demonstrates not only a show of indifference, but also his effort to show upright character, and to clean up what feels like a mess between them. When he is finished he notes that the kitchen looks new, as it did before they moved in. The implication is that it looks the way it did before they knew each other as well as he asserts they do now, and that their argument has pushed them back to a time of strangeness. He goes outside to empty the trash, and considers his relationship with his wife. Rather than taking responsibility for his defensiveness, he feels "ashamed that he had let his wife get him into a fight." He ruminates on his ideas about how "close" they are and all the time invested in their relationship, and he reacts physically to these thoughts, his neck tingling and chest tightening in a welling of emotion. This examination of his history and the ideas he has invested about himself and his wife, accurate or not, reverse the destabilizing effect of the argument, and he feels returned to himself. When he encounters two neighborhood dogs in the trash, he chooses not to throw rocks at them the way he normally would, but lets them go, returned to his self-concept as a nice, considerate guy, but alerting the reader to the disparity between his real and imagined selves.

In the last scene in the story, the husband contritely apologizes to his wife and says, "I'll make it up to you, I promise." Again, the words don't quite correlate with the argument, and suggest a greater urgency than the situation merits. When she responds with "How?" he "knew he had come up with the right answer," reinforcing the sense that this is, on some level, a game. He submits when he whispers "I'll marry you," again making the dialogue more current by using the present tense, and in so doing, heightening the tension between them. She responds with "We'll see. . . . Go on to bed." Her resistance is clearly an extension of the argument, but since they are already married, her reply has an element of flirtation, and the tension between them is clearly sexual. The man undresses and gets into bed, and his wife tells him to turn off the light before she comes in. There is a long pause before he hears her move in the dark across the room, a further extension of what is now explicit sexual tension between them. When he hears a movement and then nothing happens, his response is physical; his heart pounds the way it did the first time he was intimate with his wife, and the way it still does when he hears what sounds like an intruder in the house. In fact both are true in this closing scene; his excitement, which borders on fear, is his response to the strangeness between his wife and himself, and in the moment, in the course of what has become their game, she is a stranger. The moment recalls his assertion during their argument that people from other cultures can't really know each other the way they do. The conviction that they are close restores his sense of stability when he takes the trash out; it is fundamental to his identity that he and his wife know each other well, and when he reminds himself of this, he has a strong physical response. Now, at the end of the story, that assertion is inverted in such a way that although his wife is like a stranger to him in the moment, he has a similar physical response of excitement. Ultimately, she wins the evening's power struggle by making her husband "say yes" and, in the course of this sexual configuration, she demonstrates that much unknown goes between married partners. At the same time, the familiarity of the struggle indicates a game that is anything but new.

The argument between the man and his wife in "Say Yes" serves as a means of momentarily reinventing themselves, creating a strangeness which makes for both excitement and a threat to identity. The characters are never explicit about this; they appear to be unaware of it. They do not recognize the difference between what they believe is happening and what actually takes place. On the surface, they engage in an argument, but their shifts in language make the argument bigger than it actually is to either of them. They participate in a power struggle that, although familiar, allows them to temporarily become strangers and manifest sexual tension. "Say Yes" makes public the protagonist's private attachment to his identity and to ideas about the way his wife and his marriage are; in the course of the story, normalcy is turned on its head in what amounts to a game.

Source: Jennifer Lynch, in an essay for *Short Stories for Students*, Gale Group, 2001.

Liz Brent

Brent has a Ph.D. in American Culture, specializing in film studies, from the University of Michigan. She is a freelance writer and teaches courses in the history of American cinema. In the following essay, Brent discusses symbolic expressions of marital conflict in Wolff's story.

The 1985 short story "Say Yes," by Tobias Wolff, describes an argument between a husband and wife over the course of one evening during which they wash dishes, clean the kitchen, take out the garbage, and get ready for bed. As these chores are being carried out, the couple quarrel over the issue of whether or not he would have married her had she been black (they are both white). The way in which Wolff describes the carrying out of these chores expresses the subtle tensions building between the couple over the course of the evening.

As the story opens, the couple stands at the kitchen sink doing the dishes. The evening chore of dishwashing represents the level of equality in their relationship. Particularly, the husband takes pride in helping with the dishes as a demonstration that he consciously "tries" to be "considerate" of his wife.

> They were doing the dishes, his wife washing while he dried. He'd washed the night before. Unlike most men he knew, he really pitched in on the housework. A few months earlier he'd overheard a friend of his wife's congratulate her on having such a considerate husband, and he thought, *I try*. Helping out with the dishes was a way of showing how considerate he was.

This opening passage illuminates several elements of this couple's relationship. It describes a marriage that is specifically structured on a principal of equality, as demonstrated through a very organized system for sharing the burden of domestic chores. She washes, while he dries. The previous night, he washed while she dried. In addition, the husband takes special pride in the extent to which he consciously "tries" to be "considerate" of his wife through such efforts as "helping out with the dishes." However, the two begin to disagree over the issue of whether or not they approve of mixed race marriages between black and white people. The husband asserts that he does not approve of such unions, maintaining that this is not due to racism but because of what he believes to be the insurmountable cultural differences between black and white people. The wife, however, severely questions this stance. As the tension between them builds, during the course of this discussion, the manner in which she goes about washing the dishes becomes an outward expression of her growing anger and resentment toward her husband. As soon as he states that he thinks interracial marriage is "a bad idea," he observes a change in her facial expression that demonstrates her initial disapproval of this opinion, and indicates that she is prepared to pursue the matter. She asks "why" he feels this way, and he notices that "Sometimes his wife got this look where she pinched her brows together and bit her lower lip and stared down at something. When he saw her like this he knew he should keep his mouth shut, but he never did."

The husband's detailed observation of this change in his wife's facial expression in part indicates how well he knows her; he can accurately read the subtlest changes in her facial expressions, and is familiar with exactly the state of his wife's mind

> After the husband runs to the medicine chest to doctor her cut, he returns and squeezes the cut on her thumb, 'to see how deep the wound was,' symbolically assessing how 'deeply' the rift between the two of them has 'wounded' his wife. When he does so, 'a single drop of blood welled up, trembling and bright, and fell to the floor.'"

indicated by this change. When she again asks "why," her husband makes note of the precise manner in which she holds the bowl she has been washing: "she . . . stood there with her hand inside a bowl, not washing it but just holding it above the water." From this factual, almost photographic, description of how the wife holds the bowl, the narrative conveys a strong emotional response on her part. She is so deeply angered and disturbed by her husband's statement, and so concentrated on interrogating him about it, that she is momentarily paralyzed—her emotional reaction is so strong and her thoughts so intensely focused that she cannot even continue to carry out such a simple task as washing a bowl. The husband then tries to explain his opinion, telling her that "'I don't need you coming along now and implying that I'm a racist.'" With the wife's response that "'I didn't imply anything,'" she begins washing the bowl again, "turning it around in her hand as if she were shaping it." This image suggests that of a potter, shaping a bowl out of clay as it spins on a potter's wheel. It implies that, at this point, the wife is in control of the argument, "shaping it" to conform to her own opinions and emotional state. As the argument between husband and wife heats up, the wife's movements in washing the dishes change again. As she becomes more angry and resentful, she begins to wash the dishes more and more rapidly, neither looking at her husband nor paying careful attention to her task: "She was washing faster now, not looking at him. . . . She was piling dishes on the drainboard at a terrific rate, just swiping at them with the cloth. Many of them were greasy, and there were flecks of food between the tines of the forks." At this point, the increasing speed with which she washes the dishes is an expression of her growing fury toward her husband. She is angry with him, and so will not look at him as they talk. Her anger is also expressed through the violence with which she merely "swipes at" the dishes, as if hitting them in punishment. Her anger toward her husband is thus taken out on the dishes. In addition, the husband's detailed critical observation that the dishes she has supposedly cleaned are still "greasy," and that "there were flecks of food between the tines of the forks," expresses his own critical attitude toward her, at this point. His intense focus on the dishes, in the midst of this marital conflict, is also a way of attempting to focus his own anger upon inanimate objects, rather than directly at his wife.

When the wife cuts her thumb on a knife in the dishwater, the discussion is temporarily halted. However, the cut, and the couple's response to it, further expresses the tensions that have mounted between them. What began as light conversation in the course of performing a routine household task takes on a sharper edge that cuts deep into the relationship. The wife cuts herself when she "plunged her hands under the surface" of the dishwater. Likewise, she has plunged "under the surface" of the conversation, to its deeper implications for the marital relationship. After the husband runs to the medicine chest to doctor her cut, he returns and squeezes the cut on her thumb, "to see how deep the wound was," symbolically assessing how "deeply" the rift between the two of them has "wounded" his wife. When he does so, "a single drop of blood welled up, trembling and bright, and fell to the floor." Likewise, their disagreement has caused a small rift (or cut) between them, by touching on feelings deep within the wife which "welled up" momentarily, like the drop of blood from her thumb. Nonetheless, the wife seems to blame her husband for the cut, as if the argument itself had "wounded" her: "Over the thumb, she stared at him accusingly." Like a minor knife wound to the thumb, the "wound" incurred by the wife over their disagreement, while momentarily intense and upsetting, "trembling and bright," is not very deep, and will heal by the next day. The husband tells her, "'It's shallow. . . . Tomorrow you won't even know it's there.'" This statement expresses the husband's hope that the argument has not, in fact, caused any "deep" rift between them, and that they will both have forgotten it by the following day. And although the husband's consideration in coming to her aid is out of genuine "concern," he hopes that it will serve as a "gesture" for which she will reward him by dropping the argument: "He hoped that she appreciated how quickly he had come to her aid. He'd acted out of concern for her, with no thought of getting anything in return, but now the thought occurred to him that it would be a nice gesture on her part not to start up that conversation again, as he was tired of it."

However, the wife continues the discussion while the husband washes and she dries. At this point, the way in which the husband washes the dishes becomes an expression of his feelings toward his wife. As he begins rewashing the silverware that she had not adequately washed the first time, he does so, "giving a lot of attention to the forks." By being particularly meticulous in rewashing the forks, the husband indirectly expresses criticism of his wife—she had done a bad job of washing the forks, and so he attempts to prove himself in the right by doing an especially good job of it. But when he rinses the forks with the rinsing nozzle, the "heat" of their anger toward one another becomes manifest: "The water was so hot that the metal darkened to a pale blue, then turned to silver again." It is as if the "heat" of their temporary conflict has caused the nature of their relationship to turn from its usual high quality of closeness, as symbolized by the "silver," to a "darker," "bluer" (as in sadder) mood. However, the fact that the metal just as quickly retains its silver tone symbolizes the expectation that the relationship between husband and wife will be restored to normal before long.

Nonetheless, as the wife pursues discussion of the topic, the tension between the two comes to a head. She finally asks him the hypothetical question: would he have married her if she were black. After much protest, he finally responds "'No,'" he would not. Clearly upset by his answer, she merely says, "'Thank you,'" and walks from the kitchen to the living room. Whereas before she had expressed her anger through the manner in which she washed the dishes, she now expresses it through the manner in which she flips through a magazine while sitting in the living room. Again, the accuracy with which the husband can interpret what she is expressing through her behavior, even just hearing her from another room, demonstrates how well these two know each other: "A moment later he heard her turning the pages of a magazine. He knew that she was too angry to be actually reading it, but she didn't snap through the pages the way he would have done. She turned them slowly, as if she were studying every word. She was demonstrating her indifference to him, and it had the effect he knew she wanted it to have. It hurt him." The husband and wife thus communicate much of their conflict merely through the manner in which they perform menial tasks and handle inanimate objects. They are so effective at communicating to one another in this manner that she can successfully "hurt" her husband merely by the speed with which she turns the pages of a magazine.

The husband likewise responds to this hurtful magazine-page flipping through a retaliatory cleaning of the kitchen. Just as she sends him a message of "indifference" through the manner in which she turns the pages of the magazine, he responds with a message of "indifference" by giving the kitchen a quiet and thorough cleaning: "He had no choice but to demonstrate his indifference to her. Quietly, thoroughly, he washed the rest of the dishes. Then he dried them and put them away. He wiped the counters and the stove and scoured the linoleum where the drop of blood had fallen. While he was at it, he decided, he might as well mop the whole floor." Although he is intending to send her a message of "indifference," he is also symbolically attempting to clean up the emotional mess caused by their argument. He is especially careful to clean up the blood that had fallen from her thumb as he "scoured the linoleum where the drop of blood had fallen." In other words, to the extent that she has symbolically shed blood in the course of their conflict, he attempts to symbolically repair the damage by cleaning up the blood.

After thoroughly cleaning the kitchen, the husband takes out the garbage. Outside, he watches two dogs that have tipped over a garbage can. The dogs, one male and one female, though companions, tussle over the garbage, symbolic of the husband and wife in the midst of a quarrel: "The two mutts from down the street had pulled over the garbage can again. One of them was rolling around on his back and the other had something in her mouth. Growling, she tossed it into the air, leaped up and caught it, growled again and whipped her head from side to side." The husband and wife, through raising the unexpectedly volatile topic of interracial marriage, have symbolically tipped over a can of marital garbage. Like the dogs, they wallow in their own emotional garbage for a time. From the husband's perspective, watching the dogs, it is the female who is most aggressively attacking and struggling with a piece of trash, while the male lies on his back. The husband feels defeated, identifying with the seemingly harmless male dog that merely lies on his back in the garbage. He associates the female dog with his wife, as it more aggressively attacks and plays with a piece of garbage, growling in an intimidating manner. Likewise, whereas he had been willing to drop the whole messy matter between himself and his wife, she had rather aggressively pursued the topic—in the process creating an even greater emotional mess between them. Nonetheless, like the cut on her finger, the discoloration of the fork, and the drop of blood on the kitchen floor, the overturning of a garbage can by neighborhood dogs represents a relatively minor, temporary, and easily corrected problem. Likewise, the conflict between husband and wife in this story, while momentarily intense, is ultimately a minor glitch in an otherwise close and harmonious relationship.

The ultimately positive resolution to the conflict between husband and wife is expressed through the symbolic remarriage of the couple. As he hears her preparing for bed through the bathroom door, he leans close and whispers, "'I'll marry you.'" Although the wife is not immediately placated, the words indicate a reaffirmation of the relationship, which will no doubt survive numerous minor injuries and scatterings of emotional garbage over the course of a lasting and intimate marriage.

Source: Liz Brent, in an essay for *Short Stories for Students*, Gale Group, 2001.

Sources

Banks, Russell, Review of *Back in the World*, in *New York Times Book Review*, October 20, 1985, p. 9.

DePietro, Thomas, Review of *Back in the World*, in *Hudson Review*, Autumn, 1986, pp. 487–88.

Dyer, Jeff, Review of *Back in the World*, in *New Statesman*, January 24, 1986, p. 28.

Gilbert, Matthew, Review of *Back in the World*, in *New Statesman*, December, 1985, p. 27.

Kakutani, Michiko, Review of *Back in the World*, in *New York Times*, October 2, 1985, p. C25.

Montrose, Jeff, Review of *Back in the World*, in *Times Literary Supplement*, January 24, 1986, p. 82.

Penner, Jonathan, Review of *Back in the World*, in *Washington Post*, November 3, 1985, Book World section, p. 5.

Simpson, Mona, Review of *Back in the World*, in *New Republic*, December 9, 1985, pp. 37–38.

Wesley, Marilyn C., "Tobias Wolff" in *Dictionary of Literary Biography*, Vol. 130, Gale Research, 1993, pp. 314–322.

Further Reading

Bailey, Peter J. "'Why Not Tell the Truth?': The Autobiographies of Three Fiction Writers," in *Critique*, Summer, 1991, p. 211.
   Bailey's essay compares the autobiographical writings of Tobias Wolff, Philip Roth, and John Updike.

Lyons, Bonnie, and Bill Oliver, "An Interview with Tobias Wolff," in *Contemporary Literature*, Spring, 1990, pp. 1–16.
   This text details a lengthy and in-depth interview with Wolff.

"Tobias Wolff," in *Current Biography*, January, 1996, p. 55.
   This material offers a biographical account of Wolff's life, including his childhood and his education.

The Sheriff's Children

Charles Waddell Chesnutt

1888

"The Sheriff's Children" was one of Charles Waddell Chesnutt's first pieces of fiction exploring the insidious effect of racism on America. Collected in *The Wife of His Youth, and Other Stories of the Color Line* eleven years after its initial magazine publication, even at the turn of the century "The Sheriff's Children" stood out for its indictment of white society in contributing to the problems faced by African Americans.

Many of the other stories in the collection dealt with internal "African American" issues—that is, how African Americans dealt with the problems of race, skin color, and prejudice among themselves. Such stories, including the title story, were generally more well received at the time of the collection's initial publication, in 1899. Such issues as racial intolerance, racial violence, and particularly racial intermingling did not sit well with the American reading public or its white reviewers. Only a handful of white Americans—though esteemed literary figures—publicly praised Chesnutt's work. The majority criticized him for bringing such issues as miscegenation to the forefront and implied he would do better to return to the folktales he had previously written to such acclaim.

Chesnutt did not do so; his later works, novels, treated race issues in an even more blatant manner, and in consequence, sold fewer and fewer copies. Six years after *The Wife of His Youth* had been published, Chesnutt had officially retired from his

writing career. After decades of lingering forgotten in archives, his work was rediscovered. Today, Chesnutt is widely praised as one of the most important African-American writers of his period.

Author Biography

Charles Waddell Chesnutt was born in 1858 in Cleveland, Ohio, the son of free African Americans who had left the South a few years previously. Chesnutt spent his early childhood in the North, but after the Civil War, his family moved back to Fayetteville, North Carolina, where his father ran a grocery store.

As a boy, Chesnutt enjoyed reading at a private library and browsing in bookstores. Chesnutt dreamed of becoming a professional writer, and his first story was published in a local paper when he was only fourteen. The following year, he was forced to drop out of school and go to work as a teacher in order to supplement his family's income. Four years later, he began to teach at the Colored Normal School in Fayetteville, and he became principal of that institution in 1880. Despite his successful career, he still worked toward his long-cherished dream, partially as a means to improve racial situations in the United States.

Worsening racial conditions in the South compelled Chesnutt to move his family north to New York City in 1883, where he started a new career as a court stenographer and reporter. Soon, the Chesnutts relocated to Cleveland, Ohio, where Chesnutt had relatives and friends. He began to study law, and passed the Ohio bar exam in 1887 with the highest grades in his group.

Two years earlier, in 1885, his first story was purchased for publication. In 1887, *The Atlantic Monthly*, at the time the nation's most prestigious magazine, purchased his story "The Goophered Grapevine"; Chesnutt was the first African-American writer to be published in that magazine. Chesnutt, however, was light-skinned with "Caucasian" features, and he made no mention of his race when he submitted the story. The characters in Chesnutt's early fictions were generally white, as magazines limited their acceptance of stories with African-American characters. Chesnutt also wanted to save his treatment of African-American characters until he was a more skilled and better known writer.

Throughout the 1890s, Chesnutt continued to publish short stories. In 1899, two collections were published, as well as a biography of Frederick Douglass. *The Conjure Woman* was a collection of folktales, but *The Wife of His Youth, and Other Stories of the Color Line* featured African-American protagonists, such as middle-class African Americans in Ohio, as well as the character Tom in "The Sheriff's Children."

Literary successes encouraged Chesnutt to give up his business as a court reporter. The following year, Chesnutt published a popular novel, *The House Behind the Cedars*, as well as a series of controversial essays on the race issue. In 1900, Chesnutt embarked on a southern lecture tour, and his work in the early part of the century was instrumental in raising issues of race and exposing prejudices.

His predominantly white audiences, however, did not respond well to the increasing criticisms of racial prejudice expressed in his next two novels. He reopened his court reporting business, and by 1905 had retired from the writing profession. He continued, however, to work on novels, publish short fiction occasionally, and produce articles, essays, and speeches.

Throughout his life, Chesnutt remained a firm supporter of racial equity, working toward the goal of ending racial prejudice. He was elected to a membership in a previously all-white literary group and was cited by the National Association for the Advancement of Colored People for his pioneering work depicting African Americans.

In the late 1920s, only a few years before his death, his collection *The Conjure Woman* was republished. His work was "rediscovered" in the mid-1970s. Despite the brevity of his career, he is now considered an important author of African-American fiction.

Plot Summary

The story opens up with a description of its setting, Branson County, North Carolina. Branson County is a typical rural southern community in the post-Civil War era. The Civil War has a pervasive effect on all aspects of present-day life, but in reality, had little physical affect on the area, and its inhabitants were generally apathetic to the defeat of the South.

The biggest town in the county is Troy, a village of 400 or 500 people. Troy is a sleepy town, with little going on, until one day the villagers are shocked by the news of a murder in their midst. The victim is the widely liked Captain Walker. Some of the villagers have seen a ''strange'' mulatto near Captain Walker's house the previous night, and it is immediately assumed that the African-American man must have committed the crime. The sheriff organizes a posse and apprehends this man.

When the news of the capture spreads through the town, the men are still not happy. They feel that ''ordinary justice was too slight a punishment for such a crime.'' The gathered crowd decide to lynch the prisoner, and arrange to meet at five that afternoon to take action.

Close to five, an African American who overheard the talk runs up to the door of Sheriff Campbell's house to inform him of the planned lynching. The sheriff is an educated, wealthy, and respected man. He vows to go the jail and protect his prisoner, as is his duty. His daughter, Polly, pleads with him not to go, but he remains resolute. He leaves a pistol with his daughter in case anyone disturbs her.

The sheriff has hardly locked the jail when the crowd of men appear. They demand entrance into the jail, but when the sheriff refuses, they say they will bust the door in. The sheriff warns them that if they try, he will do his duty—he will shoot them. The men in the crowd and the sheriff all acknowledge that most likely the prisoner will be found guilty of the murder and be hanged, but the sheriff is determined to fulfill his job. While the leaders converse, the sheriff enters the prisoner's cell. The scared man pleads with the sheriff to save his life and declares that he didn't kill the captain. The sheriff unshackles the man and tells him if the men get in the jail, to fight for himself.

The men, surprised at the sheriff's resistance, decide to give up the idea of lynching the prisoner. The mob departs, and the sheriff watches them through the cell window. He does not notice the prisoner steal his revolver, and the prisoner soon levels the gun at him. The prisoner declares his intention of escaping. The sheriff says that this is little gratitude for saving his life, and the prisoner admits that while the sheriff saved him, it is only momentary; soon he will hang on the order of the court. The prisoner says he didn't kill the captain but knows he will not be able to prove it.

Charles Chesnutt

Under orders from the prisoner, the sheriff unlocks the doors of the jail, then the men return to the cell. The man then reveals that to get away, he will have to kill the sheriff. When the sheriff reveals his utter surprise that the prisoner would ''kill the man to whom you owe your own life,'' the prisoner says indeed he owes his life to the sheriff—in fact, he is Tom, the sheriff's illegitimate son, born to him of the sheriff's former slave. The sheriff remembers them now. Angry with the mother and financially worried, the sheriff had sold Tom and his mother down South, to Alabama. He had been sorry for his actions many times since. The sheriff gasps, saying in surprise, '''you would not murder your own father?''' Tom counters with logic: what ''father's duty'' has the sheriff done for him; he also points out that other white owners gave their African-American children freedom. He lashes out at the sheriff for giving him ''a white man's spirit'' in a black man's body. Then he asks if the sheriff will promise to not raise the alarm if he does not shoot. The sheriff hesitates, not knowing if he could ignore his duty. Tom declares his intention to shoot the sheriff—he could not trust him even if he gave his word to keep silent.

The two men are so deep in discussion that they don't notice Polly's entrance. Worried when her father didn't return, she had come to the jail to see if he was wounded. Seeing the gun pointed at her father, she shoots Tom with the pistol. The sheriff binds up the prisoner's wound and promises to send a doctor the next day. He also says he will not reveal that the injury came while Tom was attempting to escape, knowing that would make the prisoner's situation worse.

That night, the sheriff has trouble falling asleep. He decides that he has a duty to his son, a responsibility. He comprehends how he has failed Tom, that he may have been able to restrain the younger man, that he might have freed him and sent him North, providing him with an opportunity to make something of his life. Believing in Tom's innocence, the sheriff decides the best thing he can do for his illegitimate son is to investigate the crime and attempt to discover the real criminal. He raises the idea of letting Tom go free, but his sense of duty will not permit him to do this.

The next morning, the sheriff goes to the jail. He finds Tom sleeping on his pallet, and unresponsive. The sheriff enters the cell, where he discovers Tom's dead body. He had torn the bandage off his wound and bled to death, alone, during the night.

loyal, courageous, and independent. Thus, the children of the sheriff serve as a means to demonstrate two very distinct sides to his personality.

Polly

Polly is the sheriff's white daughter. She is courageous and independent, as indicated by her actions in saving her father's life.

Tom

Tom is the illegitimate mulatto son of the sheriff. He instantly recognizes his father, but his father does not recognize him. Tom has led a life of waste; he is clearly intelligent, yet he suffers from the lack of opportunities the white world affords. He is wise to the ways of the world, acknowledging that although he didn't kill the captain, it is almost assured that he will be found guilty of the crime. In many ways, Tom emerges as the voice of reason, acknowledging that he owes his father nothing, for his father was less than a father to him. Tom's suicide at the end of the story indicates his understanding that he has lost any minimal control he ever had over his own life.

Characters

Sheriff Campbell

Sheriff Campbell is the protagonist of the story. He is a man of social standing and wealth, and he is respected in his community. The sheriff is strongly ruled by his sense of duty; it leads him to defend the prisoner from the mob, even at a threat to his own life; it leads him to refuse to allow Tom to escape, even when he believes Tom is innocent. Through the conversation between the sheriff and the prisoner—the father and son—more is revealed about the sheriff's background and personality than had been previously. The reader learns that the sheriff is a passionate, bullheaded man, and also that despite his seeming morality in defending the prisoner, he has acted in ways that might seem unacceptable and surprising; that is, in selling his son and the boy's black mother instead of securing his son's freedom. This neglect of his son directly implicates him in the way the son turned out in life. Yet, as a counterpoint, the sheriff has also raised a daughter who is

Themes

Race and Racism

The themes of race and racism are integral to ''The Sheriff's Children.'' The story takes place in the postbellum South, when African Americans, although free, were hardly considered equal to whites. The mulatto Tom is brought in as a suspect for the murder of a white man on circumstantial evidence; ironically, only after his capture does it emerge that there actually is evidence linking him to the dead man—a coat that he stole. Tom claims not to have killed the man, but he also recognizes that the society in which he lives will condemn him unfairly. The white men who make up the lynching mob also recognize this truth, as does the sheriff; they all acknowledge that there is no actual need to lynch Tom at the present time, for almost certainly he will be sentenced to hang for the murder.

The story reveals more about the pervasive nature of racism than just its fatal consequences. Tom's history demonstrates how African Ameri-

Topics for Further Study

- Conduct research to find out more about the trials of African Americans in the post-Civil War South. Do you think an African American stood a chance of getting a fair trial?

- Imagine that Tom had not died and that he and Polly were able to meet the next day. What conversation do you think would take place between the sheriff's children?

- What moral stance do you take on the sheriff's actions throughout the story and throughout his life, specifically, on his treatment of his illegitimate son and his mother, his chasing away the mob, his final decision about how to help Tom?

- Most of the sheriff's actions are determined by his sense of duty. To which cause do you think he has the greater duty: to help Tom or to uphold his position? Do the sheriff's past actions—those during his time as a slaveholder—demonstrate his sense of duty?

- Reread the section on Point of View in the story. Do you think this point of view helps or hinders the telling of the story? Explain your answer.

- Do you find Tom to be a believable character? Explain your answer.

---

cans were regarded even when they are no longer slaves. The fact that Tom views himself as a black man with the spirit of a white man shows that there was little conception that an African American of that period could have the same yearnings and hopes for bettering himself as a white man.

The insidious nature of prejudice is also evident in Tom's self-loathing. He knows that he looks African American on the outside, yet he feels that he belongs to the race of his father far more than that of his mother. He feels this way because there is little opportunity open to African Americans. Thus, Tom is willing to degrade his own race, as he does when he blames the sheriff for giving him a black mother.

Responsibility and Morality

The story raises issues of responsibility and morality—and to whom these are owed. The sheriff considers himself to be a responsible person; he bases his life decisions on what he believes to be his "duty." Yet, his actions show that his sense of morality is connected to the person to whom he feels his duty derives. For instance, he takes his job as the sheriff seriously—even willingly risks his own life to protect his African American prisoner from the lynching mob—because that duty derives from the white community. However, he completely disregards his job as a father to Tom, taking no responsibility for the boy's well-being and by making his situation worse in selling him further South; he feels little responsibility toward Tom, for Tom is only an African American—at the time, regarded only as a piece of property—and thus not deserving of his careful duty.

The sheriff's sense of morality is also tied up in what is right according to the rules of society, not what should be done. After he regains control of the prisoner, he wonders what he can do to help Tom and "hypothetically" thinks that he could free him, but his mind does not even process this as an option. Instead, the sheriff resolves to follow the legal channels; he will attempt to prove that Tom is not the murderer, a nearly impossible task. The sheriff does not have the slightest comprehension of the prevailing southern white morality, which does not care if the African American is guilty or innocent, only that some African American be made to suffer because a white person has also had been made to suffer.

In contrast, Tom regards responsibility more on a personal level. When he says he will kill the sheriff to ensure his escape, the sheriff claims that

Tom has a responsibility to him because of their blood tie. Yet Tom denies this because the sheriff has not acted like a father in any sense, not even in "name only." Tom's reasoning shows his belief that sometimes responsibility must be earned, that it is not owed.

Identity

The theme of identity is important in "The Sheriff's Children." The two protagonists in the story—Sheriff Campbell and his mulatto son Tom—both undergo crises of personal identity. The sheriff derives his identity from his society; he is described at first as his neighbor might perceive him: "The sheriff of Branson was a man far above the average of the community in wealth, education, and social position," the narration begins and then continues to describe his accomplishments. The narration, however, does not delve into any personal aspects of the man's personality. Such information is only revealed through Tom when the younger man confronts the sheriff with the truth of his parentage. Through his son, the sheriff begins to see himself aside from the roles of his job: "He knew whose passions coursed beneath that swarthy skin and burned in the black eyes opposite his own. He saw in this mulatto what he himself might have become had not the safeguards of parental restraint and public opinion been thrown around him." Yet, once Tom is subdued, the sheriff turns his back on that part of himself that recognizes the more emotional level, and he again embraces the personality that only follows duty. He then decides not to set Tom free although he is convinced of his innocence.

Tom is also trapped between two identities, yet he never has the chance to confront them and make his own decision about his own identity. On the outside, he is African American but his passions lead him to believe he has the spirit of a white man. In so defining himself, Tom negates his own blackness and buys into the common belief of the time that whites and blacks are inherently different, with whites being superior.

Style

Structure and Setting

The structure of the story emphasizes the intermingling of the story and the setting, showing that one could not occur without the other. The story begins with an overview of the setting. The early description of the county demonstrates the importance of the Civil War to the life and perception of its inhabitants. As the narration states, "the war is the one historical event that overshadows all others." Although the inhabitants' perception of African Americans is not mentioned, the emphasis on the Civil War—a conflict taking place, in part, because of the fight over slavery—brings the idea of African Americans place in southern society to mind. At the time Chesnutt published the story, readers were aware, or had the capacity to be aware, that the postbellum South was a place rife with prejudice and discrimination, sometimes fatal, against African Americans.

Point of View and Narration

The point of view in "The Sheriff's Children" shifts several times. At the beginning of the story, the tale is told from an omniscient point of view; the narrator's voice is that of an editorial commentator, someone who understands the county, its history, and its inhabitants. Early on, the narrator is even self-referential: "At the period of which I write, no railroad had come to Troy." The omniscient point of view is maintained through the first two-thirds of the story. The narrator makes decisions of what details to include and which are "immaterial to this narrative."

After the prisoner levels the gun at the sheriff, however, a new element is added to the point of view, as suddenly the omniscient narrator is getting into the mind of the sheriff, revealing his thoughts; "The sheriff mentally cursed his own carelessness for allowing him to be caught in such a predicament," the narration reads. From that point on, all events are mainly funneled through the sheriff's point-of-view. The all-knowing narrator, however, still applies to facet's of the story of which the sheriff is unaware, as when Polly, unseen by him or Tom, creeps up through the jailhouse.

The narrator, however, steadfastly avoids getting involved in Tom's interior thoughts. Everything that Tom feels or thinks is revealed through his actions or his words. This narrative tactic allows the narrator not to be involved in Tom's suicide and bring it up at the end of the story as a surprise for the reader. This ending gives the story added punch.

Dialogue

The dialect and speech patterns of the different characters in the story reveal information about their backgrounds. The sheriff, as befits a man who has been college educated, speaks with grammatical correctness. He is a sharp contrast to the men who make up the lynch mob, men who do not enunciate their words (''purlim'nary), drop the final sounds of their words (''hearin'''), and use improper grammar (''Hangin' air too good fer the murderer''). These speech patterns indicate the social and educational backgrounds of the speakers, and also serve as a divider between those who misinterpret their duty and the person who is committed to upholding his duty, which is the sheriff.

The African Americans, aside from Tom, speak in stereotypical dialogue, for instance, with ''axe'' for ''ask'' and the man and the woman identifying each other as ''Brer'' (''Brother'') and ''Sis''' (''Sister'').

Tom speaks elements of both dialects. When he is afraid for his life and appeals to the sheriff for help, he deliberately takes on an inferior speech pattern; ''don't let 'em lynch me,'' he murmurs from a cowering position. As soon as he is safe and in control of the situation, he speaks as an educated person. Even the sheriff notices his fine language, comparing it favorably to that of most of the residents of the county.

Historical Context

Post-Civil War Southern Society

After the end of the Civil War, the United States government embarked on a plan called Reconstruction to rebuild the South and reunite the nation. Reconstruction lasted from 1865 to 1877. Under Reconstruction, the southern states set up new governments and revised their constitutions. By 1870, all of the former Confederate states had been readmitted to the Union. However, the new legislatures often restricted the freedoms of African Americans, a practice to which many northern Republicans objected. On a positive note, Reconstruction governments founded new social programs and organizations, such as public school systems. Southern states also spent a great deal of money repairing their infrastructure, that is railroads, bridges, and public buildings, which had been destroyed during the war.

At first, African Americans were optimistic about their future. The Fourteenth and Fifteenth Amendments gave equal citizenship to African Americans and guaranteed their right to vote. Many African Americans took part in government, serving in Reconstruction legislatures. As early as 1866, however, southern governments began passing Black Codes, which were laws that limited the freedom of African Americans. Many African Americans also remained tied to the land through the system of sharecropping, by which a sharecropper worked a parcel of land in return for a share of the crop. Under this system, most African-American sharecroppers (as well as white sharecroppers) remained in poverty. African Americans had few economic opportunities to better their lives. Many were also threatened by the Ku Klux Klan, which opposed African Americans obtaining civil rights and used violence to discourage them. As Democrats regained control of southern state governments, they began to overturn the Reconstruction reforms. For instance, they devised methods of keeping African Americans from voting by implementing poll taxes and literacy tests. Southern states also passed Jim Crow laws, which called for the segregation of African Americans. By the late 1800s, many African Americans felt the New South was beginning to look very much like the Old South.

In response to such prohibitory measures, African Americans built their own social institutions and adopted different approaches to fighting discrimination. African American leaders carried their message to African American and white audiences. In his Atlanta Compromise speech of 1895, Booker T. Washington spoke of his desire for peaceful coexistence and suggested that African Americans and whites should cooperate for economic progress. His views that African Americans should concentrate on economic advancement, and not protest discrimination, angered some other African Americans.

Ida Wells-Barnett and W. E. B. DuBois both brought greater attention to racial prejudice. Wells-Barnett urged African Americans to leave the South for the North, where there was less discrimination and violence perpetrated against African Americans. She also was a leader in the anti-lynching crusade. In *A Red Record* she printed the name of every one of the 197 African American men lynched in the United States in 1894, the reason they were lynched, and the place. Her efforts helped show that one third more African Americans were killed that year by lynch mobs than were legally executed.

Other American Minorities

Other minorities also found life difficult during this period. In 1871, the Indian Appropriation Act

Compare & Contrast

- **Late 1800s:** In 1880, the African American population of North Carolina is 531,000 out of a total population of 1.4 million. African Americans comprise almost thirty-eight percent of the state's population.

    1990s: In 1997, North Carolina's total population is just over 7.4 million. Of this figure, close to 6 million North Carolinians are white and just over 1.6 are African American. African Americans comprise almost twenty-two percent of the state's population.

- **Late 1800s:** Between 1899 and 1909, lynchings become an increasingly southern and racial phenomenon. In 1888, 137 Americans are lynched; 68 of these are white people and 69 are African Americans. By 1899, of the 106 lynching victims, only 21 are white and the remaining 85 are African American. In North Carolina, between 1882 and 1903, 15 whites and 48 African Americans are lynched.

    1990s: No lynchings take place in the 1990s, or in the several decades preceding it. However, hate crimes do persist and seem to be on the rise. Hate crimes are not restricted to African Americans, but tend to include other racial minorities, non-Christians, and homosexuals. Illustrious instances of hate crimes in the 1990s include the fatal beating of a young gay man in Wyoming and a shooting at a Jewish Community Center in Los Angeles.

- **Late 1800s:** In 1870, the United States prison population is 33,000 out of total population of 39,818,449—.08 percent of the U.S. population is incarcerated.

    1990s: In 1996, there are 518,492 inmates in prison out of a total population of over 265 million—almost 2 percent of the American population. Of these inmates, 228,900, which is approximately half, are African American.

- **Late 1800s:** In 1880, the African-American population of the United States is 6,581,000, or 13.1 percent of the total United States population. Within 10 years, that percentage has dropped to 11.9.

    1990s: In 1997, the African-American population of the United States is nearly 34 million or 12.7 percent.

- **1890s:** Cotton is the primary crop for many southern farmers. Its price fluctuates between a high of 12 cents a pound down as low as 5 cents a pound. Cotton production, however, is on the rise, and by the mid-1890s, more than 20 million acres of cotton is harvested.

    1990s: The price of United States cotton fluctuates between 47 cents a pound up to $1.13 a pound. In 1997–98, the United States produced just under 19 million bales of cotton, of which close to 7 million will be exported.

- **1890s:** By the time Chesnutt writes *"The Sheriff's Children,"* slavery has been outlawed by the Thirteenth Amendment. In the antebellum years, however, the majority of African Americans in the South were enslaved. In 1860, slaves made up thirty-four percent of the southern population, while free African Americans—around 260,000—made up about two percent of the southern population.

    1990s: Most nations throughout the world have abolished slavery although it is still practiced in some parts of Africa, Asia, and South America. The Anti-Slavery Society for the Protection of Human Rights in London estimates that forms of servitude affect more than 200 million poor people.

made all Native Americans wards of the federal government and nullified all treaties with them, thus Indian tribes lost any remaining traces of national sovereignty. Then in 1887, the Dawes Act broke up reservation lands, dividing them into individual family plots. Tribes were forced to sell any leftover land to the federal government for its resale to non-Indians. The Dawes Act proved devastating to Native Americans. Not only did they end up losing control of two out of three acres of land they had held, but under this act, the land allotment acreage was not large enough to sustain families. Many Native Americans ended up leasing or selling their land to whites.

Prejudice also rose against those Americans who were not Protestant. As more and more immigrants arrived in the country in the mid- to late 1800s, there was a rise in hate groups. Nativists—people who disliked anyone who came from another country or ethnic background—urged laws prohibiting emigration. Violent attacks were also perpetrated against Catholics and Jews.

The American Economy

The American economy was undergoing significant changes towards the end of the nineteenth century. A mining boom in gold and silver drew many Americans out West, and others chose to settle in the Great Plains, where they could find inexpensive land and rich soil for farming. The Second Industrial Revolution, which began in the late 1800s, led to a period of explosive growth in U.S. manufacturing. By the mid-1800s, the United States was the world's industrial leader. Big business grew, as did the number of new factories. Many of the immigrants who were increasingly coming to the United States in the late 1800s were hired to work at these factories. As the United States population kept growing—doubling from 1860 to 1900—the number of farms tripled. Modern machines allowed farmers to produce crops much faster than they ever had before. However, the combination of more farms and greater productivity led to overproduction and lower crop prices. By 1893, because of a stock market panic, the United States had entered a depression.

Critical Overview

"The Sheriff's Children" first appeared in the *Independent* in 1888. Eleven years later, it was included in Chesnutt's second collection of fiction, *The Wife of His Youth, and Other Stories of the Color Line*. This collection blatantly raised issues more generally left untouched, such as racial miscegenation, the divided racial identity of mixed-blood Americans, and the racial barriers that kept African Americans from fully participating in American life. The Nashville *Banner* even outright accused Chesnutt of being an "advocate of miscegenation."

Although the collection was not as well-received as Chesnutt's previous volume of folktales, W. D. Howells, the well-known literary editor and writer, praised it in *The Atlantic Monthly*. Both Howells and fellow editor Hamilton Wright Mabie declared Chesnutt a first-class realist. Wrote Howells, "It is not from their racial interest that we could first wish to speak of [Chesnutt's stories], though that must have a very great and very just claim upon the critic. It is much more simply and directly, as works of art, that they make their appeal, and we must allow the force of this quite independently of the other interest." Howells, however, recognized that this task "cannot always be allowed," and for many readers, that was indeed the primary focus.

Such was the case with Nancy Huston Banks, another early reviewer. In *Bookman*, she praised the story "*The Wife of His Youth*" but found the others "hardly worthy of mention." Her gravest criticism fell on "The Sheriff's Children" for its "shocking instance of [Chesnutt's] reckless disregard of matters respected by more experienced writers." Despite her criticism, Banks recognized the importance of Chesnutt's message: "there is no intention to deny the too probable truth of the untellable story, nor any wish to dispute its tragic importance as legitimate literary material. On the contrary, it is the recognition of that terrible truth and its might weight which cause the protest. Had the author recognized these things, it would seem that he must either have left them alone or approached them more carefully, and with greater strenuousness; that he must have felt the need of laying hold of them with far surer, firmer, larger grasp, if he touched them at all." Whereas white reviewers often focused on the difficult issues raised in the collection, particularly of sexual relations between African Americans and whites, reviewers in African-American periodicals often thanked Chesnutt for depicting the image of educated, intelligent African Americans, an image with which many white Americans were not familiar.

Chesnutt's racial message was even more apparent in the novels he published in the early 1900s, and by 1905, he had ceased writing as he failed to find an audience among the American reading public. Chesnutt's work was largely forgotten, until a new edition of *The Conjure Woman* came out in 1929. But again, the writer drew mixed opinions as reviewers looked back on his literary career. Although John Chamberlain, writing for *The Bookman*, declared that "Negro fiction in America properly commences with [Chesnutt], he still prefers the more innocuous *The Conjure Woman* to *The Wife of His Youth*; according to Chamberlain, he can accept the "queer twists" in the former collection because they come from an "old Negro Machiavelli, Uncle Julius," but he cannot accept such plot machinations in the latter collection. He did, however, find "The Sheriff's Children", which he calls "a story of North Carolina," to be "effective as melodrama."

By the end of the decade, reviewers had begun to make note of the importance of Chesnutt's prevailing message of the problems facing African Americans. While Sterling Brown pointed out certain faults of Chesnutt's in *The Negro in American Fiction*—such as a reliance on mistaken identity or the upstanding behavior and language of his "better class Negroes"—Brown recognized the "great use" Chesnutt makes of his mixed-blood characters. Brown also praised Chesnutt's decision to show even those unpleasant scenes, such as mob riots and lynching mobs. "He knew a great deal," wrote Brown, "and all things considered, he told it well." Two years later, in 1939, J. Saunders Redding wrote in his book *To Make a Poet Black* that Chesnutt's was "the most worthy prose fiction that the Negro had produced." Redding showed an appreciation for Chesnutt's mixed-blood heroes and heroines: "They represent a new approach to the Negro character in fiction," he wrote. "They argue artistically and not too obviously . . . of the way of life to which the Negro might attain were it not for the bugaboo of color."

However, Chesnutt was largely overlooked until the mid-1970s when *The Short Fiction of Charles W. Chesnutt* was published. It included most of his short stories, including some that were previously uncollected. Contemporary critics continued to appreciate Chesnutt's work. Many modern critics have focused on the theme of identity and how racial beliefs affect personal identity, which Chesnutt raises through his characterization. They also concern themselves with Chesnutt's ideas of racial miscegenation. Arlene A. Elder, in her book *Charles Waddell Chesnutt: Art of Assimilation in the 'Hindered Hand': Cultural Implications of Early African-American Fiction*, posits that this "probing examination of the ironies of miscegenation" might shed some light on Chesnutt's self-image.

Overall, the publication of *The Wife of His Youth* contributed to the rise in Chesnutt's literary stature. Today, it continues to add to his reputation.

Criticism

Rena Korb

Korb has a master's degree in English literature and creative writing and has written for a wide variety of educational publishers. In the following essay, she explores some of the racial issues raised in Chesnutt's short story.

In 1880, while he was still working as a schoolteacher in North Carolina, Charles W. Chesnutt wrote in his journal, "The object of my writing would not be so much the elevation of the colored people as the elevation of the whites—for I consider the unjust spirit of caste that is so insidious as to pervade a whole nation, and so powerful as to subject a whole race and all connected with it to scorn and social ostracism—I consider this a barrier to the moral progress of the American people: and I would be one of the first to head a determined, organized crusade against it. . . . The work is of a two-fold character. The Negro's part is to prepare himself for recognition and equality, and it is the province of literature to open the way for him to get it—to accustom the public mind to the idea; to lead people on, imperceptibly, unconsciously, step by step, to the desired state of feeling." Chesnutt stayed true to his stated mission; in much of the fiction he wrote after the folktales collected in *The Conjure Woman*, Chesnutt attempted to make white America see a new, more positive image of black America. He also asked blacks to confront their own problems and responsibilities with the question of racial issues.

"The Sheriff's Children," asserts William L. Andrews in *The Literary Career of Charles W. Chesnutt*, "constitutes Chesnutt's boldest arraignment of the South, both Old and New, for its sins of omissions against black people." Published in 1888, it was one of the first stories in which Chesnutt shifted from the folktales and local color tales that had made up his previous fictions. In writing to Albion Tourgée, a northern writer who wrote sympathetically about African Americans in the South, Chesnutt called his newest work "a

What Do I Read Next?

- Kate Chopin's *Desiree's Baby*, written in the same period as Chesnutt's fiction, also deals with the subject of racial miscegenation. Desiree, the adopted daughter of an upstanding Louisiana family, marries the son and heir to another plantation family. The couple are blissfully happy until Desiree gives birth to a son whose features show evidence of African-American heritage.

- Mark Twain's 1894 novel *Pudd'nhead Wilson* is a story about miscegenation in the antebellum South. A light-skinned slave switches her baby with her white owner's baby, with unexpected results for the entire household. The novel is noted for its grim humor and its reflections on the nature of racism.

- Charles Chesnutt's story "The Wife of His Youth" (1899) examines color prejudices among middle-class northern African Americans. The so-called Blue Blood society—made up of African Americans of light skin—isolates itself from those people of its race with darker skin until a stranger comes into their midst.

- Zora Neale Hurston's second novel, *Their Eyes Were Watching God* (1937), was both widely acclaimed and highly controversial. Hurston's lyrical prose shows the influence of African-American folklore as she tells the story of one woman's burgeoning self-reliance and identity.

- *A Lesson Before Dying* is a wrenching novel by Ernest J. Gaines. In the novel, a young African-American teacher grudgingly befriends an ignorant, uneducated African American who has been sentenced to execution for a crime he may not have committed. The teacher instills in the doomed man a new self-respect and learns about himself in the process.

- Albert French's novel *Billy* depicts the lynching of a young African-American boy in the rural south. Written in dialect, it presents a realistic and chilling portrayal of this vicious crime.

- *Cane* (1923), an experimental novel by Jean Toomer, expresses the experience of being African American in the United States. The novel is comprised of a variety of literary forms, including poems and short stories. It draws on the South's rural past and on African American folklore.

- Richard Wright's novel *Native Son* (1940) addresses the repression of African Americans by white society. It focuses on a man imprisoned for two murders—one accidental and one purposeful—who reflects on how the African American can fight submission to white society.

---

southern story," but noted that its subject was "dealing with a tragic incident, not of slavery exactly, but showing the fruits of slavery." He admitted that the story "has a moral" but denied that he took a moralistic stance: "I tried to write as an artist, and not as a preacher." Indeed, he later expressed concern that his 1899 collection, *The Wife of His Youth, and Other Stories of the Color Line*, might read too much like a sermon, but he hoped that "it might have its influence in directing attention to certain aspects of the race question which are quite familiar to those on the unfortunate side of it." Chesnutt's comments, written before the collection's publication, proved prophetic: many black reviewers praised him for showing "educated, intelligent, and refined" African Americans to white America, instead of the expected stereotypes; while the majority of white reviewers objected to his stark racial themes, and particularly to the specter of miscegenation.

Chesnutt, however, does not begin "The Sheriff's Children" on such racial topics, though they ultimately arise as the crucial aspect. Instead,

> "The man in Tom—by implication, the 'white' part of Tom—knows that he can never lead the life he wants to lead. He will never be free, never be respected, never be above quick and discriminatory judgment. That Tom should want to die is not surprising at this point, for he believes, perhaps rightly so, that his life has no hope."

Chesnutt describes the county in North Carolina where the story takes place. Even though the text focuses on the physicality, evidence is presented of the prejudice that resides so particularly in the South, for according to the narrator, "Most of the white people own the farms they till," but no mention is made of African Americans. Until a scapegoat is sought for a crime, the only mention of African Americans in the story comes with a stereotypical, idyllic description of "the yodel of some tuneful negro on his way to the pine forest." In contrast, the tragedy of the Civil War, now ten years over but still "the era from which all local chronicles are dated," is sharply evoked.

The narration then hones down its vision to the individual town of Troy. An unprecedented event has taken place, the murder of a white gentleman, a former soldier in the Civil War. A "strange mulatto" had been sighted in the vicinity and soon a sheriff's posse has caught him and brought him to prison. Although a trial is impending, for many of the residents of the town, the promise of almost certain punishment is not enough, for "a white man had been killed by a negro," and that required vengeance. They determine to lynch him that afternoon—and then the heart of the story begins.

The only man willing to stop such a crime is Sheriff Campbell. He is "a man far above the average of the community in wealth, education, and social position." He is also a man of duty with "a high sense of responsibility attaching to his office." Because of this, he "with no uncertainty in regard to his course" goes forth to defend the prisoner. The sheriff confronts the unruly, ignorant mob—one man against many—and he prevails. The mob disperses and the prisoner is safe. As Andrews writes, this scene provides "a preliminary climax" for the reader: "For once, the forces of law and decency prevail over those of racial enmity and violence."

This sense of relief, however, is short-lived. The prisoner, Tom, has picked up the sheriff's gun, and now aims it at the sheriff. Tom is determined to flee, even though it means killing the sheriff—the man who has saved his life—to ensure no alarm will be raised. The sheriff is aghast when he hears Tom's plan. "'Good God!' exclaimed the sheriff in involuntary terror: 'you would not kill the man to whom you owe your own life.'" This is when the sheriff gets an even greater surprise: Tom is his illegitimate son, born to a slave once owned by the sheriff. In a fit of anger at the mother, he one day sold her and the boy to a speculator on his way to Alabama. It seems that the sheriff has thought of his son little, despite his assertion that he had been sorry for selling the boy and his mother "many times since," for he evinces no recognition of him even though Tom points out that "You gave me your . . . features—no man need look at us together twice to see that." Such an exchange demonstrates the sheriff's failure to "see" Tom as a man, for up to that moment, he was only a "cowering wretch," a man with the stain of "yellow" skin.

The sheriff responds to the news of his own parentage by calling on Tom's sense of duty: the sheriff gave him life, thus Tom owes it to him not to take his life. Tom, however, sees the issue differently. The sheriff, he contends, has performed no "father's duty" for him. "'Did you give me your name, or even your protection?'" he asks. "'Other white men gave their colored sons freedom and money, and sent them to the free States. *You* sold *me* to the rice swamps.'" Worse than that, the sheriff gave him "'a white man's spirit, and you made me a slave, and crushed it out.'" Such words are telling, for Tom shows that he buys into the common myth of the era: that whites and African Americans are inherently different, that whites have a certain spirit—perhaps a longing for independence, education, refinement, or even passion—that is lacking in African Americans. Tom further denigrates his own mother and his own race in this soliloquy when he accuses the sheriff: "'you gave me a black mother.'" In the same breath, however, Tom valorizes the woman. "'She died under the lash,'" he says, "'because she had enough womanhood to call her soul her own.'" Tom does not comprehend that he is, in essence, attributing to his mother some of those prideful traits he had only reserved for white people.

Tom does not equate his own defiance and passion with his black mother, only with his white father. Thus he allies himself with the white race because of his inner nature—best seen in the story as passionate, fiery, and individualistic. He sees himself as "'Free in name, but despised and scorned and set aside by the people to whose race I belong far more than to my mother's.'" Although Tom's statements seem to imply a sort of reverse racism— the same dislike of African Americans that white people have—his subsequent words make it clear that part of his longing to be recognized as part of the white race is the opportunities that come with such membership. For instance, he has been educated, but what he learned at school did not help him form a career or make a better life for himself. Instead, the lesson he took with him was "'that no degree of learning or wisdom will change the color of my skin and that I shall always wear what in my country is a badge of degradation.'" Where there is shame—either internal or external—there is little chance for the individual to better his condition in life.

After Polly saves her father by shooting and wounding Tom, the sheriff spends the evening pondering Tom's words. He comes to realize that "he had owed some duty to this son of his—that neither law nor custom could destroy a responsibility inherent in the nature of mankind." With these thoughts, the sheriff acknowledges that in the South— Old and New—whites owe nothing to African Americans. Laws do not legislate equality or fair treatment, nor do the customs and accepted practices of the land. All that could cause a man like the sheriff to treat an African American—be it his son or otherwise—fairly would be his own conscience. The sheriff had turned a blind eye to any conscience, and now that it has been raised, he must deal with the consequences. However, the text also indicates that the sheriff is not to blame for his moral lapses to this point: "But the baleful influence of human slavery poisoned the very foundations of life, and created new standards of right. The sheriff was conscientious; his conscience had merely been warped by his environment." Still, other men had clearly developed their own more enlightened con-

In Chesnutt's story, a small-town sheriff attempts to hold off a mob intent on lynching a mulatto man wrongly accused of murder. African-American journalist Ida B. Wells was a leader of the anti-lynching crusade, publishing a book on the subject in 1894.

science, as indicated by Tom's comparison of his father's behavior to other former slaveowners' treatment of their illegitimate mixed-blood children— men who freed or otherwise "saved" their children.

Although the sheriff vows to help Tom, he is still so bound by the law and custom of his society. He puts these elements above human compassion. Although he is now fully convinced of Tom's innocence, he rejects letting Tom escape, and instead vows to "investigate the circumstances of the murder, and move Heaven and earth to discover the real criminal." He believes that "he could employ counsel for the accused, and perhaps influence public opinion in his favor." At this point, the sheriff is merely invoking a fantasy. The text has already made clear the fate of African Americans involved in a crime against whites—even if they were not truly involved. The sheriff's denial of reality is further demonstrated by his proposed appeal to public opinion. The sheriff, of all people, should understand the improbability of such a shift, for he faced the rabble that very afternoon and understood the mind set of the people who most wanted Tom's death.

Tom alone understands the impossibility of any positive action resulting from his interaction with the sheriff. His decision to commit suicide by taking off his bandage emerges as a strong indictment of the society in which he lives. As he said earlier, "'When I think about it seriously I do not care particularly for such a life. It is the animal in me, not the man, that flees the gallows.'" The man in Tom—by implication, the "white" part of Tom—knows that he can never lead the life he wants to lead. He will never be free, never be respected, never be above quick and discriminatory judgment. That Tom should want to die is not surprising at this point, for he believes, perhaps rightly so, that his life has no hope.

"The Sheriff's Children" stands out among Chesnutt's fiction for its grim and unusual exploration of a serious racial issue. According to Andrews, "What makes 'The Sheriff's Children' . . . unique among Chesnutt's race problem stories . . . is its redirection of the southern color question, so that the problem of the black man's presence in the South is laid before the southern white man, who, as 'The Sheriff's Children' argues, must recognize his past complicity and present responsibility if 'the problem' is ever to be solved." Sheriff Campbell, however, shows himself unequal to this task. He is cursed with an insufficient conscience, lacks spirit, and too quickly takes up the reigns of his assigned duty instead of carving out a new duty—one based, not on law or social code, but on what is right and just, what is humane.

Source: Rena Korb, in an essay for *Short Stories for Students*, Gale Group, 2001.

P. Jay Delmar

In the following essay, Delmar examines "the theme of the mask"—"how both whites and blacks are constrained to hide their true personalities and, often, their true racial identities from themselves and each other"—in "The Sheriff's Children."

The third and sixth stories in *The Wife of His Youth*, "The Sheriff's Children" and "The Passing of Grandison," illustrate the mask-theme and the mask-structure in Chesnutt's fiction, and the fact that they do so in markedly different ways makes them worthy of separate consideration here. "The Sheriff's Children" uses his mask theme negatively: hiding one's true soul leads to tragedy. "The Passing of Grandison," on the other hand, like "Her Virginia Mammy," apparently argues that mask-wearing can be a virtue if it is directed toward virtuous ends. "The Sheriff's Children" uses techniques of subtle foreshadowing to screen its conclusion. In "The Passing of Grandison," however, Chesnutt succeeds with a bold, dangerous ploy. Though he uses almost no foreshadowing, he succeeds in a nearly complete masking of the story's surprise ending.

The two major figures of "The Sheriff's Children," Sheriff Campbell and his mulatto son, are both plagued by crises of personal identity; their reactions to these crises both exploit the theme of the mask and exemplify Chesnutt's structural use of the mask concept. These achievements make a powerful story of one which might without them have degenerated into a naive, run-of-the-mill treatment of the long-lost son plot. Had Chesnutt made the revelation of the relationship between the Sheriff and the son whom he had abandoned as a child its focal point, his story would never have attained any particular significance. Chesnutt instead uses the Sheriff's parenthood as the starting point for an examination of its tragic results.

Campbell is a man who wears the mask of duty and morality. Ronald Walcott stated the case quite well when he argued that while Campbell appears to be free of the primitive impulses which seem to motivate his neighbors, he "possesses his own inhibiting personal code before which all else must pay obeisance, his Southern gentleman's concept of duty" . . . The point is that the Sheriff is not free of primitive impulses; the concept of duty which he has adopted has only hidden them. In his youth, he had fathered a child with a Black woman; later, in a fit of anger, he had sold them down the river. As the crisis of the story unfolds with his "child" standing before him—a prisoner accused of murder whom an unruly mob wants to lynch—Campbell begins to see himself for the first time without a mask, reflected in his son's eyes: "He knew whose passions coursed beneath that swarthy skin and burned in the black eyes opposite his own. He saw in this mulatto what he himself might have become had not the safeguards of parental restraint and public opinion been thrown around him." Campbell had always lived by the code of the Southern aristocracy, one which sanctioned his behavior toward his lover and child. But he had never consciously realized that he was using the code to mask his instincts from himself. Whether the passions which coursed within him were noble or not, they were his, and he should have come to terms with them. When he learns who his prisoner is, Campbell begins to get an inkling of the existence of the mask which he has worn so long.

The prisoner, though, does not really come to grips with who and what he is. He feels trapped between two racial worlds. As Mr. Ryder says, in a story which satirizes this viewpoint, persons of mixed blood "are ground between the upper and the nether millstone." They may be accepted by either the white race or the black but the former does not want them, and acceptance by the latter would be a disgrace. Ryder would prefer acceptance into the white world, and, here with Chesnutt's apparent sympathy, Sheriff Campbell's son has also selected that goal. The prisoner cries that he is "despised and scorned and set aside by the people to whose race [he belongs] far more than to [his] mother's." The mulatto rejects his Blackness, but the rigidity of white society prohibits him from taking up the white man's mask. Essentially, the Sheriff's son feels robbed of his birthright; he has grown rebellious as a result of his inability to wear a mask which appears to him to be not a mask at all but rather his true spirit. He feels that he is being forced to wear a mask of Blackness.

Whatever the merits of Chesnutt's point about the proper sphere of the mulatto, it is clear that the Sheriff's mask of duty and the mulatto's mask of Blackness are evil forces; they cause the prisoner's death and the father's failure to atone for his past misdeeds. This outcome, tragic because both figures are basically noble men whose personalities reveal weaknesses which lead to their downfall, is a part of the story's mask-structure. Two elements of the work are crucial here—the Sheriff's daughter's wounding of the prisoner and his subsequent suicide—and both are well disguised.

The first event occurs after the prisoner asks the Sheriff at gunpoint to let him escape. Paralyzed by his sense of duty, the Sheriff cannot agree to what Chesnutt unmistakably feels is a proper course of action: "It may seem strange that a man who could sell his own child into slavery should hesitate at such a moment, when his life was trembling in the balance. But the baleful influence of human slavery poisoned the very fountains of life, and created new standards of right. The sheriff was conscientious; his conscience had merely been warped by his environment." In all justice and mercy, as Chesnutt suggests, Campbell should let his son go. Even if he were guilty of murder, his chances of escaping the

> "Campbell had always lived by the code of the Southern aristocracy, one which sanctioned his behavior toward his lover and child. But he had never consciously realized that he was using the code to mask his instincts from himself."

lynch mob are minimal at best; should he somehow escape its rage, his chances of receiving a fair trial in Troy are even worse. Although Campbell is now beginning to understand these truths, he cannot break through the barriers thrown up by years of tradition. He hesitates, and his son declares that he must die.

A reader might expect such a tragic result of the Sheriff's personality since hesitation is often a mark of a tragic figure, and Chesnutt does carry Campbell to the brink of catastrophe: the prisoner "raised his arm to fire, when there was a flash—a report from the passage behind him." Just as he was about to pull the trigger, he was shot by the Sheriff's daughter. This type of masking is well known to viewers of Westerns. Whenever the hero is in danger of being bushwhacked, an unseen marksman brings the villain down. One's expectations are keyed to an "anticipated event" (the death of the hero), but the event which actually occurs (the death of the villain) is its exact opposite. Such a situation is intended to shock the viewer momentarily, and Chesnutt intends a similar effect here. Of course, the tactic can be abused. In the worst examples of grade-B Westerns, the viewer is given no hint that the hero will be saved. In better examples, though, some foreshadowing hints at the truth; the film might show the hero's sidekick riding to the rescue, then leave him until he fires the mysterious shot.

"The Sheriff's Children" provides such foreshadowing just before the girl wounds her half-brother: "So absorbed were the two men in their colloquy and their own tumultuous thoughts that neither of them had heard a light step come stealthily up the stairs, nor seen a slender form creep along the darkening passage toward the mulatto." Without this suggestion—which only makes sense after the reader learns that the Sheriff's daughter has shot the prisoner—the "actual event" would come as a complete surprise to the reader; the anticipated event (Campbell's death) makes sense, and nothing would cause the reader to doubt its probability. So great a surprise would shock the reader too much; it would tend to annoy, rather than satisfy. If the foreshadowing were too heavy, on the other hand, there would be no surprise at all. In this case that charge cannot be made. There are 162 words heavily charged with emotional energy between the foreshadowing element and the prisoner's wounding, so the foreshadowing itself does not receive too much emphasis when the reader first encounters it. Moreover, the foreshadowing passage does not necessarily suggest the shooting, since "slender forms" do not generally carry horse-pistols.

The second crucial situation in the story, the mulatto's suicide, is equally masked. After the prisoner is injured, the Sheriff bandages his arm and tells him to lie about his escape attempt if he is questioned further. These are acts of kindness which apparently bode well for the Sheriff and his son, and they are followed by almost four pages which reveal Campbell's ruminations on his past life. When the Sheriff finally decides to "atone for his crime against this son of his—against society—against God," the reader feels that the story might end on a positive note. Even though a tragic atmosphere has been already established, a happy conclusion is not completely unlikely because of the inherent nobility of the characters. The qualities which make a tragic fall tragic could also be used to avert the tragedy. Campbell is basically a good man, and his son is not inherently evil. However, Chesnutt soon lifts the mask and reveals the actual ending. The tragedy is not averted because the mulatto kills himself while his father, still hesitating, slowly arrives at the decision to aid him.

This turn is clearly plausible, and, even more important, Chesnutt foreshadows it while he establishes his false trail. First, the mulatto had spoken of death as something he did not fear when he denounced his existence as a non-white, non-Black man: "When I think about it seriously I do not care particularly for such a life. It is the animal in me, not the man, that flees the gallows." Secondly, after he is wounded the mulatto's attitude of defiant rebellion transforms itself into sullen dejection; he simply gives up. Finally, the Sheriff himself tells his son how to die. The injury is described as a "flesh wound," something normally not very serious. However, as Campbell warns his son after bandaging him, "I'll have a doctor come and dress the wound in the morning . . . It will do very well until then, if you will keep quiet." If he does *not* keep quiet . . . the conclusion is left unsaid, but the prisoner knows what his father meant. During the night, the mulatto tears his bandage off and bleeds to death. The suicide does not come as a complete surprise to the reader, then; it does fit the tragic atmosphere of the story, and Chesnutt has shown it to be a reasonable occurrence without focusing upon it as an obvious ending.

"The Sheriff's Children" uses both mask-theme and mask-structure. The Sheriff and his son fail because they cannot accept their true identities or, perhaps in the case of the mulatto, because he cannot achieve recognition for what he perceives to be a true identity. And by the use of foreshadowing Chesnutt is able to hide the story's tragic outcome, increasing its emotional impact when readers finally recognize the truth.

Source: P. Jay Delmar, "The Mask as Theme and Structure: Charles W. Chesnutt's 'The Sheriff's Children' and 'The Passing of Grandison,'" in *American Literature*, Vol. LI, No. 3, November, 1979, pp. 364–75.

Hartmut K. Selke

In the following excerpt, Selke offers an extended analysis of the short story "The Sheriff's Children," which contains what he identifies as Chesnutt's characteristic literary themes.

Charles Waddell Chesnutt vies with Paul Laurence Dunbar in being the first Afro-American author to be accepted by major American publishing houses and to win national recognition and fame. Both authors, in order to be published at all, had to come to terms with the literary forms and conventions of the Plantation Tradition whose chief exponents were Joel Chandler Harris, Thomas Nelson Page, James Lane Allen and Harry Stillwell Edwards. This literary convention stipulated that the black characters be presented as living contentedly in an Edenic South, that they be quaint, childlike and docile, tellers of exotic yarns for the entertainment of massa's children or for massa himself. It is this tradition which gave rise to the literary stereotypes of the "Contended Slave," the "Wretched Freeman," who, being deprived of the paternal care of his master, is unable to provide for himself, the "Comic Negro" and the "Local Color Negro."

Since the black writer, who wanted to break into print with his accounts of the black experience in America, had to adapt his work to the prevalent tastes of the day and to present his characters in a pastoral, harmonious setting, the only freedom left to him was that of choosing "the genre or the countergenre," as Robert Bone points out . . . . By pastoral genre is meant the "idyllic posture toward experience," by countergenre the "ironic posture."

Whereas Dunbar by and large conformed to the limitations of the idyllic posture, wearing, as it were, "the mask that grins and lies," [the line is from Dunbar's poem "We Wear the Mask," *Majors and Minors*, 1895] Chesnutt never did, even when he made use of the established forms, as for example in his "conjure" stories, in which he subtly undercut the submissive message apparently inherent in the very form. . . .

Among the themes treated most often in Chesnutt's works are (1) the inhumanity of the system of chattel slavery, (2) the incongruities of the color line as drawn within the black society itself, (3) the dual themes of passing and the ordeal of the double identity and (4) the injustices that Southern blacks have to suffer even after Emancipation, particularly during the restoration of white supremacy after Reconstruction.

At first sight, "The Sheriff's Children" might seem to be a treatment of the theme of the tragic mulatto. However, this is only one and, as shall be demonstrated, not the dominant theme of the story.

"The Sheriff's Children" was first published in the New York weekly magazine *Independent* in November 1889. The *Independent* then catered to an educated, liberal white audience. The first readers of the story were unaware of it, author's racial identity. Earlier that year Chesnutt had moved into his own, rather spacious home in Cleveland. Yet, the other stories published or written during that year evince the same sombre and combative note that characterizes "The Sheriff's Children." In "The Conjurer's Revenge" (June 1889) the narrator, Uncle Julius, denounces slavery with unwonted explicitness, calling the slavetraders stealers and sellers of men and thus seeming to invoke the Biblical punishment for the manstealer.

"Dave's Neckliss" (October 1889) is also an Uncle Julius story, although not a "conjure" story in the narrow sense. Like "The Sheriff's Children," this gruesome story exposes "the baleful influence of human slavery." Indeed, the story bears close

> "Tom, the Afro-American, is as much an heir to the political and cultural heritage left by Campbell, the Founding Father, as is Polly, the Anglo-Saxon. But whereas nobody will dare question the legitimacy of the latter's claim, the former's is generally denied."

resemblance to "The Sheriff's Children": punished unjustly by an otherwise "kind" master (this fact is peculiarly insisted on in the story), Dave is driven to insanity and suicide. The "kind" master's recognition of his own guilt and his repentance come too late to undo the wrongs wrought by a system of chattel slavery. The third story, of which Chesnutt completed the first draft in 1889, was the often revised "Rena Walden." It deals with the problem of the tragic mulatto, which is also touched upon in "The Sheriff's Children."

Chesnutt's sombre outlook may be explained by the fact that at that time he was butting his head against the restrictions imposed by the tastes of the reading public and of magazine publishers. This went so far that he even toyed with the idea of migrating to Europe. In a letter written some six months after the publication of "The Sheriff's Children" he confided [in a letter to George Washington Cable]:

> If I should remain idle for two weeks, at the end of that time I should be ready to close out my affairs and move my family to Europe. The kind of stuff I could write, if I were not all the time oppressed by the fear that this line or this sentiment would offend somebody's prejudices, jar on somebody's American-trained sense of propriety, would, I believe, find a ready sale in England.

Ten years after its original publication, "The Sheriff's Children" reached a wider audience through its inclusion in *The Wife of His Youth and Other Stories of the Color Line*. Whereas in the first collection of stories the superficial white reader could easily be deluded by Chesnutt's apparent adherence to the conventional forms of the Plantation Tradition, this second volume, at least in some of the stories, more openly strikes a note of poignant protest against the Afro-American's social and psychological predicament in the South.

In a letter to his publisher, in which he discussed promotion strategies for the volume, Chesnutt wrote:

> The book was written with the distinct hope that it might have its influence in directing attention to certain aspects of the race question which are quite familiar to those on the unfortunate side of it; and I should be glad to have that view of it emphasized if in your opinion the book is strong enough to stand it; for a *sermon* that is labeled a sermon must be a good one to get a hearing.

Whereas the book was well received in the North, Southern critics, as was to be expected, did not fail to discover the elements of "crusade" and "sermon" and berated Chesnutt for his impropriety. One critic wrote: "'The Sheriff's Children' furnishes, perhaps, the most shocking instance of his reckless disregard of matters respected by more experienced writers" [Nancy Huston Banks, in a review in *The Bookman*, New York, X, February 1900]. Criticism seems to have been directed primarily against "The Sheriff's Children" with its bold treatment of the tabooed subject of miscegenation, and not against "The Passing of Grandison," which effectively explodes the myth of the happy, docile slave, or against "The Web of Circumstance," which undermines Booker T. Washington's accommodationist contention that the acquisition of skills and property would automatically ensure recognition for the Afro-American even in the South.

The story opens with a description of the sleepy village of Troy, county seat of Branson County in North Carolina, a district so isolated that the war seems to have passed it by, had it not been for the tribute of one generation of young men that the great conflict demanded. Some ten years after the war, the citizens of Branson County are shocked to learn that Captain Walker, an old soldier, "had been foully murdered." A mulatto, a stranger in the area, is suspected of the crime and quickly apprehended. While the prisoner is awaiting judgment in the county jail, the citizens decide to lynch him. The sheriff is informed of the plan by a Negro and determines to do his duty and resist the lynch mob. He proceeds to the jail where he locks himself into the prisoner's cell. After having warded off the lynching party and having fired a shot in reply to a sniper's bullet, he is disarmed by the prisoner who then reveals his identity. The mulatto is Tom, the sheriff's son, his mother is a slave woman whom the sheriff had sold to a speculator. The son demands that the sheriff release him or else he will shoot him. At the very moment when Tom decides that he cannot trust his father and prepares to shoot him, the sheriff's daughter, Polly, who had worried about her father's long absence, comes up from behind and fires at the mulatto, wounding his arm. The sheriff dresses his son's wound, telling him that he will call a doctor on the following morning. He spends a restless night, passing his life and his failings in review and finally deciding to "atone for his crime against this son of his." When he goes to the jail on Sunday morning, he finds that his son has committed suicide by tearing off the bandage and bleeding to death.

Chesnutt's story may be read simply as a carefully wrought suspense story, which moves in steadily increasing crescendo from the opening description of the dull and somnolent community to the final twist at the end of the story. As the plot develops, the scene narrows: the first two pages are devoted to the county, the following six to the village of Troy and its inhabitants, the next seven focus on the sheriff's house as the sheriff is informed of the plot by Sam. The scene then moves to the captive's cell in the jail. The next shift back to the sheriff's house seems to suggest that there is a break in the development delineated above. [In a dissertation] William L. Andrews sees in this supposed break a flaw of plot development: "The story . . . lapses into argument and introspection which fail to sustain the tenseness of the action in the first half of the story." However, this lapse into introspection is no more than a further narrowing of the scene along the pattern of the rest of the story, only this time to the sheriff's consciousness. The constant narrowing of the scene from the "sequestered district" of Branson County to the "hamlet" of Troy, from there to a prison cell and finally to the sheriff's mind conveys a feeling of claustrophobia, of inescapability.

This gradual restriction of space has its parallel in the gradual resolution of the question of identity, which was posed at the beginning of the story. The question is first raised in the speculations "upon the identity of the murderer." But at that point in the story everything is vague, ill-defined. A "strange mulatto" is suspected of the crime. The second central character, the sheriff, is only introduced at the beginning in his function as a public officer whose duty it is to arrest the suspect.

This vagueness is carried over into the next scene. As the design to lynch the prisoner assumes shape, the townspeople remain anonymous: no names are mentioned. Naturally, a major function of this scene is to demonstrate the genesis and anonymity of mob violence. By their very speech the townspeople are characterized as dumb-witted backwoods people whose dull minds are helped along by illegally distilled whiskey and vague notions of "honor" to give birth to the dastardly plan.

The heavy hand of the omniscient narrator who edits and comments on his material makes itself felt particularly in this scene, driving home a point that does not stand in need of such commenting. The planned lynching is to the townspeople's minds "a becoming way in which to honor [Captain Walker's] memory." Their perverted notion of justice is reflected in the mocking solemnity of the narrator's language as he describes the plan: "By agreement the lynchers were to meet at Tyson's store at five o'clock in the afternoon, and proceed thence to the jail . . . ".

The following scene at the sheriff's house marks a first departure from the aura of anonymity which had characterized the first pages. The reader is informed of the sheriff's name and of his appearance. Sheriff Campbell is a "tall, muscular man," he has "keen, deep-set gray eyes" and "a masterful expression." His very stature and "attitude of a soldier" as well as his language bespeak his determination and his superiority over the rest of the townspeople. Additional information provided by the omniscient narrator corroborates this first impression. Campbell is a cultivated man, "far above the average of the community in wealth, education, and social position.... He had graduated at the State University at Chapel Hill, and had kept up some acquaintance with current literature and advanced thought."

The members of the lynch mob, too, are given a semblance of identity when the sheriff asks Sam who is coming. They are an array of self-styled doctors, majors and colonels: "'Dere's Mistah McSwayne, en Doc' Cain, en Maje' McDonal,' en Kunnel Wright, en a heap er yuthers.'" But even this identity is fleeting, as well befits a mob setting out with this purpose in mind. It is wiped away by the sheriff who declares them all to be "strangers" to him because he "did not think it necessary to recognize anybody in particular on such an occasion; the question of identity sometimes comes up in the investigation of these extrajudicial executions."

The question of identity comes up again in the confrontation between Campbell and his prisoner after the lynch mob has withdrawn. It is no longer the detective story question as to who was the murderer, a question which persists only as a vague hope of extricating the prisoner from his hopeless situation. In the course of the story every suspicion against him is dispelled in the reader as well as in the sheriff: "he no longer doubted the prisoner's innocence."

Alone in his cell with the sheriff, the prisoner undergoes an almost miraculous transformation from a "cowering wretch" who provokes the sheriff's "contempt and loathing" to a "keeneyed, desperate man . . . a different being altogether from the groveling wretch" of only a few minutes before. This transformation is possible only because Tom, the prisoner, is exclusively seen through the sheriff's eyes. He is never presented, except in his own utterances, in his own right, but remains a reflection in his father's eyes. Before the prisoner had gained control of the situation, he had remained a mere abstraction to the sheriff, a well-defined quantity that fitted into a prefabricated category. It is this refusal to look upon the prisoner as an individual human being that prevents him from recognizing his son sooner than he does.

As Tom points out to him, they have the same features: "no man need look at us together twice to see that . . .". It is obvious that the sheriff had never looked at his son. Instead he had seen "the negro" in him: "He had relied on the negro's cowardice and subordination in the presence of an armed white man as a matter of course." It is only this unwonted behavior that "caused the sheriff to look at him more closely." Even then, however, he does not recognize the prisoner, and it is only after the question "Who are you?" that the latter's identity is revealed to him.

This revelation initiates a new movement. It is the beginning of yet another question of identity. The confrontation with "this wayward spirit" who had come "back from the vanished past to haunt him" forces the sheriff to see himself as he truly is, to explore his own smug identity.

This new and central theme of the story is prepared by a change of the point of view. The first two thirds of the story bear the mark of the omniscient narrator whose presence as editorial commentator is constantly felt. This is particularly true of the three-page introduction which leads up to the action proper. Here the author even appears in the first person, explaining his materials to the reader: "At the period of which I write . . . ". In what follows, the omniscient narrator as editorializing agency is also felt, at times very directly, as in his remark that something "is immaterial to this narrative," at times less so, as in the choice of scenes which are presented in the dramatic mode. In the last third of the story these editorial interventions do not cease altogether—they are particularly obvious in the description of Poll's stealthy approach, unnoticed by both the protagonist and Tom, in the authorial comments on the sheriff's character and in the imperative addressed to the reader: "Let no one ask what his answer would have been"—but a new dimension is added. Starting with the sentence, "The sheriff mentally cursed his own carelessness for allowing him to be caught in such a predicament," all subsequent events are mainly seen and evaluated through Campbell's consciousness. From now on, to apply Henry James' words to the sheriff, "It is *his* vision, *his* conception, *his* interpretation . . . He therefore supremely matters; all the rest matters only as he feels it, treats it, meets it" [*The Art of the Novel: Critical Prefaces*, 1950].

This change of perspective is a necessary prerequisite for the soul-searching that is about to follow. The sheriff, who had hitherto appeared an impeccable character, now realizes that he "had yielded" to the temptations of an evil system when he had sold his son and his lover to a speculator. This also throws a new light on a remark made earlier in the story. Yielding to his environment, to the force of circumstances, even against his better judgment, seems to be the sheriff's particular weakness: "At first an ardent supporter of the Union, he had opposed the secession movement in his native State as long as opposition availed to stem the tide of public opinion. Yielding at last to the force of circumstances, he had entered the Confederate service rather late in the war . . . ".

This weakness also accounts for the sheriff's decision in favor of his sense of duty and against his human instincts, both when his own life is in danger and when he asks himself how he can extricate Tom from his predicament and make up for his own previous shortcomings: "It occurred to him, purely as a hypothesis, that he might permit his prisoner to escape; but his oath of office, his duty as sheriff, stood in the way of such a course, and the sheriff dismissed the idea from his mind."

It is only after the initial shock of the confrontation has worn off that the full impact of the experience becomes clear to the sheriff. "Alone with God," he again experiences "a kind of clarifying of the moral faculty . . . a state of mind in which one sees himself as God may be supposed to see him." Seeing himself as he is, the sheriff decides to atone for his sin. It is interesting to note that neither Tom nor himself see his sin in the fact of miscegenation itself, but rather in the fact that he has neglected his parental duties, his moral obligations in depriving his son of a true identity of his own: Tom has "no name, no father, no mother—in the true meaning of motherhood."

The tragedy of the story lies in the fact that the circumstances are such that the father's recognition of the son comes too late. The sheriff's personal tragedy is that his attempts at atonement are only half-hearted and incomplete and that he is finally deprived of the "opportunity for direct expiation."

As quoted above, Chesnutt had thought of *The Wife of His Youth* in terms of a sermon. "The Sheriff's Children" preaches a sermon in the sense that it induces the enlightened white reader, to whom it is addressed, to identify with the sheriff who is presented in very positive terms as a courageous, law-abiding, conscientious and educated man. The sheriff's qualities make his moral shortcomings appear in an even cruder light, and the reader, who had come to identify himself with him, is made to share in his fall and to experience a purging similar to that "clarifying of the moral faculty" that the sheriff feels. Chesnutt's is a fire-and-brimstone sermon which shows no way out of the moral dilemma. The attempt to make amends comes too late. Injustice has been done and it seems irremediable. The impact on the reader who is required to go to task with himself, is all the greater.

Yet, even after the sheriff's failings have been revealed, the sympathetic narrator speaks out in his behalf in an authorial comment: "But the baleful influence of human slavery poisoned the very fountains of life, and created new standards of right. The sheriff was conscientious; his conscience had merely been warped by his environment." Without denying any of the sheriff's guilt, he thus places it in a broader perspective, indicting a system to which Campbell has fallen prey. Again, the reader may be led to ask himself if the influence of the environment is truly a valid attenuating circumstance for Campbell and for himself.

By choosing the sheriff's point of view in the last third of the story, Chesnutt has diverted the reader's attention from Tom, the mulatto. The narrator does not perform the role of advocate for him, trying to explain his motives and soliciting compassion or understanding, as he had done in the case of the sheriff. Seen only from outside except in his own utterances, Tom's story remains untold, although the narrative offers some hints as to the dramatic potential of the theme.

[Gerald W.] Haslam detects one of the strong points of the story in the absence of this theme, which is indeed fraught with grave dangers: "By emphasizing the white father rather than the mulatto son, he [Chesnutt] partially avoided the melodramatic stereotypes which marred so much of his work".

The theme which Chesnutt partially subdued in this story is that of the tragic mulatto, which came out of antislavery fiction, as Sterling A. Brown has shown [in introductory comments to the Chesnutt entry in *The Negro Caravan*, 1969]. The mulattoes in fiction "are the intransigent, the resentful, the mentally alert, the proofs of the Negro's possibilities." The theme harbors the danger of presenting the material, in such a way that the Afro-American's humanity is measured in proportion to the "white" blood in his veins.

Upon the completion of his second draft of "Rena Walden" only a few months after the publication of "The Sheriff's Children," Chesnutt wrote to Cable on the subject of mulattoes in fiction:

> There are a great many intelligent people who consider the class to which Rena and Wain belong as unnatural.... [a] gentleman remarked to me in substance that he considered a mulatto an insult to nature, a kind of monster that he looked upon with infinite distaste.... I fear there is too much of the same sentiment for mulattoes to make good magazine characters.

Chesnutt was doubtless prompted by these sentiments when he made the sheriff's moral dilemma the central concern of his story instead of choosing the equally available theme of the tragic mulatto. Tom's major function in "The Sheriff's Children" seems to be that of the spark which sets off the crisis.

Yet, there is more to him. When Tom first appears in the story, he is ambiguously called "a strange mulatto," an epithet which is reminiscent of Chesnutt's letter. Tom is not only a stranger in his own land, unrecognized in all senses of the word and by everybody including his father, he is also an abomination in the eyes of the whites.

The dilemma of the double-consciousness as defined by W. E. B. DuBois is particularly obvious for the mulatto. DuBois wrote:

> One ever feels his twoness,—an American, a Negro; two souls, two thoughts, two unreconciled strivings; two warring ideals in one dark body, whose dogged strength alone keeps it from being torn asunder. The history of the American Negro is the history of this strife,—this longing to attain self-conscious manhood, to merge this double self into a better and truer self. In this merging he wishes neither of the older selves to be lost.... He would not bleach his Negro soul in a flood of white Americanism, for he knows that Negro blood has a message for the world. He simply wishes to make it possible for a man to be both a Negro and an American, without being cursed and spit upon by his fellows, without having the doors of Opportunity closed roughly in his face.

Tom is obviously an individual who does not possess this dogged strength and who is torn asunder by the magnitude of the conflict. He is a tortured, warped character who has come to turn his aggression against the race that the custom of the country makes him a part of, and thus finally against himself. His attitude toward his mother, who, to his mind, has become synonymous with the black race, is highly ambivalent. While he pities her and admires her for having "had enough womanhood to call her soul her own," he is at the same time ashamed of her blackness: "You gave me your own blood ... and you gave me a black mother.... You gave me a white man's spirit, and you made me a slave, and crushed it out." Tom has sought to flee his blackness, as by acquiring an education, but has found that his blackness stays with him as "a badge of degradation."

Commenting on the inappropriately refined language used by Tom, Haslam asks himself "if Chesnutt has not, in this one respect, fallen again into his habit of trying to demonstrate that mulattoes are more white than Negro." Similarly, Bone feels that "the story does not wholly escape from the stereotype of the tragic mulatto" but is redeemed by its pervasive irony. Tom does indeed seem to conform to what Brown had called the present image of the tragic mulatto: "The mulatto is a victim of a divided inheritance; from his white blood come his intellectual strivings, his unwillingness to be a slave; from his Negro blood come his baser emotional urges, his indolence, his savagery." We should, however, ask ourselves if Chesnutt did not intend to criticize Tom for his own interpretation of his situation, for his inability to turn his talents and his education to some good purpose, for his self-pitying despair.

Tom, then, is vaguely related to [Albion] Tourgée's mulatto characters towards whom Chesnutt had no charitable feelings. In the above quoted letter to Cable he writes: "Judge Tourgée's cultivated white Negroes are always bewailing their fate and cursing the drop of black blood which 'taints'—I hate the word, it implies corruption—their otherwise pure race." The only difference seems to be that Tom, distorted beyond recognition by the force of circumstance, is more sordid, his fate more sordid than that of Tourgée's characters.

This makes him very different from the saintly figures created by younger authors, figures who die a Christlike death on the cross, as in W. E. B. DuBois' story "Jesus Christ in Texas" or in Langston Hughes' poem "Christ in Alabama." Rather, Tom dies by his own hand, and the pattern of Crucifixion and Resurrection is thoroughly perverted. Yet, there is an obvious parallel in the story. The action takes place at a weekend, starting with a death on Friday morning (one page) and ending with another on Sunday morning (one page). The bulk of the story is devoted to the abortive attempt to lynch the prisoner and to the sheriff's soul-searching, which might be likened to a descent into the "hell" of his own mind where he has to face and overcome his own sinful self. But the parallel is not sustained by the characters. The whole story is pervaded by murder, near parricide, fratricide and, finally, suicide. The father cannot save the son. Instead of a resurrection, we witness the confirmation of death, of hopelessness. The Biblical allusion might be even further pursued. The death of the old soldier might be assumed to represent the sacrifice made by the nation as a whole—we are told that Branson County was robbed of "the flower of its young manhood." The redemption of the nation, however, fails miserably, ending with the death of him for whom the sacrifice has ostensibly been made.

Tom's only triumph might be that he dies of his own free will and thus in a way asserts his manhood, but it is not much of a triumph. "The Sheriff's Children" is the first sign of an angry strain in Chesnutt, more often than not subdued by his gradualist, even accommodationist, philosophy. Tom, though not possessing any of the greatness, vaguely foreshadows a later Chesnutt character, Josh Green in *The Marrow of Tradition*, who would rather die like a man than live like a dog.

The choice of the title "The Sheriff's Children" seems to be at odds with the point of view used in the story, which clearly favors the sheriff as the central character. However, the relationship between the sheriff's children opens the way to a deeper, parabolical reading of the story. It is important for this parabolical meaning that they should have no knowledge of each other's existence, or, to put it more precisely, that Polly should have no knowledge of the existence of a black half-brother. Tom and Polly do not come fully alive in the story precisely because they are made to represent more than themselves alone. They are both the heirs of a father who, by virtue of his ambivalence—he is torn between allegiance to the Union and the Confederacy—very much resembles Thomas Jefferson who managed to reconcile his authorship of the Declaration of Independence with his status of slaveholder and progenitor of mulatto children. Tom, the Afro-American, is as much an heir to the political and cultural heritage left by Campbell, the Founding Father, as is Polly, the Anglo-Saxon. But whereas nobody will dare question the legitimacy of the latter's claim, the former's is generally denied. The original sin is the father's failure to recognize his son as his heir, his having left him out of the masterplan. Polly acts out a tragic role by being instrumental in the destruction of somebody who is in reality her brother....

Source: Hartmut K. Selke, "Charles Waddell Chesnutt: 'The Sheriff's Children' (1889)," in *The Black American Short Story in the 20th Century: A Collection of Critical Essays*, edited by Peter Bruck, B. R. Gruner Publishing Co., 1977, pp. 21–38.

Sources

Andrews, William L., *The Literary Career of Charles W. Chesnutt*, Louisiana State University Press, 1980.

Banks, Nancy Huston, "Novel Notes: 'The Wife of His Youth,'" in *The Bookman*, February, 1900, Vol. 10, No. 6, pp. 597–98.

Chamberlain, John, "The Negro as Writer,'" in *The Bookman*, February, 1930, Vol. 70, No. 6, pp. 603–711.

Elder, Arlene A., "Charles Waddell Chesnutt: Art or Assimilation in the 'Hindered Hand': Cultural Implications of Early African-American Fiction," Greenwood Press, 1978.

Howells, W. D., "Mr. Charles W. Chesnutt's Stories," in *The Atlantic Monthly*, May, 1900, Vol. 85, No. 511, pp. 699–700.

Redding, J. Saunders, "Adjustment," in *To Make a Poet Black*, University of North Carolina Press, 1939, pp. 49–93.

Render, Sylvia Lyons, "Charles Waddell Chesnutt," in *Dictionary of Literary Biography*, Vol. 78, Gale Research, 1989, pp. 68–81.

Selke, Hartmut K., "Charles Waddell Chesnutt: 'The Sheriff's Children' (1889)," in *The Black American Short Story in the 20th Century: A Collection of Critical Essays*, edited by Peter Bruck, B. R. Gruner Publishing Co., 1977, pp. 21–38.

Further Reading

Chesnutt, Helen M., *Charles Waddell Chesnutt: Pioneer of the Color Line*, University of North Carolina Press, 1952.
   This book is a biography of Chesnutt written by his daughter.

Heermance, J. Noel, *Charles W. Chesnutt: America's First Great Black Novelist*, Archon Books, 1974.
   Heermance's book is a study of Chesnutt's work in association with the culture in which he lived and worked.

Render, Sylvia Lyons, *Charles W. Chesnutt*, Twayne Publishers, 1980.
   Render's text provides a solid and entertaining overview of Chesnutt's life, work, and critical reception.

Silver Water

Amy Bloom

1991

Amy Bloom's first collection of short stories, *Come to Me*, brought her immediate acclaim. Critics lauded her skill in drawing her characters, many of whom were, as Jeanne Schinto dubbed them in *Belles Letters*, "psychological anomalies." Bloom evocatively portrays these disturbed individuals amidst backgrounds rich with love, familial relationships, and essential humanity.

"Silver Water," one of the stories in the collection, was chosen for inclusion in 1992's *Best American Short Stories*. It tells about a teenager, Rose, who has a psychotic break. After ten years of fighting schizophrenia, Rose kills herself. Her struggle with the illness, the unspeakable anguish it brings to her entire family, and her eventual suicide are all hauntingly brought forth through the understated voice of Violet, who narrates her older sister's life with precise, alive words and luminous imagery. Victoria Radin wrote of the collection in the *New Statesman and Society*, Bloom's "stories are suffused with the sensual pleasures of colour, sound, scent, and love." "Silver Water" radiates with such touches, but its deeper power draws from Bloom's creation of an immensely painful situation and the love that attempts to conquer it, and yet finally has no choice but to submit to it.

Author Biography

Amy Bloom was born in 1953. She spent her childhood in Great Neck, Long Island. According to the author, she started writing stories when she started reading, but she stopped when she was sixteen. At that time, she found it difficult to write about her life when she could not even understand it.

Bloom, however, maintained her lifelong fascination with other people's stories, which perhaps explains the pull of the theater when she was younger. Bloom eventually attended graduate school and embarked upon a career as a psychotherapist. She later recalled that as she drove home after her first meeting with her training analyst, the urge to write suddenly resurfaced. By the time she reached her home, she had an entire plot for a story worked out.

Despite the interest in writing, Bloom continued to work full-time as a psychotherapist. Bloom has always been careful to completely maintain the privacy of her patients, however, and she has stated that she draws the material for her stories primarily from her own life and that of her friends and family.

Her short stories began to draw national attention in the early 1990s in such works as *Antaeus* and *Story*. Her work also appeared in *The Best American Short Stories* of both 1991 and 1992. In 1993, Bloom published the short story collection *Come to Me*. The book was a finalist that year for the National Book Award.

After her demonstrated success as a short-story writer, Bloom turned to longer works, and she published the novel *Love Invents Us*, excerpts of which originally appeared in such magazines as *The New Yorker*.

As Bloom's literary reputation has grown, she has reduced her practice. Today, she continues to divide her time between her writing, her patients, and her family, with whom she resides in Connecticut.

Plot Summary

Violet's sister, Rose, starts experiencing schizophrenia as a teenager. Violet remembers Rose before the mental illness hit her, as a beautiful, wonderful older sister. When Rose is fifteen, she has her first psychotic break. Rose's mother, a musician, realizes that Rose is "going crazy," even though the father, a psychiatrist, does not realize this. The mother takes Rose to a hospital that day, beginning Rose's ten-year odyssey back and forth to one hospital or halfway house after another.

Rose has many bad therapists and only a few good ones. The family—Violet; the mother, Galen; and the father, David—also participate in family counseling. Violet recalls the best family therapist they had, a doctor named Dr. Thorne. Under Dr. Thorne's care, Rose does much better and gains more control of her compulsive behaviors. She is able to move into a halfway house, loses weight, continues to take her medication, begins singing with a church choir, and is able to be brought back more easily when she "goes off."

After five years, however, Dr. Thorne dies, and Rose begins to lose all the progress she has made. She stops taking her medication and she gets thrown out of the halfway house after she throws another patient down the stairs. Rose's new psychiatric coverage doesn't start for forty-five days, so she comes home to live with her parents.

At that time, Violet is living an hour away from her parents. Her parents tell her that although it is hard taking care of Rose, they are managing. Violet comes home on Sunday, however, and she realizes how difficult the situation has been when she discovers that Rose broke their mother's piano bench. Her father confesses that he doesn't know how they will make it through the next twenty-seven days with Rose at home. Unfortunately, he can't put her in a psychiatric hospital, even if he and Galen pay for it themselves, because Rose's insurance policy says she must be symptom-free before her coverage begins.

Rose and Galen come home from the lake. When Galen tells Rose to go upstairs and change her wet pants, Rose begins to bang her head against the kitchen floor. Galen tries to prevent her from doing this, but Rose throws her off physically. Violet positions her body under Rose so Rose cannot hit her head anymore. This makes Rose realize what is happening. She apologizes and runs up to her room. When David comes in, Violet does not tell him what really happened or how her mother got the bruises on her face.

Throughout the evening, Rose tries unsuccessfully to control herself. Finally, Rose gets to sleep. That night, Violet wakes up at three o'clock in the morning. She goes to Rose's room, but her sister is not there. Violet goes outside and sees Rose's footprints heading into the woods. Violet finds her sister in the woods, lying on the ground, holding a bottle of pills in her hand. Violet believes that Rose says, "Closing time." Violet sits with her sister until the sun comes up. She goes back to the house, imagining how badly her mother will react to Violet's letting her sister—the "favorite"—die. Galen, however, only calls her a "warrior queen," and says Rose was one, too. Then she goes into the woods, alone, to be with Rose. When she returns, she wakes David, who calls the police and the funeral parlor. At the funeral, while her mother plays the piano, Violet closes her eyes and sees her sister at fourteen years, in the opera house parking lot with head thrown back and lovely notes rising in the air.

Characters

David

David is Rose and Violet's father. He is, in the words of Violet, a "kind, sad man." David is also a psychiatrist, yet he doesn't recognize the signs of mental illness in his own daughter. He cares for his wife and his daughter, yet he doesn't outwardly demonstrate the same emotional attachment to Rose that his wife does and, according to Violet, has less of an ability to calm her down when she "goes off." He is the one who speaks in practical terms, for instance, how it is impossible to take care of Rose after Dr. Thorne's death, and he is the one who takes care of the arrangements after Rose's suicide.

Galen

Galen is Rose and Violet's mother. She is a musician who is regarded by people in their town as eccentric. Galen is the first person to realize that Rose is suffering from a mental illness. Galen plays the piano in the countless hospitals, institutions, and halfway houses that are Rose's homes over the next ten years. Galen is very close to her daughter, and Violet even thinks that Rose is the favored child.

Addie Robicheaux

Addie sings contralto in the church choir, along with Rose. She and Rose become close, and Addie is able to help Rose when she is experiencing mental breakdowns. Addie comes over to be with the family after Rose's death.

Rose

Rose is Violet's older sister. Until her first psychotic breakdown, at the age of fifteen, she led a normal life. She was well-liked at school, showed musical talent, and was idolized by Violet. With the onset of mental illness, however, Rose's behavior grows erratic. Rose, and her illness, quickly become the focus of the family. Difficult to deal with, Rose is in and out of institutions and therapists' offices.

While under the care of Dr. Thorne, Rose makes great improvements. During this five-year period, she is able to live in a halfway house, make a friend, and sing in a church choir. After Dr. Thorne's death, Rose begins to fall apart. She stops taking her medication. She gets thrown out of the halfway house for her violent behaviors and must return home to live with her parents. There she lashes out at her family. Eventually, Rose commits suicdie with a bottle of pills. Violet finds Rose outside, dying, but she does not call for help. Instead, she remains with her until dawn.

Dr. Thorne

Known to Rose as Big Nut, Dr. Thorne is the only therapist to whom Rose responds. With his help, Rose is able to move into a halfway house, stay on her medications, lose weight, stop behaving compulsively, and join a church choir. Rose and the whole family love Dr. Thorne for the way he helps Rose. After five years of treating her, however, Dr. Thorne dies of an aneurysm, and Rose quickly loses the control he helped her gain.

Violet

The narrator of the story, Violet, is two years younger than her sister Rose. At the time she relates the story, Violet is an adult, looking back at the life and death of her sister.

As a child and preteen, she had always looked up to Rose, her beautiful, talented sister. Despite Rose's continued mental breakdowns, Violet continues to remember Rose as she once was. However, she does not ignore Rose's present condition, and when necessary, protects Rose from herself. As an adult, she lives on her own but near enough her family to continue her involvement in Rose's saga and treatment. Despite Rose's illness, the sisters share a close bond throughout their lives. It is Violet who finds Rose dying. She chooses to not save Rose from her suicide attempt. She expects that her mother will be angry with her for not saving Rose's life, but this turns out not to be the case.

Mr. Walker

Mr. Walker is the worst family therapist the family ever visits. He talks about Rose in the third person and thinks the family reacts to Rose's illness inappropriately.

Themes

Illness

The theme of illness—specifically mental illness—and how that affects everyone it touches is one of the most important themes in "Silver Water." After Rose's first schizophrenic breakdown at the age of fifteen, the illness virtually controls her life, and as the narration makes clear, it also takes over the lives of her family. The illness is seen as a family problem. Not only does the entire family participate in group counseling to help Rose, but the mother and father try to help Rose's fellow patients, as if saving others similarly afflicted will save their daughter. David, a psychiatrist, donates time to work in the hospitals and clinic that currently treat Rose, while Galen, a musician, offers salvation and peace through the only method she knows: through her music.

David and Galen, however, try to minimize Violet's involvement; they want her to be free to lead a normal life. Thus, after Dr. Thorne's death, when Rose is to spend a month and a half at home, David and Galen discourage Violet from returning home too often; her weekly Sunday visits will be enough, they say. Galen, in particular, does not want to confess to Violet just how difficult these weeks with Rose have been. Throughout the story and up through Rose's final stay at home, Violet's contribution to Rose's illness and attempted recoveries is not immediately clear, yet at the end, she provides Rose with the greatest gift of all: release from her pain.

Death

Rose's death, the event upon which the story turns, is crucial in "Silver Water." Only in death can Rose escape the terrible effects of her illness. As she tells her family the night before her suicide, she does not want to do the things she does, such as shoving her mother into the refrigerator, but she simply cannot control herself.

Topics for Further Study

- Do you think that Violet's actions at the end of the story are justified? Why or why not?

- Find out more about schizophrenia, such as who it affects, when its onset begins, how it is treated, and how treatable it is. Then write up a few paragraphs summarizing your findings.

- Violet says that Rose enjoys art therapy, and Galen often plays piano for the patients hospitalized along with Rose. How do you think these therapies would work on people with mental and emotional disorders? Conduct research to answer the question.

- Violet believes that Rose is her mother's "favorite"? Do you find evidence of her statement in the story? Explain your answer.

- What is your reaction to the family therapy session with Walker? Explain your answer.

- Do you know or have you read about somebody with problems similar to Rose's? How is this person like Rose? How is this person different from Rose?

Violet tacitly approves of Rose's suicide, and even sits besides her sister as Rose dies, as revealed by the words she uses: "I sat with her, uncovering the bottle of white pills by her hand, and watched the stars fade." It is not revealed whether Violet makes no attempt to save her sister more for her sister's sake or for her family's sake. She strongly wants to think that Rose has a very real cognizance of and culpability for her actions; "'Closing time,' she [Rose] whispered. I believe that's what she said." The story, however, seems to say that Violet's actions stem from a combination of reasoning: Rose is in pain and unhappy, and the family is in pain and unhappy. Crucially, Violet's parents do not fault her for her role in Rose's death. Her mother even evidences approval in her labeling of both of her daughters as "warrior queens." The story's final image is at Rose's funeral, yet instead of being a depressing scene, Violet concentrates on the positive. The story ends on the uplifting word "rising."

Family

One point that the story raises is the affect one member of a family has on the rest of the family. Rose's illness does not only hurt her: it hurts her mother, father, and sister. The members of this family are so inextricably intertwined. They work together to try and save Rose, and when that is no longer possible, some of them work together to help her leave the world.

Despite their closeness, each member of the family has a specific role and chooses what he or she will reveal to others. David is the one who tells Violet the truth about how difficult life is with Rose at home, while Galen wants to hide it from her younger daughter. Violet tells only the second lie of her life to her father when she does not tell him that Rose pushed Galen into the refrigerator. Violet also reveals that she has lived her life under the belief that Rose was always her mother's "favorite," to which she does not admit until the very end of the story, after she has already clearly demonstrated her love for her sister.

The story further affirms that people outside the family boundaries can cross over and truly become as close as family members. Thus, Rose's final breakdown is predicated by the death of her beloved therapist. Also significant to this point is the inclusion of Addie, Rose's choir friend, in the story's final paragraph. This elevates Addie's status more to a family member than a friend.

Style

Point of View

The story is told from Violet's first-person point of view. This means that the reader is privy only to Violet's thoughts and observations. However, this filtering does not detract from a solid understanding of Rose's life. Through Violet's eyes, the readers see Rose's overwhelming pain, sadness, and beauty. Violet chooses those details that most demonstrate what her sister goes through in the ten-year course of her illness, but she also reflects on what her sister had been: "before her constant tinkling of commercials and fast-food jingle there had been Puccini and Mozart and hymns so sweet and mighty you expected Jesus to come down off his cross and clap . . . there had been the prettiest girl in Arrandale Elementary School, the belle of Landmark Junior High." Because of Violet's clear love for her sister, the reader feels comfortable in trusting her words and her interpretations. Violet chooses fewer, yet still relevant, details to make her parents' reactions to Rose's tragedy poignant. Violet renders her parents as believable and sensitive, yet very distinct people.

Narration and Structure

Violet chooses to tell this story after her sister has died. This decision allows her greater flexibility than a straight-forward narrative would. Violet is able to include details and ideas that she might not have been aware of at the time the action was taking place. For instance, she acknowledges that the lie she told to her father about Rose's outburst in the kitchen was the second of three lies she had ever told in her life; readers thus cannot overlook its significance and will more closely reflect on the action that led to the lie in the first place.

The act of looking back on Rose's life also allows Violet to condense it. She picks out what she considers to be the more significant events and characteristics. The added perspective that Violet has because of the distance between the events and the telling of the events allows her to better shape the story, and thus better reach the reader. She can compare the outbreaks of the illness, the various doctors' treatments, and the way that the family reacts to the different episodes. In so doing, Violet highlights the changes that Rose has gone through over the years and demonstrates what a precarious hold she has on her own life and actions. This narrative style further underscores the precariousness of life itself; every change in Rose's ailment has an equivalent effect on all the members of her family.

Violet also chooses to talk about Rose as she was before the illness struck. Structurally, the story completes a full circle. Violet opens with the memory of her sister's "crystalline" voice rising in the parking lot outside of the opera house, and ends at Rose's funeral, remembering her fourteen-year-old sister, one year before her first breakdown, "lion's mane thrown back and her eyes tightly closed against the glare of the parking lot lights." This structure not only reminds the readers of the fragility of the human experience—how quickly what a person takes as the core of their life can change—

but also underscores the cyclical nature of life and death.

Symbolism and Imagery

Music provides the greatest opportunities for the use of symbolism and imagery in the story. The first line of the story reads, "My sister's voice was like mountain water in a silver pitcher; the clear, blue beauty of it cools you and lifts you beyond your heat, beyond your body." Although Violet places her sister, in these opening paragraphs, in a brightly lit parking lot, her images choose to align Rose with those of nature. Thus Rose is presented like that voice itself, like that mountain water: pure, true, beautiful, and undamaged. This link is further emphasized in the scene in which Rose dies. She chooses to go out to the woods behind the house, where Violet follows her "wide, draggy footprints darkening the wet grass."

The silver water of the title evokes the wet grass upon which Rose dies, as well as the purity of the water and the purity of Rose's voice and soul. Like rushing water, "the sweet sound [of Rose's voice] held us tight, flowing around us, eddying throughout our hearts, rising, still rising."

Historical Context

America in the Early 1990s

The decade opened with George Bush in the Oval Office. One of the most significant events of his term was the Persian Gulf War undertaken by several countries belonging to the United Nations—most notably the United States—against Iraq after its 1991 invasion of neighboring, oil-rich Kuwait. The UN forces quickly defeated Iraq, and Bush enjoyed great popularity and international praise.

At the same time, however, his administration was drawing criticism on the domestic front. A recession hit in 1990, and as the economy faltered, unemployment rose. The number of Americans living below the poverty line grew by more than 2 million in 1990. The United States was also experiencing a trade gap, particularly with Japan, and Bush and other U.S. business leaders were unable to persuade the Japanese to import more American goods. The 1991 federal deficit also surged to $282 billion. The Persian Gulf War and the bailout of the savings and loan and banking industries contributed to this deficit.

In 1992, Bill Clinton was elected president, beating incumbent George Bush and independent Ross Perot. Clinton was the first democrat in 12 years to hold the nation's top office. By the end of the year, the U.S. economy was well on the road to recovery. By the middle of the decade, Americans, on the whole, enjoyed a comparatively high level of prosperity. The United States also continued to enjoy the world's largest economy. Clinton experienced other major triumphs in the early years of his presidency, particularly balancing the federal budget and reducing the national debt. Unemployment began to go down, and the stock market boomed.

Health Care Changes?

When Clinton ran for president, many middle-class Americans felt that health insurance was out of their reach; wealthier Americans could afford high premiums, and poorer Americans were covered by Medicaid, but there was no assistance for middle-class families. One of Clinton's campaign promises was to bring affordable health care within the reach of all Americans. A bill that would support changes to this effect never even came to a vote in Congress, however. Opponents charged that such a sweeping reform would be too expensive and would also limit Americans' ability to make their own decisions. Health care has been the subject of great debate throughout the decade, particularly with the rise of HMOs and increasing costs for health care. By 1993, the United States was spending around $884 billion on health care each year.

Mental Illness in the United States

In the mid-1800s, Dorothea Dix was instrumental in the founding of mental hospitals in the United States, where ill people could get the help that they needed. Prior to her efforts, many mentally ill people were put in prisons along with criminals. These mental hospitals have remained in place through the beginning of the 21st century, however, funding for these institutions has been diminishing throughout the 1990s. Some reformers and legislators began to focus on the issue of caring for the mentally ill, both to protect them and to protect U.S. citizens. In the 1990s, a schizophrenic man in New York City pushed an innocent woman into the subway tracks, just as a train came into he station, killing her. It was later discovered that the man had been in and out of mental institutions for years and that he should have been taking medication to help control his hallucinations and dangerous impulses.

Critical Overview

Before becoming a successful author, Bloom worked full-time as a psychotherapist, and numerous critics have pointed out that her understanding of human foibles and quirks and her respect for the power of love shines through in her fiction. Bloom's collection of short stories and her first published book, 1993's *Come to Me*, was noted for its sensitivity as well as its collection of characters, many of whom suffered from some kind of pathology. Her stories focus on, among others, a transvestite, a schizophrenic, a voyeur, a delusional wife, an incestuous relationship, and a pedophiliac; as Jeanne Schinto writes in her review in *Belles Letters*, Bloom writes about characters who "exhibit all the symptoms for which people might seek psychotherapy." Indeed, therapists appear in a number of Bloom's stories. However, as Robert Phillips also notes in *The Hudson Review*, Bloom is "comfortable with the odd, the perverse, even the forbidden. Her deviants are basically people like you and me, only their needs to be loved or appreciated are more open or more extreme."

However, as Schinto points out, Bloom is as equally concerned with "the beauty beneath the bizarre," which her fine writing highlights. Another key concern for Bloom is the dynamics of family, which Anne Whitehouse of the *New York Times Book Review* notes, she writes about "with insight, sympathy and verve." Whitehouse further contends that in *Come to Me*, Bloom "has created engaging, candid and unorthodox characters, and has vividly revealed their inner lives. . . . Her voice is sure and brisk, her language often beautiful." Sally S. Eckhoff, writing for the *Village Voice Literary Supplement*, further finds that in her stories Bloom "shyly puts forth the idea that love is the religion of family life, and family life, far from being an elaborate cell from which we dream of the rest of the world, is heart's blood and inspiration."

In Bloom's exploration of family, she focuses three of her stories on the family that appears in "Silver Water." Thus, in reading the entire collection, the reader also becomes acquainted with the father as a young boy and the mother as an unhappy wife. While Daniel McGuines subtly critiques Bloom in *Studies in Short Fiction* for not writing a novel about this family, in lieu of these short stories, other reviewers were kinder to Bloom on the subject. As Whitehouse writes, the inclusion of different glimpses of the same people suggests a "complex web of relationships and concerns and how they have changed over time."

"Silver Water," which appeared in 1992's *Best American Short Stories* volume, has been called out by reviewers and readers for its many qualities. Schinto called it a "luminous story" and certainly one of Bloom's "best." Richard Eder's, of the *Los Angeles Times Book Review* called the story "stunning" and one of the collection's "small masterpieces." Victoria Radin, reviewing the collection for the *New Statesman and Society*, went a step further in calling this story of a schizophrenic who commits suicide with the aid of her sister, "ghastly." Radin also notes in an aside that the story serves as a condemnation of the psychiatric industry and the health insurance business.

In discussing the story, several critics have focused on the scene with Rose's therapist Mr. Walker—who is her therapist for all of 14 minutes—as pivotal, both for the story's rise and for the writing. Eder finds that "[T]his passage, with its breezy voice, its insights, ironies and dead-on details, is typical of Bloom at her best." Eckhoff also notes that Bloom demonstrates both "an insider's special disdain" for the offensive therapist, as well as "a writer's sense of timing."

Critics have also pointed out Bloom's drawing on images, colors, sounds, and scents. Eckhoff finds that "Silver Water" "turns on the lovely singing voice of Rose . . . whose loving little sister, Violet, craves the comfort of her music."

All of these elements make "Silver Water," and the collection from which it is taken, an engaging yet disturbing work. Wrote Eckhoff, "In *Come to Me* . . . the rare abilities she [Bloom] brings to her common ingredients make sad stories with airy spans and remarkable tensile strength. The result is a book as musical as its contents are mercurial."

Criticism

Rena Korb

Korb has a master's degree in English literature and creative writing and has written for a wide

What Do I Read Next?

- *Life Size* (1992), a novel by Jenefer Shute, tells of a young woman who has been hospitalized for another mental illness: anorexia nervosa. The novel switches between the past and the present, detailing the woman's recovery while showing the factors that led to her eating disorder.

- Bloom's collection *Come to Me* features beautifully rendered stories about people suffering from any myriad of problems and mental illnesses. "Hyacinths" tells the story of a childhood incident in which the father in "Silver Water" accidentally shoots his cousin. "The Sight of You" details the mother's affair with a handsome neighbor who wants to marry her.

- Bloom's novel *Love Invents Us* chronicles the lifetime of a woman named Elizabeth, from her abusive childhood to her dissatisfied adulthood. Along the way, Elizabeth grapples with all the typical things that make up a life, but she also steadfastly determines to keep a hold on what is important: love.

- Charlotte Perkins Gilman's short story "The Yellow Wallpaper" depicts a woman's descent into madness. Bound by the strict rules of 1890s society, Gilman's narrator finds herself unable to deal with the reality of her life, which would deny her creativity.

- *The Dark Sister* (1993) by Rebecca Goldstein tells of the relationship between two sisters. One of them, a feminist writer, is currently writing a novel about two sisters, both of whom seem to be going mad.

- William Styron's *Lie Down in Darkness* (1992) tells the story of a troubled southern family in the mid-1900s. The Loftis family experiences irreparable dysfunction as they lack the ability to forge meaningful, solid bonds with one another. The pressure of growing up in such an environment takes its toll upon a daughter, who flees to New York, where she commits suicide.

---

variety of educational publishers. In the following essay, she examines the web of complex family relationships and explores the connotations of Violet aiding Rose's suicide.

"In the tradition of Anais Nin and Sigmund Freud, Amy Blood is a practitioner of both the talking cure and of fiction-writing," writes Victoria Radin in her *New Statesman and Society* review of Bloom's first book, the short story collection *Come to Me*. Bloom had been practicing psychotherapy for eight years before she returned to her childhood love of writing and began working on fiction in her spare time. "*Come to Me* is so rich, moving and gracefully written," extols Richard Eder in the *Los Angeles Times Book Review*, "it's hard to believe she hasn't been doing this all her life." Today, Bloom, who has also published the novel *Love Invents Us*, divides her time between her therapy practice, her fiction writing, and her family. These different but equally important parts of the author manifest themselves in her stories, which maintain finely drawn characters and demonstrate a clear-eyed comprehension. As Bloom acknowledges, "all the roles affect my writing. I see a lot of different points of view because I live a lot of different points of view. Understanding has always mattered more to me than assessing, and my writing reflects that."

"Silver Water," which was chosen as one of 1992's *Best American Short Stories*, is the last in a series of three linked stories, all of which are in her collection. The stories span nearly half a century in the lives of the Silverstein family. The first story, "Hyacinths," focuses on David Silverstein as a boy; the second story, "The Sight of You," depicts the affair Galen Silverstein had when her children were young; and "Silver Water" is told from Violet's viewpoint and centers on her sister Rose,

> "Every step I took overwhelmed me; I could picture my mother slapping me, shooting me for letting her favorite die."

who committed suicide after suffering from schizophrenia for more than ten years.

As narrated, the story illustrates the close, and sometimes difficult, bonds of family. Rose resides at the center of the Silversteins, for she is the neediest. Reflecting both the love Violet has for Rose, as well as the loss that schizophrenia inflicted on Rose and the entire family, "Silver Water" opens and closes on the same image of Rose: a fourteen-year-old girl, throwing her head back in the parking lot of an opera house and letting her lovely voice free. "She opened her mouth unnaturally wide and her voice came out, so crystalline and bright that all the departing operagoers stood frozen by their cars, unable to take out their keys or open their doors until she had finished, and then they cheered like hell." Violet, who recounts her sister's life, treasures this image. "That's what I like to remember, and that's the story I told to all of her therapists," Violet says. "I wanted them to know her.... That before her constant tinkling of commercials and fast-food jingles there had been Puccini and Mozart and hymns so sweet and mighty you expected Jesus to come down off his cross and clap." Violet's memory also provides the aching reminder that, whereas once Rose drew attention for her positive attributes, now she draws attention for her abnormal behavior.

Violet briefly yet hauntingly portrays her sister before and after she became schizophrenic. Before, Rose was talented and beautiful, according to Violet—"the prettiest girl in Arrandale Elementary School, the belle of Landmark Junior High." Later, she turned into a "mountain of Thorazined fat." Still, Violet and her parents search for the old Rose inside. Indeed, elements of the old Rose do emerge from time to time, especially during the five years that Rose is under the care of Dr. Thorne. During that period, she lives in a halfway house and sings in a church choir, actions that signify a partial return to the things that had once been of most importance to her: living in a more familial environment (as opposed to an institution) and her music. Although Rose does "go off from time to time," she exhibits much greater control.

The bonds between the members of the Silverstein family are sincere and true. Even such close relationships are not perfect, and deceptions do exist, but primarily in the name of love and the desire to protect one another. Violet lies to her father about Rose roughly shoving their mother in the kitchen, only the second of "three lies in my life." Galen lies to Violet about how difficult their life is with Rose at home, telling Violet they don't need her help and she should only come home on Sunday for her regular visits (though David tells here the truth: "We're not doing all that well"). Even more crucial, Violet does not try and bring Rose back from her suicide attempt. She remains by her sister's side as Rose dies. These actions, however, are committed in the name of love. Violet does not want her father to know how Rose hurt their mother. Galen does not want Violet to feel she must give up her own life to her family's and her sister's needs. And Violet allows Rose to kill herself because that is what Rose wants. "'Closing time,' she whispered. I believe that's what she said," is Violet's summation of Rose's final words.

The difficulty of living with Rose over the years cannot be denied, thus an alternate reading of Violet's motivation points to a more selfish justification. For ten years, Rose's illness has been the focal point of the family, a focus that has been hard on Violet. The family constantly works together to help Rose, and the scene with the therapist Mr. Walker clearly demonstrates the way the family is centered on her. For awhile—during the good years with Dr. Thorne—the family does maintain some semblance of normality. Violet reveals the great gift he gives them when at college she finds a "wonderful linebacker from Texas to sleep with." The young man calls her "darlin'," just as Dr. Thorne—also from Texas—calls Rose. Essentially, however, all that work is to no avail, for after all the manageable years, Dr. Thorne's death causes Rose to revert back to lose control over herself once again.

When Rose has her first breakdown, at the age of fifteen, Violet's only recorded reaction is significant. "My mother hugged me and told me that they would be back that night, but not with Rose. She also said, divining my worst, 'It won't happen to you, honey.'" Indeed, at times, Violet's very normalcy sets her apart. When the family first meets Dr. Thorne, Rose calls him Big Nut. Dr. Thorne responds by naming all the Silversteins as nuts. Violet becomes "'No One's Nut'—a name that summed up both my sanity and my loneliness.'' It is difficult to fathom Violet's perception of her role in the family, as well as how much, if any, bitterness she holds toward Rose for usurping all the attention. She only gives one clue to her innermost secret: that she firmly believes that Rose is their mother's favorite.

By the time of Rose's final breakdown, Violet allows the reader to truly see how her parents' lives are taken over by the care they must give their daughter. As always, Rose draws all the attention. "Dinner was filled with all of our starts and stops and Rose's desperate efforts to control herself.'' Further, Rose's more extreme behavior has left Violet outside of the family dynamic. Her mother does not want to admit how hard living with Rose really is, and while her father willingly unburdens himself, after the discussion he retreats from Violet; "He stayed outside and I stayed inside until Rose and my mother came home.'' Violet's strongest sense of isolation, however, manifests itself in the scene that takes place in the kitchen after Rose lashes out at her mother, a scene that Rose has already departed. David "made my mother a cup of tea and all the love he had for her, despite her silent rages and her vague stares, came pouring through the teapot, warming her cup, filling her small, long-fingered hands. He stood by her and she rested her head against his hip. I looked away.''

Violet reveals her truest feelings about her place within the family structure as she returns to the house after Rose's suicide: "My mother was standing on the porch, wrapped in a blanket, watching me,'' Violet says. "Every step I took overwhelmed me; I could picture my mother slapping me, shooting me for letting her favorite die.'' These revelations are, in a sense, undercut by Galen's denial of their truth, yet coming so close to the end of the story and pivoting around such a crucial moment, they express some measure of truth, at last as perceived by Violet.

Violet, however, is not the only member of the family to feel isolated from the others after Rose's death. Galen "went into the woods by herself,'' and then takes to her bed until the funeral. David "picked out Rose's coffin by himself.'' Most significantly, he is left out of the final trinity—Galen, Rose's choir friend Addie, and Rose herself, whose music, voice and piano, rise together in Violet's mind's eye.

Source: Rena Korb, in an essay for *Short Stories for Students*, Gale Group, 2001.

Jennifer Bussey

Bussey holds a Master's degree in Interdisciplinary Studies and a Bachelor's degree in English Literature. She is an independent writer specializing in literature. In the following essay, she provides a character study of Rose, the schizophrenic sister.

Amy Bloom's short story "Silver Water'' is a portrait of a family struggling to cope with the mental illness of one of its members. The mother, Galen, is a somewhat eccentric musician; the father, David, is a poised psychiatrist; the younger daughter, Violet, is an English teacher by day and a poet by night; and the older daughter, Rose, is the focus of their sorrow. It is from Violet's perspective that the story is told, and although it spans only eleven pages, the story relates scenes ranging from the time the girls are adolescents through their adulthood. This perspective allows the reader to see the girl Rose was before she became mentally ill. Consequently, the reader feels the family's heartbreak as the vibrant, talented, and beautiful girl descends into psychosis. Most of the story, however, is about Rose's hospital stays and psychiatric treatments, with emphasis on the deepening sorrow of her family. As Rose sinks further into her illness, she becomes elusive both to her family and to the reader. An attentive reading of the story, however, reveals four significant facets of Rose's character: She is a foil for her parents' strengths, highlighting them but also proving their impotence in the face of her illness; she is an innocent; she is an extremely overweight woman whose obesity matches the enormousness of her problems; and she is an extremely ill person who nevertheless retains the ability to make choices.

First, Rose demonstrates that her parents' talents and abilities are powerless to help her. As a result, Galen and David are reduced to simply reacting to Rose's outrageous behavior. Never knowing what to expect creates a highly stressful environment that is an outward manifestation of Rose's unpredictable inner world.

Galen is an accomplished pianist, and Rose has a beautiful voice. The story opens with Violet's statement: "My sister's voice was like mountain water in a silver pitcher; the clear blue beauty of it

> "Although Rose is a schizophrenic character, she is drawn with realism and complexity. Bloom shows the reader that even though Rose is elusive and puzzling, she is still knowable."

cools you and lifts you up beyond your heat, beyond your body." Violet then recalls an experience from her adolescence, when the family was leaving the theater after seeing *La Traviata*. Fourteen-year-old Rose decided to show off for her sister by singing as if she were performing in an opera. Rose's voice was so magnificent that the "departing operagoers stood frozen by their cars, unable to take out their keys or open their doors until she had finished, and then they cheered like hell." When her mental illness set in one year later, however, Rose reverted to humming commercials and advertising jingles. Music is an art form built on order, yet music cannot save Rose, cannot order her mind. Despite her gift for music (inherited from her mother), there is no order in her life, and this comes to represent her mother's inability to "rescue" her from her disturbed state.

Similarly, David is a practicing psychiatrist, yet his profession is ultimately unable to save his daughter. Rose submits to seeing therapists, and the family undergoes family therapy, but neither does anything for Rose's condition. Her medications help her to keep calm, and they help quiet the voices in her head, but Rose never experiences a life-changing breakthrough.

Rose's lack of responsiveness to therapy is evident when she manipulates therapists. Her schizophrenia does not render her completely unable to understand what is happening around her, and she initiates new therapists by singing to herself and massaging her breasts. She does this with full awareness of the inappropriate nature of the behavior. It is her way of thumbing her nose at the efforts of psychiatric professionals. Her father's profession, for all its science and research, does not have the answers that will bring Rose back to normality. The only positive outcome of David's being a psychiatrist is that he has contacts who are willing to help him as he seeks the best treatment centers for his daughter.

The second significant aspect of Rose's character is that she is essentially innocent, in spite of some episodes of lewd behavior acted out for effect. Throughout the story, she is depicted as an innocent young woman trapped by her tragic situation. Violet remembers her sister in junior high school: "To me, Rose, my beautiful blond defender, my guide to Tampax and my mother's moods, was perfect." Rose's name suggests perfection, purity, and frailty, and she has been given the gift of a beautiful voice. When she sings, especially when she sings with the church choir, her gift gives her an angelic quality. When Rose approaches the church choir, the director is uncertain what to make of this "big blond lady, dressed funny and hovering wistfully at the door," but when he hears her sing, he feels "God's hand" and sees "that with the help of His sweet child Rose, the Prospect Street Choir was going all the way to Gospel Olympics." Rose's angelic gift brings comfort to those around her (as expressed in the story's opening line), yet it brings her no relief from her illness.

Rose's innocence is emphasized when she has her first "psychotic break." The family is alerted that something is wrong by her retreat into the woods behind the house. Violet explains:

> She would go out into the woods behind our house and not come in until my mother went after her at dusk, and stepped gently into the briars and saplings and pulled her out, blank-faced, her pale blue sweater covered with crumbled leaves, her white jeans smeared with dirt.

The imagery in this scene is highly symbolic. The innocent fifteen-year-old goes into the woods, a standard literary metaphor for the unknown and dangerous world (which is why woods are so prominent in fairy tales). Because Rose is frozen in place, her mother comes to rescue her among the briars (painful thorns) and saplings (pliable young trees). Rose's clothing is pale blue and white, colors that signify innocence and purity, and it is soiled by the leaves and dirt of the woods. During the evening before Rose kills herself, Galen is clearing the dinner table and humming a lullaby about the woods that she used to sing to the girls when they were very young. The reintroduction of the forest imagery reminds the reader of the contrast between Rose's innocence and the eerie woods, perhaps to prepare the reader for Rose's final scene. At the end of the story, Rose is once again found in the woods, only this time she has gone there to take her life. Again, she is a white figure in the dark woods, and even the pills she takes are white. Despite her considerable size, she seems as innocent and powerless as she was at fifteen. Violet describes finding her sister in the woods late at night: "Huge and white in the moonlight, her flowered smock bleached in the light and shadow, her sweatpants now completely wet. Her head was flung back, her white, white neck exposed like a lost Greek column." When Violet finds her sister, she is barely alive, and Violet sits with her as her life slips away. Violet says, "I sat with her . . . and watched the stars fade." The image of the stars fading attests to Rose's innocence; as her spirit leaves her body, the pinpoints of light made by the stars are outshone by the greater light of the sun.

The third significant element of Rose's character is the symbolic meaning of her weight. One of the drugs she takes is Thorazine, commonly prescribed to patients suffering from schizophrenia. A side effect of Thorazine is weight gain, so the reader can reasonably conclude that the drug intended to help Rose is responsible for her considerable size. Besides presenting a realistic depiction of a person on Thorazine, Rose's substantial weight is a visual cue offered by the author. As a teenager, Rose was thin, but as her treatment progresses, she becomes larger, just as her presence in the family becomes larger. Although many people gain weight as they get older, Rose is still a young woman, and she is the only one in the family to become grossly overweight. Her immense size is a symbol of the overwhelming challenges faced by Rose and by the family as they seek to help her. Violet describes Rose's obesity in passing, and in almost comical terms ("a mountain of Thorazined fat, swaying down the halls in nylon maternity tops and sweatpants"), but Rose's size is the physical form of all the invisible problems with which they all struggle.

The fourth important aspect of Rose's character is that she retains the ability to make decisions, despite her psychiatric problems. While she has episodes in which she is unable to control herself, there are instances in which the reader sees Rose making conscious choices about her behavior. Although the choices are not necessarily healthy, they are acts of will. When she massages her breasts in front of each new therapist, for example, she is making a conscious choice to test the new person and to entertain herself and her family in the process; it is a way to reclaim power. The reader knows

Dorothea Lynde Dix was a nineteenth-century social activist who persuaded American legislators to found thirty-two state hospitals for the mentally ill.

she is doing this willfully for three reasons. First, Violet remarks, "This was Rose's usual opening salvo for new therapists." Second, after Rose stops massaging her breasts in front of Dr. Walker, she continues to behave inappropriately, but in ways that indicate that she is engaged in her surroundings. For example, she calls the doctor "Ferret Face," and Violet notices that his features do, in fact, resemble a ferret. Third, when Rose sees Dr. Thorne, a new doctor who is a huge man, she stops massaging her breasts immediately. Later, when Rose goes through a period in which she has sex with everyone she can, she propositions Dr. Thorne. His response is sensitive and bolsters her self-esteem, and she stops having random sex. This is a conscious decision to respond to Dr. Thorne's words with a new pattern of behavior.

Rose's final choice is her suicide. Her intentional retreat into the woods to take the pills represents an act of will, not of uncontrolled psychosis. Her suicide is not an accident, which Violet knows. Because Violet knows her older sister is doing what she really wants to do by taking her life, she does not stop her. Bloom is not clear about why Rose chooses to end her life, but the story seems to suggest that Rose truly loves her family and understands what a burden she has become to them. She understands her situation well enough to know that she will never be able to function independently. In the scene in which Rose is banging her head on the kitchen floor, she only stops when Violet throws her body down to the spot where Rose is hitting her head. This causes Rose to snap out of her repetitive act because she sees that continuing will hurt her sister. Having already hurt her mother without realizing it, she breaks down in emotional apologies. Clearly, Rose loves her parents and her sister deeply, and perhaps her unwillingness to be a strain on them leads her to her final choice.

Although Rose is a schizophrenic character, she is drawn with realism and complexity. Bloom shows the reader that even though Rose is elusive and puzzling, she is still knowable. By allowing the reader to see the very human side of the character, and the heartbreaking effects her condition has on the family, Bloom creates an affecting tragic figure in Rose.

Source: Jennifer Bussey, in an essay for *Short Stories for Students*, Gale Group, 2001.

Chris Semansky

Semansky publishes widely in the field of twentieth-century culture and literature. In the following essay, he examines the idea of sympathetic identification and describes how it relates to the narrator's behavior.

The central mystery to be solved in Amy Bloom's story "Silver Water" is why the character of Violet allows her sister Rose to commit suicide. "Silver Water" attempts to realistically depict a family strained by the mental illness of their oldest child. It is told through the point of view of Violet, the younger sister who witnesses Rose's decline and ultimately decides her fate. The point of view is a significant choice, since the sisters are so close. Both are named for flowers, reflecting the fragile, ephemeral qualities of those objects. Violet shadows Rose, and is shadowed by her; and their fates, interwoven and dependent on each other, determine one's death and the other's responsibility. Because the story of Rose's life is threaded through with mental illness and ends in death, she is untenable as a narrator. By telling the story from Violet's point of view, Bloom offers as faithful and exact a version of Rose's story as possible.

The narrative voice begins by explaining that Rose was not always ill. Violet remembers a time before the "constant tinkling of fast food jingles," and the "mountain of Thorazined fat," when there was a voice "like mountain water in a silver pitcher," capable of lifting the spirits of anyone who heard it. Rose was a girl both beautiful and competent, Violet's seemingly infallible "guide to Tampax and my mother's moods." In these passages, narrated retrospectively after Rose's death, we see Violet's insistence that there was a time before—that there was more to Rose than the many therapists and doctors ever saw. In this way Violet establishes herself as the keeper of Rose's wholeness, not allowing the self that Rose was in her sicknesses to eclipse other, stronger, happier versions of Rose. As the person perhaps most responsible for Rose's death, Violet's commanding remembering of all that was good about her sister strongly indicates that Violet feels no guilt or uncertainty about her actions on the night of Rose's death.

When Rose is taken away, at fifteen, after her first episodes of psychosis, the merged nature of her and her sister's identities is made explicit. Violet's mother, divining Violet's adolescent fears, says, "It won't happen to you, honey. Some people go crazy and some people never do . . . not even when you want to." Violet's fears that she will become psychotic like Rose stem from the simple proposition that in some sense Violet cannot separate her own fate from Rose's—the most obvious eventuality to Violet is that what happens to her sister will necessarily happen to her as well. The last part of what her mother says to her on this occasion is also significant. By implying that Violet might someday *want* to go crazy herself, her mother speaks directly to the tendency toward deep identification that Violet feels with Rose. Because Rose has "gone crazy," Violet might feel that she might like to go too.

Most revealing is a scene early in the story when Violet describes an unsympathetically drawn family therapist who, unable to make heads or tails of the parents, turns his attention to Violet and asks her for an explanation of Rose's behavior. With vehemence, Violet defends her sister's obscene tactics during the session, telling the doctor that she suspects Rose's ritual rubbing of her breasts during the session has a specific goal: "Maybe she's trying to get you to stop talking about her in the third person," Violet says. In these lines it is possible to decipher that Violet's anger might be as much about the necessity of speaking about Rose in the third person as it is with the therapist. As Violet tells the story, she too must speak of Rose in the third person, no matter how strongly she identifies with her. In "Silver Water" the word "I" always refers to Violet—a narrative fact that Violet withdraws from as running counter to her feelings of identification with Rose. The therapist serves as a person on whom Violet can project her anger about the limitations of identifying too closely with her sister.

Violet's connection to her sister can also be seen in the scenes with Dr. Thorne, the Texan therapist the family loves. He is affectionate with and flattering of Rose, and Violet returns to college, feeling that Rose is at last in good hands. But on beginning classes, Violet finds, "a wonderful linebacker from Texas to sleep with. In the dark I would make him call me darlin'." She moves geographically, but psychically is still going through Rose's life with her. By taking the linebacker from Texas as a lover, Violet recreates a bulky, Texan-like Dr. Thorne that she can call her own, again mirroring her sister's life.

The tension rises in the story when an uninsured Rose comes back to live with her family until her mental health coverage begins again. Violet says that she went home every few days and called each evening, increasing her presence in her parents' home and mimicking Rose's increased presence there. Her father "quietly" gives Violet a measured and sad accounting of how they are managing. Her mother "emphatically" tells her that everything is fine, and says, "You don't need to come home so often, you know. Wait 'til Sunday, just come home for the day. Lead your life, Vi. She's leading hers." This reminder to Violet that her life need not be troubled because her sister's is again speaks to the mother's understanding that Violet loses herself when she identifies too strongly with Rose. The specificity of her words focuses the issue: the sisters' lives are separate and can function independently, if only Violet can remember that. She does not need to act in tandem with Rose.

The climax of the crisis in identity comes when Rose begins violently banging her head on the kitchen floor and throws off her mother, who is desperately trying to stop her. The mother calls to Violet to help, but Violet throws herself onto the floor, "becoming the spot that Rose was smacking her head against." This metaphor resounds. Violet, always struggling to hold her own identity in the face of Rose's overbearingly powerful impulses and actions, has now become simply a thing—a spot on the floor—against which her sister bangs. Violet's

> When Rose is taken away, at fifteen, after her first episodes of psychosis, the merged nature of her and her sister's identities is made explicit. Violet's mother, divining Violet's adolescent fears, says, 'It won't happen to you, honey. Some people go crazy and some people never do . . . not even when you want to.'"

loss of self has ebbed to its lowest point, and she is utterly dispossessed.

That night Violet wakes, feeling Rose's absence in the house. She goes outside, looking for her, and almost stumbles over her, "Huge and white in the moonlight, her flowered smock bleached in the light and shadow . . . her head flung back, her white, white neck exposed like a lost Greek column." The choice of the Greek column as a simile for Rose's neck is a fascinating one, indicating the length of the sister's history together, from the time when Rose was the "belle of Landmark Junior High" through the heart-wrenching initial episodes of madness to this moment, when Rose's despair has brought her to swallow a bottle full of pills and wander out into the woods to die. The word "lost" used to describe the column is purely meant, for now Rose herself is truly lost and Violet must decide what to do next.

What Violet does is wait for Rose to die without intervening in her suicide attempt: "I sat with her, uncovering the bottle of white pills by her hand, and watched the stars fade." Significantly, Violet turns her attention away from her sister and towards the stars, referencing their potential as indicators of the destinies of individuals, each destiny different from the next—and their remote, cold, unresponsive nature. Violet regards the stars, not her sister, and although she sits with Rose as Rose dies, Violet is separating from Rose in an act of great complexity. She lets Rose die because Rose has suffered so profoundly, and because there is no longer any place for Rose to be that is comfortable for her, that succors her and rises up to meet her. Rose has come to her last foothold and Violet lets it be her last, does not insist that Rose take another step. But the power of "Silver Water" is that it admits another reading—Violet lets Rose die because she herself must live, must move out into the world as a whole and separate being, unencumbered and disentangled, and must move past Rose to do so.

The final words in the story are a description of a pre-psychotic Rose, singing mightily in the parking lot after having attended an opera performance with her family. People getting into their cars stand frozen, listening to her voice, and Violet claims the memory and the young woman at the center of it: "I closed my eyes and saw my sister, fourteen years old, lion's mane thrown back and eyes tightly closed against the glare of the parking lot lights. That sweet sound held us tight, flowing around us, eddying through our hearts, rising, still rising." The image is vivid, the weight it carries is momentous. Violet loved Rose, saw her great power and beauty, saw her shaken off track by the senseless hand of fate, and accepted, ultimately, that she herself was not to be dealt the same blow—that her fate was separate from her sister's, and that Rose's death was the necessary act to free them both.

Source: Chris Semansky, in an essay for *Short Stories for Students*, Gale Group, 2001.

Sources

Eckhoff, Sally S., Review of *Come to Me*, in *The Village Voice Literary Supplement*, September 7, 1993, p. 5.

Eder, Richard, Review of *Come to Me*, in *The Los Angeles Times Book Review*, June 13, 1993, p. 3.

McGuines, Daniel, Review of *Come to Me*, in *Studies in Short Fiction*, Fall, 1994, p. 694.

Phillips, Robert, Review of *Come to Me*, in *The Hudson Review*, Winter, 1994, p. 765.

Radin, Victoria, Review of *Come to Me*, in *New Statesman and Society*, April 15, 1994, p. 38.

Schinto, Jeanne, Review of *Come to Me*, in *Belles Lettres*, Winter, 1993/1994, p. 28.

Further Reading

Brophy, Beth, "A Writer's Eye and a Psychotherapist's Ear," *US News and World Report*, January 27, 1997, p. 69.
   A discussion of how Bloom draws upon her work as a psychotherapist to create her fiction.

Towers, Sarah, "Inventing Euphoria," *Mirabella*, January-February, 1997, p. 24.
   An interview with Bloom focusing on her career and how she became a writer.

Tsuang, Ming T., et. al, *Schizophrenia: The Facts*, 2d ed., Oxford University Press, 1997.
   This is an introductory text on the current understanding of schizophrenia and is aimed at lay-level readers.

The Snows of Kilimanjaro

Ernest Hemingway
1936

In "The Snows of Kilimanjaro," Ernest Hemingway presents the story of a writer at the end of his life. While on a safari in Africa, Harry, the protagonist, is scratched on the leg by a thorn, and the infection becomes gangrenous and eventually kills him. Where most of Hemingway's stories feature protagonists who speak little and reflect nothing at all about their motivations and inner lives, in this story, the main character "sees his life flash before his eyes" as he realizes that he is dying. Many readers have seen Harry as a self-portrait of Hemingway himself. Reading the story this way, the reader can look into Hemingway's struggles with himself: his insecurities, his machismo, his need and disdain for women. But it is not necessary to read the story through the lens of Hemingway's biography. The story is a gripping look at a man who is facing death and regretting many of the choices he has made in his life, as well as being a memorable glimpse inside the head of a writer who is reflecting on his craft and the demands it has made on him.

Author Biography

Ernest Hemingway, as a result of his short stories, novels, and nonfiction, has become perhaps the best-known American writer of the twentieth century. In such novels as *The Sun Also Rises* and *A*

Farewell to Arms, Hemingway chronicled the lives of aimless, adventuring young adults in Europe in the early decades of the twentieth century. In other writings, Hemingway wrote elegantly and perceptively about some of his passions: bullfighting, hunting, fishing, drinking. But it is in his short stories where Hemingway best shows his mastery of style and structure and where his deepest and most enduring themes—death, writing, machismo, bravery, and the alienation of men in the modern world—dominate.

Hemingway was born, in 1899, into perhaps the most characteristically American of environments: the suburbs. His mother was domineering, and dressed young Ernest in girls' clothes when he was young (a fact that many of Hemingway's biographers and critics have noted as an explanation for his relentless machismo). He graduated from Oak Park (Illinois) High School in 1917 and immediately went to work for a Kansas City newspaper. In 1918, he enlisted in the Red Cross and drove ambulances on the Italian front in World War I until he was seriously wounded—an episode that forms the basis for his famous novel *A Farewell To Arms* (1929).

The period between the World Wars brought Hemingway fame, fortune, and great artistic success. In 1920, Hemingway moved to Paris, where he lived for much of the following decade. Hemingway became a defining figure of the famous "Lost Generation" of Americans in Paris in the 1920s, and wrote *The Sun Also Rises* (1926) as a portrait of the lives of his rootless, thrill-seeking friends who wandered from Paris to the south of France to Spain and back. During the 1930s, Hemingway wandered the world himself, spending time hunting and fishing in such locales as Kenya, Key West, Montana, and Spain. In the late 1930s Hemingway covered the Spanish Civil War as a journalist; from this experience arose his 1940 novel *For Whom the Bell Tolls*. In 1939, now an international celebrity, he moved to Cuba, but with the outbreak of war in 1939, his taste for adventuring returned and he came to Europe in 1942 to fly with the RAF and participate in the Normandy invasion in 1944.

The years after World War II, when Hemingway entered middle age, grew increasingly difficult for him. He continued to write, but only one of his books, *The Old Man and the Sea*, received much critical acclaim. He survived two airplane crashes, from which he never entirely healed, and his death was reported in the press at one point in 1954. That same year, Hemingway won the Nobel Prize for Literature, but he was declining and depressed. In 1961, he committed suicide in his cabin in Ketchum, Idaho, leaving behind four ex-wives, a number of children, and many thousands of pages of unpublished manuscripts.

Plot Summary

"The Snows of Kilimanjaro" opens on the African savanna where a man and a woman are talking to each other matter-of-factly about the man's leg, which is rotting away from gangrene. The woman is trying to make him more comfortable and make him believe that he will survive, but he seems to be enjoying the black humor of the vultures who are waiting for him to die. As she speaks to him, his resentment of her money and her upbringing comes out in his comments.

The first of his flashbacks comes at this point. In this flashback, he remembers being in World War I, then thinks about scenes in numerous winters. Details from the war and from various pleasant skiing excursions mingle in his mind. As that flashback finishes, Harry returns to the present and argues with the woman before falling asleep. When he wakes up, the woman has been out to shoot an animal for them to eat and he thinks about her, why he married her, and why he does not like her. We learn that she is a lusty woman who was married before, who had two children and lost one of those children in a plane crash. Before he slips into another flashback, he and the woman have a drink together just as the realization that he is going to die hits him.

In his second flashback, he thinks about his time in Paris and Constantinople, but all of his memories are colored by memories of the war. When he returns to consciousness, she convinces him to drink some broth and he stops thinking so harshly of her before slipping into a third flashback. In this memory, he is in the forest, living in a cabin, and then remembers being in Paris and spending time near the Place Contrescarpe. He briefly returns to the present to ask for another whiskey and soda before flashing back again, this time to the fact that he never took the time to write about many things that he wanted to write about. His flashbacks start to bleed into the real world as he asks the woman to explain why he never wrote the stories he wanted to write. He thinks about why he feels such contempt for the wealthy, a group to which this woman belongs.

In his final flashback, he thinks again about the war, this time about a man he saw die, before waking from his flashback and talking to the woman more. He begins to see Death personified, breathing sourly on him. It is then morning again, and the pilot, Compton, has arrived to take him to the city and to the doctor. Harry gets in the plane and the pilot, instead of taking him to the city, flies him right by the peak of Mount Kilimanjaro and Harry "knew that there was where he was going." In the final section of text, the woman wakes up because the hyena that has been making noise for hours stopped whimpering and has begun making another sound. As she looks over at Harry, she realizes that he has died.

Ernest Hemingway

Characters

Compton
Compton flies the plane that is meant to take Harry back to the city to save his life. He is confident and tries to make Harry feel better about his predicament. However, he exists only in Harry's dream.

Harry
Harry is the protagonist of the story. He is a writer and has had many experiences in Europe. He also very much enjoys big-game hunting. When the story begins, Harry is suffering from gangrene in his leg and he is dying in the African backcountry while waiting for a plane to take him to the city.

Helen
Harry's wife Helen, also known as The Wife, remains unnamed until the end of the story, when a delirious Harry finally refers to her by name as he dies. After Harry reaches the summit of Kilimanjaro, the previous narrative voice resumes and again calls her simply "the woman." Harry does not seem to love her, but he respects her to a certain degree for her skill with a gun. She comes from a wealthy family and Harry has contempt for that. She, on the other hand, cares for him greatly and tries to ease his suffering.

Molo
Molo is the African servant who serves Helen and Harry. He does very little in the story apart from bringing Harry whiskey and sodas.

The Wife
See Helen

Themes

Death
As the story of an imminent death, "The Snows of Kilimanjaro" is suffused not only with images of death but also with a pervading sense of death's presence. The story begins with death—"it's painless," Harry says in the first line, referring to his oncoming demise—and ends with the ironic comparison of the woman's heart beating loudly and the stillness of Harry's lifeless body. Death is symbolically figured both as the pristine whiteness of the summit of Mount Kilimanjaro and as the creeping, filthy hyena that lurks outside of Harry's tent.

Harry's attitude toward his death wavers during the story. At first, he puts up a brave and almost cavalier front, telling his wife that he does not care

Media Adaptations

- Many of Hemingway's novels and stories were adapted into films. Movies of his stories include two versions of *The Killers* (one starring Burt Lancaster and another starring Ronald Reagan) and *The Macomber Affair*, starring Gregory Peck ; movies of his novels include *A Farewell To Arms*, starring Gary Cooper and Helen Hayes, *To Have and Have Not*, starring Humphrey Bogart and Lauren Bacall, and *the Old Man and the Sea*, starring Spencer Tracy. In 1952, the studio Twentieth Century Fox produced a film of ''The Snows of Kilimanjaro'' that starred Gregory Peck, Susan Hayward, and Ava Gardner.

---

about his death and is resigned to it. He almost seems to be trying to anger her, knowing that she cares about him and that he can hurt her by seeming not to be bothered by death's imminence. But in the italicized sections of the story, Harry's bravado disappears, and he slips into the regret of a man who knows he is dying but who rues the fact that he has not accomplished what he wanted to accomplish. The gangrenous rot that is taking his leg metamorphoses, in his mind, into the poetry that he never wrote: ''I'm full of poetry now. Rot and poetry. Rotten poetry.''

Hemingway brings death into the story largely by the use of symbolism. The woman leaves the camp to go kill an animal, going out of his sight because (the narrator states) she does not want to disturb the wildlife. However, she clearly does not want to kill something in plain sight of her dying husband. The hyena, an animal that feeds on carcasses, skulks around the camp, a prefiguration of the rotting death that Harry fears. Even the relationship between Harry and his wife is a symbol of his imminent end: he says that the quarrelling had ''killed what they had together.''

But when death comes it is not rotten and lingering and painful. Rather, it is transcendent. Harry slips into a reverie in which he hallucinates that his friend Compton arrives in an airplane to take him to find medical care. As the plane takes off, it passes by the blinding white summit of Kilimanjaro. As Harry passes this image, the reader is reminded of the epigraph of the story, in which Hemingway says that ''close to the western summit there is the dried and frozen carcass of a leopard. No one has explained what the leopard was seeing at that altitude.'' Harry seems to have found something, though: a release from his earthly problems.

Artistic Creation

Harry's failure to achieve the artistic success he sought in his life is one of the main themes of the story, and in this the character of Harry comes very close to being a representation of Hemingway himself. In the italicized flashbacks, we see Harry as he was in his earlier life, especially in Paris, where he lived in bohemian poverty and devoted his energies to writing. But he consistently regrets leaving that behind. He gave up, in a sense, and began spending his time drinking, travelling, hunting, and chasing rich women. He became ''what he despised,'' as the narrator says.

His perceived failures eat away at him like the gangrene that eats his leg. At one point he explicitly equates them: ''Rot and poetry. Rotten poetry.'' He uses his verbal talents to quarrel with his wife and instead of seeking to heighten his sensations he dulls them with alcohol. In this sense, the hyena that lurks around his tent is not only creeping death but also his pangs of regret at his wasting of his artistic gifts. Ironically, it is in death that he returns to creating. As he slips away, he hallucinates a beautiful scene: his friend Compton comes to him to take him to a hospital, and as they fly away Harry catches a glimpse of the summit of Kilimanjaro, a vision that awes him by its purity. Only here, as he dies, does he take part in the kind of creation and transcendence that he has always sought.

Style

Point of View and Narration

The type of narration Ernest Hemingway typically uses, the author himself said in an interview with George Plimpton, was fashioned on the ''principle of the iceberg ... for seven eighths of it is under water for every part that shows.'' In *A Moveable Feast* (1964), his memoir of Paris in the 1920s, he expands on this. ''You could omit anything,'' he

Topics for Further Study

- Where is Mount Kilimanjaro? What country is it in and what peoples live there? What kind of wildlife has its habitat near there? Do research on this part of the world, focusing on the twentieth century and the interactions between native peoples, colonizers, and the wildlife.

- There are many wildlife parks in Africa where tourists may see such wild animals as zebras, rhinoceroses, and wildebeests. However, poachers—people who illegally hunt these animals as trophies or to sell their body parts—are a serious problem. Do research into the endangered species of animals in such nations as Kenya, Rwanda, Uganda, Zimbabwe, and Tanzania, and investigate the problems caused by poachers.

- Explore the figures involved in the "Lost Generation" of American writers and artists who lived in Paris in the 1920s, including Gertrude Stein, Josephine Baker, F. Scott Fitzgerald, Ezra Pound, Man Ray, and Kay Boyle. What brought these people to Paris? What did they accomplish there?

- In the story, Harry and Helen are on a safari in Africa. What is a safari? What kinds of wildlife do people see on safaris? Can one still go on safari today?

---

writes, "if the omitted part would strengthen the story and make people feel something more than they understood." Hemingway's characters usually bury not only their feelings about their pasts but their pasts, as well, and his narrators—usually third-person narrators who see inside the heads of the main character—join along in this act of burial. In most of his best short stories, the protagonists are carrying some deep psychological hurt that they will not even think about to themselves. Their minds are "icebergs" because the reader can see just the hint of these troubles peek forth at times, and must read extremely carefully to try to piece together exactly what is bothering the protagonist.

In this sense, "The Snows of Kilimanjaro" is a very atypical Hemingway story. In this story, the matters that trouble Harry are made clear to the reader; the narrator, who is inside Harry's head, speaks of them explicitly. But Hemingway sets these instances of introspection apart, dividing them into sections printed in italics. In all but one of the sections that are in roman type, the narration is typical Hemingway: blunt, unadorned, almost devoid of adjectives, and quite uninformative as to what Harry is feeling. The sentences are short and declarative. But when the narration drifts into the italic sections, the tone changes. The sentences grow longer and almost stream-of-consciousness, with one clause tacked on after another recording the protagonist's impression of a scene. The narrator describes scenes fondly and vividly, and uses metaphors and figurative language: "the snow as smooth to see as cake frosting," for instance.

As the story proceeds and Harry's condition worsens, the switching between unadorned narration and impressionistic, memory-laden narration becomes quicker and more frequent, until the penultimate section. In this section—the section in which Compton arrives and takes Harry away—the reader thinks they are in the "real world" until the end, when they realize that Harry is having another dream sequence. This time, though, the dream—usually delineated by italics—has bled through to the "real world," and the only clue, before the end of the dream, that it is a dream is the sentence structure. In this section, the sentences are longer, more impressionistic, more descriptive, just as the sentences in the earlier italic dream segments were. The contrast between the "real world," in which Harry's gangrene has killed him, and the dream world, in which he is flying toward the "unbelievably white" peak of Mount Kilimanjaro, is accentuated in the final section, in which the narrator returns to his short, declarative sentences.

Flashback

The flashback is a technique that Hemingway uses extensively in "The Snows of Kilimanjaro." The story is divided between present-time sections (set in roman type) and flashbacks (set in italics). In the present-time sections, the protagonist is facing his death stoically, quietly, and with a great deal of machismo. All he needs is whiskey and soda to accept his imminent death. But in the flashback sections, Harry faces his life. His flashbacks show the reader that he has had an exciting and well-travelled life, but that he is also haunted by his memories of World War I. He served in the U.S. Army in that war and saw combat on the Eastern front, in the Balkans, and Austria. The violence and death that he saw there come back to him as his rotting leg tells him that he is about to die.

Harry's past is not all negative, though. He is a writer, and in his flashbacks he thinks about his vocation and about all of the stories he wanted to write that he never took the time to begin. He has spent time in Paris with the artists and writers who lived there in the 1920s (one name he mentions, Tristan Tzara, is a real poet of the time, and another, "Julian," is a thinly-disguised portrait of the American novelist F. Scott Fitzgerald) and is familiar with the Place de la Contrescarpe, a popular bohemian locale of the time. His flashbacks also show that he is an experienced outdoorsman—necessary background to this character, so that readers do not think of him as a greenhorn who is dying out of pure inexperience.

Allusion

"The Snows of Kilimanjaro" alludes subtly to two well-known short stories: one by its structure and technique, the other by its subject matter. The first story is "An Occurrence at Owl Creek Bridge" (1891), by the American writer Ambrose Bierce. In this story, set during the Civil War, an Alabama man is being hanged on Owl Creek Bridge for espionage. As the story opens, readers see him on the bridge, having the noose put over his head. When the boards under his feet are snatched away, the rope breaks. He is able to use his bound hands to take the rope off his neck and swim away down the river as the Union soldiers' bullets hit the water by him. After swimming down the river a long way, he gets out and finds his way back home. As he arrives at his house and as his wife stretches her arms to greet him, the noose jerks at his neck and he dies instantly. The whole story has been an imaginary scene that the protagonist has lived through from the time he begins falling to the time that the rope's slack runs out. Just like in "The Snows of Kilimanjaro," the seeming salvation for the hero existed only in the hero's mind.

Hemingway's story also alludes to another well-known story, Henry James' "The Middle Years" (1893). Like Hemingway, James presents a self-portrait of a writer near the end of his life. James' Dencombe, like Hemingway's Harry, has an admirer (but in this case the admirer is male, not a wife), and this admirer gives up something important and valuable to be with the writer. Finally, like Harry, Dencombe dies, somewhat unexpectedly and ironically, at the end of the story.

Historical Context

World War I

"The Snows of Kilimanjaro" takes place in the decades between World Wars I and II. The first World War was a traumatic experience for Europe and America, for although it was fought largely in Europe it involved almost every European nation and, at the time, the European nations controlled vast areas of Africa and Asia. The war was remarkable for the sheer mass of killing it entailed. New technologies of war, including motorized vehicles, airplanes, and poison gas, were used for the first time. Probably most traumatic and senseless was the strategy of trench warfare, utilized largely in France and Belgium, in which each army dug a trench in the ground and attempted to advance to overtake the opposing army's trench by waves of soldiers going "over the top." Hundreds of thousands of soldiers died in these waves, but trench warfare only brought the war to a bloody standstill.

Hemingway saw action in the war—not in the trenches, though, for he drove an ambulance in Italy—and was wounded. Many of his characters, including Harry in "The Snows of Kilimanjaro," carry around painful memories of the war. Some of his characters, such as Jake Barnes in *The Sun Also Rises*, also carry around their physical wounds and disabilities. The war and its unprecedented gore psychologically maimed countless veterans, and often Hemingway's characters submerge their pain

Compare & Contrast

- **1936:** Kenya, where Mount Kilimanjaro is located, is a British colony.

  1999: Kenya is one of the most prosperous and stable of the African nations. It combines the colonial heritage of the British with the native traditions of East Africa. The country's leader, Daniel Arap Moi, is criticized for his efforts to thwart democracy.

- **1936:** Animals such as the zebra, rhinoceros, and elephant are plentiful in Africa. Although a number of American and European adventurers come to Kenya to hunt these animals on safaris, their numbers are not great enough to endanger them.

  1999: Many of the most unique large mammals of Africa are endangered by poaching (illegal hunting), encroachment on their habitat, and years of legal hunting. The world community has taken steps to try and help these animals survive, but a persistent world market for commodities made from these animals ensures that impoverished Africans will continue to hunt them.

- **1936:** The United States is suffering from the most deep and prolonged depression in its history. President Franklin D. Roosevelt is elected to his second term with promises to continue his "New Deal" programs.

  1999: The United States is enjoying the most prolonged period of prosperity in its history. President Bill Clinton takes much of the credit for these good times, and seeks to have his vice-president, Al Gore, elected president in 2000.

- **1936:** In Germany, Adolf Hitler is absolute ruler. German Jews are oppressed by the government; many flee the country. British Prime Minister Neville Chamberlain will meet with Hitler in 1938 and agree to Hitler's annexation of Austria and takeover of Czechoslovakia, with the condition that Hitler stop his expansionism there. In September, 1939, Hitler will invade Poland and start World War II

  1999: Germany celebrates ten years of unification after having been separated, by the aftermath of World War II, for forty-four years. Berlin undergoes massive reconstruction and seeks to be the most modern city in Europe.

---

underneath the immediate world. This submersion provided Hemingway with a real-world correlation for his "iceberg" technique of structure and narration, and often in his stories what is submerged is the protagonist's memories of the war.

Africa in the 1930s

For the first half of this century, Africa consisted almost exclusively of colonies of European nations. From the 1500s to the 1800s, the main European powers—England, France, Holland, Belgium, Portugal, and Germany—divided up between themselves control over the African continent for economic reasons. The European countries wished to take advantage of the natural—and, in the case of the slave trade, the human—resources of Africa to enrich themselves. Belgium controlled the country known until recently as Zaire; Germany and Portugal ruled the present nation of Angola; the French had dominion over much of the west coast of Africa, a region that included the current nations of Senegal, the Ivory Coast, and Algeria; the Dutch and the English fought over control of South Africa and its vast diamond mines; the English also had power over the large and very wealthy territories of Nigeria and Kenya.

Mount Kilimanjaro, the landmark that dominates Hemingway's story, is in Kenya, and this territory was a popular destination for European and American adventure tourists such as Harry who wished to hunt exotic game animals on safaris.

Beginning with World War II and lasting until the late 1970s, most of the African nations achieved independence: at times independence was granted by the European colonial powers, such as in the case of Rhodesia (present-day Zimbabwe); at times the African nation fought a war to achieve independence, as in the case of Algeria. By the 1980s, no African nation was a colony of a European power, although each nation maintained a relationship of varying closeness with its one-time colonial ruler.

Paris in the 1920s

Ernest Hemingway was a member of a group of artistic-minded young Americans who, after World War I, moved to Paris to live and write and paint and sculpt and, in writer Kay Boyle's words, "be geniuses together." Some members of this group were the writers Kay Boyle, F. Scott Fitzgerald, Ezra Pound, Robert McAlmon, and Hilda Doolittle. The writer Gertrude Stein, another American who had been living in Paris for some time, dubbed these Americans the "lost generation" partially because of the aimlessness, dissatisfaction with their home country, and refusal to assimilate into the culture of France.

Hemingway came to Paris in 1921 with his first wife, Hadley Richardson, after having been in Europe during the last year of World War I. During the time he and Hadley lived in Paris, he worked as a foreign correspondent for the Toronto *Star*. Also at this time, he lived experiences that have become inextricably linked with Hemingway, such as the running of the bulls in Pamplona, Spain. In 1923 he published his first book, *Three Stories and Ten Poems*; in 1924, his first short-story collection, *In Our Time*, appeared, published by Three Mountains Press. Small presses like Three Mountains were an essential element of Lost Generation life; many members of this crowd either ran such presses or had their work published by them. During the 1920s, Hemingway and the rest of the Lost Generation wrote, wandered around Europe, drank, and just spent time together, as a result producing some of the greatest art and writing of the century.

Critical Overview

Historically, critics have been divided on the merits of Hemingway's work. While contemporary critics praised Hemingway's mastery of form and narration, later critics took Hemingway to task for the limitations of his themes, for his perceived sexism, and for his extremely negative views of human life. Recent critical opinion has come to see Hemingway primarily as a stylist who has nothing profound or deeply original to say about the human condition, and although his influence on today's short story writers is difficult to overstate, many critics today believe that Hemingway is simply not a great writer.

"The Snows of Kilimanjaro" was first published in *Esquire* magazine in 1936, and first appeared in book form in his collection *The Fifth Column and the First Forty-Nine Stories* of 1938. At that time, critics had their first opportunity to express their opinions on the story, and most were enthusiastic. Alfred Kazin, in the *Books* supplement to the *New York Herald Tribune*, wrote that the story was simply "terrific," and Edmund Wilson felt that the ending was "a wonderful piece of writing." Malcolm Cowley, in the *New Republic*, noted that the story was "the only story in which [Hemingway] has allowed himself to be conventionally poetic."

Later critics used the story to discuss larger themes that recur throughout Hemingway's writing. Mark Schorer wrote in 1941 that "The Snows of Kilimanjaro" marked a turning-point in Hemingway's career, when his "subject matter began to change—from violent experience itself to the expressed evaluation of violence." Schorer felt that with this shift, Hemingway's powers had reached their limitations. Granville Hicks, writing in the *New Republic* in 1944, also noted a decrease of the quality of Hemingway's writing, but puts the date earlier. Such stories as "The Snows of Kilimanjaro," though, "permit Hemingway ... to pull himself together after he had given every evidence of having gone to pieces, and to declare his old powers." In 1964, the literary biographer Richard Ellman remarked that one of Hemingway's posthumous publications—the Paris-in-the-1920s memoir *A Moveable Feast*—gave the writer a chance to return to "The Snows of Kilimanjaro." "The hero of "The Snows of Kilimanjaro" regretted on his deathbed that he would never be able to describe how he lived near the Place Contrescarpe, or how he wintered in Schruns, but Hemingway carries out posthumously Harry's unfulfilled intentions." Another critic, Julian MacLaren-Ross, notes the same congruity: in *A*

Moveable Feast, "here we have again the two-roomed apartment in the rue du Cardinal Lemoine where Harry, the drunken failure dying of gangrene in ''The Snows of Kilimanjaro,'' having traded in his talent for security and comfort, also lived.''

Critics closer to the present day have examined the story closely, especially to learn more about Hemingway's attitudes toward death and writing. Joseph M. Flora extensively analyzes the story in his book *Ernest Hemingway: A Study of the Short Fiction*, and writes that it "shows us Hemingway writing a very different kind of story than any he had previously attempted.... The Snows emphasizes thought, perhaps because the protagonist can no longer avoid thinking. Ironically, the end of this African hunt has been reflection and judgment—something the African story had been designed to keep at a distance." Flora draws a parallel between this story and two etchings by the eighteenth-century English poet William Blake, noting that both artists looked at imminent death in similar ways, and allegorize it. Noting that the leopard mentioned in the story's epigraph represents Harry himself, Flora argues that the epigraph is "a compact allegory of the story." Flora also notes the irony of Hemingway describing the death of a "bad man" in a way that makes him good and that grants him transcendence. Gennaro Santangelo disagrees, feeling that this "moral redemption" symbolized by the mountain is "spurious." The story is "a nightmare version of what [Hemingway] might have been and still might be."

In their study of Hemingway's work, Earl Rovit and Gerry Brenner grant "The Snows of Kilimanjaro" a prominent place, calling it "Hemingway's one careful presentation of a non-ideal portrait of an artist" and using it to test their perceptions of Hemingway himself. Harry is "egocentric, hypocritical, and morally as well as physically rotten," but the story "elevates him to the snow-capped summit and forces the reader to accept him as a superior man." Hemingway turns the world upside-down, they argue, and readers accept it. Contrary to readers' perceptions, they come to accept Harry as a "superior man" and to feel the same contempt for his wife that he does. The wife and the hyena both, the critics argue, represent the dull, misunderstanding public against which the writer must struggle. The readers themselves are the hyenas. "It is fair to say," Rovit and Brenner conclude, "that Hemingway succeeds in this story in insulting his audience beyond endurance, in making the audience eat its own wounds, and like it."

Criticism

Greg Barnhisel

Barnhisel holds a Ph.D. in English and American literature and currently teaches writing at Southwestern University in Georgetown, Texas. He has written a number of entries and critical essays for Gale Group's Short Stories for Students *series. In the following essay, Barnhisel examines Hemingway's styles of narration and how they explain Harry.*

Although it is perhaps the least characteristic of any of Ernest Hemingway's short stories, ''The Snows of Kilimanjaro'' is often considered to be Hemingway's finest accomplishment in the genre of short fiction. Moreover, most critics agree that Harry, the protagonist of the story, is Hemingway's self-portrait, and this makes the story doubly interesting for students of this giant of twentieth-century American writing. The story recounts the death of a failed writer and a man who is at least unpleasant, if not actually the ''bad man'' that many of his critics have accused him of being. In describing Harry's death, Hemingway confronted many of the demons that haunted him: contempt for what he saw as an ignorant audience, alcohol and its numbing effects, war, and the unfulfilled promise of a vastly talented writer. Hemingway and Harry both arrive at a vision of transcendence that is ironically incongruous with Harry's decidedly degraded character.

But does this vision actually represent transcendence, or does the ending juxtaposition of the story—Harry flying toward the snow-capped peak of Mount Kilimanjaro while his wife remains in the humid tent with his rotting leg and a hyena whining outside—simply represent Harry's final fictionalizing of himself? The story relies heavily on symbolism, and critics generally have used the symbols in the story as the primary evidence for their interpretation of the moral value of Harry's end. To fully understand the story, however, readers must also take into consideration the styles of narration that Hemingway uses, for the distinction between the

What Do I Read Next?

- *The Complete Short Stories of Ernest Hemingway: The Finca Vigia Edition* (1987) collects all of Hemingway's short stories. As a body, they are truly remarkable, but the early stories—"Big Two-Hearted River," "Ten Indians," "Cat in the Rain," "A Clean, Well-Lighted Place," and many others—are haunting for the way that they embody Hemingway's "iceberg" principle of writing, in which a writer should leave out seven-eighths of the information in the story.

- Hemingway's most famous novel is *The Sun Also Rises* (1927). Its description of aimless Americans wandering around France and Spain is exhilarating, distasteful, and angering all at once.

- If *The Sun Also Rises* is the best-known fictionalization of the "Lost Generation," Hemingway's *A Moveable Feast* (1964) is the most famous nonfiction description of life in Paris in the 1920s, the milieu of such famous artists and writers as Man Ray, Gertrude Stein, Ezra Pound, and Picasso. Another excellent portrait of the same time and same people is Robert McAlmon and Kay Boyle's *Being Geniuses Together 1920-1930*, an interesting experiment in which Boyle and McAlmon alternate chapters describing their life as members of the Lost Generation. Finally, this hard-drinking crowd spent a good deal of time in bars, and Jimmie Charters was one of their favorite bartenders. His book *This Must Be The Place* (1927), features an introduction by Hemingway and tells chatty stories of the same people.

- In "An Occurrence at Owl Creek Bridge" (1891), the American writer Ambrose Bierce provided Hemingway with the structural model for *The Snows of Kilimanjaro*: a man, about to die, who miraculously escapes death and takes the reader on a flight of fancy, only to realize that he has indeed died. Another precursor story to Hemingway's is Henry James' "The Middle Years" (1893), in which a writer, near death, thinks about all he could have and should have written.

- In *Out of Africa* (1938), Isak Dineson, a Danish woman, wrote of her experiences not only with African wildlife but also with African people—a group that Hemingway leaves out of his story.

- Many critics and readers have compared the work of the American short story writer Raymond Carver to Hemingway's best work. Like Hemingway, Carver writes of characters who repress their emotions; also like Hemingway, much of the motivation for the characters is hidden. However, unlike Hemingway, Carver writes of lower-class people, primarily in the Pacific Northwest, who work, marry, and struggle through the small and great difficulties of life. Carver's best-known collection is called *What We Talk About When We Talk About Love* (1981).

---

roman type sections and the italic sections reflects the distinction between Harry's exterior persona and his interior memories.

The story moves by means of oscillation. It is structured as a pendulum that swings between two extremes, and this motion works on many levels. On a typographical level, the story moves between roman and italic type. At the same time, the text oscillates between dialogue-driven, almost adjective-free plain prose and a reminiscence-laden, run-on style of thinking about the past. Harry's attitude toward his wife oscillates between contempt or even loathing for her to affection and respect for her. Most of the symbols in the story are polarities, as well; the hyena at the end of the story and the leopard at the beginning are different extremes of the same pendulum, as are the clean white peak of the mountain and the fetid humidity of the plain.

The sections in roman type are very typical of Hemingway's writing. In these sections, the protagonist converses with his wife about the events of the immediate present and skims over the details of the past. In this, the story resembles such classic Hemingway stories as "Cat in the Rain" or "Hills Like White Elephants." But in "The Snows of Kilimanjaro"—and quite unlike many Hemingway stories—the internal thoughts of the protagonist are revealed as early as the third page: "So now it was all over, he thought . . . for years it had obsessed him; but now it meant nothing in itself." But for the most part, Harry is a classic macho Hemingway character, staring death in the face and not seeming to blink. "Can't you let a man die as comfortably as he can without calling him names?" he asks his wife. "I'm dying now. Ask those bastards," he continues, indicating the vultures who are waiting to claim his body.

The sections in roman type, such as the section discussed above, show Harry to be an egotistical, cruel, callous, and mean-spirited man. Even before readers journey into his thoughts to learn his opinion of his wife, they can already see that he holds her in contempt by the way he brushes off her efforts to be kind and caring to him. "So this was the way it ended in bickering and a drink," he thinks to himself. As the story progresses, he takes his frustrations out almost exclusively on his wife. When she tries to remind him of things he loved—hotels in Paris, for instance—he snaps back at her that "love is a dunghill . . . and I'm the cock that gets on it to crow."

Harry had been a promising young writer who fell in with a rich crowd because, he told himself, he wanted to write about them. "He had had his life and it was over and then he went living it again with different people and more money," the narrator states. However, he was seduced by their luxuries and allowed those luxuries to distract him from his true calling. "Each day of not writing," the narrator continues, "of comfort, of being that which he despised, dulled his ability and softened his will to work so that, finally, he did no work at all." To purge himself of this luxury and to remind himself of the hardships that drove him to his best work, he and his wife took this safari "with the minimum of comfort" so that "in some way he could work the fat off his soul the way a fighter went into the mountains to work and train in order to burn it out of his body."

But the presence of his wife reminds him of all of the damage he has done to his "soul," and

> Even before readers journey into his thoughts to learn his opinion of his wife, they can already see that he holds her in contempt by the way he brushes off her efforts to be kind and caring to him. 'So this was the way it ended in bickering and a drink,' he thinks to himself."

because of that he is neither able to return to his "fighting trim" or to arrive at genuine love for her. The portrait of his wife that readers have is created by the narrator, but Harry's prejudices color it, and the description of his wife becomes the battlefield on which he fights his inner conflict about who is responsible for the atrophy of his talents. "She shot very well this good, this rich bitch, this kindly caretaker and destroyer of his talent. Nonsense. He had destroyed his talent himself," he thinks to himself. The wife, on both a symbolic and literal level, represents the destruction of creativity. She has had love—the ultimate symbol of creativity—and children, but her husband died when she was young, and, later, one of her children followed her husband in death. She replaces love and fecundity with sex (through a succession of lovers) and alcohol, both of which Harry also indulges in but disdains. She has also learned to shoot and kill—two of Harry's other passions.

As the story continues the oscillation between Harry's present situation and his reminiscences accelerates, and each section becomes shorter. Harry's attitude toward his wife, as well, veers more quickly between contempt and grudging affection. Finally, the "reminiscence" section blurs into the "real-world" section as Harry imagines that Compton has come to take him to the city to be healed. Only at the end of the section, when he flies into the snow-white peak of Kilimanjaro, do readers realize that this, also, takes place in his own mind and not in the real world.

The African savanna beneath Mount Kilimanjaro serves as the setting for Hemingway's story of a dying man forced to reflect upon his life.

Although the story is much more explicit and revealing than almost any other piece of writing by Hemingway, it still leaves readers with a number of questions. The primary question is whether Harry's journey into the peak of the mountain represents transcendence. Many critics have argued that it does; Harry's wife represents the unfeeling, ignorant audience that the true artist must face, and although Harry is an unpleasant man he has been driven to be so by his failures as an artist—failures that are the fault of the misunderstanding audience. On a symbolic level, then, Harry's festering leg represents his talent, that is rotting due to a lack of understanding, and the leopard of the story's epigraph represents Harry himself: he scaled the heights only to die there. The vultures are the literary critics who await his death to metaphorically feast on him by attacking his writing; the hyena symbolizes the critics who attacked him during his life only to mourn his death. And Kilimanjaro itself represents the heights of art: the savanna is humid, rotting, hot, and teeming with life, while the mountain peak is clean, arid, pure.

Hemingway, though, does not make things so simple. Rather, he undermines this simple dichotomy between clean-high-cold and rotting-low-warm just as he undermines the dichotomy between reminiscences and "real-world" narration. The final vision of the mountain is not one of transcendence and salvation for the artist. No: the final vision of the mountain is the last manifestation of Harry's profound ability for self-deception.

The story centers on Harry's failures as an artist, and readers ask themselves why a writer as promising as Harry seems to have been ended up failing and never writing what he wanted to. The answer lies partially—not solely, but perhaps largely—in his experiences in the war. Harry's final reminiscence before the italics sections and the roman-type sections blend into one another is of the war. Specifically, he remembers a companion of his, "a fat man, very brave, and a good officer," who was wounded and caught in the barbed wire with "his bowels spilled out." Harry thinks about how he and this officer had discussed how such pain would, or should, cause a man to pass out, but how the officer did not pass out.

Harry is now in the same situation, and that is the immediate cause of the memory. But it is the larger cause of the memory, as well. The rest of Harry's memories had been of his pleasant experiences and his failure to write about them—experiences skiing in Austria, for instance, or fishing in Germany. But when the memories boil down readers arrive at one thing: the war. Harry's experiences in the war left him unable to write truly, fully, and honestly about experience because he simply could not face the horrors that he saw there. It is for this, readers then recognize, that he seeks out the wealthy, for they are best able to turn the dramas of life and death into sports and into representations of the real. The safari itself is an attempt to come to grips with the problem of death, and for this reason Harry is attracted to it, but since he has seen honest human death as closely as a person can see it he is both repelled by and inexorably attracted to it. This conflict—he must write about death, but he cannot write about it too accurately for fear that he might disturb his worst sleeping memories—drives his inability to write fulfilling work.

For this, his final vision of the peak of the mountain is ironic. Harry is powerless, drawn to life in the form of hunting, sex, and adventure, but he is also repelled by the sheer teeming, rotting, consuming nature of life. The peak of the mountain, constituted only of snow and rock, is transcendence to him. He cannot connect with life, for life, and its essential fertility, is something he needs to escape. The hyenas, the vultures, his leg, and his wife meld together as symbols of life; but they are symbols of life as something that feeds off other life—just like war itself. As he comes to the realization that life must feed off other life, he rejects life itself, and welcomes the apparition of the clean, white, sterile peak of Mount Kilimanjaro.

Source: Greg Barnhisel, in an essay for *Short Stories for Students*, Gale Group, 2001.

Sources

Cowley, Malcolm, Review of *The Fifth Column and the First Forty-Nine Stories*, in the *New Republic*, November 2, 1938, p. 367–68.

Ellman, Richard, Review of *A Moveable Feast*, in the *New Statesman*, May 22, 1964, p. 809–10.

Flora, Joseph M., *Ernest Hemingway: A Study of the Short Fiction*, Twayne Publishers, 1989.

Hicks, Granville, Review of *The Portable Hemingway*, in the *New Republic*, October 23, 1944, p. 524–26.

Kazin, Alfred, Review of *The Fifth Column and the First Forty-Nine Stories*, in the *New York Herald Tribune Books*, October 16, 1938, p. 5.

MacLaren-Ross, Julian, Review of *A Moveable Feast*, in *London Magazine*, August, 1964, p. 88–95.

Rovit, Earl, and Gerry Brenner, *Ernest Hemingway: Revised Edition*, Twayne Publishers, 1986.

Santangelo, Gennaro, "The Dark Snows of Kilimanjaro," Benson, Jackson, ed., *The Short Stories of Ernest Hemingway: Critical Interpretations*, Duke University Press, p. 251–61.

Schorer, Mark, Review of *For Whom the Bell Tolls*, in *Kenyon Review*, Winter, 1941, p. 101–05.

Wilson, Edmund, Review of *The Fifth Column and the First Forty-Nine Stories*, in *The Nation*, December 10, 1938, p.628–30.

Further Reading

Bensen, Jackson J., ed., *The Short Stories of Ernest Hemingway: Critical Essays*, Duke University Press, 1975.
This book is a good place to start a study of Hemingway's short fiction. There is an enormous mass of critical information on his stories, and this anthology gives readers an idea of the dominant strains of Hemingway criticism.

Kert, Bernice, *The Hemingway Women*, W. W. Norton, 1983.
Hemingway continues to be criticized for what many readers see as his insulting and overly simplistic treatment of women; this book is a solid introduction to the controversy surrounding "Hemingway's women" and discusses the wife in "Snows of Kilimanjaro" in particular.

Stephens, Robert O., ed., *Ernest Hemingway: The Critical Reception*, B. Franklin, 1977.
This book collects critical opinion on Hemingway from the time that his books appeared. Reading a book's initial reviews, and comparing those opinions on a work to critical opinion half a century later, is often enlightening not only as to how opinion on a writer changes but also as to how the institution of literary criticism itself changes with society.

Storyteller

Leslie Marmon Silko

1975

"Storyteller" was first published in the journal *Puerto del Sol* in 1975, and in 1981 it was collected in a mixed-genre book of the same name. "Storyteller" includes the following mix of genres: short story, poetry, and photography (and many of the poems seem more like stories than poems). The book was well-received, garnering special praise for its effect and statement as a whole. It is hailed as an important literary statement in the way that the mixing and inter-mixing of genres point to artistic practices beyond mainstream ones.

The significance of the title of this short story and book becomes clear from a consideration of their contents. Both story and book are centrally concerned with the art of storytelling and narrative, and with how stories and storytelling shape persons and communities (to tell stories that also tell stories about stories is to write "metacritical" works).

"Storyteller" depicts a clash of cultures in Bethel, Alaska, as well as the coming of age of a new storyteller in the local Eskimo community. The indigenous Eskimo community must contend with the "Gussucks" who, from the point of view of the main character, come not to live but to exploit the territory and its peoples. (The Yupik word "Gussuck" refers to any non-indigenous person; it is a derivation of the word "cossack," and thus can be dated to early Russian colonization of the area.) The main character's resistance to U.S. culture is evident from the description of her experiences at school, to which she goes for a brief time. She refuses to speak English and is whipped for her rebellion.

The young woman's identity as a storyteller is inseparable from this context of culture clash and resistance. Her story, when she begins to tell stories, appears to be of a personal nature (telling of a personal revenge). This story, however, is symbolic of the larger concerns of her community. This story about her parents' cruel death at the hands of a "Gussuck" storekeeper symbolizes her community's struggle against disdainful cultural interlopers in general. In Silko's story, the community storyteller witnesses, records and relates those events and circumstances of the most pressing communal significance or import.

Author Biography

Leslie Marmon Silko grew up on the Laguna Pueblo Reservation. This land is in the southwestern United States and was home turf to Native-American peoples before the first Europeans (Spaniards) arrived, and before the United States gained the land from Mexico. Albuquerque, the town she was born in, reflects in its Spanish name the history of the earliest European conquest of the Americas. The state she was born in, New Mexico, reflects the region's close ties to the Mexican nation southwards, the nation that only gave up the territory of New Mexico after a bitter war with the United States. Leslie Marmon Silko, of European and Keresan descent, was born a United States citizen on March 5, 1948. Silko's art and life are deeply informed by this history of cultures meeting, meshing, and clashing.

Silko and her two sisters were brought up in Old Laguna, a small town about fifty miles outside of Albuquerque. Silko went to elementary school locally and, from the sixth grade on, attended Catholic schools in Albuquerque. She completed a B.A. in English, with Honors, at the University of New Mexico in 1969, and following this she enrolled in the school's American Indian law program. Soon, however, she settled on her talent and career, and transferred to the university's M.A. program in creative writing. Silko first published while a student at the university (1969).

In 1969, the year Marmon graduated from college (undergraduate), the Pulitzer Prize in fiction went to N. Scott Momaday's *House Made of Dawn*. Momaday, like Silko, is of American Indian descent, and this book marked a milestone in U.S. letters. It won this nation's highest literary prize and its Native American themes were penned by a close cultural insider, and not a Euro-American writing, as it were, from the outside. This literary and cultural event undoubtedly helped consolidate Silko's literary path, which was to make her Native American heritage, and all the historical, political, and cultural issues this infers, absolutely central to her concerns as a writer.

Silko, very quickly, became a major and well-respected presence in U.S. letters. First published (and anthologized) were individual short stories. Her first full-length work was the 1974 book of poetry, *Laguna Woman: Poems by Leslie Silko*. This book of poems was succeeded by her first novel, *Ceremony*, in 1977. The year 1981 was an especially good one for Silko. Besides the publication of the collection of stories and poems *Storyteller* (which includes the short story of the same name), Silko received a prestigious MacArthur Foundation Prize Fellowship ($176,000 for five years). Silko continues to publish regularly, in both fictional and non-fictional modes. Her latest effort is the prodigious and ambitious novel, *Almanac of the Dead* (1991).

Plot Summary

The story begins with a young woman in a jail cell. The reason for her incarceration is not known. She is looking out of the window and sees that the sun has stopped in its course. She calls the jailer excitedly. He hears what she has to say then walks away uninterested.

Details that provide a view into the story's world are next presented ("white people" and "Gussucks" are named; the cold Alaskan world is fully sensed). Random thoughts from the girl's consciousness are presented (thoughts of "Gussuck" arrogance make her laugh). She thinks of her village and her cabin there; she thinks about the previous summer when she nailed red tin over the logs of the cabin.

The story now moves into the past. The girl's decision to go to school, out of curiosity, and

Leslie Marmon Silko

because she is tired of being cooped up with her grandmother and the old man, is recounted. Her aloneness has to do with the fact that other children avoid her cabin out of fear of the old man and woman. Already at this point in the past, the old man is enfeebled and spending winters in bed. The grandmother is gnarled and in pain due to a joint malady. She says her joints are "swollen with anger" (anger, presumably, at the disintegrating Eskimo world).

The girl hates the school, as the old man tells her she would. She is whipped for refusing to speak English, and from this detail it is understood that what the girl resists is being inducted into a culture and language other than her native one (Yupik). She returns to the village at the end of the school year to find her grandmother dead. She will never return to school. It is also learned that the old man uses the girl sexually.

The story now jumps forward in time, but still not to the present of the jail cell. The young woman has outgrown the unwelcome sexual advances of the old man. She goes looking for a "Gussuck" lover. The old man warns her that this will only lead to trouble. Also around this time, the old man begins the story that he will tell until his death; it is the story of the advance of a great bear.

The next major scene takes place in a local Gussuck store. This is where the young woman meets the "red-haired man." He sits in the back room socializing with other men. The storekeeper looks on enviously at the socializing and at the red-haired man who has the young woman come join him. They leave the store and go to the man's room. She has always been curious as to what he pins up above the bed when she can no longer see. She is careful to look this time before the item is removed. It is a picture of a woman with a large dog on top of her.

The story now jumps further back in time, to the young woman as a little girl asking her grandmother about the morning after her parents died. She says that she saw "something red" in the grass that morning, presumably near the bodies of her parents. This could be a reference to blood, but this is not certain. Her grandmother tells her how her parents died. They were sold poison, or bad alcohol, in place of the drink they thought they were buying. They were found dead the next day; the shopkeeper who sold the substance left town to escape punishment.

The story now returns to the young woman's life with the old man (during the period after the grandmother has died and just before the present time of the story). He continues with his story. His great bear is slowly but surely gaining on him. He intones stories for hours, even days on end without stop, sometimes not even sleeping nights.

The denouement of the story now begins. The young woman goes to the store and entices the storekeeper to follow her. He runs out into the cold after her, without hat or gloves. She runs out onto the iced-over river, and, as she had planned, the storekeeper falls through thinner ice. Since she is seen being chased by the storekeeper, she is questioned about his death by a state trooper. She tells the state trooper that she killed the man.

The story's last major scene is in the present. An attorney is visiting the young woman and cannot understand why she insists on taking responsibility for the crime. Eye witnesses claim that the man simply fell through thin ice, and that the girl was not near him and so did not push him. But she does not explain her motivations or thinking. The attorney therefore does not understand her and plans to defend her as someone who is "confused." In the meantime, the old man has died and villagers appear with food for the girl, just as they used to bring food to the old man. She has already begun storytelling by this time; she has become the new storyteller. The story's final scene depicts the last moments of the old man, his moment of death when the "blue glacier bear turned slowly to face him."

Characters

Attorney

The attorney is a public defender sent to look after the young woman's interests. He is perplexed that she insists on taking responsibility for the storekeeper's death. He is a sympathetic character but, ultimately, somewhat patronizing. Although the young woman does not help him understand the meaning and significance of her desire to take responsibility for her act, for his part he is quick to decide that she must be confused or of unsound mind.

Girl

See She and Young Woman

Grandmother

The grandmother seems eminently tired out by life. Her having felt its blows harshly is reflected in the gnarled and painful state of her body. Glimpses into the past suggest that she does her duty to the young woman, her orphaned grandchild, dryly and without relish. She passes on stories and nominally looks after the girl, but she does not, on the other hand, protect her from the old man's misdeeds. The unhappy nature of this household reflects the unraveling of the properly functioning traditional Yupik culture.

Jailer

The jailer angers the young woman as he refuses to speak Yupik (although he understands it). To the girl this means he is a cultural traitor, one who has capitulated to cultural conquest. He exhibits no concern for or interest in the young woman (in contrast to the community members who bring her food).

Old Man

The old man is the local storyteller at the narrative's beginning. He is old, dying, and even as far back as the story tunnels in time, he is enfeebled. His status as storyteller guarantees a certain veneration and care from his community. He is brought food, and both the grandmother and young woman seem to look after him willingly. The young woman, for unexplained reasons, also tolerates his sexual advances, despite the fact that she does not welcome them. When his death is imminent, he begins narrating a story about the approach of a great bear. This story is about the approach of his own death (and it could also signal the slow approaching "death" of his culture).

Red-Haired Man

Nobody is given a name in this short story, least of all this "Gussuck" lover the young woman takes. He is not particularly defined as a character except that his interest in the young woman seems as limited as her own interest in him. His habit of pinning a representation of a woman and dog above their bed suggests how their relationship appeals to him primarily as fantasy, and not as an interpersonal partnership or direct communion with another human being.

She

"She," also known as The Young Woman and Girl, is the main character of the story. Her character is best described as self-sufficient. She has learned to be alone from a childhood of other children running away due to her being a member of an unusual household (other children are frightened of the old man and the grandmother with whom she lives). Her self-sufficiency is demonstrated by her habit of laughing at "Gussuck" pretensions to mastery or control of nature. When she sees the disassembled parts of prefabricated houses with insulation spilling out, or when she sees machines stalled in the cold, she laughs as if she knows all along that the Alaskan freeze is the true master of all things. This knowing laughter is suggestive of superior knowledge and self-confidence. Her role in the story is to emerge as the next community storyteller, as the old man who is the current storyteller moves, at the same time, to meet his death. This process involves an act of terrible revenge. This revenge is motivated not only by the murder of her parents but also by anger at her culture's usurpation by outside cultural forces.

Young Woman

See She and Girl

Topics for Further Study

- There are, occasionally, unrealistic details in this short story (for example, at the story's beginning, the young woman is certain that the sun has stopped in its path). How do these elements relate to the plot or themes of the story?

- How does the opening and closing of "Storyteller" exemplify the plight of the protagonist in general (the young woman is in prison)?

- Research the significance of Wounded Knee, South Dakota, in Native-American history. Discuss the 1973 clash between protesting Native Americans and federal marshals, and the historic battle between U.S. soldiers and Native Americans at this site in 1890.

- Research early treaties between British colonials and Native Americans. What was the legal status of these treaties in later twentieth-century reparation negotiations and agreements?

- Persons indigenous to the American continents at the time of European conquest and colonialism were descendants of Asian peoples. How do anthropologists distinguish the various populations that stretch from Alaska to southernmost South America?

- Examine those Native-American nations divided by the Canada-Alaska border or the U.S.-Mexico border. How do these borders affect these split populations culturally?

Themes

Colonization: Territory and Culture

The Eskimo girl, along with her grandmother and the old man, represent a culture withering under the press of U.S. interests. Clearly dominant in the area are the "Gussucks," probably most of whom are U.S. citizens of European descent, who are in Bethel for the business of oil, pelts, fishing, and so forth. Bethel, of course, is official U.S. territory, and at the time that this story takes place, it is where many U.S. citizens are at "home." The region's annexation by the United States marked, for the indigenous peoples, the beginning of the end—or at least the massive disturbance—of what had been up until then largely uninterrupted tradition. The Inuit and Aleut (Eskimo) populations of the Alaskan region had no choice but to submit to the laws of the territory's conquerors.

That the traditional Eskimo way of life continues to slowly but steadily wither is subtly indicated throughout "Storyteller." For example, when the girl goes to school she appears to be the only student who even thinks to rebel against foreign ways. Yet, clearly, the school is a English-speaking school for Eskimo students run by the U.S. government: The dormitory matron pulled down her underpants and whipped her with a leather belt because she refused to speak English. "Those backward village people," the matron said, because she was an Eskimo who had worked for the BIA a long time, "they kept this one until she was too big too learn." The other girls whispered in English. They knew how to work the showers, and they washed and curled their hair at night. They ate Gussuck food. This passage demonstrates the manner in which Eskimos who have adopted U.S. ways and language might go so far as to internalize racist opinions about their own culture. Hence, the Eskimo matron refers to the village people as "backward." As for the other Eskimo girls at the school, they appear to have adopted the English language and U.S. styles and habits without question; they even whisper amongst themselves in English.

"Storyteller" is eloquent testimony to what happened following the colonization of the Americas by Europeans; namely, the decimation of indigenous ways of life and therefore of entire cultures. In this light, the approaching, obliterating, white and "final" winter that the girl expects is a metaphor for the European blanketing and cultural smothering of the indigenous American populations. This unfortunate history of empire and colonization is recently the subject of much study and debate. Up until mid-century, history books tended to recount this history in terms of an European colonization of territory, instead of it being also an attempted colonization of peoples, cultures, and ways of life.

Revenge

"Storyteller" is a tale of a young woman's revenge, felt as a grim playing out of destiny or fate. In every respect, the girl goes about her preparations in an exceedingly calm and deliberate manner, obeying some inner voice or outer force that finally informs her that "It [is] time."

She wishes to revenge her parents, next to whose dead bodies she saw "something red." Once this association between red and revenge has been made, certain details, in retrospect, become quite ominous. For example, well before the actual act of revenge itself, the girl has ritualistically nailed red tin all over her cabin. The details of her red-lined and red tasseled boots also resonate somewhat eerily. The thought that she chooses these boots precisely because they remind her of what she must do inevitably crosses the reader's mind.

The murder is planned in cold blood. The iced-over river is inspected minutely. It takes her days to get to know it intimately. She knows she can entice the storekeeper to run after her, and she knows she can excite him to the point where he will not be thinking of his own safety. Her plan unfolds without a hitch. The storekeeper falls to an instantaneous death in the freezing water, and she has guaranteed her own safety by having close knowledge of the river.

Style

Imagery

The most prevalent image in this story is that of landscape losing its boundaries. The girl and the old man await, notice, or comment upon the manner in which, during high summer or high winter, all becomes blue-green or white. Sky and land become the same color, and the line separating them on the horizon is not distinguishable. This dissolution of boundaries symbolizes a number of things in the story. If the "Gussuck" exploitative management of nature (oil drilling, killing animals for luxury coats as opposed to clothing) is compared to the Yupik living with and in nature, then this symbolism suggests how certain populations live in tandem with nature, as a part of it, as opposed to seeing it as something to be managed and used. That is, the Yupik do not live as if nature were something separate from their own being. This imagery also points to a storyteller's relationship to his or her community. There is no distinguishing a storyteller's concerns from those of the community's. When the boundaries between the two entities have dissolved, then the community knows its storyteller. This sense of boundaries dissolving could also point to a moral or ethical idea regarding the individual, his or her actions, and how the impact of these actions should be imagined. Each person must regard all of his or her actions as a studied ethical choice, as substantially impacting on the environment or others, and as having direct moral significance and repercussions. In this way, each person is enmeshed in the world such that there are no boundaries between them. This idea would accord with the story's treatment of responsibility. Even as she does not literally push the storekeeper to his death, she will not deny her responsibility for it. This meshing of distinct things could also symbolize the intermixing of cultures. The story expresses regret for the demise of the Yupik culture, but also the inevitability of this intercourse with U.S. forms. This imagery also reflects, finally, the technical achievement of the short story. The narrator is indistinguishable from the main character, and the story jumbles time, moving ambiguously through past and present. This avoidance of linear, chronological time suggests how what is important is not the young woman's voyage through time, or her own personal story, but rather her relationship to the broad world around her which has takes on significance and meaning through her community and its contact with other cultures.

Narration and Point of View

"Storyteller" is a lesson in the fine points of narration and point of view. The story is narrated by an external narrator, that is, by a voice not belonging to an actor with a role in the story. Thus, the characters in the story are referred to in the third person: "she," "he" or "they." (If the narrator were involved in, or "internal" to the story, then the first-person forms of "I" or "we" would be used.) However, this outside narrator does not necessarily provide the reader with an objective outlook on events. Instead of clearly distinguishing objective information or narrator point of view from character point of view, the two are often combined and meshed. Most often, the narrator's voice and information in "Storyteller" is imbued with the point of view and attitudes of the main character. Hence sentences such as: "There were no cars or snowmobiles that day; the cold had silenced their machines," or "The cold stopped them; they were helpless against it." The words "silenced" and "helpless" are not merely the erudite word choices of an articulate narrator. They convey also the somber pleasure of the young woman who is glad to see that the cold has stopped "Gussuck" work. She is pleased that there is something that can overcome the "Gussuck" will to extract oil from the land (i.e. render them "helpless").

Historical Context

Native American Rights Movements

It is difficult to conceive of this country's society and culture before the 1960s, yet the very visible markers of sexism and racism were everywhere. Racial segregation was the norm, and few African Americans and other non-European ethnic minorities had progressed appreciably economically or socially. Following in the footsteps of the vocal Black Rights advocates of the 1960s, American Indians began organizing at this time as well. Some actions were bold and angry, designed to capture the attention of the nation and government. For example, the American Indian Movement (AIM) seized Alcatraz Island in San Francisco Bay for a period of nineteen months in 1970–71. This same organization occupied the territory of Wounded Knee, South Dakota, in 1973. Other, less militant organizations such as the National Tribal Chairman's Association, also formed around this time (1971). This seizing of power and putting forward of demands worked to the Native Americans' benefit. They alerted a nation and a world to their admirable cultures, received monetary reparations, regained land, and recovered sacred grounds.

Multiculturalism

The prevailing notion, up until the 1960s, about the multi-ethnic nations of the Americas was that of a "melting pot," or the meshing of all the distinct cultures into a vibrant new singular one. Although, certainly, the Americas are unique precisely because of such a meshing of cultures, this is not a process that happens overnight or completely. Distinct cultures persist, whether due to the desires of the people who belong to them, or else because the world is a place of traveling people who necessarily bring their distinct cultures with them when they relocate. Now, therefore, it is more common to hear the word "multiculturalism," as opposed to "melting pot," when referring to the globally mixed regions of the world. This simply means that a nation or region need not have a single dominant culture, but can house numerous communities each with different practices and values.

Feminism

While the young woman and old man are strong purveyors of criticism against the cultural encroachments of non-indigenous populations, they are not themselves exempt from criticism within the story. The old man's casual attitude toward the young girl's body is clearly meant to disturb. And just as the girl is exploited sexually by the old man, so she seeks out "Gussucks" as sexual mates without any thought of her partner's humanity. Moreover, when she entices the storekeeper to follow her to his death, she uses her sexuality in an exploitative manner. "Storyteller" is not simply an argument about the demise of native American populations. It is also contains a feminist element insofar as feminism entails a denunciation of abusive or unequal gender power dynamics (sexism). Silko's feminism is a function of her time and place. She grew up during the progressive 1960s and 1970s, when women and other minorities asserted their rights to equal treatment, respect, and opportunity.

Critical Overview

What is known as the Native American Renaissance began in the 1970s. It is a cultural event whose name echoes another major cultural event this century, The Harlem Renaissance. The Harlem Renaissance refers to the those years in the 1920s and 1930s when African Americans constituted themselves as a political and cultural force. Similarly, in the 1970s, American Indian populations established themselves as political and cultural forces with which to be reckoned. Leslie Marmon Silko is an important literary figure in this latter Renaissance.

Until the publication of her first novel, Silko's place within the Renaissance was that of a poet and consummate writer of short stories. Her reputation was bolstered upon the publication of *Ceremony*

Compare & Contrast

- **1970s:** Affirmative action programs, designed to enhance the employment and educational opportunities of ethnic minorities and women, are set into play in the 1960s. By the late 1970s, these programs and quota systems are under attack as forms of "reverse discrimination" (that is, it is argued that the laws that protect minorities discriminate against Euro-American males).

   1990s: The passing of Proposition 209, the California Civil Rights Initiative, marks a definitive and severe blow to affirmative action in the United States. Its passing encourages other states to draw up similar propositions that make it illegal to give preferential treatment to persons based on their race or sex. One immediate result of the passing of this proposition is that Black and Latino enrollment at the California UC campuses drops considerably.

- **1970s:** Following in the footsteps of feminist and Black Rights' movements, Native Americans join together and organize major demonstrations and protests demanding civil rights, reparations for past wrongs, and the restitution of sacred lands. Political action on the part of American Indians in the 1970s ranges from the highly militant to the more traditional (armed seizures of territory to formations of negotiating bodies).

   1990s: A central global concern in the late twentieth-century is the ecological health of the planet. International political bodies such as the Green Party find their inspiration in cultures such as the American Indian ones which, despite their variations, are on the whole admired for the manner in which Nature determines social life, and not vice versa.

(1977), and attention from a wide range of critics followed from this. In fact, Silko's body of work was, by 1981, considered substantial and admirable enough to justify her receipt of a prestigious MacArthur Foundation Fellowship (the proceeds from which supported her while she wrote her second novel, *Almanac of the Dead*).

Whereas Silko's short stories, "Storyteller" preeminent among them, are known for their tight form and compositional finesse, *Ceremony* is occasionally critiqued for its compositional looseness. *Almanac of the Dead* is similarly critiqued for compositional weaknesses and has fared poorly in reviews, mainly because critics react negatively to its ethnic militancy and its central themes of cultural decadence and apocalypse. This does not mean, however, that it is not taken seriously; in fact, it is the subject of numerous scholarly articles.

"Storyteller" is seldom discussed as a single story; more often, it is an element in a larger discussion about the mixed-genre work of which it is a part. This mixed-genre work, *Storyteller*, contains story-poems, poems, photographs of relatives and the New Mexican landscape, and short stories. Some of the narratives, like "Storyteller," seem contemporary; others seem closer to traditional Laguna narratives. For those critics who wish to classify the collection, it is often considered to be autobiography. But if it is, it is a highly unusual one by mainstream standards. But this difference is, precisely, the text's point and strength. Silko is a major figure in the Native American Renaissance because she takes her heritage seriously and weaves its traditions into works that are still contemporary in flavor. The literary critic Linda Krumholz, in "Native Designs: Silko's 'Storyteller' and the Reader's Initiation" describes "Storyteller" in this way: "The Native American autobiographical subject is created amid a community of voices that relate, interact, and define one another....Thus 'Storyteller' is an autobiography in which the 'I' has been recast as 'the storyteller,' one who finds her identity through her role for and in the community, which shifts the reader away from a traditional Western location of the 'I' (as central and clearly differentiated) for author and reader." For Krumholz, the photographs of relatives and landscape demonstrate Silko's intention of diffusing herself amongst family, community, and place. Much of the scholarly work on Silko's fiction, like Krumholz's essay, explores its incorporation of Native American traditions and beliefs.

The importance of landscape and place is a central aspect of "Storyteller," and essays about this story often examine it in light of the centrality of landscape and place within Native American tradition. In the essay "Where I Ought to be: A Writer's Sense of Place," Louise Erdrich (another major literary figure of the Renaissance), explains why landscape and place is so important: "In a tribal view of the world, where one place has been inhabited for generations, the landscape becomes enlivened by a sense of group and family history. Unlike most contemporary writers, a traditional storyteller fixes listeners in an unchanging landscape combined of myth and reality. People and place are inseparable." Silko expresses this same view in the introduction to *Laguna Woman*: "I grew up at Laguna Pueblo....This place that I am from is everything I am as a writer and human being." The young woman and old man's intense relationship with place and landscape in "Storyteller" is understandable in this light, and they are, therefore, authorial *alter egos*. That is, these characters tell the reader something about how Silko thinks about storytelling and herself as a storyteller. As Linda Krumholz says, "'Storyteller' epitomizes a metacritical text; every piece can be read for the story it tells and for its story about storytelling and the role of stories."

In an essay entitled "To Tell a Good Story," Helen Jaskoski agrees with Krumholz's view: "Through all her writings Silko has been engaged in developing a theory of story and storytelling as constitutive of human identity and community, and these short stories, on the nature of story, are some of her earliest meditations on the theme." Jaskoski focuses, in her essay, on "the nature of language and its function in maintaining identity." For Jaskoski, the manner in which the Yupik girl rejects English at school is a crucial detail. This signifies the girl's sense of how the "hostile" world of foreigners is "bent on dissolving the outlines of her own identity," an identity that is intimately bound up with her own "language" (Yupik).

Jaskoski remarks, as do many critics, on the unusualness of the setting of this short story. It is the only narrative of Silko's that reflects the time she spent in Alaska (while she was writing *Ceremony*): "'Storyteller,' the first short story to appear in *Storyteller*, seems an odd source for a book that is permeated with loving familiarity with the American Southwest." Jaskoski calls "Storyteller" a "brooding" fatalistic tale and considers another short story in the volume, *Geronimo*, to be its "comedic companion piece."

Criticism

Carol Dell'Amico

Carol Dell'Amico teaches English at Rutgers, the State University of New Jersey, where she is currently working on a dissertation. This essay explores imagery in Silko's short story, such as the use of the color red and the motif of landscape losing its boundaries.

The most pervasive motif in Leslie Marmon Silko's "Storyteller" is that of landscape losing its boundaries. A "motif" is the reoccurrence of a literary device (for example, an image, symbol, or scene), not necessarily to achieve precisely the same effect or meaning each time. For example, landscape losing its boundaries in "Storyteller" is first alluded to in the first paragraph of the story: "She told herself it wasn't a good sign for the sky to be indistinguishable from the river ice....The tundra rose up behind the river but all the boundaries between the river and hills and sky were lost in the density of the pale ice." As the young woman's thoughts make clear, this instance of a loss of horizon is "not a good sign." Yet, as the story progresses, this landscape motif proves not always to signal something definitively "bad." Later, for example, it is the indicator of when the young woman must act out her revenge: "On the river bank in the distance she could see the red tin nailed to the log house, something not swallowed up by the heavy white belly of the sky or caught in the folds of the frozen earth. It was time." Whereas at the beginning of the story this special state of nature is visited upon the girl and her region, in this latter instance it is a state of nature that "speaks" to her personally. Or, to put this another way, in the first instance she passively reads the signs and in the second, nature is implicit in her own designs. "Storyteller," therefore and rather cleverly, manages to suggest the very essence of a literary motif in the image that is repeated: landscape losing its bounda-

What Do I Read Next?

- *The Man to Send Rain Clouds: Contemporary Stories by American Indians* (1974), is an early short story collection of the Native American Renaissance. It takes its title from one of Silko's stories. Edited by Kenneth Mark Rosen.

- *Ceremony* (1977) is Silko's first novel. It is the story of a young American Indian who returns from WWII and who must sort out his experiences, his adult world, and his relationship to his ancestry and heritage.

- *Yellow Woman and a Beauty of the Spirit* (1996) is a collection of essays by Silko. The book is subtitled "Essays on Native American Life Today." Silko expounds on topics ranging from Native American legal battles to Native American culture and art.

- *Love Medicine* (1984), by Louise Erdrich, won the 1984 National Book Critics' Circle Award for Best Work of Fiction. It is a highly readable and often funny text set on a North Dakota reservation; it tells the stories of three interrelated families.

- *Last of the Mohicans* (1826) by James Fenimore Cooper is one of this nineteenth-century author's novels about the North American frontier. Cooper popularized a particularly American-style adventure tale that was internationally popular during his time. Native American characters figure prominently in his novels, and they afford the contemporary reader a glimpse into attitudes and notions of the past.

---

ries suggests ambiguity and indistinctness, and a repeating motif is always an highly ambiguous literary effect. This narrative ploy points to the mechanics and method of "Storyteller" as a whole. Almost all of Silko's technical expertise in this story is mustered to suggest indistinctness, ambiguity, and shifting meaning.

Next to landscape losing its boundaries, the use of the color red, or things red, is perhaps second in suggestive importance. Things red are associated with her parents' death and her plans for revenge, even if always ambiguously or indirectly so. The story takes place during winter time, and although there are some references to the past that include descriptions of summer's green grass, the reader's impression of the story's world is that of overwhelming whiteness. This is reasonable, to be sure; the story is set, after all, in Alaska during winter, and it is also a story about the imminent demise (winter) of a culture to the encroachments of various "white people" or "white" cultures. For this reason, on the few occasions that red objects or references to the color red occur, they strike the reader at once.

The first reference to the color red is when the young woman thinks how she has "nailed scraps of red tin over the logs" of her cabin the previous summer. She has done this "for the bright red color, not for added warmth the way the village people had done." This detail distinguishes the young woman intriguingly from other villagers, but it is unclear at this juncture why she has done this (given that she is uninterested in the extra warmth). This sense of reading something significant, but having little clue as to its significance, is felt again upon noting the strange, seemingly random details of her boots having "bright red flannel linings" and "red yarn tassels" (and her lover having red hair).

However, these disparate references to red are pulled together finally when the story broaches how her parents died: "'Grandma,' she said, 'there was something red in the grass that morning. I remember.'" Then, later in the story: "'I heard sounds that night, grandma. Sounds like someone was singing. It was light outside. I could see something red on the ground.'" In keeping with the rule of ambiguity, it is never learned what this "something red" is in "Storyteller." Most readers probably first think of

> Once a storyteller's sense of him or herself is indistinguishable from the community's fate, then he or she will tell truly meaningful stories. Also along these same lines, this collapsing of boundaries could signify the Native American belief in there being only 'one story.'"

blood, but then might very well wonder how this might be so if the father and mother were poisoned, indicating a bloodless death. Another reasonable conjecture is that this "something red" is a nearby, discarded item of clothing or other debris that sticks illogically but persistently in the girl's mind. In any event, the color red is profoundly associated with her parents' death, and so the story's other references to red take on meaning in retrospect. The "red lining" of the boots now suggest the red and tender interior of the body or stomach, which in her parents' case was undoubtedly scarred and torn by the poison. The "tassels" suggest flowing blood, and, therefore, death or murder again. The color red is threaded through the story like the intertwining themes of death, crime (murder), and revenge.

Perhaps most interesting of all in terms of color imagery is the manner in which the mysterious references to "something red" manage to affect the collapse of boundaries between past, present, and future. This effect is achieved by one very strategically placed reference to "something red" quite late in the story. This strategic repetition of the phrase occurs well after "something red" has been used in association with the parents' murder. It occurs, specifically, right after the young woman has lured the storekeeper to his freezing death: "She stood still. The east bank of the river was lost in the sky; the boundaries had been swallowed by the freezing white. But then, in the distance, she saw something red, and suddenly it was as she had remembered it all those years." Unanswerable questions tumble forth upon reading this passage. "Remembered" what? Her parents' bodies lying on the grass? Is this red she sees the red tin on her cabin? But, surely not, as it has been learned that her cabin is "miles" distant from the town where she now is. Is she, then, having a vision, perhaps of the past, or is she simply seeing some other red thing or somebody else's red tin? Whatever it is that she sees, this sentence about "something red" and about remembering takes the reader back in time to the original death scene. And this association, taken in conjunction with the ambiguously worded notion that "it was as she had remembered it all those years," elicits the most crucial question of all, namely: did she see this moment in the future that morning? Was the "something red" she continuously believes she saw in the past in fact her vision into the future—a vision of this very moment of seeing "something red" in the distance immediately upon completing her long awaited revenge for her parents' murder? The answers to these questions, finally, cannot be known. But one result of this ambiguity and inclusion of "something red" in a past, a present, and, possibly, a future, is the collapse of the reader's sense of strict chronological time. Past, present, and future lose their distinctness because they are not treated as clearly separated categories in the story. The reader simply cannot know where to definitively situate a "something red."

Silko's story is, in many details, ambiguous, and its imagery and jumbling of time suggests the collapse of usually distinct realities and levels. This imagery and ambiguity could mean any number of things, given the content and themes of the story. Clearly, the story opposes the indigenous Inuit population from the "Gussucks" (the Euro-Americans). The Gussucks exploit nature, and the Inuits live with it in harmony. In this respect, the story's imagery and form could be said to advocate harmonious living with nature, or the blending of human life and society into the rhythms of nature. It could also signify, conversely, the inevitable result of foreign presence in the area, namely, the blending of cultures. Another possible meaning to ascribe to these effects pertains to the nature of storytellers and storytelling. Once a storyteller's sense of him or herself is indistinguishable from the community's fate, then he or she will tell truly meaningful stories. Also along these same lines, this collapsing of boundaries could signify the Native American belief in there being only "one story." That is, the entire world's fate is of a piece, with each person and each nation's acts affecting the rest of the world. If "everything is connected," then there are "no boundaries" between anything. As for the story's treatment of time, this could reflect the centrality of notions of cyclical time in Native American cultures. This is nature's time, and the time of seasonal reoccurrence, as opposed to the linear, chronological time of past, present, and future. Also of significance in this regard would be the Native American closeness to the past, or the past's profound relevance in the present. Traditionally, Native Americans keep their ancestors very much "alive," if only in historical memory. It is to Silko's credit that her stories are so dense with overlapping meanings. It is for this reason that she has the reputation of being a consummate writer of short stories. She does not waste a single word.

Source: Carol Dell'Amico, in an essay for *Short Stories for Students*, Gale Group, 2001.

Helen Jaskoski

In the following essay, Jaskoski provides a look at the use of allegory in relation to the "essentialist position" in "Storyteller."

"Storyteller," an arctic allegory set in the forbidding reaches of the Yukon River, seems a strange choice as title story for *Storyteller*, a miscellany suffused with familiar scenes of Silko's beloved Southwest and the intimacy of a family album. The chilling remoteness of "Storyteller," on the other hand, the anonymity of its characters and its lack of connection with the autobiographical or mythical materials in the rest of the book, indicates a special role for this story. Silko herself has noted that this story has a particular significance within the body of her work: "Nowhere is landscape more crucial to the outcome than in my short story 'Storyteller' ("Interior"). This comment emphasizes the necessity of seeing all her fiction in relation to landscape and place.

Every place is in some sense contested ground, and this is nowhere more so than in places where people of different values, cultures, and lifeways live within what is supposed to be shared physical and cognitive space. Mary Louise Pratt has introduced the term *contact zone* as a way "to refer to social spaces where cultures meet, clash, and grapple with each other, often in contexts of highly asymmetrical relations of power, such as colonialism, slavery, or their aftermaths." Since the fifteenth century the Western Hemisphere has been such a contact zone, and Silko's writings meditate

> "Every place is in some sense contested ground, and this is nowhere more so than in places where people of different values, cultures, and lifeways live within what is supposed to be shared physical and cognitive space."

on the exigencies of American Indian life within such geographical, political, cultural, and psychological borderlands.

While Silko comments on how "Storyteller" elaborates the concept of relationship between people and place, even to the extent of seeing the landscape as an essential character in the story, this short story also introduces other critical themes that pervade all her writing. Language is an abiding preoccupation, and "Storyteller" takes up language in two senses: the language of individual and communal self-creation that is storytelling, and the language—and silence—that creates boundary, identity, and personal power within a multidimensional, polyglot contact zone.

The text traces the thoughts and memories of a Yupik woman as she waits in a jail in the arctic bush to be interrogated regarding the death of a storekeeper. This place is a sparsely populated, climatically rigorous world where newcomers are all "Gussucks," a Yupik word derived from "Cossacks" and reflecting the historical fact of Russian traders, explorers, and missionaries having been the first Europeans to move in on the region. The landscape is so crucial that it comes to have the force of a character; Silko observes in her own commentary on the story: "The Yupik woman knows the appetite of the frozen river. She realizes that the ice and the fog, the tundra and the snow seek constantly to be reunited with the living beings that skitter across it" ("Interior").

The fatal impotence of those who understand neither the land nor their own desire leaves them literally overwhelmed. A thoughtless urge to gratify his sexual cravings sends the Gussuck storekeeper heedlessly across the ice in pursuit of a woman he has assaulted. She, however, has seen that the man is so enslaved to his lust that he cannot withstand her manipulation of it. The storekeeper's personal desire expresses the overwhelming cupidity of the whole Gussuck world, a perverse malignity of longing and frustration. At the moment of his attack the woman remembers that "[h]e hated the people because they had something of value . . . something which the Gussucks could never have. They thought they could take it, suck it out of the earth or cut it from the mountains; but they were fools. . . ."

The desire to take, to appropriate, to consume drives the colonial enterprise even as it impels the individuals caught up in the corporate project, and a naive overestimation of their power proves to be their undoing. The demise of one storekeeper swept away by the current rushing underneath the river ice is but a single moment in the fate of the whole project, a destiny inscribed in the tracings of the disappeared drilling rigs: "But the imprints and graves of their machines were still there, on the edge of the tundra above the river, where the summer mud had swallowed them before they ever left sight of the river. . . ."

As Kathryn Shanley's analysis demonstrates, "Storyteller" reveals how the relationship between sexual, material, and psychological covetousness lies at the heart of the colonial enterprise. An insatiable and perverse lust to possess and consume urges the Gussucks to this inhospitable place. As the old man has explained to the protagonist, the outsiders first came for the fur-bearing animals and the fish. Their appetites have depleted these resources, he tells her, and "[n]ow they come for oil deep in the earth. But this is the last time for them." Compressed within these ominous words are 400 years of colonization through trade, religious conversion, and resource extraction, from the first visits of Russian sailing ships through the construction of the Alaska pipeline. The old man's prophetic utterance returns to the woman's memory as she looks out the window of her jail cell and sees the sun about to glaze over in an apocalyptic final freeze.

The protagonist, on the other hand, is not greedy for material goods or for power over others. Rather, it is curiosity, a hunger for knowledge, that drives her. A restless inquisitiveness sends her to find out what the boarding school is like, regardless of the old man's warnings; curiosity and something resembling boredom take her in the direction of the Gussuck drillers: "She wondered what they looked like underneath their quilted goose-down trousers; she wanted to know how they moved. They would be something different from the old man." The same impulse sends her back to the red-haired oil driller with whom she has copulated, so she can find out the particulars of his pathetic fetishism. Curiosity about sex, or about Gussuck life in general, is only one expression, and not the most important one, of her desire and need. In contrast to the acquisitiveness and power hunger of the Gussucks she encounters, it is hunger for knowledge, closure, and a fullness of understanding that motivates the girl. Most of all she yearns for a satisfactory account of her parents' death, for completion of the story her grandmother has told her in tantalizing fragments. In the end, she herself enacts the completion of the story and then turns to recount her experience and her parents' as her own story, assuming the storyteller's place left vacant by the death of the old man.

"Storyteller"—as the title suggests—offers a meditation on storytelling that continues throughout the whole of the book, as well as throughout Silko's writings and lectures. The short story "Storyteller" contains many stories within it, but most are presented in attenuated, fragmentary form. At the heart of the central conflict of the plot are the stories of how the protagonist's parents met their death. A storekeeper had given one explanation, it seems, but the woman's grandmother believes that his story is a lie; the grandmother tells "the story as it must be told" of how she tried unsuccessfully to convey the truth to the authorities. But the girl senses that the grandmother's story is unfinished, the explanation incomplete, and she continues to search for "something red lying on the ground" that will satisfy her craving for explanation and closure. There are also competing accounts of the death of the man who pursues the protagonist: one story, which the protagonist's attorney wants her to tell, and the counterstory that she insists is the only valid account, the story that "must be told as it is."

Another story, alluded to only briefly, is the old man's warning of what will happen to the young girl if she goes to boarding school; also briefly mentioned is the story he tells her of what will happen if she joins him in bed, a story that she eventually discovers is a lie. At the end of "Storyteller," the villagers who have come to see the protagonist listen to her begin a story in words implying that this will be the tale we have just read, enclosing its events within a circle of storytelling. Woven fragmentarily throughout the narration of "Storyteller" is the old man's story of the hunter and the bear; it seems to be an ancient story that somehow—it is not clear how—must be implicated in the sordid contemporary events revolving the woman, her family, and the Gussucks. There is, finally, the whole story composed of and reflecting on all these stories, the text of "Storyteller" itself. The threads that link these stories together are the recurring motifs of language and identity, power and desire....

It is impossible to extract from this disrupted narration a clear chronology of events in the woman's life, nor is there any indication of how much time passes between episodes. The reader has no way of knowing how long after her parents' death and the storekeeper's disappearance it was that the protagonist heard the grandmother's story of what happened, nor how long again before she went to the boarding school, although apparently she was much older than the other students. How much time passes between her return from boarding school and the events that finally bring her to the jail? Critics often after to the protagonist as a "girl," but she could be a mature woman: several times the story refers to years passing.

All this ambiguity about chronology and sequence contributes to the mythic, allegorical texture of "Storyteller." The characters—the grandmother, the old man, the storeman (or men), the jailer, the dormitory matron, the village people, and the protagonist girl/woman—all have the archetypal anonymity of mythical personages. The girl, her grandmother, and the old man, like the supernaturals of the old stories, live at a distance from ordinary human interaction. They are marginalized and isolated at the edge of the village, treated with suspicion but respected by the villagers as central in some mysterious way to the community's continuing life. The old man "had not fished or hunted with the other men for many years, although he was not crippled or sick"; this is strange and otherworldly behavior in a precarious subsistence economy. The villagers come to visit him, as if approaching an oracle or a healer, to listen to his stories and leave their offerings in exchange.

Kenneth Lincoln has sought a specific mythical connection for Silko's story in the Greenland Eskimo myth of the Mistress of the Sea as related by Knud Rasmussen. In "Storyteller" the grandmother's rage and physical suffering do call to mind the powerful, angry, mutilated girl in Rasmussen's retold legend However, the Greenland story pays homage to the elephant seal as a principal of fecundity and regeneration, a sense entirely absent from the apocalyptic vision of "Storyteller": the watery raptures of the Greenland shamans, who dive deep into the sea in their sacred trances, are unthinkable in the unnamed village of "Storyteller," which lies "many miles upriver" from a town that is itself upriver from the Yukon delta. In Silo's story, those who enter arctic waters drown. The quality of myth also tends to efface the question of whether one or two storekeepers are present in the story. In the end the "facts" about the number of storekeepers become secondary to what the story has to say about the endemic and corrupting rapacity of colonialism.

"Truth" is less important than story. Only once do we find the word *truth* in "Storyteller"—when the protagonist recognizes that "what the old man said was true"—but as with the absence of so much of the stories that are alluded to, the text does not contain what the old man said, and so that particular truth is withheld. What "Storyteller" offers is a fundamental opposition not between lying and truth, but between lying and story. For the protagonist there is only one story that is not a lie. Her intransigent insistence on her truth as the only truth, her story as the only story, corresponds with her equally rigid insistence on her own language. In boarding school, she understood language as her defense against encroachment on her selfhood, and she recalls now how "the dormitory matron pulled down her underpants and whipped her with a leather belt because she refused to speak English." The assault on her language, carried out as a physical assault on her body, prefigures the Gussuck men's sexual deviance and the Eskimo jailer's reliance on English. She insists absolutely on her own language. In this character's ruthless refusal to compromise, there is potential for the heroic, even the tragic.

The dramatic potential in the text is qualified, however, by its intense focus on a single point of view. For all the story's mythic resonance, it is thoroughly modern in its strict reliance on the narrative device of unified point of view. The natural world of the story comes filtered through the liminal consciousness of the protagonist, whose awareness fixates on the apparently imminent disintegration of the whole of nature: "She told herself it wasn't a good sign for the sky to be indistinguishable from the river ice, frozen solid and white against the earth. The tundra rose up behind the river but all the boundaries between the river and hills and sky were lost in the density of the pale ice." The passage echoes the sense of disorientation and loss of boundaries that Silko herself recalls from her experience of living in the region: "Here the winter landscape can suddenly metamorphose into a seamless, blank white so solid that pilots in aircraft without electronic instruments lose their bearings and crash their planes into the frozen tundra, believing down to be up. Here on the Alaskan tundra, in mid-February, not all the space-age fabrics, electronics, or engines can ransom human beings from the restless, shifting forces of the winter sky and winter earth" ("Interior"). This is what the protagonist pictures in the apocalyptic vision she has in her jail cell: "That was how the cold would come: when the boundaries were gone the polar ice would range across the land into the sky...."

This monotone world lacking outline, perspective, and landmarks reflects the problematics of moral navigation in the story. The storeman pursues the woman to his death apparently because he wants to violate her, which she attributes to his jealousy of the oil drillers she has been free with. Yet self-defense is an issue never raised by the attorney, who only mentions accident and the view that "her mind is confused." She herself does not relate her actions to self-defense. Nor does craving for retribution figure as her motive. The realization of her project is the story she begins to tell to the villagers, a story that, like the old man's story of the hunter and the bear, will both fulfill and consume her. . . .

In her uncompromising repudiation of the Gussuck world the protagonist bears a strange resemblance to that other model of passive aggression as the sign of personal integrity, Herman Melville's Bartleby the Scrivener. Like Bartleby, who "prefers not to" do one thing and then another, until it seems that existence itself impinges too heavily on his sense of self, the Yupik woman steadfastly resists interaction with the world on any terms but her own. It is true that the ending of "Storyteller" finds the woman telling her story to the villagers who have come to hear it, suggesting continuity and perhaps regeneration; however, the example of the old man, whose place she has taken, and who ended his own days like Bartleby, communing with no one but himself, qualifies that suggestion.

For the protagonist of "Storyteller," truth is single and absolute, and the only way for her to maintain identity and integrity is to set impregnable boundaries around her language, her story, and herself, excluding all that would compromise her isolate vision. She hears her grandmother's voice telling her that "[t]here must not be any lies," and

"I killed him," she says of the storekeeper, "but I don't lie." There is no room here for ambiguity, compromise, contestation, revision, qualification, or any alternative possibility: this is a frozen certitude, as rigid and as lethal as the frost that threatens to immobilize the sun. The protagonist of "Storyteller" is an icon of essentialism, and the story is an allegory on the essentialist position, an allegory that will be tested and contested in the remaining stories in *Storyteller*.

Source: Helen Jaskoski, *Leslie Marmon Silko: A Study of the Short Fiction*, Twayne Publishers, 1998, pp. 13–22.

Bernard A. Hirsch

In the following essay, Hirsch conveys a connection between the "oral tradition" and the "written word" in "Storyteller."

"I was never tempted to go to those things . . . ," said Leslie Marmon Silko of the old BAE reports ". . . I . . . don't have to because from the time I was little I heard quite a bit. I heard it in what would be passed now off as rumor or gossip. I could hear through all that. I could hear something else, that there was a kind of continuum. . . ." That continuum provides both the structural and thematic basis of *Storyteller*. Comprised of personal reminiscences and narratives, retellings of traditional Laguna stories, photographs, and a generous portion of her previously published short fiction and poetry, this multigeneric work lovingly maps the fertile storytelling ground from which her art evolves and to which it is here returned—an offering to the oral tradition which nurtured it.

Silko has acknowledged often and eloquently the importance of the oral tradition to her work and tries to embody its characteristics in her writing. This effort, as she well knows, is immensely difficult and potentially dangerous, and this awareness surfaces at several points in *Storyteller*. She recalls, for instance, talking with Nora, whose "grandchildren had brought home / a . . . book that had my 'Laguna coyote' poem in it":

> "We all enjoyed it so much [says Nora] but I was telling the children the way my grandpa used to tell it is longer."
>
> "Yes, that's the trouble with writing," I said. You can't go on and on the way we do when we tell stories around here. . . .

"The trouble with writing," in the context Silko here establishes for it, is twofold: first, it is static; it freezes words in space and time. It does not allow the living story to change and grow, as does the oral tradition.

Second, though it potentially widens a story's audience, writing removes the story from its immediate context, from the place and people who nourished it in the telling, and thus robs it of much of its meaning. This absence of the story's dynamic context is why, in writing, "You can't go on the way we do / when we tell stories around here."

But Nora does a wonderful thing. She uses Silko's poem to create a storytelling event of her own. In this sense Silko's poem itself becomes a part of the oral tradition and, through Nora's recollection of her grandfather's telling, a means of advancing it as well. The conversation with Nora is important in *Storyteller* because it reminds us of the flexibility and inclusiveness of the oral tradition. Even writing can be made to serve its ends.

Storyteller helps keep the oral tradition strong through Silko's masterful use of the written word, and the photographs, to recall and reestablish its essential contexts. The photographs are important because they reveal something of the particular landscape and community out of which Laguna oral tradition is born, and of specific individuals—of Aunt Susie, Grandma A'mooh, Grandpa Hank, and all those storytellers who have accepted responsibility for "remembering a portion . . . [of] the long story of the people." The photographs, however, as Silko uses them, do more than provide a survival record. As we shall see, they involve the reader more fully in the storytelling process itself and, "because they are part of many of the stories / and because many of the stories can be traced in the photographs," they expand the reader's understanding of individual works and also suggest structural and thematic links between them.

The photographs also are arranged to suggest the circular design of *Storyteller*, a design characteristic of oral tradition. The merging of past and present are manifest in the book's design, as is the union of personal, historical, and cultural levels of being and experience, and through such harmonies—and their periodic sundering—the ongoing flux of life expresses itself. The opening photograph, for instance, is of Robert G. Marmon and Marie Anayah Marmon, Silko's great-grandparents, "holding [her] grandpa Hank." The second picture, three pages later, is of Aunt Susie—of whom Silko is the "self-acknowledged, self-appointed heir"—and Leslie Silko herself as a child. These photographs do not merely locate Silko within a genealogical context or even that of an extended family, but within a continuous generational line of Laguna storytellers as well. The last three photographs in the book bring us full circle. The first of these comes at the end of the book's written text; it is of the adult Silko and was taken among the Tucson Mountains where she now lives. The second is of Grandpa Hank as a young man after his return from Sherman Institute, and the third is of three generations preceding her, including her father as a boy, Grandpa Hank's brother, and her great-grandfather. Though there is clearly an autobiographical dimension to *Storyteller*, Silko's arrangement of photographs at the beginning and end of the book subordinates the individual to the communal and cultural. Her life and art compels us, as does the literature itself, to acknowledge the ongoing power of Laguna oral tradition in her writing.

This cyclic design, of course, is not merely a function of the arrangement of photographs. It derives primarily from the episodic structure of *Storyteller* and the accretive process of teaching inherent in it. Each individual item is a narrative episode in itself which relates to other such episodes in various ways. Oral storytelling, Walter J. Ong tells us, "normally and naturally operated in episodic patterning . . . episodic structure was the natural way to talk out a lengthy story line if only because the experience of real life is more like a string of episodes than it is like a Freytag pyramid"; and it is real life, "the long story of the people," that is Silko's concern. Moreover, the telling of her portion of the story, and of the individual stories which comprise it, involves, like all oral storytelling, a teaching process, one in which the varieties of genre and voice Silko uses are essential.

In *Storyteller*, the reader learns by accretion. Successive narrative episodes cast long shadows both forward and back, lending different or comple-

> In a Sun-Tracks interview, Silko said of 'these gossip stories': 'I don't look upon them as gossip. The connotation is all wrong. These stories about goings-on, about what people are up to, give identity to a place.'

mentary shades of meaning to those preceding them and offering perspectives from which to consider those that follow. Such perspectives are then themselves often expanded or in some way altered as the new material reflects back upon them. This kind of learning process is part of the dynamic of oral tradition. Silko uses it in *Storyteller* to foster the kind of intimacy with the reader that the oral storyteller does with the listener. Such a relationship is born of both the powerful claims of the story, in whole and in part, on the reader's attention and the active engagement by the accretive process of the reader's imagination. This process in effect makes the reader's responses to the various narrative episodes a part of the larger, ongoing story these episodes comprise while simultaneously allowing the episodes to create the contexts which direct and refine these responses. In this way the stories continue; in this way both the story and the reader are renewed.

It is impossible within the limits of this paper to explore the workings of this process over the entire length of *Storyteller*, yet the interrelationships between the various narrative episodes and photographs throughout is so rich and intricate that any attempt to formally divide the work into sections or categories would be arbitrary at best, of necessity reductive, and at worst misleading. Still, there are groups of narrative episodes that seem to cluster around particular themes and cultural motifs which I believe can be meaningfully seen as representative of the overall design and method of the book.

II

N. Scott Momaday has said: "We are what we imagine. Our very existence consists in our imagination of ourselves.... The greatest tragedy that can befall us is to go unimagined." It is apparent throughout *Storyteller* that Silko would agree, and she reminds us that in the oral tradition, "sometimes what we call 'memory' and what we call 'imagination' are not so easily distinguished." In "The Storyteller's Escape," the old storyteller's greatest fear as she waits for death is that she will go unremembered—unimagined. *Storyteller* itself is a self-renewing act of imagination memory designed to keep storytellers as well as stories from so tragic a fate. The book's opening section, which I will arbitrarily call the "Survival" section, establishes this particular concern. Embracing 5 reminiscences, 4 photographs, 2 traditional Laguna stories, the short stories "Storyteller" and "Lullaby," and the poem "Indian Song: Survival," this section explores from various angles the dynamics and meaning of survival, both personal and cultural, for tribal people in contemporary America.

Silko visually establishes continuity through the photographs. The first two, described earlier, reveal in their depiction of three generations of Silko's family genealogical continuity, but especially important in primarily the second and third photos is the idea of cultural transmission. Such transmission involves more than the passing of stories from generation to generation, essential as that is. It involves the entire context within which such passing occurs, and this includes both the land and the relationship, beyond blood ties, between teller and hearer. That is why, to tell the story correctly, Silko must bring us into the storytellers' presence, to let us somehow see them, learn something of their histories, and most of all, to hear them tell their stories.

These elements are certainly present in the book's title story, "Storyteller," which is at the hub not only of the "Survival" section but of the book as a whole. Explaining, in Silko's words, "the dimensions of the process" of storytelling, this tale, set not in Laguna but in Inuit country near Bethel, Alaska, is at once dark and hopeful, embracing all that has come before it in the book and establishing both the structure and primary thematic concerns of what follows. It is a tale of multiple journeys that become one journey expressed through multiple stories that become one story. At its center is a young Eskimo girl, orphaned, living with a lecherous and dying old man, the village storyteller, and his wife, victimized by Gussuck and "assimilated" Eskimo men, and determined to avenge herself against the Gussuck storekeeper responsible for her parents' death.

Speaking of his use of "three distinct narrative voices in *The Way to Rainy Mountain*—the mythical, the historical, and the immediate"—Momaday says: "Together, they serve, hopefully, to validate the oral tradition to an extent that might not otherwise be possible." A similar mix of voices occurs in "Storyteller"—indeed, throughout the book as a whole—and to similar effect. Against the backdrop of the prophesied coming of a "final winter," the girl comes of age and the old man, the mythic voice, begins his story of the great bear pursuing the lone hunter across the ice.

He tells the story lovingly, nurturing every detail with his life's breath, because it is the story that makes his death meaningful. The story is an expression of sacred natural processes, ancient and unending, of which his death is a part, processes Silko will treat later in the book in such works as "The Man to Send Rain Clouds" and the poem "Deer Song." But most importantly the story, in the intensely beautiful precision of the old man's telling, becomes the girl's legacy, a powerful vision by which she can unify the disparate aspects of her experience to create herself anew in profoundly significant cultural terms.

She recalls having asked her grandmother, the old man's wife, about her parents, and her grandmother told how the Gussuck storeman traded them bad liquor. The grandmother is the historical voice. Her story and that of the giant bear become linked in the girl's imagination. Once, while listening "to the old man tell the story all night," she senses her grandmother's spirit. "It will take a long time," the old woman tells her, "but the story must be told. There must not be any lies." At first, she thinks that the spirit is referring to the bear story. She "did not know about the other story then...."

This "other story" is in truth the conclusion of her grandmother's story, a conclusion that will make it the girl's story. As it stands, in the inaction of civil and religious authorities and in the storeman's continued existence, the story of her parent's death has not been properly told. The Story is life and in life it must be completed. And the story of the giant bear "stalking a lone hunter across the Bering Sea ice" tells her how. "She spent days walking on the river," getting to know the ice as precisely as the old man had described it in his story, learning "the colors of ice that would safely hold her" and where the ice was thin. She already knew that the storeman wanted her and thus it is easy for her to lure him out onto the river and to his death. Though he appeared to chase her out onto the ice, it was she who was the bear.

The attorney wants her to change her story, to tell the court that "it was an accident," but she refuses, even though to follow his advice would mean freedom. Hers is the "immediate" voice, the voice that carries the old stories into the present and locates the present within the cycle of mythic time. Through the story, life derives purpose and meaning and experience becomes comprehensible; also through the story, and through her fidelity to it, the girl recreates herself from the fragments of her own history.

Her emergence whole and intact from her experience is, in this respect, like Tayo's emergence in Silko's 1977 novel *Ceremony*, a victory for her people; given the immediate context in which the title story is placed in *Storyteller*, it is, like all stories in the oral tradition, a ritual. The girl's role as a culture-bearer, for example, receives significant emphasis from the surrounding material.

Following "Storyteller" there is a picture of Marie Anayah Marmon, Grandma A'mooh, reading to two of her great granddaughters, Silko's sisters. She is reading, apparently, from *Brownie the Bear*, a book, we later learn, she read many times, not only to her great-granddaughters but to Silko's uncles and father. Accompanying this photograph is a reminiscence about Grandma A'mooh, whose name Silko, as a child, deduced from the woman's continual use of "'a'moo'ooh' / ... the Laguna expression of endearment / for a young child / spoken with great feeling and love." That love is evident on the faces of the old woman and the little girls; it is also clear that although she is not in this captured moment telling a story from the oral tradition, she has turned the occasion, much as Nora did with the printed version of Silko's coyote poem, into a rich oral storytelling experience.

We come to the title story by way of several other narrative episodes, beginning with Silko's brief reminiscence and history of Aunt Susie, her father's aunt. Aunt Susie

was of a generation
the last generation here at Laguna,
that passed down an entire culture
by word of mouth
an entire history
an entire vision of the world ...

In its rhythms and repetitions, Silko's telling here assumes the quality of a chant and in this she reinforces not only Aunt Susie's role as culture-bearer but her own as Aunt Susie's cultural heir. Their relationship provides a necessary context within which to consider the girl and the old man in the title story. That relationship is complicated in several ways, but this context, along with the photograph that follows "Storyteller," highlights her role as the storyteller-successor to the old man.

For Silko, how a story is told is inseparable from the story itself. The old man's bear story exerts its hold on the girl's imagination through his intensely precise, chant-like, dramatic telling and retelling of it. Silko recalls a child's story Aunt Susie told about a "little girl who ran away," and she insists that we hear it as Aunt Susie told it: "She had certain phrases, certain distinctive words / she used in her telling. / I write when I still hear / her voice as she tells the story." In her own telling Silko uses poetic form with varying line-lengths, stresses, and enjambment to provide some of the movement and drama of oral storytelling. She also provides several italicized expository passages to evoke the digressive mode of traditional storytellers and the conversational texture of their speech. When the little girl asks for "yashtoah," for example, we are told that

> "Yashtoah" is the hardened crust on corn
>   meal mush
> that curls up.
> The very name "yashtoah" means
> it's sort of curled up, you know, dried,
> just as mush dries on top....

"This is the beauty of the old way," Silko has said. "You can stop the storyteller and ask questions and have things explained."

Aunt Susie's story, in some respects, is a sad one about a little girl who, feeling unloved because she does not get what she wants, decides to drown herself. Attempts by a kindly old man and her mother to save her fail and the child drowns. Grieving, the mother returns to Acoma where, standing on a high mesa, she scatters the girl's clothes to the four directions—and "they all turned into butterflies— / all colors of butterflies." This is a child's story and whatever truths it may teach it should evoke the child's capacity for wonder and delight. Aunt Susie succeeded brilliantly in this respect. She brought the characters to life, the mother's tenderness and the prophetic foreboding of the old man "that implied the tragedy to come":

> But when Aunt Susie came to the place
> where the little girl's clothes turned into butterflies
> then her voice would change and I could hear the
>   excitement
> and wonder
> and the story wasn't sad any longer.

The child learns something of pain through such a story, but she learns too of life's perpetuity, that from death itself can emerge beautiful life. She learns of the delicate balance in which all things exist, a balance forever threatened and forever renewed.

But harsh realities, having been delicately yet honestly prepared for by Aunt Susie's story, dominate, appropriately enough, the two recollections leading directly into "Storyteller." The first offers a brief history of Silko's great-grandparents, and we learn that Robert G. Marmon married a Pueblo woman and "learned to speak Laguna"; but "when great-grandpa went away from Laguna / white people who knew / sometimes called him 'Squaw Man'." The second recollection is of the Albuquerque hotel incident in which Marmon's two young sons, because they are Indians, were not permitted in the hotel.

"Storyteller," is fed by the various motifs and concerns of the narratives leading into it and it recasts them in new ways. In that sense it is as much a retelling as an original telling. It is not merely a story of survival but, like the bear story within it, a survival story itself. It is unsparing in its treatment of the nature and consequences of discrimination and unqualified in its vision of the capacity of oral tradition not merely to survive discrimination but to use it as a source of power. However, as the narratives that follow "Storyteller" suggest, the oral tradition is only as strong—or as fragile—as the memories that carry it and the relationships that sustain it.

Silko's remembrance of Grandma A'mooh, which follows "Storyteller," is warm and moving, yet painful as well. Grandma A'mooh, as her name suggests, was love itself to Silko. She loved the land, her people, her granddaughters, and the stories that evolved from them, yet it was thought best, in her later years, to remove her from all that sustained her and have her live with her daughter in Albuquerque. The daughter had to work, so much of the time Grandma A'mooh was alone—"she did not last long," Silko tells us, "without someone to talk to"....

"Indian Song: Survival," like the narrative episodes which precede it, concerns what survival is and what is needed to survive, but it considers these ideas from a somewhat different perspective than the others. It is in the first-person and this heightens the intimacy of the sustaining relationship of the individual with the land the poem explores. The poem moves in a sequence of spare yet sensual images which express at once the elemental and regenerating power of this relationship, and Silko's versification, like that of most of the poetry in *Storyteller*, is alive with motion and the subtle interplay of sound and silence. It is a "desperation journey north" she describes, but it is marked by neither panic nor haste.

"Mountain lion," Silko writes, "shows me the way." He is her guide as he has been for Laguna hunters throughout the time, and his presence helps to establish the true nature of this journey. It is a journey to reestablish old ties, ties essential to survival in any meaningful sense. As the journey continues the "I" becomes more inclusive as the speaker becomes increasingly able to merge with the nature around her. Asked at poem's end "if I still smell winter / . . . I answer:"

> taste me
> I am the wind
> touch me,
> I am the lean brown deer
> running on the edge of the rainbow. . . .

The "desperation journey" has become a journey of self-discovery, of finding one's being entire in the land. Now she can travel spirit roads.

The wholeness of the relationship emerging from "Indian Song: Survival" enhances our understanding of what, precisely, the young girl in "Storyteller" accomplishes. Her life has been a desperate journey and her final awakening involves the reestablishment of a vital, intimate connection to the land. This is what the bear story requires of her. The poem also intensifies further the poignancy of Grandma A'mooh's last days by compelling us to learn again the value of what, for her own "good," had been taken from her.

Silko follows "Indian Song: Survival" with a painfully enigmatic story from Aunt Susie, a Laguna "flood" story in which a little girl and her younger sister return home to their village after a day's play only to find it abandoned except for "the old people / who cannot travel." Their mother and the others went to the high place to escape the coming flood. If "Indian Song: Survival" concerns the establishment of vital relationships, this story tells of their being sundered. There is a beauty in the girl's devotion to her sister as there is pain in their mother's leaving them and these elements, devotion and separation, are central to the short story, "Lullaby," which follows.

If, as Momaday said, the greatest tragedy is to go unimagined, the title of Silko's "Lullaby" is in one sense bitterly ironic. Having been robbed of her grandchildren, Ayah, the old Navajo woman at the heart of the story, sings a song for them, a song that she remembers having been sung by her mother and grandmother. It is a beautiful song expressing with delicate economy the world view in which she was raised, and its closing words doubtlessly provide some consolation:

> We are together always
> We are together always
> There never was a time
> when this
> was not so. . . .

But we cannot forget that there are no children to hear it and, though Ayah's "life had become memories," those memories seem dominated now by the loss of children—of her son Jimmie in the war and the babies to the white doctors. For Silko, to go unremembered is to go unimagined, and in that sense Ayah's is a tragic story. Grandma A'mooh, in her last years, was taken from her grandchildren but she does not go unremembered. Such a fate, though, seems likely to befall Ayah, for her babies are taken not simply to make them well, but to make them white.

The "Survival" section, however, does not end on a hopeless note. Ayah's "lullaby" expresses a timeless harmony and peace which are reflected in the photograph which closes the section, taken from the sandhills a mile east of Laguna. The land seems whole and eternal here, and where that is so the people, and the oral tradition, will survive.

III

But today, even the land is threatened. A photograph in what I will call the "Yellow Woman" section of *Storyteller* is of the Anaconda company's open-pit uranium mine. "This photograph," Silko tells us, "was made in the early 1960s. The mesas and hills that appear in the background and foreground are gone now, swallowed by the mine." This photograph deepens our understanding of many things in *Storyteller*: of the importance of the photographs to the stories, for one thing, and of Silko's father's love of photography for another. "He is still most at home in the canyons and sandrock," she says, "and most of his life regular jobs / have been a confinement he has avoided." Some might think less of him for this, but Silko stifles this tendency—first by the story of Reed Woman and Corn Woman that precedes the reminiscence about her father and second by his photographs themselves, one of which is that of the now vanished mesas and hills. Moreover, his photography intensified his love of the land and enabled him to relate to it in new and fulfilling ways. We learn, for instance, that

> His landscapes could not be done
> without certain kinds of clouds—
> some white and scattered like river rock
> and others
> mountains rolling into themselves
> swollen lavender before rainstorms. . . .

Clouds, as we know, are a source of life itself to the land, and for Lee H. Marmon they bring to it a profound and varied beauty as well. Essential to the continuity of physical life, the clouds are no less essential to his spirit in that they help him express through his art his particular vision of the land and by so doing, to define himself in terms of it. Equally important, in these times, is that his artistry can help others, be they Indians removed from the land or people who have never known it, to develop a richer, more meaningful sense of the land than is held by such as those who run Anaconda. It is precisely the development of such a relationship—to the land, to the spirits that pervade it, and to the stories that derive from it—that occupies the "Yellow Woman" section of *Storyteller*.

"The Yellow Woman" section, comprised of the short story "Yellow Woman," 4 poems, poetic retellings of two traditional stories, 4 reminiscences, 4 photographs, and 2 "gossip stories," is framed by "Yellow Woman" and "Storytelling," a poem consisting of six brief vignettes based on the abduction motif of the traditional Yellow Woman stories. As does "Storyteller" in the "Survival" section, "Yellow Woman," and the traditional stories from which Silko's version evolves, establish the primary structural and thematic concerns of this section.

Based on the traditional stories in which Yellow Woman, on her way to draw water, is abducted by a mountain kachina, Silko's "Yellow Woman" concerns the development of the visionary character. This is hinted at in the story's epigram, "What Whirlwind Man Told Kochininako, Yellow Woman":

> I myself belong to the wind
> and so it is we will travel swiftly
> this whole world
> with dust and with windstorms. . . .

Whirlwind Man will take her on a journey beyond the boundaries of time and place, a journey alive with sensation and danger which promises a perspective from which she can see the world new and entire. This in effect is what happens in the story. Like the prophets and visionaries of many cultures, Indian and non-Indian, the narrator travels to the mountain where she learns to see beyond the range of mundane experience. She recalls that, at Silva's mountain cabin,

> I was standing in the sky with nothing around me but the wind that came down from the blue mountain peak behind me. I could see faint mountain images in the distance miles across the vast spread of mesas and valleys and plains. I wondered who was over there to feel the mountain wind on those sheer blue edges—who walks on the pine needles in those blue mountains. "Can you see the pueblo?" Silva was standing behind me. I shook my head. "We're too far away." "From here I can see the world. . . ."

The pueblo, which comprised her whole world before, is, from the perspective of the mountain, but a barely discernible part of a much larger whole. With Silva, on the mountain, she has entered the more expansive and truer realm of imagination and myth.

When we can see imaginatively, William Blake has said, when we can see not merely with but through the eye, "the whole creation will appear infinite and holy whereas it now appears finite and corrupt. This will come to pass by an improvement of sensual enjoyment" (*The Marriage of Heaven and Hell* . . .). This is the narrator's experience. She follows a strong impulse in running off with Silva; desire moves her to leave the familiar, secure world of the pueblo and her family to walk a new and daring road. She opens her story in the morning, after she and Silva first made love:

> My thigh clung to his with dampness, and I watched the sun rising up through the tamaracks and willows . . . I could hear the water, almost at our feet where the narrow fast channel bubbled and washed green ragged moss and fern leaves. I looked at him beside me, rolled in the red blanket on the white river sand. . . .

She does not awaken to the proverbial harsh light of morning awash in guilt, but to a newly, more vibrantly alive world of sensation within and around her. But this is a world which, like Silva himself, is as frightening in its strength and intensity as it is seductive, and when Silva awakens she tells him she is leaving:

> He smiled now, eyes still closed. "You are coming with me, remember?" He sat up now with his bare dark chest and belly in the sun. "Where?" "To my place." "And will I come back?" He pulled his pants on. I walked away from him, feeling him behind me and smelling the willows. "Yellow Woman," he said. I turned to face him, "Who are you?" I asked.

Last night, he reminds her, "you guessed my name, and you knew why I had come." Their lovemaking made her intuitively aware of another, more vital level of being, one which had been within her all along, nurtured since childhood by her grandfather's Yellow Woman stories—and she knew she was Yellow Woman and her lover the dangerous mountain ka'tsina who carries her off.

But imaginative seeing on this morning after is threatening to the narrator, for seeing oneself whole demands eradication of those perceptual boundaries which offer the security of a readily discernible, if severely limited, sense of self. The narrator clings to that historical, time-bound sense of self like a child to her mother's skirts on the first day of school. "I'm not really her," she maintains, not really

Yellow Woman. "I have my own name and I come from the pueblo on the other side of the mesa." It is not so much "confusion about what is dream and what is fact" that besets her here as it is the fear of losing that reality which has heretofore defined her—and him. As they walk she thinks to herself:

> I will see someone, eventually I will see someone, and then I will be certain that he [Silva] is only a man—some man from nearby—and I will be sure that I am not Yellow Woman. Because she is from out of time past and I live now and I've been to school and there are highways and pickup trucks that Yellow Woman never saw. . . .

Jim Ruppert is right, I think, when he says that the narrator "struggles to . . . establish time boundaries and boundaries between objective reality and myths," and that struggle is part of the learning process she undergoes in the story. Newly awakened to her own imaginative potential, she has yet to discern the proper relationship between experiential reality and the timeless, all-inclusive mythic reality of her grandfather's stories.

Her desire, however, is stronger than her fear. After they reach his cabin, eat, and she looks out over the world from the mountain, Silva unrolls the bedroll and spreads the blankets. She hesitates, and he slowly undresses her. There is compulsion, this time, on his part, and fear on hers, but she is held to him more by her own passion than by his force. When she does leave, during their confrontation with a rancher who, rightly, accuses Silva of stealing cattle, it is at his command. "I felt sad at leaving him," she recalls, and considers going back, "but the mountains were too far away now. And I told myself, because I believe it, that he will come back sometime and be waiting again by the river."

She returns home. Yellow Woman stories usually end that way. And as she approaches her house, A. Lavonne Ruoff tells us, "she is brought back to the realities of her own life by the smell of supper cooking and the sight of her mother instructing her grandmother in the Anglo art of making Jell-O." The details here suggest a world governed more by routine than by passion, a world somewhat at odds with itself, as mother instructing grandmother suggests, and a world no longer receptive to the wonder and wisdom of the old stories. Having sensed this, she "decided to tell them that some Navajo had kidnapped me." But the unnamed narrator here, like the unnamed Eskimo girl in "Storyteller," keeps the oral tradition alive by going on her own journey of self-discovery—a journey born of acknowledging the rightful demands of passion and imagination—and by intuitively accepting the guidance of her grandfather's stories. Her life itself has become part of a visionary drama to be completed by Silva's return, and within that context it has gained fullness and meaning. Her recognition, in the story's final sentence, that hers is a Yellow Woman story—and that she is Yellow Woman—reveals as much. She has come to see herself, in Momaday's words, "whole and eternal" and like Momaday when, on his journey, he came out upon the northern plains, she will "never again . . . see things as [she] saw them yesterday or the day before."

Cottonwood, which follows "Yellow Woman," is in two parts, each a poetic rendering of a Laguna Yellow Woman story; taken together, these poems and Silko's story provide a richer, more inclusive perspective than they do separately on both the relationship between oral tradition and the written word and Silko's use of the Yellow Woman character.

The focus in "Yellow Woman" is on the unnamed woman narrator. She tells her own story, which concerns her evolving consciousness of who she is, and though that story has definite communal implications, its focus is interior and personal. *Cottonwood*, however, though undeniably Silko's creation, derives directly from the oral tradition and retains that tradition's communal perspective. Neither "Story of Sun House" nor "Buffalo Story," the poems that comprise *Cottonwood*, deal with character development or internal conflict any more than do the stories on which they are based. Rather each poem underscores the communal consequences of Yellow Woman's action, and in each case those consequences are positive. Given the narrator's references within "Yellow Woman" to the grandfather's Yellow Woman stories—indeed, Silko's story ends with such a reference—the *Cottonwood* poems, placed where they are, suggest that however offensive her actions may be to conventional morality, the narrator brings from her journey with Silva a boon for her people.

"Story of Sun House" ends as follows: "Cottonwood, / cottonwood. / So much depends / upon one in the great canyon." It is this tree, "among all the others" where Yellow Woman came to wait for the sun. Like the lone cottonwood, Yellow Woman too has been singled out, and much depends upon her as well. She is called by the Sun to journey to Sun House, and this involves the loss of what is familiar and secure and dear:

> She left precise stone rooms
> that hold the heart silently

> She walked past white corn
> hung in long rows from roof beams
> the dry husks rattled in a thin autumn wind.
> She left her home
> her clan
> and the people
> (three small children
> the youngest just weaned
> her husband away cutting firewood)....

The sacrifice is great, and in the spare yet powerfully evocative images of these lines Silko conveys the intense pain of separation. Her versification here, with "home," "clan," and "people" isolated in separate lines and children and husband further isolated in parentheses to the right, makes such pain almost palpable, as does the southeastward movement of the verse as it mirrors her journey toward the sun. Such "drastic things," however, "must be done / for the world / to continue." Harmony between the people and the spirit powers of the universe is necessary to existence and, through her marriage to the Sun, Yellow Woman perpetuates this harmony. The "people may not understand" her going; the visionary is invariably misunderstood. But that does not deter her, for she goes "out of love for this earth...."

The narrator in "Yellow Woman," too, restores an essential harmony through her going— a going which is also likely to be misunderstood. Her experience in living the reality revealed in her grandfather's stories has shown her the oneness of past and present, of historical and mythic time, and of the stories and the people. More, she has given the people another story and that, too, "must be done / for the world / to continue...."

Yellow Woman brings about good in "Buffalo Story" as well, and in a sense its link with Silko's short story is even stronger than that of "Story of Sun House." Like "Sun House," it enriches the short story by locating it for the reader within the necessary cultural and communal context, but "Buffalo Story" is itself enriched by the individualistic perspective cast forward upon it by "Yellow Woman." "Buffalo Story" follows the abduction storyline somewhat more closely than does "Story of Sun House" and evokes the sexual aspects of the traditional Yellow Woman stories more insistently. During a time of drought, when game is scarce and crops cannot grow, Yellow Woman, looking for water for her family, comes to a churning, muddy pool. At first she fears that a great animal had fouled the water. Then

> She saw him.
> She saw him tying his leggings
> drops of water were still shining on his chest.
> He was very good to look at
> and she kept looking at him
> because she had never seen anyone like him.
> It was Buffalo Man who was very beautiful....

She has ventured far from her village, as has the narrator in "Yellow Woman," and the intense sexual pull Buffalo Man has on her here recalls that of Silva on the narrator. When Arrowboy, her husband, finds her asleep and calls to her to run to him so that they might escape the Buffalo People, to whose country Buffalo Man had abducted her, "She seemed to / get up a little slowly / but he didn't think much of it then." Her slowness here, he later learns, is not due to fatigue. After he kills all the Buffalo People, he tells Yellow Woman to go tell the people that there is meat, but she refuses to come down from the cottonwood which they had climbed to escape the Buffalo People's pursuit. Arrowboy sees that she is crying and asks her why:

> "Because you killed them,"
> she said.
> "I suppose you love them,"
> Estoy-eh-muut [Arrowboy] said,
> "and you want to stay with them."
> And Kochininako nodded her head
> and then he killed her too....

Paula Gunn Allen, while acknowledging the underlying centrality of oral tradition in the lives of tribal people, nonetheless maintains that "the oral tradition is often deceptive in what it makes of the lives of women." She says that

> so cleverly disguised are the tales of matricide, abduction and humiliation that the Indian woman is likely to perceive consciously only the surface message of the beauty, fragility, and self-sacrificing strength of her sisters though she cannot help but get the more destructive message that is the point of many tribal tales.

Such a "destructive message" is at least potentially present in the "Buffalo Man" story in Boas' *Keresan Texts*, but Silko casts the killing of Yellow Woman in "Buffalo Story" in a much different light. In Boas' version, when Arrowboy explains to Yellow Woman's father why he killed her, the Chief says, "Indeed? ..." "All right," said he, "never mind." His response seems to justify the killing. In "Buffalo Story" her father, though implicitly accepting the justice of what was done cries and mourns. Moreover, in Silko's rendering we are told that "It was all because / one time long ago / our daughter, our sister Kochininako / went away with them" that the people were fed and buffalo hunting began. Yellow Woman here is not an adultress who deserted her people but rather remains "our daughter, our sister," whose journey, like her journey in "Story of Sun House," brought good to her people.

The context here established by the written word—Silko's short story—is essential in helping us to see Yellow Woman more completely than do the traditional stories alone, just as those stories in turn provide the necessary cultural context for "Yellow Woman." Through the narrator's telling in Silko's story, the individual dimension predominates and personal longings are shown to be as powerful and worthwhile as communal needs. Silko well knows, as the *Cottonwood* poems make clear, that individual sacrifice is at times crucial to community survival. But, as "Yellow Woman" reveals, individual fulfillment can be equally important to a tribal community, especially in the modern world where acculturation pressures are perhaps greater than ever before. Silko shows us, in this opening sequence of the "Yellow Woman" section, that personal and communal fulfillment need not be mutually exclusive—that they in fact enhance each other. And, by extension, the same is true of oral tradition and the written word as ways of knowing and of expression. To attain this harmony requires a powerful and inclusive vision, one receptive both to internal and external demands and the diverse languages which give them meaning. The development of such a vision, and of the network of relationships to the land, the people, the stories, and oneself it fosters, is, as I have said, the controlling idea of what I have called the "Yellow Woman" section of *Storyteller*, and it is expressed in various ways in the narrative episodes that follow.

The five short pieces that follow "Yellow Woman" and the *Cottonwood* poems focus on learning to see the land rightly and developing the proper relationship to it. This learning process is implicit in the narrator's experience in "Yellow Woman," both in her journey with Silva up the mountain and in the precise, evocative detail in which she describes particular aspects of the landscape; it becomes refined describes particular aspects of the landscape; it becomes refined and expanded in these brief narratives. In the first one, a poem entitled "The Time We Climbed Snake Mountain," the narrator is a teacher who knows the mountain intimately and knows that "Somewhere around here / yellow spotted snake is sleeping": "So / please, I tell them / watch out, / don't step on the spotted yellow snake / he lives here. / The mountain is his." "Them" are never identified, but that is unimportant because this kind of teaching has been going on for thousands of years. It is a simple lesson in perspective and respect.

What follows is a personal reminiscence which in a different way reinforces this lesson. It is of Silko's girlhood when she first learned to hunt, and through her telling we learn something of how she began to acquire the wisdom she hands down in "The Time We Climbed Snake Mountain." Hunting alone one day Silko saw, or thought she saw, a "giant brown bear lying in the sun below the hilltop. Dead or just sleeping, I couldn't tell." She "knew there were no bears that large on Mt. Taylor; I was pretty sure there were no bears that large anywhere," and she also knew "what hours of searching for motion, for the outline of a deer, for the color of a deer's hide can do to the imagination." Almost paralyzed with caution and curiosity, eager to examine the bear up close but unsure if it is dead or is just sleeping or is at all, she walks, "as quietly and as carefully as I probably will ever move," away from it. As she goes she looks back, still unsure of what she has seen, and "the big dark bear remained there. . . ." "I never told anyone what I had seen," Silko laughingly recalls, "because I knew they don't let people who see such things carry .30–30s or hunt deer with them. . . ."

That the bear impressed itself deeply on her imagination, however, is apparent as she recalls another hunting trip which took place two years after the first one. Her uncle had killed a big mule deer, and, as Silko went to help him, she realized that it was the same time of day as when she saw, or thought she saw, the bear:

> I walked past the place deliberately. I found no bones, but when a wind moved through the light yellow grass that afternoon I hurried around the hill to find my uncle. Sleeping, not dead, I decided. . . .

At this point, there is no longer any doubt in her mind that the bear was real; and her use of poetic form further suggests that this place where she saw the great bear has become part of an inner as well as an outer landscape. Through an act of imagination she has learned a profound truth from the land which intensifies her bond to it.

The photograph which separates these two reminiscences reinforces this idea. In it, laid out on the porch of the old cabin in which Silko and her hunting party stayed on Mt. Taylor, are five mule deer bucks, prayer feathers tied to their antlers, Silko herself, and her Uncle Polly. She and her uncle had just finished "arranging the bucks . . . so they can have their pictures taken." Given the "special significance" of photographs to her family and to the people of Laguna, the careful arrangement of the deer, and the prayer feathers, we are prepared for the subtle revelation in her second reminiscence. Her vision of the bear, like the deer, was a gift to help the people survive. It was the intimate expression of the land to her imagination of its own spiritual integrity and that of its creatures. Through the mystery and wonder of her seeing, the land, impressed itself indelibly upon her memory.

Two photographs follow the second bear reminiscence. The first, discussed earlier, is of hills and mesas that no longer exist and, placed where it is in *Storyteller*, the photograph movingly conveys the need, more important now than ever before, for all people to know the land as the place that gives us being and the source of our profoundest wisdom. It reminds us, as does *Storyteller* as a whole, about the oral tradition—of the fragility of what was once thought whole and eternal and of how much all life ultimately depends on imagination and memory. The second photo, taken from the east edge of Laguna looking toward the west, enhances this idea by showing us the place from which the stories in *Storyteller*, old and contemporary, arise. What follows is a series of such stories and reminiscences unified not by subject or theme but by the shared landscape that nurtured them. They express the richness, diversity, playfulness and humor of Laguna oral tradition. Like the first of these two photographs, they also express its fragility.

The first story which follows these photographs is a poetic retelling of a hunting story Silko, when a child of seven, heard from her Aunt Alice. It flows smoothly out of the photograph of Laguna in that it endows a particular portion of the land with mystery and wonder, and by so doing makes it a gift of and to the imagination. Though she heard this story six years before she saw the great bear on a hunting trip, the story flows out of her recollection of this experience as well; and by using cyclic rather than chronological structure, she more strikingly evokes, as with the "Yellow Woman" and *Cottonwood* sequence, the timeless significance of the oral tradition to the understanding of human experience. Told, as are other such stories in the book, in the conversational accents and occasional expository digressions of the traditional storyteller, the story is again of Yellow Woman, here a young girl and a fine hunter who, having gotten seven big rabbits in a morning's hunting, comes upon "a great big animal" who asks for one of her rabbits, which he immediately devours. The animal's demands escalate with his appetite and they are rendered by Silko in a compellingly dramatic sequence as the animal, having demanded and received all the girl's rabbits and weapons, insists upon her clothes as well. Rightly fearful that she herself will be next, little Yellow Woman fools the animal into letting her remove her clothes in a cave too small for him to enter. Knowing, however, that her escape is at best temporary, she calls upon the twin Brothers, Ma'see'wi and Ou'yu'ye'wi, who kill the animal with their flint knives. They then cut the animal open, pull out his heart, and throw it. At this point in the telling the legend melds with contemporary reality, myth enters experience, as we are told that the heart landed "right over here / near the river / between Laguna and Paguate / where the road turns to go / by the railroad tracks / right around / from John Paisano's place— / that big rock there / looks just like a heart, / . . . and that's why / it is called / Yash'ka / which means 'heart'. . . ."

By telling this story to her seven year-old niece, who is disappointed at not having been allowed to join her parents on a hunting trip, Aunt Alice both entertains and teaches. She raises the child's self-esteem by showing her that young girls can be skillful and clever hunters, alerts the prospective young hunter to the unexpected dangers that at times confront a hunter, reassures her that such obstacles, however dangerous, may be overcome, and perhaps most importantly, helps her niece to see the land with the same sense of wonder and joy with which she heard the story. A part of the landscape heretofore ordinary and unremarked has by means of the story been made precious to the child. Six years later, when she sees the giant bear, Silko will have her own hunting story to tell—and Aunt Alice's story will be recalled anew, recreated as it is here, richer and truer than ever.

The story told by a loving aunt of a special place engenders a reminiscence of another place which is special because of the woman who may, or may not, be buried there. With this reminiscence Silko shifts her focus from the land per se to the people—more precisely, to how people get remembered. This reminiscence concerns two women. Silko's great-grandmother, Helen, was born of an old traditional family, and Silko recalls that "even as a very young child / I sensed she did not like children much and so I remember her / from a distance . . . ." Much dearer to memory is a woman Silko never knew, old Juana, of whom Silko learned from the stories of Grandma Lillie, one of Helen's daughters. Juana, who "raised Grandma Lillie and her sisters / and brothers," was not born into a "genteel tradition" as was Grandma Helen. A Navajo, "Juana had been kidnapped by slavehunters / who attacked her family...." Stripped of her family, of whom no trace remained, her language, and her heritage, Juana "continued with the work she knew" and was eventually hired by Silko's Grandpa Stagner to care for his family. Silko recalls going on Memorial Day with Grandma Lillie to take flowers to Juana's grave. The graveyard where she was buried was old and the "small flat sandstones" which served as grave markers were mostly broken or covered over; as a result Grandma Lillie could never be certain if they found her grave—"but we left the jar of roses and lilacs we had cut anyway." Juana's actual presence, like the giant bear's in the earlier hunting story, is ultimately irrelevant. As the bear lives in Silko's imagination, so Juana lives in her, and in Grandma Lillie's heart, where they have more perfect being. Though orphaned young, Juana is restored through the stories to a family, language, and heritage.

Juana is remembered for her loving kindness, but that is not the only way people get remembered. The tone shifts rather suddenly from the reminiscence about Juana to two "gossip" stories, both of them rich in humor and irony. The first story, of a man caught en flagrante in a cornfield by his wife and her two sisters, and Silko's telling of it—in which she uses the storyteller's conversational tone and shifts the point of view from the two lovers to the wife and sisters and then to the man alone—express a delicious comic blend of conspiracy, anticipation, antagonism and resignation. She dramatically sets the scene: "His wife had caught them together before / and probably she had been hearing rumors again / the way people talk." The lovers planned to meet in the afternoon, when it was so hot that "everyone just rested" until evening, when it was cool enough to return to work. "This man's wife was always / watching him real close at night / so afternoon was / the only chance they had." When they were caught the woman left, and the man had to take the inevitable chastisement alone. His "wife would cry a little," her sisters would comfort her, "and then they would start talking again / about how good their family had treated him / and how lucky he was. / He couldn't look at them / so he looked at the sky / and then over at the hills behind the village." Though the man's inability to look at the women may suggest guilt, his wandering gaze has something of boredom in it, as if he were merely playing a role in an ancient and rather tiresome domestic ritual. His manhood is not spared, as the women are quick to remind him that his lover "had a younger boyfriend / and it was only afternoons that she had any use / for an old man":

So pretty soon he started hoeing weeds again
because they were ignoring him
like he didn't matter anyway
now that
that woman was gone....

The irony here is rich. The man, it seems, is important to his wife and relatives, and perhaps to the community as a whole, only by virtue of his infidelity. It is this by which he lives in a communal memory, enriches the storytelling life of the people, and gains mythic dimension. Apart from that context he "didn't matter."

"Then there was the night," Silko gleefully continues, whetting our appetite for the story of old man George who, on a trip to the outhouse, "heard strange sounds / coming from one of the old barns / below." Checking, "just in case some poor animal / was trapped inside," the old man is shocked to discover Frank,

so respectable and hard-working
and hardly ever drunk—
well there he was
naked with that Garcia girl—
you know,
the big fat one.
And here it was
the middle of winter
without their clothes on!...

Silko's tone here expresses two points of view simultaneously. George, to say the least, is surprised to find a man like Frank in this situation and Silko, as storyteller, relishes the irony. Further, she creates the proper context here by giving us, through her "you know" aside, a sense of her immediate audience—another young person, perhaps, to whom Frank would be cited by conventional morality as an example to follow. "Poor old man George / he didn't know what to say," and his befuddlement is comically rendered in the story's closing lines: "so he just closed the door again / and walked back home—he even forgot where he was going / in the first place." But he'll remember Frank and the Garcia girl.

It may at first glance seem strange that these stories are followed by a brief recollection of Grandma A'mooh and the way she read the children's book *Brownie the Bear* to her great-granddaughters, especially since "Storytelling," which follows, consists of six vignettes largely in the same vein as the "gossip" stories. This reminiscence, however, mentioned earlier in another context, is wonderfully appropriate here. Taken in conjunction with the "gossip" stories that surround it, it reminds us again of the variety and inclusiveness of the oral tradition. It also underscores Silko's intent throughout *Storyteller* to convey the dynamic relationship between the oral tradition and the life it expresses. The life of a community, or of an individual, does not arrange itself into precise categories, literary or otherwise, nor does it follow neat, unbroken lines of development; and Silko, by juxtaposing different kinds of narratives and subjects, helps us to see vital, rewarding connections that might otherwise go unnoticed. Remember, too, that her emphasis in the "Grandma A'mooh" reminiscence is on how a story is told. A good story cannot exist apart from a good storyteller. Much of the fun of the "gossip" stories, as we have seen, is in Silko's manner of telling them. Grandma A'mooh

> always read the story with such animation and
>   expression
> changing her tone of voice and inflection
> each time one of the bears spoke—
> the way a storyteller would have told it. . . .

Her telling makes the story live, recreates it in effect with each repetition. This is what Silko, in the "gossip" stories as well as in others, tries to do, to give a sense of the flux and immediacy of life lived. Too, it is her telling which links Grandma A'mooh to past generations of storytellers—as it does Silko.

The six vignettes in "Storytelling," all variations on the Yellow Woman abduction stories, bring what I have called the "Yellow Woman" section of *Storyteller* full circle. The first of these is Silko's abbreviated rendering of the opening of the "Buffalo Story," when Yellow Woman goes for water:

> "Are you here already?"
> "Yes," he said.
> He was smiling.
> "Because I came for you."
> She looked into the
> shallow clear water.
> "But where shall I put my water jar?". . . .

In this version Yellow Woman is apparently expecting Buffalo Man, and though coercion might be implied when he says he came for her, her response is willing, even coy and playful. The tone of the fifth vignette is quite similar:

> Seems like
> its always happening to me.
> Outside the dance hall door
> late Friday night
> in the summertime.
> and those

> brown-eyed men from Cubero,
> smiling.
> The usually ask me
> "Have you seen the way the stars shine
> up there in the sand hills?"
> And I usually say "No. Will you show me?". . . .

Silko alerts us as "Storytelling" begins that we "should understand / the way it was / back then, / because it is the same / even now." The traditional stories, Silko is saying, both here and throughout *Storyteller*, offer profound and necessary insights into contemporary experiences. Specifically, the "Yellow Woman" stories, especially Silko's renderings of them, are among other things open, unqualified expressions of woman's sexuality. This is not to say that, because the traditional stories are abduction stories, Silko is dealing in rape fantasies. Quite the contrary. In her versions the coercive element, though present, is not the controlling one. Yellow Woman is at all times in charge of her own destiny. She understands and accepts her sexuality, expresses it honestly, and is guided by her own strong desire. We see this in Silko's short story, "Yellow Woman," in the *Cottonwood* stories, and again in these two "Storytelling" vignettes. By focusing in these little narratives not on the love-making but on the prelude to it, Silko establishes the sexual integrity of both the mythic and contemporary Yellow Woman, and conveys with playful subtlety the charged eroticism between them and Buffalo Man and "those / brown-eyed men from Cubero" respectively.

Yellow Woman's sexual integrity gets a broadly comic touch in the fourth vignette, where Silko inverts the traditional abduction motif. The F.B.I. and state police in the summer of 1967 pursued a red '56 Ford with four Laguna women and three Navajo men inside. A kidnapping was involved, and the police followed a trail "of wine bottles and / size 42 panties / hanging in bushes and trees / all along the road." When they were caught, one of the men explained: "'We couldn't escape them' . . . / 'We tried, but there were four of them and / only three of us'. . . ."

But sexual honesty, especially a woman's, is, as we have seen, likely to be misunderstood. In the first *Cottonwood* poem, "Story of Sun House," the Sun tells Yellow Woman that even though their union is necessary for the world to continue, "the people may not understand"; and the narrator in "Yellow Woman" must make up a story for her family about being kidnapped by Navajo. In fact, the abduction motif of the Yellow Woman stories proves useful, or almost so, in a number of situations. "No! that gossip isn't true," says a distraught mother in the third "Storytelling" vignette: "She didn't elope / She was *kidnapped* by / that Mexican / at Seama Feast. / You know / my daughter / isn't / *that* kind of girl." As was stated earlier, however, there cannot be a good story without a good storyteller, as the contemporary Yellow Woman of the sixth vignette learns. "It was / that Navajo / from Alamo, / you know, / the tall / good-looking / one," she tells her husband. "He told me / he'd kill me / if I didn't / go with him." That, rain, and muddy roads, she said, are why "it took me / so long / to get back home." When her husband leaves her, she blames herself: "I could have told / the story / better than I did. . . ."

In a *Sun-Tracks* interview, Silko said of "these gossip stories": "I don't look upon them as gossip. The connotation is all wrong. These stories about goings-on, about what people are up to, give identity to a place." What she argues for here is in effect what the "Yellow Woman" section is all about: a new way of seeing. Seen rightly, such stories are neither idle rumor nor trivial chatter, but are rather another mode of expression, a way in which people define themselves and declare who they are. Thus it is fitting that the "Yellow Woman" section, and this essay, conclude with a photograph taken of some of the houses in Laguna. Here, after all, is where the people live their lives and it is this sense of life being lived, of life timeless and ongoing, changing and evolving, contradictory and continuous, that Silko expresses with grace and power through her melding of oral tradition and the written word in *Storyteller*.

Source: Bernard A. Hirsch, "'The Telling Which Continues': Oral Tradition and the Written Word in Leslie Marmon Silko's 'Storyteller,'" in American Indian Quarterly, Vol. 12, No. 1, 1988, pp. 1–25.

Sources

Jaskoski, Helen, "To Tell a Good Story," an essay in *Leslie Marmon Silko: A Collection of Critical Essays*, edited by Louise K. Barnett and James L. Thorson, University of New Mexico Press, 1999, 87–100.

Krumholz, Linda, "Native Designs: Silko's 'Storyteller' and the Reader's Initiation," an essay in *Leslie Marmon Silko: A Collection of Critical Essays*, edited by Louise K. Barnett and James L. Thorson, University of New Mexico Press, 1999, 63–86

Silko, Leslie Marmon, *Laguna Woman*, Greenfield Review Press, 1974.

Erdrich, Louise, "Where I Ought to Be: A Writer's Sense of Place," in *The New York Times Book Review*, July 28, 1985: 1+.

Further Reading

Seyersted, Per, *Leslie Marmon Silko*, Western Writers Series, 45, Boise State University, 1980.
>This text offers a short biography of Silko. It is good for information about her social and cultural milieu and early writing days. No other biography, as yet, exists.

Brown, Dee, *Bury My Heart at Wounded Knee; an Indian History of the American West*, Holt, Rinehart & Winston, 1970.
>Brown's book is a classic in Native American letters. It is a moving account of U.S. history from the point of view of Native Americans.

Lincoln, Kenneth, *Native American Renaissance*, University of California Press, 1983.
>Lincoln's book provides an overview of the figures, goals, and achievements of the Renaissance.

Anzaldua, Gloria, *Borderlands/La Frontera: The New Mestiza*, Spinsters/Aunt Lute, 1987
>Anzaldua's book is a cultural and feminist theory that speaks to the cultural "borderlands" of the U.S. Southwest. Anzaldua describes cultures forming at the borders and exchanges of distinct cultures.

Wong, Hertha Dawn, "Contemporary Innovations of Oral Traditions: N. Scott Momaday and Leslie Marmon Silko," in *Sending My Heart Back across the Years: Tradition and Innovation in Native American Autobiography*, Oxford University Press, 1992, 153–99.
>This dense chapter details how the two writers engage with the oral traditions of their cultures. An attempt to deal with the issues inherent in writing published print literature about oral storytellers.

Women in Their Beds

Gina Berriault

1996

Gina Berriault's short story "Women in Their Beds" was published in a collection of the same name in 1996, when the author was seventy. This volume of new and selected stories represented a breakthrough for Berriault, who had worked steadily at her craft for forty years but, up to this point, had received little critical attention. *Women in Their Beds* was widely praised in the press and won a number of prestigious national literary awards. In his effusive review of the collection, Lynell George of the *Los Angeles Times Book Review* writes, "In stories that are part trance, part cinema, Gina Berriault writes about the beds we make and are forced to lie in."

The title story, set in San Francisco in the late 1960s, describes the experiences of a young actress, Angela Anson, who has a day job as a social worker at the county hospital. She carries out the duty of assigning patients on the women's ward to beds at other institutions, but otherwise resists her role as a cog in the bureaucracy, identifying strongly with the downtrodden and lonely women on the ward. Meditating on the patients, Angela makes imaginative connections between the destinies that all women share, forming a theory that women are "inseparable from their beds." "Women in Their Beds" has a dreamlike logic that blurs the boundaries between self and other, fact and feeling, drama and reality. The story showcases Berriault's greatest strengths as a writer: the precise beauty of her language, the vivid comparisons she draws between perception

and reality, and the enormous compassion with which she represents her characters.

Author Biography

Berriault was born in Long Beach, California, in 1926, the youngest of her Russian-Jewish immigrant parents' three children. Her father worked as an ad solicitor and a writer for trade magazines. Berriault began to write stories on her father's typewriter when she was still a child. She was, from a young age, independent and self-motivated. In an interview with Bonnie Lyons and Bill Oliver in the *Literary Review*, she describes transcribing passages from great literature when she was a child, "to see the words coming out of my typewriter. It was like a dream of possibilities for my own self."

The family fell on rough times in Berriault's teenage years. When they lost their house, Berriault dreamed of earning enough with her writing to buy the family a farm. Her mother began to go blind when Berriault was fourteen. Her father, whom Berriault describes to Lyons and Oliver as a "mentor for my spirit," died when she was in high school. At this point Berriault had aspirations of being an actress, and a teacher had offered to pay her tuition at a drama school, but Berriault declined in order to help support the family by taking over her father's trade writing business. After high school she received no further formal education, but remained an avid reader and dedicated writer while she worked at odd jobs including clerk, waitress, and journalist.

Berriault began to publish her short fiction in popular and literary magazines in the late 1950s and her first novel, *The Descent*, was published in 1960. Though she gained little popular attention, her work was much admired by fellow writers. She began to earn a living as a writing teacher and was also the recipient of a number of fellowships. Berriault published three other novels and several volumes of short stories. She adapted one of her best known stories, "The Stone Boy," as a screenplay in 1984. In 1996 she published *Women in Their Beds*, which collected new and selected stories. This book won her great accolades, including the PEN/Faulkner Award, the National Book Critics Circle Award, and the Rea Award for the Short Story. With this book, the fruit of a forty-year career, Berriault finally rose from obscurity and came to be credited as one of the finest writers of her generation.

Berriault was by all accounts a private person, and little personal information about her has been made available. Her marriage to musician J. V. Berriault produced one child—daughter Julie Elena, born in 1955—and ended in divorce. Berriault lived most of her life in northern California, where she died in 1999.

Plot Summary

The story opens with Angela Anson—the protagonist—and two of her friends joking around by calling each other by the names of famous fictional doctors over the loudspeaker of a city hospital where they are all employed as social workers. It is San Francisco in the 1960s, and the events of the story take place against the background of the Vietnam War and the counterculture youth movement. Angela, who is a struggling actress, has been working on the women's ward of the hospital for only a few days. She has no credentials to work as a social worker. The atmosphere on the ward—where Angela's task is to report to the elderly and infirm women the public institutions where they will next be sent—has a strong impact on the sensitive young woman, who sees in the patients a reflection of the condition of women at large. She is not sure she will be able to stand the job.

Angela delivers to one middle-aged alcoholic woman the news that she will be sent to an undesirable "home" called Laguna Honda. The woman responds that her daughter will prevent it, but the daughter never comes to advocate for her mother. This makes Angela think back on visiting her own mother in a hospital ward in another city and the grief involved in the severing of mother-daughter bonds. Angela tries to reassure the woman that there might be other options, but this is futile. Later she sees the woman thrashing in her bed in the midst of alcohol withdrawal, which looks to Angela like the woman is trying to run away.

She talks to another patient who reminds her of a sickly old aunt she visited as a child who, her mother told her, had once been beautiful. She tries to picture the women on the ward as they had been when they were girls, but she can't. She tells this to Nancy, the head nurse, who doesn't understand why she would bother.

Gina Berriault

Angela tells Dan her theories about women and beds. That night, against hospital rules, she helps a teenage girl who has just attempted suicide to use a bedpan. She recalls her own suicide attempt at sixteen. She then goes to visit the psychiatric ward where she observes a psychiatrist, whom she calls "The Judge," determine where patients should be assigned upon admission, and remembers having waited on him when she worked as a caterer.

Angela accompanies a dwarflike woman as she is discharged from the hospital. She is a cleaning woman who had gotten pneumonia. Her young son, who has an extra finger on each hand, had stayed at the hospital with her because there was no one else to care for him. A young doctor asks to see the cleaning woman's hands and questions her about her son's birth defect. She explains that they were cursed. Angela later complains to Lew about the doctor's lack of insight into his patients' lives. Lew cautions her never to take a deep breath while at the hospital.

An old Gypsy woman who is a patient on the ward offers to read Angela's palm, telling her that she will live a long life and asking her if she is a "wayward girl." The next morning the Gypsy woman has taken a turn for the worse. Her numerous children and grandchildren gather around her.

When Angela returns to the ward later that afternoon the Gypsy woman has died. Her children ask for a candle. Angela looks around the hospital for one and even goes to the corner grocery, but cannot find one.

That night, in her own bed, Angela imagines telling the women at the hospital about her life and choices. She describes her life in terms of different beds in which she has lain—the linty bed she shares with her current lover in a basement apartment, the bed she shared with her first lover when she was fourteen, a bed at a home for unwed mothers. She thinks about the son she gave up for adoption in comparison to the devoted son of one of the patients. She imagines herself as an old woman on the ward, describing her life to a young social worker and meditating on the significance of beds in women's lives. Then she sees a candle in her bedroom and thinks about bringing it to the hospital.

The next morning she enters the women's ward holding the lit candle. Nurse Nancy asks her about it and she says it is for the Gypsy woman's children. Nurse Nancy dismisses this. When Angela says that other women on the ward might appreciate it, the nurse says that they haven't even noticed that the Gypsy woman is gone. The story ends with the nurse blowing out the candle and touching Angela ambiguously on the elbow and back.

Characters

Alcoholic Woman

One of Angela's patients is an alcoholic woman in her fifties. Angela surmises that she "must have run away from home at nine and kept on running." Angela tells her that she has been assigned for transfer to an undesirable public institution. The woman says that her daughter will come to the hospital and prevent it, but the daughter does not come. This reminds Angela of her relationship with her own mother and the grief of mother-child separation.

Angela's Lover

Angela's current lover is a painter. She is not in love with him. She describes him as a "friend, who is as much in need as myself of a friend to lie down with, make love with, share the rent with, share soup with, break bread with, and lie down with again." Sharing these things with him makes life easier but does not mitigate the loneliness she feels.

Angela Anson

Angela is the protagonist of the story, which is dominated by her outlook on the world. She is a struggling young actress living in bohemian San Francisco in the 1960s. She takes a job as a social worker on the women's ward of the city hospital and is deeply affected by her interactions with the patients there. Her job is to inform them of the next public institution where they will be sent, the next "bed" to which they have been assigned. However, she is unable to maintain any kind of clinical detachment, imagining pasts and futures for the women and bending hospital rules to accommodate their emotional needs. She starts to meditate on the relationship between women and their beds as a summation of the female experience, one that transcends her differences from the downtrodden women on the ward. In each of the sick women, she sees parts of herself—her past, her future, her relationships with her mother and her abandoned son. Angela's ability to see into the interior lives of the women patients is connected to her vocation as an actress, which requires imagining oneself as another person.

Cleaning Woman

Another of Angela's patients is a cleaning woman who has just recovered from pneumonia. She is so small that Angela, with her theatrical way of seeing the world, perceives her as a dwarf and a symbol of deprivation. A doctor questions the woman about her son, who has an extra finger on each hand. He asks to examine her hands, foreshadowing the Gypsy woman's reading of Angela's palm. The doctor is looking for a scientific rationale and doesn't understand her explanation that the extra fingers are due to a curse.

Dan

Dan is one of Angela's friends and coworkers. He has a master's degree in political science, has dissident views on Vietnam, and writes a political column for an underground weekly. Angela describes him as having "the kindest heart, the hardest head." He is witty and playful, joking with Angela and Lew at the hospital by calling them over the intercom by the names of famous fictional and historical doctors. She tells him some of her ideas about women and beds.

Gypsy Woman

An old Gypsy woman on the ward has a special fascination for Angela. Described as a "Gypsy queen," she is a powerful image of womanhood. The Gypsy Woman offers to read Angela's palm and tells her she will have a long life, then asks if she is a "wayward girl," which Angela attributes to her clothing and jewelry rather than her palm. This stands in contrast to the doctor's request to see the cleaning woman's hands; the Gypsy woman represents a more intuitive form of knowledge.

The next day the Gypsy woman takes a turn for the worse and her children and grandchildren, whom Angela admires, gather around her. Even though she dies, she avoids the isolation and disappointment that the other women exude. "Fear wasn't her bedmate here, Faith was and probably always would be."

The Judge

The Judge is the name Angela gives to the doctor who screens psychiatric patients upon admission to the hospital. His title suggests that this administrative power has a mythic force behind it. He assigns patients to their next "bed" and thus—according to the metaphorical logic of the story—to their destiny. Angela remembers meeting him in a different context: at a wedding reception where she had worked as a caterer. She observes his demeanor and imagines how she would play a judge on stage.

Lew

Lew is one of Angela's friends and coworkers. Like Angela, he is an actor. With Dan, he plays the prank of calling fake names over the intercom. She shares with him some of her critical and despairing ideas about the women's ward. Lew seems to "know everything before it was told him," but listens to her anyway. He advises her not to breathe too deeply at the hospital, suggesting that he understands how its atmosphere may be dangerous to her state of mind.

Nurse Nancy

Nurse Nancy is the head nurse on the women's ward. She discourages Angela from imagining the patients as girls or bringing them candles. A part of the cold medical system, she lacks Angela's imagination and therefore, also, her empathy for the patients. She is the only woman character with whom Angela doesn't establish a connection, except, perhaps, in the ambiguous closing lines, when she touches Angela "to assist her to stay on her feet and point her in the right direction" or, perhaps, out of "complicity."

Suicidal Girl

During one of Angela's shifts, she helps a young girl with a bedpan, though she is not supposed to do this in her capacity as a social worker. The girl has recently bungled a suicide attempt, and Angela is curious as to why she did it. She identifies with the girl's awkwardness, remembering her own secret suicide attempt as a teenager. Later, she visits the psychiatric ward, curious to see where the girl's next bed will be.

Young Doctor

A young doctor approaches the cleaning woman as she is about to be discharged from the hospital and asks to see her hands, curious about the medical cause of her son's extra fingers. He is described as "hyperactive" and "intense." Angela gets angry with him for his insensitivity toward his patients. He is blinded by his enthusiasm for medical knowledge, unable to see the complex ailments of his patients' spirits.

Themes

Sex Roles

The story is explicitly about women, but it touches on sex roles only indirectly. Berriault does not compare women's roles in society to men's so much as she explores women's common life experiences. At the hospital, Angela observes women in crisis and transition as she assigns them to new places, or "beds," at public institutions. Seeing the various women on the ward, all in their beds, makes Angela think back on formative moments in her own life—a visit with her mother, a suicide attempt, her first lover, the birth of a child. This leads her to form a theory about women's place in the world. "Now I see women as inseparable from their beds," she tells Dan. "Maybe beds are where women belong. Half the women in the world are right now in their bed, theirs or somebody else's, whether it's night or day, whether they want to be or not." She intimates that women are determined by the beds that they have chosen—or are made—to lie in.

Because men also get sick, have sex, and sleep, the idea that women are specially destined for beds must be understood as a metaphorical comment on women's place in society. Women are "inseparable from their beds" because the activities associated with them play a large role in forming women's identities. Beds are intimate places, where relationships with others are consummated, confirmed, contested, or sorely missed. Daytime rationality doesn't apply in beds, and things in beds have a dream-logic. Intimacy and irrationality are associated with femininity. This can be powerful, as in the case of the Gypsy woman who commands destiny through palm reading, but more often women go from bed to bed passively, not in charge of their own fates. Angela compares the rows of beds on the women's ward to those she sees on television of soldiers in Vietnam. "Over that other scene there was always a terrible struggle in the air, but in this women's ward there was a yielding to whoever was watching over them and to the medication that must seem like a persuasive stranger entering their most intimate being for their own good."

Life Cycle

When she starts working at the hospital, Angela tries to imagine the women on the ward when they were young, to "come to their rescue by reviving them as girls again." Later, she imagines herself as an old woman in a hospital bed: "Some night, some day, there'll be Angela Anson herself in your row, and what will I say to soften the heart of the social worker who I'll dislike at first sight?" By thinking of women's lives in terms of their beds, she sees connections between them at all points in the life cycle. The bed is a site of birth, sex, childbirth, sickness, and death. All of these are particularly important in determining who women are and how they experience the world.

These various transitions, which take place at different points in the life cycle, are to some degree interchangeable according to Angela's way of thinking. She sees similarities between these "beds" and imagines women moving through them continually. "Just remember the beds where you wished you weren't and the beds where you wished you were,

Topics for Further Study

- In the story, Angela develops a theory that beds have special significance to women. Summarize Angela's ideas about why women are "inseparable from their beds." Do you agree or disagree with her view of women's lives?

- Berriault offers the metaphor of "women in their beds" as a way of thinking about common experiences that all different kinds of women share. Try to come up with a symbol for the common experiences that all different kinds of *men* share. Explain why you chose this symbol.

- At the hospital, Angela, Lew, and Dan communicate by paging each other using the names of famous fictional and historical doctors. Berriault opens and then punctuates the action of the story with these names. Identify the doctors to whom Berriault alludes. Discuss how one or more of these figures reflects the themes of the story.

- Angela is an actress posing as a social worker. She often thinks about the hospital as if it were a kind of stage. How does Angela use acting techniques to help her understand the patients on the women's ward? Do you think that she overdramatizes things or is, in her own words, "carried away by her role"?

- "Women in Their Beds" takes place in San Francisco in the 1960s, against the backdrop of the antiwar movement and the other associated social protests. Do some research about the kinds of criticisms that young people leveled against social institutions in the counterculture movements of the 1960s. How does this context enrich your understanding of the story?

---

and then name any spot on this earth that's a bed for some woman," she says. She comes to see it as misguided that women try to control their lives by choosing the right bed, when their fates are so inescapably determined by their place in beds in general—including, ultimately, in the bed that is the grave. As a young woman, Angela looks back on previous beds and forward to prospective ones with some despair. She sees the women—the "dear alones" at the hospital—and, picturing her own end in a hospital bed, feels powerless before her fate.

Creativity and Imagination

Angela and her consorts, Dan and Lew, make light of their day jobs at the hospital by calling for each other using the names of fictional and historical doctors over the intercom. This is not the only way in which Angela treats the hospital as if it were a stage. She performs the clinical duties of a social worker—informing women of the next bed to which they have been assigned—but with the imagination of an actress. The hospital is an institution dominated by a rational and pragmatic mode of thought, as represented by Nurse Nancy, while Angela is creative and intuitive, attentive to the patients' injured "karmas" rather than their physical ailments. Angela sees human drama everywhere. She imagines life stories "unfolding" like the portable hospital beds. She envisions one patient as a dwarf "because of her theatrical tendency to recognize types from bygone centuries" and imagines an entire history for another: "This one . . . must've run away from home at nine and kept on running. The nights of her life on a bar stool till 2:00 AM and the last hours of the morning with a new-found friend, down in the dubious comfort of his bed." Part of what makes her capable of such flights of imagination is that her identity is very fluid; she identifies powerfully with the women she cares for, seeing correspondences between their lives and her own. For example, she has an imaginary conversation with this patient's daughter—who has never come to the hospital—sharing her feelings of grief about her own mother. While Angela might not be very tuned in to "reality" as a doctor or nurse would understand it, she has special insight—closer to that of the Gypsy—based on her intuitive and empathetic outlook.

Style

Narration

"Women in Their Beds" is narrated in the third-person—that is, from the point of view of someone who is not involved in the situation described. However, this narrator has a perspective very closely aligned with that of Angela Anson, the deeply absorbed protagonist. The narrator has complete access to and knowledge of Angela's inner thoughts and feelings, but not those of any of the other characters. Frequently, the narration switches from third-person description to Angela's interior monologue. The boundary between the narrator and Angela is very fluid, as is the boundary between Angela and the patients she encounters, and the effect is moody and introspective.

The narration reflects Angela's state of mind in great detail, while representing the external reality only in a fragmentary way. For example, when one patient begs Angela to advocate for her to be allowed to go home, Angela's speech is briefly quoted: "I'll ask again." Then the narration dips into Angela's consciousness, recounting her memory of an asking an arrogant doctor to help, exploring her motivation for doing this, and going on to describe how this patient has "humanized" her by reminding her of a visit to a sick aunt when she was a child. The scene concludes with Angela's thoughts about trying to imagine the patients as young girls. For Angela, the connection she feels with the women and the sorrow, pity, and insight that they evoke take precedence over the external and pragmatic concerns of the hospital. The narration closely reflects these priorities.

Structure

The plot of "Women in Their Beds" is not structured conventionally through the introduction of conflict, which rises in tension to a climax, then reaches resolution in a denouement. In fact, Angela's inner conflicts regarding her day job as a hospital social worker are relatively similar when she questions how long she can last at the job at the story's opening and when Nurse Nancy blows out the candle at the story's close. However, "Women in Their Beds" does have a structure—albeit a less traditional one. Like the experience of the women who move from bed to bed, the structure of the story is based on a pattern of repetition, contrast, and comparison. Objectivity (a view of truth as external and verifiable) is repeatedly contrasted with subjectivity (a view of truth based on personal, inner experience). Angela's empathetic and subjective view is set against that of the cold and distant medical personnel again and again. For example, when Angela sees the cleaning woman's hands, she imagines them curled around mop and vacuum cleaner handles, while the doctor examines them with only the science of genetics in mind. The story is also structured by the repeated comparison between "self" and "other," moving back and forth between Angela's experiences and those of the women on the ward. Angela encounters a series of women patients in their beds and relates parts of their lives to her own. Then, back in her own bed, she imagines herself as one of them. The story ends with death—the Gypsy woman's death and the symbolic death of empathy and imagination as represented by the blowing out of the candle. But in death there is still irresolution; as Angela sees it, the grave does not offer a grand conclusion, but is just another in a series of beds.

Symbolism

"Women in Their Beds" is named for Angela's symbolic way of thinking about the commonalties between women's lives. Her ideas about women and their beds are multifaceted. Beds are associated with sleep and dreams. They are an illogical space where ego boundaries become fluid. The women Angela meets are dreamlike figures, symbolizing aspects of her own past and future. As Angela assigns institutional beds to the women on the ward, she thinks about how women lack agency in their own lives. She forms a theory that women are "inseparable from their beds." Beds represent women's role in society, which is bound by their biological destiny and their most intimate relations with others. This relates to women's roles as sex objects and as child-bearers—both of which are potentially sources of power and joy but, in Angela's experience, more often sources of impotence and loss. The beds where women lie—for sex and sleep, in labor and sickness—sum up their fates. Beds suggest passivity: "And what about the beds you thought you'd chosen yourself? Do they now seem chosen for you? Destiny's hand patting them down. *Lie here, Lie here.*" On the women's ward, Angela glimpses her own fate, determined by the set of feminine roles that beds symbolize.

Beds are the dominant symbol in the story, but not the only one. According to Angela's way of thinking, things are always more than they seem, thus symbolism permeates the story. For example, the candles that the Gypsy woman's "archangelic" children request have great symbolic meaning for Angela. She does not know the particular role they play in the family's death ritual, but she has an implicit understanding of the importance of ritual. She identifies the candles with her own alternative lifestyle—she and her friends always light them. Candles represent a form of comfort and healing that the bureaucratic hospital is completely unable to offer. When Angela brings the candle to the hospital she is offering a symbol of the connection she feels with the women, most of whom are severely isolated, and of the continuities she sees among women and between life and death.

Historical Context

Youth Counterculture

"Women in Their Beds" takes place in the late 1960s, a period of great social upheaval in the United States. In 1966, the largest generation of Americans—the crest of the baby boom—reached legal age, and a youth-oriented counterculture was born. While the majority of these young people went on to college, work, marriage, and family, as had the conservative generation that came before them, an increasing and visible number began rebelling against the social rules and norms that governed American life. They were the counterculture, which means counter to or against the established, mainstream culture. These youthful rebels, often known as hippies, were critical of what they described as the Establishment—institutions including the police, schools, businesses, organized religion, and the traditional nuclear family. The characters' mockery of the doctors' status through their intercom prank can be seen in light of this antiestablishment outlook. Angela's more somber critical perspective on the bureaucratic hospital authorities is also counterculture in spirit.

Sometimes hippies' social criticisms were politically motivated; members of the youth counterculture were active in the powerful antiwar and civil rights movements of the era. (In the story, Dan writes articles expressing his dissident views on Vietnam.) Others hippies were more individual and philosophical in their approach—preaching peace and love, using drugs such as marijuana and LSD that were thought to broaden the mind, and adopting permissive sexual practices. Though based on strong criticisms of the greed and isolation of mainstream American life, the hippie movement was generally positive and even utopian in spirit. Young people believed that if they opened their minds and hearts they could bring about a true social revolution. Though Berriault sets her story at the heart of the hippie movement, she does not share this optimistic outlook.

The Sexual Revolution and Feminism

Berriault writes of her protagonist, Angela, "Anyone could spot her for a working hippie, a counterculture actress, a wayward girl." She is an actress living with her lover in San Francisco. San Francisco—and, in particular, a neighborhood called Haight-Ashbury or The Haight—was a center for the early counterculture movement. Few of the antimaterialist, anticapitalist hippies had steady jobs, so they lived modestly and shared what they had. Angela implies that she is living with her lover in order to share, among other things, the rent of their small basement apartment. The sexual permissiveness that would allow such an arrangement was central to the hippie movement, which promoted free love. When the Gypsy woman calls Angela a "wayward girl" she refers to her sexual accessibility.

One of the reasons it was possible for the idea of free love to come into currency was the development of the birth control pill. The Pill, which, when taken daily, is nearly 100 percent effective in preventing pregnancy, was approved by the FDA (Food and Drug Administration) in 1960. By 1967, about twenty percent of women of childbearing age were on the Pill. Use of the Pill among the women of the baby boom generation was even higher. On the Pill, young women were liberated from their fears of an unwanted pregnancy, giving rise to a much higher level of sexual experimentation. (Abortion, however, remained illegal until 1973.) Premarital sex became more common and, arguably, the Pill gave women a greater sense of social and sexual autonomy than they had ever before experienced. By those who saw their generation as ushering in a new age, the new, freer attitudes toward sex were celebrated as part of a Sexual Revolution.

The concept of free love was premised on the positive potential of permissive sexuality. At the same time that hippies began to preach free love, a "second wave" of feminism was forming that criticized sex roles in and out of the bedroom. (The "first wave" was in the 1920s.) In 1963, Betty Friedan's *The Feminine Mystique* gave voice to the dissatisfactions of a generation of housewives. By the end of the decade, women had won legal battles over wage parity and sex discrimination in the workplace. They also had begun to question the way they conducted their most intimate relationships. A slogan of the second-wave feminist movement was "the personal is political." Though it was largely a middle-class movement, one of the bases of its philosophy was the struggle against the universal oppression of women.

"Women in Their Beds" does not take up a specifically feminist agenda, but it does reflect the ideas about women circulating at the time. Angela lives her life as a "liberated" participant in the Sexual Revolution, but she recognizes the ways in which she shares with all women the burdens and pains of her sex role, which she sees as a kind of destiny. In contrast to the tenor of the feminist movement at large, Berriault is gentle in her representation of men in the story. Women are, on some level, oppressed—but men are not their oppressors. In a *Literary Review* interview with Bonnie Lyons and Bill Oliver, Berriault commented on her view of gender politics: "I've known and still know a fear of men's judgments and ridicule and rejection. At the same time I've been acutely aware of the oppression and abuse and humiliation that men endure and struggle against, the same that women endure and now know they don't have to endure. In other words, I'm a humanist, I guess."

Critical Overview

Berriault began to publish her fiction in the late 1950s, earning the praise of a few critics and the loyalty of a small but devoted group of readers. Her stories and novels portray a wide range of characters, but share a concern with situations of isolation and loss and themes contrasting subjective and objective views of the world. Some early reviewers found her writing too gloomy and criticized her novels for their lack of narrative momentum, but she was also admired for her ability to create complex, believable characters and to plumb the depths of the human heart. Her short stories, in particular, were singled out for their precise form and deep feeling. Berriault continued to write for over forty years in relative obscurity. She had the dubious honor of being viewed as a "writer's writer"—admired by her literary peers and considered by them to be one of the most unappreciated talents of her generation.

In 1996, when Berriault was seventy, she came out with *Women in Their Beds*, her third collection of short stories. The book, containing thirty-five new and selected stories, represented the best of Berriault's long career and, at last, brought Berriault into the literary spotlight. The collection won a number of prestigious national awards, including the PEN/Faulkner Award, the National Book Critics Circle Award, and the Rea Award for the Short Story. It was widely reviewed with practically unanimous high praise. Critics commended Berriault's ability to represent such a broad range of characters—male and female, young and old, rich and poor—with such accuracy and empathy. *Nation* reviewer Gary Amdahl expresses his admiration for Berriault for creating characters who are so different from most readers. "[Berriault] creates characters whom we emphatically do not recognize—or whom we recognize, rather, only in ways that have nothing to do with superficial similarities." Others also compliment Berriault's ability to enable readers to see the world from her diverse characters' points of view. The "elevation of the particular to the universal is the hallmark of Berriault's finely wrought stories," writes Donna Seaman in a *Booklist* review. In addition to reflecting the author's capacity for empathy, the collection was often praised for the beauty of its writing. "In these 35 stories, one struggles to find a sentence that is anything less than jewel-box perfect," writes Tobin Harshaw of the *New York Times Book Review*.

Several reviewers singled out the title story as representative of the Berriault's greatest talents. Seaman posits that "Women in Their Beds" "contains all the key elements of her metaphysical, compassionate fiction." Lynell George concluded his review in the *Los Angeles Times Book Review* with these comments, riffing on Berriault's own overarching metaphor: "Ghosts, impostors, pariahs, Berriault's characters move like somnambulists through their lives. These are the beds, prompts her protagonist from the title story, 'Where you wished you weren't and the beds where you wished you were. . . .' Memory recalls the rote particulars, but Gina Berriault's great gift is summoning the pitch and roll of restlessness within which we lie in them."

In an autobiographical statement appearing in editor John Wakeman's *World Authors, 1950–1970*, Berriault chooses to describe her motivation for writing rather than the events of her life.

> My work is an investigation of reality which is, simply, so full of ambiguity and of answers that beget further questions that to pursue it is an impossible task and a completely absorbing necessity. It appears to me that all the terrors that human beings inflict on one another are countered to a perceptible degree by the attempts of some writers to make us known to one another and thus to impart or revive a reverence for life.

Berriault goes on to list some of the writers who she believes achieve this feat. More than twenty years later, reviewing *Women in Their Beds* for the *Nation*, Amdahl praises Berriault for the very life-affirming quality that she spoke of admiring in others. "Berriault does not imitate, cater, affect or posture," he writes. "She deepens reality, complements it, and affords us the bliss of knowing, for a moment, what we cannot know."

Criticism

Sarah Madsen Hardy

Madsen Hardy has a doctorate in English literature and is a freelance writer and editor. In the following essay, she explores Berriault's representations of superstition in her story.

> *So she was ... Dr. Curie ... discoverer of so much that was undetectable and that might not even exist.*

Angela Anson, the sensitive young protagonist of Gina Berriault's "Women in Their Beds," doesn't like going to work. In fact, she is not sure that she will last at her job as a hospital social worker for more than a few days. And it's not just because the job assigning patients on the women's ward to their next "beds" at various public institutions is depressing, or because she is afraid that it will be discovered that she lacks the credentials for the job, though these things are also true. Angela suffers from a feeling of dread that is both more personal and more cosmic. She comprehends—and vicariously experiences—the frightening emotions of the patients themselves. For example, she implicitly understands one alcoholic patient's dread of an institution called Laguna Honda because of her own superstitious idea of the place, where she imagines ghostly "pale faces floating on deep black waters" whenever she drives by.

"Women in Their Beds," is structured, in part, through the contrast between pragmatic and superstitious outlooks on the world. The hospital setting is a space of science and bureaucracy, both of which are ultimately pragmatic in nature—that is, concerned with empirical rules of cause and effect. This cold practicality is represented by the figure of Nurse Nancy, who discourages and disapproves of Angela's lack of clinical distance from the patients. When Angela describes trying to imagine the patients when they were girls, Nancy asks pragmatically, "Why would you ever think to do that anyway?" In contrast, Berriault often describes Angela's feelings and perceptions in magical or, at least, specifically nonrational terms. A superstition is a belief held resulting from ignorance of the laws of nature or from faith in magic or chance. Superstitions rely on the belief in connections between things that can be empirically proven *not* to exist. For example, the common superstition, "Don't step on a crack or you'll break your mother's back," or Lew's less explicit warning to Angela about the dangerous atmosphere of the hospital, "Never take a deep breath in here." As represented by these examples, superstition often involves fear resulting from such irrational beliefs. The word "superstition" has a somewhat negative connotation, defined in opposition to a rational, science-based concept of truth that has been dominant in Western culture for centuries. However, most people hold some beliefs that are not strictly rational and certainly not provable—for example, the beliefs that go into any kind of religious faith or spirituality.

In "Women in Their Beds," Berriault explores a world of unprovable connections. She refers to superstition throughout the story, developing the idea through a pair of references to palmistry, otherwise known as palm reading. Palmistry, a superstitious practice that predicts a person's destiny based on the creases and lines in the palm of his or her hand, resonates with Angela's interest in tapping into the life histories of the patients, and embroiders on the story's theme of destiny as an unfolding series of beds. In two parallel and contrasting incidents, a palm is "read." In the first, a young doctor asks to see the hands of one patient, a cleaning woman, in order to discern the reason for her son's birth defect. In the next, another patient, an aged Gypsy woman, offers to read Angela's palm. The doctor and the Gypsy represent two opposing ideas of fate—one based on the empirical science of genetics, the other on the superstition and faith.

In the first scene, Angela is in the midst her own kind of intuitive "reading" of the cleaning woman, interpreting her diminutive stature as a symbol of

What Do I Read Next?

- *Conference of Victims* (1962), an early novel by Berriault, offers an indirect and ironic view of the effects of a man's suicide on those closest to him.

- *The Infinite Passion of Expectations: Twenty-Five Stories* (1982) is an acclaimed earlier collection of Berriault's subtle and compassionate short stories, some of which are reprinted in *Women in Their Beds*.

- *Girl, Interrupted* (1994), Susanna Kaysen's memoir of her psychiatric hospitalization in 1967 at age eighteen, questions the boundary between what is normal and what is deviant.

- *Dusk and Other Stories* (1989), a collection of lyrical short stories by James Salter, explores relations between men and women and takes up themes of memory and loss.

- *The Gate of Angels* (1990) is a short novel by Penelope Fitzgerald. Set at a hospital in 1912, this doctor-nurse love story is also an inquiry into different ideas of truth.

- *The Shawl* (1990), by Cynthia Ozick, includes the title story and a short novel centering on the same character—a woman now living in Florida and confronting her loss thirty years after her infant daughter died in a Nazi concentration camp.

---

deprivation, when a young doctor runs up and demands to see her hands. Angela first thinks that the doctor is talking to her—"Was there some new scan that doctors had, a scientific palmistry for detecting liars and imposters and actors?"—which suggests Angela's identification with the patient, their shared intimidation by medical authority. But the doctor is interested in the patient's hands because he has noticed that her son has a strange birth defect, leaving him with an extra finger on each hand. The "scientific palmistry" he wishes to perform is informed by the laws of genetics—which can be understood as a rational method for predicting a person's fate. His zeal for uncovering the objective cause for the birth defect renders him oblivious to the woman's overall condition. "Can you tell me . . . why your son has six fingers?" he demands, blind to the life history that Angela intuits as she gazes at the woman's humble hands, "curved to the shape of mop handles, vacuum cleaner handles."

The answer the patient offers him literally stops him in his tracks. She tells him that her mother cursed her and her child. Curses depends on a superstitious idea of cause and effect, one that doctors, educated in the laws of nature, would dismiss as sheer ignorance. However, when Angela describes the events to Lew, it is the doctor she describes as "simpleminded." "Doctors don't know what they're getting into when they get to be doctors," she says. She is critical of the young doctor's insensitivity to his patients as human beings as opposed to organisms and his blindness to the spiritual profundity of their suffering. She herself gleans from the cleaning woman's modest stature, her humbly curved hands, and her mother's curse, a life of poverty, indignity, and severed bonds of love.

What Angela does to her patients—glimpsing into their souls, imagining pasts and futures in her brief interactions with them—is not unlike palmistry. But in the next scene a patient turns the tables and glimpses into her soul. A ninety-six-year-old patient, described as a "Gypsy queen," offers to read Angela's palm—in order to flatter her, Angela surmises. She speculates that the Gypsy's "reading" of her as a "wayward girl" has more to do with her clothes and grooming than it does with the lines in her palm. But, nevertheless, Angela's waywardness lies at the heart of her lonely condition.

While Angela affects a skeptical attitude toward the reading, she is moved by what she hears of her destined long life, both admiring and fearing the Gypsy's power.

The Gypsy is not, like the cleaning woman, humble before the hospital authorities. She is not passive in the face of the bureaucracy of which Angela nominally is part. Instead of allowing her fortune to be "told" by the pragmatic logic of the health care system, takes control and tells Angela's fortune. This refusal to be passive is the secret of the Gypsy's life force, one that Angela also identifies with her brood of beautiful "children of whatever generation" who remain, after the Gypsy's death, as a testimony to intimacy and continuity throughout the life cycle. The "archangelic" children transcend the pragmatic gloom of the hospital atmosphere, "Unreal, their garments biblically splendid as that coat of many colors, and all with golden skin." They are an extension of the Gypsy's spiritual health and her power. The Gypsy's faith in that which is unprovable dignifies the superstitious feelings that dominate the women on the ward and inhabit Angela when she works there.

It is Angela's job on the women's ward to facilitate patients' transition into their next "beds." When the Gypsy's children ask for a candle, she understands implicitly that this is part of a ritual of transition, and seizes the chance to invest her bureaucratic job with a bit of spirituality. Angela experiences the hospital as a place of dread, from which she wishes she could magically disappear, but also, at the same time, as a holy place. Angela (whose name is derived from *angel*—a spiritual being) uses a light step at the hospital, one she saves for "museums and churches, sanctified places that always made her feel unworthy." Thus, it makes sense to her to try to convert the hospital into a place of ritual. There are no candles to be found there, however, and the only reason the "bona fide" social workers could imagine for needing one is utterly pragmatic: "Maybe the light had gone out in the lavatory." When she returns with one the next day, Nurse Nancy blows it out, telling her that the other women won't appreciate it, "They've got their own problems." The impractical candle that Angela searches for, and ultimately brings to the women from her own home, represents the connection between each of the isolated women's "own problems" and the unifying, healing power of faith.

For Angela, the women's ward is a place where she can make a leap of faith and connect to some-

> 'Can you tell me . . . why your son has six fingers?' he demands, blind to the life history that Angela intuits as she gazes at the woman's humble hands, 'curved to the shape of mop handles, vacuum cleaner handles.'"

thing larger than she is. By referring to God as "an Audience of One who never blinked," Berriault draws a parallel between Angela's dramatic sensibility and religious faith. Angela seeks truths that are based on faith and feeling rather than observation and verification. It is largely through Angela's vocation as an actress that she is able to perceive the women patients' injured "karmas," their unobservable, nonmedical injuries. Acting requires the capacity to imagine oneself as another. The women's ward offers her a chance, as suggested by the dream she has of her mother berating her, to learn about herself through the suffering of the patients. This openness to other women's souls is a chance for knowledge but also a threat to Angela's delicate sense of self. Angela, like most of the women on the ward, lives a life in which connections keep coming undone. The women's lives "must be unfolding before their eyes, in there, and they're unfolding mine," she thinks. "They're unfolding me." She needs to be healed as much as they do.

Source: Sarah Madsen Hardy, in an essay for *Short Stories for Students*, Gale Group, 2001.

Chris Semansky

Semansky publishes widely in the field of twentieth-century culture and literature. In the following essay, he discusses the ways in which Berriault's story embodies the author's idea of "the eternal moment."

Although she has written numerous screenplays, novels, and essays, Gina Berriault says that she finds her true voice when writing short fiction. On the dust jacket of her collection of short stories *Women in Their Beds*, she has this to say about the form: "[Short stories] are close to poetry—with the fewest words they capture the essence of a situation, of a human being, and they attempt to capture the eternal moment."

In the searching, elliptical title piece of that same collection, Berriault captures that eternal moment in showing readers the women's ward of a county hospital in San Francisco during the Vietnam War years. She replicates the then-common televised sight of wounded soldiers in makeshift hospitals with eerie inexactitude: the wounded are all women, and the war which has cost each so dearly has been waged within rather than without. Some are withdrawing from alcohol, some have attempted suicide, all bear the weight of poverty and emotional torment. In the hospital, the social workers are untrained, including out-of-work actors and writers, and the doctors are young interns who sometimes charge their patients with making their own diagnoses.

Angela Anson is the character Berriault creates to give the reader a view of this "captured situation," to guide readers into the story's deepest recesses. The point of view is third person, but the reader has complete access to Angela's thoughts as she moves through the women's ward. Her own suicide attempt at sixteen and her past experiences with her bedridden mother and aunt give Angela a pressing reason to come to terms with the essential meaning of a woman in a bed. Berriault tugs and pulls at the image of the vertical, attended woman, treating it as a conundrum or a sign, and asking, through Angela and the women she encounters on their backs: what brings a woman to a bed, and what is her world once she arrives there?

One cannot help recalling the "rest cures" once pressed upon women who stepped outside their tightly constructed gender roles. For women too passionate or too aware, bed rest was recommended as antidotal—the most vigorous will could be sapped by simply disallowing the possibility of rising from a bed for indefinite durations. In titling her story "Women in Their Beds" and in dwelling on numerous images of women living in a helpless and immured world, Berriault alludes to the seminal work of Charlotte Perkins Gilman's, "The Yellow Wallpaper," as well as to contemporary works such as Susan Sontag's "Alice in Bed."

Angela Anson walks the ward, charged with explaining to the women where they will go once they are discharged—as she thinks of it, "the dispersal of the deranged." The beds in the ward have a way of appearing and disappearing, of multiplying in the night or magically subtracting themselves, creating a "shocked atmosphere like that after a quake." This atmosphere resonates throughout the ward: "*What's happening here?* The question on each face upon a pillow. A quake of the mind, a quake of the heart." Like life elsewhere, each moment in the ward is surprising, unrehearsed, and potentially shattering, and the question that rings out of each human being is one of wonder. But unlike life elsewhere, these women are cast adrift in a world where they have become defined almost solely as burdens to others, and where their own helplessness is the only certainty on which they can depend. The physical instability of the beds echoes the tenuous interior lives of these female patients.

Angela and her fellow employees play a game that sets up another kind of echo in the story. A point that is felt acutely by Angela—who calls herself a "confidante without credentials," and despairs of doing anyone any good, even for a fleeting moment—is the falseness of their qualifications as social workers. The game, which is to call to each other over the paging system using code names, pokes fun at the idea of expertise. The names they use for one another, Dr. Zhivago, Dr. Jekyll, Dr. Curie, Dr. Freud, bear a ring of authenticity as they sound down the grim corridors, but for any inmate listening closely enough, the ridiculousness of hoping for serious help from any of the local authorities is made manifest. Berriault uses the calling of these names over the paging system as a device for breaking the story into pieces, for showing the passage of time, and for calling readers back to the sensory life of the ward from Angela's thoughts. The names, each in their turn, bring to mind heights of romance, gothic terror, female will, and the psychopathology that underlines the need for the hospital in the first place and the undulating rows of women's beds that line it in the second. Angela's own epithet is "Dr. Curie." She finds it curiously apropos, since she sees her work in the hospital as being that of a "discoverer of so much that was undetectable and that might not even exist."

The ward itself is "pale" and "quiet," like a woman grown acquiescent after her own rest cure. Angela moves through it gently, trying to imagine lives for the women better than the ones they've had. Her hope is to see that they are not overlooked. As she works, she finds that the ward affects her in ways she would not have predicted. She comes to see that its unlucky people and vulnerable pain make it a meaningful place on its own terms, and give it a sanctity different from the ordinary life that those a short walk beyond its threshold might be able to claim. In fact, its peculiar atmosphere makes her feel unworthy. She unconsciously delivers to her fellow social workers a representation of herself so filled with a longing to merge with the patients that they chastise her and tell her she is not St. Teresa of Avila, and that kissing lepers' wounds is not part of her job description. But the difference between Dr. Curie—the name her coworkers chose for her—and St. Teresa, is less than one might think. Both figures moved willingly toward sickness, be it radiation or leprosy, as a path to enlightenment. In this way Berriault underlines one of the subversive processes open to women in their search for self-fulfillment and development—a movement toward the weakening of the self to bring on knowledge.

At night Angela dreams of her mother, bad dreams in which she is being berated. She guesses that she is to blame for never knowing enough about her mother, who may have wanted to reveal herself, to unfold herself, but was unable to. Angela looks at the women in the ward whose lives, "must be unfolding before their eyes, in there," and believes that "they're unfolding mine. They're unfolding me [as well]." She remembers herself as she stood at her mother's bedside in some other hospital. In her mind, she speaks to a daughter who fails to come to see her own mother in the ward. "Your heart sinks down and leaves your breast and may never come back. But when you're out in the street again it comes racing back, bursting with grief." The period of nonfeeling Angela describes during her own long-ago visit to her mother is a common occurrence in the county hospital for those who are forced to stand beside a woman who is in bed, raising the specter of helplessness. In one instance, a woman in bed pleads with Angela to intervene with a doctor. But the doctor remains arrogant, with "impatiently jiggling knee" and "disposing gaze." So there is only Angela herself to overcome the nonfeeling that separates the healthy from the unhealthy. Angela alone must "humanize herself" and face the consequences of witnessing something she would rather not see.

On the woman's face Angela superimposes the face of her own Aunt Ida, one of the legion of women in beds, and remembers that her mother told her that this same withered aunt had been the most beautiful of all her five sisters. As a child Angela was pierced with disbelief, and now, in the ward,

> "In this section we see Angela achieve the 'eternal moment' that Berriault says the short story can provide. The moment is transcendent because Angela's identification with the women is complete; her own suffering and the suffering of her mother and aunt, which resurfaced for her during her stint as a pseudo-social worker, have been painfully acknowledged."

looking into the eyes of this woman at her elbow, she is likewise unable to believe that this woman "had ever been other that she was now, had ever been young, a girl, twelve, sixteen, eighteen, in that flowering time." In the most abstract sense, Angela avoids the truth the moment offers up because it implicates her: if others can wither and grow old and become burdensome, so can she. But more specifically, she perhaps sees a trajectory that mimics too closely the one she has already begun. It was at sixteen, a year she specifically mentions when looking at the pleading woman, that Angela attempted suicide, an attempt that she had convinced herself was childish and awkward, and that she now recalls "fondly." This jarring idea of closure on her past is upended by her vigorous attempts to picture all the women on the ward "when they were young, wanting to come to their rescue by reviving them as girls again."

Berriault plays with the sexual nature of the image of a woman in bed, writing that "in this women's ward there was a yielding to whoever was watching over them and to the medication that must seem like a persuasive stranger entering their most intimate being for their own good." Later, Angela asks a fellow employee if he has ever been to the French cemetery where Colette is buried. She tells him that the monument above the writer's grave resembles a bed, which suggests to her that cavorting on beds is "where women belong," whether living or dead, sick or well. She invokes Hamlet's mother and Desdemona as examples of women inseparable from their beds. Her contact with the women in the ward has made her think about destiny, which she sees as the force moving people—women in particular—from one bed to the next, without their consent and sometimes to their sorrow. In this way a subtle implication is made that a woman's sexual life is her destiny, and that the beginnings and endings of love affairs are the major currents of change.

The epiphany in "Women in Their Beds" occurs when Angela is lying beside her lover, reworking the meaning of the lines: "I in my bed of thistles, you in your bed of roses and feathers." In her actress's life she has said these lines before, but until she went to work at the county hospital she believed they were no more than a simple expression of jealousy, one woman reporting on her lost lover as being another woman's gain. But Angela's recent experiences have left her unable to see her life in terms of personal losses and gains; the line reworks itself in her mind and she understands that should she in fact be the one with the bed of roses and feathers then she would only be relegating someone else to the bed of thistles. She moves away from the duality of good and bad, me and her, and toward an understanding of collective suffering that is irrefutable. "Just remember the beds where you wished you weren't, and beds where you wished you were, and then name any spot on this earth that's a bed for some woman at this very hour. . . . If I'd wished for a bed of roses and feathers, and *I did, I did*, now I don't want it so much anymore." In this section readers see Angela achieve the "eternal moment" that Berriault says the short story can provide. The moment is transcendent because Angela's identification with the women is complete; her own suffering and the suffering of her mother and aunt, which resurfaced for her during her stint as a pseudo-social worker, have been painfully acknowledged.

In the final scene in "Women in Their Beds" a distressed Angela walks up and down the aisles of the women's ward carrying a white candle in a wooden holder. The light, she thinks, is "for any woman leaving at any time." Leaving the ward? Leaving this life? Leaving one particular bed to go to another? The reader knows only that she is stopped by the head nurse, who blows out the candle after questioning the intent of the ritual and finding it inadequate. "And Nurse Nancy blew out the flame, with a breath that failed to be strong and unwavering but did the job anyway. Lightly then, a touch at Angela's elbow and at her back, touches to assist her to stay on her feet and to point her in the right direction." By helping her "stay on her feet" the nurse strikes a note against the helplessness of women in their beds, and Angela is left faltering but still upright as the story closes.

Source: Chris Semansky, in an essay for *Short Stories for Students*, Gale Group, 2001.

Sources

Amdahl, Gary, "Making Literature," in *Nation*, June 24, 1996, pp. 31–32.

George, Lynell, "Secrets Accidentally Spilled," in *Los Angeles Times Book Review*, May 26, 1996, p. 7.

Harshaw, Tobin, "Short Takes," in *New York Times Book Review*, May 5, 1996, p. 22.

Lyons, Bonnie, and Bill Oliver, "Don't I Know You?: An Interview with Gina Berriault," in *Literary Review*, Vol. 37, Summer, 1994, pp. 714–23.

Seaman, Donna, "The Glory of Stories," *Booklist*, March 15, 1996, p. 1239.

Wakeman, John, ed., *World Authors, 1950–1970*, H. W. Wilson, 1975.

Further Reading

Berriualt, Gina, *The Lights of Earth*, North Point Press, 1984.
   Because little biographical information on the author is available, readers interested in Berriault's life may want to read this semi-autobiographical novel. The novel centers on a San Francisco writer struggling with loss and grief.

Dickstein, Morris, *Gates of Eden: American Culture in the Sixties*, 2d ed., Harvard University Press, 1999.
   Dickstein characterizes the youth culture's drive to experience the world in a new way and analyses a number of important sixties icons. This sophisticated yet readable study of the period was nominated for the National Book Critics Award.

Ehrenreich, Barbara, and Deirdre English, *Complaints and Disorders: The Sexual Politics of Sickness*, Feminist Press, 1991.
   Ehrenreich and English consider the relationship between medical and social views of women, arguing

that medicine reflects gender oppression. This work of sociology is quite accessible to general readers.

Hamilton, Neil, *The ABC-Clio Companion to the 1960s Counterculture in America*, ABC-Clio, Inc., 1998.
An evenhanded and comprehensive overview of the rise of the 1960s counterculture focusing on cultural and political changes in American society. Four hundred A-Z entries make this book a useful research tool.

Glossary of Literary Terms

A

Aestheticism: A literary and artistic movement of the nineteenth century. Followers of the movement believed that art should not be mixed with social, political, or moral teaching. The statement "art for art's sake" is a good summary of aestheticism. The movement had its roots in France, but it gained widespread importance in England in the last half of the nineteenth century, where it helped change the Victorian practice of including moral lessons in literature. Edgar Allan Poe is one of the best-known American "aesthetes."

Allegory: A narrative technique in which characters representing things or abstract ideas are used to convey a message or teach a lesson. Allegory is typically used to teach moral, ethical, or religious lessons but is sometimes used for satiric or political purposes. Many fairy tales are allegories.

Allusion: A reference to a familiar literary or historical person or event, used to make an idea more easily understood. Joyce Carol Oates's story "Where Are You Going, Where Have You Been?" exhibits several allusions to popular music.

Analogy: A comparison of two things made to explain something unfamiliar through its similarities to something familiar, or to prove one point based on the acceptance of another. Similes and metaphors are types of analogies.

Antagonist: The major character in a narrative or drama who works against the hero or protagonist. The Misfit in Flannery O'Connor's story "A Good Man Is Hard to Find" serves as the antagonist for the Grandmother.

Anthology: A collection of similar works of literature, art, or music. Zora Neale Hurston's "The Eatonville Anthology" is a collection of stories that take place in the same town.

Anthropomorphism: The presentation of animals or objects in human shape or with human characteristics. The term is derived from the Greek word for "human form." The fur necklet in Katherine Mansfield's story "Miss Brill" has anthropomorphic characteristics.

Anti-hero: A central character in a work of literature who lacks traditional heroic qualities such as courage, physical prowess, and fortitude. Anti-heroes typically distrust conventional values and are unable to commit themselves to any ideals. They generally feel helpless in a world over which they have no control. Anti-heroes usually accept, and often celebrate, their positions as social outcasts. A well-known anti-hero is Walter Mitty in James Thurber's story "The Secret Life of Walter Mitty."

Archetype: The word archetype is commonly used to describe an original pattern or model from which all other things of the same kind are made. Archetypes are the literary images that grow out of the "collective unconscious," a theory proposed by psychologist Carl Jung. They appear in literature as incidents and plots that repeat basic patterns of life. They may also appear as stereotyped characters. The "schlemiel" of Yiddish literature is an archetype.

Autobiography: A narrative in which an individual tells his or her life story. Examples include Benjamin Franklin's *Autobiography* and Amy Hempel's story "In the Cemetery Where Al Jolson Is Buried," which has autobiographical characteristics even though it is a work of fiction.

Avant-garde: A literary term that describes new writing that rejects traditional approaches to literature in favor of innovations in style or content. Twentieth-century examples of the literary *avant-garde* include the modernists and the minimalists.

B

Belles-lettres: A French term meaning "fine letters" or "beautiful writing." It is often used as a synonym for literature, typically referring to imaginative and artistic rather than scientific or expository writing. Current usage sometimes restricts the meaning to light or humorous writing and appreciative essays about literature. Lewis Carroll's *Alice in Wonderland* epitomizes the realm of belles-lettres.

Bildungsroman: A German word meaning "novel of development." The *bildungsroman* is a study of the maturation of a youthful character, typically brought about through a series of social or sexual encounters that lead to self-awareness. J. D. Salinger's *Catcher in the Rye* is a *bildungsroman*, and Doris Lessing's story "Through the Tunnel" exhibits characteristics of a *bildungsroman* as well.

Black Aesthetic Movement: A period of artistic and literary development among African Americans in the 1960s and early 1970s. This was the first major African-American artistic movement since the Harlem Renaissance and was closely paralleled by the civil rights and black power movements. The black aesthetic writers attempted to produce works of art that would be meaningful to the black masses. Key figures in black aesthetics included one of its founders, poet and playwright Amiri Baraka, formerly known as LeRoi Jones; poet and essayist Haki R. Madhubuti, formerly Don L. Lee; poet and playwright Sonia Sanchez; and dramatist Ed Bullins. Works representative of the Black Aesthetic Movement include Amiri Baraka's play *Dutchman*, a 1964 Obie award-winner.

Black Humor: Writing that places grotesque elements side by side with humorous ones in an attempt to shock the reader, forcing him or her to laugh at the horrifying reality of a disordered world. "Lamb to the Slaughter," by Roald Dahl, in which a placid housewife murders her husband and serves the murder weapon to the investigating policemen, is an example of black humor.

C

Catharsis: The release or purging of unwanted emotions—specifically fear and pity—brought about by exposure to art. The term was first used by the Greek philosopher Aristotle in his *Poetics* to refer to the desired effect of tragedy on spectators.

Character: Broadly speaking, a person in a literary work. The actions of characters are what constitute the plot of a story, novel, or poem. There are numerous types of characters, ranging from simple, stereotypical figures to intricate, multifaceted ones. "Characterization" is the process by which an author creates vivid, believable characters in a work of art. This may be done in a variety of ways, including (1) direct description of the character by the narrator; (2) the direct presentation of the speech, thoughts, or actions of the character; and (3) the responses of other characters to the character. The term "character" also refers to a form originated by the ancient Greek writer Theophrastus that later became popular in the seventeenth and eighteenth centuries. It is a short essay or sketch of a person who prominently displays a specific attribute or quality, such as miserliness or ambition. "Miss Brill," a story by Katherine Mansfield, is an example of a character sketch.

Classical: In its strictest definition in literary criticism, classicism refers to works of ancient Greek or Roman literature. The term may also be used to describe a literary work of recognized importance (a "classic") from any time period or literature that exhibits the traits of classicism. Examples of later works and authors now described as classical include French literature of the seventeenth century, Western novels of the nineteenth century, and American fiction of the mid-nineteenth century such as that written by James Fenimore Cooper and Mark Twain.

Climax: The turning point in a narrative, the moment when the conflict is at its most intense. Typically, the structure of stories, novels, and plays is one of rising action, in which tension builds to the climax, followed by falling action, in which tension lessens as the story moves to its conclusion.

Comedy: One of two major types of drama, the other being tragedy. Its aim is to amuse, and it typically ends happily. Comedy assumes many forms, such as farce and burlesque, and uses a variety of techniques, from parody to satire. In a restricted sense the term comedy refers only to dramatic presentations, but in general usage it is commonly applied to nondramatic works as well.

Comic Relief: The use of humor to lighten the mood of a serious or tragic story, especially in plays. The technique is very common in Elizabethan works, and can be an integral part of the plot or simply a brief event designed to break the tension of the scene.

Conflict: The conflict in a work of fiction is the issue to be resolved in the story. It usually occurs between two characters, the protagonist and the antagonist, or between the protagonist and society or the protagonist and himself or herself. The conflict in Washington Irving's story ''The Devil and Tom Walker'' is that the Devil wants Tom Walker's soul but Tom does not want to go to hell.

Criticism: The systematic study and evaluation of literary works, usually based on a specific method or set of principles. An important part of literary studies since ancient times, the practice of criticism has given rise to numerous theories, methods, and ''schools,'' sometimes producing conflicting, even contradictory, interpretations of literature in general as well as of individual works. Even such basic issues as what constitutes a poem or a novel have been the subject of much criticism over the centuries. Seminal texts of literary criticism include Plato's *Republic,* Aristotle's *Poetics,* Sir Philip Sidney's *The Defence of Poesie,* and John Dryden's *Of Dramatic Poesie.* Contemporary schools of criticism include deconstruction, feminist, psychoanalytic, poststructuralist, new historicist, postcolonialist, and reader-response.

D

Deconstruction: A method of literary criticism characterized by multiple conflicting interpretations of a given work. Deconstructionists consider the impact of the language of a work and suggest that the true meaning of the work is not necessarily the meaning that the author intended.

Deduction: The process of reaching a conclusion through reasoning from general premises to a specific premise. Arthur Conan Doyle's character Sherlock Holmes often used deductive reasoning to solve mysteries.

Denotation: The definition of a word, apart from the impressions or feelings it creates in the reader. The word ''apartheid'' denotes a political and economic policy of segregation by race, but its connotations—oppression, slavery, inequality—are numerous.

Denouement: A French word meaning ''the unknotting.'' In literature, it denotes the resolution of conflict in fiction or drama. The *denouement* follows the climax and provides an outcome to the primary plot situation as well as an explanation of secondary plot complications. A well-known example of *denouement* is the last scene of the play *As You Like It* by William Shakespeare, in which couples are married, an evildoer repents, the identities of two disguised characters are revealed, and a ruler is restored to power. Also known as ''falling action.''

Detective Story: A narrative about the solution of a mystery or the identification of a criminal. The conventions of the detective story include the detective's scrupulous use of logic in solving the mystery; incompetent or ineffectual police; a suspect who appears guilty at first but is later proved innocent; and the detective's friend or confidant—often the narrator—whose slowness in interpreting clues emphasizes by contrast the detective's brilliance. Edgar Allan Poe's ''Murders in the Rue Morgue'' is commonly regarded as the earliest example of this type of story. Other practitioners are Arthur Conan Doyle, Dashiell Hammett, and Agatha Christie.

Dialogue: Dialogue is conversation between people in a literary work. In its most restricted sense, it refers specifically to the speech of characters in a drama. As a specific literary genre, a ''dialogue'' is a composition in which characters debate an issue or idea.

Didactic: A term used to describe works of literature that aim to teach a moral, religious, political, or practical lesson. Although didactic elements are often found in artistically pleasing works, the term ''didactic'' usually refers to literature in which the message is more important than the form. The term may also be used to criticize a work that the critic finds ''overly didactic,'' that is, heavy-handed in its delivery of a lesson. An example of didactic literature is John Bunyan's *Pilgrim's Progress.*

Dramatic Irony: Occurs when the reader of a work of literature knows something that a character in the work itself does not know. The irony is in the contrast between the intended meaning of the statements or actions of a character and the additional information understood by the audience.

Dystopia: An imaginary place in a work of fiction where the characters lead dehumanized, fearful lives. **George Orwell's** *Nineteen Eighty-four,* and Margaret Atwood's *Handmaid's Tale* portray versions of dystopia.

E

Edwardian: Describes cultural conventions identified with the period of the reign of Edward VII of England (1901-1910). Writers of the Edwardian Age typically displayed a strong reaction against the propriety and conservatism of the Victorian Age. Their work often exhibits distrust of authority in religion, politics, and art and expresses strong doubts about the soundness of conventional values. Writers of this era include E. M. Forster, H. G. Wells, and Joseph Conrad.

Empathy: A sense of shared experience, including emotional and physical feelings, with someone or something other than oneself. Empathy is often used to describe the response of a reader to a literary character.

Epilogue: A concluding statement or section of a literary work. In dramas, particularly those of the seventeenth and eighteenth centuries, the epilogue is a closing speech, often in verse, delivered by an actor at the end of a play and spoken directly to the audience.

Epiphany: A sudden revelation of truth inspired by a seemingly trivial incident. The term was widely used by James Joyce in his critical writings, and the stories in Joyce's *Dubliners* are commonly called "epiphanies."

Epistolary Novel: A novel in the form of letters. The form was particularly popular in the eighteenth century. The form can also be applied to short stories, as in Edwidge Danticat's "Children of the Sea."

Epithet: A word or phrase, often disparaging or abusive, that expresses a character trait of someone or something. "The Napoleon of crime" is an epithet applied to Professor Moriarty, arch-rival of Sherlock Holmes in Arthur Conan Doyle's series of detective stories.

Existentialism: A predominantly twentieth-century philosophy concerned with the nature and perception of human existence. There are two major strains of existentialist thought: atheistic and Christian. Followers of atheistic existentialism believe that the individual is alone in a godless universe and that the basic human condition is one of suffering and loneliness. Nevertheless, because there are no fixed values, individuals can create their own characters—indeed, they can shape themselves—through the exercise of free will. The atheistic strain culminates in and is popularly associated with the works of Jean-Paul Sartre. The Christian existentialists, on the other hand, believe that only in God may people find freedom from life's anguish. The two strains hold certain beliefs in common: that existence cannot be fully understood or described through empirical effort; that anguish is a universal element of life; that individuals must bear responsibility for their actions; and that there is no common standard of behavior or perception for religious and ethical matters. Existentialist thought figures prominently in the works of such authors as Franz Kafka, Fyodor Dostoyevsky, and Albert Camus.

Expatriatism: The practice of leaving one's country to live for an extended period in another country. Literary expatriates include Irish author James Joyce who moved to Italy and France, American writers James Baldwin, Ernest Hemingway, Gertrude Stein, and F. Scott Fitzgerald who lived and wrote in Paris, and Polish novelist Joseph Conrad in England.

Exposition: Writing intended to explain the nature of an idea, thing, or theme. Expository writing is often combined with description, narration, or argument.

Expressionism: An indistinct literary term, originally used to describe an early twentieth-century school of German painting. The term applies to almost any mode of unconventional, highly subjective writing that distorts reality in some way. Advocates of Expressionism include Federico Garcia Lorca, Eugene O'Neill, Franz Kafka, and James Joyce.

F

Fable: A prose or verse narrative intended to convey a moral. Animals or inanimate objects with human characteristics often serve as characters in fables. A famous fable is Aesop's "The Tortoise and the Hare."

Fantasy: A literary form related to mythology and folklore. Fantasy literature is typically set in nonexistent realms and features supernatural beings. Notable examples of literature with elements of fantasy are Gabriel Garcia Marquez's story "The Handsomest Drowned Man in the World" and Ursula K. LeGuin's "The Ones Who Walk Away from Omelas."

Farce: A type of comedy characterized by broad humor, outlandish incidents, and often vulgar subject matter. Much of the comedy in film and television could more accurately be described as farce.

Fiction: Any story that is the product of imagination rather than a documentation of fact. Characters and events in such narratives may be based in real life but their ultimate form and configuration is a creation of the author.

Figurative Language: A technique in which an author uses figures of speech such as hyperbole, irony, metaphor, or simile for a particular effect. Figurative language is the opposite of literal language, in which every word is truthful, accurate, and free of exaggeration or embellishment.

Flashback: A device used in literature to present action that occurred before the beginning of the story. Flashbacks are often introduced as the dreams or recollections of one or more characters.

Foil: A character in a work of literature whose physical or psychological qualities contrast strongly with, and therefore highlight, the corresponding qualities of another character. In his Sherlock Holmes stories, Arthur Conan Doyle portrayed Dr. Watson as a man of normal habits and intelligence, making him a foil for the eccentric and unusually perceptive Sherlock Holmes.

Folklore: Traditions and myths preserved in a culture or group of people. Typically, these are passed on by word of mouth in various forms—such as legends, songs, and proverbs—or preserved in customs and ceremonies. Washington Irving, in "The Devil and Tom Walker" and many of his other stories, incorporates many elements of the folklore of New England and Germany.

Folktale: A story originating in oral tradition. Folktales fall into a variety of categories, including legends, ghost stories, fairy tales, fables, and anecdotes based on historical figures and events.

Foreshadowing: A device used in literature to create expectation or to set up an explanation of later developments. Edgar Allan Poe uses foreshadowing to create suspense in "The Fall of the House of Usher" when the narrator comments on the crumbling state of disrepair in which he finds the house.

G

Genre: A category of literary work. Genre may refer to both the content of a given work—tragedy, comedy, horror, science fiction—and to its form, such as poetry, novel, or drama.

Gilded Age: A period in American history during the 1870s and after characterized by political corruption and materialism. A number of important novels of social and political criticism were written during this time. Henry James and Kate Chopin are two writers who were prominent during the Gilded Age.

Gothicism: In literature, works characterized by a taste for medieval or morbid characters and situations. A gothic novel prominently features elements of horror, the supernatural, gloom, and violence: clanking chains, terror, ghosts, medieval castles, and unexplained phenomena. The term "gothic novel" is also applied to novels that lack elements of the traditional Gothic setting but that create a similar atmosphere of terror or dread. The term can also be applied to stories, plays, and poems. Mary Shelley's *Frankenstein* and Joyce Carol Oates's *Bellefleur* are both gothic novels.

Grotesque: In literature, a work that is characterized by exaggeration, deformity, freakishness, and disorder. The grotesque often includes an element of comic absurdity. Examples of the grotesque can be found in the works of Edgar Allan Poe, Flannery O'Connor, Joseph Heller, and Shirley Jackson.

H

Harlem Renaissance: The Harlem Renaissance of the 1920s is generally considered the first significant movement of black writers and artists in the United States. During this period, new and established black writers, many of whom lived in the region of New York City known as Harlem, published more fiction and poetry than ever before, the first influential black literary journals were established, and black authors and artists received their first widespread recognition and serious critical appraisal. Among the major writers associated with this period are Countee Cullen, Langston Hughes, Arna Bontemps, and Zora Neale Hurston.

Hero/Heroine: The principal sympathetic character in a literary work. Heroes and heroines typically exhibit admirable traits: idealism, courage, and integrity, for example. Famous heroes and heroines of literature include Charles Dickens's Oliver Twist, Margaret Mitchell's Scarlett O'Hara, and the anonymous narrator in Ralph Ellison's *Invisible Man.*

Hyperbole: Deliberate exaggeration used to achieve an effect. In William Shakespeare's *Macbeth,* Lady Macbeth hyperbolizes when she says, ''All the perfumes of Arabia could not sweeten this little hand.''

I

Image: A concrete representation of an object or sensory experience. Typically, such a representation helps evoke the feelings associated with the object or experience itself. Images are either ''literal'' or ''figurative.'' Literal images are especially concrete and involve little or no extension of the obvious meaning of the words used to express them. Figurative images do not follow the literal meaning of the words exactly. Images in literature are usually visual, but the term ''image'' can also refer to the representation of any sensory experience.

Imagery: The array of images in a literary work. Also used to convey the author's overall use of figurative language in a work.

In medias res: A Latin term meaning ''in the middle of things.'' It refers to the technique of beginning a story at its midpoint and then using various flashback devices to reveal previous action. This technique originated in such epics as Virgil's *Aeneid.*

Interior Monologue: A narrative technique in which characters' thoughts are revealed in a way that appears to be uncontrolled by the author. The interior monologue typically aims to reveal the inner self of a character. It portrays emotional experiences as they occur at both a conscious and unconscious level. One of the best-known interior monologues in English is the Molly Bloom section at the close of James Joyce's *Ulysses.* Katherine Anne Porter's ''The Jilting of Granny Weatherall'' is also told in the form of an interior monologue.

Irony: In literary criticism, the effect of language in which the intended meaning is the opposite of what is stated. The title of Jonathan Swift's ''A Modest Proposal'' is ironic because what Swift proposes in this essay is cannibalism—hardly ''modest.''

J

Jargon: Language that is used or understood only by a select group of people. Jargon may refer to terminology used in a certain profession, such as computer jargon, or it may refer to any nonsensical language that is not understood by most people. Anthony Burgess's *A Clockwork Orange* and James Thurber's ''The Secret Life of Walter Mitty'' both use jargon.

K

Knickerbocker Group: An indistinct group of New York writers of the first half of the nineteenth century. Members of the group were linked only by location and a common theme: New York life. Two famous members of the Knickerbocker Group were Washington Irving and William Cullen Bryant. The group's name derives from Irving's *Knickerbocker's History of New York.*

L

Literal Language: An author uses literal language when he or she writes without exaggerating or embellishing the subject matter and without any tools of figurative language. To say ''He ran very quickly down the street'' is to use literal language, whereas to say ''He ran like a hare down the street'' would be using figurative language.

Literature: Literature is broadly defined as any written or spoken material, but the term most often refers to creative works. Literature includes poetry, drama, fiction, and many kinds of nonfiction writing, as well as oral, dramatic, and broadcast compositions not necessarily preserved in a written format, such as films and television programs.

Lost Generation: A term first used by Gertrude Stein to describe the post-World War I generation of American writers: men and women haunted by a sense of betrayal and emptiness brought about by the destructiveness of the war. The term is commonly applied to Hart Crane, Ernest Hemingway, F. Scott Fitzgerald, and others.

M

Magic Realism: A form of literature that incorporates fantasy elements or supernatural occurrences into the narrative and accepts them as truth. Gabriel Garcia Marquez and Laura Esquivel are two writers known for their works of magic realism.

Metaphor: A figure of speech that expresses an idea through the image of another object. Metaphors suggest the essence of the first object by identifying it with certain qualities of the second object. An example is "But soft, what light through yonder window breaks?/ It is the east, and Juliet is the sun" in William Shakespeare's *Romeo and Juliet*. Here, Juliet, the first object, is identified with qualities of the second object, the sun.

Minimalism: A literary style characterized by spare, simple prose with few elaborations. In minimalism, the main theme of the work is often never discussed directly. Amy Hempel and Ernest Hemingway are two writers known for their works of minimalism.

Modernism: Modern literary practices. Also, the principles of a literary school that lasted from roughly the beginning of the twentieth century until the end of World War II. Modernism is defined by its rejection of the literary conventions of the nineteenth century and by its opposition to conventional morality, taste, traditions, and economic values. Many writers are associated with the concepts of modernism, including Albert Camus, D. H. Lawrence, Ernest Hemingway, William Faulkner, Eugene O'Neill, and James Joyce.

Monologue: A composition, written or oral, by a single individual. More specifically, a speech given by a single individual in a drama or other public entertainment. It has no set length, although it is usually several or more lines long. "I Stand Here Ironing" by Tillie Olsen is an example of a story written in the form of a monologue.

Mood: The prevailing emotions of a work or of the author in his or her creation of the work. The mood of a work is not always what might be expected based on its subject matter.

Motif: A theme, character type, image, metaphor, or other verbal element that recurs throughout a single work of literature or occurs in a number of different works over a period of time. For example, the color white in Herman Melville's *Moby Dick* is a "specific" *motif*, while the trials of star-crossed lovers is a "conventional" *motif* from the literature of all periods.

N

Narration: The telling of a series of events, real or invented. A narration may be either a simple narrative, in which the events are recounted chronologically, or a narrative with a plot, in which the account is given in a style reflecting the author's artistic concept of the story. Narration is sometimes used as a synonym for "storyline."

Narrative: A verse or prose accounting of an event or sequence of events, real or invented. The term is also used as an adjective in the sense "method of narration." For example, in literary criticism, the expression "narrative technique" usually refers to the way the author structures and presents his or her story. Different narrative forms include diaries, travelogues, novels, ballads, epics, short stories, and other fictional forms.

Narrator: The teller of a story. The narrator may be the author or a character in the story through whom the author speaks. Huckleberry Finn is the narrator of Mark Twain's *The Adventures of Huckleberry Finn*.

Novella: An Italian term meaning "story." This term has been especially used to describe fourteenth-century Italian tales, but it also refers to modern short novels. Modern novellas include Leo Tolstoy's *The Death of Ivan Ilich*, Fyodor Dostoyevsky's *Notes from the Underground*, and Joseph Conrad's *Heart of Darkness*.

O

Oedipus Complex: A son's romantic obsession with his mother. The phrase is derived from the story of the ancient Theban hero Oedipus, who unknowingly killed his father and married his mother, and was popularized by Sigmund Freud's theory of psychoanalysis. Literary occurrences of the Oedipus complex include Sophocles' *Oedipus Rex* and D. H. Lawrence's "The Rocking-Horse Winner."

Onomatopoeia: The use of words whose sounds express or suggest their meaning. In its simplest sense, onomatopoeia may be represented by words that mimic the sounds they denote such as "hiss" or "meow." At a more subtle level, the pattern and rhythm of sounds and rhymes of a line or poem may be onomatopoeic.

Oral Tradition: A process by which songs, ballads, folklore, and other material are transmitted by word of mouth. The tradition of oral transmission predates the written record systems of literate society.

Oral transmission preserves material sometimes over generations, although often with variations. Memory plays a large part in the recitation and preservation of orally transmitted material. Native American myths and legends, and African folktales told by plantation slaves are examples of orally transmitted literature.

P

Parable: A story intended to teach a moral lesson or answer an ethical question. Examples of parables are the stories told by Jesus Christ in the New Testament, notably "The Prodigal Son," but parables also are used in Sufism, rabbinic literature, Hasidism, and Zen Buddhism. Isaac Bashevis Singer's story "Gimpel the Fool" exhibits characteristics of a parable.

Paradox: A statement that appears illogical or contradictory at first, but may actually point to an underlying truth. A literary example of a paradox is George Orwell's statement "All animals are equal, but some animals are more equal than others" in *Animal Farm*.

Parody: In literature, this term refers to an imitation of a serious literary work or the signature style of a particular author in a ridiculous manner. A typical parody adopts the style of the original and applies it to an inappropriate subject for humorous effect. Parody is a form of satire and could be considered the literary equivalent of a caricature or cartoon. Henry Fielding's *Shamela* is a parody of Samuel Richardson's *Pamela*.

Persona: A Latin term meaning "mask." Personae are the characters in a fictional work of literature. The persona generally functions as a mask through which the author tells a story in a voice other than his or her own. A persona is usually either a character in a story who acts as a narrator or an "implied author," a voice created by the author to act as the narrator for himself or herself. The persona in Charlotte Perkins Gilman's story "The Yellow Wallpaper" is the unnamed young mother experiencing a mental breakdown.

Personification: A figure of speech that gives human qualities to abstract ideas, animals, and inanimate objects. To say that "the sun is smiling" is to personify the sun.

Plot: The pattern of events in a narrative or drama. In its simplest sense, the plot guides the author in composing the work and helps the reader follow the work. Typically, plots exhibit causality and unity and have a beginning, a middle, and an end. Sometimes, however, a plot may consist of a series of disconnected events, in which case it is known as an "episodic plot."

Poetic Justice: An outcome in a literary work, not necessarily a poem, in which the good are rewarded and the evil are punished, especially in ways that particularly fit their virtues or crimes. For example, a murderer may himself be murdered, or a thief will find himself penniless.

Poetic License: Distortions of fact and literary convention made by a writer—not always a poet—for the sake of the effect gained. Poetic license is closely related to the concept of "artistic freedom." An author exercises poetic license by saying that a pile of money "reaches as high as a mountain" when the pile is actually only a foot or two high.

Point of View: The narrative perspective from which a literary work is presented to the reader. There are four traditional points of view. The "third person omniscient" gives the reader a "godlike" perspective, unrestricted by time or place, from which to see actions and look into the minds of characters. This allows the author to comment openly on characters and events in the work. The "third person" point of view presents the events of the story from outside of any single character's perception, much like the omniscient point of view, but the reader must understand the action as it takes place and without any special insight into characters' minds or motivations. The "first person" or "personal" point of view relates events as they are perceived by a single character. The main character "tells" the story and may offer opinions about the action and characters which differ from those of the author. Much less common than omniscient, third person, and first person is the "second person" point of view, wherein the author tells the story as if it is happening to the reader. James Thurber employs the omniscient point of view in his short story "The Secret Life of Walter Mitty." Ernest Hemingway's "A Clean, Well-Lighted Place" is a short story told from the third person point of view. Mark Twain's novel *Huckleberry Finn* is presented from the first person viewpoint. Jay McInerney's *Bright Lights, Big City* is an example of a novel which uses the second person point of view.

Pornography: Writing intended to provoke feelings of lust in the reader. Such works are often condemned by critics and teachers, but those which can be shown to have literary value are viewed less harshly. Literary works that have been described as pornographic include D. H. Lawrence's *Lady Chatterley's Lover* and James Joyce's *Ulysses.*

Post-Aesthetic Movement: An artistic response made by African Americans to the black aesthetic movement of the 1960s and early 1970s. Writers since that time have adopted a somewhat different tone in their work, with less emphasis placed on the disparity between black and white in the United States. In the words of post-aesthetic authors such as Toni Morrison, John Edgar Wideman, and Kristin Hunter, African Americans are portrayed as looking inward for answers to their own questions, rather than always looking to the outside world. Two well-known examples of works produced as part of the post-aesthetic movement are the Pulitzer Prize-winning novels *The Color Purple* by Alice Walker and *Beloved* by Toni Morrison.

Postmodernism: Writing from the 1960s forward characterized by experimentation and application of modernist elements, which include existentialism and alienation. Postmodernists have gone a step further in the rejection of tradition begun with the modernists by also rejecting traditional forms, preferring the anti-novel over the novel and the anti-hero over the hero. Postmodern writers include Thomas Pynchon, Margaret Drabble, and Gabriel Garcia Marquez.

Prologue: An introductory section of a literary work. It often contains information establishing the situation of the characters or presents information about the setting, time period, or action. In drama, the prologue is spoken by a chorus or by one of the principal characters.

Prose: A literary medium that attempts to mirror the language of everyday speech. It is distinguished from poetry by its use of unmetered, unrhymed language consisting of logically related sentences. Prose is usually grouped into paragraphs that form a cohesive whole such as an essay or a novel. The term is sometimes used to mean an author's general writing.

Protagonist: The central character of a story who serves as a focus for its themes and incidents and as the principal rationale for its development. The protagonist is sometimes referred to in discussions of modern literature as the hero or anti-hero. Well-known protagonists are Hamlet in William Shakespeare's *Hamlet* and Jay Gatsby in F. Scott Fitzgerald's *The Great Gatsby.*

R

Realism: A nineteenth-century European literary movement that sought to portray familiar characters, situations, and settings in a realistic manner. This was done primarily by using an objective narrative point of view and through the buildup of accurate detail. The standard for success of any realistic work depends on how faithfully it transfers common experience into fictional forms. The realistic method may be altered or extended, as in stream of consciousness writing, to record highly subjective experience. Contemporary authors who often write in a realistic way include Nadine Gordimer and Grace Paley.

Resolution: The portion of a story following the climax, in which the conflict is resolved. The resolution of Jane Austen's *Northanger Abbey* is neatly summed up in the following sentence: "Henry and Catherine were married, the bells rang and everybody smiled."

Rising Action: The part of a drama where the plot becomes increasingly complicated. Rising action leads up to the climax, or turning point, of a drama. The final "chase scene" of an action film is generally the rising action which culminates in the film's climax.

Roman a clef: A French phrase meaning "novel with a key." It refers to a narrative in which real persons are portrayed under fictitious names. Jack Kerouac, for example, portrayed various his friends under fictitious names in the novel *On the Road.* D. H. Lawrence based "The Rocking-Horse Winner" on a family he knew.

Romanticism: This term has two widely accepted meanings. In historical criticism, it refers to a European intellectual and artistic movement of the late eighteenth and early nineteenth centuries that sought greater freedom of personal expression than that allowed by the strict rules of literary form and logic of the eighteenth-century neoclassicists. The Romantics preferred emotional and imaginative expression to rational analysis. They considered the individual to be at the center of all experience and so placed him or her at the center of their art. The Romantics believed that the creative imagination reveals nobler truths—unique feelings and attitudes—than those that could be discovered by logic or by scientific examination. "Romanticism" is also used as a general term to refer to a type of sensibility found in all periods of literary history and usually considered to be in opposition to the principles of classicism. In this sense, Romanticism signifies any work or philosophy in which the exotic or dreamlike figure strongly, or that is devoted to individualistic expression, self-analysis, or a pursuit of a higher realm of knowledge than can be discovered by human reason. Prominent Romantics include Jean-Jacques Rousseau, William Wordsworth, John Keats, Lord Byron, and Johann Wolfgang von Goethe.

S

Satire: A work that uses ridicule, humor, and wit to criticize and provoke change in human nature and institutions. Voltaire's novella *Candide* and Jonathan Swift's essay "A Modest Proposal" are both satires. Flannery O'Connor's portrayal of the family in "A Good Man Is Hard to Find" is a satire of a modern, Southern, American family.

Science Fiction: A type of narrative based upon real or imagined scientific theories and technology. Science fiction is often peopled with alien creatures and set on other planets or in different dimensions. Popular writers of science fiction are Isaac Asimov, Karel Capek, Ray Bradbury, and Ursula K. Le Guin.

Setting: The time, place, and culture in which the action of a narrative takes place. The elements of setting may include geographic location, characters's physical and mental environments, prevailing cultural attitudes, or the historical time in which the action takes place.

Short Story: A fictional prose narrative shorter and more focused than a novella. The short story usually deals with a single episode and often a single character. The "tone," the author's attitude toward his or her subject and audience, is uniform throughout. The short story frequently also lacks *denouement*, ending instead at its climax.

Signifying Monkey: A popular trickster figure in black folklore, with hundreds of tales about this character documented since the 19th century. Henry Louis Gates Jr. examines the history of the signifying monkey in *The Signifying Monkey: Towards a Theory of Afro-American Literary Criticism,* published in 1988.

Simile: A comparison, usually using "like" or "as,"of two essentially dissimilar things, as in "coffee as cold as ice" or "He sounded like a broken record." The title of Ernest Hemingway's "Hills Like White Elephants" contains a simile.

Social Realism: The Socialist Realism school of literary theory was proposed by Maxim Gorky and established as a dogma by the first Soviet Congress of Writers. It demanded adherence to a communist worldview in works of literature. Its doctrines required an objective viewpoint comprehensible to the working classes and themes of social struggle featuring strong proletarian heroes. Gabriel Garcia Marquez's stories exhibit some characteristics of Socialist Realism.

Stereotype: A stereotype was originally the name for a duplication made during the printing process; this led to its modern definition as a person or thing that is (or is assumed to be) the same as all others of its type. Common stereotypical characters include the absent-minded professor, the nagging wife, the troublemaking teenager, and the kindhearted grandmother.

Stream of Consciousness: A narrative technique for rendering the inward experience of a character. This technique is designed to give the impression of an ever-changing series of thoughts, emotions, images, and memories in the spontaneous and seemingly illogical order that they occur in life. The textbook example of stream of consciousness is the last section of James Joyce's *Ulysses*.

Structure: The form taken by a piece of literature. The structure may be made obvious for ease of understanding, as in nonfiction works, or may obscured for artistic purposes, as in some poetry or seemingly "unstructured" prose.

Style: A writer's distinctive manner of arranging words to suit his or her ideas and purpose in writing. The unique imprint of the author's personality upon his or her writing, style is the product of an author's way of arranging ideas and his or her use of diction, different sentence structures, rhythm, figures of speech, rhetorical principles, and other elements of composition.

Suspense: A literary device in which the author maintains the audience's attention through the build-up of events, the outcome of which will soon be revealed. Suspense in William Shakespeare's *Hamlet* is sustained throughout by the question of whether or not the Prince will achieve what he has been instructed to do and of what he intends to do.

Symbol: Something that suggests or stands for something else without losing its original identity. In literature, symbols combine their literal meaning with the suggestion of an abstract concept. Literary symbols are of two types: those that carry complex associations of meaning no matter what their contexts, and those that derive their suggestive meaning from their functions in specific literary works. Examples of symbols are sunshine suggesting happiness, rain suggesting sorrow, and storm clouds suggesting despair.

T

Tale: A story told by a narrator with a simple plot and little character development. Tales are usually relatively short and often carry a simple message. Examples of tales can be found in the works of Saki, Anton Chekhov, Guy de Maupassant, and O. Henry.

Tall Tale: A humorous tale told in a straightforward, credible tone but relating absolutely impossible events or feats of the characters. Such tales were commonly told of frontier adventures during the settlement of the west in the United States. Literary use of tall tales can be found in Washington Irving's *History of New York,* Mark Twain's *Life on the Mississippi,* and in the German R. F. Raspe's *Baron Munchausen's Narratives of His Marvellous Travels and Campaigns in Russia.*

Theme: The main point of a work of literature. The term is used interchangeably with thesis. Many works have multiple themes. One of the themes of Nathaniel Hawthorne's "Young Goodman Brown" is loss of faith.

Tone: The author's attitude toward his or her audience may be deduced from the tone of the work. A formal tone may create distance or convey politeness, while an informal tone may encourage a friendly, intimate, or intrusive feeling in the reader. The author's attitude toward his or her subject matter may also be deduced from the tone of the words he or she uses in discussing it. The tone of John F. Kennedy's speech which included the appeal to "ask not what your country can do for you" was intended to instill feelings of camaraderie and national pride in listeners.

Tragedy: A drama in prose or poetry about a noble, courageous hero of excellent character who, because of some tragic character flaw, brings ruin upon him- or herself. Tragedy treats its subjects in a dignified and serious manner, using poetic language to help evoke pity and fear and bring about catharsis, a purging of these emotions. The tragic form was practiced extensively by the ancient Greeks. The classical form of tragedy was revived in the sixteenth century; it flourished especially on the Elizabethan stage. In modern times, dramatists have attempted to adapt the form to the needs of modern society by drawing their heroes from the ranks of ordinary men and women and defining the nobility of these heroes in terms of spirit rather than exalted social standing. Some contemporary works that are thought of as tragedies include *The Great Gatsby* by F. Scott Fitzgerald, and *The Sound and the Fury* by William Faulkner.

Tragic Flaw: In a tragedy, the quality within the hero or heroine which leads to his or her downfall. Examples of the tragic flaw include Othello's jealousy and Hamlet's indecisiveness, although most great tragedies defy such simple interpretation.

U

Utopia: A fictional perfect place, such as "paradise" or "heaven." An early literary utopia was described in Plato's *Republic,* and in modern literature, Ursula K. Le Guin depicts a utopia in "The Ones Who Walk Away from Omelas."

V

Victorian: Refers broadly to the reign of Queen Victoria of England (1837-1901) and to anything with qualities typical of that era. For example, the qualities of smug narrow-mindedness, bourgeois materialism, faith in social progress, and priggish morality are often considered Victorian. In literature, the Victorian Period was the great age of the English novel, and the latter part of the era saw the rise of movements such as decadence and symbolism.

Cumulative Author/Title Index

A

A & P (Updike): V3
Achebe, Chinua
   Vengeful Creditor: V3
Aiken, Conrad
   Silent Snow, Secret Snow: V8
Allende, Isabel
   And of Clay Are We Created: V11
An Occurrence at Owl Creek Bridge (Bierce): V2
And of Clay Are We Created (Allende): V11
Anderson, Sherwood
   Death in the Woods: V10
   Hands: V11
   Sophistication: V4
Araby (Joyce): V1
Atwood, Margaret
   Rape Fantasies: V3
Axolotl (Cortazar): V3

B

Babel, Isaac
   My First Goose: V10
Babylon Revisited (Fitzgerald): V4
Baldwin, James
   Sonny's Blues: V2
Bambara, Toni Cade
   Blues Ain't No Mockin Bird: V4
   Raymond's Run: V7
Barn Burning (Faulkner): V5
Barth, John
   Lost in the Funhouse: V6
Barthelme, Donald
   Robert Kennedy Saved from Drowning: V3
Bartleby the Scrivener, A Tale of Wall Street (Melville): V3
Bates, H. E.
   The Daffodil Sky: V7
Battle Royal or *The Invisible Man* (Ellison): V11
The Bear (Faulkner): V2
The Beast in the Jungle (James): V6
Beattie, Ann
   Janus: V9
Berriault, Gina
   The Stone Boy: V7
   Women in Their Beds: V11
Bierce, Ambrose
   An Occurrence at Owl Creek Bridge: V2
   The Boarded Window: V9
Big Blonde (Parker): V5
Blackberry Winter (Warren): V8
Bliss (Mansfield): V10
Blood-Burning Moon (Toomer): V5
Bloodchild (Butler): V6
The Bloody Chamber (Carter): V4
Bloom, Amy
   Silver Water: V11
Blues Ain't No Mockin Bird (Bambara): V4
The Blues I'm Playing (Hughes): V7
The Boarded Window (Bierce): V9
Borges, Jorge Luis
   The Garden of Forking Paths: V9
   Pierre Menard, Author of the Quixote: V4
Bowen, Elizabeth
   The Demon Lover: V5
Boyle, Kay
   The White Horses of Vienna: V10
Boys and Girls (Munro): V5
Bradbury, Ray
   There Will Come Soft Rains: V1
Butler, Octavia
   Bloodchild: V6
Butler, Robert Olen
   A Good Scent from a Strange Mountain: V11

C

Camus, Albert
   The Guest: V4
The Canterville Ghost (Wilde): V7
Capote, Truman
   A Christmas Memory: V2
Carter, Angela
   The Bloody Chamber: V4
Carver, Raymond
   Cathedral: V6
   Where I'm Calling From: V3
The Cask of Amontillado (Poe): V7
The Catbird Seat (Thurber): V10
Cathedral (Carver): V6
Cather, Willa
   Neighbour Rosicky: V7
   Paul's Case: V2
The Celebrated Jumping Frog of Calaveras County (Twain): V1
Cheever, John
   The Swimmer: V2

Chekhov, Anton
   The Lady with the Pet Dog: V5
Chesnutt, Charles Waddell
   The Sheriff's Children: V11
Children of the Sea (Danticat): V1
Chopin, Kate
   The Story of an Hour: V2
A Christmas Memory (Capote): V2
The Chrysanthemums (Steinbeck): V6
Cisneros, Sandra
   Woman Hollering Creek: V3
Clarke, Arthur C.
   The Star: V4
A Clean, Well-Lighted Place (Hemingway): V9
Connell, Richard
   The Most Dangerous Game: V1
Conrad, Joseph
   The Secret Sharer: V1
A Conversation with My Father (Paley): V3
Cortazar, Julio
   Axolotl: V3
Crane, Stephen
   The Open Boat: V4

D

The Daffodil Sky (Bates): V7
Dahl, Roald
   Lamb to the Slaughter: V4
Danticat, Edwidge
   Children of the Sea: V1
de Balzac, Honore
   La Grande Bretèche: V10
The Dead (Joyce): V6
Death in the Woods (Anderson): V10
Death in Venice (Mann): V9
The Death of Ivan Ilych (Tolstoy): V5
The Demon Lover (Bowen): V5
The Devil and Tom Walker (Irving): V1
The Difference (Glasgow): V9
Dinesen, Isak
   The Ring: V6
   Sorrow-Acre: V3
Disorder and Early Sorrow (Mann): V4
The Door in the Wall (Wells): V3
Dostoevsky, Fyodor
   The Grand Inquisitor: V8
Doyle, Arthur Conan
   The Red-Headed League: V2
Dubus, Andre
   The Fat Girl: V10

E

The Eatonville Anthology (Hurston): V1
Eliot, George
   The Lifted Veil: V8

Ellison, Ralph
   Battle Royal or *The Invisible Man*: V11
   King of the Bingo Game: V1
Everyday Use (Walker): V2
Everything That Rises Must Converge (O'Connor): V10

F

The Fall of the House of Usher (Poe): V2
Far, Sui Sin
   Mrs. Spring Fragrance: V4
The Fat Girl (Dubus): V10
Faulkner, William
   Barn Burning: V5
   The Bear: V2
   A Rose for Emily: V6
Fever (Wideman): V6
Fitzgerald, F. Scott
   Babylon Revisited: V4
Flaubert, Gustave
   A Simple Heart: V6
Flight (Steinbeck): V3
Flowering Judas (Porter): V8
Freeman, Mary E. Wilkins
   A New England Nun: V8
   The Revolt of 'Mother': V4

G

Gaines, Ernest
   The Sky is Gray: V5
Galsworthy, John
   The Japanese Quince: V3
The Garden of Forking Paths (Borges): V9
The Garden Party (Mansfield): V8
Gardner, John
   Redemption: V8
The Gift of the Magi (Henry): V2
Gilchrist, Ellen
   Victory Over Japan: V9
The Gilded Six-Bits (Hurston): V11
Gilman, Charlotte Perkins
   The Yellow Wallpaper: V1
Gimpel the Fool (Singer): V2
Girl (Kincaid): V7
Glasgow, Ellen
   The Difference: V9
Glaspell, Susan
   A Jury of Her Peers: V3
Gogol, Nikolai
   The Overcoat: V7
A Good Man Is Hard to Find (O'Connor): V2
A Good Scent from a Strange Mountain (Butler): V11
Gordimer, Nadine
   The Train from Rhodesia: V2
Grand Bretèche, La (de Balzac): V10
The Grand Inquisitor (Dostoevsky): V8

The Grave (Porter): V11
The Guest (Camus): V4
Guests of the Nation (O'Connor): V5
A Guide to Berlin (Nabokov): V6

H

Half a Day (Mahfouz): V9
Hands (Anderson): V11
The Handsomest Drowned Man in the World (Marquez): V1
Han's Crime (Naoya): V5
Harrison Bergeron (Vonnegut): V5
Harte, Bret
   The Outcasts of Poker Flat: V3
Hawthorne, Nathaniel
   The Minister's Black Veil: V7
   My Kinsman, Major Molineux: V11
   Young Goodman Brown: V1
Head, Bessie
   Snapshots of a Wedding: V5
Heinlein, Robert A.
   Waldo: V7
Hemingway, Ernest
   A Clean, Well-Lighted Place: V9
   Hills Like White Elephants: V6
   In Another Country: V8
   The Short Happy Life of Francis Macomber: V1
   The Snows of Kilimanjaro: V11
Hempel, Amy
   In the Cemetery Where Al Jolson Is Buried: V2
Henry, O.
   The Gift of the Magi: V2
Hills Like White Elephants (Hemingway): V6
The Hitchhiking Game (Kundera): V10
A Horse and Two Goats (Narayan): V5
How I Contemplated the World from the Detroit House of Correction and Began My Life Over Again (Oates): V8
Hughes, Langston
   The Blues I'm Playing: V7
   Slave on the Block: V4
A Hunger Artist (Kafka): V7
Hurston, Zora Neale
   The Eatonville Anthology: V1
   The Gilded Six-Bits: V11
   Spunk: V6

I

I Stand Here Ironing (Olsen): V1
In Another Country (Hemingway): V8
In the Cemetery Where Al Jolson Is Buried (Hempel): V2
In the Garden of the North American Martyrs (Wolff): V4

In the Penal Colony (Kafka): V3
Irving, Washington
   The Devil and Tom Walker: V1
   The Legend of Sleepy Hollow: V8

J

Jackson, Shirley
   The Lottery: V1
Jacobs, W. W.
   The Monkey's Paw: V2
James, Henry
   The Beast in the Jungle: V6
   The Jolly Corner: V9
Janus (Beattie): V9
The Japanese Quince (Galsworthy): V3
Jeeves Takes Charge (Wodehouse): V10
Jewett, Sarah Orne
   A White Heron: V4
The Jilting of Granny Weatherall (Porter): V1
The Jolly Corner (James): V9
Joyce, James
   Araby: V1
   The Dead: V6
A Jury of Her Peers (Glaspell): V3

K

Kafka, Franz
   A Hunger Artist: V7
   In the Penal Colony: V3
Kincaid, Jamaica
   Girl: V7
   What I Have Been Doing Lately: V5
King of the Bingo Game (Ellison): V1
Kingston, Maxine Hong
   On Discovery: V3
Kipling, Rudyard
   Mrs. Bathurst: V8
Kundera, Milan
   The Hitchhiking Game: V10

L

La Grande Bretèche (de Balzac): V10
The Lady, or the Tiger? (Stockton): V3
The Lady with the Pet Dog (Chekhov): V5
Lamb to the Slaughter (Dahl): V4
Lawrence, D. H.
   Odour of Chrysanthemums: V6
   The Rocking-Horse Winner: V2
Le Guin, Ursula K.
   The Ones Who Walk Away from Omelas: V2
The Legend of Sleepy Hollow (Irving): V8
Lessing, Doris
   Through the Tunnel: V1
The Life You Save May Be Your Own (O'Connor): V7
The Lifted Veil (Eliot): V8
London, Jack
   To Build a Fire: V7
Lost in the Funhouse (Barth): V6
The Lottery (Jackson): V1
Lullaby (Silko): V10

M

The Magic Barrel (Malamud): V8
Mahfouz, Naguib
   Half a Day: V9
Malamud, Bernard
   The Magic Barrel: V8
The Man That Corrupted Hadleyburg (Twain): V7
The Man to Send Rain Clouds (Silko): V8
The Man Who Lived Underground (Wright): V3
The Man Who Was Almost a Man (Wright): V9
The Management of Grief (Mukherjee): V7
Mann, Thomas
   Death in Venice: V9
   Disorder and Early Sorrow: V4
Mansfield, Katherine
   Bliss: V10
   The Garden Party: V8
   Marriage á la Mode: V11
   Miss Brill: V2
Marmon Silko, Leslie
   Storyteller: V11
Marquez, Gabriel Garcia
   The Handsomest Drowned Man in the World: V1
   A Very Old Man with Enormous Wings: V6
Marriage á la Mode (Mansfield): V11
Mason, Bobbie Ann
   Residents and Transients: V8
   Shiloh: V3
The Masque of the Red Death (Poe): V8
Mateo Falcone (Merimee): V8
Maupassant, Guy de
   The Necklace: V4
McCullers, Carson
   Wunderkind: V5
Melanctha (Stein): V5
Melville, Herman
   Bartleby the Scrivener, A Tale of Wall Street: V3
Merimee, Prosper
   Mateo Falcone: V8
The Minister's Black Veil (Hawthorne): V7
Mishima, Yukio
   Swaddling Clothes: V5
Miss Brill (Mansfield): V2
Mistry, Rohinton
   Swimming Lessons: V6
The Monkey's Paw (Jacobs): V2
Morrison, Toni
   Recitatif: V5
The Most Dangerous Game (Connell): V1
Mphahlele, Es'kia (Ezekiel)
   Mrs. Plum: V11
Mrs. Bathurst (Kipling): V8
Mrs. Plum (Mphahlele): V11
Mrs. Spring Fragrance (Far): V4
Mukherjee, Bharati
   The Management of Grief: V7
Munro, Alice
   Boys and Girls: V5
My First Goose (Babel): V10
My Kinsman, Major Molineux (Hawthorne): V11

N

Nabokov, Vladimir
   A Guide to Berlin: V6
Naoya, Shiga
   Han's Crime: V5
Narayan, R. K.
   A Horse and Two Goats: V5
The Necklace (Maupassant): V4
Neighbour Rosicky (Cather): V7
The New Dress (Woolf): V4
A New England Nun (Freeman): V8
The News from Ireland (Trevor): V10

O

Oates, Joyce Carol
   How I Contemplated the World from the Detroit House of Correction and Began My Life Over Again: V8
   Where Are You Going, Where Have You Been?: V1
O'Brien, Tim
   The Things They Carried: V5
O'Connor, Flannery
   Everything That Rises Must Converge: V10
   A Good Man Is Hard to Find: V2
   The Life You Save May Be Your Own: V7
O'Connor, Frank
   Guests of the Nation: V5
Odour of Chrysanthemums (Lawrence): V6
O'Flaherty, Liam
   The Wave: V5

Olsen, Tillie
  I Stand Here Ironing: V1
On Discovery (Kingston): V3
One Day in the Life of Ivan Denisovich (Solzhenitsyn): V9
The Ones Who Walk Away from Omelas (Le Guin): V2
The Open Boat (Crane): V4
The Open Window (Saki): V1
Orwell, George
  Shooting an Elephant: V4
The Outcasts of Poker Flat (Harte): V3
The Overcoat (Gogol): V7
Ozick, Cynthia
  The Shawl: V3

P

Paley, Grace
  A Conversation with My Father: V3
Parker, Dortothy
  Big Blonde: V5
Paul's Case (Cather): V2
Phillips, Jayne Anne
  Souvenir: V4
Pierre Menard, Author of the Quixote (Borges): V4
Poe, Edgar Allan
  The Cask of Amontillado: V7
  The Fall of the House of Usher: V2
  The Masque of the Red Death: V8
  The Tell-Tale Heart: V4
Pomegranate Seed (Wharton): V6
Porter, Katherine Anne
  Flowering Judas: V8
  The Grave: V11
  The Jilting of Granny Weatherall: V1
Pushkin, Alexander
  The Stationmaster: V9

R

Rape Fantasies (Atwood): V3
Raymond's Run (Bambara): V7
Recitatif (Morrison): V5
Redemption (Gardner): V8
The Red-Headed League (Doyle): V2
Residents and Transients (Mason): V8
The Revolt of 'Mother' (Freeman): V4
The Ring (Dinesen): V6
Robert Kennedy Saved from Drowning (Barthelme): V3
The Rocking-Horse Winner (Lawrence): V2
Roman Fever (Wharton): V7

A Rose for Emily (Faulkner): V6
Roselily (Walker): V11

S

Saki,
  The Open Window: V1
Sartre, Jean-Paul
  The Wall: V9
Say Yes (Wolff): V11
Scott, Sir Walter
  Wandering Willie's Tale: V10
The Secret Life of Walter Mitty (Thurber): V1
The Secret Sharer (Conrad): V1
The Shawl (Ozick): V3
The Sheriff's Children (Chesnutt): V11
Shiloh (Mason): V3
Shooting an Elephant (Orwell): V4
The Short Happy Life of Francis Macomber (Hemingway): V1
Silent Snow, Secret Snow (Aiken): V8
Silko, Leslie Marmon
  Lullaby: V10
  The Man to Send Rain Clouds: V8
  Storyteller: V11
  Yellow Woman: V4
Silver Water (Bloom): V11
A Simple Heart (Flaubert): V6
Singer, Isaac Bashevis
  Gimpel the Fool: V2
The Sky is Gray (Gaines): V5
Slave on the Block (Hughes): V4
Snapshots of a Wedding (Head): V5
The Snows of Kilimanjaro (Hemingway): V11
Solzhenitsyn, Alexandr
  One Day in the Life of Ivan Denisovich: V9
Sonny's Blues (Baldwin): V2
Sontag, Susan
  The Way We Live Now: V10
Sophistication (Anderson): V4
Sorrow-Acre (Dinesen): V3
Souvenir (Phillips): V4
A Spinster's Tale (Taylor): V9
Spunk (Hurston): V6
The Star (Clarke): V4
The Stationmaster (Pushkin): V9
Stein, Gertrude
  Melanctha: V5
Steinbeck, John
  The Chrysanthemums: V6
  Flight: V3
Stockton, Frank R.
  The Lady, or the Tiger?: V3
The Stone Boy (Berriault): V7
The Story of an Hour (Chopin): V2
Storyteller (Marmon Silko): V11
Swaddling Clothes (Mishima): V5

The Swimmer (Cheever): V2
Swimming Lessons (Mistry): V6

T

Tan, Amy
  Two Kinds: V9
Taylor, Peter
  A Spinster's Tale: V9
The Tell-Tale Heart (Poe): V4
There Will Come Soft Rains (Bradbury): V1
The Things They Carried (O'Brien): V5
Through the Tunnel (Lessing): V1
Thurber, James
  The Catbird Seat: V10
  The Secret Life of Walter Mitty: V1
To Build a Fire (London): V7
Tolstoy, Leo
  The Death of Ivan Ilych: V5
Toomer, Jean
  Blood-Burning Moon: V5
The Train from Rhodesia (Gordimer): V2
Trevor, William
  The News from Ireland: V10
Twain, Mark
  The Celebrated Jumping Frog of Calaveras County: V1
  The Man That Corrupted Hadleyburg: V7
Two Kinds (Tan): V9

U

Updike, John
  A & P: V3

V

Vengeful Creditor (Achebe): V3
A Very Old Man with Enormous Wings (Marquez): V6
Victory Over Japan (Gilchrist): V9
Vonnegut, Kurt
  Harrison Bergeron: V5

W

Waldo (Heinlein): V7
Walker, Alice
  Everyday Use: V2
  Roselily: V11
The Wall (Sartre): V9
Wandering Willie's Tale (Scott): V10
Warren, Robert Penn
  Blackberry Winter: V8
The Wave (O'Flaherty): V5
The Way We Live Now (Sontag): V10
Wells, H. G.
  The Door in the Wall: V3

Welty, Eudora
 Why I Live at the P.O.: V10
 A Worn Path: V2
Wharton, Edith
 Pomegranate Seed: V6
 Roman Fever: V7
What I Have Been Doing Lately
 (Kincaid): V5
Where Are You Going, Where Have
 You Been? (Oates): V1
Where I'm Calling From
 (Carver): V3
A White Heron (Jewett): V4
The White Horses of Vienna
 (Boyle): V10

Why I Live at the P.O. (Welty): V10
Wideman, John Edgar
 Fever: V6
Wilde, Oscar
 The Canterville Ghost: V7
Wodehouse, Pelham Grenville
 Jeeves Takes Charge: V10
Wolff, Tobias
 In the Garden of the North
  American Martyrs: V4
 Say Yes: V11
Woman Hollering Creek
 (Cisneros): V3
Women in Their Beds
 (Berriault): V11

Woolf, Virginia
 The New Dress: V4
A Worn Path (Welty): V2
Wright, Richard
 The Man Who Lived
  Underground: V3
Wunderkind (McCullers): V5

Y

The Yellow Wallpaper (Gilman): V1
Yellow Woman (Silko): V4
Young Goodman Brown
 (Hawthorne): V1

Nationality/Ethnicity Index

African American

Baldwin, James
  Sonny's Blues: V2
Bambara, Toni Cade
  Blues Ain't No Mockin Bird: V4
  Raymond's Run: V7
Butler, Octavia
  Bloodchild: V6
Chesnutt, Charles Waddell
  The Sheriff's Children: V11
Ellison, Ralph
  Battle Royal or *The Invisible Man*: V11
  King of the Bingo Game: V1
Hughes, Langston
  The Blues I'm Playing: V7
  Slave on the Block: V4
Hurston, Zora Neale
  The Eatonville Anthology: V1
  The Gilded Six-Bits: V11
  Spunk: V6
Toomer, Jean
  Blood-Burning Moon: V5
Walker, Alice
  Everyday Use: V2
  Roselily: V11
Wideman, John Edgar
  Fever: V6
Wright, Richard
  The Man Who Lived Underground: V3

American

Aiken, Conrad
  Silent Snow, Secret Snow: V8
Anderson, Sherwood
  Death in the Woods: V10
  Hands: V11
  Sophistication: V4
Baldwin, James
  Sonny's Blues: V2
Bambara, Toni Cade
  Blues Ain't No Mockin Bird: V4
  Raymond's Run: V7
Barth, John
  Lost in the Funhouse: V6
Barthelme, Donald
  Robert Kennedy Saved from Drowning: V3
Beattie, Ann
  Janus: V9
Berriault, Gina
  The Stone Boy: V7
  Women in Their Beds: V11
Bierce, Ambrose
  An Occurrence at Owl Creek Bridge: V2
  The Boarded Window: V9
Bloom, Amy
  Silver Water: V11
Boyle, Kay
  The White Horses of Vienna: V10
Bradbury, Ray
  There Will Come Soft Rains: V1
Butler, Octavia
  Bloodchild: V6
Butler, Robert Olen
  A Good Scent from a Strange Mountain: V11
Capote, Truman
  A Christmas Memory: V2
Carver, Raymond
  Cathedral: V6
  Where I'm Calling From: V3
Cather, Willa
  Neighbour Rosicky: V7
  Paul's Case: V2
Cheever, John
  The Swimmer: V2
Chesnutt, Charles Waddell
  The Sheriff's Children: V11
Chopin, Kate
  The Story of an Hour: V2
Cisneros, Sandra
  Woman Hollering Creek: V3
Connell, Richard
  The Most Dangerous Game: V1
Crane, Stephen
  The Open Boat: V4
Dubus, Andre
  The Fat Girl: V10
Ellison, Ralph
  Battle Royal or *The Invisible Man*: V11
  King of the Bingo Game: V1
Faulkner, William
  Barn Burning: V5
  The Bear: V2
  A Rose for Emily: V6
Fitzgerald, F. Scott
  Babylon Revisited: V4
Freeman, Mary E. Wilkins
  A New England Nun: V8
  The Revolt of 'Mother': V4
Gaines, Ernest
  The Sky is Gray: V5
Gardner, John
  Redemption: V8

Gilchrist, Ellen
  Victory Over Japan: V9
Gilman, Charlotte Perkins
  The Yellow Wallpaper: V1
Glasgow, Ellen
  The Difference: V9
Glaspell, Susan
  A Jury of Her Peers: V3
Harte, Bret
  The Outcasts of Poker Flat: V3
Hawthorne, Nathaniel
  The Minister's Black Veil: V7
  My Kinsman, Major Molineux: V11
  Young Goodman Brown: V1
Heinlein, Robert A.
  Waldo: V7
Hemingway, Ernest
  A Clean, Well-Lighted Place: V9
  Hills Like White Elephants: V6
  In Another Country: V8
  The Short Happy Life of Francis Macomber: V1
  The Snows of Kilimanjaro: V11
Hempel, Amy
  In the Cemetery Where Al Jolson Is Buried: V2
Henry, O.
  The Gift of the Magi: V2
Hughes, Langston
  The Blues I'm Playing: V7
  Slave on the Block: V4
Hurston, Zora Neale
  The Eatonville Anthology: V1
  The Gilded Six-Bits: V11
  Spunk: V6
Irving, Washington
  The Devil and Tom Walker: V1
  The Legend of Sleepy Hollow: V8
Jackson, Shirley
  The Lottery: V1
James, Henry
  The Beast in the Jungle: V6
  The Jolly Corner: V9
Jewett, Sarah Orne
  A White Heron: V4
Kincaid, Jamaica
  Girl: V7
  What I Have Been Doing Lately: V5
Kingston, Maxine Hong
  On Discovery: V3
Le Guin, Ursula K.
  The Ones Who Walk Away from Omelas: V2
London, Jack
  To Build a Fire: V7
Malamud, Bernard
  The Magic Barrel: V8
Mason, Bobbie Ann
  Residents and Transients: V8
  Shiloh: V3
McCullers, Carson
  Wunderkind: V5
Melville, Herman
  Bartleby the Scrivener, A Tale of Wall Street: V3
Morrison, Toni
  Recitatif: V5
Nabokov, Vladimir
  A Guide to Berlin: V6
Oates, Joyce Carol
  How I Contemplated the World from the Detroit House of Correction and Began My Life Over Again: V8
  Where Are You Going, Where Have You Been?: V1
O'Brien, Tim
  The Things They Carried: V5
O'Connor, Flannery
  Everything That Rises Must Converge: V10
  A Good Man Is Hard to Find: V2
  The Life You Save May Be Your Own: V7
Olsen, Tillie
  I Stand Here Ironing: V1
Ozick, Cynthia
  The Shawl: V3
Paley, Grace
  A Conversation with My Father: V3
Parker, Dorothy
  Big Blonde: V5
Phillips, Jayne Anne
  Souvenir: V4
Poe, Edgar Allan
  The Cask of Amontillado: V7
  The Fall of the House of Usher: V2
  The Masque of the Red Death: V8
  The Tell-Tale Heart: V4
Porter, Katherine Anne
  Flowering Judas: V8
  The Grave: V11
  The Jilting of Granny Weatherall: V1
Silko, Leslie Marmon
  Lullaby: V10
  The Man to Send Rain Clouds: V8
  Storyteller: V11
  Yellow Woman: V4
Singer, Isaac Bashevis
  Gimpel the Fool: V2
Sontag, Susan
  The Way We Live Now: V10
Stein, Gertrude
  Melanctha: V5
Steinbeck, John
  The Chrysanthemums: V6
  Flight: V3
Stockton, Frank R.
  The Lady, or the Tiger?: V3
Tan, Amy
  Two Kinds: V9
Taylor, Peter
  A Spinster's Tale: V9
Thurber, James
  The Catbird Seat: V10
  The Secret Life of Walter Mitty: V1
Toomer, Jean
  Blood-Burning Moon: V5
Twain, Mark
  The Celebrated Jumping Frog of Calaveras County: V1
  The Man That Corrupted Hadleyburg: V7
Updike, John
  A & P: V3
Vonnegut, Kurt
  Harrison Bergeron: V5
Walker, Alice
  Everyday Use: V2
  Roselily: V11
Warren, Robert Penn
  Blackberry Winter: V8
Welty, Eudora
  Why I Live at the P.O.: V10
  A Worn Path: V2
Wharton, Edith
  Pomegranate Seed: V6
  Roman Fever: V7
Wideman, John Edgar
  Fever: V6
Wolff, Tobias
  In the Garden of the North American Martyrs: V4
  Say Yes: V11
Wright, Richard
  The Man Who Lived Underground: V3
  The Man Who Was Almost a Man: V9

Antiguan

Kincaid, Jamaica
  Girl: V7
  What I Have Been Doing Lately: V5

Argentine

Borges, Jorge Luis
  The Garden of Forking Paths: V9
  Pierre Menard, Author of the Quixote: V4
Cortazar, Julio
  Axolotl: V3

Asian American

Kingston, Maxine Hong
  On Discovery: V3

Nationality/Ethnicity Index

Austrian
Kafka, Franz
 A Hunger Artist: V7
 In the Penal Colony: V3

Canadian
Atwood, Margaret
 Rape Fantasies: V3
Mistry, Rohinton
 Swimming Lessons: V6
Mukherjee, Bharati
 The Management of Grief: V7
Munro, Alice
 Boys and Girls: V5

Chicano
Cisneros, Sandra
 Woman Hollering Creek: V3

Chilean
Allende, Isabel
 And of Clay Are We Created: V11

Colombian
Marquez, Gabriel Garcia
 The Handsomest Drowned Man in the World: V1
 A Very Old Man with Enormous Wings: V6

Czech
Kafka, Franz
 A Hunger Artist: V7
 In the Penal Colony: V3
Kundera, Milan
 The Hitchhiking Game: V10

Danish
Dinesen, Isak
 The Ring: V6
 Sorrow-Acre: V3

Egyptian
Mahfouz, Naguib
 Half a Day: V9

English
Bates, H. E.
 The Daffodil Sky: V7
Bowen, Elizabeth
 The Demon Lover: V5
Carter, Angela
 The Bloody Chamber: V4
Clarke, Arthur C.
 The Star: V4
Conrad, Joseph
 The Secret Sharer: V1
Eliot, George
 The Lifted Veil: V8
Far, Sui Sin
 Mrs. Spring Fragrance: V4
Galsworthy, John
 The Japanese Quince: V3
Jacobs, W. W.
 The Monkey's Paw: V2
Kipling, Rudyard
 Mrs. Bathurst: V8
Lawrence, D. H.
 Odour of Chrysanthemums: V6
 The Rocking-Horse Winner: V2
Lessing, Doris
 Through the Tunnel: V1
Orwell, George
 Shooting an Elephant: V4
Saki,
 The Open Window: V1
Wells, H. G.
 The Door in the Wall: V3
Wodehouse, Pelham Grenville
 Jeeves Takes Charge: V10
Woolf, Virginia
 The New Dress: V4

Eurasian
Far, Sui Sin
 Mrs. Spring Fragrance: V4

French
Camus, Albert
 The Guest: V4
de Balzac, Honore
 La Grande Bretèche: V10
Flaubert, Gustave
 A Simple Heart: V6
Maupassant, Guy de
 The Necklace: V4
Merimee, Prosper
 Mateo Falcone: V8
Sartre, Jean-Paul
 The Wall: V9

German
Mann, Thomas
 Death in Venice: V9
 Disorder and Early Sorrow: V4

Haitian
Danticat, Edwidge
 Children of the Sea: V1

Indian
Mistry, Rohinton
 Swimming Lessons: V6
Mukherjee, Bharati
 The Management of Grief: V7
Narayan, R. K.
 A Horse and Two Goats: V5

Irish
Bowen, Elizabeth
 The Demon Lover: V5
Joyce, James
 Araby: V1
 The Dead: V6
O'Connor, Frank
 Guests of the Nation: V5
O'Flaherty, Liam
 The Wave: V5
Trevor, William
 The News from Ireland: V10
Wilde, Oscar
 The Canterville Ghost: V7

Japanese
Mishima, Yukio
 Swaddling Clothes: V5
Naoya, Shiga
 Han's Crime: V5

Jewish
Babel, Isaac
 My First Goose: V10
Berriault, Gina
 The Stone Boy: V7
Kafka, Franz
 A Hunger Artist: V7
 In the Penal Colony: V3

Jewish American
Malamud, Bernard
 The Magic Barrel: V8
Ozick, Cynthia
 The Shawl: V3
Paley, Grace
 A Conversation with My Father: V3
Singer, Isaac Bashevis
 Gimpel the Fool: V2
Stein, Gertrude
 Melanctha: V5

Native American
Silko, Leslie Marmon
 Lullaby: V10
 The Man to Send Rain Clouds: V8
 Storyteller: V11
 Yellow Woman: V4

New Zealander
Mansfield, Katherine
Bliss: V10
The Garden Party: V8
Marriage á la Mode: V11
Miss Brill: V2

Nigerian
Achebe, Chinua
Vengeful Creditor: V3

Polish
Conrad, Joseph
The Secret Sharer: V1
Singer, Isaac Bashevis
Gimpel the Fool: V2

Russian
Babel, Isaac
My First Goose: V10
Chekhov, Anton
The Lady with the Pet Dog: V5
Dostoevsky, Fyodor
The Grand Inquisitor: V8
Gogol, Nikolai
The Overcoat: V7
Nabokov, Vladimir
A Guide to Berlin: V6
Pushkin, Alexander
The Stationmaster: V9
Solzhenitsyn, Alexandr
One Day in the Life of Ivan Denisovich: V9
Tolstoy, Leo
The Death of Ivan Ilych: V5

Scottish
Doyle, Arthur Conan
The Red-Headed League: V2
Scott, Sir Walter
Wandering Willie's Tale: V10

South African
Gordimer, Nadine
The Train from Rhodesia: V2
Grand Bretèche, La (de Balzac): V10
Head, Bessie
Snapshots of a Wedding: V5
Mphahlele, Es'kia (Ezekiel)
Mrs. Plum: V11

Welsh
Dahl, Roald
Lamb to the Slaughter: V4

West Indian
Kincaid, Jamaica
Girl: V7
What I Have Been Doing Lately: V5

Subject/Theme Index

*Boldface terms appear as subheads in Themes section of story.

1960s
- *Mrs. Plum:* 130, 135, 137
- *Storyteller:* 262-263
- *Women in Their Beds:* 285, 291

1970s
- *Storyteller:* 262-263

1980s
- *Say Yes:* 188, 192-195

A

Abandonment
- *Hands:* 109-110

Adultery
- *The Gilded Six-Bits:* 51-52

Adulthood
- *Marriage á la Mode:* 115-117, 123, 125-126

Adventure and Exploration
- *The Gilded Six-Bits:* 53

Africa
- *Mrs. Plum:* 130-138, 144-146
- *The Snows of Kilimanjaro:* 245-246, 249-251, 254-255

Alcoholism, Drugs, and Drug Addiction
- *Women in Their Beds:* 285, 291

Alienation
- *Say Yes:* 191

Alienation and Loneliness
- *Hands:* 97
- *Roselily:* 172

Alienation and Loneliness of Growing into Adulthood
- *Battle Royal* or *The Invisible Man:* 22

Allegory
- *My Kinsman, Major Molineux:* 154, 156, 160-164
- *Storyteller:* 269-270

Alliteration
- *Roselily:* 178-179

Ambiguity
- *Storyteller:* 265-266

American Northeast
- *Hands:* 96-97, 102
- *My Kinsman, Major Molineux:* 149-150, 153-156, 161-163
- *Roselily:* 172-174

American Northwest
- *Battle Royal* or *The Invisible Man:* 19, 22-25, 29-31

American South
- *The Gilded Six-Bits:* 53-54
- *A Good Scent from a Strange Mountain:* 61, 65-66
- *Roselily:* 169, 171, 173, 175
- *The Sheriff's Children:* 206-207, 214

Anger
- *Mrs. Plum:* 141-143
- *Say Yes:* 202-203
- *Storyteller:* 262

Apartheid
- *Mrs. Plum:* 130-132, 136-138

Apathy
- *Say Yes:* 203

Appearances and Reality
- *The Gilded Six-Bits:* 43

Hands: 98

Artistic Creation
- *The Snows of Kilimanjaro:* 246

Asia
- *A Good Scent from a Strange Mountain:* 60-62, 65-71, 75-77

Atonement
- *The Grave:* 81-82
- *The Sheriff's Children:* 221, 224-226

B

Beauty
- *A Good Scent from a Strange Mountain:* 74-77
- *Silver Water:* 230, 232-234, 238
- *Storyteller:* 273-275

Betrayal and Forgiveness
- *The Gilded Six-Bits:* 43

Betrayal
- *The Gilded Six-Bits:* 39, 41, 43-44

Bildungsroman
- *Mrs. Plum:* 135, 138

Black Arts Movement
- *The Gilded Six-Bits:* 45, 48
- *Roselily:* 169, 174-176

Bloomsbury Group
- *Marriage á la Mode:* 121

Buddhism
- *A Good Scent from a Strange Mountain:* 62, 65, 68, 74-76

Subject/Theme Index

C

Change and Transformation
   Marriage á la Mode: 119
   Roselily: 172

Childhood
   Marriage á la Mode: 123, 125, 127-129

Christianity
   The Grave: 81, 86
   Roselily: 171-174, 183-185

City versus Country
   My Kinsman, Major Molineux: 153

Civil Rights
   Mrs. Plum: 133

Civil Rights
   Battle Royal or *The Invisible Man:* 23, 25-26
   Roselily: 171, 174-175

Colonialism
   Storyteller: 256, 260-261

Colonization: Territory and Culture
   Storyteller: 260

Coming of age
   The Grave: 81

Coming of Age
   My Kinsman, Major Molineux: 152

Communism
   A Good Scent from a Strange Mountain: 60-61, 67, 74, 76

Creativity and Imagination
   Women in Their Beds: 289

Crime and Criminals
   The Sheriff's Children: 207-208, 212
   Storyteller: 275, 277, 281-282

Cruelty
   Battle Royal or *The Invisible Man:* 17, 19, 22-24, 28-29
   The Sheriff's Children: 205, 209, 211, 213

Cubism
   Marriage á la Mode: 121-122

Cycle of Life
   And of Clay Are We Created: 5

D

Dance
   Battle Royal or *The Invisible Man:* 19, 27, 32-34

Death
   Silver Water: 231
   The Snows of Kilimanjaro: 245

Death
   And of Clay Are We Created: 1-3, 6
   A Good Scent from a Strange Mountain: 60-62, 66, 68-83
   The Grave: 86, 90-92
   The Sheriff's Children: 208, 216-220, 225-226
   Silver Water: 230-234, 237, 240-248
   The Snows of Kilimanjaro: 251, 253-259
   Storyteller: 262, 265-270, 273-274, 281
   Women in Their Beds: 286, 288-291

Depression and Melancholy
   Silver Water: 231-232

Description
   Battle Royal or *The Invisible Man:* 35-37
   The Sheriff's Children: 224

Dialect
   The Gilded Six-Bits: 40, 45, 47-48, 54-58

Dialogue
   The Gilded Six-Bits: 55, 57-58
   Say Yes: 200

Divorce
   Say Yes: 193

Dreams and Visions
   Battle Royal or *The Invisible Man:* 20, 22-23, 26
   Hands: 96-98, 103-104
   The Snows of Kilimanjaro: 247
   Storyteller: 273-274, 277-280

Duty and Responsibility
   The Sheriff's Children: 207-211, 217-219

E

Emotions
   And of Clay Are We Created: 3, 6-7, 10-15
   The Gilded Six-Bits: 55-58
   Hands: 99, 107, 111-113
   Marriage á la Mode: 121
   Mrs. Plum: 140
   My Kinsman, Major Molineux: 166-167
   Say Yes: 191, 199-200, 203-204
   The Sheriff's Children: 220, 225
   Women in Their Beds: 296

Essay
   Battle Royal or *The Invisible Man:* 22, 25-26
   Roselily: 174-176

Eternity
   Storyteller: 274-275, 280, 283
   Women in Their Beds: 296-298

Europe
   A Good Scent from a Strange Mountain: 61, 66-68
   Marriage á la Mode: 116, 119-123, 126
   My Kinsman, Major Molineux: 150, 154-156
   The Sheriff's Children: 222
   The Snows of Kilimanjaro: 248-250

Evil
   The Sheriff's Children: 223-224

Exile
   And of Clay Are We Created: 7
   A Good Scent from a Strange Mountain: 64-65
   Mrs. Plum: 135

Exploitation
   Storyteller: 261-262

Exposition
   Battle Royal or *The Invisible Man:* 29-31

F

Family
   A Good Scent from a Strange Mountain: 64
   Silver Water: 232

Farm and Rural Life
   The Gilded Six-Bits: 51-54
   The Grave: 84-85, 91-92
   The Sheriff's Children: 206, 212-213

Fate and Chance
   Roselily: 183-185
   Silver Water: 241-242
   Storyteller: 264, 272, 275, 281-282
   Women in Their Beds: 289-295

Fear and Terror
   The Grave: 90, 92
   Hands: 94-96, 99, 102
   Storyteller: 272, 277, 280
   Women in Their Beds: 293, 295

Femininity
   The Grave: 81, 83-84

Feminism
   Storyteller: 262-263

Femme Fatale
   My Kinsman, Major Molineux: 165-166

Folklore
   The Gilded Six-Bits: 51-54
   Storyteller: 271-275, 278-280, 283

Foreshadowing
   The Sheriff's Children: 218-220

Freedom
   Roselily: 180-182

Friendship
   Marriage á la Mode: 120

G

Gender Roles
   The Gilded Six-Bits: 48, 50-51
   Women in Their Beds: 292

Subject/Theme Index

Ghost
  Roselily: 181
God and Religion
  Roselily: 172
God
  Hands: 107-108
  Roselily: 171-172
Greed
  Storyteller: 268-269
Grotesque
  The Grave: 87, 89
  Hands: 97, 99
Growth and Development
  Mrs. Plum: 134

H

Happiness and Gaiety
  The Gilded Six-Bits: 39-40, 44-45
  A Good Scent from a Strange Mountain: 77
  Marriage á la Mode: 116, 118-119, 125-127
Harlem Renaissance
  The Gilded Six-Bits: 39, 47
Hatred
  Battle Royal or *The Invisible Man:* 20-22
  The Sheriff's Children: 209, 212-213
  The Snows of Kilimanjaro: 252-253
Heaven
  A Good Scent from a Strange Mountain: 62, 64, 66
Heroism
  The Gilded Six-Bits: 52-53
  The Snows of Kilimanjaro: 248, 250
Historical Periods
  My Kinsman, Major Molineux: 154
History
  Battle Royal or *The Invisible Man:* 21, 23, 26, 28
  The Gilded Six-Bits: 45-46
  The Grave: 78
  The Snows of Kilimanjaro: 249
  Storyteller: 261, 264
Homelessness
  Storyteller: 256, 260-262
Homosexuality
  Hands: 94, 98-99
Honor
  My Kinsman, Major Molineux: 162
  The Sheriff's Children: 223
  Storyteller: 280, 282
Hope
  Battle Royal or *The Invisible Man:* 22, 28-29
  Hands: 96-100

Human Condition
  Hands: 112
Humanism
  Mrs. Plum: 137-138
Humor
  The Gilded Six-Bits: 55, 58
  Storyteller: 280-282

I

Identity
  The Sheriff's Children: 210
Ignorance
  Battle Royal or *The Invisible Man:* 33
Illness
  Silver Water: 231
Imagery and Symbolism
  Battle Royal or *The Invisible Man:* 23, 26-29, 35-37
  The Gilded Six-Bits: 45, 51-54
  A Good Scent from a Strange Mountain: 75, 77
  The Grave: 83, 86
  Hands: 99-100, 104-105, 110-112
  Say Yes: 202-204
  Silver Water: 239
  The Snows of Kilimanjaro: 245, 247, 251, 253-254
  Storyteller: 261, 266
  Women in Their Beds: 288, 290-292
Imagination
  Storyteller: 272-273, 277, 279-281
Immigrants and Immigration
  A Good Scent from a Strange Mountain: 60-61, 67-68
Individual versus Nature
  And of Clay Are We Created: 5
Insanity
  Silver Water: 240-241
Irony
  And of Clay Are We Created: 6-7
  Battle Royal or *The Invisible Man:* 23, 25-27
  My Kinsman, Major Molineux: 153-154
  Storyteller: 281
Islamism
  Roselily: 169, 171-172, 175-176, 184-185

K

Killers and Killing
  A Good Scent from a Strange Mountain: 74
  The Sheriff's Children: 207-209, 216, 220
  Storyteller: 276, 278-280

Kindness
  My Kinsman, Major Molineux: 149, 151-154, 166-167
Knowledge
  Battle Royal or *The Invisible Man:* 20, 22-23

L

Landscape
  A Good Scent from a Strange Mountain: 73-74
  Hands: 96, 98-99
  My Kinsman, Major Molineux: 153-155, 161-163
  Silver Water: 230, 233, 237-239
  The Snows of Kilimanjaro: 248-255
  Storyteller: 261-271, 274-277, 280-282
Law and Order
  Battle Royal or *The Invisible Man:* 19, 23-24, 28
  Mrs. Plum: 130-138, 145-146
  My Kinsman, Major Molineux: 165-166
  The Sheriff's Children: 207-211, 214, 216-220, 223-226
  Storyteller: 258, 260, 263, 273, 278, 282
Life Cycle
  Women in Their Beds: 288
Limitations and Opportunities
  Battle Royal or *The Invisible Man:* 22, 24, 26, 28
  Hands: 111-113
Literary Criticism
  The Gilded Six-Bits: 54
  Hands: 101
  The Snows of Kilimanjaro: 254
  Storyteller: 263
Loneliness
  Hands: 94-99, 104-109, 112-113
Lost Generation
  The Snows of Kilimanjaro: 250
Love and Marriage
  Say Yes: 191
Love and Passion
  The Gilded Six-Bits: 44
Love and Passion
  And of Clay Are We Created: 1-2, 7, 9-15
  The Gilded Six-Bits: 41, 43-45, 55-56
  A Good Scent from a Strange Mountain: 73
  Hands: 107-113
  Marriage á la Mode: 119-120
  Mrs. Plum: 138-141
  Roselily: 170-173
  Say Yes: 190-192
  Silver Water: 228, 232, 234-237

Subject/Theme Index

Storyteller: 273-278, 281
Women in Their Beds: 286, 288, 291, 296-298

Loyalty
My Kinsman, Major Molineux: 162-164
The Sheriff's Children: 226
Women in Their Beds: 286, 292

M

Magic Realism
And of Clay Are We Created: 7

Marriage and Family
Marriage á la Mode: 118

Marriage
The Gilded Six-Bits: 48-51
Marriage á la Mode: 119, 123, 127-129
Roselily: 170-174, 179-185
Say Yes: 191, 193, 196-197, 202-204

Memory and Reminiscence
And of Clay Are We Created: 4

Memory and Reminiscence
A Good Scent from a Strange Mountain: 60-61, 66, 68
The Grave: 80-83
Roselily: 182
The Snows of Kilimanjaro: 244-249, 253-255
Storyteller: 271-276, 280-282

Memory and the Past
A Good Scent from a Strange Mountain: 64

Mental Instability
Silver Water: 229, 231, 233, 237-240

Middle Ages
My Kinsman, Major Molineux: 154-156

Modernism
The Grave: 83-86

Money and Economics
Battle Royal or *The Invisible Man:* 17, 19-26
The Gilded Six-Bits: 41, 43-51

Monologue
Roselily: 179-181

Morals and Morality
The Grave: 86
The Sheriff's Children: 214-215, 218-219, 225-226
Storyteller: 270

Murder
A Good Scent from a Strange Mountain: 60-62, 65-67, 76-77
The Sheriff's Children: 208-209, 212, 214, 216-217, 223, 226

Music
Silver Water: 229-234, 237-238

Myths and Legends
The Grave: 87-89
Storyteller: 269, 272-273, 277-278, 281-282

N

Narration
And of Clay Are We Created: 1-3, 6-7, 10-15
Battle Royal or *The Invisible Man:* 19-23, 26-37
The Gilded Six-Bits: 54, 56, 58
A Good Scent from a Strange Mountain: 60, 68-69
Hands: 99-100, 105, 109-112
My Kinsman, Major Molineux: 150, 152-155
Roselily: 172, 174, 176
Say Yes: 189, 192, 195, 199-200
The Sheriff's Children: 221, 223-225
Silver Water: 232, 240-241
The Snows of Kilimanjaro: 247-251, 254
Storyteller: 256, 261-264, 269-274, 277-279
Women in Their Beds: 290, 292

Nation of Islam
Roselily: 171, 174

Nationalism and Patriotism
A Good Scent from a Strange Mountain: 60-61, 66

Nature
Battle Royal or *The Invisible Man:* 22, 36-37
The Gilded Six-Bits: 52, 54
Hands: 96, 99, 109-111
Marriage á la Mode: 126-129
Mrs. Plum: 143
My Kinsman, Major Molineux: 156, 164, 166
Silver Water: 233, 238
The Snows of Kilimanjaro: 255
Storyteller: 257, 261, 263-264, 267, 269, 274-275

North America
And of Clay Are We Created: 7-8
Battle Royal or *The Invisible Man:* 23, 25-27
The Gilded Six-Bits: 45-46
A Good Scent from a Strange Mountain: 68
Say Yes: 192-194
The Sheriff's Children: 212-213

Novel
And of Clay Are We Created: 1, 7-9
Battle Royal or *The Invisible Man:* 22, 25-28
The Gilded Six-Bits: 47-48
My Kinsman, Major Molineux: 149, 154-156

Nurturance
Storyteller: 270, 272, 276, 280

O

Old Age
My Kinsman, Major Molineux: 165-166
Storyteller: 259-262, 268-270, 273-274

Order and Disorder
My Kinsman, Major Molineux: 152

P

Painting
Hands: 109-110
Marriage á la Mode: 121-122

Patience
Women in Their Beds: 284-286, 290, 293-295

Perception
Hands: 110-113
Storyteller: 276-278

Personal Identity
The Sheriff's Children: 210, 213-214, 222-224
Storyteller: 283

Personification
The Gilded Six-Bits: 51-52

Philosophical Ideas
Women in Their Beds: 291-292

Picaresque Novel
The Gilded Six-Bits: 51, 53-54

Plot
Hands: 100, 102
The Sheriff's Children: 222

Poetry
Roselily: 176-179
The Snows of Kilimanjaro: 248, 251
Storyteller: 270-279

Point of View
And of Clay Are We Created: 6
A Good Scent from a Strange Mountain: 64-65
Marriage á la Mode: 120, 123
Mrs. Plum: 135
Say Yes: 192
The Sheriff's Children: 210, 223-224
Silver Water: 240
Storyteller: 256, 261-262

Politicians
The Grave: 85
My Kinsman, Major Molineux: 160-163
Say Yes: 194-195

Politics
My Kinsman, Major Molineux: 152

Politics
    And of Clay Are We Created: 3, 7-9
    Battle Royal or *The Invisible Man:* 23-28
    The Gilded Six-Bits: 46-48
    A Good Scent from a Strange Mountain: 61-62, 65-70, 73-77
    The Grave: 85
    Mrs. Plum: 130, 132, 134, 136-138
    My Kinsman, Major Molineux: 154-155, 161-163
    Say Yes: 193-194
    The Sheriff's Children: 213
    Silver Water: 233
    The Snows of Kilimanjaro: 249
Postmodernism
    The Grave: 84-85
Power of the Individual
    Battle Royal or *The Invisible Man:* 22
Psychology and the Human Mind
    Hands: 94, 100-102
    The Sheriff's Children: 210, 222
    Silver Water: 228-229, 232, 234, 237-241
    The Snows of Kilimanjaro: 248
    Storyteller: 267-268
Public versus Private Life
    Mrs. Plum: 134

R

Race and Racism
    The Sheriff's Children: 208
Race
    Battle Royal or *The Invisible Man:* 18, 21-31, 35
    The Gilded Six-Bits: 43-47
    Mrs. Plum: 131-138, 145-146
    Roselily: 174-175
    Say Yes: 190-194
    The Sheriff's Children: 207-223, 226
    Storyteller: 260, 262-264
Racism
    Battle Royal or *The Invisible Man:* 21
    Say Yes: 190
Racism and Prejudice
    Battle Royal or *The Invisible Man:* 17, 21-30, 35-37
    The Gilded Six-Bits: 45-47
    Mrs. Plum: 136
    Say Yes: 189-191
    The Sheriff's Children: 205, 208-211
Recreation
    Battle Royal or *The Invisible Man:* 34-37

Redemption
    The Grave: 81
Religion and Religious Thought
    And of Clay Are We Created: 6, 8
    A Good Scent from a Strange Mountain: 64-65, 70
    The Grave: 82
    Hands: 108
    Roselily: 171-172, 175-176, 184-185
    Women in Their Beds: 295
Remorse and Regret
    The Snows of Kilimanjaro: 243, 246, 250-251
Responsibility and Morality
    The Sheriff's Children: 209
Revenge
    Storyteller: 261
Revenge
    Storyteller: 257, 261, 264-266
Roman Catholicism
    And of Clay Are We Created: 6, 8
Romanticism
    My Kinsman, Major Molineux: 154

S

Satire
    Marriage á la Mode: 115, 120, 122-123
Schizophrenia
    Silver Water: 228-229, 233-234, 239-240
Science and Technology
    And of Clay Are We Created: 5-6
    Women in Their Beds: 294
Search For Knowledge
    Battle Royal or *The Invisible Man:* 20, 22, 25, 29
    Mrs. Plum: 134-135, 138
Self-realization
    Storyteller: 275, 277, 279
Setting
    The Grave: 79, 84
    Marriage á la Mode: 124-126
    Mrs. Plum: 138
    My Kinsman, Major Molineux: 150, 152, 154-156
    The Sheriff's Children: 210
Sex
    Hands: 98
Sex and Sexuality
    The Gilded Six-Bits: 49-51
    The Grave: 91-92
    Hands: 96, 98-100
    Storyteller: 272, 274, 276, 278, 282
    Women in Their Beds: 288, 290-292

Sex Roles
    Women in Their Beds: 288
Sickness
    Silver Water: 228, 231-233
    Women in Their Beds: 290
Sin
    The Grave: 83-84
    The Sheriff's Children: 221-222, 226
    Storyteller: 269-270
Slavery
    Battle Royal or *The Invisible Man:* 18, 23-26
    The Sheriff's Children: 209-210, 215-217, 221-222, 225-226
Social order
    The Grave: 83
Social Order
    The Grave: 83, 85
Solitude
    And of Clay Are We Created: 12-13
Soothsayer
    Hands: 111, 113
    Women in Their Beds: 293-294
South America
    And of Clay Are We Created: 1, 7-9
Spiritual Leaders
    Roselily: 170-172, 179-184
Spirituality
    Women in Their Beds: 293, 295
Sports and the Sporting Life
    The Snows of Kilimanjaro: 243-244, 248-249, 255
    Storyteller: 272-274, 279-281
Storms and Weather Conditions
    The Snows of Kilimanjaro: 251-255
    Storyteller: 276, 278-279
Structure
    Battle Royal or *The Invisible Man:* 21, 27-28
    Hands: 109-111
    The Sheriff's Children: 219-220
    The Snows of Kilimanjaro: 248-249
    Storyteller: 272, 280
Superstition
    Women in Their Beds: 293-295
Survival
    Storyteller: 271-272, 275-276

T

The American Dream
    Battle Royal or *The Invisible Man:* 22
The Grotesque
    Hands: 97
The Individual and Society
    The Grave: 85

Time and Change
Storyteller: 274, 277, 283
Tone
Battle Royal or *The Invisible Man:* 22, 26-27
Hands: 113
Storyteller: 281-282

U

Uncertainty
Battle Royal or *The Invisible Man:* 32, 34
Hands: 103-105
Understanding
Storyteller: 271, 275, 280
Upper Class
Battle Royal or *The Invisible Man:* 17, 19, 22-23, 28-29

W

War
A Good Scent from a Strange Mountain: 64
War, the Military, and Soldier Life
And of Clay Are We Created: 4, 7-8
Battle Royal or *The Invisible Man:* 23-26, 36
A Good Scent from a Strange Mountain: 60-62, 66-68, 75-77
The Grave: 84-85
The Sheriff's Children: 210-211, 223-226
The Snows of Kilimanjaro: 245, 248-251, 254-255

Wealth
The Gilded Six-Bits: 40, 43-46
Wildlife
Battle Royal or *The Invisible Man:* 35-37
The Grave: 80-81, 86
Mrs. Plum: 141-143
My Kinsman, Major Molineux: 151-167
The Snows of Kilimanjaro: 245-246, 251-255
Storyteller: 274-276, 279-282
World War I
The Snows of Kilimanjaro: 244, 248, 250
World War II
The Snows of Kilimanjaro: 249-250